First published in Great Britain in 1998 by
ANCHOR BOOKS
An imprint of Forward Press Ltd
1-2 Wainman Road, Woodston,
Peterborough, PE2 7BU
Telephone (01733) 230761

HB ISBN 1 85930 578 4
SB ISBN 1 85930 573 3

Printed and bound in Great Britain by
The Bath Press, Bath

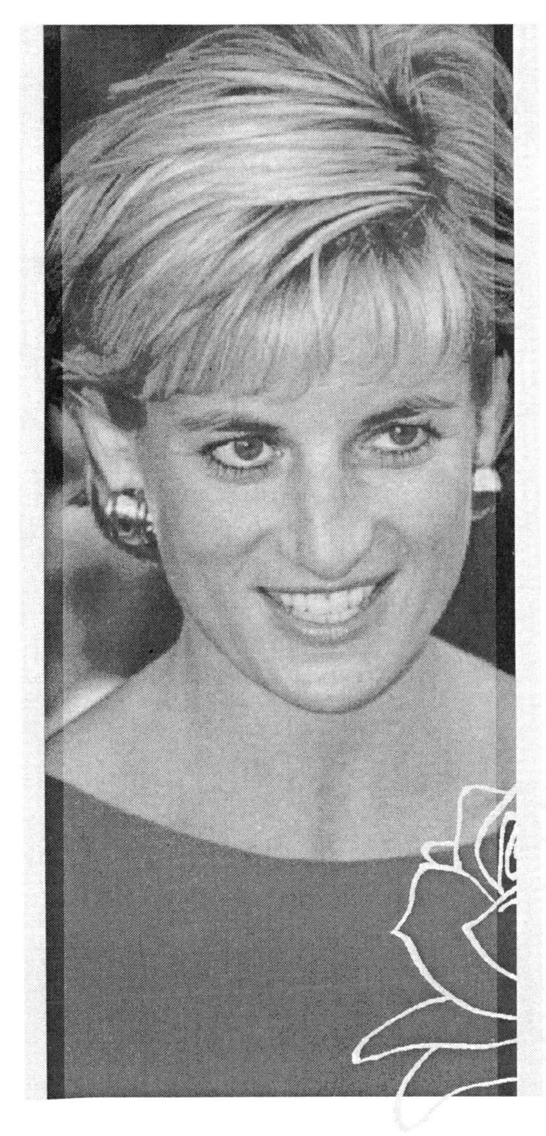

ANCHOR BOOKS

Poems for a Princess

In Memory of Diana, Princess of Wales 1961-97

Edited by:
Heather Killingray, Andrew Head, Chris Walton, Simon Harwin

Foreword

The tragic death of Diana, Princess of Wales sent waves of shock, grief and regret around the world. The eruption of anguish in this country manifested in mountains of flowers, floods of tears and a rising tide of anger.

Many people were taken by surprise at the depth of their own feelings and those of others. What was it about this young woman that had captured the hearts of millions of people around the world?

The poems in this book express and explore our collective sadness and disappointment; illuminating Diana's 'special brand of magic' and giving all the reasons why Diana, Princess of Wales was indeed the people's princess.

Heather Killingray
Editor

Index of Poets

The Queen Of Hearts

How will we remember you?
We will remember, in a quiet moment in time.
The people's princess, loved and adored,
Taken from us, suddenly, a tragedy, a crime.

How will we remember you?
In our hearts, you will remain.
You cared, for all the little children,
Compassion for others, in suffering, in pain.

How will we remember you?
Shock and horror, at your tragic loss.
Our ambassador, for human rights,
We weigh up, the price, the cost.

How will we remember you?
For your beauty, world famous, renowned.
Charitable work, carried out, with a joke, a smile,
Through the years, you became, the jewel in the crown.

Shirley Thompson

Golden Days

It's a splendid day in early spring,
I can hear the cuckoos and the linnets sing,
Overcome by apple blossom and bright sunshine,
Machiko and I descend the long incline.
Princess Diana has come to open a home,
And London Road is jam packed full with a throng.
We wait for the four car motorcade,
And Diana cheerfully smiles and waves,
Later, resplendent with hair so gold,
Each waiting hand she clasps and holds.
Such days are in the past now, and in the past remain,
Will such golden days for England ever come again?

Nigel David Evans

A Fond Farewell

The nation has gathered,
Upon this sad day,
To say goodbye to a friend.
Like seeds we are scattered,
As each in our own way
But we are loyal right up to the end.

The memories we share,
Of those happy days,
We'll have 'til the end of time.
Those moments so rare,
And your special ways,
Keep coming back into mind.

Princess Diana with you,
Our hearts will remain,
As we say a tearful goodbye,
With feeling so true,
We just wish to say,
That we love you with so much pride.

So it's just left to say,
Just how sorry we feel,
As we bid you a fond farewell.
But maybe someday,
With feeling so real,
We'll remember how for you we all felt.

Paul Secrett

A Tribute To Diana, Princess Of Wales

Diana, Princess of all the people,
Your charm and beauty was so graceful,
The best are taken to live above,
But never forgotten for their love.

You will now live on within your sons,
You were the greatest of all mums,
Rest in peace with your special friend,
May your happiness now never end.

Angie J Gibbs

And The World Cried Too

August thirty-first nineteen ninety-seven,
Was a tragic day for Britain,
When our Princess was taken to heaven,
Such a sad loss,
To those she loved and knew,
Such a sad loss,
To those like me and you.
She touched the world with magic,
Made problems lighter with her smile,
She gave love to everyone,
That stretched from mile to mile,
Nobody can express,
All the inner pain we feel,
It's an enormous emotion,
That we can't seem to reveal,
But it wasn't just tears from Britain,
From the flowers and gifts we knew,
That the young and the old and
the rich and the poor,
And the whole world cried too.

Caroline Hartley

Diana

(She was a very special Lady, who will be greatly missed.)

Like a rosebud, small and shy,
You raised your head and faced the world,
The bud it bloomed and showed its colour,
A delicate beauty for all to behold,
The bloom so open, so full of life,
Touched the world with tenderness,
But just when the rose was at its most radiant,
Along they came and cut it down,
Its life extinguished, just like a flame,
Never, ever to bloom again.

Tina Elener

A Tribute To A Princess

The suffering and pain which we all feel,
We ask ourselves will it ever heal?

The loss of a Princess which we all have
to bear,
Our Queen of Hearts you really did care.

The outcome of this tragedy leaves us sad and
broken-hearted,
You were too young to leave us Di, your life
had barely started.

Your life an inspiration but so tragically short,
A reason for this death in our minds we've
all sought.

Your need to live in peace, well what can
we say?
God took you for a happier life to a place
far away.

We have to come to terms in the time which
we bide,
While we know you are safe at
Our Father's side.

This poem, a gesture to you which I send,
Your life beautiful Princess, did it really
have to end?

Jayne M Lysyj (15)

Untitled

Pavements are the flower bearers
Gun carriage, coffin's throne
For a Queen that never ruled England
Though English hearts she won.

A London City standstill
Never seen before
A million mournful faces
Build a city wall.

A tribute to a princess
Whose fairy tale died
Extinguished, leaving darkness
A nation knelt and cried.

Siân Kelly-Scott

Diana A Princess

Golden hair, sad eyes, gorgeous smile, coy look
Features of a Princess from a story book
Alas this is not fiction
It is a real Lady, with a love addiction.

Into railway sidings, late at night would go
For loving secret meetings, with her Royal beau
From these secret meetings, romance grew
and grew
Until Her Royal Prince said, 'I really do love you.'

A ring upon her finger, with the world she
shared her joy
She really thought at this time, she had
got her boy
A wedding later followed, a day of regal grace
That look of loving feelings showed upon her face

Out of that Cathedral, stepped our Lady Di
She had now become a Princess, looking
oh so shy
It had always been a dream, a Prince for her
to marry
As time went by along came sons, William
and Harry.

A veil of mist now shrouds that face
No smile, no laugh a slower pace
The marriage now is at an end
It would appear it will not mend.

Her Royal Highness, she is no more
But still she's loved by rich and poor
Now she's Diana Princess of Wales
She's free to seek out other males.

At last she finds a real good friend
Her heart can now, start to mend
That laughing smiling face is back
As they are hounded by a paparazzi pack.

On an early August morning
Di meets death, there was no warning
Into a tunnel dark and black
Her car flips over on its back.

Now a nation deep in mourning
Flowers, prayers, yes it's dawning
Diana Princess is no more
As she enters through, heaven's door

Farewell my Princess, you were the best
I pray for you as you're laid to rest
I promise that, I shall not weep
As your body lies in the ground so deep.

Ray Jacks

The Rose Princess

As shadows of grey shrouds over the Vale,
the heavy silver clouds gently float,
and sparkled rain falls for every crystal tear.

The empty sky, not a bird free in flight,
swaying trees whisper silently in the distance,
the whimpering sighs of the gasping world.

The air is crisp and clean, so sharp,
a life so precious, so lonely,
burning time can never take away the pain.

Winter chills are blowing near,
as every wave on the ocean waves,
soft snow will soon fall,
for our beautiful rose princess.

Endless questions are often unanswered,
as we gather our spirits together.

We celebrate one so filled with love,
for all the land can never forget,
the beautiful rose princess.

Strong and spirited,
loving and giving,
capturing and melting hearts.

But now we stand - one body,
one nation - forever.

Gone but never forgotten,
to our beautiful rose princess.

Donna Joanne Kinsey

For Eternity

I never met our Princess although,
strangely, somehow
Since her death 'tis almost like I've come to
know her now;
In the last few days from seeing her on the TV,
There were many things she did quite
unobtrusively,
Things that weren't reported at the time when
they were done,
Like sharing with the people her sense of
joy and fun,
Ordinary people at work, and in their homes too,
For them, if the need arose, doing what
she could do,
Giving to those who had lost it, for the
future, hope,
Helping them see, after all, that with life
they COULD cope;
Cheering up the elderly, the homeless
and the sad,
All despite the personal problems she also had;
To raise funds for charity she gladly lent
her weight,
Happily encouraging all those less fortunate;
Dealing with the landmines' scourge,
she made us all aware
Of the lives these fearful weapons, if not banned,
lay bare,
Although her humanity in EVERYTHING she did,
Beneath royal protocol would simply not be hid;
Stripped of being HRH, no scrap of difference
made,
In fact helped increase for her the people's
accolade;
Showing she was vulnerable, just like you and I,
Only served to heighten our feelings for Lady Di;
A Princess she may have been, yet one
of us no less,
Having to deal with life's problems,
ups and downs, and stress;
However, for living it was clear she had a thirst,
Likewise, as a loving mother, her two boys
came first;
But, out of the blue, then came that dreadful
August day
When, to be with Him, The Lord spirited
her away;
Who though could have known the grief and
sadness left behind?
Who, just the right words to express
their feelings, could find?
Why was it Diana had been given such a cup?
Surely it was a bad dream from which we'd
soon wake up;
Yet we had to face the truth, our Queen of Hearts
had gone,
Whilst, down her path, we must do our best to
follow on,
Giving of ourselves like Christ who, all those
years ago,
On a cross gave Self for us, that in Him we
might grow;
And, though we see darkly now, His risen light
will guide,
Helping us to know that, even now, He's at
our side
'Til, when in His Father's house, our mansion
is prepared,
And love, in all it's fullness, for eternity
is shared.

Richard Beeson

Queen Of Hearts

The Queen of Hearts you've gone forever,
To everyone's surprise,
No-one could believe the news,
Nearly everyone cried,
Those who never shed a tear,
Mourned in a different way,
Everyone showed some respect,
By giving flowers for your grave,
No-one will forget you,
Your love for the world was strong,
You made everyone feel special,
As if they could do no wrong,
Princess Diana why did you go,
The world needs your special kind of glow.

Marie Evans

Just A Short Time

You came to us in a fairytale way
When you married Prince Charles on your wedding day.
You wanted your husband to love you so much
It showed in your kiss, it showed in your touch.
Prince William was born how proud we could see
Prince Charles, Princess Diana and William made three.
You both were still together when Harry came along
But your feelings were changing, love wasn't so strong.
You were criticised for speaking, about the pain that you felt
But that's just how women work, with pain they've been dealt.
It wasn't that you were cunning, you just wanted to say
To the people you loved, Charles turned me away.
The boys both adored you that was plain to see
When you took them both out like a normal family.
You had so much to do, some days must have been tough
But you never stopped caring when the going got rough.
You were looking for love when Dodi came along
He made you feel wanted, was that really so wrong?
You'll always be with us, but wherever you are
I hope you're with Dodi, and your Dad's not too far.
At last you're at peace, and as free as a bird
But it's taken your Death, life's really absurd.

Judith Stevens

Diana

Shadow lost
life cruelly snatched
death's dark calling

A nation shocked
grieving, weeping
tears are falling

Spirit released
full of shining splendour
a spark of hope

Angel of mercy
illuminating hearts
giving us the will to cope

Your short life
a burning beacon
lifting the gloom

Spreading love
a sea of light
dispelling doom

A catalyst
uniting nations
gathered mourning

Never forgotten
etched in memory
a new age is dawning

The people's heroine
worshipped woman
of many parts

Rest in peace
beloved Diana
Queen of Hearts

Paul Birkitt

A Tribute To Diana, Princess Of Wales

Those years we have known you are endearing
So beautiful so kind
Looked the whole world over but just not find
a Princess such as you
Now grief is on our mind
You were God's messenger always there on call
You grew up and married before hearing
your public call
You have won our hearts Diana even in your
last breath
Nothing takes you from us
Not even the stillness of death
You lived your life at a fast pace and always
beat the clock
Now you have died tragically and we must bear
the shock
We will look to family in our future days
Giving them the love you have shown in so many
different ways
We will watch our every move and discourage
nasty deeds
Remembering your kindness how you thought
of others' needs
Life was not so good for you indeed it was
quite rash
It plummeted you through Paris streets and stole
you in a crash
Family is there for you and friends there are
so many
How fate dealt that twisted blow it really is
uncanny
Charles will go on loving the children indeed
he is so caring
He just knows and so do we that you will still
be sharing
Bye Diana too young to sleep - All we can do is
give you flowers before falling down in grief.

Rosaleen and family

Diana, More Than A Princess

A queen that never was,
You will forever be,
Within our hearts,
As a queen should be.

At one with the people,
Everyone united in their grief,
The hands of friendship,
Shared in spontaneous applause.

Without pomp and ceremony galore,
Beauty to behold,
As unique as a flower,
Reigning as nature intended.

Silence in expression,
Disbelief in the facts,
As accident too common to know,
Awake to the mercy of fate.

Tears may flow from guilt or sorrow,
Ignorance excused if unborn,
Too many if onlys,
A future lost in memories.

Sorry for doubting your sincerity,
Humble to your actions unknown,
Let me grieve alone,
And pray for your accession into Heaven.

Neil Fisher

A Moment To Live
(In Tribute To Diana Princess of Wales)

It is for a moment . . .
we live,
It may seem longer . . .
but no!
Time passes by so quick,
No time to forgive,

So take a look at life,
Before it passes you by,
No longer on earth,
But in Heaven above the sky.

Jessica Wright

Princess Diana

Like a beacon shining bright,
you turned the darkness into light.

Your smile as radiant as the sun,
brightened the hearts of everyone.

You blessed us with your caring touch,
and we loved you very much.

Then like a snowflake's fleeting stay,
God's angels carried you away.

Our lives are poorer without you,
Queen of Hearts, so loving and true.

We as a nation shed many tears,
and we'll cherish memories of your short years.

I wish I had met you but it was not to be,
for others needed you much more than me.

The millions of flowers may fade away
but your youth and beauty forever will stay.

You are the brightest star in the sky,
and I hope I meet you in the sweet by and by.

Pamela Eckhardt

A Tribute To Diana

An unstoppable tide of tears flowed
As a nation's grief was felt across the land
Its soul, its heart now broken
As tragedy was now at hand
A light once bright
Had now been extinguished from within
As one by one they came remembering a princess
Whose lasting love upon a nation
Had won our hearts.

A W Harvey

To HRH The Princess Of Wales

Always you awakened the world
to your regal charm and grace.
Like gems in bright light
you would sparkle and delight,
to captivate each soul and heart.
But your outer and inner beauty
combined made you stand out
as the unique jewel in the crown.
True, you were a shining example for
others how to behave.
So regal you were in every way,
how you walked, talked and smiled.
HRH was all over you stamped.
Once you were destined to become
the future Queen of the UK.
Now as such, in the nation's hearts
and minds, forever you will stay.

Lucy Carrington

Princess Diana

You were a special lady, who radiated love
And cheered hearts of those you touched.
Your warm smile and caring personality
Shared with your courage and sincerity,
Earned love and admiration from everybody

But now you have gone to the heavens above
Cruelly taken along with the man you loved.
Our hearts ache for such a tragic loss
A vast raincloud, wet tears of grief,
Releasing sadness, as our eyes openly weep.

Tides of time will hopefully stop the pain
But not the boundless love that we hold,
That shall survive and need not be told.
May you now have peace and eternal rest
Our much missed - 'People's Princess'.

Stephanie Bones

Diana, Princess Of Wales

D iana Princess of Wales -
I n each mind a fond memories prevail - of
A heart which was loving and filled people's need -
N o prejudice of colour or creed.
A Princess of beauty, charm and such grace -

P ut sick people at ease with a single embrace -
R eaching out often a kind helping hand - to the
I njured, maimed - who could not stand.
N othing daunted or held her back -
C ourage and energy she did not lack -
E yes so beautiful and blue - witnessed
S ights of what landmines can do.
S uffering humanity she helped without pause -

O pining that banning of mines be the laws.
F un-loving, generous with a lively quick wit

W herever she went a dark corner she lit
A bove and beyond a dutiful call - her deep
L ove for people never ceased to enthral.
E legant, modest - a Lady unique -
S tilled now - her heart - but thro' her works to us speaks.

Marian Curtis Jones

Diana

Diana, the day you died
I feel in some strange way
It was a blessing in disguise
For if you had lived
And Dodi died
I can only imagine the tears
You would have cried.
Now Heaven is holding you
In its arms
Keeping you from all life's harms
No longer will we see
Your beautiful face
But in our hearts
You will always have a place.

Debbie Allen

Diana, Princess Of Wales 1961-1997

She came upon the scene with a shy coy look in her eyes,
The radiance of her smile took everyone by surprise,
The freshness of her youth with her determined ways,
Revitalised the Royals through out all her days,
The love in her heart was there for everyone,
Not just her sons saw her full of fun,
She had compassion, for people on the street,
Each heart was touched with love, by people she did meet,
Her work for Charities, The Homeless and those with AIDS,
Gave others hope and love in many different ways,
She had her own struggles and even faced divorce,
Yet she carried on and did things by choice,
Her work to abolish landmines and the damage they bring,
Gave everyone a new prospective - she was inspiring,
She was England's greatest ambassador and countries from abroad,
Took her in their hearts and lingered on her words,
Yes she had style and grace with a warm look in her eye,
She was the Queen of Hearts - yet I'm wondering why,
Why she wasn't given privacy in her private life as she pleaded for,
She was constantly in camera - often by the score,
When you give so much love and friendship - was it too much to ask,
For a few minutes' peace and quiet to get on with your task,
And now she's gently sleeping safe in God's good care,
Gently protected, Unique, and so very rare.

Christine Helen Cruse

A Flower Lost Forever

(Inspired by the untimely death of
the Princess of Wales, Diana)

A flower lost forever
But the perfume lingers on
A life as sweet as music
So you'll not forget the song
A world lost in its hunger
For the greedy ones to feed
Forgetting love's humanity
The wanting and the need
A touch of someone's caring
Wearing heart upon her sleeve
So short a stay of kindness
Why in God's name should you leave?
Your work, a worldwide effort
Sowing seeds of hope and love
Too good to live in this life
You were wanted up above
But though your smile's a memory
It's a smile that will not die
It was blessed with every angel's kiss
And though we're bound to cry
We won't forget you princess
You were special to us all
And though we cried the loudest
You responded to God's call
So dear flower lost forever
Let your perfume linger on
You'll be with us now forever
So you haven't really gone.

David Whitney

In Memory Of Diana, The Princess Of Wales

May your golden smile and heart.
Light our darkest path.
For the lost, sick, and homeless,
God bless, our people's Queen from the people
Who loved her dearly. . .

Diane Godbold

Lady Sunshine

Lady Sunshine what has happened to you
You came here with so much to do
Lady Sunshine you were so unaware
Of the evil which lay everywhere

You had a touch of innocence about you
That the tougher kind took in their stride
And as I sit here writing about you
I cannot understand why you have died

For I see so many around taking all they can
They never think of giving a thing
I think you learned a long time ago
Something they may never know
Simply the joy that giving can bring

Lady Sunshine you looked so well
With your beauty and insecurity
There were times when you stumbled and fell
I know it wasn't easy to know life wasn't easy
Princess of our time
Your beauty will live on Lady Sunshine.

Valerie Marshall

Together Forever

Two bright stars shine from the night sky
One is Dodi and the other Di
Two smiling faces above the clouds
Now away from photographing crowds
And as they walk hand-in-hand
Across a beach of golden sand
It's such a shame no-one will see
Just how happy Di and Dodi will be
Together forever in eternal rest
Proves that God only takes the best.

Allison Jones

All We Had

You lived. You loved. You cared. We lost.
Media. News Pictures Cost.
Natural love. Mother Earth.
Ambassador. A World of Worth.

You took the stars. You shared them out.
Presented hope. Enlightening doubt.
A fairy tale. A dream come true.
Heart of a Nation. A picture of you.

Your love reached out. Touched with care.
Disfigured lives. Decay. Despair.
Famine. Disease. Relics of War.
Love for these and many more.
The Aged. The Young. Humanities Need.
The World has lost to Inhuman Greed.

Two boys at home, who've lost a mother.
Irreplaceable. Like no other.

Now and Forever you'll always be,
Our 'Queen of Hearts'. Eternally.

Where Jesus walked, Diana went.
Where Jesus Loved, her love she spent.

HRH The World's Princess Diana
1961-1997

Gossamer wings. A pale blue sky
Heaven on Earth. Never Goodbye.

Linda Dickerson

Dear Diana

Dear Diana you gave so much
You seemed to have the magic touch
Your eyes so blue and full of light
Your smile made a grey day bright

You cared about other people
Less fortunate than you
People with AIDS the poor
Children, these are just a few

But sadly your life came
To an abrupt end
The world lost the people's friend
But although you may be gone
Your spirit lives on

So don't be blue, but carry on
All Diana's good work will be done
And give William and Harry too
The strength and courage to start anew.

J Pearson

Diana

We saw a chrysalis transform
Into a moth.
Slender
Tender
Resplendent in
Beauty
And frailty.

We praised her work
For victims
Of AIDS
Grenades
The underprivileged
The suffering
The dying.

We longed to claim her
As our own.
We fought
And bought
Every picture
Indiscreet
And revealing.

Now she is dead
Crushed in a car
Slaughtered
And martyred.
Her blood
Is on our hands.
We bought the newspapers.

Frank Henry

For The Love Of Diana

The heavens wept with us today
There are not words enough for what
I need to say.

A downpouring of rain
An outpouring of pain.

Please let the light and warmth
That radiated, permeated
Be enough to lift us all
And inspire us.
For I fear the world is now a darker place.

There are two among us,
Who I hope can feel our love
For their loss is immeasurable,
But I know they carry the same goodness
That will keep her spirit alive

An outpouring of pain
A downpouring of rain

The heavens wept with us today.

Vivienne M Wright

Farewell To A Princess

She was goodness she was kindness
She was gentle she had love
The good Lord sought to take her
To a new world up above

And because of all the hardships
She faced down here on earth
She was given the chance of staying
Or going forward to re-birth

She chose the later option
And a partner to share it with
And together they're in Heaven
United they both will live

It's a better place they are now
With peace and love and caring
Far from the human beings
That made their lives despairing

No longer can those plague them
That made their lives a hell
Lessons learned, maybe!
We bid you both farewell.

Jean McDonnell

Princess Diana

In the year of nineteen sixty-one
A beautiful baby girl was born
Engaged to your Prince Charming
How you looked a darling
Charming like Cinderella on your marriage
Travelling in a horse and carriage
William and Harry were your boys
Bringing you both happiness and joys
Diana you cared for Dodi with your heart
But far too soon you were to depart
A whole world will remember
That bleak day in September
Diana we have memories to treasure
More than any words can measure

Ann Burton

Our Princess

To our Princess, a devoted Mother
Your first priority, wherever you might be.
Our Princess, you loved your sons above all other,
That was plain for us all to see.

Your smile and devotion spread far and wide,
Our Princess you spread your warmth around,
When problems engulfed you, you did not run
and hide
Another visit to the needy, a comfort in this
you found.

Our Princess you are now in heaven above,
Leaving us feeling empty and blue,
But we will smile and remember your love
Queen of Hearts, Our Princess, we will miss you.

Margaret Phillips

A Poet's Homage To Princess Diana

*In the early hours of Sunday morning,
31st August 1997 a Nation's heart was
torn apart, as Princess Diana was tragically
killed. A great, great, loss, leaving people
unbelieving stunned and shocked, who would
show a bereavement never again to be
repeated and recorded in British history.*

*As a World War Two battle-hardened
Infantry veteran, I never cared for Royalty.
So what makes an ordinary man like me,
forsake his usual Saturday morning beer,
stay at home and shed a tear?*

*Did a Nation deserve one so dear?
How can humans sink so low to seek
and photo some intimate times of our
Princess without compassion or fear?*

*The Tabloid newspapers who in your short life
hounded and did their utmost to find and print
what they considered the worst of you.
On your death, tried to atone and print the
very best of you.*

*The millions of ordinary people, who never
realised you were part of their family until
you died. They paid their deep respect,
watched you go, and cried. Throwing their
flowers on the passing hearse, with a love
so deep, to a Rose, who's alas so fast asleep.*

*Being human we will forget our Diana for
periods of time, but to forget you forever,
Impossible! The mention or sight of the words,
Leprosy or AIDS, will instantly trigger off
a mental image of Princess Diana holding
the hands of the victims of AIDS or Leprosy,
providing a powerful weapon against
people's ignorance and fear. Then a tear
will appear at the corner of our eye, and
future generations should know the simple
answer, why.*

*Princess Diana seemed to draw on a powerful
inner strength that her unhappiness appeared
to give her, which ignited a bravery few of us
ever acquired, enabling her to impart a love
to the less fortunate in our society, of which
the compassionate people in the world
very much admired.*

Tom Bull

Farewell Princess Of Wales

*A nation mourned the loss,
this sad September day.
Of a star, cruelly extinguished,
to shine, in the Milky Way.*

*This beautiful English Rose,
never meant to grow old.
Whose legend will endure forever.
Because the Lord, broke the mould.*

*Such scenes never before witnessed,
in London's teeming streets.
An overpowering silence,
as the Princess's cortege progressed.*

*Diana's boys, William and Harry,
followed their mother's coffin,
on which a wreath of lilies,
bore the simple word 'Mummy'.*

*Union flag at half-mast,
the palace declares consent.
People Power, the die is cast.
Protocol, uniquely, absent.*

*A horse-drawn carriage,
escorted by Welsh guards and Troopers.
Abbey bells, pealed in homage,
as poignant as the mourners.*

*Princess Diana's last journey,
in the flower strewn hearse.
Through silent crowds,
of those she loved.
Remember, the happy nursery nurse.*

Raymond Baggaley

A 'Legend' In Her Lifetime

Our Lady Diana, we grieve today.
A nation 'heartbroken' God plucked you away.
Everyone loved you, a beauty to behold
'Lord' carve her name with pride in letters of 'gold'.

Your 'smile' haunts us forever, a star shining bright
Our own 'special Princess' hand-in-hand with her 'knight'.
An ocean of tears, like we've NEVER seen.
An abundance of flowers, NEVER have been.

The world has lost a 'Diva' regardless of creed or race.
And we have lost an 'Icon' that can NEVER be replaced
We commend to you this Precious-soul,
For her to achieve her Ultimate Goal.

We pray the world come together as 'One'
Diana's work fulfilled and second to 'None'!
In DEATH she deserves her peace and her rest.
In LIFE dear Lord she was simply 'THE BEST'!

Dilys Parry

Queen Of Hearts

Princess Diana, Queen of Hearts
A human being, a mother like most of us,
You did us proud, you stood up for your rights
You did not give in, you held on tight.
Your heart ruled for your children and the world,
Many a hand you held.
Pleasure, comfort to the needy you gave
Happy you made them with your smiles or a wave
Never to be forgotten, in our hearts you will stay
You have shown us the light of day.

Maria Smith

A Tribute To The Late Diana, Princess of Wales 1961-1997

Darling Diana, you were loved by all
So young and pure, a sweet young girl
Pomp and Regality became your life
When Charles, Prince of Wales took you for his wife
Life was not easy and as time went on
You had two sons, a loving mum
You became the focus of attention
With difficulties not to mention
Your work here on Earth must be done
Love and care you showed to everyone
God gave you the courage to bounce back from your sorrows
With strength to go on and face your tomorrows
A wonderful Lady, however oppressed
You never gave in - you did your best
You will be remembered with pride and love
As you rest in peace in your home above.

Evelyn A Evans

Our Princess Diana

You were Princess, of Thurnscoe, just for a day
You were special, like an angel, we wanted you to stay
Laughing, talking freely, you showed you cared a lot
About downtrodden people in a mining village forgot.
No pit wheel turning, just shops and houses boarded up
Tin cans and rubbish near your feet but you didn't even look.
You lit up our grimy village like a ray of sunshine
In Thurnscoe, for once everything was divine.
You were our Princess, of Thurnscoe, just for a day
You were special Diana, you've left a memory that won't fade away.

Lillian Johnson

Princess In The Sky

(Diana's final goodbye)

The light behind the stars I'll be
Forever young, bright and free,
Not black and white or from afar
Instead I'll shine like a bright new star.

And in my own true light I will gleam
Not from a front page or on a screen,
And my thoughts and feelings will be my own
Not the right of a camera lens or microphone.

Up here I'll feel no need to ever hide
And I'll have Dodi right by my side,
So please dry your tears, don't cry and mourn
For I've been given the chance to be reborn.

God's issued me with my final break
A gift I feel in my heart, I must take,
Family and friends I'll miss and leave a memory of love,
And for my sons I'll forever be an inner voice from above.

So do not view it as a tragedy for me to die,
For I can now be a Princess in the sky.

Vicky Dillingham

Fond Memories Of Diana, Princess Of Wales (1961-1997)

Her smile, so bright, 'neath sparkling blue eyes.
Warm greetings, hugs and gestures keen.
Love and compassion evoking sighs
From the strong, or faithless their God unseen.

Diana sought-out and conquered evil all.
Children, too, recognised her special Grace.
Fame and glory disdained them, she.
Her sacrifice upheld an Angelic face.

Brian Harris

Princess Of Smiles

A light was snuffed out in the world tonight,
A brightness extinguished for ever.
A warmth has been snatched so cruelly away.
Chilling all like a glacial river.

Her beauty and brightness shone out to all,
Like a beacon glows in the dark,
Her caring and kindness her love for all men,
Radiated straight from her heart.

So young and so vibrant; so full of life,
A beautiful person inside,
Then - gone in an instant of madness we're left
With our memories which never will fade.

To the world, a Lady of Royal Line,
A Duchess, a Princess of Wales,
For us on the street forever she'll be,
Diana, Princess of Smiles.

Margaret J H Goudie

Diana

Something so precious has been taken away,
it happened in a sad and awful way.
You are greatly loved and we'll all miss you,
you'll be watching us all especially your two.

You did a lot for the world and not everyone knew then,
Just how special you were rather like a mother hen.
My thoughts and thousands of others are with your two sons,
They will be without the love and the arm of their mums.

Thank you for giving all the love that you gave out,
People are all thankful without a doubt.
You're the People's Princess Lady Diana,
The Queen of our hearts forever.

We love you and miss you.

Marie O'Kane

Poem For Remembrance To Diana, Princess Of Wales

With a smile, with the air of grace,
She came into this life to become the
Princess of Wales,
The work she did will be remembered,
The kindness she showed the people
and societies,
The boys she leaves and the future King,
Diana 'Queen of Hearts' has gone but will
not be forgotten,

Hassle, stress, pestering is all they got,
The photographers would not leave her alone,
The face covered worldwide magazines,
the fashion hit the headlines,
The life she had with Prince Charles went
so quickly,
The boys older now, can remember their
mother with all their own personal memories,
William, Harry, and Prince Charles may you
all find peace.

Janet Robinson

In Memory Of Princess Diana

The Princess of Wales and our nation's Rose,
Why you left us, nobody knows.
A light in our hearts, that has now burnt out,
We'll always remember you, without a doubt.

The Queen of Hearts, full of sunshine
and light,
You fought for the people, never gave up
without a fight,
You helped out the world, though it brought
you pain,
You gave so much, but had nothing to gain.

You disappeared like early morning dew,
This is for you Diana, we love you.

Kirsty Davies

Diana: A Requiem

Diana was the Goddess of hunting poised
in flight,
And now her modern-day counterpart has
gone to eternal light,
No-one knows what's wrong or right
or what happened that fateful night,
God's ways are not given to us to understand,
Why should He take such an angel; such
a delight,
When the news broke,
I got such a fright,
Like a bolt from the blue, a hideous surprise,
I could feel the tears jolt in my eyes,
Let the funeral bells toll throughout the land,
Surely this was never planned,
One thing for sure,
Diana had allure,
For troubled souls, and rich and poor,
She only had to flash that shy,
beguiling smile,
You were truly the Queen of style,
Ashes to ashes, dust to dust,
You had no-one in whom you could trust,
I went to sign the book of consolation,
To say goodbye from an ever grateful nation,
My sorrow can find no placation,
So from one of humble station,
I write this hymn to you, my pen's creation,
Away from pressman's allegation,
It baffles me,
It must baffle them;
Now you wear Heaven's diadem,
It must have been one of your dearest joys,
To bring up your beloved boys,
In truth, without you we are not alone,
As long as Prince William sits on
England's throne.

Alan Pow

She Deserved Respect And She Got It

A quiet calm, invaded me
the depth, to yet, I have never felt
'twas here, so deep inside my soul
that throbbed, pulsated, in agony
twas a hurt so fierce that none could help
except for to sit in its mournful presence
to ponder, to wonder, to try to absorb
and to question the reasons why?

And there we stood in silent reverence
we mourned as one, a throbbing unity
a chain of emotions reaching throughout
the land
an agony of shock that ran from nation to nation
a silence that stemmed from the roots of despair
a silence that hung like a man from the gallows
a silence that said more than words ever would
a silence that only pain could effect

As our eyes fiercely followed her casket of abode
we allowed us to dwell on the memory of her
and the meaning of life, of her sadness
and hopes
of her insecure feelings yet her abundance of love
of her desire for life, and her spirit of freedom
of her tortured and passionate love for her boys

This then we turned and watched them walk
down the path of dignified heartache
so slow, as grief marked their every step
so weary, as pain sat on burdened shoulders
so bitter, at the loss of one so rare
so sad as their grief spanned the ocean wide
yet astounded by the love, her people showed
and proud to know she was really Queen

Esther Austin

Princess Diana

She's my inspiration to be a hero.
If we all could be like her
The world would never fall apart.
If everybody did some charity deed
The world would pull together to be one.

One day I'll cry a tear for you, my dear.
Today I am too shocked to know the full.
It's not just me to suffer, England alone,
But the whole Nation.

What is the world going to be without you?
Nobody knows.
If only we could share that last moment together,
Just to show exactly how much I care about you.

I wish I could have met you as you are my
inspiration.
You were the one to break down the barriers
Between old and young, sick and dying.
You were never above the rest
But shed a tear when sorrow affected
You were the only one to care about all.

Not only were you an inspiration to me,
but to others too.
How are we to cope with no Patron Saint
of so many charities and sufferers?

Who shall take your role as the only one to care?

Rest in peace
As we all remember the good things you did,
And hope to continue.

You were a hero to the Nation
A carer, a friend, a mother - but few to name.
You shall be sadly missed.
But most of all you were an inspiration,
A hero to remain.

Samantha Malster

Life Of A Princess

Born in the golden pastures of serenity
Deep in the English countryside
A baby girl became a 'Lady'
Not knowing to what great heights she'd ride
They called the babe 'Diana'
The name of the Goddess of Hunting
Little did they know, that years later
She would wed midst a sea of 'bunting'
Kings and Queens from all over the world
Were present at her wedding
For she had married a Royal son
Her doomed future not suspecting
She gave this man two handsome sons
The people simply adored her
For she was the light in a Palace so dull
But not a Courtier loved her
As years went on her beauty grew
Many hurts and slurs came upon her
Her spirit broke her heart was pained
Her Prince had found another
The world cried out their words of love
Through all her pain and sorrow
But then she found another man
To love her and her boys in the morrow
But in a shocking twist of fate
Life ended for both in a carriage
But Paradise has been given by God
As they received a truly Heavenly marriage.

Moira M Michie

Vocation

They tried to constrain me
But my dance sprang from within,
Propelling, impelling me to reach out to
the other,
Stretching and expanding the limits of heart
and soul,
Embracing, enfolding, and finally encompassing
Suffering humanity across the world.

Glenna Towler

Memories Of A Beautiful Princess

As beautiful and graceful as a swan,
She brought happiness into this world.
Now she has sadly departed,
From this world, to a beautiful paradise.

Memories of her good deeds are in our minds,
Her warm and tender ways.
To find another woman like her is impossible,
She was so beautiful and unique.

The whole world mourns for our lovely princess,
How quickly she left us in torment.
Our world will never be the same,
But she will be remembered eternally.

She brought smiles to even the saddest of faces,
The warmth in her heart could have lit
a thousand fires.
And like her kindness stay alight forever,
Warming up the entire world with her love.

She was never selfish, everyone else was put
before herself,
She was such a generous, thoughtful person.
In our hearts she will remain forever,
Alive and full of passion.

She shone with beauty and radiance,
We all loved and admired her.
But we never did show her how much we cared,
And now it is too late.
Memories of a beautiful princess.

Lisa Frost (14)

Queen Of Hearts

Rough autumn came too soon and seized
The rose of summer
Before her petals were unfurled
In mellowed splendour,
A rose encapsuled in our hearts
Forever vibrant,
The Queen of Hearts of all the world!

Denise Margaret Hargrave

Diana

My tribute to Princess Diana is in praise
of her warm human side,
In dealing with sick children, Diana let her
heart be her guide,
Her hugs, were a legion, as was sitting
on her knee,
Comfort was passed by a handshake, I think
you will agree,
I did admire her courage, when let down by
so-called friends,
Those hurtful remarks remembered, to her
journey's end,
Princess Diana, was a loose cannon,
a dangerous woman I recall,
No-one jumped in to defend her, least of all
the Royals,
When Princess Diana, was going through
a bad patch all sorts of rumours grew,
But Diana, in a witty speech said, her head
was not down the loo!
Princess Diana's greatest treasures, was not
a glittering tiara, or a sparkling diamond ring,
No, her greatest treasures, were
Prince William and Prince Harry with their
boyish grins,
The hush of the crowds, the applause, with
flowers being thrown on the hearse,
This is unusual, or perhaps a new trend,
this is Britain at its best,
Princess Diana was beautiful, had charm, and
dress sense, with style of her own,
No wonder those flowers kept arriving as soon
as her death was known,
God gave peace, Princess Diana, you are
now and forever in his care,
Buried on an island, your family's choice
away from the camera's glare!
Special flowers had a card that said 'Mummy'
as on her coffin they lay,
Their sad tribute to Diana, and
Prince William and Prince Harry's worst day,
So who's sorry now? Who back-pedalled
when they saw the tributes of flowers laid down
Who's sorry now?:

Dinah Matthew

August 31st 1997

Today is a day of great sadness
Our Princess Diana has died,
Thousands of people laid flowers
And millions more of them cried.
Her life had been filled with sadness
She married the heir to the throne,
She gave him two wonderful children
But the press couldn't leave her alone.
Princess Diana our Queen of Hearts
Was loved both at home and afar,
Her tireless work for charity
Had made our Princess quite a star.
Her private life was unhappy
Rejected by Charles from the start,
But she had to be strong fro her children
When Prince Charles had broken her heart.
For once in her life she was happy
When Dodi Al Fayed made her smile,
He took her away from her troubles
Where she was content for a while.
When leaving a restaurant in Paris
With Dodi her 'knight' by her side,
And hounded again by photographers
Set out for that last fateful ride.
Our modern day Mother Theresa
Courageous and strong to the end,
Lives on happily high up in heaven
With Dodi, her real special friend.

Nicky Handley

Diana, Always

In our hearts
in our minds
forever with us
for all of time.
You were an angel
a gift from above
you gave us happiness
and so much love.
You were our saviour
our hopes and dreams
you will always be
remembered
for your smile that
beamed.
You gave so much
to people everywhere
you really did
truly care.
You were full of laughter
full of fun
your heart was as bright
and as big as the sun.
You were an example
of how kind we could be
we must carry that on
now that your spirit
is free.
But how will we cope
and who will show us the
way
when you left us
it darkened our days.
There is a pain
in our hearts
hurt in our souls
all we have left
is a big empty hole.
We won't be the same
now you're not here
all we are left with
is our sorrowful tears.
The world will miss you
for the loss of a friend
I cannot believe it has come
to an end.
It isn't right
you should be here
you had so much to give
for so many years.
You will always be with us
when we look in
our hearts
but surely this wasn't the
time
you were meant to part.
We will miss you
for the rest of all time
the good that you did
we will keep in our minds.
You were a Legend
whose life will live on
because you're not here
doesn't mean that you're gone.
We will love you forever
and keep every part
for you are quite simply
Queen of
Our
Hearts.

Diana, Princess of Wales
You will be missed.

Caroline Amess

Diana

Diana our bright and shining star,
The people's own beloved queen,
We thought nothing could mar,
What has now become a dream.

For in our hearts you'll always stay,
Forever shining through,
And whatever comes our way,
We always will love you.

We know that life must go on,
Though our love will never cease,
And now that you are gone,
Diana rest in peace.

Sheila E McMillan

To The People's Princess

(To Diana, Princess of Wales.
May you and Dodi rest in peace. Always to be remembered forever in our hearts.)

Silence the cameras
Close up the lens
There will be no more pictures of you again
Hold the papers
Let nothing else be said
Now the world knows that you are dead.
Dressed in black
The mourning starts
Pay tribute to the Queen of Hearts
Gone now to a better place
No more intrusions will you face
Farewell from me to England's best
Now finally let the cameras rest.

Anita Farrington

The Melody Lingers

Vulnerable and young
Her melody will continue
to be sung

She touched hearts
From every race and age

Wherever she went
With her support, charm and encouragement

A devoted mother
Though a troubled wife
With the help of therapies
Battled through to succeed

And as we look up to the skies
To mourn and pray
We must confess . . .
Too late
We valued in her brief life
Our compassionate
Princess!

Tamar Segal

Princess Of The People

Rest in peace our gracious Princess
Your work is over now
They must have missed you up above
We'll meet again somehow

Oh Princess of the people
You passed by us today
All the people they were holding flowers
Which were strewn across your way

And our hearts were filled with sadness
Which we've never known before
Sorrow for your children who have lost their mother
And we've no Princess anymore

For the length of your procession
You never were alone
Your people adorned your hearse with flowers
All along your route to home

Never be a sadder day in London
For your funeral so many have come
What a cruel reminder we are mortal
But Lord Thy will be done

God bless you our Diana
Your death tore us apart
But you'll always hold a special place
In every person's heart.

Fred Tighe

A Star Shines Brightly

Diana, Princess of Wales,
fair lady of children's fairy tales
though no longer with us in the flesh
you still live on in hearts and minds afresh.
And when I look out at the stars tonight
and see one twinkling,
bigger and brighter than the rest.
I call it the Diana star,
reflecting your image from afar
and that is the one, I love the best

Doris Dobbins

A Burning Candle

A burning candle that burns bright,
giving out light, and spreading knowledge
is truly a magnificent sight.
Over time as it burns slowly,
you can see that the light it gives out is for you,
it's to make your life brighter.
But as this candle completely melts, I think of
only one thing, and that is the bright light that
comes from the candle represents the 17 years of
your life that you gave to our country -
United Kingdom.
The joys of watching people smile and the
sorrow that comes from the world, is enough
to make, anyone think twice about dedicating
their life to help others, so I just want to say . . .
The bright light that you gave out over the
years, will always live in the hearts of those
people you have touched and helped!

Jyoti Patel

Forever In Our Thoughts (William and Harry)

We feel your loss
We feel your pain
In grief and sorrow
We extend a wrap of warmth
A sadness has engulfed us all
Man, woman and child alike
To you both our sympathy lies
Words we offer in comfort
Our love and compassion will remain loyal
Be brave, be strong
Our thoughts are with you both always
One may take comfort from the other
May our flowers and cards cushion the pain
We the public share your grief.

Helen Nelson

Diana - England's Rose

You were great
and you were kind
There's nobody else like you
we could ever find.

You filled people's hearts full of joy,
you could do this to anybody,
it might have been man,
woman, girl or boy.

You could brighten and lift
people's spirits, through their
illnesses, wounds and pains,
just by talking to them or calling their names.

Diana, you had a special talent that
nobody else had,
I'm sure you made people very happy
and very glad.

But now it is so sad, that you have to die,
and so we have to say
farewell Diana, and goodbye.

So, last of all, I have to thank you
Diana, for what you have done on earth
and I have to say, you have been the kindest,
most wonderful woman since your birth.

Jamie Redding (12)

A Prayer For A Princess

Our Lady,
You have touched us with your spirit of
grace and love.
Breathed life on us anew;
Freely, you showed us how to give,
In our hour of need, help us to find the strength
to tread in your path and in our own way, make
the World a better place.

Maureen Owen

The Fairy-Tale Princess

Shy and vulnerable, she entered our hearts,
Marrying a man of great power.
Now, when we feel this sadness inside,
We recall that memorable hour.

She stole the hearts of everyone,
From the United Kingdom to Perth.
She was the Eighth Wonder of the World,
Loved by everyone on this earth.

She went beyond the line of duty,
To help anyone in need,
The sick she would look after,
The hungry she would feed.

Even in the times of pain,
She put on a smile.
Always in the 'Public Eye',
Always under trial.

The nicest person you could ever have met,
Tried to help everyone she saw,
But this caring nature that she had
The 'Press' saw as a flaw.

She had smiling, sparkling eyes,
Her face never showed a frown.
But the 'Press' did all they could
To put our Princess down.

They would never let her,
Live her life the way it should be.
They tried to control her all the time.
They would not let her be free.

Now, for this fairy-tale Princess,
Our nations mourn together
For this wonderful woman,
Who will be remembered forever.

Her two sons are left behind
To face the struggles, the pain.
We pray for them, they're in our hearts,
As our tears fall like rain.

Our beautiful Princess Diana
Who will never be replaced,
Was taken from us, when for the first time
it seemed,
With happiness she was graced.

So now our Fairytale Princess,
Is looking after us from above.
The mother, the helper, the carer, the sharer,
The peacemaker, the dove.

Rachael Taylor (15)

The Passing Of A Princess

I woke up on Sunday
And they said that you had gone
I just couldn't believe it
It's so terribly wrong.

I read in the paper
The real awful truth
And saw from the pictures
The heart-wrenching proof.

I'm so sorry Diana
That your life had to end
You were a saviour to us all
A true loyal friend.

Our hearts are all broken
And deeply distressed
Because you were so wonderful
Just simply the best.

So now you're in heaven
With Dodi your friend
I wish you both eternal happiness
That will never end.

Now your beautiful face
We will never see again
It has left us all crying
And so full of pain.

So rest now sweet Princess
Your memory lives on
We will never forget you
Even though you have gone.

Gary Long

Princess Diana

Diana was a lovely girl,
Her last weeks she spent in a whirl.
Prince Charles never loved her from the start
That's one of the reasons for deciding to part.
In her marriage there wasn't much joy
Only when she gave birth to each boy.
Her sons will feel grief and pain
But they are young and will live again.
She showed her sons the other way of life
How others live through trouble and strife.
She hoped one day when 'Wills' was King
Things she taught him would mean something.
She was good and showed kindness true
Spent time with the crippled, sick and
homeless too.

Doing it alone how she planned
Trying hard to get landmines banned.
Pictures taken and gowns she wore,
She fitted the name Princess more and more.

It was a terrible and tragic way
How her end came, that awful day.
Nations were shocked and full of tears
This day will be remembered for many years
For Diana was loved by almost everyone
And won't be forgotten now she's gone.
The good die young so they say
But sad as it is, God has just had his way.

The sun shone down with no sign of showers
And no-one has ever seen so many flowers.
As we watched your coffin go slowly by
We had no tears left so we couldn't cry.
People lined your path from beginning to end
Everyone there was saying goodbye
to a friend.
And as you passed there was no sound
Diana, and both your boys did you proud.
Your brother in tribute to you
Let his true feelings come boldly through.
His thoughts and what he said surely will be
Written to go down in history.
Back home and which is for the best
Your body has now been laid to rest,
In surroundings so beautiful and serene,
It's surely the fit place for the people's Queen.

Gwen Smith

Diana
Queen Of Hearts

On 6th September 1997
Is when our Princess went up to heaven
Up in the sky her star will glitter
Leaving many below feeling angry and bitter
Why do you take the beautiful ones?
Leaving behind two heartbroken sons
She was so full of life, too young to depart
To us she was the Queen of Hearts
No-one will ever take her place
Such a caring Lady such a beautiful face
A daughter, a sister, a mother, a wife
She did so much good, in her short life
The Nation's in mourning, under a cloud
Princes William and Harry stood regal
and proud
They can't understand why she had to die
Only in private do they sit and cry
Forever her memory will linger on
Although in our hearts we know she has gone
To a far better place up in the sky
God bless you and keep you Princess Di.

Sue Hamilton

Diana - The Legend

Most caring person who ever lived,
Diana our best friend,
Now lay in tranquillity,
The legend will never end.

We thank thee Lord for Diana,
Who held the world in her arms,
Helping those in need,
And using her great charms.

Her warmth always surrounded us,
And never would let go,
Even in the darkest nights,
Diana's love would glow.

Those people whom you met,
You'd be utmost in their mind,
Remembered for your smiles,
And for being ever kind.

We all say farewell,
As our beloved Diana departs,
YOU achieved what you wanted,
You are the Queen of Hearts.

Christopher Downs (13)

Portrait Of Diana

Such beauty beyond imagery
captures the eye
Reassures me of love forever
In embracing arms
I hold you so dear

Tears for you
colour my world
As I follow in your footsteps
never to grow old,
And the picture is seen - vividly!

Francis Paul Farnworth

Diana

Gentle Lady, whose love and affection,
Has captured the world.
Leaving humanity, speechless by,
Your premature and unwarranted demise;
Numbed and saddened to a degree unknown
by many,
Your absence has, united the world in sorrow,
Leaving people thinking hard as to why?
These dreadful things need happen.
An emptiness and a great Miss-you-ness,
Overshadows each one of us at this time.
Unable to comprehend the reasons as to why,
You were snatched away from us too soon.
Recalling your radiant smile,
The sparkle in those beautiful blue eyes,
We cry, realising we shall see them no more;
Touched by your unceasing concern for the
sick and needy,
Remembering how many people you brought
new hope to.
You always gave all of yourself during
these times,
We can only be thankful for the years you
graced our world,
Even though we wish with all our hearts,
it could have been for longer.
Still in your tender years, such a perfect
image to behold;
Both externally and internally,
Unforgettable, 'Sweet Princess' you will
remain in our hearts,
Remembered always for your tender,
loving touch.

Amanda-Lea Manning

Hug

Gone now
I feel only sorrow
Concern
For your children
For their tomorrow
You would not wish
Anyone to hate
Or retaliate
With a simple hug
You showed how easy
It is to love
To forgive
You were not perfect
You did not hide
In a pretentious world
You walked amongst us
A Queen disguised as a Princess
Gaining back the love you showed
Tenfold
Not knowing you were
Our special shining star
Diana, Princess of Wales.

J Robson

Sombre Days

September morn,
sun arising changing our lives
leaving us in mourning.
A gift from heaven you cupped our hearts,
but now . . .
You depart.
Can we ever again, be the same?
Full of hope,
full of love for one so special.
Our doubts,
our fears are trebled without guidance to
light the world's path healing.
Our Diana.
Divine Invincible Angel of Nation. Amen . .

T A Peachey

Tribute To Diana

How great a woman
Could walk on earth.
An angelic smile, with divine beauty.
Kind and thoughtful.
An angel in disguise.
Caressing the sick, to give them hope
Giving them love, for what they had lost
An angel we suddenly lost.
The sky darkened, as we shed a tear.
For the tears that we shed
A stream of flowers, began to appear.
Flooding the land, from end to end,
With a heavenly scent.
The stars above
Shall become, eternal flames
Burning the dark sky, into light.
Hearts begin to bleed.
As she's laid to rest
God bless her soul
For ours, she once blessed
Her name, we shall not forget
As it's carved, deep in our hearts.
With elegance and harmony.
The choirs sing, as people pray.
Remembering an angel.
For whom, her name, we'll remember.
DIANA.

Richard Wolfendale

Diana Princess Of Wales

D is for Devotion and affection
I is for Inner love and kindness
A is for Assurance and confidence you gave
N is for Nobody was too high or low to whom
you gave your love too
A is for All the people who you brought love and
kindness to in your life.
Our Diana

Ronald Finnighan

A Friend Of Friends

A heart so very heavy
With love and interpretation
For those that were reached out to,
In many different ways

No matter what the suffering
A helping hand, and a cuddle
Wasn't far away when needed
To ease a plight of compassion

From one side of the globe to the other,
The work was never-ending,
But oh, what pleasure it brought
In helping different charities along the way.

This life is now no more
Laid to rest in God's Kingdom
With lots left still to achieve,
But sadly, cannot be completed

All our memories will linger
For a Princess dearly missed,
And maybe through the following years
Will we come to terms with our loss.

S J Davidson

A Tribute To Diana Princess Of Wales

A beautiful fairytale princess
From a fairytale country,
You were a dream come true,
An inspiration to its people;
Now a loss to the world
The saintly Queen of Hearts
You sure moved mine
You touched my hand, you smiled serene.
Now an angel in the sky
Smile down on me
And fill me anew, I miss you so much,
I cherish your memory
And I always will.
God bless you.

Catherine Mary Smerdon

To Diana

How dark this night,
Even the stars are weeping.
The moon, aware of earth's great tragedy
Hides, silent,
In deference to that brighter light
That only yesterday illumined the world.
How short a time since darkness came.
Impossible to think it was but yesterday,
It seems, in grief and tears, to be a lifetime.
Oh how earth grieves.
Flowers and candles like a girdle round the earth
Speak of love.
Were ever hearts and minds so stunned,
Blood so chilled as on this day.
As one the nation mourns.
The bonds of grief unite like bands of steel.
Heart against heart folk stand
United in pain and a million different memories.
Surely love like this will soar to Heaven's gates.
Rest well sweet Diana, assured that in death
As in life, every heart is yours
And ever will be.

Peggy Adams

A Tribute To Princess Diana

You gave your all,
To the people.
Even when in distress
You found this gave you,
Strength to carry on -
To love others
To give them hope and joy
To help the sick and elderly
To get the Ban of Mines
Your inspiration to others,
Will be remembered -
The whole World over
A True Mother
The Queen of Hearts
Now in God's hands at Peace.

Gladys Davenport

Diana - The People's Princess

Diana was a princess everyone loved,
now God has seen fit to take her above,
but why take her so young and in her prime?
Surely God, it was not really her time?
There was so much more she could have done,
and what about William and Harry, her
precious sons,
right now they must feel that their lives
are undone,
wondering why God has taken their
precious Mum,
They loved her dearly, that much is true,
so why did you take her God, to be with you,
for once she had found happiness in her life,
and I think Dodi would have taken her for
his wife.
It's such a shame that they should die,
and only you, God, will ever know why.
She as gentle, loving, kind and true,
and now God, she rests with you.

Anne Adams

For A Princess

I behold an angel in a golden sky.
With a halo of love,
She looks down to see
The grand bouquets spread throughout a
grieving world.
She smiles,
Her heart beaming with joy.
She has compassion for those in tears -
She has compassion for those whose ills
She has helped to heal.
A light has departed from the Earth,
But in the heavenly fields a new soul is born.
We know
Her memory will never die.
We know
Her spirit is eternal - shining - at peace . . . .
For evermore.

Keith Barnard

Eternal Love

In love divine for the world to see
Our Princes Diana meant so much
to you and to me.

God Almighty graced her
With a caring wonderful nature
Whose very Angel Personality
Gave love and hope to humanity.

Dear Diana, our Fairy-tale Royal Princess
In her great gift and role as a wife and a Mother
Showed in this greatest gift from God above
Mother love for Prince William and Prince Harry
Also in love for children everywhere
In them she will be loved and remembered
Forever

Joy and Sadness tinged her life
Yet, she held her head up high
In dignity Brave Caring Diana reached her goal
Blessed by Mother Teresa
In her gift for help to the Rich, the Poor
and the Needy

A candle of love that will always be aflame
In her Epitaph wonderful Diana
is loved and remembered in Eternal
love for everyone

. . .

Most of all she touched the lives of people all ages
Now our Princess is resting peacefully
In Jesus forever more
In her beloved island home carpeted in a million
flowers
Where she is free and bluebirds sing
Such love shown by humanity to our
Princess of Hearts
And in Children everywhere praying and giving.

Maureen J Archibold

The People's Princess

Sunday morning the people cry,
The news-flash said we've lost poor Di.
Her short blonde hair and eyes of blue.
The Country of England don't know what to do.

Killed in a car crash on their way home.
Diana and Dodi were not alone.
The love they had no-one could have more.
The paparazzi closed their door.

Poor William and Harry heard Charlie say.
'My grown up boys Mummy's gone away'
She adored her boys from head to toe.
Our sweet Diana why did you go?

You worked so hard for your charities.
Everyone worshipped you, they fell to their knees,
Why did our God take you away,
William and Harry have so much to say.

We'll miss you Di with all our heart.
Your memory and us will never part.
'Cos every day we'll think of you,
William and Harry of them too.

We said goodbye on Saturday,
The black limousine drove you away.
A place of rest you are today.
Your own little island far away.

No more photos will they get of you,
They'll leave you alone, what you asked them to do.
So rest in peace our sweet Princess,
Your memory lives on, you were the best.

M Craven

Diana, Our Princess Of Wales

A friendly smile, a warm embrace,
A loving Mum, a beautiful face,
And on this day the sunshine beams
As you sail away to your Isle of Dreams.

Sandra Sharp

Diana The Lady We Love

First a Lady, then a Princess,
To all of us you were the best.
We'll never see one like you again,
You'll always be with us, and with us you'll reign.
Supreme on high you're not alone,
You sit with God on your Princess' throne,
To watch over us the people you love,
We look to the heavens and know you're above.

We know you were our Queen of Hearts,
And was dedicated to every part
Of everything that you stood for,
The sick, the homeless and the poor,
You will forever be in our minds,
You found such joy with all mankind.
To have that snatched away from you
In your short life you were good and true.
So goodnight Diana and God bless
You're safe in God's hands and there you'll rest,
For all of your eternity,
To be at peace and harmony.

Edna Adams

Diana

D iana you were the finest jewel in England's golden crown.
I n your short life Princess of the People you shone.
A lways ready to show the world you cared.
N ow and forever your goodness and beauty will still live on.
A s heaven claims back its brightest star to wear.

Pauline Christina Knight

Diana

Light shining like a star
People you touched, felt your warmth

You a giver not a taker
Maker of dreams you made them come true

High or low, always you inquired
Wanted to know, caring

Light's gone out
You've faded away

Someone's selfishness
Makes the words hard to say

You so young, leaving sons
A Nation grieves, sorrow is their tomorrows

You touched millions, with your leaving
Song written about you, words happy and sad

You with the smile, pleasant with your presence
Somehow had to leave and go to heaven.

Dennis Turner

Diana

(Tribute to Diana Princess of Wales written
especially for the Princes William and Harry)

Diana was like a butterfly
She spread her wings and learnt to fly
She fluttered her wings from heart to heart
Bringing love and beauty to worlds apart
With so much love she did much good
Proud to be doing what she could
But much too soon to Heaven she's flown
Leaving us all but not alone
In years to come and you should die
Then off to Heaven you will fly
Who will be waiting at those pearly gates
With arms outstretched and smiling face
Your mother Diana all beauty and grace
To hold you forever in her embrace.

With much sadness and love.

Jean

Nos Star

The thunder roared,
The lightning flashed,
The mountains called out!
There's something wrong.
Then, the bad news -
'Yes, she has gone,'
The Lady of our land . . .
The choir in the valley stopped singing . . .
The Welsh were weeping because,
The Lady of our land has gone . . .
Bless you, Lady of the land . . .
But, Diana, we will never forget you . . .
So, we will lay the flag of our land
to the steps of heaven for you,
The Lady of our land . . .
The Welsh all love you, because you are
Diana, our Princess,
Always in our hearts . . .
We will carry your memory with pride and joy,
FOREVER,
You will always be,
The Lady of our land . . .

Richard Beck (14)

To Princess Diana

Angel to the sick and suffering,
comforter of those in pain,
loved by everyone who knew you,
shall God give us your like again?
Yours, indeed, an ageless beauty,
reflected in both word and deed,
love, compassion, understanding,
sympathy for those in need!
Let us learn from your example,
though, at first, we don't succeed;
who could possibly replace you?
Follow your unselfish creed?

Noel Egbert Williamson

Lady Di

You came into our lives a Princess
You leave with shock and wonder.
We thought you had finally found
happiness in Dodi.
But your happiness was short-lived.

At least you were with the one you loved
when tragedy struck.
We all hope and pray that you are with him now
and for evermore.
The only sadness is for your two sons who are left
behind to cope with the loss of their beloved
mother and friend.

Our thoughts and prayers are with them both
you gave so much to so many people
those who were lucky enough to meet you can
only begin to feel the loss that William and Harry
feel.

You were an inspiration to many and you will
never be forgotten
You always put people especially the old, the
young and the sick first -
Even though you suffered so much unhappiness
you were always there for other people.

I never had the chance to meet you but I feel that
I know you.
But I still feel very unhappy about the very tragic
way you had to die.
They always say the good die young . . .
God knows he has got one of the best in you
I hope and pray that wherever you are, you are
with those you loved who have left this world and
entered the next.

I hope that Princes William and Harry can learn
to accept your death given time.
Taking a little comfort in the fact that you were
happy.
That you had finally found some happiness with
Dodi.

At least now you are out of the way of the
photographers forever, you can be what you want
when you want.
The ones who followed you should be made to
pay but they won't be!
They deserve the strongest punishment available
but if you were here you would probably forgive
them as you were that kind of person.

You will be dearly missed by everyone
Our beloved Lady Di.

Lisa Hobden

Angel

Diana, you were taken from us
While still in your prime
We never said a proper goodbye
Before you were gone, forever this time.

But you gave us two special people
Your pride and joy, your two sons
And in your memory we will look
After them as you would have done.

For you gave the ordinary people
Love which meant so much
You were a Royal Princess
Who had the human touch.

Heaven reclaimed the angel
It had given us in 1961
An angel full of warmth and love
And always full of fun.

The world will always be a much
Sadder place without you near
Although your body is in Heaven
Your spirit will always be here.

Ian Fowler

Compassion Lost

My heart bleeds for an angel past
And flags the world over fly at half-mast
For faces sad and tears that fall
Like rain down cheeks both large and small
For hearts that ache and throats turned dry
And people saying why, oh why
For days turned grey as voices say
'Diana we love you so'
When no-one cared a toss, good seed
did you sow
So gently did you do God's work ever humble
to a fault
You used your station and position over
obstacles to vault
Your voice your smile worked wonders to
enhance the sick on earth
From heaven you came I'm sure into your
Royal birth
Now sadly gone but not forgot and never
could you be
You had to go this World to show
TO CARE is to be free.

John Bryan

Diana - Princess Of Wales

What sad news as dawn breaks today.
The world grieves for our lovely
Princess Diana.
Hearts broken, tears falling,
bewilderment too.
Why should she be taken in this
tragic manner?

For one who has helped and encouraged
so many,
She has been dealt a blow, she could
never deserve.
Princess of the people, loved the world over.
Severed from life in her springtime, her gift
was to serve.

Her humility shone through like a beacon,
She lit up so many lives on her way.
Forever in our memories, Diana -
Queen of Hearts.
It is for her special family and loved ones
we pray.

Gwyneth Cleworth

We Are Numb

You have been dead but a few brief weeks
and we are numb.
Thoughts of you unbidden come
Of how you were so short a time ago.
Life and laughter, that happy glow
And loving smile
All ours for just a while.

But we must carry on from day to day,
Press on regardless, as we used to say.
And maybe in our dreams sometime when
We least expect it you might come home again,
To smile and hold our hands
And maybe then our loss we'll understand.

Eileen M Lodge

Diana

Slowly you entered our hearts
filling them with love
Treading where no woman
before you had dared
Reaching out to embrace
the world's untouchables,
the forgotten, the sick,
and giving so much to so many
until there was no more to give
An empty shell
wasted by man's heartless greed
Yet still you filled
a gaping wound with yours
'Midst mountains of fragrant petals
The nation's hearts beating as one.

Kay Rainsley

To Diana

Today I went to sign the condolence book for you in the Town Hall in Leigh,
I couldn't believe the queues there were, waiting so very patiently.
No-one grumbling, no pushing, no jostling, to get to the front of the queue,
All, everyone wanted was a chance to write down their thoughts on you.
You were lovely and admired so much by people young and old everywhere,
Because you weren't afraid to step into the unknown and you were a princess who really did care.
We'll miss you more than words can ever say,
But for some reason God decided to take you away.

D Ridings

Tribute To Diana

I am not ready yet for the sun to shine
or to join with the laughter of others
I am not ready
yet to smile beyond polite
or to hold any sense of meaning to life
I am not ready
yet to notice any sparkle of nature's glory
a sunrise or darkness are the same
Life continues because I breathe
I have no will nor reason
I am not ready
yet to fully live without her in this world
She whom this nation loves
and I who love her too.

B S Hansen

Diana, Princess Of Wales

Dear Princess Di, the world and I
will mourn your loss, and wonder,
Whose fateful hand destroyed your life,
And tore our heart asunder.

No words of mine, however fine,
Could enhance your charm, and beauty,
The love and tenderness you displayed,
Outshone the light, of duty.

This nation's grief, will not be brief,
Though time may ease the pain,
For a nation's tears, will outlive the years,
At the mention of your name.

Your memory will live, for evermore,
In the hearts of the needy, and the poor,
Those were the ones, who day by day,
Heard your message, heard you say.

Give out more love, and end the pain,
We will not see your like again.
But as sure as there's a heaven above,
There you will find peace and love.

Edna Hunt

Dreams Of Light

You were the light in someone's shadow
offering laughter
Just one smile from you and they had
the light that you offered them.
Even though you have left
Your spirit lives on as each day passes.
If you look at the sky, we can see
the light that you gave others, carries on.
You were such a wonderful person
that God decided you had finished your duty
You have your freedom at last,
free as a bird.
Beautiful as a swan.

Mel Leggett

Our English Rose

An English Rose, as you were known
A perfect bud, had not yet grown
The sweetest scent upon your face
A loving smile - to any race,
The kindest colour, was in your heart
An eternal glow that won't depart
The warmest person one could know
Who made the hearts of many glow,
No riddled cancer - to you, seemed fair
For in your arms your cradle care
No saddened child you'd turn away
But hold them in a loving way
A memory true to any soul
To aim and reach their highest goal
No-one was lowly - not to you
A smile a tear would shine on through
An English Rose, that is no more
Beheld your heart forever more
This country that will mourn for thee
But oh Diana - now, you are free!

Fiona Gilpin

Diana

One true English rose
pure in heart and mind
born with no thorns
only goodness and kindness that shone from within
loved by oh so many people
born to be our Queen
yet was not to be
but you gave us two heirs
and your kindness will live on
from the love you have given them
and in every heart around the world
our Queen of Hearts you have become
the flowers placed in London Town
and all around the world when you died
showed that you were loved by everyone
So Diana, Queen of our Hearts
rest in peace now on your island in the lake.

Pauline Haggett

An Epitaph To A Real Lady

You were the one; the only one
We loved and adored, our
Treasured icon, so courageous;
Defying all adversities in a glance.

Beautiful; compulsive and ever watchful
You used your situation
For the wealth of millions,
For what does it take to give a smile
Or love to any man or woman, form or creed?

Our beloved Lady, you are
Gone now to a better place
And lay in grace and peace
Away from the ever-present and
Perverse evils of a sometimes too fast and
Modern world, that understood you
So well, yet never quite left you alone?
Goodbye our Lady, and may your spirit carry
Onward through time,
In our hearts, forever
As a lesson in love epitomised.
Goodbye.

Sue Jackett

The Bruise-Laden Sky

I think about you and I cry.
I dream about you
and so does the bruise-laden sky.
You at last found true love
and thanked whoever was above.
Together you made a handsome pair
him so dark, you so fair,
but then your happiness was taken away
and we had to face a cold dark day.
Now we walk around with eyes full of tears.
We'll remember you for years and years.
When in secret we have a cry,
we'll think of that cold dark day
when there was a bruise-laden sky.

J M Smith

Eulogy To A Princess

Diana, our loving Princess of Wales,
Your memory will remain evermore,
In our hearts and minds it will never fail,
For you were a special person, to adore,
Time and again you will return, in all ways,
Your good works to prove you were here,
For so many, they brought better days,
As you dispelled their worries and fear.

Your achievements inspired us all,
For your dream of a fairer world,
Throughout our lives, your vision to recall;
We shall strive on, your flag unfurled,
Until the innocent shall survive,
And shall not needlessly be slain;
God's little children enabled to thrive,
Not allowed to endure endless pain.

We will never forget our angel of light,
Though you have gone so far away,
Your vision will shine thro' the darkest night,
And carry us forward, by your golden ray.

Julia Eva Yeardye

In Memory . . .

Fragility, yet strength,
Borne from suffering.
Tender empathy,
Exuding compassion.
Joy tinged sadness,
Bearing hope.
Irradiation of life,
Poured out for many.
Intangible beauty,
Beheld in wonder.
Bright dancing sunbeam,
Cast now in shadow.
Cherished in memory,
Through tears with closed eyes.

Graham Wickens

Peace, Love And Diana

(Dedicated in loving memory for Diana,
Princess of the people Queen of our hearts)

Thank you God from high above
For creating Diana for us to love
You picked her out from all the rest
Because you knew we'd love her best

Her gentle touch that gave us hope
Her courage showed us how to cope
She tried to help us where she could
She cared for us, she understood

You knew the joys that she would bring
She made us laugh and cry and sing!
Compassion that she'd never hide
Whenever she was by our side

Beauty that no Rose could touch
We loved Diana very much
Her smile that once lit up the room
Leaves a nation, now in gloom

Our Queen of Hearts she'll always be
Remembered for eternity
For watching us where once she'd been
A golden Angel stands, serene.

Nikki George

Poetic Tribute To Diana

I loved her looks
I loved her ways
I loved her caring
I loved the days
When in the papers
Her face I would see
Great pleasure and comfort
Would be given to me.
To read the news now
Seems a trifle by far
For the light has gone out
On my favourite Star.

A K Swann

God Lent Us An Angel

God lent us an Angel,
Diana was her name,
Then one day he took her back,
To Heaven from whence she came.

Her love and warmth lit up our world,
Her smiles and charm shone through,
Diana was the Queen of Hearts,
Our love for her just grew.

We never thought she'd leave us,
God only takes the best,
Diana how we miss you,
Now you're laid to rest.

God's taken back his Angel,
We're left behind to grieve,
A nation that's in mourning,
Why did she have to leave?

The thirty-first of August,
Will always spring to mind,
It was the day Diana left us,
This world she left behind.

We'll always remember our Diana,
She's in our thoughts to stay,
Sleeping in a better place,
God bless, sleep tight, we pray.

Amen

Susan May Downs

Tribute To Diana

One tear fell from heaven.
And the whole earth cried.
Stunned into silence
So young so beautiful
'Dear Diana,'
Touching hearts by mere chance.
Those shy eyes, my princess
Given to work, and so did.
With time for all
Dear, Dear, Diana.

Mick Philpot

Chronicle Of Memories

Your name incites fond memories
a teenager so innocent and shy,
a fairytale wedding,
a spectacular dress,
veiled, was your beautiful smile.

Adoringly we watched you grow,
such startling beauty and grace,
your elegance was unsurpassed
and your vibrancy as a mother admired.

You camouflaged your sadness well,
we knew nothing of your pain,
then we learned of your own self-doubts,
your secret ills and loss in love,
It broke all our hearts that we could not help.

Dying children cradled in your arms,
your hands touched a man with AIDS,
your compassion truly knew no bounds,
you addressed our ignorance and fears,
we the guilty, hung our heads in shame.

You are dead.

Stunned silence befalls us all,
a nation and a world are in mourning,
seas of flowers and oceans of tears
for a cherished princess,
but forever now a Queen in Heaven.

Jacki McEneaney

A Tribute To Diana
(The nation's Queen of Hearts)

Your kindness was a loving word
Your kindness was a helping hand
Loving persons beneath her rank
Performing so many difficult tasks
Visiting the sick, young and old
She succeeded with flying colours,
To me she was not only the Queen of Hearts
But a saint in disguise
May she rest in peace
Never to be forgotten.

Gilbert Harford

Diana

From that clay
there came no sign.
Almost a child
and enjoying
the flattery of photos,
the hugs of children
the laughter
of true friends.
Changing with the years
as springtime wife
a baby breeder
then unrequired
thrust into suffering.
Reactions all askew
staircase falls
Bulimia
and careless men.
Claustrophobic
you burst
outwards to hold
the broken child
to touch the AIDS stricken.
Nursing the legless one
of selfish wars,
the Christ-missed children
you though scorned
and hounded,
you from naive clay
surprised us all.
Death in a flash
came too soon
but now peace
a nation holds your hand.

Alan Graham

Diana - (Voice Of The World)

Such a need for life -
Such a loss in death -
The world lost its voice -
When she lost her breath.

W G Royce

Final Journey Of A Princess

A heart-warm sea of emerald and cerulean
flowers
Surged hard against cliffs of rock-cold faces,
Thawing hard-frozen facades,
Drawing salt water from grief-stricken stone.

The bloom-scented air,
Loaded thick with bursting silence,
Weighed down with solid sorrow,
Trembled as a southerly wind blew.

And out from the petalled sea,
Floating on waves of white blossoms,
Gently steered by motherly wind,
A golden mermaid came forth.

A red rose river led her northward,
Led her home. And as flowers parted,
A radiance rippled outwards in her wake,
Rippled outwards to cliff faces, halting
salty erosion.

And, long after the river had run dry,
Long after the sea-bed had been unveiled
to sky's eye,
Long after the southerly wind had breathed
its last,
A radiance rippled outwards in her wake.

Bruno D'Itri

Untitled

There is a feeling of emptiness inside,
a sadness that wraps itself around us,
in our moments of silence.
We dare not think,
for to think brings tears.
We must remember the smile,
the beautiful eyes,
the kind heart.

Richard Irvine

Many Years Of Love

Many years of love, of anger and of pain,
Many years of sorrow, of hope and of blame.
Many years of pictures, we felt we knew you well,
Many years of being betrayed, of 'kiss 'n' tell'.

Many years of caring, the joy that you brought,
Many years of sheer hard work, the battles
that were fought.
Many years of comfort for the old and the meek,
Many years of giving love to the young and
the weak.

Many years of friendship for ones you
hardly knew,
Many years of grace and beauty that were
unique to you.
Many years of pride for your precious ones,
Many years of laughter with your growing sons.

Now not so many years you had,
Too far and few between,
But in our hearts for many years,
You'll always be our Queen.

Susan W Robinson

Memories

You only have one Mother
Patient kind and true
No one in this whole wide world
Will be as true as you.

We hold you close
And there you will stay
Within our hearts
To walk with us
Throughout our lives
Until we meet again.

You are still with us
Still in our thoughts
And always in our hearts
But there you only have one mother
Till death do we part.

Janet Brown

Diana Princess Of Wales

Diana Princess of Wales
You will never be forgotten
You're one in a million we all love you
Those little children you went to see
Hold them in your loving arms for a cuddle

People with AIDS you held their hands
You gave them love and comforted them
You visited the homeless with your sons
People will miss you our loving Princess

In Paradise together you and Dodi
Praying now you'll both
Be able to Rest In Peace
You've left behind sweet memories

Lisa Wyatt

Diana

A Rose
Whose petals
Will never
Wither
A Rose
Whose scent
Remains
Forever
A light
But hidden
From view
Who shines
Brighter
Now
Than ever
Somewhere
In Eden
The only place
For a rare gem.

Simone Ryder

The Blossoming Of Diana
The White Rose

Diana you came into our lives
as a shy violet hiding your beauty amongst
the leaves. We knew you were there your
perfume filled the air around us.

Like a snowdrop you bowed your head
but your pure beauty still shone through.

Your sparkling eyes as blue as the
forget-me-not shone with compassion.

Your tall slim figure like the lily
which you loved.

As fragrant as the exotic orchid
you wore in your hair.

You were always there.

As the English Rose your beauty grew.
Rising above the cruel thorns
to emerge into the sunlight.

So will you always be remembered
as we covered you with flowers
to rest in peace in the garden
of your home.

Safe in the Arms of God.
And always in our hearts.
Rest in Peace. English Rose.

Pauline Morris

Diana's Lullaby

Once in every million years
the world is steeped in shame.
Its people cry a million tears
as love reveals its name

Once in every million years
a new bird sings its song
and though death deals its mighty blow
the melody lives on.

The melody is soft and sweet
to new-born babies' ears,
Diana's loving lullaby
to wash away the tears.

And time and tide mean nothing now
The strength is in the song.
Her lullaby of life and love
Forever marches on.

Margaret Wendt

The Silent Scents Of Remembrance

(Written after a visit to the Palaces of Kensington and Buckingham and St James and to Harrods, 3.9.97)

I will always remember
The sombre silence
The incredible quiet
Enveloping such crowds of ordinary people
The silent vigil and gentle tears of everyone
around me
The sharing of sorrow in whispers with
complete strangers
The very serene homage that I felt so privileged
To be part of.
I will always remember
The scented air
Perfumed with musk and frankincense and myrrh
from so many candles
The deep and unforgettable scent of so many
white lilies
The sweet aroma from such a sea of flowers
Pervading the Park and Palaces and along
The Mall and in front of Harrods
Drifting from the trees and the railings and from
the ground and the pavements
Into the hearts of her people and beyond.

I will always remember.

Barbara Keeling

BBC1 London, September 6th 1997

Today, we in our millions, saw
The scarlet tunics and the gold
Which found no place in her.
We saw the million sombre faces
Of the shocked and silent crowd
Who had come unbidden
To mourn her loss
As the cortege cast long shadows
In the low September sun.

We heard the minutes counted
By one lonely tolling bell,
The slow clop of unhurried hooves
Which gave us time to ponder
As she passed:
The jingle of the harness,
At times, the sound of muffled weeping.
The grind of heavy wheels
Across Horse Guards Parade.

And, amidst it all,
High above the trappings,
The jewel, which was Diana,
Glowed in the autumn light,
Wrapped in the Royal Standard,
Crowned by the waxen white
Of her loved ones' flowers,
As we said goodbye
To the funny, fragile, loving girl -
The queen who never was
Save, as she wished to be
In our hearts, this day
And in a special way,
For ever.

John Matthews

A Fond Farewell To Our Queen Of Hearts

The nation awoke with a painful thunderbolt
Realisation was too far away as numbness filled our senses.
As the news broke:
'Diana, Princess of Wales is Dead'.
We knew this was a cruel lie,
The people did not have a Princess of Wales;
We had a Queen of Hearts
And we knew our Queen could not be dead.

But the truth became ever apparent
As the flowers of hope poured into Kensington Palace.
A united hope that she is happy now,
A dream the nation must share forever;
That Diana; Queen of the People is at last,
Where and with whom she wants to be.
We cannot deny; the end was all too tragic,
But we must believe in sweet Destiny.
We must hope and pray our Queen is now free.

They may have stripped her of the HRH title,
But to the people; to the country;
Diana was above and beyond royalty.
For she knew how to communicate,
How to care, how to love - how to make things happen.
Some say Diana was alienated from the Royal Family,
I think the nation believes this too.
In reality; there will never be another Diana.
Farewell Queen of Hearts - You did make a difference.
With love; Your family of millions. x x x

Matt Valentine

The Smile Of Love

A shy young girl worked at a nursery
Loving children, all of her life,
She met, and was courted by a Prince
Who then made her his wife.

It was a fairytale wedding
A beautiful bride on that July day.
With plenty of laughing and cheering
And a kiss, on the balcony - so gay.

A son was born soon after
Who would eventually be Heir to the Throne.
Two years later, he had a brother,
So now, he was no longer alone.

Their mother loved them deeply
She shared their sorrows and joys.
Love and happiness radiated from her,
When she was with her two boys.

Divorce and unhappiness followed,
Her life went a different way.
Her love for the young, the aged, the sick,
Was seen in her caring, each day.

Her life was to end so sudden,
Her love, still never fails.
To touch the hearts of the people,
Diana, Princess of Wales.

Joan Smith

Diana

A sweet earthly angel
On a mission of love
Was guided in goodness
By the Lord up above.

A symbol of sainthood
On an errand of hope,
A tutor of love
Showing kind ways to cope.

The people adored her,
The whole world her domain,
Some critics maligned her
And inflicted great pain.

And God's great dilemma
Was to let her remain
Or shield her from heartache
While the world mourns in shame.

Arch Lang

A Princess - And A Mother

On the sixth day of September
Whole Nations said goodbye
To a mother of two children,
Known to all as Princess Di.

People in their millions
Flocked to the Palace gate,
Hardly able to believe
The cruelty of fate.

To sign books of condolence
They stood and queued for hours.
The love she gave out they returned
With tears, poems and flowers.

And money, to her charities.
Because she was so kind,
In her memory, they will continue
The work she left behind.

In Westminster Abbey,
The words of Saint Francis' prayer,
Told that from sadness she brought joy,
Gave hope where there was despair.

We will remember a Princess
In the years to come.
But, our two young Princes
Will just remember their mum.

Pamela Evans

Simply Diana

Diana was an English Rose,
A rose beyond compare,
With beautiful complexion,
And hair so very fair.

She really was a Princess,
Spreading joy where'er she went,
Reaching out to those in need,
No barriers would she heed.

Then there was the pleasantest job,
The one she loved the best,
The one she did most willingly,
Of being a loving Mum.

Her own life sometimes wasn't fun,
But she came smiling through,
And brought to people's notice,
Things that they would rather shun.

Now she's no longer with us,
And we all feel in despair,
Especially her family,
Who loved her more than all.

But her memory will linger on,
Of the causes she has fought,
Of her comfort, care and laughter,
And her legacy of love.

Matthew J Prescott (12)

Happiness

Happiness is yellow
It tastes like melting toffee
It smells like cut grass
It is a bowl of juicy fruit
It sounds like birds tweeting,
and thinking of the beautiful
Princess Diana.

Mark McFall (10)

The Princess Of The Lake

Lady Diana Spencer, sweetest rose, home-grown,
was picked by Charles - Heir to the Throne.
She became his wife in a fabulous gown,
and the crowds rejoiced over London town.

Sons, the young princess came to bear.
Harry and William, like his mother - fair.
Whilst his wife blossomed out in every way,
the Prince of Wales contrived to stray.

Bejewelled and lavishly gowned she went,
beautifying people's lives as if heaven-sent.
A touch, a glance, embrace or smile,
brought the sick and weary hope - awhile.

She traversed the world, her all she gave,
performing acts of kindness, so calm and brave.
Stripped of her title, and finally free,
from an adulterous marriage, seeped in
acrimony.

Dawned the day everyone knew by her glow,
the 'People's Princess' was romancing a beau.
Named - Dodi Al Fayed, of Egyptian blood he,
but dark stars predicted, this love couldn't be.

They died together long before their time,
amidst a mangled fusion of metal and grime.
Dressed forever in black, golden hair
nowhere grey,
inside leaden coffin, the 'Queen of Hearts' lay.

Folks bereaved wept and wailed, extolling her
worth.
Flowered shrines grew enmasse upon the
sad earth.
Candles burned from shore to shore,
for the angelic one who'd smile no more.

Now she rests at peace beneath a mound,
on an isle within her family's grounds.
No soul her place can ever take,
Diana - Lady of the Lake!

Rena Soloman

Sunday 7th September 1997 'Afternoon'

The sea of people in the Mall
Moved forward to the Palace.
Walking by the scented flowers, piled high
Posies, teddy bears, cards and sprays.
Lighting candles on the way,
Heads of children bent together
Reaching out to lay their wreaths.
All the messages say her name in love
And every photo of her beauty sends
A dart of pain, for they know
We shall ne'er see her face again.
While passing by a tree along the Mall
Its age had seen all sights of pageant,
Through happy times and the sad,
By my feet I heard a sound, - 'plop'!
And looking down I saw a leaf had dropped.
It shimmered, tinted by the delicate hues
of autumn.
I dared not pick it up nor touch its frailty.
The tree had wept and so did I.

Marlene Sarah Jones

Dear Lord Up Above

Dear Lord up above,
Please open the golden gates
For a very special angel,
An angel so beautiful and kind,
Give her golden wings
To match her heart of gold,
Plant a perfect rose,
With golden petals.
Let it bloom and grow,
Plant it in a special spot.
Don't ever let it die.
Live on forever Diana
As the perfect rose you are,
Bloom on forever Diana
Open up your petals,
Like that golden smile, we all knew.
Please call this rose
'The Golden Angel Rose'.

S Bale

Princess Diana

Diana you were the people's princess
Oh how we loved you so
Both the old and young alike
When you married Charles it was like a fairy tale
And unto you two sons were born
Who are now without a mum
You had many difficult and troubled times
In your short-lived life
But you were a very lovely person
Always reaching out to others
In their time of need

Young children you adored
And they loved you back
Your work was all worthwhile
You were making changes for the good
Then just as you had found love
And happiness in your life once again
God saw fit to take you away
The world will surely grieve for you
You will never be forgotten dear Diana
Your memory will always stay.

Pamela Jewell

Litany Of Diana

We will remember your courage
We will remember your caring
And compassion in all its strength
We will remember you Diana
Princess of Wales
Queen of Hearts
Rose of England
Help of the Needy
Comforter of the Sick
Refuge of the Homeless
Lover of Children
Friend of the World.

WHAT MAN COULD HAVE DONE MORE

Mary Seddon

The People's Princess

Our dear beloved Princess,
Was a very special soul,
She shared the grief of others,
And made it her life's goal,
She touched the hearts of millions,
And held babes in her arms,
Was truly quite unique and kind,
The Nation loved her charms,
Countless thousands paid respect,
To our Princess whom we love,
May God Bless her and her friend,
Now both, in Heaven above,
She wanted to make folks aware,
Of the suffering of many,
Whether we are rich or poor,
Or don't possess a penny,
It did not matter to this child,
Her kindness was a light,
That radiated from her heart,
And helped make this world bright,
So I make this a tribute,
To our Regal Princess Di,
You touched so many people,
With that sparkle in your eye,
Prince William and Prince Harry,
Are her two sons she adored,
May they follow in her footsteps,
With that love she always poured,
Then the Nation will stand by them,
And will love them like their Mum,
May God help them feel her presence,
For she'll always be their chum,
I pray that those two children,
Will be strong and will possess,
The courage of their Mother,
Who was a loving, kind, Princess.

Janette Campbell

Our Eternal - The Princess Diana

She walked like a model,
And smiled like a friend,
She was beauty itself,
A new Royal 'trend'.

She had the grace of a Queen,
And the style of a star,
Charisma and charm
A bodyguard and car.

A life full of sadness,
But her heart full of hope,
We loved 'Our Diana',
She showed she could cope.

Diana showed us so much,
How to fight with your heart,
How to share all your love,
How to have a new start.

Her strength was admired,
Her beauty adored,
Her bravery recognised,
For landmines outlawed.

With a new man in her life,
Di looked happy at last,
Until a Harrods' chauffeur,
Drove a car much too fast.

A fatal crash,
One August night,
Killed our Diana,
And turned out our light.

The whole world was in grief,
At the news she was gone,
But we all know in our hearts,
Her memory lives on.

Olivia Lambeth

A Queen Of Hearts

She was ours for just a little while
Our own Princess of Wales
Now sadly, we are mourning
In the Hills and in the Vales

Nations followed in her steps
To try to get wrongs righted
Our Ambassador of care and love
Wished the World to be united

She trod where others feared to tread
Despite any objection
Did a job that needed doing
And she did it . . . to perfection

A Joan of Arc of modern times
She battled on with zest
Fighting for the sick and needy
Complying with each quest

Her time with us was limited
Like a beautiful butterfly
She flew away and left us
Now we're left to wonder . . . Why?

We'll remember her as she would wish
Over the coming years
'A Queen of Hearts' without a Crown
Whilst the World wears a Coronet of Tears.

Bell Ferris

Only A Minute

It's over; just like that - no more
My soul is raw
I can't believe
My eyes - my ears
This thing - this death that takes your life.
An end to strife -
No shining light
To warm our nights.
Your beauty echoes ever on
You will live on
In hearts of ours
For love goes far.

Elizabeth Mitchell

Diana

Sleep well, sweet gentle Princess,
You've more than proved your worth;
Not just to God in Heaven,
But to all of us on Earth.
Your loving glance and tender touch,
No matter where you went,
Plainly showed to all the World,
That you were Heaven-sent.
So rest in peace, sweet Princess,
Now God has called you home;
No-one could e'er forget you,
Nor all the love you've shown.
As you, sweet gentle Princess,
Upon your island lie,
Like petals, we will blanket you,
With love that cannot die.
You shared with us your everything,
Your blessings, sorrows, joys,
Leaving us the legacy,
Of your two precious boys.
Sleep well, sleep well, Diana,
Our brightest shining star,
You made our World a better place,
Yet shimmer still afar.

Betty Taylor

Farewell To Diana

I saw the clouds scurrying along the sky
to say a last farewell to Diana.
The sunlight shimmered on the lake
breaking into a thousand fragments
like the hearts that break for Diana.
A white rose sheds dewdrop tears for Diana.
Stars shone brightly in the depth of
night,
to pay homage to Diana, and yet
though we lived through the darkest of nights
then came the dawn and the breeze with the
dawn whispered rest in peace, all is well with
Diana.

Lindy Ess

A Princess, An Angel, A Friend

Diana, was an Angel
Sent from God above,
She was the one, who helped the world,
And whom, we love so much.

She taught us, to be good,
She helped, when times were bad,
She was there for everyone,
For this we're all so glad.

Diana, still an Angel
Is in the skies above,
There she can see all of us,
And still give out her love.

Because of our Diana
I know that I have learned
To give, and to be kind.
And all the people, around the world
May have these words in mind.

To our dear Diana may you
Rest in peace. Amen.

S Kirkley

Diana

All your people wept for you.
They cheered for you, to show they care.
They prayed and sang for you,
To show you on your way,
To meet and guide
The angels in heaven

You will be greatly missed
By the poor, the maimed and ill,
You touched us all.
With your strength to fight,
People will carry on
Your good work for the needy,
Knowing you are watching,
Making sure your work
Continues the way you would want.

Don Jeffery

Parting Song For Diana

Sweet angels carried thee to thy rest
And with music was borne into
Heaven's realm
Passing along a perfumed path of love
To stay within a scented bower
England's beloved loveliest flower
The moon to watch over you at night
The sun to shine on your beautiful place
At last away from prying sight
Those bowing trees protect your grace
We'll miss forever your radiant face
Our tears will be like the rain from above
Covering you gently with our cloak of love
Dearest Diana compassion's best
Sweet angels carried you to rest
You caused a nation's heart to beat as one
Laying wreathes and cards reluctant to leave

You who'd gone
You are not here
But haven't gone
Your love lives on.

Elizabeth Ruskin

September Sadness

When the world stood still
and the stars went dim
The leaves on the trees
hung silent and still
Something happened to the world
like a knife in the heart
Such pain - such sadness
no words can impart
It's not fair to take her
she had love to share
It's not fair - we need her
to show us she cared.
Life can be ugly and so unfair
Was she too beautiful for us mortals?
Did heaven need her - too much to share?

G Tominey

To Diana

It was such a sad
And tragic day
When God sent his Angels
And took you away
He saw you were tired
And did what he thought best
So he took you to Heaven
Where he knew you could rest

You were the Queen of our hearts
And the strength of our nation
A person so caring
A great inspiration.

A people's Saviour
The sweetest love song
The memory of you
Will always live on.

A bud that never opened
If you only knew
What a difference you made
To this world
And how much this world loved you.

Samantha Jayne Eley

Princess

To hear such news that tragic day
A life so sadly snatched away
Time stood still in disbelief
While nations joined to share their grief

A solemn silence filled the air
The whole world wept in true despair
For our Princess was gone forever
Though in our hearts forgotten never

Even though now worlds apart
She's still the Queen of all our hearts
A true Princess one of their kind
Such tender warmth so hard to find

As time goes on and tries to heal
The emptiness and pain we feel
We'll think of her in celebration
With love for all her dedication

Though out of sight not out of mind
Sometimes this life is so unkind
A life we proudly once embraced
Now can never be replaced

Goodbye Diana, Princess of Wales.

Lindsey Newrick

Lament

Farewell Diana beloved.
Sharp fragments of past joys
Pierced our hearts, when your night fell
Upon the disbelieving world.
There can be no response
To mournful yearning,
Eternity has wrapped His
Heavenly mantle about you,
Protecting, loving, forgiving.
Sweet rest dear Princess.
Your earthly journey brief,
Will never be forgotten.

Cynthia Beaumont

O' Beloved Diana

O Beloved Diana, you outshone
even the brightest of stars. We
will hold you ever dear in our
hearts for you will never fade.

O Angel of grace, charm, kindness
and all good, how we grieve
at our loss unable to bear this
wretched day that lies before us.

O Sweet joy of ours, now you are
in heaven's realm, peaceful at last,
never to be forgotten, evermore to be
cherished.

Samia Chacko

A Tribute

Goodbye to our lovely Diana
Our own Princess of Wales
Who had been so kind-hearted
After all those damning tales

You lived your life for your two boys
As any mum would do
Which makes us want to hold on
To the memory of you

Sadly, we miss you
Since that fateful day
You answered the ultimate call
And tragically went away

Now that you're gone
Like a bird on the wing
Your never- fading love
Will guide us on the way

Your legend will live forever
For your humanity and will to win
As people to you were people
Not just anything

Samantha

In Memory Of Diana, Princess Of Wales

She walked in beauty,
Bright as any star,
Touching the world, with love,
As she passed by,
This 'Queen of Hearts', God lent us,
For a while,
To warm and brighten,
Earth's dark corners,
With her smile,
But though no more, her happy face,
We'll see,
Through death, she'll reign,
Queen of all hearts, forever,
In our memory.

Barbara I Grove

In Memory Of Diana, Princess of Wales

I'd like to be a mender
of all the broken hearts

I'd like to be a seamstress who
sews the things in life that
fall apart

I'd like to give smiles to those
who have no fun
I'd like to be a refuge into which
they could run

I'd like to be the water
in a dreaded drought
I'd like to have a heart
in which you'd find no doubt

I'd like to reach my hand out
for those who are about to fall
There's not one thing I'd like to be . . .
I'd like to be them all . . .

Lorraine Day

Rose In Paris

A Rose was crushed in Paris
Taken when blooming in kindness, love
and maturity,
Victim of circumstance, machine and mankind
And now blame is sought,
Is it this, is it that, is it him?
All are hounded in the hunt for retribution,
They all must pay.

God wanted this Rose in his garden
He took perfection and replanted it on high,
A blameless Rose was needed, an example
to us all,

The Rose will bloom forever
It would not have wanted 'blame',
Let the Rose rest in peace and tranquillity
Let love and forgiveness reign.

Gillian Ackers

To Diana

Our very first Princess of Wales,
Your name will live on from beyond the grave,
Because to us you were always so brave,
Someone so good, someone so kind,
Someone like you is hard to find,
The people loved you your family too,
Everyone who was in contact with you,
You were a Princess, a friend and a mother,
For to us there will never be another,
And Lady Diana you were a first Lady,
Always helpful and kind to the sick
and the needy,
And you, our Princess, though we never met,
When you spoke to us our hearts they
would melt,
But now for us our Princess has gone,
What can we do, can the world go on?
The world at a standstill, the grieving
the same,
At a wonderful person, Diana by name,
But all is not gone, all is not lost,
We'll love you forever, whatever the cost,
And now Diana as you rest in peace,
On your special island - a beautiful place,
And maybe someday when our journey
will end,
Our lovely Diana, with the Angels descend,
'Tis there we will find our Princess above,
Waiting for us, she'll shower us in love.

Iris McFarland

My Tribute For Princess Diana Is . . .

Deep is the loss we feel,
In our hearts you will always be.
All the world mourns you.
No-one will ever replace you,
Always to be remembered.

Rest in peace sweet Princess.
Goodnight and God bless.

Victoria Hogan

Earth's Rainbow Of Love

Like a torch across the sky
Shooting stars added to dreams untold
Thunder and lightning gave warnings
A Rainbow circled the earth

Like an angel with wings outstretched
Clouds rolled by echoes of love moving
Like magic all around

Heartbeats brought tears
People's thoughts stood still
Flowers forever blooming
The world dreams for-ever-as with love

Voices with feelings will ring
Bells will chime, memories will
always be there
Life as with love brought happiness
Passing - brought sorrow

The green grass and hills with
Flowers ever blooming
A loss never to be forgotten.

J S Mitchell

Our Princess

You were a bud
That opened in bloom
You married a prince
Yet your dream was shattered
But we all loved you Diana
That's what mattered
But now our flower has gone
But to the world you were the one
Whom we loved and adored
How we will miss you
That beautiful flower
That died
Now you have gone
How all the world cried
You will be sadly missed
We send you our love
Sealed with a kiss.

P M Wardle

Lady Di

A gun carriage rolled through a sea of tears
Shed by millions, on either side of
its procession
A week before our Lady riddled with fear
Left us in awe; proving there is no exception.

Death pulls on every wrist, as our sands
run out
And God plucked love, just like the last rose
Ghost fingers of the inevitable had chosen
their night
But our Lady will shine, wherever love blows.

Heaven will make a better avenue of
resting place
A place where our media, cannot knock twice
Where the archangels hover, leaving no trace
Of human quilt; which to them mere mice.

Don't cry Lady Di, your fears are cradled
by us
Your Princes shall grow, and reflect through
your majesty
Time will heal all for them, although
they'll cuss
But be proud with this world to have shared
in your destiny.

Goodbye England's Rose, alone at last
in peace
May your spirit mingle, with the
brightest saints
A globe has mourned; now it shall blow kiss
Toward your sacred island, where whispers
are Heaven sent.

George Livingston Shand

Rest A While

Rest a while
On the lull of the evening,
Let the ebb tide of the day
Wash away any sadness.
Let the memories
of the day's goodness
resonate within you
As you drift towards
The dimming of your day.
For if you hold in your heart
A cherished memory,
What more could you have asked for?
Rest a while
On the lull of the evening,
Let the ebb tide of the day
Wash away any regrets.
Let the memories
Of the love you feel
Envelop you
As it eases your passage
Into the embrace of your night.
For if you have loved
And been so loved,
What more could you have hoped for?
So rest a while
On the lull of the evening,
Let your goodness
Let your love
Return on the tide
Of someone else's day.

Jacqueline Gilbert

A Picture Of Tragedy

Diana, Princess of Wales
Our Queen that never was
The prima donna of our country
With eyes of adoration
Revealing your love for Dodi
Your dignity, warmth and caring
Was the realism of life
You touched the hearts of all nations
As no one had done before you
You invigorated the sick, and wounded
The ones others deemed untouchable
In life, you were a saint
In an evil, corrupt, and greedy world
We will mourn your loss, Diana
And forever, have tear-stained cheeks
As our ruby red eyes still weep for you
Your diamond sparkling eyes, and smile
Have gone from reality
Prevail on Diana
In the hearts of all nations
We beg of you
Live on in heaven
For the love of Dodi
You will live on in death
Deep within our hearts,
Forever more.

RIP Diana, and Dodi.

Sylvia M Coulson

Diana Sweet Princess

How many tears must we shed to bring you back?
Oh why did you have to leave us, when you touched our hearts in a special way?
We will never forget your warm loving caring, and the smile and joy you brought to people's lives.
Rest in peace Sweet Angel.

Darren Hennessy & Family

Diana The World's Princess

You were the jewel in the crown.
And there was no one who could compare
With such a loving person as you.
Even though you have gone
On this sad August day
You will never be forgotten.
In our hearts you will always shine
Above anyone else.
When the world needed you
You came and helped
With your loving arms and words of kindness
Right from the beginning you chose your path to follow.
So beautiful you were,
With a great shyness. But you were loved
In every corner of the world.
But you were sadly taken.
In your young life
You will always be remembered by all
That you will always be the jewel
Whose gem sparkled in the crown.

Ann Best

On Your Island Of Dreams

A scented rose, the striking lily,
Blue delphinium eyes in enhanced repose.
Lie within a magnificent sentinel array of flowers
Upon your Island of Dreams.

Do not be afraid, the Royal Court protagonists
And one-eyed pack should be pitied and forgiven.
The People's Coronation of Wreaths
Will not wither, in time they will gently blossom.

Do not weep sweet young princes,
Mummy would not want to see you cry.
She is with you, just listen inside.
Diana is within all her people.

Jackie Goldsworthy

Lady Of The Lake

You are our Lady of the Lake,
Lying on your lonely island,
With the flowers all around.
Lady of the Lake.
And the lilies and the roses and the sweet,
sweet wind
That blows the smoke of candles in my eyes.
And the anger and the anguish and the deep,
deep grief
As the nation cries.

He's just a beggar in the street,
Lying in his lonely doorway,
With the rubbish all around.
Beggar in the street.
And the litter and the dustbins and the sour,
sour wind
That blows the dust of London in his eyes.
Oh the anger and the anguish and the deep,
deep grief
As a beggar cries.

She went to him and held his hand
Gave him hope and found him shelter
Thawed the ice inside his heart.
She held his hand.
And now he brings the lilies to her palace gates
And wipes the tears of sadness from his eyes
As the sea of flowers rises from the deep,
deep grief
As a nation cries.

For the lovely Lady Di.

Janna Eliot

Without You

(This poem has been created for Princess Diana)

Tomorrow will come without you,
How can I face it,
The people you helped,
The people you loved.

You had more love then anyone,
You had love to give,
You got people through their hard times,
You put everyone before yourself.

You touched so many hearts,
You never gave in,
The next day won't be the same,
I wish you didn't have to go.

Please Lord keep our Princess safe,
Please give her all the love you can give,
We will miss her every day within.

Kate Susan Douglas (15)

We Came From Miles Around

We came from miles around,
'Your funeral was great!'
The message in our feelings attempting
to relate;
Our love for you,
Our hate for them
How strong emotions were.

The sky has picked a rose today;
This country's finest flower.

But where had all this started,
In England's finest hour?
You didn't hold the wheel then,
it wasn't in your power.

Always an outsider, always one of us,
reaching to the heights and hearts,
that others could not touch.

The people won't forget you
your life was not in vain
in Heaven as on Earth,
ever to remain.

Of all the pledges made this day,
your brother held the word.
When any other statement,
would have seemed absurd.

You've died and gone to Heaven,
of this we can be sure.

But which way up Heaven is,
we'll never know,
no more.

Philip Isle

Diana
Princess - Super Star

Born infinitely blessed, she wore an easy grace
that lingered in the mind,
the kind of form and face possessed
by rarest chance, to last a lifetime's span:

a single glance could fell the strongest man,
with women too, held captive by her eyes.

There seemed no limit to such charm as hers,
A God-grown gift, designed to scorn the spite
of passing years:
like peerless crystal, shining and unflawed,
she drew whatever light was there to find,
and adulation grew.

Then, somewhere in the shadows,
mischief stirred,
cruel rumours gathered pace and
spread distrust,
with brutal thrust of words combined to shame
the blameless life, by fortune made so sweet.

Sorely, she felt sharp chill of malice in the air,
yet, with disarming flair,
as swiftly charmed away the hate,
to halt wild spate of gossip in its run,
for no barbed, vengeful story, could denigrate
to dust,
the glory and acclaim - so fairly won.

June White

Gentle Diana

Thank you Diana,
You've done a life's work,
so now the Lord has called you home.
They say the good die young!

Gentle Princess,
Madonna to the modern world,
distressed by every cruelty,
distressed by every hurt.

God bless you, Diana,
Princess of Wales,
for all the work you've done to help
the victims in this world.

Gentle Diana,
Queen of all our hearts,
rest you now in splendid state,
but also rest in peace.

Patricia Tilling

Funeral Of Diana, Princess Of Wales

(Written while watching the television
broadcast)

Silence, oh the enveloping silence
So overwhelming. So emotional.

Only the horses' hooves
Clicking of brass against leather
Soldiers precise marching shoes on tarmac
and the every minute muffled bell
accompanied a gun-carriage coffin
on a bright sunlit unique occasion.

White tulips and lilies
Placed on top of the Royal Coat of Arms
never realised how the World
would focus on their simplicity.

How many tears fell from public and private eyes
during that monumental procession
through London streets,
that showed unimaginable respect towards
an individual
who also showed great respect
and interest
and compassion and love
to those of lesser upbringing?

A sadder moment in history never existed . . .?

John Ernest Day

Compassion

Compassion is a name for love and it's there within you all,
usually it doesn't surface until you hear an anguished call,
or sometimes it's in response to a brother who's in need;
It shouldn't matter who it is, his colour or his creed.
Because you're all God's children, each sister and each brother,
the greatest gift you can give to Him, is to show compassion to each other.
You have had a good example in the child you called Diana,
She showed a deep compassion in a very loving manner.
Her love was unconditional, she gave it to all in need,
to the sick and the homeless, to all warning, she paid no heed;
she touched the hands of lepers, hugged victims of AIDS too,
this was to be a lesson, it's what she came to do.
She broke down many barriers and kept God's natural law,
because she was who she was, she could open many a door;
she could show her deep compassion because she'd also know the pain,
it's easier to understand if you've walked through showers of rain.
Because she did what she did, she's reaping what she's sown,
compassion keeps just pouring in, from brethren she's never known.
Gaze at this phenomenon, it's human nature at its best,
watch it through the coming years, for time will be its test.
To take on human form and walk upon your Earth,
means you aren't perfect, your faults are there from birth.
It was the same with that dear child, but know, she did her best,
that's all Our Father asks of you, as you come up against each test.
Make it your responsibility to show compassion wherever you can,
to nature and to animals, as well as your fellow man.
You find it very easy to comfort a distressed child,
but how hard is it to succour your foe, when he has made you wild?
Sometimes the hardest tests in life make you feel abused,
you erect a wall around yourself and sit there, feeling used.
These feelings can turn to selfishness, compassion can be well covered,
but however deep, it's always there, waiting to be recovered;
it's then, when something touches you, your heart begins to melt,
a wakening to that deep love, for that is what you've felt.
For some, it is the first time that they've been moved to pray,
a simple prayer for Diana, is what they came to say.
Share this deep emotion, do God's work wherever you can,
extend a hand, a comfort, give love to your fellow man.
Each show of compassion is personal, some of you have seen at first hand,
but you have also seen the power when single acts join as a band.
Never forget this valuable lesson, love's the greatest power of all,
and whenever the opportunity arises, use the compassion that's within you all.

Beryl Cosgrave

Diana

A nation of tears, how one person in death can give so much grief to so many people, the castle ruins of life then the searching, to rebuild the outer walls.

The sweet smell of the rain bringing new love to the flowers of life, tree branches opening up their hearts, calling in all nature's love.

Fighting out of the thickets, the country lane at peace and love, no one in life should be empty of love, such a small word that can put into life what no other word can.

If there is someone in life that can hold you, look into your eyes, romance you with the power of love, taking you on a journey of passion, trust lighting candles in your life, never to be blown out.

The calling of time we can't understand, the towers of the castle rebuilt, a new love of life starting, why the angry clouds, drizzling rain, the flagpole broken apart, the new flag of life wet and drooping, this love should never a dreadful word, died.

Garrett John

A Young Man's Princess

Although I never met Diana
I felt I knew her so well
And since I was young
She's been in my heart

Beautiful from the first day I saw her
And gorgeous to her last
She graced my young life
Now she'll never leave

I was there to bid farewell to her
My tears ran down London's streets
Along with every man's, woman's and child's
The homeless and our future King's.

The country she brought together
Will remain strong in her name
Just as the world remained silent
To remember and respect her . . .

Gordon S Allen

Silence

Silence!
Only the birds singing lovely humming sounds,
No sound of cars in the air,
People moving quietly,
Noses sniffing,
Sniff, sniff
Scent of flowers,
Fills the air.
Silence!
Only the people talking,
In hushed whispers all around,
People weeping,
Feet moving,
Slow and steady down The Mall.
Silence!
Bouquet upon bouquet,
A million bunches lay on the ground.
The wind flutters amongst the cards,
With one thought,
They all say,
We really miss you,
Diana, Princess of Wales.
Silence!

Jennifer Packham (9)

Diana - Queen Of Hearts

She was the most beautiful woman the world's ever seen,
A woman one day we hoped would reign as our Queen,
Though a truly loved Princess in our hearts we could see,
That this woman as Queen was never to be.

But how did we know then the fate that was to befall,
That in her young years she would be snatched from us all,
That the heart that she gave in so many ways,
Would stop beating for her on that one fateful day.

From the innocent young girl she gained worldly acclaim,
She married her Prince and took on his name,
She gave him the son that one day would be King,
She gave her all to his life, she gave everything.

But dark clouds were looming and pressures too hard to bear,
And the love in her life was no longer there,
But the load on her shoulders she knew she could carry,
For her much adored sons, Princes William and Harry.

So she travelled the world across seas, across land,
Helped the children and sick by the touch of her hand,
With warmth and affection she would brighten their day,
And give a bit of herself in her own special way.

But God knew that this was a woman he could help from above,
And in his good wisdom gave her a man for friendship and love,
And for that very short time she was happy and free,
Her happiness glowing for the whole world to see.

But still she was hounded for that updated news,
No-one heeded her pleas or respected her views,
So are we all a little guilty and partly to blame,
For taking her life and exploiting her fame.

Now from life into death she is laid down to rest,
For the world, for her family she just did her best,
And we hope that in Heaven her soul she's now sharing,
With someone she loved who is tender and caring.

So let's pause for a moment and think for a while,
Remembering her beauty, her caring, her smile,
And the role that she played in so many parts,
To remember her truly, as our own 'Queen of Hearts'.

Josephine Giles

Diana Princess Of Wales

Pain, pain and more pain
can make one's life seem in vain
To overcome this hopeless task
Diana did more than was asked

To help the poor the old the sick
through her own experience of the rich
No-one will know the loneliness she endured
it now comes out, be assured

By helping others in their pain
gave her courage much more to gain
Inspired her life behind the beauty
the facade of abuse, supposed duty

She bucked the system in a way
giving pleasure, just to say
Help is there you're not alone
stricken faces with no home

True kindness of giving, no-one knowing
so many times, her only way of showing
A charmed life some might say
the pointing finger comes back your way

She never wore a judge's cap
any child lay on her lap
In God's eyes she did her best
now her soul is laid to rest

Kindness comes in many guises
in her heart she chose the wisest
Her epitaph can only be
in helping others sets you free . . .

Jean Tennent Mitchell

Tribute To Diana

Gap too wide for another to cover
Deep the loss for her sisters and brother
With them the world poured out their grief
Shedding tears of sadness seeking relief

Diana where possible showed kindness and love
He for knowing the Lord God up above
Killer uncaring stole away her young years
Sons with future without mother so dear

Born she was of high standard blood
Faced her enemies for longer than should
Quietly alone she sat in deep sadness
Late her portion of joy with gladness

Diana her name shall not fade away
Of the last day of August what can we say
Stunning she was in all of splendour
Expression of adoration her boys too remember

Hannah Birch

A Sea Of Tears Out Of Sadness

Today there is a sea of tears around the world
Tears from the inner soul, are like open prayers
Each tear, has a thought of compassion, of love,
a feeling of losing a friend, whose young life came
to an end.

Today God has sent a sea of flowers from each
and every heart, an aroma of love fills the air.
The velvet petals, alikened to the GRACE which
Diana shared, soft and gentle to those for whom
she cared.

Today the world stood still to share peace and
sadness, of at times an unseen angel behind
the scenes.
To the poor, afflicted, tiny children, she was
a Queen.
Today the atmosphere was of God, all around,
the hurting he upheld, the unbelieving believed.
Today we came together to mourn a Mum, who
loved and adored her sons.
Today the sons followed their Queen, who gave
them love and hugs and life's perspective.

Today the air stood still, the coming of change in
the human heart, the remaking of history the
new young King, the common part, the scenes of
which young and old will never see again.

Days ago Diana's soul had returned to her
Heavenly Home but her gentle spirit is in the air.
Loved, not forgotten, her seeds and fruits shall
live on forever in the nation's heart.

B Fletcher

Sleep Now, Sleep

(Dedicated to the memory of Diana -
The Princess of Wales)

When the famous die one feels sadness
Yet this is different.
A figure of debate, controversy, pity.
She touched our lives
She touched the world.
Why does such beauty and love leave us now?
Maybe this earth did not deserve her
Maybe Deity requires her.
A fairy-tale Princess who cared, who noticed.
Supporting foundations donating her time,
Such time which now seems precious.
Her beacon of light shines forever.
An indelible mark left behind,
Not surpassed for centuries.
The world was your family you nurtured
and hugged,
For decades will pass when we'll crave for
your goodness.
But the angels will sing to their wondrous arrival
They'll value this asset not drag through
the gutter.
Sleep now, sleep.
The pain is over, the parasites have gone.
Your prophecy foretold a legend now born.
A figurehead of souls
The real 'Queen of Hearts'.

Nicholas William James

Princess Of Smiles And Tears

Diana was a jewel
That shined so bright
She had that distinctive demeanour
Turning darkness into light

There can never be another
No other could take your place
The Queen of Hearts the world over
So alluring and full of grace

You left us oh, so sorrowful
We loved you oh, so dear
Our People's Princess
We all now shed a tear

Forever we will think of you
Time may help ease the pain
God in heaven care for our Diana
Until the time we meet again.

P J Knightly

Diana Princess Of Love Remembered

D iana
I can
A nd will
N ame you
A gain

P rincess
R ighteousness,
I will sing your
N ame,
C herish your
E ntity, to
S weep away
S orrow.

O bituary;
F orever

L over
O f the
V ictims of
E arth.

R emembered,
E very time
M an is unjust.
E very time
M an is intrusive,
B eckoned by greed.
E very time
R eason is lacking.
E very time
D eath is sudden!

Linda Coleman

Beloved Diana

In memoriam, in sympathy
Beloved Diana
Princess of hearts

Diana
Pure in soul
Pure in heart
tainted by life
touched with love

'twas divine intervention
dark forces to part
hosts of angels
save a light of the world so bright
light shines forth - triumphant
to herald thy way
be guided and let thy spirit rise

In your life's path and people's
there is a lesson for all
some may rise now but some may still fall
mirrors of love, mirrors of lust
mirrors of sorrow, now mirrors of dust

Who are we?
We the hypocrites who dare to point and judge
judge oneself
then be silent

In loving memory
We search our souls.

Lynne Stuart

A Dark September Day

They filled the streets of London,
Two million or more,
A nation sharing in its grief,
As never known before.

For she the lonely bell did toll,
The hollow click of hoof.
So near and yet so far away,
We did gaze in disbelief,
At the power of love and touching,
Of a gentle life so brief.

But she beyond this sombre day,
Will always twinkle bright,
Forever she the Princess,
Who turned darkness into light.

Ken Lowe

Diana

Diana,
Bright Star of our firmament.
So cruelly torn away from out our midst,
By those whose sole desire was gain,
For a photograph or two.
So great your fame,
Throughout this globe, that we call Earth.

Beauty, compassion, kindness,
And the common touch,
Were those reflections of your soul;
That meant so much,
To all who met you on life's way.
Great or small, disabled, maimed
Or sick. Homeless, bereaved or just simply lost.
You gathered them within your love;
Gave them comfort rare.
And did not stop to count the cost.

Now, in ever-flowing stream they come,
Their grateful thanks to say,
With flowers, a word or more,
And patiently wait for many hours,
In winding queues, outside the doors.
To enter on each open page,
Their own small tributes,
To a miracle of our age.
In their own words.
Diana, queen of our hearts.
God in His mercy grant you peace.

Stella J Jefferies

Glittering Star

Diana a star that shone
And glittered briefly
She came painfully innocent
Into our lives
Pure in heart
Loved complete
But was hurt in return
And found no one could help
Her through those early times
Brought tears to our eyes
When we saw her so sad
With mixtures of emotions
She valiantly fought back
To become maturer and wiser
No one could damage her sweet soul
She befriended the weakest of our race
And left behind a glitter
That had turned to gold
And inherited in the air we breathe.

Vivienne Doncaster

Diana

A million images frozen in time
couldn't capture the essence of you.
Diana.
The billions of tears shed for loss of your life
can't equate with the grief the world feels.
Diana.
Countless words may be written on whole
forests felled
but they won't express how the world loves you -
Diana.
Our sorrow's intangible - soft as night air
and the fragrance of mountains of flowers.
Diana.
You may now lie alone - but be sure we're
all there.

All hearts bleed . . .
for the Queen of our hearts.
Diana.

Patricia Finney

May Flowers Grow

May flowers grow,
Colourful, radiant, from ashes below

May they flow,
Freely, lovingly, from head to toe.

Each sombre day, though disbelieved.
Mourning hearts, broken, grieved.

Tears, thoughts, anger come seeping in,
Sorrow, sadness, here within.

We've listened, learned, the people churned.
Young heart and soul, sadly burned.

Explain!
I cannot do.

The Nation was and will, remember You.

Mr & Mrs L Smith

A Beacon Of Light

When the sun rises in the morning,
It illuminates and warms the day,
And within, our spirits lifted,
We face another day.

Diana was a sun,
Whose warmth and light like stardust fell,
And touched the hearts of the world.

A daughter, a wife, a mother,
No task too much to bear,
She loved and cherished so deeply,
How could she be short-changed?

To learn by her life and example,
Is all her spirit can ask,
Give hope to the hungry and needy,
Show the world you're 'a beacon of light'.

Cindy Mitchell

Queen Of Hearts

You were once a lady quiet and shy,
But now you're a star that shines in the sky.
I hope you're happy with Dodi by your side,
You'll now no longer have to hide.
You were a great person and a brilliant friend,
I can't believe this is really the end.
You helped the sick with just a touch,
All I say is Diana we miss you so much.
Just one comfort for us today,
Is that Diana you're not far away.
We hope from this it won't happen again,
Right now in heaven you'll suffer no pain.
I still can't believe this is really true,
I loved your work and admired you.
You were very special and one of the best,
I hope that in heaven you'll finally get a rest.
I know you'll brighten up your place,
With that beautiful smile upon your face.
Your life was special you had little fears,
And I'll now no longer have to hold back the tears.
You helped a lot of people, in different parts,
You're not just a princess but a
Queen of Hearts.

Tanya Gilmore (13)

Diana, Now Departed . . .

There's now a pain in many hearts
Because our sweetheart's gone . . .
This happens when a friend departs
And takes the light that shone . . .
The light of love within her smile,
Her kind words now and then,
Her sense of joy, her sense of style . . .
The darling of most men!
She truly tried to do good works,
When others looked away!
Yet underneath, where sorrow lurks,
She suffered in dismay . . .
She tried to change the world itself,
Campaigning for the poor . . .
Regardless of her private wealth,
Their plight could not ignore!
Yet loneliness must find release -
Or else life has no soul . . .
And yet the hounding would not cease -
It got out of control!
Pursued by those that photograph,
For profit, pure and plain,
Diana found her epitaph,
'The fast lane is insane!'
We love her still, beyond death's grasp -
Our Princess, smiles and all . . .
And to our hearts kind memories clasp . . .
For even the mighty fall . . .

Denis Martindale

Diana

No words can express how we're feeling today,
we all just feel like locking ourselves away,
but under all the mourning, just stop and foresee,
Diana's up in heaven with her friend Dodi.

When midnight falls look up to the sky,
you will see two stars, one Dodi, one Di,
together in happiness they will keep,
as they dream in an eternal sleep.

Haley Rose Cox (12)

Diana

Diana I never met you
But admired you from afar
A Princess made in Heaven
A bright and shining star
You shared your love with everyone
Touching people's hearts
Giving hope and understanding
How sad we had to part.

June Jones

A Tribute To Diana

(This is for William and Harry and their Father, Charles, in thanks for letting us see and know an angel like 'Diana')

You were not just an English Rose,
You were the scent, the fragrance,
A bouquet of every flower,
You were every woman, every mother,
Each attribute complementing the other,
Your beauty and kind heart were only
Just a part,
Of the role you were to play,
On the stage of life yesterday,
The luminary star of many,
There's no comparison no not any,
A sapphire that sparkled passionately and bright,
You tried so hard to make everything right,
Your goodness permeated all,
Even the regalities so benign and formal,
Oh yes you normalised the abnormal,
And threw the mask of formality away,
You told the truth and had your say,
Now the stage is bare the star is gone,
And now it's the audience who are all alone,
No more photographs or invasion,
No more spectacles or sensation,
The throne of life was yours the Queen of Love,
Your spirit is free now and flying like a dove,
Its lightness will not be too heavy to carry.
For your brave and beautiful sons
William and Harry,
Nothing anyone can do or say,
Can portray the emotions we try to convey,
Only olay 'Diana' olay . . .

Peggy Keogh

Diana

We saw her as a blushing bride,
with a dashing Prince by her side.
We saw her sharing all her joys,
in the love she gave to her two boys.
We saw her looking sad and drawn,
her married life tattered and torn.
We saw her looking stressed and thin,
a battle that she fought to win,
We saw her touch the sick and infirm,
wanting to help, wanting to learn.

We saw her cortège with disbelief,
ordinary people showing their grief.
We saw her brother, her sons and Charles,
walking behind her on the last half mile.
We saw their sorrow, so heavy the pain.
Lives touched, never to be the same.
We saw her placed in the hands of the Lord,
a wonderful person so greatly adored.
Our love for her will never cease.
God Bless Queen of Hearts, Rest in Peace.

Jenny Bowles

Diana Queen Of Hearts

You're in a place not far from here
But all our hearts go with you dear
You showed us all what love's about
You shall remain there is no doubt
You're in our hearts, you're in our minds
There is no other of your kind
Your life was short, but not in vain
You helped the world to ease its pain
Up in the sky there shines a light
The brightest light that shines at night
Upon this star is where you fell
Goodnight Princess a fond farewell.

Sweet dreams Diana
May you rest in peace.

Rachelle, Jordan & Shannon Wilcox

A New Star Shines

Around the world a light's gone out
That shone so very bright
One thing of which there's no doubt
A new star shines in heaven tonight.

A caring heart in a world of pain
No battle was too great
A shining sun through driving rain
Why couldn't heaven wait?

A loving mother of two young boys
She gave them a special gift
A mother's love, her heart, her joys
Let time help their spirits lift.

Gone to a better place
A world with no more pain
God can now bask in her wonderful grace
While we remember her name.

The time has come to say goodbye
To our Queen of Hearts, our Lady Di.

Gareth Evans

A Princess In Heaven

A country's loss means Heaven's gain,
Will all this praying ease the pain?
Your character blossomed like a flower in bloom,
But nobody guessed God would take you so soon.
Such a wonderful lady I wish I had met,
Now your memory lives on and I'll never forget;
William and Harry couldn't wish for another,
But now they face life away from their mother,
You're with them in spirit,
They know in their hearts,
That Heaven nor Earth could tear you apart.
You did so much for those in need;
God tried you and you passed the test,
The nation hopes you'll find your peace;
And finally come to lay in rest.

Natalie Rhian Davies (17)

Why Does The Nation Mourn?

Why does the nation mourn
for a solitary soul
So small amongst the death of millions every day?

Why does the nation mourn
As we lay wreaths and each single rose?
We lay them for one who embodies our own soul's longing.
We weep for each injustice born;
We weep for each dying child she held;
for the limbless,
the foodless,
the hopeless,
the homeless.
All the camera caught images we beheld
through her eyes we mourned.

Why does the nation mourn?
We mourn our own lost-ness,
our divorces,
our families
torn apart by argument
and words which can never be taken back.

We mourn for our own children - innocents left alone - someday -
Maybe?

Why does the nation mourn?
We mourn the pain of death's early call
The reality too close.
We mourn death itself;
Through your eyes, your beauty;
Skin unwrinkled for death's timely call.
We mourn love aborted when it just began
We mourn for what we know too well.

Why does the nation mourn?
Because the mirror of death
faced each one
and instead of a Princess
we saw ourselves.

Wynne Stearns

Poem For A Princess

A vulnerable flower in a field of corn
We give thanks to God for the day you were born
Like a shining light you carried our hopes
Your warmth was around us you helped us
to cope.

For the sick and the old, the young and the frail
You never forgot them, nor faltered, nor failed
You gave of yourself to ease others in pain
Relentlessly, tirelessly, time and again.

From a shy young girl to the Queen of our hearts
Fate took you from us and tore us apart
We must let you go and in God's faith
we trust . . .
That his love is forever and he will love you for us.

We will never forget you our sweet 'Lady Di'
We know you are watching us all from on high
Just as you were you always will be . . .
Treasured by all - your 'big' family.

God Bless you dear Diana,
Loved Always

Maria Daines & family

Untitled

The gates of Heaven stood open
God did what He thought was best
He took our Princess by the hand
And whispered 'Come to rest'
And through a silent thought
And with a falling tear
Goodnight Princess Diana
Our Queen of Hearts
Who was loved so very dear.

David Coombes

Reign In Heaven Our Queen Of Hearts

You were the core of our great kingdom,
You were the flame of inspiration and of grace.
You willingly reached out and touched so many
troubled hearts,
Regardless of disability, creed or race.

You toiled and built countless bridges,
You walked where others would not dare.
You generated warmth throughout our nation
and world,
You showed the forgotten how much you cared.

You gave comfort to the less fortunate
when they despaired and could not cope.
You gave to them a new-found purpose,
Dignity and an everlasting sense of hope.

You gave so much of yourself, Princess Diana,
Even though you endured suffering and
intense pain.
Never once did we see you falter,
Never once did we hear you complain.

The admiration and love for you was greatly
underestimated.
When the news of your untimely death was
broadcast,
Millions wept openly in disbelief.
I'm certain your spirit will continue to guide and
embrace your beloved boys,
Especially at this time of profound grief.

Sandra Edwards

Diana

D ivine and heavenly messenger
I ntrepid and sometimes shy,
A lthough you did leave
N o need to grieve
A ngels don't simply just die.

Brian Edwards

Diana

You were a shining Beacon
A candle in the dark
Another Florence Nightingale
Another Joan of Arc

A woman of compassion
Of beauty and of fame
Who touched so many people
One we'll never see again

And we will long remember
This sad and fatal day
When Heaven gained an Angel
But took a Saint away

You'll no more need to suffer
And never need to cry
For you are in a better place
Far above the sky

And in the darkest night
You'll still be the brightest star
Though you're no longer with us
You're never very far

For we will not forget you
As this life you depart
You're still the People's Princess
Diana Queen of Hearts

'In life you touched many people
In death you embraced us all'.

Sheila Peacock

Diana

You touched the heart of the nation,
The most beautiful thing in creation,
All the flowers that have been laid,
All the tears that have been cried,
Will build you a golden stairway,
To your mansion in the sky.

Meg Turnbull

The People's Princess

A country in mourning, a world in shock,
A treasure lost - will 'they' still mock?
That her smile's a memory is too much to bear,
What she meant to us we were unaware.

She showed compassion beyond her years,
Still helping others, whilst shedding tears.
She touched people's lives with her love and her smile,
Holding a hand, chatting for a while.

She took risks, made mistakes - that was part of her charm.
But like another who was crucified, she took a leper by the arm.
What our lives will be without her, I cannot comprehend.
My own sorrow is so great, will my pain ever end?

Take care of her boys, Lord, give them sunshine not rain.
Forgive those whose ignorance caused misery and pain.
Reunite the two lovers in your heaven above,
So they can share peacefully their everlasting love.

We can try to emulate her in our own humble way,
Give a hand to a stranger, have a kindly word to say.
Show compassion to beggar, forgive those who have sinned,
Rekindling the flame of the
CANDLE IN THE WIND.

Deryn Barrington

In Memory Of Diana, Princess Of Wales 1961-1997

In August nineteen ninety seven
An Angel winged her way to Heaven
There to sit at God's Right Hand
Watching Her beloved land

She shared Her life with the sick and poor
Her heart an ever open door
Shared our troubles, worries and strife
Taken in the prime of life

Ne'er to set herself apart
She really was The Queen of Hearts
Now She watches from afar
A shining light, undying star

Now our Di, is with the best
With Her Dodi She can rest
Away from all life's hurt and pain
Safe and sound they will remain

At last She's in a gentle sleep
I pray the Lord Her soul to keep
When your eyes lift to the sky
Remember our BELOVED DI

Paul Mason

Princess Diana

And we who are left behind can ne'er forget
That compassion you bore for the unfortunates that you met.
Your hands reached out when others turned away
Dear Diana look down on us this day.

The sick, the maimed, the poor you did embrace
You touched all our hearts with your love and grace
You were, and always will be 'our shining ray'
Dear Diana look down on us this day.

Maureen Rice

A Thought Of Love

It's no good trying to shift the blame
As you can plainly see
Things that happen every day
Are truly meant to be
There's only one who knows our fate
He lives way on high
And no-one knows who will be next
We shouldn't even try
Be it princess or pauper
A beggar or a king
And whether you're good or bad
It doesn't mean a thing
So if you've lost somebody
A good friend or a spouse
Don't live in sorrow and torment
They're all safe in God's House
So let's remember our Princess
A saint to all by far
Just look in the sky at night
You will see a brand new star
Maybe not just one star
There may be even two
A Princess so in love and happy
Dodi's up there too
Remember all things she has done
She gave love and understanding
And helped the sick by handling
But now she's gone, who will fill the void
Who will do the good work, in which she was employed
Who will handle world problems
And do it without fuss
This is where you can help
It's really up to us
Let's assemble the world powers
Make all the problems cease
Let all know, her efforts weren't wasted
So she can rest in peace
Let's remember all things good
The smile, the eyes, the dress
And there'll only ever be one
Our Di the People's Princess.

G W Whalley

Tribute To Diana

The world has lost its Princess
But Heaven's gained a Queen
And now embraced with Dodi's love,
So peaceful, so serene.

My heart is broken, filled with pain,
Aching for your sons,
For now the world's gift to you,
Is to cherish your little ones.

Your beauty and your elegance,
Your eyes and your sheer grace,
Your love for each and everyone,
We never will replace.

For you Diana, there's no more hurt,
No doubts, no sorrow, no pain,
You truly were an angel,
Our loss is Heaven's gain.

And as we lay you down to sleep,
We'll always wonder why.
Did God come to take you home,
Why did you have to die?

Farewell Diana, our sweet Princess,
Your beauty we will miss.
To you, I send, with my love,
A silent goodnight kiss.

So may you now Rest in Peace,
Be free as the sweet dove,
Remembered with such tenderness,
With joy, with hope, with love.

Goodnight, Diana.

Carole Dyer

Dear Diana

I thank you for your inspiration
And the feelings of hope you gave to me
Such love and dedication
Even at times when you were so unhappy

Who will show us the way to peace
Now that your light has gone out
How do we make the fighting cease
Now you are no longer about

The human race has lost its heart
Pain and sorrow everywhere
For we thought you'd never part
Somehow life does not seem fair

Two sons without a mummy
How will they learn to cope
Will their lives become more sunny
As each day they grow up

I thank you for your inspiration
And what you have done for humanity
I thank the Lord in jubilation
Your life came to touch me

Always in my heart
Goodnight and God Bless

Lea Potter

Diana - Queen Of Hearts

Your dream will never die,
Your fight will never end,
Alas, it is only now I truly realise,
You always were a friend.

Your light has gone out,
But your eternal flame burns bright,
We see you in our hearts,
Although you are no longer in our sight.

Goodbye England's rose,
The Cinderella story has been torn apart,
Tears have been shed, flowers thrown,
For Diana, Queen of Hearts.

Steven James (17)

Heaven's Touch

Bereft of our Princess, we grieve in silence,
A nation now as one, in our despair;
You leave behind such emptiness and sorrow,
A void we cannot fill, without you there.
Yet, in your shortened life, you gave so freely
Of love, compassion, strength, and human care;
You drew respect and friendship from your people
A shining star, so special and so rare.

So, now that God has called you to His kingdom,
A Paradise where hearts are freed from strife,
We thank Him for the gift of you, Diana:
He gave us beauty when He gave you life.
In losing you, we lose so very much -
Through you He showed us, briefly,
Heaven's touch.

Julie Martin

Princess Of The People

Sweet dreams Princess and yet while you sleep
Your people gather to mourn you and weep
For you have achieved what no other could do
Uniting all nations in their grief for you
You have left your light shining
compassion the name
Forever to burn, like the eternal flame
As the pages of history begin to unfold
Yours is the message that will always be told
Stand up when you're down but be sure
when you do
That love and compassion are flowing from you

So for you bells will ring throughout
every church and steeple
As last respects are paid to the
Princess of the People

Veronica Hill

Farewell To A Unique Princess

Out of our darkness, you brought us light.
Where you saw injustice, you put things right.
You were not afraid to touch the untouched
A word or a smile from you meant so much.
You enhanced the lives of all that you met
Such love and compassion, we'll never forget.
The love in your eyes, the smile on your face
The caring you showed us, no-one can replace.

You'd had so much heartache in your young life,
So much unhappiness, trouble and strife.
But still you found time to care for all others.
To hug a sick child, comfort Father or Mother.
You taught us all that life is such fun.
But wherever you went, always, good things
were done,
No-one else ever gave us such inspiration,
You were loved and respected from nation
to nation.

And just when we all hoped you'd found
happiness,
Fate has taken you from us, and we're in distress.
Why the Lord had to take you we can't
comprehend
Why He needed our Princess, our Darling,
our Friend,

Now all we can do is to spend these last hours.
Waiting in sadness with candles and flowers,
Our eyes filled with tears as we watch you depart,
Farewell, Diana our dear Queen of Hearts.

Sally Bailey

When Teardrops Fell For Princess Di

Autumn sunshine clear blue skies,
As gentle as your caring eyes
A nation stood with so much pride
Our love for you we could not hide.

Teardrops fell like autumn rain
Our hearts so heavy filled with pain
We never shared the pains you had,
In days gone by it seems so sad.

A Princess filled with love and care,
Your life and time with others shared
You touched the hearts of all you met
Your gentle deeds we won't forget.

You travelled far with so much speed,
To give your help to those in need.
Your work on Earth will see the gains,
For all your suffering and your pains.

You carried out our Saviour's plans,
To show the world how life was planned.
The Lord must need you by His side,
He placed you there the night you died.

G D Eccleston

Diana

This wasn't how the fairytale was meant to end,
With broken hearts that will never mend,
With shattered dreams and forgotten vows,
Hasty words and now haunting rows,
Separate lives that bought about fate,
Happiness that came too late,
After years of sorrow, grief and pain,
At last a chance to smile again,
No time to enjoy a new-found love,
The fairytale ends in the Heavens above,
A world left stunned in disbelief,
Sadly united in heartfelt grief,
A lesson learnt that brings tears to the eye,
And our brightest star will now shine in the sky.

Denise J Woollard

Untitled

No words were ever written
That could express such pain,
Such an overwhelming sadness
Yes our loss is Heaven's gain
The whole world mourns your passing
United in our grief.
So much love was felt for you
So much love, beyond belief,
No-one will ever forget you,
All this love will travel through,
All time, all space, to eternity,
To surround and comfort you.
Never again will you feel alone
You have Dodi at your side
His loving arms embracing you
Together you'll abide.
Now we have to say goodbye
Goodnight, sweet dreams, God Bless,
Our very own Diana
The People's Princess.

Patricia Bott

Diana's Legacy

Are you looking down from heaven
At our mourning and our grief?
You who made an everlasting mark
Although your life was brief.

We saw you as our princess
On the television screen
And didn't know how much you cared,
Your kindness went unseen.

But you left for us a legacy
That everyone must share
Of how to treat our fellow men
With tender loving care.

So, though you had to leave us
And we miss you very much,
When we help the sick or dying
May we feel your gentle touch.

Doreen Noble

Simply Di

The world has lost an angel
With a heart so pure and true
Our friend our true companion
Someone we all felt we knew.

We cannot explain the heartache
All the pain and all the sorrow
You gave us love you gave us hope
You gave us a tomorrow

There's now a star at night so bright
It shines with grace and style
We all know that it is you above
The star that shines your smile

Now rest in peace our Queen of Hearts
Our Princess and our friend
You'll always be remembered
Until time comes to an end.

So sad you cannot stay with us
A saddened world you leave
Forever we'll remember you
Till the end of time we'll grieve.

Alan Lankester

For Diana

Heaven has our Princess
The Lord He has her soul
The suffering of others
To relieve was her main goal.

So fair of face and graceful
She always did her best
To ease the pain of others
Now she is at rest

The sadness of the people
Will linger on in time.
To us she was an angel
And now a saint in time.

She's left us a fine legacy
In the form of two dear sons
And a host of happy people
From all the deeds she's done.

Farewell our lovely Princess
God Bless and Rest in Peace
For we know that you are watching
And see us as we weep.

K Pickup

Diana, Princess Of Wales

A shining light has just gone out,
but we won't scream and we won't shout
We'll just remember a smiling face
A lady, so full of grace

Our tears will fall and we will weep
Our Princess has gone to sleep
All too soon you went away
But in our hearts you'll always stay

The happy face's full of love,
But you were taken up above
All your life you did your best
So goodnight Diana, sleep and rest.

Julie Richards

To William And Harry

The loss you have is so very great,
but don't forget there is a gate,
that leads beyond the pain that's here,
your mum is there and she can hear.
You have your dad he is the one
that both of you can lean upon.
You have two families they both have loss,
that doesn't mean that words will cross,
it's only what the papers say,
you'll have to take it day by day.
I lost my dad when I was ten,
Life does go on you'll live again,
Your mother's missed in every way,
but don't forget you'll meet one day.

Janice Carter

Thoughts And Feelings

So many thoughts rushing through my mind
With a jumble of emotions tumbling behind.
I thought no, not Diana!

I cried all morning when I heard the news,
I felt as if I'd lost someone I knew.
Such desolate thoughts.

I thought of William and Harry, how must
they be feeling?
How could they take it in? - Their heads
must be reeling.
I wondered - did they really want to be
seen in public?

I felt astounding sadness on her funeral day
Seeing all those flowers, many strewn
along her way.
So beautiful but devastatingly sad feelings.

Her brother's words in the Abbey were just
so true,
She was magic, unique, full of love and
caring too.
I felt anger at how she'd been treated by
certain people.

On the day of her funeral I thought, how come
the world looks the same?
On the radio they said 'We'll never see her again'
That shocked me - I think that was the saddest
thought of all.

When I saw her moving image shown on TV
I was startled for a moment thinking can it be
She's not really dead at all, they've got it wrong?
But then I heard again the words of Elton's song
And all the feelings of sadness came rushing back.

But then I thought - the history books will
celebrate her memory
And hundreds of years from now future
generations see
Just how much Diana meant to you and me.
I like that thought best of all - I think I'll keep
it close to me.

Frances Browning

My Tribute To Diana
'Your Light'

The night the Lord put out your light
The furthest star shone ever bright
And as we look to skies above
With hearts of sorrow and with love
We search inside to ask God why
Why He thought it best you die
Your life itself was heaven-sent
Now God's took back the life he lent
The reasons we will never know
But sleep assured we loved you so

From all of those you left behind
You fill our thoughts, distract our minds
The grief, the sorrow oh so real
Cannot express the hurt we feel
And as we think of your fair face
We remember you and your sweet grace
At every dawn of every day
We think of you in a special way
For even death could never part
or take away our Queen of Hearts.

Julie Doran

A Heart Full Of Love

From stars that twinkled in night skies,
He put a sparkle in her eyes,
From flowers in blossom he took the dew,
He put in her tears unselfish and true,
From the warmth of sunshine up above,
He filled her heart with care and love,
From morning dawn with fair winds blowing,
He endowed her a smile refreshing, glowing,
She was sent from Heaven to do good things,
Now she's left us on angels' wings,
The World in unison does weep,
Rivers of tears form oceans so deep,
Forever in Paradise she will remain,
Will we see her like again?

Reg Summerfield

Tribute To Diana Princess Of Wales

The nation mourns for her today
That special lady who passed away,
She taught the world to laugh and cry
But did she really need to die?
She touched the hearts of all she met
The Princess of the World will not forget.
What is the reason? Who is to blame?
Someone will hang their head in shame
Her troubled life has reached its end
The broken hearts we hope will mend
That those who loved her will never forget,
The joys she brought to all she met.
Now Diana will cry no more,
For the sick the needy and the poor,
She'll rest in peace in the world above
With the promise of God's undying love.

RIP Diana Princess of Wales.

Jackie Douglas

Goodbye Diana, Princess Of Wales

Goodbye Diana, fair Princess,
You were our only Queen of Hearts,
And always there you will remain,
Even as your sweet smile departs.

Goodbye forever shining light,
You lit up our lives with your grace,
And ever will your image stay,
In our memory, your kind face.

Goodbye so soon to all your truth,
You departed prematurely,
And now we stand alone in shock,
Your life, taken so cruelly.

Goodbye then, our beloved Di,
We wish you happiness above,
You left us gifts, your heart and soul,
But more than this, you gave your love.

Donald V L Macleod

Diana

(Dedicated in memory of Diana,
Princess Of Wales)

Diana, Princess of Wales,
And self-styled 'Queen of Hearts'.
In Royalty and Charity,
You faithfully played your parts.

A fairy-tale wedding.
Two outstanding boys.
Your life was marked with sorrow,
As well as all the joys.

Hounded by the media,
Until that fateful day.
When you returned to Jesus,
Happy, in a loving way.

You will always be remembered,
And money will be found.
To do the work you started,
Moving land mines from the ground.

AIDS, the Ballet and Red Cross,
All knew you as a friend.
Though many did not understand,
This new Royal trend.

Now you are in Heaven,
With Angels at your side.
This Earth will never be the same,
For those who spied and lied.

Your son one day will be our King,
King William he will be.
A different sort of Monarch,
For all the World to see.

C H De Meza

A Poem For Diana, Princess Of Wales

The world is mourning full of pain.
Their tears they cannot hide.
Shock and grief they can't explain
Our Queen of Hearts has died
Thousands of people camping out,
Quiet and disbelieving.
The tragic news they all doubt.
'It can't be true' they reason.
Dodi and Di - so full of life
They cared and loved each other.
She wanted to be a loving wife;
Already a special mother.
But for fate she could have been
Our last hope and prayer
Upon the throne as our Queen
So regal and so rare.
Millions of flowers commemorate
The passing of Diana.
The love and impact she has made
We will never forget Diana.

H E Anning

Heavenly Father

Heavenly Father

Thank you for the
life of Diana, Princess of Wales,
the flower of love we failed to
see until the flower died.

May the seed of love she sowed
take root in us and blossom
with a fragrance of compassion
spread abroad in our hearts.

May we who seek to do thy will
take on the same nature as this
flower that her death will not be
in vain.

Through Jesus Christ Our Lord,

Amen.

Joyce Taylor

Fatality

Shock, horror,
Disbelief,
A sea of fragrant blooms,
Scattered,
Spilled out like those lives lost,
Upon the pavement everywhere,
To bring relief.

Impact, stillness,
Lives are wrecked,
Now loss is clothed in words of grief,
Anger,
Felt at what may have been avoided,
Is now with flowers decked.

Suddenly,
Tragedy,
Surely, by God not planned,
Stolen,
Untimely and unfair,
Ended,
With seatbelts unfastened,
Agony.

We owe,
Responsibility,
To other lives,
Caring,
Not to exceed in speed,
Nor to take chance or ruthless risk,
In death daring.

Yet in their lives, the good outweighed
the bad,
Best to remember this and not be sad.

Kathleen M Scatchard

In Memory Of Diana Princess Of Wales

I can picture the lovely island
Wherein your body rests
But your soul is safe in heaven above
And numbered with the blest.

No, I never met you here on earth
But I'll meet you up above
And thank you for the folk you helped
As you served them with your love.

You touched the leper, nursed the weak
You sought the homeless on the street
You travelled miles and miles afar
Your love for the maimed you did not bar.

Heaven is richer by you being there
For those in pain your love did share
God filled your heart with love for all
The old, the young and the very small.

God saw your work on earth was done
So He called you to His heavenly home
You did the work you loved so well
With Him forever more you'll dwell.

You were not there to see the crowd
The day that you were laid to rest
The flowers and the tears that were shed
And the pain in every human breast.

But you'll always be remembered
For the lovely things you've done
My prayer is this, that God will guide
Your two young lovely sons.

Your love, your charm, your gentle ways
Will live with me through all my days
Your visits to our northern isle
We'll never forget your winning smile.

Diana, I would love to paint your picture
That's something I'd like to do
But in the poem that I've just made
I have painted a picture of you.

Tom Lucas

Diana

At last you were in love and loved
Until that dreadful night
When fate took you and Dodi
And you lost your fight for life.

Two young princes without a mother
Wanting to cry out loud
Even though their hearts were breaking
They still stand tall and proud.

Your mother, brother and sisters,
Bereft, and shocked, and distressed
Amazed at a world's reaction
At losing Diana their Princess.

You had a heart so full of love
Gave comfort to all you touched
A kind word, a look, a beaming smile,
For mankind you loved so much.

It took your death, for us to see
A world united in grief,
The flowers and tributes across the globe
To a caring angel, are beyond belief.

If ever there were saints on earth
You were truly one
Now go to sleep and rest awhile
Charles will look after your sons.

Goodbye our own Diana,
What a difference you did make,
For compassion, and love we'll remember you
Rest in peace and safety,
Dear Princess of the Lake.

Eileen Waldron

Your Diana

She bloomed like a rose
In a garden of weeds,
Her smile simply nurtured the soil.
The good Lord He needed
The smile of your rose,
He relieved her of all earthly toil.
Your loss is profound
For your light has gone out,
Her smile will be missed for a start,
She's left you forever,
Forget her? No, never.
Is she not Queen of the Heart?

The bouquets, the blessings,
The prayers on the street,
From thousands of people she never did meet,
They saw in Diana
A girl set apart,
The love that was needed to fill empty hearts.
The homeless will miss her
And the people with AIDS,
The poverty-stricken who knew better days,
She knew they were helpless
In different ways,
Your Diana, simply amazed.

Watch over your nephews
Who are missing their mum,
They'll need a compassionate guide.
In their darkest of moments
Just give them a hug,
They'll be happy with you by their side.
Diana is taking
Her final recline
On the wooded and tiny wee isle,
Where angels will sing
And rejoice among stars
When they see your Diana's bright smile.

Jim Wyer

Diana

A light went out in my life that day
And not only I will feel this way
You were a person so unique
Admired by many, you were loving and sweet
Kind and thoughtful, with time to spare
For those lost souls in great despair
You were a lady loved so very much
And those whose hands you could not touch
You found a place right in their hearts
Be you at home or in foreign parts
You were a mother with a love so great
Would have been Queen but for the hand of fate
There are thousands now who stand and stare
With tears in their eyes because they care
There are flowers flowers all the way
And more arriving every day
The sadness comes because we had to part
But you will be remembered forever
Our Queen of Hearts.

Edna Garbett Barratt

To Diana

You had beauty, along with grace
You had a lovely smiling face.
Warm, compassionate, loving too
That's why the people cared for you.
But, suddenly, now you've departed
You left a nation broken-hearted.
William and Harry are grieving too
But we know your love
Will see them through.

Brenda Holland

Why Does It Hurt?

Why does it hurt
When I thought I didn't care
When your movements didn't matter
And your interests I didn't share.

Why does it hurt
When your children I see
Out there with the public
Putting a brave face on for me?

Why does it hurt
When your public cry out loud
Putting flowers on the pavement
Making me feel proud?

The truth of the matter
Is that I really care
I just somehow never knew it
And the public's remorse I share.

The hurting is still there
Although you're now in peace
Farewell Diana
Your torment now to cease.

Robert Vella

Legacy Of Love

Diana, you touched the un-touchables,
Loved the un-loveable,
Walked where others feared to walk,
Had time to care; had time to share,
Time to smile and time to talk.
To all those in need, a true friend indeed;
Sick children cradled; time for disabled,
Millions of people were blessed;
We wonder, and wonder, and wonder again,
Why did the Lord take the best?
The Battle fought, the Victory won,
We are only remembered by what we have done;
You will always be with us, your example lives on,
Lord, help us to follow,
Till our life's work is done.

William J Bartram

For Princess Diana

We didn't know your loss, not until you were gone,
Until we saw your coffin silently pass along,
You gave your heart and soul, but you were only lent,
For God was in need of an angel, He called and so you went.

But we paved your way with flowers right up to Heaven's door,
and lit your way with candles, for the Princess we loved and adored.

You broke the heart of a nation the day you left for home,
we didn't know or guess that the 'Good' only come on loan.

But we will remember you always, for love is a circle of light,
not eclipsed at all by the deep black night.

Kathleen Cliff

A People's Princess

A lways remember, we love you

P rincess Di, you were a lady true
E nding suffering was your plight
O pening eyes to see the light
P ushing for landmines to be gone
L aughing and cuddling with a little one
E xtinguishing prejudice against AIDS and Gays
'S saying and doing, those were your ways

P ublic understanding is what you sought
R enowned love and affection is what you got
I n your short years, you achieved so much
N o-one will forget your soft gentle touch
C ruelly your life has come to an end
E xcept in our hearts where you're always a friend
S ilent tears roll down every face
S eeing you go to your resting place.

Natalie Baxter

Princess Diana, Queen Of Our Hearts

You were part of our lives for seventeen years,
And during that time, you dried many tears,
From children at play school to derelicts
on streets,
From lepers to paupers - They fell at your feet.

You also cried so many tears of your own,
At times you felt desperate, unloved and alone,
But darling Diana, you were never alone,
We loved you as though you were one
of our own.

Your beauty, compassion and caring ways,
Will live in our memories for the rest
of our days,
A Fairytale Princess, so tender and true,
Could you ever imagine what we all thought
of you?

May we learn from your life what you tried
to show,
To love one another, be it friend or foe,
Dear Father in Heaven, please hear
our prayer,
And keep dear Diana in Thy loving care.

The tributes, the flowers - the mourning
was vast
You left us a legacy which forever will last
Forgive us, Lord when we cry from the pain
Of knowing we won't see Diana again.

Forgive us, too, when we question Why?
Why did our Diana have to die?
Grant Diana, and Dodi eternal rest,
It broke all of our hearts when you reclaimed THE
BEST.

An English rose, lent, not given,
To grow on earth, but to bloom in Heaven,
Resting in peace, now, where the good
people go,
God Bless you, Diana, we all loved you so.

Avril Goodall

Grace And Favour

The world welcomed royalty's wedding -
Archbishop, cathedral and queen -
Which ravished all loyal eyes, shedding
Warm tears as they stared at the screen.
Romance reigned invincible, bringing
Its bounty to hamlet and home,
While Kiri Te Kanawa's singing
Rose clear to Wren's resonant dome.

Though luck may be fickle, deceiving
When future diminishes past,
This honeymoon had us believing
The prologue - so perfect - would last.
Life's credit, not giving but lending,
Distrained in due course on the debt:
Diana, your idyll was ending
In sad disillusion's regret . . .

Publicity's feverish clamour
Grew loud with each outgoing breath:
Sensational scandal and glamour
Pursued you and hastened your death.
Forgotten those marital troubles,
Remembered the causes you served:
Love's traumas have vanished like bubbles
And left you the praise you deserved.

Fate's hammer-blow sounded no warning,
Raised no antecedent alarm;
We nurse a numbed emptiness, mourning
Your beauty and effortless charm.
The tears of a suffering nation
Are tributes that nothing can still:
The well of our deep desolation
Only time's healing waters might fill.

Giles de la Bédoyère

Diana

Our lovely princess so caring and true,
What on earth will we do without you?

Your beautiful face and lovely smile,
Made every day seem all worthwhile.

Your loving ways and gentle touch,
These things and more, we'll miss so much.

To have such a princess, we were
truly blessed,
Even though the Royals couldn't care less.

Giving out more happiness, than you
got by far,
What a special Lady you were and still are.

No-one on this earth could ever take
your place,
We'll never again see your sweet smiling face.

But we'll always remember and never forget,
Even though unfortunately, our paths
never met.

And you'll still be with us, in spirit and soul,
Looking down from Heaven and guiding
us all.

For you thought just as much for the sick and
the poor,
Never too pompous to knock at their door.

You brought joy to people, too many to say.
The dying clung on, to live another day.

You are the sky, the stars, the moon,
Oh, why did you have to die so soon?

We hope you'll live on, in the sons that
you love,
And pray, you'll watch over them, from
Heaven above.

I never, ever thought I'd feel like this,
But not seeing you, is something I'll miss.

Our lovely princess, so caring and true,
What on earth will we do without you?

Gina Gizzi

The Lady Of The Lake

(In Loving Memory Of Diana,
Princess Of Wales)

The light of youth has passed like a fever,
And yet we saw and learnt the greatest lesson of
our lives.

We were with you in the days of your glory,
the world was with you in your death.

The feet of the war-horse drummed upon the
cities of the world,
the kings of the world dragged behind your
chariot, and the people of the world behind your
laws and deeds.

But sadly, for us,
The princess of the world smiles no more.

We searched, but you were gone,
You were in Paris by day and gone by night,
But not all is lost, your star shines Bright,
It illuminated the world - for it is the power of
your light.

Through all your memories, this has been
your path,
A solitary existence amongst the
beautiful stars.

God has saved you from the cruelty of
the world.
You were unique and there are no others like you
to be found.
For only a being who has peace with himself is
capable of joining you.

For now you shall taste the blissful wine of peace,
And tomorrow the earth shall speak,

'She is with me, my jealous breasts will hold her
forever, in peace.
The Lady of your Hearts.'

Laila Al-Bulushi

Our Loss

Everyone is crying, everyone is sad,
They are crying for 'Our Princess',
The best we've ever had.
We couldn't believe it happened
We can't accept it's true.
We need someone to tell you
We loved and respected you.

We all ask 'Why, did it happen?'
But will we ever know
Why, you our beautiful princess
To another world had to go?

Were you afraid or frightened?
Or did you never know
That day, that last Black Sunday
Would be, the last you'd know?

We pray that you are happy,
We hope it's lovely there
We picture 'Dodi' beside you
Giving you everlasting care.

Don't fear for your boys Di
Just look down from Heaven above,
And be proud of the boys you groomed Di,
They have grown, full of your love,

You'll never be forgotten,
Your people won't let you die,
They love and respect you,
And worship you on high.

We can deny, that this has happened
We can pretend it isn't true.
And then we face reality
And realise, we miss you.

But we will meet in a much better place.

Delma Price

Dedicated To Diana, The Princess Of Wales

You touched the hearts of
so many
The poor, the weak,
the needy.

You had compassion
You had grace
You were the innocent victim,
of a brutal chase.

You were admired
You were despised
You were a saint in the
people's eyes.

When times were tough,
you stood above and
showed us all,
you were good enough.

You were remarkable
You were adorable
You were the nation's
sanctity

You had a heart of
gold,
a mind so bold.

You were an angel
of the night,
a bird in full flight.

As time goes by and
people cry
We worship you,
above the sky.

With love,

Georgio Makasis

Diana

You were our vibrant English rose
who transcended rules and wooden prose
who softly opened troubled doors
to comfort souls and embrace our flaws.

You were our fawn with elfin eyes
that joyfully skipped across our skies
who kissed us all with perfumed light
that shone so briefly, yet so bright

So graceful in your times of sadness
you gently bore our unhinged madness
and purified cold, spiteful air
with the fragrance of your loving care

You were the girl across the road
an angel with a gentle ode
whose wistful harp cried out in vain
for love to melt your lonely pain

You were our dove whose fragile wings
though glanced by cruel and poisoned slings
caressed our wounds without a glove
and healed our hurt with tender love

But now our youthful dove lies dead
and her coffin wrapped in royal thread
was borne in slow, majestic grief
through a London knifed with disbelief

Accompanied by the mournful march
of polished boots and scarlet starch
white lilies wept upon her cage
in autumn's sharpened, sunlit rage

And in reverence at the Abbey gate
the ghosts of Kings and Queens did wait
whose hands reached out in noble tide
to anoint their nation's spiritual bride

Without you there's no playful breeze
no trees to climb, no leaves to tease
but the scent of your intoxication
will soothe us with your kind intention

So in your tranquil island bed
may you rest your fair and gentle head
and find the peace to 'freely sing'
and dip your toes in a moonlit ring.

You were Diana, Princess of Wales
the princess of all fairy tales
who left our crown a sparkling gem
in the heir to our Jerusalem.

Duchy Of Cornwall

Compassionata

One look, one smile, one touch,
How it came to mean so much
From a Goddess of the modern age,
Who took her place on a global stage.

Surrounded by a sea of adoring faces,
Made up of different creeds and races,
Soothed by every heartfelt word
That from her loving lips they heard.
Diana had answered the call,
To go out and embrace them all.

The children's Angel of Peace,
The sufferers' release.
Oh! How good of God to bring
One of whom such praises we can sing.
One like us in so many other ways,
Who helped to soften the final days
Of those who had given up on life,
Victims of abuse and strife.

At last they had someone who cared,
And knew the relief of a trouble shared.
And even those that she did not meet
Took her to their hearts in town and street.

Now we have lost the people's friend,
How sad such goodness had to end.
For everyone left behind,
Justification we cannot find.

M Mayes

Your Light Will Shine Eternal

God lent to us an angel
You were the chosen one
So vibrant and so innocent
When the fairytale begun

You wed your own Prince Charming
Your precious boys were born
But hiding in the shadows
was the ever-present thorn.

It twisted and it turned
until the marriage fell apart
And you were left alone
to mend your aching broken heart.

Then suddenly you realised
You were the pawn among the kings
So you pulled your life together
and moved on to better things.

To the old folk and the homeless
to the dying and the feared
You touched their lives with happiness
and our love for you just seared.

Finally true love found you
so your heart could now run free
But destiny decided it was
not for us to see.

So God recalled His Angel
to return to Him above
Never to be lonely
but to share eternal love.

No prying eyes can see you
your foe no longer hound
So rest in peace Diana
with the new love you have found.

But never has our nation
felt such sorrow or such pain
And never will our nation
feel this depth of grief again.

For you were the people's Princess
and our love will never end
Your light will shine eternal
to each of us a friend.

God in all His wisdom
snatched you from our tender touch
But He'll never take you from our hearts
WE LOVE YOU FAR TOO MUCH.

Angela Connor

The Picture

The world, one day, would glance upon,
A picture that was new!
And it would study hard its find,
To analyse its view.

The frame was dark, and heavy wood,
To give the canvas strength.
And oh! What coloured oils were used,
All throughout its length!

Such beauty man had never seen,
Nor ever would again!
Compassion hung in every shade,
But never stayed the same!

Love ran through, on brushstrokes wide!
And Truth shone there so bright!
And Tenderness caressed each scene,
As gentle as the night!

The subject of this painting was,
The suffering of Mankind.
The destitute, the poor, the sick,
Were lovingly entwined!

Each simple soul was much enriched,
To be included in,
This deeply moving Masterpiece!
The picture called 'Diana'!

James Bull

Tribute To A Friend

(Lady Diana Spencer)

She changed all our hearts,
Brought cheer to our lives,
Wisdom to husbands, strength to wives.

This beautiful Princess,
Taken too soon,
The light had now dimmed,
From the pale yellow moon.

And now as we mourn her,
With grief and great loss,
Perhaps, we should pause, and count
The true cost.

She showed how each one,
Could reach out in love,
To those who had nothing,
Except God's perfect love.

So by her example, her beauty and grace,
Let us in honour, remember her face,
That shone like an angel,
Her heart full of love,
She now is at peace,
With her Father,
Above.

David Grant

Diana's Inspirations

Diana's inspirations and never-ending love.
An Angel sent from Heaven,
to change the world for God.
Her hopes, her dreams, her laughter,
will always carry on.
Oh! How she touched the hearts of everyone.

L Nicholls

Goodnight Candlelight

A flower with her petals
Blossoming each day
A butterfly who spread her wings
To quickly fly away

Who brought us so much laughter
And made a smile spread wide
And if the world was at war
She'd weaken the divide

A free but troubled spirit
Who searched for happiness
Each golden opportunity
With joy she would caress

She helped so many people
Who could not help themselves
And wiped each tear of sorrow
Brought on by great ill-health

It did not seem to matter
That she would sometimes feel
So sad and oh so lonely
Who yearned for love so real

And when she finally found it
When things were going her way
The candlelight stopped burning
She slowly passed away

The Princess left her mourners
All wondering 'Oh why?'
And almost every person
In the world had to cry

Goodbye Princess Diana
Wherever you may be
I hope you've found the love you craved
For all eternity.

Deborah Gorman

Diana 1961 - 1997

A wonderful mum and princess
Whose love in our hearts we hold dear
Over a million bouquets is our gift to you
A petal for every tear.

Your efforts did not go unnoticed
You had a heart of gold
Its magic you spun around the world
Like a rose, its petals unfurled.

You touched the heart of everyone
Both here and afar
And brought to light the grief and pain
The suffering of war.

There's not a person on this earth,
Who can ever take your place.
You turned the eyes of everyone,
To help the human race.

Now God enfolds you in His arms,
Our prayers reach out to you,
On earth you were our Queen of Hearts
God bless, we all loved you.

E Jones

God's Gift

God looked down
And with a smile
Lent us Diana
Just for a while
With hopeful intent.
We took her to heart
Without ever thinking
That one day we'd part,
The pain of life
She carried so well
The heartache she felt
No one could tell,
She gave us her all
Compassion and love
That God looked down
From Heaven above,
Her beauty and grace
Her light how it shone
In one fleeting moment
Diana was gone.
A golden soul
So radiant and bright
Sits on God's right side
Tonight.

Michael J Hayes

Compassionate Companion

The heavenly gates are open wide
For Diana and Dodi side by side
Our hearts are broken now you are gone
Leaving behind a sun that shone
Compassionate companions to all who are in pain
But in our hearts you will remain
Happiness and joy to Dodi and Di
As all here on earth cry out goodbye
Work on earth done and sorrow departs
Farewell, adieu, be still at peace
Our Queen of Hearts.

Mary Sutherland

Untitled

God sent us down an angel
His duties to perform
This was done with dignity
And she took the world by storm
Now that He has called her
To His home away up high
The brightest star that shines at night
Will be our darling Di.

Rest in peace.

A E Board

Diana

The world will seem an empty place
When we no longer see her face,
Now that she is but a dream
This is how the world will seem:

Like a candle with no wick
Like a clock that doesn't tick,
Like a fire without coal
Like a mint without the hole;

Like a forest without trees
Like a beehive without bees,
Like a doughnut without jam
Like mint sauce without the lamb;

Like a tunnel with no light
Like a boxer with no fight,
Like a TV with no screen
Like a palace with no queen.

She stood out amongst the rest
And never failed to try her best
To comfort those who were in pain;
She could not live her life in vain.

She fought through all the madness
Despite her pain and sadness
And, with the love she freely shared,
She showed the world she really cared.

Her smile will live forever more
But we will miss her, that's for sure,
Despite her role of many parts
She really was a Queen of Hearts.

As far back as we can see
Her happiness was not to be,
Now that she's found her release
I pray that she may rest in peace.

Theodosia Soteriou

We Stand And Weep

(In Memory Of Diana, Princess Of Wales)

We stand and weep,
She was not ours to keep,
And tho' she stayed for but a while,
Through her deeds she made us smile.

And, as we stand and stare
at her coffin, she is not there,
Her soul is in the morning mist
and in every life she kissed.

We stand and weep,
she was not ours to keep,
An angel lent from Heaven above,
Who came to earth to show us love.

Do not weep,
She is ours to keep,
Though we are now so far apart,
Her loving deeds stay in our hearts.

Nia Lloyd Williams

In Memory Of A Princess

Head bowed
A nation stood
In silent prayer
To remember a Princess
No longer here
Its grief
Its sorrow
Now felt throughout the land
As the world stood back
To reflect in quiet reverence
As each tear fell
So the flowers grew
From the heart they came
As a token and tribute
To a Princess who cared
Whose love within our hearts
Will always remain
A burning flame.

A Harvey

A Tribute To Diana

The tenor bell was tolling the whole world shared our grief,
The show of adoration was quite beyond belief,
The gift that was Diana had been cruelly snatched away
The nation showed just how it felt by queuing night and day.
The sea of tears, the written words, the bouquets large and small
A feeling of togetherness enfolded one and all.
She thought ignorance and prejudice were not worth very much
And though she was of noble birth she had the common touch.
She was frequently a rebel, this jewel in the crown
And there were those amongst us who thought she'd let us down.
But the attitude of millions now proved this to be wrong
As they showed exactly how they felt with prayer, verse and song.
It's often said that tragedy promotes something that is good
And a wind of change is blowing where Royalty once stood.
Now protocol and precedent seemed to be swept away
And simplicity and silence were the order of the day.

Now all the hype is over and you've been laid to rest
Your family have made a vow that they will do their best
To guide your boys and say the hounding of the press will cease
And so in your small island grave your soul can Rest in Peace.

Joan Whitehead

Diana, Princess Of Wales

The world seems to have stopped for a few minutes today.
Our beloved fairy-tale Princess has passed away.
Never again to feel that gentle touch, that warm embrace,
never again to gaze upon that truly beautiful face.

Who shall we wave our flags for, now she has gone,
how patiently we would wait, on the crowded concrete streets.

Just to wait for a glimpse of that radiant smile, her serene grace.

She could love, and pacify that wriggly child,
clutch gently that elderly person's hand, her unhurried pace.

We will never forget this truly special English rose.

Now may she rest in peace, the chapters of her life on earth are now at a close.

Heather Lynes

Princess

She touched our hearts
with all her love,
Now she is in Heaven above,
God reached out
and touched her hand,
She took it, now she is in God's land,
Never has there ever been
A Princess fit to be a Queen,
Ever so shy, ever so coy,
She filled our hearts
with so much joy.

A Henry

Diana

Time shall not lessen
The impact of your passing
Oceans of teardrops
Won't wash away the pain
In memory we'll cherish
Your face so sweetly smiling
Diana we'll never
See your like again

So thanks for the memories
The sunshine and the laughter
Thank you for guiding
We who blindly grope
Thank you for sharing
Our suffering and sorrow
Thank you for showing
That there is always hope

So rest there with JESUS
Stroll through Heaven's garden
Play with the children
On Canaan's golden shore
Goodbye to the sweetest
Who made life so much brighter
Diana in memory
You'll live for evermore.

John Johnston

Our Nation Mourns

The nation is mourning
It's all for you
Why did you leave us
Grieving for you
If all of our tears could
Bring you back
You'd never have left us
As tragic as that
You were our young princess
So rare that is true
Dear God how we wish
It were all so untrue.

Susan Kelly

Never Enquire

Never enquire too closely into the nature
of Beauty
You should not have pointed that unwavering eye
onto her smile
For it needed the well-spring of bubbling thought
to survive

You should never have pried into the hidden
places of Beauty
For she was human as you are human
It was cruel to expose those little murky pools to
public gaze.

All of those questions you should never
have asked
For she could not have explained herself
to you
And the trying just tangled the real and true into
false briars of words

Why try to make yourself a product of Beauty?
You could not have gift-wrapped the kisses she
gave where you would not
Or hugs, the sharing of giggles, teasing hours
and whispered confidences.

You cannot hold, or understand the glint of water
around the oar
The dappling of light on flowers laid
under trees
These also have the name of Beauty, but probing
them will not bring her back

You should never enquire too closely into the
nature of Beauty
For true Beauty's nature is too subtle
To endure the grasping, groping clumsiness of
such as you.

Sandra Peddle

My Tribute To Diana, Princess Of Wales

Sleep on Princess
A dreamless rest of peace
Beneath a counterpane
Of flowers where worries cease.
No longer troubled
At your journey's end
When the whole world
Is grieving for a friend.
We who are left
Must face the great unknown,
While you who rest
Have journeyed safely home.
You've left behind
A legacy of care
Which, by your example
And courage we should share.
No ugly barriers
Of colour, class or creed
Only compassion
Where there is pain and need.
The homeless rehoused,
The landmines all banished,
The sick given hope
And prejudice vanished.
We, in our frailty,
Are vulnerable and lost
Sadly too late
We now must count the cost.
Often the truth
Distorted in the mind
Instead of trust
Which waits for us to find.
On wings of angels
Soaring high above
God in His wisdom
Only asks for Love.

Vanda Gilbert

God's Flower

One day God looked upon us
From Heaven in the sky,
He sought a special flower
To grace His home on high.
The flower that He looked for
Was gentle, straight and true,
Unselfish, caring, beautiful,
That flower, Di, was you.
God plucked the flower from this world
And placed it in the sky,
And left us all down here on earth
Asking 'Why, oh why?'
Now our most precious bloom has gone,
Whose like we'll see no more,
And as we mourn our tragic loss
We ache right to the core.
But though we'll miss you terribly
And we're all stunned and sad,
We know you're smiling down on us
And we'll try not to feel bad.
Though you were only loaned to us
For just a few short years,
You'll watch us all from Heaven
And help us dry our tears.
In Heaven life's eternal,
So this flower that God chose,
Will bloom through all four seasons
Our cherished English rose.

Helen Hines

Diana

Her life on earth is ended.
Eternal life begun.
The brightest light in Heaven
Shines down on everyone,
Always the beauty and smile will remain,
Whilst her love beams down from afar,
God's hand will guide her now,
Forever to be a star.

Joyce Dee

An Ode To A True Princess

Your eyes they sparkle in the stars
which shine at night so bright
Your smile it brightens up the moon
which lights our sky at night.

Your hair it glistens in the sun
which warms us to the skin
Your heart gives life into the sea
so deep yet still within.

You are the clouds so pure and white
you are the green of grass
And through the trees you are the breeze
so gentle as you pass.

You are the sweetness of the dew
on petals in the morn
You are the breath a new-born gasps
you are the break of dawn.

You are the rainbow arching out
encircling us with love
Our guardian angel of the skies
still caring from above.

Your passing on was not in vain
we will carry on your fight
You have achieved what you set out to do
you made the world unite.

You will never be far from our thoughts
and this we shan't forsake
Sleep well Princess Diana
Our Lady of the Lake.

With love,

Sindy Malpas

Diana Princess 'Gloria'

An emblem of immortal love,
A flower beyond compare,
The gift sent down from Heaven above,
This maiden sweet and fair,
That God may touch our hearts again,
New hope the world has given,
Millions have felt that searing pain,
Crying to God in Heaven.

O touch our hearts, dear God above,
Our tears not yet subdued,
Diana darling of our love,
In all our hearts abide,
Help us to know the pain we bore,
When Diana went to Heaven,
O Lord, help us to love you more,
Through homage we have given.

We felt your Holy Spirit's power,
In silent adoration,
May we from that most hallowed hour,
Accept our soul's salvation,
Teaching us how our Saviour died,
Through bitter pain and sorrow,
How on a cross was crucified,
That we His love may follow.

Now let Diana's love and care;
Compassion freely given,
In us show kindness everywhere,
Until we meet in Heaven,
No greater virtue can behold,
As history tells life's story,
A wonder ever to be told,
Diana Princess 'Glory'.

Ernest Stephen Swan

Dear Heavenly Father
(Reference St John 11 vs 25-26)

Dear Heavenly Father,

We thank you for the life and work of Princess Diana for the love and compassion she gave to others, for the new awakening of love shown to one another through the grief that touched everyone, we pray that we could go on in the realisation that we need to be humble and kind and consider other people, please help us Lord.

Most of all we thank you Lord for your compassion and your great love, the agape love shown on the Cross at Calvary where you suffered and died, but rose again from the dead and all who believe in you though they be dead yet shall they live and whosoever liveth and believeth in you shall never die, thank you Lord for your word.

In Jesus' name,

Amen

Dorothy Price

The Problem That Wouldn't Go Quietly And Died As A Result Of Her Fame

A people's Princess
The most looked at woman in the world
A media Princess
Who understood the power of touch, of hug
That gesture that was always more eloquent
than mere words

And as the fairy tale fractured
She laid open the workings of monarchy
Of hereditary privilege
Refusing to accept a husband's infidelity
A quest for depth in a world of superficiality

The clothes she wore
The water she drank
The charities she supported
In the hearts of those she touched
She will continue to glow, forever young

Dying for a world's need
To carry on looking
Diana Frances
A people's Princess
A Queen of Hearts.

B A Stone

Diana
(This is my tribute to Diana, the 'People's Princess)

Princess Di you've gone to Heaven
Away from prying eyes
Where you will be so happy
Far beyond the skies,
Your father there to meet you
With friends and family
And you all will live forever
In peace and harmony.

W Nicholson

Sleeping Princess

She sleeps in peace on her island green
By the quiet lapping water
Far away from the spotlight's glare
And the cameras'eyes that sought her
Our Princess, our Golden Rose, yes
But first
Precious mother, dear sister,
much loved daughter.

Kath Finney

Princess Diana - A Tribute To A Special Lady

A candle flickered in the dark,
a ray of hope was seen
But now a nation breaks its heart,
all hope a shattered dream,
A word, a smile, a simple touch
Princess Diana you'll be missed so much.

You taught us compassion
for all that we meet
The rich and the famous,
or the poor on the street;
You taught us that life was a gift
we could share
With those less fortunate
who have no one to care.

Just like a flower blossoms so bright
Princess Diana you were a guiding light;
You taught the young princes
all they should know
To set them up right for each day as they grow.

Your life had a meaning, a lesson for all
That no matter what our start in life
like you we could stand tall,
Your life was just beginning
to turn itself around,
You'd put the past behind you
and your feet on firmer ground.

They say the good go early
I guess this must be true,
For the world lost an angel today
when God took you;
He took you back to rest in peace
and left a void untold
A world of broken hearts
mourning a heart of gold.

There'll never be another who'll
reach so far and wide
No one will ever understand why
suddenly you died.

You'll always be the Queen of Hearts
as long as we shall live,
You taught us that compassion
is a lovely gift to give.

Pat Ferris

Diana, Forever In Our Hearts

You're not here anymore, what can we do about it?
I just can't understand, why we need to fight it.
I feel so sad, I feel so lonely, can we save you, oh, if only
A thousand people are to blame, the papers ought to feel the shame
A Nation without a hand to hold, we always knew you had a heart of gold
Words can't express the way we feel, the loss of a Princess, oh so real
In the hearts of many you were our Queen
Most of your work seemed to go unseen
To care for the needy, the sick and the dying
Why did the press have to go on lying?
So they got their story in the end, but did they have to kill our friend?
Why do pictures mean so much?
Are we a world that's out of touch?
A million questions, no answers why,
so many good people have to die?
Life goes on, it always must, but sometimes God I lose my trust.
My trust in you to put things right, are we still precious in your sight?
Today has been a solemn day, so much love to take away
People in the streets upset and crying, their love for DIANA never dying.

J Garrington

Diana

To the world she was a princess
But to us she was a friend
To William and Harry a mother
On whom they could depend.
To give them hugs and kisses
Lots of happiness and love
To them I say she's still with you
Watching over from heaven above.

Although her troubles were many
And she was often in despair
She still found the strength and courage
To show how much she cared.
Loving, giving, caring, sharing
A smile and a tender touch
To all she met on life's long path
These gestures meant so much.

We gave you our hearts
And you gave us yours
Until our dying days
You'll live in our hearts forever
No-one can take our memories away.

Brenda Young

Goodnight

Goodnight to our star that sparkled world-wide.
To our guardian angel,
To your magical smile,
Goodnight to our Princess,
Queen of our Hearts
Though you are in Heaven
You'll never be far.

Goodnight to your arms
That were open to all
To the joy that you gave
And the lessons you taught
I'll not say goodbye to you, just goodnight
For I'll see you one day
When the timing is right.

Debbie Greaves

Diana

You impressed us all with your charm and grace,
You cheered those you met with your smiling face,
You helped the helpless, the poor, the sick,
In a life so sadly short and quick,
You gave your all for those in need -
Of every nation, race and creed,
You touched our hearts with your unique beauty,
You always did what you thought your duty,
Yet, reviled by some for doing so,
Your care and kindness are what WE know.
Our tragic loss is Heaven's gain:
Queen of Hearts! Long shall you reign.

Colin Janes

Island In The Lake

(For Diana - Princess Of Wales)

Upon an island in the lake,
One sleeps, eternal, will not wake,
But from the island reaches out,
The brightest light without a doubt.
In life, the nation touched by love,
Pray as her soul takes flight above,
Sped by a thousand golden wings.
The breezes whisper, Elton sings.
A candle's fragile flame that shone,
Snuffed out by Death, and now is gone,
Cast to an island, rest in peace,
Half a troubled life, now ceased.
Princes, quiet, reflect and pray,
Shadows lengthen from today.

Liz Rotheram

A Tribute To Diana

Like the sun, the stars, the moon at night
Diana was our guiding light
She smiled and laughed, she loved to touch
In her short life she gave so much.

Around the world she spread her care
For young and old she was always there
It was as if she knew, she could not stay
To teach us all, to show the way.

To love, to touch, to hug, to heal
These things she taught us all to feel
A part of her will always be
In all of us in memory

She left behind two precious sons
One soon will be a man
Then we will have a King of Hearts
From our Queen of Hearts, Diana.

We live on in our children.

Christine Jane Franklin

Diana Frances Spencer August 31st 1997

Heart freeze.
Time cease.
Mouth wide open -
Disbelief.
Has NOT happened - Nightmare scene.
Life, please wake me - Devil's Dream!

Tears, wet millstones, well with pain
in eyes where truth has dawned, insane.

Our prisoner, without a cage,
Victim - of this corrupted age -
Is FREE at last, intrusions - passed.

This Lady was ahead of Time.
Her passing's Ours
Her absence - mine.

Heart free,
Timed release.
Shine Forever.
Rest in Peace.

Peter Ransome

In Memory Of Diana

We never can forget you Di
The way you used to be
Loving, caring, sharing,
For all the world to see.

A light went out
The day she died,
Her lover Dodi
By her side.
They died together
So in love

And now we know
They're in Heaven above.

E Kirkby

Sonnet On The Death Of Diana, Princess Of Wales

The sun is dimmed within the dome of Heaven,
And on the world a veil of sorrow lies,
We mourn with tears from hearts so deeply riven
For one who has cast off her mortal ties;
A lamp went out on earth with her demise,
The shining beacon that lit up the day
Is now no more, yet she will still rise
To greater heights of love, forever stay
Within the nation's memory and heart,
Revered and worshipped, even, for her grace,
Her understanding of the common part,
Her warm humanity, her smiling face;
Though crushed and broken lies the English Rose,
Fresh, on another shore, her beauty grows

Betty McIlroy

Princess Of The Lake

Of noble line from Tudor time,
Like a simple bud of briar she rose,
From naive skirt to wondrous gowns.
She filled the world with rapturous prose.

Princess of the common people,
Duchess of Cornish land.
She won the people with a smile,
And held the ailing hand.

For causes she held just,
She campaigned wide and near.
Above apathy and ignorance,
To raise their profile clear.

In the window of the world,
An unjustly direct light.
Stole away her privacy,
Made restless, troubled night

Of royal lineage are her sons,
A blessed gift so plain.
Cruelly a light extinguished,
As it rose up high again.

And her royal dignity,
Through her sons did flow.
As they paid their last respects,
To a candle once aglow.

A bunch of flowers,
A simple posy hold.
Lay it in remembrance,
Multiply ten millionfold.

Surrounded now by liquid moat,
In the church of her home's land.
A shrine of royal pilgrimage,
A place to hold her hand.

K P Watch

Diana

DIANA the queen of everyone's heart,
Young life cut short, body torn apart
Her new world beginning, was not to be,
Blood shed on roadway, Parisians could see.

DIANA spread happiness, wherever she went,
Compassion she gave, from Heaven God-sent,
A touch, a smile, showing shy radiant face,
We shall not forget, no one else can replace.

DIANA so gentle, sensitive true,
Whoever she met, for her only you,
To sick, to dying, to young, to old,
Her charisma she spread, a sight to behold.

DIANA a mother, her sons were her life,
Two boys so young, have now to bear strife,
One heir to the throne, she was his guide,
Now what awaits, without her by his side.

DIANA her life, held love, yet great sadness,
Married a prince, at first there was gladness,
She was born a sweet angel, right from the start,
Gone now, not forgotten, this rare loving heart.

Muriel Rodgers

Diana Dream

Floral isle on England's green,
Diana, sleep, Diana, dream.
Leaves are falling all around,
Birdsong makes a joyous sound.
Floral isle on England's green,
Diana sleep, Diana, dream.

Whispering winds, like spirits, sigh.
Perfumed flowers wave goodbye.
Through dark grey skies shine golden rays,
Remember only love filled days.
Floral isle on England's green,
Diana sleep. Diana dream.

K Bradley

Condolence She

Not for her the thump of feet upon the street,
The pomp of military sounds
But the steady tenor of the bell
To the tap of horses' hooves
Brings police before behind,
Now protected from the people
Who loved her to destruction.
I see the bearskins and the lilies
And wonder at the silence of the crowd.
So tolls the bell for bodies moving
For she represents a younger people
Who have not known the fear of war
Only love destroyed in life.
What anger stalks the streets
That such a life should be snuffed out.
She no saint but fully living
Of low esteem but so adored,
Touched by love but never seeing
The crowd who came to see the pall.
Then to the Abbey came the people,
Not the great and good so proud
But friends and those who felt her love.
Comes the body, oh, so slowly!
Through the dappled shade of trees
Witnesses to others long since gone,
So much a part the pageantry of death.
I see the bodies of the broken people,
Some in chairs but touched by love,
Some in tears and held by others
But all united in the pain of love.
Now comes the Queen and all her people
To watch the shadow of the past go by
And think of what she could have been.
There goes our doubt about the Crown,
Homage paid before the body
Of a strange and tortured person.
Still comes the carriage measured tread.
I see a husband, wife in holding
Together locked in strangled grief.
Comes father, sons and older prince
Behind the Guards around the coffin.
Throwing flowers the people pray,
Wondering what it is that she would say.
'I vow to thee, my country, all earthly
things above.'
What now for monarch
When so exposed to 'crucify'
From all devouring people,
Represented but fomented
By press machine,
A Babel of hypocrisy,
In the interest of the nation.
So passes she and Dodi Fayed.
'Don't cry for me, young Britannia'.

Sandy Landale

Diana, Queen Of Hearts

We shared your life for many years
We'd see you on the news.
You soon became a mega star
You got such great reviews.

They'd follow you around the world
To every state affair,
Just to get a glimpse of you,
To see what dress you'd wear.

The Princess of the people,
You gave your special care,
Your charisma and compassion
You'd not hesitate to share.

A woman with so much to give
So generous and kind.
You touched us all, the young, the old,
The sick, the maimed, the blind.

Our memories of you are filled
With love, respect and pride.
A trillion hearts were broken
On that fateful night you died.

Though you're no longer with us
Your spirit will remain,
Your smile a ray of sunshine,
Your tears the falling rain.

A nation joined as one in grief
You'll stay within our hearts.
A legend in our lifetime
Diana, Queen of Hearts.

Lydia Martin

Dedicated To Diana, Princess Of Wales

How can it be, who can explain
Taken cruelly from us in the name of fame
The grief we feel, the utter despair
If only you'd known how much we care
Your strength was an example to young
and old
As we slowly watched your life unfold
We admired your courage, your
beautiful grace
You made this world a better place
And yet so suddenly, your bright light diminished
So much left to give, so much left unfinished
An Ambassador for our country you
sought to be
An Ambassador for the world is what we see
You've achieved it all, rest now, fly free

Deborah Jensen

In Memory Of Diana, Princess Of Wales

Such goodness there has never been,
And she will never know our love.
Compassion felt for old and young.

Diana, Gift from One above.

The little babies fondly nursed,
And ailing folk put so at ease,
Good causes fought with all her strength,
All she sought was just to please.

Such sadness in those clear blue eyes,
But now she's with her Saviour true.

Our love we send to both her sons,
May they feel her love, whate'er they do.

Sadly missed and she has left
a void never to be filled.

God bless her always.

Doris A Pearson

My Tribute To Diana - Princess Of Wales

Caring, compassionate, loving; so kind,
Such a charisma this girl's left behind.
How can we forget this young Mother of two
Whose love for her boys was both constant
and true.
Her fun-loving spirit - her radiant smile
Are memories to cherish and keep all the while.
An affectionate person, sensitive too,
Her charitable works always ready to do.
She had a warm, gentle nature as
everyone knows.
With exquisite beauty - a real English Rose.
Countless numbers adored her; she had
sparkle and charm,
And that sweet, rare ability to pacify, calm.
Even the shyest would respond to her touch
And the fact that she cared really helped
them so much.
It just did not matter; race, colour or creed
She responded and aided myriads in need.
We'd be wise just to follow the example she set
Showing so much concern for the people she met.
She has proved to us all that love never fails,
Our lovely Diana - the Princess of Wales.

Winnie Goodson

Diana

You will never grow old, or grey, or bent,
Feel no more sorrow or discontent,
No more pain, no need to hide,

From photographers always by your side,
You will not see your boys grow into men,
See them marry, have children.
No more will you laugh, or dance, or sing,
But we thank you so much for our future king,
He's so much like you, so he has a good start,
God bless you Diana, 'QUEEN OF OUR HEARTS'.

Jackie Whittaker

Legacy Of A Princess

Come my friends let's sit awhile,
let's sit awhile and talk.
Let's shed the difference of our lives,
and forget our different walks.

Let's speak of things that yet to be,
and things that might have been.
Let's talk of things long in the past,
and things we've never seen.

Let's talk of things that went amiss,
and things that yet to right.
But let's not dwell on ifs or buts,
just put our wrongs to flight.

But if we cannot sit and talk,
or make past mistakes amends.
Then at least let us sit awhile,
let's sit awhile as friends.

And if I give my ready hand,
my hand in friend to thine.
Then I would only happy be,
for yours in warmth to mine.

And if you need a shoulder,
I will offer you my heart.
But if you're sick and dying,
then I'll sit until you depart.

For I have tasted all your tears,
and I have felt your sorrows.
I only wish I had the answer,
to brighten all your morrows.

For it matters not to me,
if you're noble or down trod.
For why should it offend me,
if it matters not to God.

This then was the life,
the life of one who cared.
Who felt the other's pain and sorrow,
who broke the rules and dared.

Not for her the rank or file,
nor high brow or low.
Inform or healthy rich or poor,
nor skin brown or yellow.

Now our treasured Princess is gone,
and our grief will never end.
Yet the saddest thing of all,
is that the world has lost a friend.

M A Varris

An English Rose

Sunbeams dance on your resting place, filtering
through simple fronds of lace.
Visions remain of your lovely face,
- Diana - our Princess of Love.

Your life was brief, too soon you'd gone,
but in our souls you still linger on,
You gave us hope, where there was none,
- Diana - our Princess of Love.

Lacking perfection, being mortal born,
- for even a rose, has stems of thorns,
Still England saw you, with crown unworn,
- Diana - our Princess of Love.

People listened, as you gave voice,
Your laughter let the world rejoice,
When we lost you, where was the choice,
- Diana - our Princess of Love.

When Heaven called, you could not stay,
breaking our hearts - you went away,
We all must lose, we all must pay,
- Diana - our Princess of Love.

An island of flowers, is where you sleep,
our sorrow hurts, it runs so deep,
Some day we'll smile, but now we weep,
for Diana - our Princess of Love.

R Halford

Diana

With a smile from your face
And a touch from your hand
You brightened the lives
Of the whole of this land.

A nature so gentle
A heart filled with love
You were sent for a reason
From God up above.

A soul of compassion
A spirit so free
You were loved by a nation
And always will be.

Above all these things
Was your role as a mother
You were loving and giving
There just can't be another.

May you rest in peace with angels
In God's loving, tender care
May your goodness, love and smile live on
Through William, your heir.

Teresa Low

Another Angel In Heaven

The brightest lights never
Shine long enough -
And this was so with you.
Too caring for this world;
Too special, too human,
Too beautiful for words.
You're where you belong now -
Where you'll live forever.
Another angel in Heaven, yet
Your spirit is still with us.

Steve Jeffery

For Princess Diana

To us you were the Queen of Hearts.
And now our lives are torn apart,
Your caring charm and smiling face,
No one will ever take your place,
You loved and laughed and suffered sorrow,
You gave hope to the people for tomorrow,
You put your life upon the line,
Walking through the fields of mines,
Talking, touching, reaching out,
All walks of life you cared about,
Today the flags at 'half mast fly',
The question we all ask is 'Why?'
The sick and well. The old and young,
United by the love for one,
Standing together in disbelief,
Crying together and sharing their grief,
Together they stand hour by hour,
To write their condolence, to lay down a flower,
They openly mourn and say their 'goodbyes',
To the world's 'Queen of Hearts'
To 'Our Princess Di'.

Pauline Horsham

Diana - Princess Of Wales

The time you spent upon this earth
Was filled with so much good
The whole world now is mourning
Their grief is understood.

They think about your two dear sons
Who are left without a mother
And then reflect the work you did
There'll never be another.

Now that you've been laid to rest
No words can do you harm
Apart from all the work you did
You had that special charm

No prejudice of race or creed
Skins yellow, black or white
When you went to higher realms
Out went a shining light.

Maisie Sampson

Diana
The People's Princess

The nation bared its anguished heart,
Each simple blossom played its part,
Each tear that fell, along the way
A fount of sorrow and dismay.

Sad equine hoof-beats tolled the knell
More poignant than the ancient bell
To mark the passing, share the grief,
Sorrow and sadness, disbelief.

Welsh Guardsmen marched with measured tread,
Flanked the cortege, guard foot and head.
These too will mourn and miss the Rose
But silently in barracks close.

Her broken body laid to rest
Among the blooms the nation blessed.
Her spirit is a legacy,
Memorial and memory.

We will keep faith with you Princess,
The love you gave we can't assess.
Within our hearts you will remain
People's Princess with world acclaim.

Sidney A Gadd

Beauty Within

Who was this person, this shy young girl?
We watched for the woman inside to unfurl
And when she did through the heartache
and pain
Of a loveless marriage so hard to explain
She emerged so beautiful inside and out
She produced two sons whom she loved without
doubt
And gave freely to others her time and
her love
But all that she got in return was the shove
By the media and sceptics whose hounding
gave strife
Hell-bent on destroying this wonderful life
And now she has gone through no fault
of her own
I'm sure she now basks in the love she
has shown.
Diana we were inspired and all in your debt
But your one shining light we will never forget
And may your good works carry on in
your name
Your true vocation, the reason you came.

Joan Twine

God's Angel

Her love is but a breath away,
her kindness near at hand
I see her shining eyes,
beneath the halo's golden band.
The lowly people felt her hand touch
their saddened hearts.
Her smile helped many souls in pain
her healing love to share,
God touched her loving heart
and whispered come with me sweet dear,
Your love will sprinkle from the stars,
and on the earth bestow
God sent an angel for a while
His loving hand to show.

V N King

A Tribute To Diana, Princess Of Wales

'Princess of the People' is the mantle
which you wear,
And with your sudden passing the loss
is ours to bear.
Your many caring facets, like a diamond
shining yet,
Never will be dimmed, for we shall
not forget.
A Lady born to be a Princess, who played
so many parts,
You did indeed become a Queen,
the Queen of all our hearts.

Marjorie Hone

Our Angel In Disguise

God sent to us a messenger,
An angel in disguise,
In all this world, we did not share,
More wonderful a prize.

She helped the sick, she helped the poor,
No-one could show more care,
Her loving smile, her tender glance,
Brought comfort everywhere.

Her work had only just begun,
She had so much to do,
Our little angel in disguise,
A fairytale come true.

We did not need to know her,
We loved her just the same,
Then one tragic morning,
Death's young angel came.

And now she's gone to Heaven,
Our Darling Princess Di,
You've taken her away from us,
But God, please tell us, 'Why?'

John Napier Williams

Pain

Even God sometimes
Makes mistakes,
Takes for Himself
The brightest star,

Leaves mankind bereft
Clothed in sackcloth and ashes,
Numb, cold, old,
Children weeping for
Loss of gentle hands
That caress;

A darker world
With one star less.

Lily Izan

Death Of A Princess

On the Festival of the Mooncakes
I swam in a Blue Lagoon,
And on high
The sun-soaked sky
Filled with a choir of bird song,
Emperors, as they soared,
Of their Paradise Kingdom.
On the shore
The breeze flicked
The leaves of the coconut trees,
Whilst at sea
Distant sails dipped
A toe in an Ocean
Of Dreams.

On the Festival of the Mooncakes
I swam in the Blue Lagoon,
On high
In the darkened sky
A bird
Clipped her wings
On the edge of the sun;
And a silence fell on the Kingdom.
On the shore
Nothing stirred
In the leaves,
Whilst at sea
Distant sails slipped away
Beyond the horizon.

On the Festival of the Mooncakes
I swim in a Lake of Salt Tears,
Birds fly high
In the sky,
Out of reach.
Orchid petals
Settle
Onto the beach
Stained
By the warm rains.
The world holds its breath
Waiting
To catch the tread
Of her final footsteps.

Sandra Davies

Diana - The Hunted

You, appeared, so timid, so shy,
Like a doe emerging from the forest.
Eager to learn how others live in the world around you,
But nervous, always alert, looking over your shoulder,
Watching for the hunters who stalk you.

You - grew, into a beautiful creature,
A wonder in the eyes of all who saw you.
Your beauty and charm, warmth and love,
Attracted the attention and the interest of the whole world,
And from all over the world, the hunters came.

You - gave, of yourself so freely,
Eager to help the troubled, the sick and the dying,
Trying to publicise the plight of downtrodden and poor.
Your compassion, your touch, and your love,
Only made them hunt you more.

You - loved, your sons with passion,
And you taught them how to care.
You showed them how real life is lived,
By real people, everywhere.
But as you turn a corner, the hunter he is there.

You - lived a life so public,
And the hunt it rarely ceased.
From dawn to dusk and day to day,
You became their sole obsession,
The hunters' 'guns' were aimed your way.

They never, ever let you be.
As they pursued you underground,
Relentlessly they fired their shots.
As you lay wounded and dying the firing never stopped.
They just wanted more and more and more . . .

You left us all so suddenly,
Without a goodbye, a wave, or a smile.
The Father outstretched his arms, to an angel,
Who was engulfed in the peace and tranquillity she so truly deserved.
Free from the hunters at last.

Diana, you were beautiful.
You gave so much more than all the rest.
On this sad day a bright light went out,
And a darkness filled our world.
But through the sorrow and our pain,
We will never forget you.
You were, the 'Queen of all our Hearts'

Carol Harris

Diana

An angel on earth you are no more,
the Lord took you back, don't cry anymore.
He put you here to bring love and compassion,
and the world loved you more than one could imagine.

A mother to all, not only your boys, whom you so adored,
we are sorry your privacy was so ignored.
the world will unite and cradle them in its arms,
to your boys will come no harm.

Don't cry anymore, the Lord calls to you,
I have found you a man, who loves you too.
Two angels in Heaven you must be, to get away from the paparazzi,
who so cruelly took you to your death,
I know the world will never forget.
A legend, a saint on earth we were blessed,
your life here not the happiest.
But still you gave love, life and cheer,
to all who had so much to fear.

No-one, could ever replace,
our Princess with whom we were graced.
A lady whom we will love forever more,
of this I am truly sure.

But sadly it's time to say goodbye,
to the Queen of Hearts,
our beloved Di.

T Williams

Diana
A Special Gift From God

She was an earthly butterfly of beauty
Colours intermingled
On the wing she soared
through earthly life.
She beautified our lives
with her delicate beauty and gossamer wings.
She touched our lives
with her simplicity.
She moved us with her love.
Our butterfly has taken flight
Her delicate wings have soared the corridors of
space
Through the realms of light
She has come to rest.
She has reached the breathless peace
and tranquillity of eternity.
She is free from the bonds which clipped her
earthly wings
And God has welcomed her into His
loving hands
And breathed his breath of eternal love
over her
And all Heaven rejoices
Diana has arrived home
Safe in the arms of her Lord.

Julie Howard Moore

England's Treasure

On an island in a lake
They buried England's treasure,
Not silver gold or diamonds
But love beyond all measure.
To those who had a share
Before it vanished from our eyes,
Nothing can compare
It's their most important prize.
This treasure of the people
We shall see no more, and yet,
The brilliance, and value,
We never will forget.

Barbara Jones

And So She'll Sail

Diana you're not here anymore,
But sail on the 'whitest cloud'
Smiling lovingly at the people you owned
Not dressed in a tear-soaked shroud.

Diana you were worshipped,
For the people you did care,
From rich and famous people
To paupers everywhere.

You gave out love for nothing
And were so genuine,
Touching people's faces,
Around you birds would sing.

Now those little birds are famous,
All white and called 'a dove.'
And just like you so peaceful and warm
But from you they found their 'love'.

Gaynor Jenkins

Diana Princess Of Wales

You did so much for others
From every walk of life
A ray of hope and comfort
To lift them from their strife
This power you had within you
Shone like a glowing sun
Bestowed not on selected few
But shared for everyone
You were born to be a Lady
A Princess and a Queen
It's all too unbelievable
No more will you be seen
And though not Queen of country
Of that you were apart
Much more than that to everyone
you were the Queen of Hearts
Pray God may you be happy
In peace and lasting love
As you take your place in Heaven
With the angels up above

Elizabeth Fraser

A Tribute To Diana, Princess Of Wales

Oh why did Fate bestow no care
On one so lovely and so fair?
She smiled and thought of those in need
Imparting love in word and deed.
The world stood still that tragic morn
When Life went out at the coming dawn
Her charm and beauty knew no bound
Happy best with folk around.
She was so precious - more than gold
Now our hearts are sad and cold.
We're filled with sorrow to see her part
She truly was the world's sweetheart.
As radiant as the morning sun
As lovely as a rose
Will we ever see her like again?
'Tis God that only knows.
May she rest in Heaven, and there abide
Sadly missed by all world-wide.

Bernard Sweeney

To Diana

Diana,

I was unable to bring you flowers
But my tears were from the heart,
And though we never ever met,
Of my life you were a part,
You were the 'People's Princess'
So caring and sincere,
The love you showed to everyone
Was so unconditionally clear,
And though fate has been unkind to you
And taken you so young,
The compassion that you gave this world
Will be forever sung,
You will never be forgotten
It will be written down in time,
The beautiful 'Princess of Wales'
Our hearts will be your shrine.

Dianne Woods

Diana

Her smile could soothe their sorrow,
All promises she kept,
As she comforted the dying,
Her blue eyes wept.

She admired strength and courage,
And she needed the same,
While her gift of true compassion,
Eased the guilt and blame.

In life she had been troubled,
The people knew her pain,
And she tragically was taken,
As true love grew again.

It's her sons the nation cry for,
They must be so proud,
Knowing that their mother's love,
Is remembered by the world.

As flowers, prayers and poems,
Are offered up to voice,
What Diana meant to everyone,
For her life we should rejoice.

Bobbie Hurdman

Guilt

In the week that
Should not have been,
When we all prayed
To cancel time,
And covered up
Death's clumsy work
With flowers,
A people wept
For past insults
And shoddy deals
It let happen,
That were avenged
Not with hate, but
Compassion.

Joan Kelly

Untitled

The cardboard box is this girl's home
When darkness fell you would come

When you took the sick man's hand
How you made us understand

The child you held within your arms
You sheltered from life's further harms

Their bodies maimed, their pain not healed
Their suffering you have revealed

For all the care that you had shown
Others tried to bring you down

The shy young Di we taught to cry
We didn't listen I don't know why

We stood and watched as they hounded you
As if there was nothing we could do

The Royal protection taken away
We didn't agree, why didn't we say?

Our hearts are heavy our pain is deep
For William and Harry we now weep

You must have thought that we weren't there
But we did love you, we did care

And now we'll pledge this on your death
To protect your boys with our last breath.

Joy Beswetherick

To Diana, Princess Of Wales

No more sadness, no more crying,
No more critics, no more sighing
No more hurt and no more pain
Will ever grieve your heart again.

For you now joy, eternal love
For you now peace in Heaven above
For us your love to play its part;
Long live your work, O Queen of Hearts.

Trish Walton

Diana

Diana such a rare bloom
Flowering so sweetly
Her smiling face cleared the gloom
To cheer us completely

The days seem so dark and bare
Seems there's nothing left to gain
Now that she isn't there
Never to see her face again

She has left us something so rare
Two young oaks, sturdy and strong
To grow among the flowers with care
Given to us, to stay where they belong

Sleep on in tranquil dreams
Never again to feel pain or sorrow
For you it seems
A long time to eternal tomorrow.

E Taylor

Diana RIP

Those bridal scenes of bliss blazed on TV;
our toddler twigged: 'It's Cinderella! See!'
And there, for sure, the root of her allure:
a glass-slipper world of happiness so pure,
of cheers forever, endless bells and chimes,
transmuting our foul world to her sublime.

But her good fairy fouled up; fluffed the script:
the glass was cracked; the idol's robes
were ripped.
We came now to deride, to jeer her fall -
just like the rest, another flawed mortal.

So now we have a lifetime left to rue
those mocks and jests, Diana, we made at you.

Andrew Cunningham

Women Of Love

(A Tribute to Diana, Princess of Wales and Mother Teresa)

A week, not very long,
But in this short space of days
So many things can happen
In so many dreadful ways.

We wake to a world of tragedy,
A world where nothing is fair,
A world of so many people
Where so little of them care.

So why do we have to lose
Two women so many loved,
Who cared for everyone they knew
The poor and sick were their beloved.

One was a regal princess,
The other just a nun,
But even with their differences
The two of them were one.

So goodbye Diana and Teresa,
Two women so good and so strong.
I hope you meet in Heaven,
The place where you both belong.

Amanda McStay

Diana

A gentle hug, a tender touch
to show us that you cared so much,
A kindly word or fond embrace
a loving smile upon your face.

To young and old, sick and lame
you showed compassion just the same.
You touched our lives in different ways
bringing sunshine to our darkest days.

For each of us that still remain
your life and death were not in vain,
A true princess who earned respect
one that the world will not forget.

Giovanna Gallo

Diana The Crown Jewel

The Jewel in the Crown is dead now,
But her memory lingers on.
She lit up so many lives,
Still loved, though her spirit has gone.

Bouquets and bunches of flowers,
Each with a loving word,
Given by people who love you.
Though now you're as free as a bird.

Looking on us mere mortals,
From your place on high.
Listening to the 'sound of silence',
And hearing a soft, low sigh.

A world cries out in sorrow,
'Why did you have to go,
Oh why did GOD allow it,
Oh why?'. . . We'll never know.

Frances R Morgan

In Memory Of Princess Diana

With a friend by her side
to heal her sorrow,
And to return the sparkle
in her eyes.

Her company was soon sought after,
helping where it was most required.
As she travelled around the world
young and old were all inspired.

She showed true compassion
when seeing so many injured people
Always a cuddle, and a smile
for the children she loved so dearly.

On departing saying goodbye
with her wondrous sparkling eyes.
There is no one to replace her
but; no doubt she is still working

From Heaven above
with God by her side.

Mollie Elborough

Princess Diana 1961 - 1997

To us you were a shining star
Kind and honest, strong and bright
A burst of sunshine from afar
To those who couldn't see the light.

A Princess with a heart of gold
Once a wife and twice a mother
There's never been one quite like you
And we'll never see another.

On the night you went away
A candle in our world burned out
The angels have your soul today
You're safe forever, free from doubt.

Princess, we won't forget your work
We have your memories to keep
Your love has touched so many hearts
It's here for us, now that you sleep.

Steve Rouse

Promise To A Princess

At your wedding I watched you glide
down the aisle
Capturing the world with your gleaming
smile
I was only a child, watching wide-eyed
How my vision was blurred,
when I heard that you'd died.

Despite my grief and tears of despair
You made me realise how much I care
About you, and the princes you left behind
And other issues affecting mankind.

Diana, your inspiration has filled me with love
And I promise to you, and our God above
That your death will never be in vain
And all you've achieved, I'll help to maintain.

Thank you for showing me how to give
What life is about, and how to live
REST IN PEACE PRINCESS, you've played
your part
You now live forever inside my own heart.

Wendy Pearce

The Last Journey Home

The bell is tolling slowly in the sunfilled morn,
The horses proud and strutting,
Soldiers march forlorn,
The coffin draped in sadness trundles on
its way,
The crowds stand by in silence, not one word to
say.
Flowers in their thousands strewn along
the road,
Laying a path of colour before the
burdened load.
Five heads bowed in mourning tread the painful
miles, lost now in their memories,
grief replacing smiles.
The journey's nearly over now,
the Abbey's up ahead,
Opening wide its loving doors to welcome in the
dead.
And after all the hymns are sung, and all the
words are said,
They'll lay you down beneath the soil in earth's
eternal bed.

Laura Smith

Star Of Diana

You shone like a star in the sky, so bright,
sent from above to show us the light.

Sharing your love to young and old,
helping the needy, aged and cold.

Sent as an Angel from God above,
to carry on His work and teach people to love.

Oh what an Angel you turned out to be,
gone but not forgotten by millions like me.

The North Star the brightest in the sky,
is now the star of Diana and we all know why.

God Bless you Diana, may you rest in peace.

Carolyn Taylor

The People's Princess

We thank you my Lord for giving us,
Diana Queen of Hearts,
We're sorry she has left us,
in our minds, she'll never part,
Sleep in peace dear gentle lass,
your final journey's made,
Deep in the cold bare earth,
your mortal shell they've laid.

You know now sweet Diana,
that your love had conquered all,
You broke the Royal barrier,
that kept you from walking tall,
You gripped our nation's heart,
with your stately regal grace,
The grief your mourners felt today,
etched deep upon their face.

When you look down from Heaven,
let your gentle heart be proud,
While they play the gentle music,
join the angels, and sing out loud,
May God take care of your gentle soul,
so you'll live forever more,
As gentle angels sing their song,
from the book of God's own score

You've left your trials and tribulations,
upon this dismal land,
God took you to his mansions,
when he took your fevered hand,
Our lovely sparkling English rose,
that shines with a haloed light,
Will flash across the endless skies,
and light the darkest night.

Through avenues of painted trees,
o'er a sea of scented flowers,
Passed this classless gentle maiden,
who loved with a gentle power,
This regal princess without the name,
was a beautiful scented rose,
She was laid to rest in her haven,
this queen that God had chose.

Goodbye our sweet and bonny maid,
home in your Heavenly bower,
Our Queen of Hearts now laid to rest,
our gracious scented flower,
Sleep in peace dear Queen of Hearts,
God blessed your immortal life,
Our Lord has granted eternal peace,
away from your mortal strife.

Sandy Laird

Diana

You lived, you loved, you cared,
All these gifts with us you shared,
You were never distant, you were never vain,
You sought to see that we would gain.

You didn't confine your work to home,
You helped the world where'er you'd roam,
Where there was hunger, you would appear,
Where there was pain, you'd dry a tear.

You fought a cause each living day,
You trod a path where landmines lay,
You spoke to those whose hearts were hard,
But you were always a winning card.

A winning card for many parts,
A winning card, the Queen of Hearts,
Heads of state who spoke to you,
Knew their duty and what to do.

You did your duties with care and grace,
You made our world a better place,
Yet still we feel our life so poor,
We wish you'd lived a few years more.

For in our life you played your part,
Many times you lightened a heavy heart,
How often you eased the pain of fear,
As you hugged a child stained by a tear.

Now you have gone, our life is grim,
You're at God's side, to stand by him,
But your efforts were not in vain,
We'll tell you all, when we meet again.

James T Wray

Dedicated To Prince William And Prince Harry

The whole wide world is weeping
For our princess - good and true,
And everyone is whispering -
'Diana - WE love you.'
Your courage, strength and wisdom -
Your sympathy and grace,
Your kindness, love and beauty -
As you travelled place - to - place,
You mixed dignity with laughter -
You mixed joyful times with tears -
And brought opposing sides together -
And cast away their fears.
The whole world will miss your presence
And your courage all the way.
Your smile to cheer the homeless -
In silence we will pray.

Dorothy Reade Scott

Carer Of All Nations

Princess of Wales - our Diana
Carried so well, her poise and glamour
Yet world-wide amongst people she'd walk
Stopping to listen, and to talk

No matter what their ailments be
Cancer, AIDS or leprosy
Her outstretched hand and gentle touch
To so many, meant so much

Her sparkling eyes, her loving smile
Would melt their problems for a while
Her short life, spent in charity
To ease the lives of you and me

Though the world mourns, her untimely death
Will carry on to all depths
The good work for which Diana strived
Keeping her, very much alive

Princess of the People - 'Diana'

June Bishop

A Tribute To Diana, The Princess Of Wales

What can one say, that hasn't been said
We've heard today
Diana is dead.

The shock sets in. Papers are read.
Paris, an accident.
Diana is dead.

What had she done to deserve all of this?
Courted. Married. Sealed with a kiss.
Our Diana.

That unison,at St Paul's,not
Westminster Abbey
Didn't it all make us so very happy
We LOVED Diana.

We all took time off, to see her marry.
She then gave birth to William and Harry.
Caring mother, Diana.

Oh, dear lady. What have you done?
In bearing two children. Heirs to the throne.
Disillusioned Diana.

Managed. Manipulated. Wanting a change.
The royal family. Set in a rage
Rebellious Diana.

A PEOPLE'S person. that's what she was.
Sometimes causing us to count the cost . . .
To keep her.
Expensive Diana.

We always got our money's worth.
When we saw her 'sally forth'
Where PEOPLE MATTERED.
Brave Diana.

This last day in August. What a sad day,
When you were tragically taken away
From us . . . Diana.

Go rest in peace. You've earned your part
In our, and every nation's heart.

Goodbye, Diana.

F S Fell

We Will Love You Always

We will miss you
The world and I,
Your beauty, your smile, your forever glow.
You suffered so much
But still you gave
Your heart, your warmth, your forever love.
You touched our hearts,
Our souls and minds,
You showed compassion and respect,
You're precious, you're loved,
You are special to us,
We will love you always,
We will miss you so much.

Guide your sons through their lives and make them strong.
May you both sleep peacefully.
We will remember you always . . .

With love

Lisa Ramirez Langley

The Loss Of A Princess

The loss of a princess
Her memory lives on
With kindness she helped all
Such courage, so strong.

This country so speechless
As news fills the air
Our nation so proud
Of a princess we share.

This world loves our princess
And her fairy-tale life
From a shy young girl
To a prince's wife.

We've grown with our princess
With every new test
She proved she's a royal
Our nation's best.

James L Wood

Diana, Princess Of Wales

(Prayer by Pastor Adrian Prior-Sankey,
Scout Chaplain, at the lighting of a beacon at
Huish Woods Scout Campsite near Taunton,
on the evening of the day of the funeral -
6th September 1997.)

Heavenly Father, on this sad occasion
we gather in the gloom of our grief
to seek Your light and comfort.

As we ignite this beacon we ask your blessing
on all who mourn the passing of
Diana, Princess of Wales.

May the light of Your love shine brighter
in our hearts and lives as a consequence
of the examples she set us - in her service
among the wide spectrum of humanity
and in her encouragement to make your
world a better place for all whom You
desire should live in together in peace.

We pray again for your comfort for those
who were closest to Diana, the princes
and her immediate family and close friends.
May they also know the love and affection
of Your people, at this time and the years ahead.

Now, again, we give our thanks for the life
of one whose compassion burned so brightly
but which is now so tragically taken from us.
Help us and others not to forget,
but to learn the lessons You would teach us
today and in the days to come.

Sanctify this symbol and take us forward
with hope we ask for we bring our prayers
in the name of Jesus, Your Son,
the Light of the World.

Amen.

A Path Of Flowers

I also stood in that vast sombre silent crowd
With wet cheeks and tear-filled eyes,
Head bowed
I stood among all kinds of folk,
Some frail some young and spry
Alongside a road,
To see our princess' cortege go by
I saw a thousand flowers,
Bouquets or just a single bloom
Tossed towards that procession,
That came and went too soon
I saw a carpet of flowers,
Upon the road there lay
And I thought of another procession,
On another day
Where sprays of palms were laid,
Before a donkey's feet
Where Jesus rode amongst the crowd,
Along a narrow street
He helped the poor and needy,
Until His untimely loss
When God wanted Him in Heaven,
And He died upon the cross
And the world was a better place,
For His being here
And the people loved each other more,
And felt His presence near
Our princess had a way with children,
And their troubles understood
She had compassion and feelings,
And was forever doing good
But God wanted her in heaven too,
And took her to His side
She made the world a better place,
And it was for us she died.

Keith Coleman

Weep Not

Thousands of words have been written,
about how beautiful you are.
How your loveliness shines through,
like a bright and rising star.
but I'm sure if you were here,
you would say something like this.
To comfort us in mourning
the loss of our princess . . .

'The time has come for me to go,
this journey's at an end
But weep not . . . don't shed a tear,
don't be sad my friends.
This path I tread is dimly lit,
but when I'm safely through the door.
The glory of my Lord will shine
on me for evermore.
So weep not . . . my friends don't weep,
for I am in safe hands.
The Lord is lighting up my way
into a better land.
I know it's hard to leave you,
but the time has come to part.
Weep not . . . my friends don't weep,
just keep me in your heart.'

Teresina N Fullard

Ode To Diana

Goodnight Diana
our sweet English rose
no longer to see your
elegant pose
the passion and love you
gave to us all

So goodbye Diana
may your star never dim
The legend you left us
will live in our hearts

So sweet dreams Diana
the 'Queen of Our Hearts'
may you rest in peace.

Frank John Mcbain Neish

To Diana, The People's Princess

Farewell Diana, the Princess of Wales,
Our sorrow is deep and hard to bear,
We have lost a dear and cherished friend,
Who was caring and warm with love to share.

With her passing a light is quenched,
Dimming our lives, leaving greyness behind,
Her beauty and glamour brightened the days,
She was compassionate, tender and kind.

In their millions, all colours, religions and creeds
Gazed at the procession in stunned disbelief,
Our princess, adored the world over had gone,
Now we mourn, our faces etched with grief.

On a mellow September morning,
To the haunting ring of horse's hoof,
We paid our tributes and sad goodbyes
Amidst an ocean of blooms that told the truth.

So farewell our beloved Queen of Hearts,
We give thanks for the gift of two lovely boys,
Princes William and Harry to remind
Of your sweetness,
A poignant reflection to restore our joy.

Patricia Petres

In Appreciation Of Diana, Princess Of Wales

You were here for just a little while
Like a brightly shining star,
With beams that stretched across the world
To countries near and far.

The people's princess, and friend of all
The lame, the sick and the blind
There's so many going to miss you
In this land you've left behind

You've left a legacy behind you
That time will never dim
And you'll take your place in history
As the mother of a king

And so Diana sleep in peace
In 'God's Eternal Rest'
Death opened the door to life everlasting
And your home among the blessed.

Mary Woods

God Speed, Diana

A nation mourns a lost princess
who gave comfort in distress,
who gave less fortunate a chance
without 'pomp and circumstance'.

Who flew in the face of adversity
and opened her heart for the world to see,
others gained strength from affinity
to transcend their own misery.

To her boys she was devoted
and so to glory now promoted,
still she is their overseer
protecting them with love so dear.

But we rarely showed you how we felt
even though our hearts would melt,
every time you hugged a child
or took a frail hand and smiled.

We didn't know just what we had
until you'd gone, and it's so sad,
but I hope you're looking from above
and feeling all your nation's love.

So although the world is weeping
we give you now to God's good keeping,
and hope you find in His domain
the rewards you earned on this mortal plane.

Sue Vernau

Diana

She was the golden girl - destined to be queen
Her eyes like shining stars
Showered warmth and love and sadness
On those from near and far
She captured hearts of people
And kept them close to hers
She tuned in to their sorrow
And took away their cares.
To those with AIDS she gave BACK their dignity
To the homeless and the addicts
She gave her love and sympathy
To the aged and little children
And to those with leprosy
She touched their hands and hearts
And went where others would not be
The hardened politicians could not
Ignore her power
They must remove the landmines
Must do this in her honour
Alas that she was taken, from us so suddenly
But forever she'll be near us
To help allay the fear
For by her good example,
Always will show the way
And teach so many others
What true humanity can mean.
For to hearts universal
DIANA forever will be queen.

Norah E Nash

Diana - Princess Of Wales

No more shall see your smiling face
Feel the magic in your touch
So many people, who adored you
Charities you've helped so much

You came into our lives
A princess whose life we shared
You made the world take notice
By showing people that you cared

You touched so many people's hearts
It's sad that you are gone
Our prayers are with your family
That they may all be strong

May good come out of sorrow
Lessons learnt along the way
For the memory of 'Our Queen of Hearts'
Who in our hearts will always stay

Karen L Young

A Princess Sleeps

A princess sleeps upon an island
Lain to rest
Where she loved best

A princess sleeps upon an island
Her loving light
Still shines so bright

A mother sleeps upon an island
She need not fear
For those left here

A mother sleeps upon an island
She prepared them well
Their strength will tell

A beauty sleeps upon an island
So fair of face
So full of grace

A beauty sleeps upon an island
A heart that glows
A love that shows

A princess sleeps upon an island
Her love lives on
In everyone

Barbara Osborne

Peace Perfect Peace

How lovely it is just to lie
Beneath a clear blue summer sky
To rest in peace and listen to
A linnet, lark and sly cuckoo.
Wandering here, quite by chance
I see the mayflies' courting dance
While lazy cattle chew the cud
A sound of someone chopping wood
I think I'll rest here for a while
To dream of you my loves and smile
Now all my dreams just fade and flee
I must awake it's time for tea.
My heart it is so strangely still
Not dancing like a daffodil
My breath it too it seems has flown
No more the words of love be sown.
A shame it is, they seem to say
That I should pass away this way
I've left you loves without goodbye
I'm sorry this will make you cry.
Oh scatter what is left of me
Remember things that used to be
I'll wait till we are side by side
On Heaven's endless green hillside.
Take heart my loves this had to be
My place beside this crystal sea
Upon my head a glorious crown
My dress, an everlasting pure white gown.

T Powell

Prayer In Memory Of The Princess Of Wales

Dear Father
Teach us to value small things.
The warmth of a smile, the touch of a hand
and the uplift that a kind word can bring.
Show us how to reach out to others,
regardless of caste, colour or creed, and fill
our hearts with the love and compassion
shown by Jesus and may we like Him
not count the cost. Amen.

F L Brian

Diana's Legacy

Today the nation stands numb,
deep in shock and disbelief,
A hush descends and unites
our hearts wracked and bowed in grief.

She brought such joy and comfort,
her smile touched a broken heart,
Her hand gave reassurance
to someone falling apart.

She gave of her compassion
where she saw the need for love.
Her heart was filled with pity
that she couldn't give enough.

She didn't seek the headlines,
she never liked all the fuss;
She just wanted the world to know
she was really just like us.

She sought those shunned by the world,
she thought they deserved it;
They felt that she understood,
she said that they were worth it.

The flowers keep on coming
but they'll soon wither and fade,
When tangible tributes cease
still in our hearts they'll be laid.

Her message is so simple
that we'll cherish her memory,
She showed us how to truly care,
her love is her legacy.

Mary Care

A Special Princess To All Mankind

Oh so sad was everyone to hear
how you were taken from us.
We couldn't believe at first until
it was thrust upon us.
Your smiling face, your beauty and your grace,
No one could ever take your place.
You were our diamond in the crown.
We didn't like to see you put down.
Your spirit was shining, fiery, glowing but
also generous, warm and kind.
Adored by all, rich and poor, a special princess
to all mankind.
You always showed concern for others despite
your own heartfelt inner pain.
So many times you met the people,
often standing in the pouring rain,
but never once did you complain.

Diana, you wanted to be our Queen of Hearts
but we knew you had a heart of gold.
No one was too sick, too young, or too old
for you to hug and to hold.
Your life was so short lived, a tragedy because
you had so much love to give,
It gave many the will to live.
Gently, now the breeze whispers your name
as we see all the flowers laid down in vain.
Nothing will bring you back to comfort
those in pain.
Rest now on your flower scented island
in the lake,
Knowing you gave us your love
and made the world a happier place
for all our sake.
We'll support the causes you worked for
so hard
because the difference you made,
Will be remembered with so much regard.

Pauline Palmer

An Angel Passing Through

Let the sun shine for the princess
on her final journey home
Let the people line the streets
so that she may not ride alone
Let the scent of summer flowers
fill the air with perfume sweet
As the teardrops fall like raindrops
on the ground beneath our feet
And then let us all remember
in so many different ways
Her kindness, strength and goodness,
and the difference she has made
All the joy she gave to others,
despite her own unhappiness
The warmth and true compassion,
of a fairy-tale princess
The poor, the sick, the dying,
felt the touch of healing hands
The universal strength of love,
that all can understand
Remember, yes remember,
her legacy of love
Two bonny boys, a prince, an heir,
her gift to all of us
The good die young, or so they say,
I guess this must be true
For surely all of us have glimpsed,
an angel passing through.

Suzanne Burkill

Lady Of The Lake

Resting now in peaceful sleep
sweet rose of England,
upon an island deep with perfumed flowers,
no harsh words or unkindly slurs
can now hurt your loving spirit,
swaying trees in gentle breeze
endlessly whispering words of love
for you that have been spoken,
from so many hearts that were broken,
rippling waters now guard and surround you
as in flowing countless tears that were shed,
so many memories of you as darting sunbeams
in our minds will hold you dear
for all times.
Your image living on in two proud sons,
their smiles and tears will mirror
your radiant beauty for endless years.

So sleep on peacefully Lady of the Lake,
for the love you showed to countless people
will carry on through the hearts of the nation,
in love and admiration for you and your children.

Rita Maher

Diana

In the cold light of day,
The heartache, the sadness prevails,
The disbelief, the emptiness,
The nation's pain is overwhelming.

DIANA, the name brings warmth,
The world understood your language,
You understood their pain,
What we would give to turn the clock again.

DIANA, your sons were taught humility,
They learned to give love openly,
How to take love willingly, how to care.
What will happen Diana now you're not there.

DIANA, how will the world survive,
Without your love, without your hopes
for those with none,
Our fairy-tale princess, why must the story
end sadly.
Time won't change what we had,
Our memories of you will always live on.

Patricia Andrews

Diana Dreams

In my dream I see the highest mountain,
a snowy mountain where my children play.
I share their fun, I hear their joyous laughter,
and, just before I have to go away,
I tell them that I love them.

I dream I see a shining, turquoise ocean
and somewhere out there true love waits for me.
I swim through rippling tides of new emotion
and, knowing that I have to go away,
I tell him that I love him.

Today, surprised, I see a sea of people,
and snowy mountains where the flowers lay.
I see the tears, I feel the poignant silence,
and know, although I have to go away,
they love me as I love them.

Kate Cheasman

If Tears Could Build A Stairway

If tears could build a stairway,
And heartaches make a lane,
I'd walk right up to Heaven,
And bring you back again.
It's hard to hide the heartache,
When someone speaks your name,
Our lives go on without you,
But things are not the same.
A heart of gold, a smiling face,
Diana - no-one will ever take your place
You were the 'People's Princess',
Helping those in need,
Our Princess of Wales, our Queen of Hearts
Fond memories of you, we will always keep.

Caroline Brown

Diana

Today the world stopped
And time stood still
The impact on my life
Means that I never will

Living is everything
Love is for all
I want to stand and wonder
At the vastness of it all

The sky I can touch
And get lost in its blue
The water so clear
Cleanses through
The greenness of grass
The strength of the trees
The humanness of you
Brings me to my knees

I want to live
I want it all
Living
Breathing
Your Spirit of Love
Hears my call

Gentle Diana
Loving and true
The world
All peoples
Will never be the same
Because of you!

Thank you

Charlotte Anne James

Diana, Princess Of Wales

The nation's a poorer place today
Since you were taken far away
Your greatness was felt throughout the world
As love, thought and kindness to all you unfurled.

The brightest star in Heaven tonight
Is yours Diana - shining bright
Though borne too early, your life half done
Whilst here your qualities were second to none.

You gave to all such love and compassion
Encouraged hope and caring in such a fashion
That even the downtrodden, the meekest, believed
That life held much more than
what they perceived.

You bought joy and happiness to the young
and the old
A kinship to the sufferers of whose hands
you would hold
Lepers and victims of landmines sought solace
The need to be aware, you chose not to miss.

You possessed and emitted an aura
You had a genuine and pure Midas touch
It's clear to see why all who knew you
Deeply loved and admired you so much.

May your goodness live on in each one of us
May we continue the work you begun
You're our Princess of Hearts and will remain so
Your being enriched all our lives. Everyone.

There has never been anyone to surpass you
And it's doubtful there ever will be
Such great beauty and grace comes once only
May you find true happiness in Heaven. R.I.P.

Susan Merrifield - (Cornwall)

Diana

Fool that I am, I know that I'll cry
On some far distant day remembering Di
But surely such tears are not a disgrace
When I see, in my mind, her warm smiling face.
An angel on earth? No, she'd never agree,
She too had her faults, like you and like me.
Yet the image was there, felt strongly by all,
She'd touch a hand lightly,
And tough men would fall
For her charm,
And children stood waiting for hours,
Both eager and shy to offer her flowers,
And melt to her smile, then her laughing
Goodbye -
A memory of childhood, slowly to die!

So was she for real, or did I just dream
Of this girl who perhaps might have
Lived to be queen?
But, whatever the story, pray her troubles
May cease,
And in her last sleep, find the sweetest of peace.

Pamela E Williams

Diana's River Of Tears

Blessed were the tears that flowed as a river
to the sea
Searching for an answer that's denied
to you and me
Guided by a hand of fate through many a
vale and down
Sparkling like a precious jewel set in a
tiara crown
Flowing into oceans that surround our
planet's lands
Sending forth this message:-
'The answer is in our hands'
Those tears will help mankind to complete
Diana's dream
The world now have the answer via river,
sea and stream.

Cyril Doy

Diana - A Mum Just Like You And Me

Diana, Diana, the world loves you so
Why on earth did you have to go
They say the Lord takes the very best
At least now you have a place to rest

You taught the world a lesson that's true
On how to love people so dear to you.
You're in our hearts both night and day,
But nothing can take this pain away.

As days go by and nights draw close,
It's the boys we now fear for most.
To have them now in our mind,
This is one thing they can't put behind.

They must be brave, they must be strong.
As this lesson seems so wrong.
They simply cannot run and hide,
They're on a pedestal world-wide.

She was the Queen of Hearts that's true,
But at the end of the day
She's a mum just like me and you.

S Christian

A Lasting Tribute To Diana

Love had no boundary in your short life.
Comforter, protector, guardian of strife.
Arms outstretched to ease all pain
Perplexity and anguish was the cause of
such strain.

An eternal ray of hope to the homeless
and dying.
A compassionate listener who found relief
in crying.
Encountered and consoled those with leprosy
and AIDS.
Proved the stigma that surrounded them
could gently fade.

Cradled victims of land mines in tender arms
Broken bodies of war, the cause of all harm.
To Heaven sent; in peace at last.
Diana our saviour, our Queen of Hearts.

Sheila Barry

The Day We Said Goodbye

For a week, the music talked instead of singing.
On the day a gun carriage came,
church bell ringing.
Past the perfume of flowers, drifting up above.
So many bouquets given with sympathy,
true love.
The roses with the one word 'MUMMY'
Surpassed the loss felt by so many.
On the day we said goodbye.

This time carried down the aisle of the Abbey.
We remembered when she walked and smiled,
so happy.
Elton John's Candle in the Wind,
made us all cry.
The world will be a little dimmer without Di.
A spontaneous clap after a loving
brother's speech.
To the world with compassion she did reach.
On the day we said goodbye.

Harrold Herdman

Diana

Your lilies shone white and bright
As they glided by in the morning sunlight
Swept along by a nation's grief.

Their bobbing heads were to me a symbol
Of the light your life will leave behind.
Like you the lilies shone.

The horses neighed and tossed their heads
The big wheels turned - inside we bled.
But your proud lilies shone.

The choir sang a sad lament
All inside bowed their head.
But beneath grand arches your lilies shone.

On the motorway they were swept along
To your resting place of quiet tranquillity -
Your bright and brave shining lilies.

Pauline Smith

To England's Rose

Princess Diana - so caring and kind
Wonderful memories you've left behind -
Holding a hand, caressing a cheek
Bringing some love to a life that was bleak.
Going to places society shunned
Opening a hospice, supporting a fund.
We loved you Diana, you made our lives bright
But all that was shattered one dreadful night.
We'll never stop loving you tho' you are gone
Your beauty, your courage, your caring live on,
And now your dear sons - your joy and your pride
Will need our support without you by their side.
Rest assured we will give it - life has to go on
And we'll help them to live it - as you would
have done.
So now dear Diana, safe in Heaven above
Your beauty undimmed as you rest in God's love,
You'll never grow old with life's worries and woes
You'll always remain England's beautiful rose.

Doreen Wright

Princess Of Love

A chill wind blew through the world and said,
Diana Princess of Wales is dead,
Stars dimmed and the silver moon was wane,
Will we ever see her like again.

An English Rose we all heard sung,
Handkerchiefs filled with tears were wrung,
Tender eyes that shone with Love,
Look after her God in your Heaven above.

Her heart went out to the disabled and poor,
Eternity will love you forever more,
A Princess you were for the world to cherish,
Our thoughts Diana will never perish.

Your style, your heart, your pristine grace,
Our hearts are embedded with your
beautiful face,
You earned top marks in the loving scales,
God Bless the lady called Diana,
Princess of Wales.

Bill Milne

Diana - 1961-1997

Sleep, my dear, we'll meet again,
For now, no sorrow, no tears, no pain,
Within our minds, we hold your face,
Within our hearts, you keep your place.

Sweet, sweet child, so tragic, forlorn,
United in grief, your nation mourns,
We cry the tears you would never show,
Our love for you just overflows.

You were only lent from Heaven above,
To share your smile, your open love,
Now you return to take your place,
You've earned your wings,
You've earned God's Grace.

And as we look towards the sky,
We see your light shine there on high,
Sad we are, that we had to part,
Farewell Diana, our Queen of Hearts.

Brenda Barker

Di In The Sky

Congratulations God
On your sixty-one creation
Of a perfect lady
Who won the heart of a nation
With unconditional love
Her compassion became unfurled
And genuine understanding
Diana she was Princess of the world
She would caress the poor and sick
On less important shores
To the old she was Mother Teresa
To the young a Santa Claus
Were you a little envious God
When from a sea of flowers
You trawled the lovely rose
Who for ever should be ours
Indelible must now be added
To the rainbow in the sky
As a divine enduring epitaph
To the prolific Lady Di

Tedward

Diana
My Tribute

The sorrow you left behind
The world so full of grief
The love you gave so kindly
Was way beyond belief.
The sick, the needy, the dying
You helped in every way
You did your best to comfort them
And take the pain away.

Your boys must be so proud
Of a person such as you.
A devoted mum, a caring one
Someone so warm and true.
Rest now Diana
The rest of your days
Beneath the glowing sun
So peaceful and so beautiful,
A goddess to everyone.

Jean Dennis

Diana

We are sorry you have left us,
We know not the reason why.
You left us in the prime of life,
And couldn't say goodbye.
Your sons will always love you,
Fond memories will be had.
Of their loving mother,
Whose leaving made them sad.
But one day in the future,
When time has eased the pain.
I know that they will realise,
One day you'll meet again . . .

Doreen Blackwell

The Last Rose Of Summer

Drowsily, I stirred . . .
'I think you'd better listen to the news!'
Rang an urgent voice in my ear
Disbelief clawed my throat
tightening in a vice-like grip
as sickening truth dawned slowly . . .

The world is stationary
hanging in cobwebs of confusion
flowers drooping in a veil of tears
eclipsing out the sun
a light switched off.

Your life, Diana was transitory
Your thoughts fragmented
You flew too close to the cutting edge
of fame and fortune
An icon of beauty yet a fox on the run
until you could run no more
trapped by the four winds of N E W S

And the winds of change are here
for people look softer as I watch TV
grief-stricken and
not trapped within a press prison
by the paparazzi
The world weeps and bids farewell
to a Princess who pioneered for change

Shock-waves fall like a gargantuan wave
as we pick up the pieces of
our lives; learning life is ephemeral
And making each day count
as though it were our last . . .

We won't forget your sparkle, your charm
your charisma and your laughter
through the memory mists of time
and eternity
For now we see through a glass darkly . . .

One day we'll know why you had to
depart so early
so young
so vibrant
and your memory
will burn in our hearts
like a candle
which can never be extinguished
in a wild, wild wind!

Farewell.

Judy Studd

Our Princess

It is the people's beloved Princess,
That we have now laid to rest,
So many people in mourning shroud,
All around the Abbey crowd,
The Royal family patiently wait,
Outside the Royal Palace gate,
Waiting for the procession to pass,
Of that humble darling lass,
Six king's horses shining black,
There was nothing that this funeral did lack.
Pulling along a gun-carriage so green,
Such splendour so seldom seen,
Twelve Welsh Guards dressed in red,
With shining busbies on their heads,
Oh how our hearts and faces grew pale
As we thought of our Diana, 'Princess of Wales'.
This is really beyond belief,
A nation united in so much grief.
Millions of people all standing there,
In an awful silence that is hard to bear.
So many flowers along the road,
Thrown from the ever-growing crowd,
Never has this world known,
Such despair and grief to be shown.

Janet Allwright

Diana . . .

Like the petals of a rose,
So you unfolded,
Your scent filled all our heads,
The colours of you - exploded.
Like the rain,
You drenched a universe,
So gentle within the storms,
With eyes of rainbows
That glistened to their end,
The crock of gold
Your golden heart.
You flowed as a river,
Within our hearts - a sea,
We offered you an ocean,
So many flowers to see . . .
But, all too late
For you are love
Our Queen for evermore,
What sorrow kept you
So locked
Behind the palace doors . . .?

Allison Harris-White

Goodnight Sweet Princess

Goodnight sweet princess,
Please sleep well,
We'll never forget,
The day you fell.

Your life an example,
To us all,
You held your head high,
As you walked tall.

Although your problems,
Hit you hard,
Your wonderful smile,
Was never marred.

Much love you possessed,
Inside your heart,
To each and every one of us,
You gave a part.

Victoria Gray (16)

A Nation Mourns

Quietly they came in their thousands
With saddened hearts, tears welling in their eyes,
The nation's people had gathered together
To mourn their Princess's sad demise.

With reverence they brought messages
of sympathy,
Laid a dense carpet of flowers on the ground
As the glow from the candle's light flickered
On the sorrowful multitudes around.

The dedicated compassionate Diana
Lost her young life in such a sudden tragic way,
The whole world was shocked to hear
the sad news
On that fateful unforgettable day.

We pray that her family will be strengthened
In the knowledge the good Lord chose
Diana, Princess of Wales, Queen of our Hearts
To adorn Heaven's garden with a beautiful
English rose.

Barbara Sowden

For Diana

She loved the world, it's plain to see
She gave her love to you and me,
She asked for nothing in return
We really have a lot to learn.

Her boys were always her pride and joy
She wanted them to see
Ordinary people, just like you and me.

Her beaming smile, her outstretched hand
Could be seen throughout the land
She hugged the sick, the poor, the lame
She did not ask for any fame.

The paparazzi followed her
She had no peace of mind
They took away her freedom
No privacy could she find.

Despite it all she found her love
Dodi Al Fayed
Together they found happiness
Perhaps sent from above.

Her life was in the public eye,
Now people ask the question why?
In Paris on that fateful night
Someone, somewhere, turned out the light
On our Diana, our Princess
Could anything be so senseless.

At last she has the peace she craved
On her island of flowers
She'll never be forgotten
She was special - she was 'ours'.

Kim Braley

For Diana . . .

For your honesty and truth
For your style and grace,
For your love and compassion
That would light up a face,
For the way reached out
To touch every hand,
For the way you moved
Every heart in the land,
For your love for your sons
Harry and Wills,
For the way you felt
For everyone's ills,
For uniting a world
So often uncaring,
For your strength and courage
For your selfless sharing,
We'll no longer see
Your smiling face,
Without you here
It's a colder place,
May you find the peace
You so dearly deserve,
And feel the love
Of all those you served,
And even though now
We are so far apart,
You will forever be
Here in our hearts

N J Palmer

An English Rose

Your gentle touch, a fond embrace, the people were your heart,
Your tireless work for charity, was only just the start,
Compassion with all your kindness, your charm, your smiling eyes,
Beauty and style you possessed, the nation's greatest prize,
You will forever remain a symbol, like jewels in a crown,
For like the Queen Egypt, your name will be renown,
Tears still flow on every cheek, for a goddess who was a guide,
Wherever we are, whatever we do, you will always be at our side,
There are many, many roses, though flowers are much the same,
It is only a matter of time itself when one will bear your name,
They picked you out an island, safe from prying eyes,
Alone with mother nature's gifts, under clear blue skies,
Surrounded by clear still waters, through those darkest nights,
A shrine sheltered by trees, away from the camera lights,
Goodbye sweet princess and be proud, for the people will carry your banner,
You will always be our favourite child, 'you belong to the world DIANA'.

J R H Graham

Shone She So Brightly

Oh great luminous solar light,
wouldst humanity be as true, steadfast
as thou eternally art, yet blight
rampage amongst controversial blasts.

Yet, the loving Queen of Hearts comparest
to thy brightest, to thy firmament.
Isolation in a cold void, yet sharest
the Queen of Hearts her special sentiments.

Alas, Welsh humanity grieveth, they weepest
for their golden Princess of Wales
who now, in Althorp grounds sleepest -
privately, here intrusive paparazzi fail.

Holdeth fast in the hearts, oh Wales;
she, who uniquely lovest,
leavest her legacy, yea not in fairy tales
but in life, this is Diana's bequest.

Let her people, (yea all people) exhorteth
the great commandment, the universe
crieth out for the Queen of Hearts
who purveyeth encouragement and worth.

Yet we asketh 'Why risest thou not,
oh solar quest?
Why hidest thou thy light from broken hearts?
Oh, then shinest not, forever rest;
be still, joinest one forced to part.

Shinest, yea shine, if only the future king
purveyeth a princess's first love, to care.

Lloyd Noyes

Thoughts On The Life And Death Of Diana, Princess Of Wales

Alas! A lass - a great Princess
Whose life was shrouded in distress,
Wedded to Royal Prince was she
But lasting love was not to be.

Unfaithfulness will soon divide
When solemn vows are set aside;
The match so dreamlike at the start
Is shattered when they sadly part.

Soon do we find the onward course
Could only end up in divorce,
Then was she free, as one might say,
Without restraint to make her way.

A suitor she was pleased to meet
Who came and swept her off her feet.
The press gave chase in frantic dash
Which ended all in gruesome crash.

Life was snuffed out so suddenly
By this most awful tragedy;
As all the world the tidings hear
Folk near and far will shed a tear.

When Abbey funeral takes place,
A sea of flowers the pavements grace
And books of condolence will swell
With messages of fond farewell.

O what a sorry tale is this,
Does it give hope of heavenly bliss?
That heart of gold - will it hold sway
When Righteous Judge shall have His say?

The world may say good works suffice;
The Word of God points otherwise,
That what we need most in the end
Is just to have a ROYAL FRIEND.

An earthly Prince we would not crave
But HEAVENLY KING with power to save:
This only will bring joy and peace
When this our mortal life shall cease.

L F Waller

Diana

A tragedy that held no earthly reason.
Revealed itself that very dreadful day.
We thought at first someone was being callous
and prayed that somehow it would go away.
Reality gave way to gutted feelings
and hearts were torn and shred and cast aside
and soon the world's entire population,
were stunned to hear their Queen of Hearts
had died.
A fairytale without a fair conclusion,
amid the pomp and splendour and the love,
while on her own, away from the confusion
an angel winged her way to Heaven above.
Each step was scrutinised in lines of duty
but some intruded in her privacy
and just like them we watched her soul emotions,
exposed for all the greedy world to see.
Sleep well Diana, no-one there can reach you.
No flashing cameras or intrusive pries.
It's just a shame that while we watched intensely
we overlooked the sadness in your eyes!

Sheila M Birkett

Diana: The Fairytale Princess

A princess whom I never met
Died tragically an untimely death
She touched so many with her heart of gold
There's no one else like her in the world.

Our very own Lady Di
An English rose who was so shy
And then so glamorous she became,
It shot her to such worldwide fame.

When at last she found true love
God decided from above
To take this angel that he sent
As she had only just been lent,
To show us how to live today
By expressing our love in every way,
To every race, colour and creed
In a world of chaos and greed.

She is now a star at night
Shining down so very bright
She has forever left a mark
Our very beautiful Queen of Hearts.

Shine on Diana and Dodi too,
May God forever look after you.

Sinéad Rattigan (16)

A Kensington Night

Stars above, candles below.
Trees hung with poems and toys.
I'm trying to read them
From the candles' glow.
The air is thick with perfume
From a million flowers.
People are staring in disbelief,
Just wandering around for hours and hours.

Reading messages from around the world,
The cards wide open and sheets unfurled.
Eyes are pouring out a thousand tears,
Enough to last a thousand years.
For dear Diana, who is no more.
Who touched our hearts to the final core.
For this lady of grace who thrilled millions of children
Just by the sight of her smiling face.

For a friend we did not know.
For the love we could not show.
For a loving mother, forever mourned.
For 'HRH' once there, now pawned!
So, the highest price was paid,
For a princess . . . betrayed.

Jennifer A Taylor

Diana . . .

Diana . . .
If they'd said we'd feel so empty inside,
We'd have shrugged it off, wondering who
they meant.

Diana . . .
We're 'very British', with stiff upper lip,
For hundreds of years, no emotion
was evident.

We were never prepared to miss you so much,
Remembering your smile and your gentle touch
On the cheek of a child, an old lady's hand,
The comfort you gave to a dying young man.

All these things, your charm, your grace,
Have carried you on to a better place
More special than we here can give,
But within us all, your dreams will live
on.

The floral path you travelled upon
Back 'home' - in silence - sings our song
Of praise, for all the saddest of tears
You've wiped away throughout the years.

Diana . . .
Now God has given you a special place,
Your island of peace, but still you remain
within our hearts.

Diana . . .
You live on in William, he has your eyes,
Your smile -
We'll never be apart.

Janice Trueman

A Very Special Lass

This a very special female person,
Wrongly likened by some as a mere
candle in the wind
More like a magnet to the world's people,
A burning flame with pure compassion
of a Godly kind

Diana was never a stiff uncompromising
pillar of white wax, but with her magical
smile lit up the day or night
Never a flickering light, but a passing
through burning flame to him who is
THE WAY AND THE LIGHT

Some say Diana only attended events
but in every society in the world there
are people we do not touch
This proud mother of two sought them out
then she reached out to them and she
missed not very much

Observed by the world's people with pleasure
and pride,not a rose or candle but an
emotional soul of class
Beloved mother of two sons enchanting sweet,
beautiful, generous will never be forgotten
this special lass

James Burns-Swan

A Tribute To Diana Princess Of Wales

You were born to fame but not to reign
Even though you had a Royal name
Your life was sad, it seemed unfair
Thousands now just stand and stare
Without your love to touch our lives
Happy emotions have taken a dive
Flowers that are a symbol of beauty and love
For a Princess whose life has flown like a dove
Your loss to this world will never repay
As we watch your funeral on this sad day
Your joy and beauty are over and gone
As Elton John sings your song
You leave behind sad little hearts
Who now must go on to make a fresh start
You'll never be forgotten for you had many a fan
We love you dearly Our Princess Diana.

Muriel Magee

The People's Princess

Tears were shed by millions
Even Mother Teresa shed a tear
She died with her friend
United in life, separated by death
Riches, glamour, fame and travel
They had it all, yet their clocks stopped
They had so much to live for
Now we have our memories
She cared for those in need
She gave time and comfort to the dying
She had world vision of peace and hope
Her sons will miss her, her nation weeps
She gave her all for the good of mankind
Her name will live on, her truth will be victorious
Her toil was not in vain
In Heaven she will comfort both the young and the old.

The poor and the rich
Diana your spirit will live on forever
God will bless you and hold you close.

Keith A Davis

Sweet Diana

Lovely Princess Diana,
So fair was your face,
We will miss your kindness,
And your elegant grace.

Queen of our hearts,
Compassionate and kind,
A more loving friend -
We never will find.

A true loving mother -
To your two lovely boys,
May they grow up remembering
All the happiness and joys -

You showered them with love, warmth -
And gentleness too,
Our hearts feel for them -
Such credits to you.

At times you were sad,
Had tears in your eyes,
We all wanted to comfort you -
Our most cherished prize.

So goodbye sweet Diana,
Your life wasn't in vain,
May God bless and keep you -
Till we meet again.

D M Jennings

Diana - Queen Of Hearts

Never again to see your face,
No more to feel your fond embrace.
Gone too sudden at the prime of your life,
May you rest in peace, free from worry and strife.
We will never forget you, for compassion you showed.
Your love for all people was ethereal and flowed.
A Lady who enthused in so many parts,
But to all us mortals, you were our Queen of Hearts.

Pauline Hall

In Memory Of Princess Diana

A gift from God was Princess Di
And in our thoughts she will not die
Though she died in a terrible way
With us all she will always stay.

A Princess sent from Heaven above
To leave us all with a gift of love.
A love that God alone can give
If we believe in Him, we live!

If her work is not to be in vain
Awake, oh Nation and hear the refrain
United in her death, united in sorrow
But have we thought what will
happen tomorrow?

Life is short and we will need to stand
Together in love across this land
We have to trust in God and He will bring
us through
To an everlasting life, His word is truth.

Princess Di had compassion for people in need
But God is the one who sows that special seed
To help those who suffer from all kinds of pain
And the Lord's death alone was not in vain.

The praise and glory all belongs to God alone
For without His help we are completely forlorn
Praise the Lord for Diana Princess of Wales
May she rest in peace, now and always.

Terry Thompson

Diana

One so bold and so wise,
Taken from beneath our eyes,
A fairy Princess through and through,
About her death we have no clue,
On an island she now rests,
Away from slander, lies and press,
The Queen of people's hearts she said,
Now our Queen of Hearts is dead.

Stuart Robertson (15)

To Precious Diana Queen Of Hearts

You reached out and touched
so many hands.
You made the world a better place
in every land.
Your patience and kindness
was always on view
Your troubles of life
We learned from the news.
We realise now that it's too late
You've finally found your real true mate
Now all we can do is make amends
Is to reach out and touch
And make everyone friends
And remember how precious
You were to the world
And wonderful stories of you
Will be told.

Nellie Gibbs

A Tribute To Diana

So special, so pretty, so proud. No love
did you hide.
Everyone who knew you. No matter what
they did
Felt the greatest love within you. The love you
never hid.
We couldn't see the sadness. Which hid behind
those smiles.
We saw the love and kindness, shown through
those lovely eyes.
No-one could ever take your place. Of this
I'm very sure.
You were a very special person. Who could have
asked for more.

Edith Bebbington

Diana

Princess Diana, Queen of our hearts,
Firmament star with compassion,
Underdog's Royal Ambassador,
World renowned leader of fashion,
At age thirty-six you have succumbed,
Crash victim of much too much speed.
Lively teenagers have lost their mum,
Deprived at a time of great need.
Steadfast and loyal to all your friends,
Your mortal existence no more,
Loveable, shy, you'll be remembered
Funny, vital friend of the poor.
Your violent destruction has shown
How precious is the gift of life.
From landmines children have lost their limbs
Or have been killed when war is rife.
Ever warm-hearted you've cuddled them close,
Victims of AIDS you have greeted.
Leprosy sufferers have felt your touch,
Inspired to rest undefeated.
For years you have had your detractors,
Orthodoxy's followers prim.
Their unspoken wish you'd disappear
Has been fulfilled in ways most grim.
A paragon of kindness and love,
You were a Saint many will say,
Betrayed, vulnerable, beautiful,
Eternally at peace we pray.

Hywel Davies

Diana Princess Of Wales

Goodnight my sweet Princess,
May you rest in peace.
You're a new Angel in Heaven.
You certainly were England's rose,
May God use you as a rose for his garden.
God bless you
Diana.

Samantha Jayne Miles (9)

Forever

Delicate, sweet and serene,
Immaculate and kind.
A Lady born to reign supreme.
Noticing others, strong will to bind
A nation together with dutiful mind.

Quietly pondering, thinking,
Using her position in linking the
Evil use of landmines into
Everyone's home via television,
Noting amputees' wounds with horrific precision.

Obvious to all the love that she shared,
Forever Diana's legacy, showing that she cared.

Healing time and eternal heartbeat,
Every breath a gift of loving hope.
A tiny zephyr disrupts the flame and heat
Rushes soberly into every heart. An antelope
Traverses across the plain, pursued. . . it leaps.
Silence. One light extinguished, the whole
world weeps.

Joanna Moore

Diana

Her consistency of love for others never faltered once,
Her generosity was immense for each and everyone,
She gave courage to those in need,
A true Princess of love indeed,
Her beauty was inside and out,
Loved by all without a doubt,
The tireless way in which she cared,
Her feelings of love she always shared,
Now we weep one and all,
And silently our teardrops fall,
Never will there ever be,
A Princess loved as much as she.

Bunty

Diana

You inspired us through your sadness
You inspired us through your smile
You inspired us when you 'lived with us'
But now you've 'left us for a while'

Your eyes that sparkled like the stars
Your laughter and your style
We loved the way you looked at us
But now you've 'left us for a while'

Diana - you made us listen
You embraced us with your smile
Your compassion for humanity
But now you've 'left us for a while'

So short your life with us on earth
But it's just a tiny part
Through you we surely can believe
That this is just the start

You may have had unhappiness
Confusion in your soul
But now your spirit will live on
Your life completely whole

One day we'll surely meet with you
Again we'll see your smile
And never will our hearts forget
You've only 'left us for a while'.

Jean Stewart

Diana

The world has lost a lovely star,
The crown has lost its fairest jewel,
But two pearls are left behind,
To shine in future days.

You showed your love to one and all,
A friendly smile for young and old,
The sick the dying felt your touch,
Now they have lost their guiding light.

Two boys are left to grieve and cry,
A mother they cannot replace,
We feel your pain and share your tears,
Her spirit must live on in you.

Ashelene Watson (14)

The Princess

I'll tell you about a Princess
Who was once called Lady Di
Her hair was the colour of sunshine
Her eyes as blue as the sky
She met a Prince called Charles
He was nicknamed Action Man
He asked for hand in marriage
And the fairytale began
Her wedding gown was gorgeous
Silk, lace, and frills
She had two lovely children
She named them Harry and Wills
She appeared on the covers
Of all the magazines
More famous than the famous
And all the catwalk queens
She wore the finest clothes
The best that money could buy
But she was so unhappy
And was even seen to cry
She thought that she'd be Queen
And sit upon the throne
But the fairytale ended
And she was all alone
They took away her title
HRH no more
But still she visited the sick
The dying and the poor
Then at last she found new love
With Dodi Al Fayed
But now the world's in mourning
Our Princess Di is dead.

Kathleen Lever

Diana

We can't believe it happened
It came as quite a shock
To think that you and Dodi
Whose hearts were interlocked
Will be no more around us
No more to see you smile
You didn't deserve this ending
You were much too good to die
A legacy of love you left behind
To all who were in need
The nation mourns you Diana
You were a friend indeed
But now that you have gone
We will always remember you
Through the love you have shown the world
Rest in peace and God bless you.

EPILOGUE

We must all of us remember
We are only here on loan
And when Our Father calls us
We will make that journey home.

V A Bonello

To Diana - With Love

We'll miss your face,
We'll miss your grace,
We'll miss your smile,
We'll miss your style,
We'll miss those eyes!
So kind and wise.
We'll miss the fashion,
We'll miss your compassion,
We'll miss the love you gave,
To everyone it's true.
But most of all Diana
- our Princess,
We'll miss seeing you.

Joan Fowler

Dear Sirs

I was so sorry
And particularly upset sirs,
For both your own two sakes,
Your mother's passing deeply stirs.

I watched your courage today
At the sad sight of the funeral,
I saw you keep your cool
And dignity was wonderful.

You will have many teaching
The two of you to have the strength,
So needed at present
Please know that time will heal at length.

My lines to you are simple
Yet my heartfelt wishes know no bounds,
I can only feel glad
Your mother's now in her home-grounds.

The country has done her proud
As she, likewise, always did for it,
For her Queen and country
Your mother did more than 'her bit'.

Dear sirs, take life in both hands
And grasp the cherished memory of,
Our Princess Diana
And pray, keep her deep caring love.

Barbara Sherlow

Diana

God saw her footsteps falter
Her task was now too much
She gently went around the world
With a smile a kiss and a touch
She touched the hearts of all she met
The world owes their all an unpaid debt
There'll not be another who can compare
The gift she had was beautiful and rare
Her sons will miss her now they're apart
But one thing is sure she's left them her heart.

Hazel Richards

Diana Princess Of Wales

Diana words cannot express how we feel,
We only know pain maybe time can heal,
You gave so much love and so much joy
We could never want to or try to ignore.

Diana to us you were compassionate and kind
All that you achieved here on earth
Will be forever in our minds
You were a genteel lady so precious and true
No-one we know could ever replace you.

Whatever the colour, race or creed,
From the old to the young the ill and diseased
You showered them with love
That they so greatly did need
Diana we know that you cared very much
We could see it in every move, smile or touch.

I hope Diana, you see all of our love
I know you will be smiling down from above
Please give us the strength to carry on,
It will be hard Diana now that you're gone
Be at peace, and be happy in God's kingdom above
Diana queen of our hearts and all that was good.

We could not have loved you any less
Goodnight, rest in peace, and God bless

Please God take care of OUR SWEET, OUR KIND,
OUR BEAUTIFUL PRINCESS.

Collette Treacy

Remembering Always

Engraved in our hearts,
Your name will always be,
A tender loving person,
For all the world to see.

Anyone who saw you,
Remembers you with awe,
For those who never met you,
You were their guiding star.

Dodi brought you happiness,
In the last few months of your life,
So now in God's paradise,
I will remember you as man and wife.

Margaret Walker

Diana My Princess

Diana, I adored you, my love for you, you'll never know,
Through your suffering, sadness and despair, I can never show
That I felt the pain in your heart, the loneliness, the strife
I know - from that fairytale wedding, I have followed your life
With your inner beauty, you captured the world
It's absurd that your private life should be hurled
under the cruel lenses which you were doomed to depart,
You touched people and lives, you spoke from deep in your heart
The warmth and compassion in your eyes
gave hope and happiness to those in need, no-one can disguise
AIDS victims, children, elderly, no-one did you deprive
of your reassurance that they deserved to survive.
Behind your suffering, your love was endless, a gift so rare,
Courage, endurance, devotion, no one can ever compare
With your work on the Earth, you stood like a rock,
Happiness you finally found, snatched away, unbelievable shock.
A fate so cruel, life is so unfair - two boys without a Mother
The love and eyes of adoration can be replaced by no other.
I pray now you are resting in peace and happiness
Diana, you will always be my Queen of Hearts, my Princess.

Nicola Shanahan

Tribute To Diana - Princess Of Wales

Diana you were a shining star
Visiting and comforting those from afar
Your loving smile, grace and charm
Resting now where you can come to no harm
Your work took us to special places
Memories of smiling faces.

The old, the young, the rich, the poor
You'd be waiting at their door
To hold their hands and give a smile
And stay with them a little while
So please remember while we're apart
You'll always be our Queen of Hearts.

Don't worry about your lovely boys
They'll get lots of support, cuddles and toys
They will remember all the times you had
The fun, the laughter and the sad
So in their hearts you will always stay
To be remembered every day.

The whole world has shown such grief
For a special Princess, it was so brief
But in our hearts the memories will stay
To be told to those not around today
So loving God up above
Please take care of the one we loved.

C Heritage

Diana

Thrust into the public eye
for all the world to see.
An unknown girl, so shy
A princess soon to be.

We shared the joy of a happy bride,
the first ever public kiss.
A prince so proud at her side,
to share the wedded bliss.

Next her greatest role to be
of a loving, caring mum;
She expressed her love so openly
and shared her sense of fun.

Then sadness touched her life,
her every tear we shared;
No longer to be a wife.
How deeply we all cared.

She gave her time so freely
to the homeless and the poor.
Her kindness showed through clearly;
Alas! To be no more.

A beauty so warm and yet, so shy.
An ageless, timeless treasure.
The girl we knew as Princess Di,
locked in our hearts forever.

E Thompson

We Will Remember

We will remember always the tenderness
of your smile
As you cradled in your arms a sick or forlorn child
We will remember always how your loving caress
Gave comfort to the dying and hope
to those distressed
We will remember always lovely Diana Queen of
all our hearts
She was unique there will never come another
And we pray God will guide the young Princes
Who were proud to call her mother.

Hugh Todd

Diana

God lent you to us for such a short while
But long enough to adore your smile
Then you were so kind
You left a part of you behind
In William and his brother
To whom you were a wonderful mother
You were so kind to young and old
And babies you simply had to hold
So why? We would like to know
You were much too young to go.

M Hunt

To Our Queen Of Hearts

The light has gone from your lovely face,
No other person can ever replace,
The smile - the look - the touch of your hand,
To millions your death was so tragic and sad.

We will remember you with each passing day,
Dear Lord why did you take her away,
We loved you so much,
No words can express,
The feeling of sorrow and deepest regret.

You touched the hearts of the sick, young and old,
Your presence in Heaven will give life to the fold,
Your radiance shone like the stars in the sky,
An angel on earth now in Heaven up high.

Please God look after her,
and Diana if you're looking down,
To us you were the Jewel in the Crown.

Edna Driver

Queen Of Hearts

The Lord wanted an Angel
So he took you away
Sunday 31st August was that tragic day.

The world and its people
still cannot believe
And for many more months will still mourn
and grieve.

She was a symbol of kindness
of faith hope and love
sent to help others from Heaven above

Intrusion of your privacy
will now cease
we pray for you Diana, that you may
rest in peace.

Darina Davies

To A Star - A Poem

When God sent down a glittering star
To spread his love both near and far
It took the form of someone high
And became our beautiful 'Lady Di'
Her young life was mixed with joy and remorse
The parents split and the inevitable divorce
She carried on regardless with effort and guile
The eyes full of sparkle and mouth with a smile
Her love for a prince was sincere and loyal
Why oh why did he turn out a royal
She was destined to settle and finally marry
Then came her treasures both Wills and Harry
Her marriage turned sour, full of misery and bliss
Hardly a word no time for a kiss
She thought of her parents, the unhappy days
So Di and husband went their own separate ways
A new world had beckoned the quest of new lands
The challenge of new glory she grabbed with
both hands
The world was her oyster to spread love and
good cheer
People with AIDS or leprosy she cuddled without fear
Visits to the sick and handicapped she'd
regularly combine
And the maimed and crippled of the dreaded
landmine
As if she was guided by the Lord up above
She spent her days spreading her love
We were all just realising what good she had done
When the crash took her young life and now she
has gone
So the glittering star went back up to God
But not before she gave us the nod
To continue her work, we've been given many starts
And dedicate it to Diana 'The Queen of our Hearts'

D Cummins

A Queen Of Hearts

She was ours for just a little while
Our own Princess of Wales
Now sadly, we are mourning
In the Hills and in the Vales

Nations followed in her steps
To try to get wrongs righted
Our Ambassador of care and love
Wished the World to be united

She trod where others feared to tread
Despite any objection
Did a job that needed doing
And she did it, to perfection

A Joan of Arc of modern times
She battled on with zest
Fighting for the sick and needy
Complying with each quest

Her time with us was limited
Like a beautiful butterfly
She flew away and left us
Now we're left to wonder . . . why?

We'll remember her as she would wish
Over the coming years
'A Queen of Hearts' without a Crown
Whilst the World wears a Coronet of tears.

Bell Ferris

A Tribute To Diana

The nation has never known such sorrow
Diana will be in our thoughts today and
Every tomorrow
We cannot believe she has gone from our sight
But shall all think of her as a star shining bright
Diana was an angel sent to us in disguise
Sent on loan to show nations how to be wise
The love she had so deep in her heart
Makes it much more painful for us to part
But now with Dodi and God above
Her sons forever in her heart will love.

Margaret Sanders

Sleeping Beauty

Dearly departed, your race is run.
In perfect peace you rest.
Amongst the playground of your childhood fun.
No climbing trees today, you sleep beneath
their gentle sway.
Around, the beautiful flowers, a sea of glory,
you abound.

Perfume, fills the air above,
Resting, amongst the beauty, the birdsong sound,
Incensed by the whole world's love.
Now with your Prince of Peace,
Christ, up above, in Heavenly grace.
Every wish you hoped for, for wars to cease,
Selfless, you strived with smiling face.
Strived to make this world a better place.

Oh yes! You were beautiful, dutiful too!
For all beings, whatever colour, race or creed.

Welcoming, caring, hugging, even the HIV.
Amongst the landmines' limping amputee.
Everyone adored you, loved you like a friend.
Sleep on, Sleeping Beauty, our love will never end.

Peter W P Turner

Our Rose

A pretty bud bloomed into a Rose
As she opened out her petals
We looked in wonder as we tried to take in
The depth of her beauty.

She whispered kindness on the wind
She filled the air with sweetness
She bent and swayed in life's storms
Yet her compassion never faltered.

Tragedy struck down our blossoming Rose
Right in her glorious prime
But we'll all hold dear our memories
Of a Rose beyond compare.

Alison Shand

Farewell Darling Diana

Who will ever forget that sad Sunday we lost our Princess so fair?
The brightest and best of all, she was loved beyond compare.
The whole world was shocked and sorely stunned that day
When a terrible car crash took Diana's life away.

You were beautiful not just of face, but also heart and mind
The best of humanity shone clear, to those you left behind,
Compassion, time, and tender love you always gave so free,
Those lovely eyes the mirror of your soul, so plain to see.

To the simplest of people, sick, dying or sad
With great affinity dear Lady, you gave all you had.
'Though often despondent with your own problems too
You put others first Diana - so exceptional of you.

Giving comfort with an understanding word or kindly look
The warmest smile, the gentlest hug, these are what it took
To place you deep within our hearts, for all you did so well
Queen of Hearts you will remain, as passing time will tell.

It's Saturday and in London today, two million people or more
Join two billion throughout the world, to mourn for one they adore
This sea of flowers and messages all through the week has gown
'Midst a sea of tears for you Diana, sweet bird sadly flown.

Her Majesty and family bow heads as your cortège goes by
The awesome scene is of disbelief to every tearful eye
So silently the two-hour walk proceeds with solemn faces
Then your cherished brave sons walk behind you, in the last heartbreaking paces . . .

To the Abbey, for a heartfelt service, so moving and unique
For our most unique Diana, to mark this poignant week.
Then on your final journey, tears and flowers all the way,
Along the last long miles to your resting place, but we feel the need to say -

'Wish we still had you with us, lovely beacon of light,
That was cruelly extinguished upon that dreadful night.
How could anyone have allowed this to happen to you - how?
Those who caused your death should serve a sentence now.'

Your resting place is beautiful, in a lake on an island so green
So peaceful, so quiet, so lovely, for an angel so serene
No more hounding, hurt or pain of this life, will you have to face
For, England's most graceful and sweetest rose, you've gone to a far better place.

Even now on Sunday, after laying you to rest,
Crowds have not gone home, but from north, south, east and west
STILL COMING! More than ever yet, how deeply touched they are
STILL placing flowers in sympathy, at the loss of a magic star.
Many lives will be less bright now, without this shining star
But their loss is Heaven's gain, and a new star shines afar.

Please God, give Wills and Harry strength and courage to endure
Life without their darling Mother, whose love was deep and pure.
Guide those closest to her boys to mould them as she'd do
Inheriting qualities of love and kind compassion too
Their memories of happy times with Mum let time never erase
Pondered in their hearts through life, those precious early days.

Irreplaceable LADY in every sense of the word
We thank God for you as we ask our prayers to be heard
Farewell darling Diana, with dear Dad and Dodi, rest,
We ask humbly of God, please grant you His best.
Give her evermore in Your Heavenly dwelling
Divine love and happiness, all others excelling. x x x

Pearl H Duke

Diana - The Angel

She walked through life, with beauty and grace,
with always a smile on her lovely face.
She was happy again, after years of sadness,
her life was taken, in a moment of madness.
No-one expected she would be taken just yet.
She had such an effect on those whom she met.
The sick and the dying, the young and the old,
they held out the hands she just had to hold.

She loved her two sons, William and Harry,
and then she loved Dodi and they hoped to marry.
But fate intervened and took them away,
never to live for another day.
Their families are mourning, the people are sad,
we have lost the best Princess that we ever had.
God gave us an angel, sent from heaven above,
to teach the whole world compassion and love.

Born to be Queen, but not of our land,
our 'Queen of Hearts', with a helping hand.
She worked so hard for what she believed,
quite unaware, how much pain she relieved.
A beautiful woman both inside and out,
and a wonderful mother, without a doubt.
Heaven, we know, is a beautiful place,
so she will now walk in death,
with beauty and grace.

Shirley A Bramley

When The Tears Have Gone

Numbness fills my heart and soul
Knowing you are gone from this cruel bitter
world of ours, never to return.
We'll never see your smiling face as it brightened
up our day, or hear your sincere wishes spoken
to the nation ever again.

As your body lies adorned by people's flowers on a grave across the lake, your soul I know is in heaven with your new found love 'Dodi Al Fayed'. There you have found peace at last away from the public's continuous gaze.

Diana you were not only a Princess, but an angel of mercy as well, lent to us by our Heavenly King to be a messenger for him. To show us all how to behave for people less fortunate than ourselves.

I hope deep down in my heart your Memorial will raise needed money for charities that you had shown so much love.

When the tears have gone, we will continue to hold your memory inside, and pray that your children can give as much love to us all, as you have shown in your short life, here on earth, may God bless You, 'Princess Di'.

Maureen Connolly

An Angel On Loan
In Loving Memory Of Diana

An angel sent to earth on loan
Has now been called to go back home.
No more of her beautiful, happy, smiling face.
We won't forget the courage, faith and love she gave.
Having time and love for everyone it's
Hard to take in that she has gone.
But one comforting thought on her journey
Home, she won't be travelling all alone.

Jean Lamb

Diana, The People's Queen Of Hearts 1997

Princess Diana,
You were the people's Queen of Hearts.
Darkness has fallen now you have gone.
You gave everyone hope, I'm one!
All over the world people are sad now you have gone.
Perhaps to a better place, that we do not know?
People all over the world have lit candles in hope and remembrance of all the good work you have done, and now sadly much more work is being done now you have gone, why? We don't know why, only God knows? Your boys William and Harry will carry on your work for you, as you taught them well, to be like you and me the ordinary people. The world had a coronation on the 6th September for you Diana. The Queen of people's hearts, and what a day it was! Never will we see the like again. Flowers of all colours and size, toys, cards and much more. People showered flowers for you in places everywhere to show how much we really cared for you Diana. The people's Queen of Hearts, and what you have done, if only you were still alive to see what you achieved. Perhaps you're a bright light up there and its shining down on everyone, all over the world to help us all.
God bless you Diana the Queen we never had. May you now rest in peace forever.

X X X

K Parsons

Our Shining Example

She sleeps upon an island green,
A Princess born to be a Queen,
She lived for all the world to see
A shining example to you and me.

With smiles and laughter, bright and gay
She stopped upon her busy way.
To cheer the lonely and the sad,
To share with them the love she had.

We should all remember her grace and truth,
This Princess gone, still in her youth.
And strive to follow, day by day,
Her shining example on our way.

For in our hearts she will always stay,
Loved, and remembered every day.

R Perry

Beautiful Angel

(Diana, Princess of Wales
1st July 1961 - 31st August 1997)

I could hardly believe it
When I heard the news today,
How could it be true
How could she be taken away?

The People's Princess
Our Queen of Hearts,
Some didn't even know her
But still they're torn apart.

Finally she found happiness
She was again in love,
But cruelly cut so short
Now she's up in Heaven above.

A truly beautiful lady
Who everyone will miss,
For everyone to leave her alone
Was her only simple wish.

But now she's gone forever
Leaving so much behind,
But her memory will go on living
Her loving smile will always shine.

For Diana is in Heaven
And she's the brightest star in the sky,
But still the world asks itself
Why take Diana? WHY?

She'll always be remembered
Though her absence is hard to take,
But now she's watching down on us from Heaven
And what a beautiful angel she will make.

Casey Ball

Earthly Angel

Diana we loved you oh, so much
Lift up your hand for me to touch
This world alone was not for you
Our tears are falling like the dew
Our hearts must share the love you gave
Though they are broken we must be brave
You were a beautiful climbing Rose
To be cut down in your prime
The flowers are laid like soldiers in rows
To be gathered up in a very short time
You were the brightest beacon of light
Forever shining day and night
Sadly that light has diminished forever
Go travel through the darkness together
Unto a new life, a new beginning
Take heed dear Diana, the bells are ringing
The angels are singing
Go forth no-one can harm you now
Continue to shine your light in heaven
Princess we are thinking of you
Dear angel we all love you
Peace be with you.

Lucy Atwell

Tears For A Princess

All over the world the feeling's the same,
Overwhelming grief, loss and pain.
Diana's death has touched young and old,
She was a beautiful girl, with a heart of gold.
It was a terrible shock when the news came through,
Nobody actually knew what to do.
Tears started coming, they were in everyone's eyes,
As the nation started planning their last sad goodbyes.
Books of condolence were signed everywhere,
People finding their burden was so hard to bear,
You just can't believe it, you hear everyone say,
The tragic events that unfolded that day.
Then came her funeral, thousands were there,
I'm sure she would never have realised, so many would care.
They camped out for nights just to get a good place,
As it eventually passed by, at a very slow pace.
Her boys walked behind, what a sad sight to see,
That's when it really hit home for me.
Why had this to happen to someone so young,
She was only thirty-six and so full of fun.
God take care of Diana we pray,
We hope her and Dodi are happy today.

Doreen Andrews

The Princess Of Wales

(Dedicated to Diana, Princess of Wales
We all love you)

Diana, oh Diana what a tragic way to end,
Your life we could never mend.
Your kindness we shall sorely miss,
You made poor people's life a bliss.
A sad moment for us all it is,
Your life brought happiness joy and fizz.
But now your life ends in sorrow,
I shall also think the same tomorrow.
You were so unbelievably fine,
I can't think of a more sorrowful time.
You shall be deeply missed Diana forever.

James Hassall (10)

Diana, Princess Of Wales

Everyone can remember, each person can recall
The special look, the touch of your hand, your smile,
It tells us all
You were our Princess and our friend
It's so sad your life had to end.
But we won't forget you
Your memory will not fade
Although the flowers wither on the place where you are laid.
Farewell lovely lady
In our hearts you will stay
Our special memory of you
Will never fade away.

Barbara Froggatt

Dear Diana

Dear Diana, so short a life
With more than its share of stress and strife
Hounded for photos wherever she went
no escape from photographers, who were hell bent

Not all the media were at fault
Thank God we knew Her, through a moderate cult
her beauty and compassion they just shone through,
the mirror of her soul, Her eyes so blue.

Your two little sons 'God breathed on them too'
William a mirror image of you.
Dodi he brought new happiness to you
These are the memories I will always hold true.

Your death was almost too much to bear
for one so young, it doesn't seem fair
but the help you have started for all mankind
we will follow in your footsteps, and walk
close behind.

Now you are gone, flown away like a dove
leaving behind you a legacy of love
you have found your reward now and you are
at peace
May the good work you started multiply and
NOT CEASE.

Anne Jessop

A Tribute To Diana

Dear Diana, how many hands did you hold
with care,
How many hearts did you save from despair.
But who was there to hold your hand
When life's timer was fast running out of sand.

Did you not know of the love here for you,
Those who did not, would count only a few.
From all over the world, if you could but see,
Tributes, flowers, love notes pinned on a tree.
Not just women and children but grown men too,
Are grieving and weeping in silence for you.
So I say this Diana, you died not in vain,
For people now care about others in pain.

Ada Ferguson

Surely A Lady

Diana, Princess of Wales of some degree,
With which we all must agree.
Princess of the nation, and the people too,
With a heart of care and love for you.
Reaching out to help to alleviate distress,
To lift up the fallen caught in life's wilderness.
Her life often sad, coping with so much despair,
To overcome and win the fight, 'gainst much unfair.
Her battle was won, in the service nobly given,
Helping millions to share on earth a taste of heaven.

John Waddington

Untitled

When Diana was 19 she married a prince,
Looking back just a short while, think what's
happened since.
She had two sons named William and Harry,
Now the grief of the world they must carry.
She met a man named Dodi, there was love
in the air,
When we look back on her sons' childhood she really
did care.
Princess Diana, was the Queen of Hearts,
Now her sons' lives are torn apart.
In heaven she is in God's keep,
Now forever she will peacefully sleep.

Sarah Bullock (13)

Diana
'Our Nation's Golden Child'

You were the only heart
that felt us all.
You will never leave
our mind and soul.
Loving, caring and precious were you,
anything for others you would do.

A beautiful Princess
there was only one.
Princess Diana, now you're gone,
a gift you have left
to love one another,
every race, sister and brother.

We will remember you every day,
by giving and sharing in every way.
Good Night and God Bless,
you are in our hearts forever.
Your courage your goal will last
Forever.

Beverley Mansley

Diana, Princess Of Hearts

With your warm smile and good intent,
happiness was left wherever you went.

You loved the people young and old,
this showed you had a heart of gold.

You were never out of the public glare,
this to us never seemed very fair.

For although your work needed people's awareness,
you needed your privacy nevertheless.

Our thoughts go out to William and Harry,
right now they are sad, but one day we hope
they will be happy.

You have been taken from this world,
that seems quite rotten,

But PRINCESS DIANA! You will never be forgotten.

Carolyne, Chas, Stephen (7) & Rachel (4) Mowforth

Diana Princess Of Wales

Sleeping peacefully under the trees by the lake
There did our princess leave us for a heavenly state
The queen of our hearts whom we all held so dear
The hardest of hearts cannot help shed a tear

Whose wonderful smile will now bring light to us all
Bring hope love and joy as our lives sometimes fall
We felt that you were one of us sharing life's pain
A remarkable young lady, your life was our gain

We grieve at our loss, it's a sorrow that's shared
We weep for her sons and their pain that's unheard
Who now will make us aware of folk dying of AIDS
Stop the landmines, if her memory should fade

Let us remember the smiles, the hugs for the young
Let us all partake in her work still to be done
Part of her life that's in her two wonderful sons
The nation rises a last goodbye your race is won

A S Flack

Untitled

God misplaced an angel,
to earth she did stray.
Became a fairy princess,
her magic to display.
She taught us all a new song,
love neighbour as thyself.
Greedy hands abused her,
to enhance their wealth.
She cried out to heaven,
God took her by the hand.
He dried her tears, healed the pain
then he took command.
God flew her back to heaven,
we on earth bowed down.
God placed upon her platinum head
a well earned golden crown.

L D McLellan

Diana

Princess Diana you have been a gift from above
you taught us how to live and showed us God's love
This is His commandments to love Him and
one another
your love brought unity among nations like sister
and brother
your smile your love and compassion
shall always be remembered in all nations
you have been sent from God up above
He always takes the righteous ones,
when He thinks it's enough
He takes them to Himself to share His presence
and love
In the presence of angels in paradise above
I thank God for you for your short life
you have been through so much pain and sorrow
yet so much compassion and love you gave and sown
Diana if only you can see your harvest
as you lay in peace and rest
a harvest of unity and love among nations
God used you mightily in life and in death
if only you can see your harvest
I know your heart will sing and be glad
God's infinite wisdom who can understand
in your life and in death we see God's mighty hand
and one day Diana we shall meet again
But until then, rest in peace Queen of Hearts
who has been a Princess a gift from above

Tanya Benton

Goodbye England's Rose

When others turned away
When others did not care
An angel wiped away the tears
And answered every prayer.

A golden smile had she
A portrait from a pose
A blessing to us all
Known as our English Rose.

So Diana go most regal
Most loving and most true
With all God's humble blessings
In the knowledge we love you.

Robert Young

I Haven't Left, I'm Here

Lord,
I need to speak with you
of something that just can't be true.
We've lost a special lady
one, the whole world knew.
I have prayed and asked her Lord
'Diana please don't go'
The world and I have lost a friend
we all do love her so.

I couldn't bear to sleep last night
my heart has ached and cried
I never will believe it Lord that she has left and died
The world is now in darkness
the lights went out the day she left.
It's now our turn to give her peace and eternal rest.

Lord,
She did so much for many
I can do nothing to repay
Apart from pray her memory never goes
away.
There is this selfish feeling. I just can't let her go.
So Lord I really beg you
Let her memory live, shine and glow.
Tonight I thought I heard her voice
'I haven't left I'm here'
and Lord I believe she is. To guide us through
our fears.

Diana we never part from those we really love
You were so very rare,
and I for one will always feel your presence
everywhere.

Sue Turner

A Love As Pure As Gold

Princess DI,
We loved you so,
You always showed us your care,
I admired the way you glowed and shone
A loving role model, a loving face.
So deep within our hearts you touched us,
With your love, you showed you cared
A special person to everyone,
A special person who was there.
We will miss you with all our hearts,
The wonderful things you did
For us, for your children,
Your family and friends
Never forgetting your kindness.
We will always remember you,
Never forgetting your smile
No-one can compare to you,
Our Princess Di.
The love you shared among us,
I will never forget
And so with the rest of the world
The love we felt inside us
A love as pure as gold.
No-one can ever replace you,
You, our 'Queen of Hearts',
Never forgetting your love
Which will always stay in our hearts.

Avegayle Terrado (15)

Tribute To Lady Diana

One short spell of happiness.
One brief spell at play.
Her tragic life came to an end,
On that eventful day.

There was an understanding,
In life she played her part.
The things that she did best,
Came straight, right from the heart.

Hers was a life of sorrow,
And one of kindly deeds.
The people took her to their hearts,
And she fulfilled their needs.

Although she was in public life,
She walked through life alone.
Her life so short came to an end,
Now she's safely home.

Mary Murphy

Tribute To Diana

The lines of communication are full of the
dreadful news
our lovely Princess Diana has died
Oh why oh why did we all have to lose
the lady who filled us with such pride
Her elegance and style, her charm and grace
captivated us all through the years
Now she's gone to a higher place
and a whole nation is united in tears
Tears for her two sons, her family and friends
and the incredible loss they must feel
Her premature departure from all of their lives
so overwhelmingly surreal
The princes were blessed with a very special mother
who gave them wisdom, courage and fun
She will always be with them in their hearts
and memories
to see them through the years to come
All over the world flowers and candles adorn
the concrete
and the garden of grief grows each day
Poignant messages of condolence make the
picture complete
but so heart wrenching to survey
Now we await the day when we must bid farewell
To our extremely special Princess Di
To a lady who gave us so much
we were cherished to be given you - goodbye.

D L Petterssen

To Diana With Love

As she lay in peace
The world, we mourn
Her goodness and kindness
From us was torn.

She dared to be different
But kept her grace and charm
Tried to rid the world of disaster
And protect us from harm.

A natural beauty
Born with class
A saint among royals
She loved with her heart.

She was the nation's friend
Brave and strong
We still love her
Although she's gone.

No words can describe
What a mother she was
The way she loved her boys
For them we pray to God.

She was a fighter
A believer too
Helped many people
Like me and you.

She believed in them
Gave them a chance
Gave them hope
And a second glance.

When at last happiness,
She tried to find
The press were there
Showing the public eye.

This tragic life
Was suddenly ended
She died as she lived
With the press, in her face
We'll always remember her
As the goddess of the human race.

She is the queen of our hearts
The people's princess
We hope she'll find happiness
Now she's been laid to rest.

Diana, the Princess of Wales, can never be replaced.

Danni Turner

A Nation In Mourning

The world has lost a princess
A burning candle has lost its flame
A light has gone out across the world
That will never be lit again.

You've helped the people in Angola.
You helped to ease their pain.
You touched their lives so greatly in such a
wonderful way.
You will be remembered with great affection each
and every day.

And for all the wonderful things you've
done for charities in Britain and abroad
You will be remembered in our hearts and forever
be adored.

So now we will try to put our grieving hearts at ease
for now no-one can harm you and you'll be left to
rest in peace.
God has gained an angel whose beauty can't be
defined
You may be out of sight but you'll never be
out of mind.

And now as you begin your very last journey home.
There will be a nation showing so much love I wish
you could have known!

Diana you're irreplaceable you're our Queen of
Hearts and our saint,
Goodbye sweet princess may you forever
rest in peace.

Rosalyn John

Our Diana

Diana you were but a shy, young maid
When, with Charles, you were first displayed -
It was the day of your engagement, I remember,
The time the Royal household had gained
another member.

On the day of your wedding you were a
beautiful bride,
A treasure forever for Charles, by his side,
And as the years passed by you were blessed
with two sons,
From when your life seemed to become such fun.

But suddenly we knew, sadly, it wasn't to last
And you decided to put Charles in your past,
Seeking love and affection from your 'Charity bid'
And of your hope to become 'Queen of Hearts'
you had opened the lid.

The last few weeks of your life you appeared
to find love
And why this had to be denied by the 'One above'
Will leave everyone questioning forever more,
And especially your sons, too, of that I am sure.

As you passed through Althorp Gate my heart
felt like lead,
I still can't believe that 'Our Princess' is dead -
The light has gone from our life and TV
Never again your radiant and caring smiles to see.

I adored you, Diana, and hoped that we'd meet -
And although my memories are all very sweet,
I am saddened too much to think this can't be,
But I'll hold you as a 'daughter' eternally.

Margaret Rushby

Diana

D is for devoted, to everything she did.
I is for irreplaceable, to a world in which she lived.
A is for angel, looking down from the sky.
N is for never, having to say goodbye.
A is for answers, why did she have to die.

Paula Ringer

Grieve Not For Me

Grieve not for me for I was lent to you for just
a while,
To comfort you in sadness I gave to you my smile.
For all the sick and suffering whom I loved so
very much,
I offered them my warmth and compassion
in my touch.
But then God beckoned me to Heaven up above
Because He said He needed me to spread His word
of love.
And so I will continue as you would want me to
And one day when you join me I will meet again
with you.
My sons I leave in treasured hands as I know you
love them too,
Give them the support in the years ahead in
everything they do.
I did not want to leave them, that was the
hardest part,
For I will always love them so and keep them in
my heart.

Betty Whitcher

Diana

I look up at the sky
and ask myself why oh why
It was so unfair you had to die
the whole nation they did cry
It seemed so unreal
I think everyone would feel
that you deserved a long and happy life
to be free of trouble and strife
Your lovely sons are very sad
but one thing makes me glad
You now have the peace you deserve
memories of you we will preserve
although you are far away
in our hearts you will stay
Sleep well, Princess Diana
AMEN

Donna Holmes

Poem For Diana

She was a gift to all of us,
In our memory she will always stay,
Because, every day in her own way,
She showed everyone the way.

Her time was so precious, whatever came that day,
She dealt with, in an overly acceptable manner,
I wonder if we could have done the same,
And still made speeches, without a stammer,
Think about it.

People the world over, simply loved her,
Why, you might say, why, was she so special,
Because, my friends, she did her share,
Of caring for others in genuine love, until,
That day she was taken away.

So suddenly, she was gone, with her friend,
Leaving behind, her beloved boys,
So, so sad her tragic end,
But they will remember all of the joys,
Always in their hearts will be,
Memories of a mother, a friend and advisor,
Of everything that life can give,
And take, but through it all,
You have no choice, but to live,
Until you receive your call.

In our hearts Diana you will always stay,
Your people will remember you when they pray,
Peace and happiness is wished for you now,
And in the church, our heads we'll bow.
GOD BLESS AND KEEP FOREVER OUR PRINCESS
OF WALES AND QUEEN OF HEARTS.

Joyce Seddon

The Sorrow Of Two Princes

Two princes left behind to grieve
the passing of their mother
must now stand tall and brave and strong
and comfort one another.

And I believe she'll stay with them -
her spirit's very strong -
and guide them gently on along
campaigns to end what's cruel and wrong!

Patricia Tilling

Legacy Of Diana

Beautiful sweet Diana rest in heavenly peace
Knowing your precious legend will never cease
The willingness to help others less fortunate
and alone
Comforting the sick and dying despite unhappiness
of your own
Unleashed thoughts to improve lives of young
and old
New stories every day most eagerly being told
How much your short life touched others in
tender embrace
Just the radiance of a smile lit the gloomiest place
Around the world people left grievously shedding
many tears
Thankful for having known of you in such
troubled years

Pavements of London became carpets of
perfumed flowers
Laid by thousands queuing in sunshine and
heavy showers
Messages of sympathy along with many of these
Cuddly toys and ribbons hung from trembling trees
Time slowly marches on and hopefully all will find
Diana's legacy lingers on in the two sons left behind
Queen of people's hearts Diana so gladly wanted
to be
Surely much adoration and mourning for no other
will we see
A fairy-tale without a happy ending seems so
very wrong
So slumber in dream kissed sleep as your memory
lives on.

M M Davey

A Tribute To Diana

One day I shook hands with the Princess of Wales
A day I will cherish - a day to remember,
I first saw her car as it passed me close by,
Just a wave, she was gone, on that day in September

But later I stood, just to see if I could
Catch a glimpse of a Princess known simply as Di,
The children in front started waving and cheering,
And then she appeared and passed her car by.

She walked down the drive as the children all smiled,
Their hands stretching out to touch if they could,
A handshake, a smile and a word here and there,
A thrill for each child - then before me she stood.

Her eyes were so blue as they looked into mine,
Her handshake was firm, and I'd nothing to say
But 'Hello,' for my mind was a blank from the start,
Just a word and she'd gone, but it brightened
my day.

And now as the nation is mourning her loss,
I weep for the Princess know simply as Di,
Remember her kindness, her love and her caring,
Her radiance has gone and we wonder just why.

A bright star has glittered and waned in the heavens,
But beautiful memories we'll always retain.
For her spirit lives on in our hope for the future,
The Queen of our hearts she'll forever remain.

M Turtle

Diana

God lent us an angel
Just for a little while.
To show us how to love and care
She made the people smile.

Diana set a shining example
Of how people should really be.
To love and share and care
And hug definitely.

So she's done her work here on earth
And made it a better place
Now God has taken her home
Because he needed her more
But she's left us two wonderful princes
Whom the nation adores

Rest peacefully our princess
Your people will watch over them.

Julia M Powell

Diana, Our Princess Of Wales

It seemed that she had everything,
To the great big world outside,
The country girl who won the heart of a prince,
Then became his blushing bride.

The simple things in life, are what
Meant the most to her,
Her beloved family, her privacy,
Various charities and the poor.

She never really cared
For her riches or her wealth,
But more for those without a home,
Those less fortunate, or in bad health.

She won the hearts of everyone,
From the youngest to the old,
Now, how much we all will miss her,
Never can be told.

For on that fateful night,
We lost her, her chauffeur and her friend,
But one as elegant, as beautiful as her,
The world will never see again.

Though with Dodi, she never lived
To fulfil that fairy tale,
We will always fondly remember and love,
Diana, our Princess of Wales.

Lorraine O'Shea

The People's Champion

A silent witness I look on,
Along with a nation, your passing I mourn;
For the world is now a much emptier place,
Without you, our Princess, to embrace.
How could it be, that one so pure of heart,
At such a young age, should have to part.
The people's champion you became,
You helped to alleviate so much pain.
You became a victim of your deeds,
Not one of selfishness or of greed;
But of giving and sharing, loving and caring,
Never aloof or condescending.
From AIDS to Palsy to the evil landmine,
You unselfishly gave, your precious time.
A few kind words, a gentle touch,
To those who were suffering, this meant so much.
Never giving a thought for yourself,
Into others' problems you would deeply delve.
When you held the dying in your arms,
For your own safety, you had no qualms;
The love you showed was pure and true,
A gift you gave to many, not just a few.
Never did you ask, for anything in return,
The respect of the world, you did not demand but earn.
The media brought you into our lives,
You were always there with us, morning and night.
An Ambassador last, a mother first,
In public or private, your life was cursed.
You became so popular, with your deeds so great,
That your very being, was to seal your fate.
The paparazzi invaded your life,
As if they had, some God-given right;
Not for one moment, were you left alone,
Whether holidaying abroad, or with your children at home.
But now you have eternal peace,
The kind before, you found only in sleep.
We will never forget you, though you have gone,
Your words and your deeds, will forever live on;
For we shall always have, our memories and dreams,
Of a fairytale Princess, who in our hearts, will 'always be Queen'.

Peter Redpath

In Memory Of Diana, Princess Of Wales

Diana, you were lovely,
Not only in your face,
Your heart was filled with love,
Compassion and grace.

The world misunderstood you,
As we all too often do,
But you had the courage to
Speak out, and the gift to see it through.

We knew that you were hurting,
Deep down within your soul,
But you were taken from us,
We were unable to console.

As that haunting bitter-sweet
Refrain so eloquently sung,
A 'Candle In The Wind' it said
And you were oh! So young.

There surely is a message here
For all of us to ponder,
When we think of all the need
In the great big world out yonder.

The outcast, the unwanted,
The broken, and the lame,
You loved them all the same,
I think it fills the rest of us
With guilt and real shame.

If something good can come from this,
If it touches every heart,
Then surely from this tragedy,
We may help, make a start.

J Lea

Diana

Words are oh so many.
Deeds are oh so few.
Diana carried hers out.
Have I, has the world, have you?

Brenda Kelly

Untitled

I said a prayer to God today
To tell him you were on your way
So he summoned his angels one by one
To welcome our Princess home

I said a prayer to God today
To plead with him to let you stay
He said your time on earth was through
There was work in Heaven for you to do.

I said a prayer to God today
To pick the sweetest rose and lay
It gently on the Isle of Peace.
Where our beloved Princess sleeps

God answered the prayer I said today
He knew that you were on your way
For he had your loved ones by his side
As he opened the gates of Heaven wide

Smiling softly as you walked through
Our Lord held out his hand to you
As the gates of Heaven gently close
We know God picked the sweetest Rose.

Pauline Brown

Untitled

Out is the fire, out is the flame
Can the world ever be the same again
Her beauty, her youth, compassion and care
The way that she loved, beyond compare.
A daughter, a sister, a mother, once a wife
Special indeed to have touched a life
Was happiness for her ever to be
Apart from her boys, her immediate family
Then holidays, love, a meal at the Ritz
Off into the night, she loved him to bits
A surge of power, a flash of light,
An error of judgement, DIANA, goodnight.

Valerie Breithaupt

Ode To Diana

Weeping willow weep;
as we bring her home to rest
to the place she loved the best.
Our sacred flower this earth caress,
then you need weep no more.
Weeping willow weep;
like dew on the last summer rose,
like autumn leaves that fall,
like mocking birds that call,
then you need weep no more.
Weeping willow weep;
like a river of no return,
like an aching heart that yearns,
like a candle flame that burns,
then you need weep no more.
Weeping willow weep;
as you watch beside the lake,
soon her soul will gently wake.
Then you will stand so tall
you need not weep at all.

Lilian Cherry

Do Not Cry For Me

My dear people, do not cry for me,
now that I have gone.
But, do as you saw me do,
to help my work live on.
If anyone is in despair,
put your arms around them,
show them that you care.

Words do very little for those in distress,
Actions are much better, give a sweet caress
The love that you showed me,
share with others, make them free.
Just a small gesture, a touch, a smile, a kiss
For those who have never had it,
it is pure bliss.

In my heart you will all remain,
Please don't let my work be in vain.

Lesley Lister

Rose Of England

In the garden of Althorp House
Lies a beautiful English rose,
The wind and the rain, caress her,
As she sleeps in sweet repose.

For Diana was a princess
Her qualities were rare
Her caring ways and compassion
Were everyone's to share.

Although we never met her
Overwhelmed with grief we are
No-one can ever replace
That bright and shining star.

You had so much to give us
You taught us to understand
What the meaning of true love is
To give and not demand.

We will remember the day we lost you
It was such a tragic day
You had to die, to show men
How to change their ways.

So sleep on dear Princess
In the garden you loved so dear
And when the rain falls upon you
It is angels shedding tears.

Mary Seddon

Untitled

God reached down and extended his hand,
And took you away to a better land,
Up to the clouds and heaven above,
To look after, protect you and give you his love,
To a place where we can harm you no more,
He's given you the key to heaven's door,
Your brand new life has now begun,
And you've finally found your place in the sun.

Lisa Crosby

Tribute To Diana Princess Of Wales

She showed the world
The way to care,
To help another and -
Their troubles to share.
She gave love to others
Who she felt were in need.
Such depth of feeling
In her eyes you could read.
Love is a thing -
No amount of money can buy,
It costs nothing to give -
If we all try.
Maybe the world can learn
From her tragic loss,
To give of oneself and -
Not consider the cost.
No one can ever take her place,
Most of us will remember
Her lovely face.
Her tender smile, her loving touch.
This world will miss her -
Very much.

Alma A Dodds

Diana

If there's a heaven up above,
Look after our princess, whom we love.
I'll never forget when you were lying in your bed,
And I came in and told you, 'DIANA WAS DEAD.'
Those greedy photographers we'll never forgive,
For Diana is gone, and they live on.

And to your tender loving sons,
We'll never forget them Wills and Harry, who
One day will marry, you too will love
Your children, like your mum did with you,
You too, like your mum will be such fun,
Keeping her special, ever burning. loving flame alive,
In you, and your children's children forever.

God bless you sweet princess.

R J and M E Boyd

Diana - Reflections

Born to high estate she seemed to wear privilege as a casual garment without display,
Moving among her fellows, content to share the common birthright of humanity.
Her smile dissolved barriers.
Children clung to her and the rejected felt reinstated by her touch.
Folk were at ease with her.
In her company the tongue-tied found words and the inarticulate needed none
For her intuition read the tale of pain in a troubled face.
She understood.
Sadness and uncertainty were no strangers to her.
Had she known loneliness, longing for the comfort of a mother's arms, the sympathetic ear or word of wise advice?
Perhaps,
The restraints of royalty bore heavily upon her.
May not the exotic bird, aviary reared, look sometimes with longing at the sparrows scratching in the dust outside?
How much more the wild bird caged?
Self-wounding, she had beat her frail wings against the rigid bars of protocol.
The glare of spotlights troubled her and she sought escape.
The hunters' nets closed in on her seeking to entrap,
To hold her in cruel exposure.
The crowds surged forward, seeking booty.
They who fed on scandal as maggots on rotting flesh did not mean to harm her.
'Father forgive them, for they knew not what they did'.
She was young and made mistakes.
The hasty word or ill-conceived venture brought stinging rebuke.
Of course she did wrong - as who does not?
Leave judgement to the All-Seeing One.
Perhaps her very fallibility endeared her to a stumbling generation,
One which had torn down life's signposts in the name of freedom,
Giving to the young freedom to lose their way.
For a while she lost hers.
Then the compass of her heart directed her.
She would become a voice to the voiceless, a champion of those who could not help themselves.

Perceiving her goal she advanced with fervour and courage.
She could not know how short would be her time.
How sadly short!
Short but enough.
Enough to wake some flicker of awareness - of duty to those so long ignored.

Hold fast the vision now!
Keep faith.
Let not rank weeds of apathy obscure the trail she blazed.
Follow the course.
Build on her beginnings.
Therein, perchance, we may build her memorial.

V E Godfrey

Diana

You came into our lives like a breath of fresh air,
The brightest star in a cloudless night sky,
So young and innocent,
A fairytale princess with a Prince Charming.
We thought you would be our queen.
Loved by millions from all over the world.
Wherever you travelled you touched people's hearts,
Touching, kissing, hugging the young, old and sick,
Caring came so naturally.
You live on through two boys, whom you so deeply loved,
In their laughter, their smiles, their tears and their hearts.
No one can hurt you now Diana, as God's angels watch over you.
So don't be lonely, we will never forget,
Our princess, we once thought would be queen.

J L Fielding

Queen Of Hearts

(In memory of a true princess)

Oh sweet Lord on high above
Why did our angel die
Show her your eternal love
And wipe our tears dry

When all the world is crying
And it is for you they weep
You gave them dignity in dying
And joined them in their sleep

And as you walk through broken dreams
While other children cry
You will hear their frightened screams
And wipe their tears dry

Goodbye my lovely, goodnight God bless
You stole our hearts away
Those laughing eyes and tenderness
For innocents to play

I will always walk with thee
Through all life's weary trials
Whilst thou always walk with me
Those dark and lonely miles

Goodnight, God bless my sweet princess
You've left that we might start
All bathed in grief's togetherness
DIANA, our Queen of Hearts

R Finch

Epitaph To Diana Princess Of Wales

Love thy neighbour as thyself
as Diana sought to do.
Her loving smile and warm compassion
helped so many to pull through.

Thank God for giving us Diana,
the un-crowned 'Queen of our hearts';
She gave of herself magnanimously,
inspiring others to play their part.

Diana enriched our lives immeasurably;
She died needlessly due to man's greed.
Let us all work to honour her memory
by reaching out to help those most in need.

Without doubt a humanitarian,
loving mother, an ambassador for peace;
Diana, in eternal tribute,
may we all strive your goals to reach.

Malcolm F Andrews

Diana - A Special Princess

It was the thirty first of August
Nineteen ninety seven
The Lord decided he would take Diana
Up to heaven.
The timing seemed so tragic, for once she seemed
So happy,
Finding strength from her new love,
A man she knew as Dodi.
He also died and now the two are joined as one
In soul,
No-one can hurt or tarnish them,
No more lies can be told.
Diana touched the hearts of each and
Everyone she met,
Giving love, compassion that no-one will forget.
Making friends with all no matter what their
Race or breed,
Searching out the homeless with so many mouths
To feed.
The young, the old, the sick, the well,
No matter who they were,
She had a place for all of them,
A place in her heart to share.
Goodbye Diana from all of us may you enjoy
Your special love,
As you shine down, the brightest star,
Shine down from up above.

Janette Halliday

RIP Princess Diana

Diana you will be
Sadly missed,
Through all those lives
You touched and kissed.
Diana you could never
Be replaced,
Through all those times
In life you faced.

You were an inspiration
Through your charity work,
Even though you died that
Morning in your Merc.
With Dodi in the car you
Cared,
Your last week with him you
Shared.

You died on the day of
Rest,
The press no more will
Be a pest.
When you were a girl
You were very shy,
Now that's gone we shall
All cry.

You were bubbly, caring
Charmful and witty,
Not to mention you were
Extremely pretty.
Delicate, graceful and
Incredibly smart,
These are the features that
Make the Queen of Hearts.

Dawn Martin (12)

My Inspiration!

I lay awake in bed tonight
and felt the urge that I should write
one thousand words are in my head
but most of all the words 'Not dead'

This is one that has come to me
although I know not what the words
will be.
I seem to be full of fire
I do not slow, I do not tire
I feel so alive and full of drive
I do not know whose words are these
I just feel full of sense to please
I cannot stop, I do not want to
In Diana's memory I promise not to.

Could this be where my fate lies?
To see the world through Di's eyes
for I now too
feel the yearning
to show I care,
to love and be warming
and once I can accomplish these
then I too,
will feel the joy to please.

I wonder why she's chosen me
in my soul she seems to be
I have never felt so inspired,
to write these words - I do not tire
could she somehow be telling me
now that her spirit has been set free
I feel so close, I cannot describe
the words that are floating around inside
I feel a great urge to pass on these,
and ask you to listen if you please!

C L Brownless

Diana, Princess Of Wales

Diana, you were beautiful in every possible way,
God in his wisdom, took you away from us today,
we just cannot believe it, you are missed so much,
a caring person, everyone you loved and touched,
birds no longer sing, and the sun no longer shines,
all the ones you have loved, that are left behind,
your gentle hands have helped to heal our wounds,
we all mourn your passing, you have left us
too soon,
Diana, Princess of Wales, loved her sons with pride,
with all the love and affection she had inside,
heaven has another angel, to outshine all the others,
an example to us all 'Queen of Hearts',
a loving mother,
our hearts go out to William and Harry,
from now on,
Diana was adored by all, but now,
sadly, you are gone.

Josephine Elliott

Untitled

Once a young, shy girl with so much love to give,
We took you to our hearts as the prince's wife.
And though there was so much for you to learn,
You emerged with honours from the School of Life.
You showed us people need love and care,
No matter what their state of health,
Colour or creed.
The evidence of your work is round us everywhere.
You tried to be at any place there was a need.
Now that you're gone, a nation sadly mourns,
Your vital presence is already greatly missed.
We will remember your tireless good work,
Your words of comfort and the lives your
Kindness kissed.
One more star is in the sky tonight.
You touched so many that you never even met,
And yet, we all knew you as a constant friend,
And in your honour, we will not forget.

S E Seagrave Pearce

Untitled

To you Diana
An ambassador of love
Sent to earth
From heaven above
They say that beauty
Is the depth of skin
But you had a beauty
Even greater within
A wonderful woman
With a compassionate face
A person impossible
To replace
You filled our lives
With happiness and joys
Seeing your devotion
To your two lovely boys
They will miss you
How much?
Who could know?
But your spirit will be there
As they grow
What stronger a force
Than a mother's care
Challenge that, you
Cynics, if you dare
You'll live on within our life
Giving us strength during
Trouble and strife
You found love with Dodi
A man of passion
Who loved your inner beauty
And your love of fashion
Your memory will always
Remain in our hearts
You reached the world
In its remotest parts
Bless you Diana
May you both rest in peace
Our love for you
Will NEVER cease.

Christine Hughes

The Gift

Out of the sorrow
And in your hearts
'Your mum and you'
Will never part

Your mum
Had that gift
To make you smile
When you were
Sad and lonely,

And gave her love
And heart to you only,

The world
Was a better place
For her
Saving grace.

William and Harry,
In life
You will never part.
God bless.

Bill Crossan

For Diana - The Queen That Never Was

As I gaze at the darkened skies,
I see a lone star shining so bright,
Jesus has welcomed our princess this night,
Diana was so loyal, so loving, so kind,
Helping the needy as much as she could,
Fulfilling her dreams, yet taken from us,
So soon we all know,
A short time is better, than no time at all,
I now pray for you, with all of my love,
Diana I miss you and remember,
You'll always be my Queen of Hearts,
So rest in peace with the angels above.

Carl Ball

A Tribute To A Princess

I still read the headlines in utter disbelief
Coming to terms with your passing . . . such grief
We keep asking ourselves can this really be true?
Why . . . such a tragic end for someone as
wonderful as you . . .

Princess Diana . . . an icon of our years
We followed your life, tears and fears
We watched your fairytale . . . turn for the worse
Where your love was doomed like some
ancient curse

But yet, you remained so compassionate . . .
so strong
Working with your charities and the world
gone wrong
You said that people needed to be loved for
what they are
And you made others feel that you were never
that far

A royal princess you might have been
but even a commoner's heart you would win
You will be remembered not only for your
glamour and fashion
But for your heart filled with love and
genuine compassion

You reached out to millions, from the young
to the very old
You gave people hope and courage to go on,
we're often told
Your captivating smile, warmth and shy glance
Could melt anyone's heart and place one in a trance

I feel so much pain thinking of you dying in the cold
Whilst the paparazzi just took photos . . .
actions so bold
Even in your dying moments you didn't have
any peace
But was surrounded by vultures vying for
their 'piece'

Only one consolation is that you are in a place
of love
In GOD'S safe hands up above

Sandra Galistan

Thoughts Of A Grandma
10am on 31.8.97.

The morning star has been extinguished!
A glowing light, a beacon bright,
A shining example of human warmth
And love - is no more!
She was saintly, ordinary, royal, so popular
Beloved, extraordinary, ambassador and mother -
Such a good mother -
Mother of a future king and his brother.
Now she has gone - so suddenly.
A car crash in Paris - chased by the paparazzi
On seven motorbikes!
Terrible! Criminal! Horrendous tragedy!
Incomprehensible!
A nation in shock - why?
The grief is unbearable -
Worldwide disbelief -
International despair -
Personal - her loss is so personal.
My princess will be missed forever,
I am numb -
I weep for Diana
I weep for her boys

Pauline Andrews

Babies

Shining like the stars above,
She takes your hand in her glove,
In golden light, with eyes so bright
Her babies cry all through the night

Our Princess Diana, Queen of Hearts far and wide
Take our love and tears into the tide
The world has lost one so bright
And her babies cry all through the night

Remember how she held your hands,
Warm and in her glove
Remember her and share the love
Shining down from up above.

Natasha De Sousa

Untitled

Early on a Sunday morning,
My daughter phoned to say,
That Princess Di and Dodi,
Had been cruelly taken away.

The nation started crying,
'It's not true, it's all a lie,
Our Princess Di and Dodi,
Were too beautiful to die.'

When it finally started to sink in,
We thought of William and Harry,
What a terrible burden,
Their young shoulders had to carry.

Please, please cry, please shed a tear,
When you walk behind your mother,
She is the only one you'll have,
There will never be another.

They say in church you shed your tears,
And for that we are all glad,
The healing tears are what you need,
They'll help when you are sad.

Now sleep on dear Diana,
Your two boys will be fine,
Your family will make sure of that,
So now let PEACE BE THINE!

Margaret Jones

Diana - Our Queen Of Hearts

One rainy Sunday in August
I heard that you had died
My daughter told me the sad news,
In total shock and disbelief,
We comforted each other and cried
No more of your loving smile
Or those lovely blue eyes
We will all miss your gentle touch
Your voice, to ease a baby's cries.
You were an inspiration
To all people far and wide.
But deep down 'Diana'
Your own pain, you tried to hide.
Finally you met happiness with Dodi
Your life was looking bright
Then God went and took away
Our only shining light.
God bless and keep you both in his care.
For two very special people like these,
Are very, very rare.

Goodnight, God bless
Love,

Rose, Samantha and Stacey

Simply The Best

As the nation unites to count the cost,
A charming lady it has lost.
Diana full of grace and charm,
To the people she did no harm.

She travelled to so many lands,
She shook the leper by the hand.
To many people she gave them a hug,
The little ones her coat did tug.

She was showered with so many flowers,
She saw so many people in sunshine and showers.
We saw the sunshine in your smile,
As you stopped to chat awhile.

And now as Diana is laid to rest
We say Diana you were simply the best.
You brought us much happiness and many joys,
We pray God will take care of Diana's boys.

David Reynoldson

Diana

The days go on in sadness, yet,
Our lives they must go on,
To cherish our dear Princess,
Whose face was true and shone.

Her life was always hectic
With plenty much to do
Caring for the weak and sick
Princes William and Harry too.

We sit, stare and listen
To all that is said and done
Diana will always glisten
We can't believe she's gone.

One day we'll all meet again
With happiness and rejoice
When God does take away our pain
We'll hear her gentle voice.

Diana was a mother
And a sister too
She will always be remembered
By folk like me and you.

When we have our private thoughts
Each night and every day
Let us all remember
Diana showed us the way.

We all did love her dearly
She clearly was the best
We all mean this sincerely
Our Princess may you rest.

Sammy Hagar and children
Tina, Tanya, Tara, Timothy and Tamara

Princess Diana

Everyone in the world is in shock and grief,
Her short life now seemed oh so brief,
She was unique, loved by everyone and adored,
The Queen of Hearts, happy and self assured,
There had been sadness and trouble in her life,
But she'd helped many others through illness
And strife,
Like a flame she shone bright,
To take her away is just not right,
She held out a hand to give a magic touch,
No words said, but the thought meant so much,
She was the world's most famous and adored
Princess,
At least her last weeks were full of happiness
And not distress,
She will never be forgotten, in our memories
She will stay,
Not just for now, tomorrow, but for every day,
God will now surely return the love that
She has given,
The cameras, flash bulbs, press have now
Been driven,
God will now welcome her with open arms,
Hold out his hands and take her palms,
You've done so much, and shown others the way,
Your good work will continue, we shall pray,
Your eternal flame will never go out,
Your love has not been wasted,
Of that there is no doubt,
So now Diana, rest in peace
As we must say goodbye,
Until one day we'll all meet again way up high,
Like a star in the sky, your light shines bright,
With wings spread on a journey through
Life's flight,
But nothing ever really ends,
Our thoughts, prayers and love to you we send.

Trudy Lapinskis

To Diana

Oh my Diana, snow white lily, rose of
heaven and earth.
Sweet spirit, sister of this lonely universe,
whose Empire is the name you wept upon.
In our heart's memory we suspend to thee these
votive wreaths of beautiful memories.

Poor captive bird, who from thy narrow cage,
poured out such love and kindness that might have
assuaged the rugged hearts that imprisoned you.
We're not deaf to all your rightful yearnings,
through their own cold powers, to speak
in feeble warnings.

This shall be my rose and poem to thee.
Whose petals by my tears are dead indeed.
But soft and fragrant is the blossom,
Oh my princess it has to thorn to wound thy bosom,
because you have beheld the form of love.

With unrelaxing speed the whole world heard
of your death,
with vision and love they have cried aloud,
sleep or death shall not divide us long,
we know the cause of your departure,
our love for you is far too strong.

Oh dream of youth, oh breath of heaven,
it is a woe too deep for tears.
Which night and time have quenched for ever,
Oh death's white and winged steed took away
our flower and trampled down the weed.

Goodbye our princess of the people,
may you be forever in God's arms sleeping,
both our birthdays are written in the sky
we were both born years apart,
the first day of July, we will be linked together
until I will die.

Elizabeth Clancy

Diana, Princess Of The World's People

A tender touch, a friendly smile,
Was always to be your style,

Many pathways stretched before you,
For you did choose the very one to

Our hearts, and in our minds we
Knew you loved us so naturally and free,

Then suddenly you were not there for us,
We were broken-hearted every one of us,

Flowers were all we had to show the heavens,
The tears as raindrops fell to floods and ravines

Which flowed to a sea of love,
To set free the brightest dove

Of peace and goodness ever imagined on earth,
By mere mortals living around the breadth and girth

Of our Mother Earth.

Bruce Allen

Princess Diana

Words are not enough to express how I feel,
it's hard to believe you are not here,
you touched so many hearts
with a kind word and a smile,
You brought sunshine into our lives,
and gave us hope
when we gave up caring,
Your sons are so beautiful
just like you
I myself know what they are going through
You brought them up in such a way
that they remind us of you
with each passing day.
Now our country has lost a princess
and Heaven has gained the most
beautiful queen.
Our 'Queen of Hearts'.

Samantha White

Diana

Beauty, an aura a golden glow
Emanating, dazzling all who saw,
Compassion from the depths of her heart
flowed out,
To touch every soul that she happened to meet.

A privilege and honour, they all agreed,
From the dignitaries, workers down to waifs in
the street,
She treated them all to kindness and grace.
Faith, love and sorrow mirroring o'er her face.

She gave her all to the ones most in need,
The sick and the dying, the maimed - any creed,
Her presence warmth and caring enough for
them all
Their troubles and problems she showed to
the world.

She proved to us all that we should not have fear
Of sickness and death, that we should draw near,
To those who are suffering, to help where we can,
No matter what age or what colour the hand.

They'll never forget her, throughout the world,
Her image portrayed holding aged and child,
Soothing the suff'ring wherever she could,
With kind words and gestures,
but most of all Love.

Margaret J H Goudie

An Ode To A Rose

To our darling Diana
The Princess of Wales
Who blossomed into the most
beautiful rose,
I will never forget your smiling face,
or the two buds you left behind to
blossom and bloom in your place.

D Wickens

Goodbye England's Rose

You touched the hearts of many people
Across the world your love you shared
You brought the nation close together
To let the people know you cared

For all you cared for, all the help you gave
We could see you were born a fighter
We have watched, listened and learned from you
We now see that our future is brighter

With you beside us we would never give up
For you would guide us through the hard parts
When days were tough you would keep us strong
You are our Queen of Hearts

In person we thank you for all your support
What you gave was a comforting manner
For charities, illnesses and lives torn apart
God sent an angel and called her Diana

Although with our eyes we cannot see you
The love in our heart still grows
The angels do call and you must go
With love, goodbye England's rose

In loving memory of Diana, Princess of Wales

Steven Tanner

Untitled

You were a special princess
There will never be another
A princess who was so very kind
And a loving mother.

You warmed the hearts of everyone
When you were very daring
Walking through those minefields
It showed you were so caring.

You have worked wonders in this world
That others could not do
You have helped thousands of people
They owe their thanks to you.

A princess of understanding
Always nimble on your toes
A lovely pretty princess
A lovely 'English Rose'.

But now you're up in Heaven
Looking down on all of us
You might be saying to yourself
What is all the fuss?

So rest in peace my angel
We are very sad
But I know you are so happy
Up there with your Dad.

R W Cox

Dearest Diana,

We're writing this little poem for you,
Because we feel so sad and blue.
Your caring, sharing, loving ways,
Your kindness, and your smiling gaze.
We will now and forever miss you so.
We'll never forget you, NEVER, NO!
Diana, the Princess, you played your part,
But to all of us, you are Queen of Hearts.

God bless you
Rest in peace.

Elaine, Chris, Elizabeth (5)
& Andrew (3) Reeve

Diana, The Brave

Not in cold stone, nor slabs of wood,
For neither could capture that which was good,
No sculpture could render the essence we craved
Our hearts must remember, Diana, the Brave.

Friend to the lost, in a world full of greed,
A symbol of hope to those most in need,
Think of the homeless, the hungry, the victims she saved,
The poor shall remember, Diana the Brave.

Still now sad hearts, for she is at rest,
Her work here is done, a work that was blessed,
A touch of her hand was all that she gave,
The sick shall remember, Diana, the Brave.

Not in cold stone, or Memorial Park,
To remember the beautiful, Queen of our Hearts,
Remember her light, in a world that was grey,
We will never forget you, Diana, the Brave.

Mike Smith

Dearest Diana

To say you're missed, is an understatement
It tears us apart inside
We flush a range of feelings
The tears we cannot hide.

The pain grows within us
The anger it does show
The nation is shocked and grieving
We don't want to let you go.

You left the earth so quickly
We never did say goodbye
Your death was masked with tragedy
And all we do is cry.

The people's princess, the Queen of Hearts
Is what they are calling you
I for one must agree
After seeing all the things you'd do.

You were always someone special
And never a thought away
I'll remember you forever
And hold you dear each day.

Helen Pearce

Kensington Revisited

(A fond remembrance of Diana, Princess of Wales 1961-1997)

We took our American friends back to
Kensington Palace that day in May.
Then to tea at the Orangery.
It was all so very British.

A leisurely stroll through the gardens
In the heat of late afternoon.
Back on the main road our steps
Quickened.

We saw two outriders, a
Large black car was moving very slowly.
She bent forward. Her smile and wave
Was just for the four of us.

A double take, suddenly we realised this was
Our own princess, truly a vision of loveliness,
Graceful and every inch the
Embodiment of royalty.

A gasp of recognition and
Joyfully we waved back.
Our step was lighter for
This brief encounter.
The memory lingers on.

Now she has gone to her Maker.
The whole world is saddened for her
Tragic passing. Would the outriders had
Been with her in Paris that fateful night.

Two boys have lost
Their loving wonderful mother.
Let us hope that her pathetic critics realise
How much, and how often, they debased our
Priceless, National Treasure.

Hilary Moore

Diana

You were in the news almost
every day,
Giving a constant fashion
display,
Your superb figure was second
to none,
And before you died you were
having fun,
Visiting places far and wide,
With Dodi Fayed by your
side,
Travelling the world by boat
and jet,
Mixing with the upper set,
What else could we expect
from you?
You looked a dream and
reigned supreme,
Wherever you went the newsmen
flocked,
To photograph your latest
frock,
Now you've gone, the world's
in shock,
Our beloved princess,
Britain's Rock,
We will never forget you,
our beautiful Di,
You're the brightest star, in
the sky

Lucy Scholey

Queen Of Hearts

(This poem was inspired by the wave of love for
Diana, Princess of Wales, after her sudden death,
31st August 1997)

She wanted to be called the Queen of Hearts
And won a deep devotion giv'n to few.
Her warmth, compassion and her ringing laugh
Attracted love and admiration too.

'I was in prison and you came to Me.'
'When I was hungry, then you gave Me meat.'
'Do this for others and it is for Me.'
He spoke and her obedience was complete.

Diana, Princess, mingled with the crowds,
Picked up the children, touched the troubled soul.
She comforted, relieved their suffering,
And those who met her felt they were made whole.

She loved the poor, the outcast, the distressed.
She visited the prisoners and the ill.
She followed Our Lord's teaching and she tried
In all her ways to do His Holy Will.

A light is out; extinguished is a flame.
Who will continue all the work begun?
She cared so much that landmines should
be banned,
The world a better place to raise her son.

The silent mourners watched as the hearse passed
And tossed their flowers - tokens of their love.
Diana left this earth a poorer place
And went to her eternal home above.

Joyce M Turner

The Queen Of Hearts

The Queen of Hearts
Went so many yards
To save the lives of so many
Now she has gone
Her love lives on
And shall remain in the hearts of so many.

Danielle Garster (10)

Shining Star

Because of everything you did endeavour,
you will be in our hearts forever,
and with all the love you gave,
and all the hearts you saved,
you shone like a star in the sky,
but even though we try, not all can say goodbye.

Rebecca Dobb (14)

Diana

They say the good die young,
and sadly this is true.
But to take you so suddenly
when you still had so much to give and do.
You gave the frail and weak the will to live
to the injured you gave hope
If not just by your presence
it would be with a laugh or joke.
You are in all our hearts
and you brightened all our days
You changed so many people's lives
in oh so many ways.
You were an angel loaned by God
to teach us to care and love.
Now God has taken back His angel
to watch us from above.
Let's hope we've learned your lessons well
and your life has not all been in vain
That we bring love and joy into the world
and not the grief and pain.
You were the 'People's Princess'
a truly special English Rose
A star that nestles in the heavens
that everybody knows.

Wendy Cooper

Diana

Diana you are beautiful
Just like the stars in the sky
Even up in Heaven
You'll smile as the world goes by

You'll still pass down your feelings
So beautiful they were
Although you are up in Heaven
In our hearts
You are still here on earth.

Your two sons one day will be reunited
With your 'Dear Diana' in the sky,
Until then your work will achieve
So you 'Dear Diana' can rest in peace.

J Davis

The People's Flower

From the tiniest of seeds a plant began to grow
Lovingly fed and watered, till leaves began to show.
Slowly pushing through the ground it started on
life's way
Tenderly loved and nurtured, protected every day.
Soon the floweret appeared, when from its
site profound
It was then transplanted out upon some strange
new ground.
Where its sweetness soon was seen by all who
passed it by
Hanging down its dainty head and looking oh so shy.
Then the plant was moved again although not far
from there
It seemed to thrive much better and gained a
beauty rare.
Anyone who ventured near when it was fully grown
Found themselves surrounded by a perfume
all its own.
Yet this place still wasn't right, which rather spoiled
the bloom,
It looked too overcrowded, in want of much
more room.
So once more the plant was moved this time to
foreign parts
And blossomed quite profusely, its name?
'The Queen of Hearts'.
Suddenly the stem was cut, that it would die
was plain,
But in the people's memory that flower will
still remain.

Marie D Hollingworth

Princess Diana

Pomp and splendour all forgotten
Home they brought the sweet Princess,
Buried like a village maiden,
In the fields she loved the best.
Pure and beautiful they gave her
To a high and noble Prince,
And her simple faith sustained her
Till she died by sad mischance.
To her childhood home they brought her
Lord and Lady, Prince and Queen,
To the island where they laid her,
Low among the rushes green.
Where the willows cast their shadows,
Where the wild flowers bloom unseen,
There, no noisy throngs disturb her,
In a peaceful pastoral scene.
Then they laid her wreaths around her;
By the gentle breeze caressed,
Innocent of all emotion,
May her spirit there have rest.

Eirlys Hawkins Edwards

Diana

You were always there Diana
With the people who needed care Diana
You were always thinking Diana
Of the people you could help Diana
In far away countries East or West.
You tried your hardest to do your best.
Your two lovely boys Harry and Wills
To them and us the world stood still
We prayed and we cried
When you were taken away.
But in our hearts you will always stay.
So when the world stops crying
Loving and giving
That's when the world will stop living.

F M Kitching

Diana, Princess Of Love

D evotion you showed to sick children you met,
You were and always will be the 'People's Princess'.

I ntuition to know the troubles and strife
That ordinary people have suffered through life.

A ttention kindness love and caring
The 'Queen of Hearts' was never sparing.

N atural compassion for the weak young and old.
The irreplaceable beautiful English rose.

A ngels came down from Heaven above.
They took you away the nation's 'Princess of Love'.

Christine Robinson

Princess Diana

The news came out you passed away
The disbelief continued throughout the day.
Pictures of you flooded the world.
Carpets of flowers spread far and wide
With words of sorrow that you had died.
Your care and compassion went through
the people's hearts.
You graced the world with your
charm and beauty.
Time stood still for a while,
Then songs of praise rang out aloud.
The memories of you will linger on
as night to day for evermore.
The people came from far and wide
to watch you go where the stars shine.

Dot Langan

'Diana', A Princess Loved

The flame of life extinguished, Diana you have gone,
To your final resting place, but your memory will live on,
Your beauty and grace are world-renowned,
Both to the rich and to the poor,
Your fight for the homeless, also leprosy and more,
All people worldwide love you,
Some though, you've never even met,
Others know Diana, your love they shan't forget,
AIDS sufferers everywhere know they too have your love,
A love which is now in Heaven, with the Lord above,
For little children everywhere, Diana you're a star,
Up in the blue, blue Heaven, shining from afar,
A waste of life still filled with love,
A love which will last for ever more,
Your fight for the landmines, is one we can't ignore,
Diana, lovely Diana, now Heaven is your home,
I hope you find true happiness
Through this very sad release
Our 'Princess of the People',
Diana, 'rest in peace'.

John Webb

Princess Diana

Your life had spells of sadness,
And yet you gave so much,
You had so much compassion
For the people whom you touched.

You stretched your hand
Out to them all.
The lepers and the ones with AIDS,
The love you felt was on your face
When little babies you embraced.

You've left behind two fine young boys
Who will be lost without their Mum,
But they will be so very proud
Of all the good things you have done.

We never will forget the care
You showed to people everywhere,
The light you shone is shining still
Within our hearts,
And always will.

Mary Rule

Queen Of Our Hearts

Diana, Princess of Wales
Queen of Hearts throughout the world
A beautiful lady who cared for others
She was also a loving and caring mother
Her life was a mixture of ups and downs
We have seen her smiles, also her frowns
She was more than a princess, that we could see
She was a nice human being, just like you and me
Unique and wonderful, charming and true
Not only a Princess of Beauty outside
But on the inside too.
Hew new relationship with Dodi Fayed
Made her happy and content
From her smile you could tell.
What happened today was a real tragedy
To lose her young life in such a way.
It has broken the hearts of all, I can say
All over the world the people will mourn
The loss of a princess with a heart of gold.
A princess whose smiling and caring ways
Will have her remembered for many a day
Diana, the Princess, the 'Queen of our Hearts'
She will be remembered for all she has done
By all of the people whose hearts she has won.
Rest in peace, Diana, our 'Beautiful Princess'.

Christine Stirling

Princess Of Love

A little star from up above
Fell on her head, for us to love
The little star was for Princess Di,
She touched our hearts
And caught our eye.

For us there could, be no other
A beautiful Princess
A loving Mother.

We shed our tears
She was the best
At Althorp House
She's laid to rest.

We will always, remember our Princess Di
When we're alone, we will sit and cry.
No-one else could take her place
For what she did, for the human race
We love her now, although she's gone

Goodbye Diana,
Our Beautiful One.

Abbey Flack

A Human Angel

This world will be a sadder place,
Without her beautiful, smiling face,
Those eyes so blue and hair so fair,
She showed this world, her love and care.

She gave comfort to the sick and dying,
With a shy smile and inside quietly crying,
Offering up a silent prayer,
Hoping that someone would always be there.

To her sons, she was a caring mother,
Her love for them was like no other,
She has left them a gift, a legacy,
Of love, humbleness and serenity.

She will be remembered in the coming years,
Not with sadness or with tears,
But with love, for playing her part,
A human Angel, a 'Queen of Hearts'.

Patricia White

So, So Sad

D on't know this feeling, it's awful strange, see
I cannot explain what is happening to me,
A ppetite half gone, deep thoughts, devotion,
N o real words to describe my emotion,
A lways thought grief was for friends and family,

P atriotism maybe, but I suppose that depends,
R ight now I feel as if I've lost a sister,
I s this correct? No ! But somehow I shall miss her,
N ewspaper portraits of glistening eyes bright,
C ar headlights beaming right through the night,
E ssences of freshness, hope and charity you brought,
S olitude and loneliness, the establishment you fought,
S crutiny and sorrow, sometimes made you forlorn,

O f course, we won't know how much, your heart was torn,
F or me it seemed, all that changed the day you fell in love,

W ith Dodi Al Fayed, maybe an angel from above,
A nd all good things come to an end, but not before it starts!
L eaving us the way you did pierces so many hearts,
E ternity is so, so sad you'll never 'ever, ever' be replaced,
S orely missed, always loved, you 'made a difference' in this space.

Goodnight, sleep tight

Mike

Diana, Princess Of Wales

Our greatest sleeping beauty
has left the world alone,
who will look after us now Lord?
Who will give the poor a home?
She brought us peace and strengthened us
and made us realise that it's true,
So let's help William and Harry
to let them make it through.

She shone a light from her heart
and cared for everyone,
But the very sad thing about it
is that she died so very young.

So please be silent for just a minute
to think about her tragic end,
So just think about it
this is the only thing
that she can't mend!

Katherine Jenkins (11)

Princess Diana, The People's Princess

You were a light burning so bright,
Now it has gone,
But you are still here,
In our hearts forever strong.

Your kind smiling face,
And your warm loving touch,
Is what the world remembers,
We will all miss you so much.

You had heartache and pain through the years,
But now you will shed no more tears,
At last you found happiness with the man that you love,
Only now it is eternal in the Heavens above.

Your loss to the world is so sad, we will be
Thinking of you now and forever,
You are in our hearts always and forever.

C D Gaywood

Diana

Four happy people in a car,
Travelling through a tunnel.
Suddenly excited bikers
Either side, thrusting papers
At the passengers, and driver,
Thoughtless, shouting, blocking sight
Of the bollards and narrow space.
Suddenly the car swung right
Speeding to avoid the bikers
Struck hard at a central bollard.
Only one survived.

Oceans of flowers
Brightening walls, grey roads
But not the sad hearts
Of people mourning
A Princess, beautiful,
Hardworking, kind, helpful
To all, irrespective
Of colour, race, gender,
Crashed with friends
Speeding through a tunnel,
To England.

M K Wickrema

Untitled

Still we mourn, still we grieve,
That our beloved Princess had to leave,
Who will bring joy, hope and love?
Our Diana will, from Heaven above.

We all lost a Princess, the boys lost their Mum,
But we will carry out her wishes in the years to come.

We are richer for knowing our Queen amongst Queens,
Be happy Diana on your
ISLAND OF DREAMS.

Annette Steele

A Letter To Heaven

Dear God up above
Tell Diana we send our love
Tell her here on Earth
We really cared
Wish she were here
So we could share
We never realised
The effect, she had
On our lives.
To bid her last farewell
Under a grieving spell
Strangers from other lands
Came hand-in-hand
United in their stand
For a Princess
Whom we all loved
Now with you up above
Tell her, in our hearts
She will always remain
A Princess, friend
Who'll forever reign
Put your arms around her, Lord
Give her love and tender care
Something she would do
Were she still here
With a final adieu
We give our love to you.
With love and tender care
From the people in despair.

N Healy

Diana Of The Lake

On your lonely green island in the lake
you sleep in peace.
The sun will shine, the little waves break
when the wind sighs.

Birdsong at morning, moonlight at night
the patter of rain,
but your bright enthusiasm, your golden light
will never shine again.

You lit a flame that will forever burn,
we must never forget
your care for the sick, the deprived, and learn
to follow your dream

So, goodbye 'Diana of the Lake'
Rest in peace.

Marge Chamberlain

Diana

Someone vital has left our lives but her presence lingers on
Not just in the hearts of her friends and those who knew her long,
But in the hearts of those whose lives she lifted with a touch,
A word here and there, a gentle smile - that showed us that she cared so much.

Maybe we were selfish and took all she had to give;
We forgot that she was human too and had her life to live.
We hounded her through kindness because we wanted to know more
Of this lovely special lady and never really saw
That sometimes she was hurting too, that she felt just the same
As those who could be lifted by the mention of her name.

A young and caring Princess, Diana was her name
Has given love to all the world which will never be the same.
She taught us how to think of those who suffered so much more
Than we did - the sick, the sad, the poor.
We know that her heritage of love will never ever cease,
And so, Princess of the People, may you always Rest in Peace.

Maggie Pendaw

To Those Who Loved Diana Look Upon Your Wall

Look upon her portrait, that
Hangs upon your wall,
Feel the love and passion,
That rests within her soul;
You placed your love and honour,
Upon this lovely maiden,
So elegant and graceful,
So courtly and so tall:

She's forever in your memory,
The love endowed upon her;
You gave to her your all.
She's no longer with you,
Except within your soul;
Hold onto your lovely dreams;
Never let her go;
Your dreams are for eternity;
Our angels told us so.

George Ponting

Jewel In The Crown

You truly were our only jewel in the crown
Now we have only tears in which we'll
surely drown
Where before we had your beautiful smiling face
Now you are gone, in our hearts there's an
empty space
A wonderful shining gem you were to the nation
Full of love and compassion, a most
unique creation
And when you wore your heart on your sleeve
In your honesty we could always believe

When we heard of your most untimely calling
The whole Nation's tears started falling
We will always remember all the good things
you did
But now lovely Princess a peaceful rest to you
we bid.

Lesley J Line

Diana

The world's greatest Star
You helped all of those around you
No matter how near or far
The help you gave to those in need
Shone out like a sparkling star
You brightened the lives of others
Their faces shone so bright
Even through a dreary day
They brightened up at night
I am sure your work will be continued
After this our saddest day
With William and Harry we are with
Them all the way
You will never be forgotten
In this country and afar
God bless you forever,
Diana, our brightest Star.

George Moneypenny

A Tribute To Diana

Your smile was like the sunshine bursting through on
a rainy day.
Your smile was for all the children to help ease their
pain away.

You gave your time so willingly, fighting for what
you believed.
Though people made false promises you were never
once deceived.

Your work will keep on growing with every passing
day.
Although your smile has gone for ever,
In our hearts you will always stay.

Louise O'Neill

Diana Princess Of Wales . . .

How perfect the grace
That wondrous smile
How lovely the face
That encaptured rank and file
With poise and perception
Warmth with no exception
Nothing too great
Nothing too small
You entered the scene
Answering the call
With comfort and care
And a sensuous air
To ease pain and distress
Our loving, caring, beautiful Princess . . .

Now gone from our lives, to be a shining star
We will look to the night sky, to where you are
Your memory will not fade, for what you achieved
For we will remember the day,
when the nation grieved . . .

John Franks

Diana

The nation lost its *Daughter*
the day that we lost you
the country recoiled in horror
couldn't believe it was true
At first you were *Insecure*
not sure how to play your part
but soon you came to realise
you had power to touch our heart
Happiness when your children *Arrived*
and you had so much love
I'm sure you are watching them
from your seat above
Your life was too short *No doubt*
and we were all so sad
but when we think of all your good
it makes our heart feel glad
We thought you were an *Angel*
and to your people you're no less
always you'll be remembered
as DIANA, the 'People's Princess'.

Joy Benford

Queen In Our Hearts

A lovely Princess inside and out
A friend to everyone without a doubt
A beautiful smile, a shake of the hand
Your magic spread all over the land
You'll always be Queen in our hearts

A direction you had, with so much to achieve
We do feel lost and so many will grieve
Your spirit will live, I'm sure in us all
We'll think of England's Rose and stands
proud and tall
You'll always be queen in our hearts

Now you are free from torment and pain
Free as a Dove and at peace once again
We'll have peace in our hearts and do
as you wished
Oh England's Rose you'll be sadly missed.

Kathy Dring

A Sonnet To Princess Diana

You're the Princess of Hearts, body and mind,
You will be remembered, forever, by all mankind,
All with whom you worked and gave time will
miss your vision,
Who could take your place and continue
your mission,
You were outstanding, with a beauty fair,
And set the trends in fashion and hair,
In your awe, people would freeze,
Oh! Diana, you knew how to put them at ease,
Your life, was, so tragically taken,
The whole wide world, so totally shaken,
So why do the good have to die young?
When your life had only just begun,
But in our hearts and minds your memory prevails
Diana, Princess of Wales.

Leon Hubbard

Diana

A voice for all the voiceless ones -
The outcast and alone;
The homeless and rejected ones
You treated as your own.
There was no rank, there was no class,
Just people in their need.
You showed your care, you showed your love -
The 'Queen of Hearts' indeed.

Your touch restored humanity
To those we turned aside.
You showed what needed to be done
And all the risks defied.
From your own pain you comfort brought
And love in action showed,
And by your care to hurting ones
New self-esteem bestowed.

May we complete what you began
And seek that love to share,
Knowing that everyone on earth
Is worthy of our care.
The lessons from your so short life
May we be quick to learn.
May all our hearts, and all our lives
With that same passion burn.

A S Clifton

Diana

D iana, you lit up our lives,
I n helping others to survive.
A n endless smile and deep concern,
N o-one but you could make heads turn.
A bundant was the care you gave,

P assing crowds to whom you'd wave.
R emembering the down-at-heel,
I nviting ill your hands to feel.
N ow you are gone our lives seem bare,
C an we cope now you're not there.
E ven though you're laid to rest,
S omehow you'll always be the best.
S adness fills the world around,

O n that sad day there was no sound.
F aithful people, heads bowed low,

W eeping as you passed by slow.
A lthough you've gone, you are still here,
L ove won't leave you do not fear.
E ach day we'll still remember you,
S o rest in peace, we all love you.

Gill Ward

Diana

You were an Angel, sent down from God above
To bestow upon the world, the gift of perfect love
Healing hands, the sick you did touch
The homeless, the needy, you cared so much
Constantly campaigning, to make us all aware
Of the plight, of those injured by landmines . . .
Hidden where?
Tragically taken, your death will not be in vain
The World laments, Heaven's gain
Crystal tears, as the Nation weeps
At the loss of our Princess, so Perfect, so Dear.

Susan L Metcalfe

A Tribute To Diana

She's gone from amongst us
A bright shining star
Diana the Princess
We adored from afar
Her short life has ended in sorrow and pain
To me she would have been a beautiful queen
Her two little boys she loved and adored
A loving mum sadly no more.
All children she loved with a love sincere
No matter what colour race or creed.
So I wish I could wake from this horrible dream
But I am not dreaming it's all so real
Our beautiful Diana we'll see no more.

Margaret Walker

Diana

Your respect for others
And your great sense of fun,
For the hearts of this nation
You certainly won.

The sadness inside
Didn't stand in your way
And the obstacles and heartaches
Didn't keep you at bay.

Visiting dying people around the world,
You touched their souls,
You inspired and loved them
Which gave them hope for their goals.

A shining example,
Though insecure yourself inside,
And the stripping of your HRH title,
Opened the photographers' gates wide.

The harassment which followed,
Finally led to your death,
We just didn't believe it and we
Took a great breath.

The week that followed
Of the shallow and the blamed,
Bowed their heads
For your life that they claimed.

But you will never be forgotten
And we'll rise up and carry a banner,
And spread just one word that means so much
And that is 'Diana!'

Debbie Twine

A Poem For Diana

We, the unknown, who are lucky
We, the unknown, who are plain
We live our lives in obscurity
But no one knows the pain

But you, who were so public
You, who were not plain
Lived in a constant spotlight
And everyone knew your pain

I pray you now are tranquil
I pray your sons feel the same
Safe in the arms of God's love
The world will not be the same.

Lorna Sim

Forever Our Princess

The nation mourns,
for the loss of our Princess,
who in making lives happy,
had so much success.

Our friend has gone,
the grief we feel,
our silent despair,
will never ever heal.

A beautiful woman,
so strong yet so weak,
an amazing gift,
so kind, so unique.

Taken from us,
at such a young age,
leaving two boys,
with such heartache and rage.

What really happened?
It's so unfair,
now you are gone,
believe it, do we dare?

All the world's a stage,
beautifully you played your parts,
Diana, you truly were,
The queen of all our hearts.

Where do you walk now,
nobody knows,
but we will walk again with you,
goodbye for now, England's rose.

Kelly White

Diana - Gone But Not Forgotten

No ceremonies to perform,
Just remember her as she was born,
For the things she did the best,
And to disregard the rest.

There's no time to give in,
Although this time, sorrow brings,
Remember the happy days,
And keep her love always.

No tears, for she has gone,
But remember all she's done,
And keep her good works going,
And the care and love flowing.

To hold each happy moment,
And all the time we spent,
Living our lives together,
For the love will last forever.

Bruce Ripley

Thoughts For William And Harry

I thought of you both this morning
as I have done all this week,
I imagine how you're feeling
as you struggle with your grief.

Just remember all the good times
and all the fun you had.
The fairground rides, McDonald's
sunshine hols and all those hugs.

Your mother loved you so much
by your side she will always stay,
her arms will never leave you
as you travel along life's way.

A million thoughts are with you
from a nation who really cares.
Your loving and compassionate Mum
will live in our hearts for years.

Margaret Gibson

The English Rose

To Diana, our very own English Rose,
A Lady of beauty and dignified pose,
So caring and gentle, and so full of fun,
Admired and loved by everyone,
But Diana's not gone, she is just sleeping.
She wouldn't expect us all to be weeping.
If you look to the sky, you will see a star,
It's our Diana, looking down from afar.
She was a Princess with a heart of gold.
She cared for the sick, the young and the old,
She cared for the needy and those full of stress
So sleep gentle Princess,
Goodnight and God Bless.

T Woods

Lovely Diana

Our lovely Diana
Queen of the sky
Why oh why! Did you have to die?
So many hearts broken in two
You know we thought the world of you
Did the children need a new nurse?
Someone to care when they got hurt?
Did you hold them in your loving arms?
Did they succumb to your many charms?
Let's keep alive her memory
This treasure we won't forget
Her special way with children
Will be with us a long time yet.

Rachel Cresswell

A Poem For Diana Princess Of Wales

You were the Queen of my Heart,
But now you've gone to depart.
If only you could have known before,
How much we all love and adore,
You and all the work you've done,
And how you were a loving mum.
This was the most tragic end,
And now there are millions of hearts to mend.
We all did love you and now we must leave you,
Going to the place where nobody can touch you.
You understood children like me,
And now you have left, oh can't you see . . .
You were the Princess you were the Queen,
You were the other one, the one in-between,
You were the healer, you were the friend,
You were the helper who would never offend.
But most of all you were like darts
Firing love into people's hearts,
For you, Diana, Princess of Wales,
You, will always be the Queen of our Hearts.

Georgina Wise (11)

A Pain So Deep

A pain so deep, it's rarely felt,
Hearts are broken, stood weeping tears,
A light blown out, no longer there the ice to melt.

A people's princess she was to one and all,
A love so strong it glowed all around,
So genuine and caring she stood tall.

Elegance and beauty with a heart of gold,
A special friend to those she knew,
Kind and caring never would she be bought or sold.

Two precious sons she gave to us all,
To follow in her footsteps, to be strong and lead,
They will carry on the kindness and goodwill
never to fall.

The end it came too soon, to bring her peace of
the white dove,
An eternal flame to glow in our hearts,
Gone forever now our Princess in an endless love.

To rest at last without the cameras haunting,
Total privacy for evermore, no need for running,
Where she has gone there will be no more taunting.

Rebecca Simmonds

Goodbye, England's Rose

To a beloved Princess
Who rose way, way above the rest
A heart so loving and with tender care
Brought precious moments for one and all to share
Your work is done,
You did your best,
Now you've gone to have a rest.
We loved you then,
We love you still
So take our hearts on this last journey,
I know you will
To live with God
Who picked you to be the best.
Goodnight, God Bless
Dear Princess.

D C J Jones

That Fateful Day

(Written on the morning of the sad demise of Diana, Princess of Wales)

The thirty-first of August
Year nineteen ninety seven
The day our lovely princess died
And God welcomed her to Heaven

All lights on earth went out that day
But the stars shone bright above
As angels greeted her with joy
We mourned our own lost love.

Gwynn Watt

England's Rose

Born first of July nineteen sixty one,
The life of Diana had only just begun.

Raised at Park House her brother and sisters in tow,
They played with the future Princess and didn't even know.

With the death of their grandfather they moved away,
To an estate called Althorp where her family did stay.

At the age of nineteen she met the Prince of Wales,
This took place in Sussex amongst the hay bales.

On February twenty-fourth nineteen eighty one,
Was the date of their engagement known by everyone.

St Pauls Cathedral was where their marriage was to start,
Watched by the nation thrilled to the heart.

June twenty-first saw the birth of a son,
The people cried tears of joy for a new life had begun.

His name was Prince William, an heir to the throne,
In the eyes of the public he would become well-known.

Three years later saw the arrival of another,
Prince William was finally to have a brother.

Prince Harry was his name a second son of a proud mum and dad,
They knew he would grow to become a handsome young lad.

Diana was loved for her charity work in all parts,
That's how she became our Queen of Hearts.

Visiting victims of AIDS, leprosy and landmines,
Laughing and joking making them shine.

Along came Dodi Al Fayed her last ever love,
The nation unaware that they were wanted up above.

Then came the tragic day when Princess Di bowed out,
The day the nation will never forget without a doubt.

Many felt the light had gone out of their hearts,
All the memories of her will never ever part.

Our thoughts are with Princes William and Harry on this day,
For the pain they feel in time will gradually fade away.

Rest in peace Diana for the whole of the nation knows,
On that fateful day we lost our English Rose.

Lisa Burgess of Handforth

'Diana' - Princess Of The People

When I heard the news that Sunday morn
I felt so sad and all forlorn
I tried to go about my daily chores
But felt the light blocked through closed doors.

Diana Royal, Princess of Wales
Smile and beauty by all was hailed
Your love and compassion for the common man
I'm sure was all part of God's special plan.

The way you cradled those tiny mites
Because you were touched by their plights
These acts came from your very soul
Knowing for them life had taken its toll.

You gave your princess a wonderful start
Love and devotion straight from your heart
Your memory they will always treasure
Missing you always, forgetting you never.

Dear Angel of Mercy take your rest
For on this earth you stood the test
A shining example to all walks of life
At last free from sorrow and all strife.

S Bradshaw

Goodnight Sweet Princess!

Words cannot express how sad the nation feels today,
You will always be remembered for your kind and loving ways.
You put a smile on so many faces,
Visiting the sick and needy in so many places,
Just as you found happiness your life ends on earth,
but in heaven you and Dodi will re-birth,
You brought joy to everyone especially your two
Lovely sons, who today are so proud to have you as their Mum,
'Cause to everyone you are the number one.
No-one can replace our beautiful princess, who's happy in heaven, now safe and at rest.
No-one ever will forget the special person you are,
you were a princess, a saint, now an angel at last.

Goodnight sweet Princess.

Jenny Coyle (17)

Diana, Princess Of Wales

Where are you dear Diana,
Can you see the Nation cry,
Can you hear the anguished voices
Questioning 'Why?'

You did so much for many
In this harsh and hostile World,
With a look, a touch, a gesture,
Hope and love unfurled.

Our thoughts are with your family
They may help in some way,
But, Diana, Queen of Hearts,
In our hearts you'll always stay.

We hope you rest in peace now
Wherever you may be
And that somehow your work continues
Let Love be your Legacy.

A P Stevens

The Colours Of Diana

So young you appeared in blue on his arm,
The sapphire and diamonds mirrored your charm.
So sweet and naive we held you close that year,
As you emerged from St Paul's we all raised a cheer.
Your work took you tirelessly from home to abroad,
The sun would shine and the rain it poured.
Your visits so special to everyone there,
Each patient knew: here was someone to care.
You brought with you sunshine, like a beacon of light
Into people's hearts, you shone so bright.
You dazzled us, glittering, shining like a star,
Your gowns in New York told of who you are.
A sparkle of hope you gave to the dying,
Their spirits lifted to know you were trying
To brighten their day, to make them feel good,
You gave so much love in any way you could.
Dressed in red, your head held high,
Now happier in life, no longer shy.
You always carried flowers, you are an eternal rose
Whose beauty will live on in us, as your days come to a close.
Your life is spread before us now, a sea of dazzling hue,
If only you could see that all our love still shines for you.
A nation in black mourns you like no other,
Not only to your boys but to us you were a mother,
Embracing us no matter what, when others feared to touch,
We want to tell you now how you meant so very much.
A life with so much left to live, so tragically cut short,
We know that in your final hour, the bravest ones they fought
To save you, to restore your energy and zest,
But now in death we hope you will be allowed to rest.

Avril Reay

Our Queen Of Hearts

This is a very sad day
For people everywhere
Princess Diana died today
With the man who really cared
They are both together now
No man can ever part
She cared for everyone here
She was our Queen of Hearts
She cared for the sick and for the poor
People with AIDS and many more
We pray for her sons she left behind
And hope they will be given peace
We pray the laws will now be changed
And paparazzi will eventually cease
We know she is still living on
Working from heaven above
She is still looking down on us
And sending all her love
So let's give thanks for her short life
The life an angel brings
She's holding hands with our Lord
As He gives her, her deserving wings
Today we feel sad so very sad
And I will tell you why
Today we lost a very dear friend
We lost our precious Di.

Linda Field

Wind-Blown Petals

The permanence of plastic blooms
would not express so much
as wind-blown petals left to bless
a dead princess's touch.

Barbara Smoker

Diana 1961-1997
On This Day August 31st '97

On this day
Diana died.
On this day,
The world it cried.

On this day,
The world stood still.
On this day
You left a gap
No-one else can fill.

On this day,
No-one could believe,
The entire, overwhelming,
Shock we feel.

On this day
A woman of substance,
Passed on by
All we can do,
Is sit and cry.

Andrea Edwards

Diana Princess Of Wales

Another star shines in the Heavens tonight
Why oh why? People cry in the night
Of sorrow and pain she had her share
A person who shone was England's crown
She was sad and happy and always chained
A smile so bright and then a frown,
She wanted freedom to love not be restrained
The world loved her through her tears and stress
They wanted her to have happiness
She has left a void too deep to fill
Her eyes are closed her heart is still
Her hopes her dreams will never be
Her boys growing up she will never see
But on her last journey of tear-filled miles
People will always remember her brilliant smiles.

J Straker

Diana - The Mother

She was a mum, just like me,
The love for her boys was plain to see.
Two boys with heads bowed low,
The nation sharing their sorrow.
Together they walked behind, on her final journey.
Flowers, a card, bearing one word 'Mummy'.

Watching the boys, their loss was so real,
I cannot imagine the ache they must feel.
The nation has lost a princess, a friend,
No-one really knows what happened at the end.

Boys, I hope the memories you cherish will ease your pain,
And the love that surrounds you, will help you smile once again.

Ann Elizabeth Hurley

For Diana Princess Of Wales

From a stark underpass in Paris,
With the first chill thrust of dawn,
Came the news of the death
Of a beautiful Princess,
Who held the wide world in thrall.

Diana of the loving heart,
May you be given peace.
And may love like yours,
So freely given,
Evermore increase.

Ron Delacruz

A Poem For the People's Princess

The Journey of Life cut painfully short
The Sorrow we feel for the Love that she sought
Love and Compassion the gifts that she brought
Now just Contemplation and silent thoughts.

R J Oldroyd

Diana - Flower Of England

Princess Diana Flower of England your life's work here is done
Drawn to an end so tragically with so many things just begun
We stand aghast and tremble for no one can take your place
Never more shall we see your majesty, your beauty and your grace.

Oh Diana if you could but see, the nation brought to tears
They cried for you, they cried for your boys and they cried for your suffering years
And into your path they threw their hearts, they threw their flowers and love
Not wanting to believe that you had been called to the Realms of Glory above.

And the world looked on in numbness at our nation washed in tears
As we paid our respects and bade you farewell at the passing of your years
With us they too had witnessed, your compassion for the sad and forlorn
Watched you reach out with love, to the castout, the broken, the torn.

From deep within came the love that you gave, from a heart that suffered so much
And to watch from afar was enough for us all, to feel your special touch
And the nation knows a light has gone out, a light that lit up the world
A light that will never be seen again, though eternity be unfurled.

You touched our hearts like no other could, before you or beyond
You brought joy and happiness to all you held, creating love's special bond
And that bond shall not be broken with the passing of the years
It will grow and blossom and bear much fruit, nurtured by a million tears.

God bless.

Colin & Margaret James

Heart-Rending

You have passed through time
Diana, touched hearts like mine.
Your beauty, always to be young
Your mission just begun.
To those who struggled in need
You reached with heart-warming deeds.
A touch, a smile
Oh so fragile.
Simply to do good
You were often misunderstood
Flashing white lights stripped you bare
Your heart was only to care.
Your dignity assured
The Royal Standard flag caressed
The People's Princess.
Now you rest with heaven's best.
The People's Princess, Queen of Hearts

Anthony Keyes

God's Flower

When Diana walked thru the Heavenly gate
She told the Press there 'You can wait.'
God He knew for sure
Diana wanted to see the poor.
She gave a little frown
I am ordinary, I don't need a crown.
The angels cheered from their cloud
They were so very proud.
She wanted to help God, could tell
'Let's visit the poor down in Hell.'
God used His magic power
To make a special flower.
And the name He chose
He called it His English Rose.

Colin Allsop

Farewell Beloved Princess

It was in her eyes, in her eyes,
A multitude of grief and sighs.
Married in hope and early betrayal,
Forsaken, hurting and so dismayed,
Searching in agony of grief,
Oh how to find some light relief.
A broken and compassionate heart,
Such a longing to play her part
For the lame and lost for whom she cared,
And all their miseries she shared.
But set aside, yes set aside
By one she loved and how she cried.
She cried with tears that could not flow
And on and on she had to go -
Functions, visits, opening fetes,
Crowded diaries with duty dates,
Seeking, seeking how to stop hurting
Whilst all around the press were skirting.
But, dear reader, don't blame the press,
Backtrack to what began this mess,
Go back to the very beginning
She more sinned against than sinning.
Royal protection suddenly lost,
Another's sin to pay the cost,
All she hoped for now quite frail
And not allowed to weep or wail.
The need now to defend herself
With loss of stature, threatened health.
Lovely Diana now at peace,
Now your agonies will cease.
With Our Lord's mercy and His grace
You will be in a better place.
Woe to the Church which kept silent on sin
Responsible for the state you were in.
What can be said in honour of thee?
The axe must be laid to the root of the tree
To convict of such hypocrisy.

Pearl Kumar

Goodbye Sweet Princess

Your timeless beauty, your ardent grace
You helped to make this world a beautiful place
The words of comfort, the hands you held,
Your light shone bright around the world.

From the rich and famous to the layman and poorer
We have all been blessed by your healing aura.
Can this world endure such tragedy,
When it was you alone that gave such clarity.

Our Queen of Hearts, our sister friend,
Will our sadness ever end?
Is there a soul on earth, that didn't love her?
Could you have been our 'Holy Mother'?

Forgive our ignorance of the past
Of that we may never alter
As Venus be the goddess of Love, you must
surely be her daughter.
Amongst the angels in Heaven, your star
will shine the best
Goodbye sweet Princess, may your soul be at rest.

Jacqui Green

Diana

Princess of life
A lady of love
With hands of hope
Spreading peace . . .

'Thou art, our white dove'

Innocence, grace
and a childlike smile
You've captured us all
with your beauty and style.

The work that you've done
and breath that you gave . . .
the sick and the wounded
those lives you have saved.

Two people in love
in peace, you'll remain,
for eternal embrace

'at last'

In the Palace of Heaven . . .
OUR QUEEN will reign.

Amanda Southern

Dodi And Di

Dodi and Di, now departed
So many people left broken-hearted,
Why did it happen? No-one knows
But at least together are their souls.
Up in Heaven high above
No more pain, but so much love
Together now they are free
Happy so happy as they can be.
Away from people spying and prying
Are they the cause of their dying?
So many hearts are left broken
So many words left unspoken
For both their families, we must pray
Their memories of them will always stay.

My love to both families,

Julie Mahoney

It Was A Tragic Parting

It was a tragic parting
too tragic to forget.
Those who loved you dearly
are the ones who won't forget.
So we will hold you close within
our hearts, and there you will remain
to walk with us throughout our lives
until we meet again.
So rest in peace dear Diana and thanks
for all you've done.
Pray that God has given you
the crown you've truly won.

E Peel

Our Diana

Tears on my pillow, I cried each night
The world has lost its guiding light
You showed the world how to love and care
For God to take you away, it's not fair
For the children it was to be hugged or kissed
By them alone you will be sadly missed
For those who suffered you gave your tender touch
To others your smile meant so much
A nation mourns a loss of a special treasure
For me to have known you would have been
a pleasure

Our Diana is now at rest
The world she is in must be the best
The human race must continue Diana's fight
To stop suffering, wars, and put things right.
With broken hearts, so full of sorrows
Never, never, forget our Diana in our tomorrows.

Rowan Lee

The Blooming Of A Rose

In the shade of the realm was a rosebud so shy
Which slowly blossomed, catching our eye
An innocent bloom - a true English rose
With such beauty, everybody knows
Full of compassion a quality rare
For the sick and the poor she really did care
Her inner beauty outwardly showed
Surrounded by an aura she positively glowed
Poise and serenity this rose did possess
Showing love for us all - the people's princess
Though some of her days were often grey
Dutifully she smiled, hiding dismay
But this princess - on earth - had too few years
We mourn her loss and still shed our tears
Now in heaven's garden she eternally grows
Princess Diana - our English rose.

Val Farrell

Queen Of Our Hearts

We know she's up in heaven
Watching, looking down
And God was there to meet her
To present her with her crown
And there she is an angel
Just like she was before
God was so impatient
To get her to his door.

Diana Queen of Hearts
How dearly we'll miss you
You left us here behind
Where folk like you are few
The world has lost its only queen
A mother to us all
When you had to leave us
That shining star did fall.

But you'll never be forgotten
The joy to hearts you brought
You'll always remain with us
In every single thought
The world will be a sadder place
Now that you have left.
To take you away from us
Was God's greatest theft.

But God took you up into His house
And angel now you'll be
You shone your light way up high
For all of us to see.

So Diana Queen of Hearts
This poem I wrote for you
Just to let you know
How dearly we'll miss you.

With my deepest sympathy.

Patrick Hennessy

Farewell To Our Princess

A bright light has gone out in the world,
Flowers came from everywhere, grieving all around,
People in their millions brought the country to a stop,
Silence was golden, you could hear a pin drop,
They lined the route to say farewell,
To take our princess home,
Back to the angels from where she had come,
A carpet of flowers strewn,
But you can see her from afar,
Looking down from heaven as a -
Brand new shining star.

Veronica Harding

Diana, A Vision Of Pure Perfection

The magic of a princess
is just so hard to find
That when you look at Diana
You come to realise why.

Gaze into her loving eyes
Past the radiant complexion
You then see why she was chosen.

'A vision of pure perfection'.

Rachel Whitford (14)

Untitled

Oh God, you've taken our Diana
And what's the reason why?
She's done such wonders in this world
And now you've let her die,
There must be some good reason
Why you need our princess there
Perhaps you want an angel
To give her love elsewhere!

Ronald Waller

Lost

Your passing has taught this world a lesson,
Your life has taught this world to care,
Your love has taught this world emotion,
At Heaven I stand and stare.

Your beauty was there for all to see,
Your eyes they shone so bright,
Right now the world has stopped to see,
Our Princess is out of sight.

In life you were the victim,
In death the people's Queen,
In Heaven you can look down and see,
In life, what you had never seen.

Yesterday you were the Queen of Hearts,
But peace you were not given,
Today the world cries oceans,
As our Queen finds peace in Heaven.

Although you're gone, you're still around,
Memories so clear to see,
Thank God that they will never hound,
His favourite child who tried to flee.

The light has tragically disappeared,
The world in disbelief,
I hope you find what you had sought
As this world sits numb in grief.

Everyone you touched in life,
The tears, the loss, the scream,
Is this really happening?
They hope it's all a dream.

Your sons and family in our thoughts,
The pain they feel, we do,
Together we unite in sorrow,
For the one who was one of few.

Diana, Diana, you'll never die,
Your love is in the air,
Alive forever in our hearts,
Now your love this world can share.

Melville Campbell

Farewell Diana

Farewell Diana - Princess of Wales
You will be sadly missed in the towns and the vales
Beautiful princess no longer doing good in the land
Walks with God now, hand in hand.

It is such a shame you will never have known
The love for you that has been shown
Candles lit and flowers laid
A kind tribute the people paid.

We love and miss you is the message in the card
We cannot believe you're gone
The world will seem a darker place
Without the light that shone.

Anita Wonnacott

Diana

She came like a flower in summer
blossoming, shining so bright,
Her petals soft and warm
still brightly shone at night.

But this flower has lost its petals
but not in vain it's known
Each one touched by her softness
in love and companion has grown.

Julie McKenzie

A Poem For A Princess And Her Love

Diana you came to us
from a star in heaven
and now you have returned
to re-kindle a star with Dodi
shining upon us like a magic light
Burning brighter each night
together forever to show
us the light.

S Corrigan

Diana

Diana was the queen of our heart,
And now our world's been blown apart,
A massive void never to be filled,
Was caused the day Diana was killed.

She was an angel from above,
Who gave everyone the same kind of love,
She didn't care what people said,
She cared about AIDS and landmines instead.

She wasn't perfect, but then who is,
But performed her duties with bubble and fizz,
She loved all the people whatever their ills,
But mainly her love was for Harry and Wills.

Her cheeky grin, her beautiful face,
The world will be a worse off place,
You'll be remembered till the world does cease,
Diana, I hope you can now rest in peace.

Kevin Rounce

A Tribute To Diana

On this last day of August, nineteen ninety seven
Lovely Princess Diana, was sent up to heaven
There's a hush everywhere, in the towns and the vales
Everyone's mourning, our Princess of Wales.

Gracious compassionate, full of humility
She strived to help others, to the best of her ability
Without any warning, struck down in her prime
She won't be forgotten, she's a saint of her time.

We'll always remember, her kindness and empathy
To the sick and the needy, she showed them
her sympathy
An Ambassador for Britain, and example
to womanhood
Giving her time humbly, doing nothing but good.

Sheila Ware

Untitled

Diana, Princess of Wales,
a real life princess in fairy tales,
With your heart and soul you always cared,
with so much enthusiasm you forever shared,
Comforting all those with troubles and strife,
you accomplished so much in such a short life,
Loving your sons, Princes Harry and William,
We all agree you were a mum in a million,
The whole country will mourn and shed many tears,
The pain and the loss we shall feel for years,
Diana and Dodi are now laid to rest,
Why is it God only takes the best?

The Hutchinson Family

Diana 1961-1997

To a very special lady,
Whose smile never ended,
Whose tears never lied,
Whose thoughts and happiness was always shared,
Whose love was for all,
Someone who cared and spoke from her heart
To the people of the nation, the people of the world,
Through the good times and the bad - she always
Came through,
Her loving nature and beautiful smile that
Will always be remembered and will never die,
Her spirit will live on forever,
Goodnight sweet lady,
Diana - Princess of Wales.

Victoria Mitchell

Diana

Queen of Hearts, that's who you are,
now you're safely with the shining stars,
looking down at us, watching us all,
we will never forget you at all,
no-one can ever replace you Diana
for you are England's beautiful carer
we thank you, love you, miss you Diana
but mostly of course we'll never forget you.
Diana, Princess of Wales you are
our England's rose.

Joanne & Nathan

Diana Remembered

Tall slim and elegant
humorous witty intelligent

Beautiful smile and eyes of sapphire blue
that's how I will always remember you

A Queen of Hearts of this land
I once had the honour of shaking your hand

Always willing to help those in need and despair
you took the time to visit them anywhere

Your tragic death was so very very sad
If only things had been different what a
Queen of England we would have had

Why do the good die so young for goodness sake
God bless you Diana and rest in peace
on that beautiful island in the ornamental lake.

Paul Ronald Adkins

Diana

Diana, our princess, the one we love
Now you reside in Heaven above
Taken from us, by the cruel hand of fate
The world is in mourning, but now it's too late
To show you how much, you meant to us all
From the rich and the famous, to the man on
the dole
For William and Harry, the hurt and the pain
Their mother is gone, their lives not the same
To wake up each morning and face a new day
Without you to guide them and show them
the way
The love and compassion that showed
in your eyes
For the sick and the injured, could not
be disguised
Not false and pretentious, but honest and
true
Like a light in the darkness, the memory of you
I feel like I knew you, but we never met
Now this is my tribute, lest we forget . . .

Glenn Briggs

Landmines

Landmines
Laid in battle and left to maim or kill
And in times of peace there are other
destructive forms
Too late - exploding flashes have taken
their toll
Of yet another victim - an innocent soul
Lethal pressures where one must so
carefully tread
Or else one false move and another dead
In a web of disaster
Regardless of wealth or rank, servant
or master
The enemy is relentless
And we must be ready to play our part
For we no longer have the luxury
Of a sacrificial Princess with a heart.

Tamar Segal

Diana - Princess Of Hope

In this world of devastation,
Diana gave hope to every nation.
She turned the dark, into light,
And fought for all she believed was right.

For all humanity, she did care,
And for each needy case, she was there,
To AIDS victims, she gave her hand,
And fought to get landmines banned.

Children she loved, like a mother to all,
And for the sick, she was always on call.
To common folk, she gave her heart,
Diana was loved, from the very start.

Never could anyone take her place,
A true princess with an angel's face.
Her heart of gold, and a quality so rare,
Not a soul in this world, to her could compare.

Her time was so short on this earth,
Just thirty-six years, from her birth.
But in those years, she gave so much love,
Now she rests in heaven above.

Diana will be missed by so many,
How words could express . . . there just
aren't any.
Her memory will live, forever more,
To a new world of caring, she has opened
the door.

Elaine Sturman

Untitled

A million tears won't bring you back
I know because I've cried,
Neither will a thousand words
I know because I've tried.
If roses grow in Heaven
Lord pick me one with care
And place it in Diana's hand
To show that I still care.

Doreen Aylieff

Remembering An Angel

An angel with style
An angel with grace
An angel who put a
Smile on a poor little face

An angel who cared
And shared all her love
An angel in pain that
She floated above

An angel who gave hope
To us all
An angel whose compassion
Would never fall

An angel whose presence was
Dearly felt
An angel who made a
World's hearts melt

An angel in Diana we
will never forget
An angel we all loved
But never met

An angel taken before her
Work was done
An angel who lived for
The love of her sons

An angel now in heaven
Looking down from above
An angel of hearts
Never to be forgotten but
Always loved.

T Newman

A Tribute To Diana

Here today, gone tomorrow,
All the world filled with sorrow.
Diana has gone, her memories live on,
So in love, so at peace, Diana.

The Maye Family

Heaven Has A Princess

When the angels came to take you,
It even broke their hearts,
To imagine life without your smile,
We just do not know where to start.
Heaven has always been a special place,
And now you have made it complete
No-one will ever fear death now
Because one day we know we will meet
The pain we have in our hearts
The tears will always flow,
That sparkle in your eyes, your beautiful smile
Will always be a special memory that will
never go
We did not know how much we loved you
Until the day we lost you
But the love we have in our hearts for you Diana
Will always be true
I know that you are in heaven now
And that you are looking down
The sun will always be your smile
And the stars will be your crown
The love you have given us
Will never ever go away
The angels may have you now
But your love and your smile will always stay.

Mandy Tott

Diana - Our Special Friend

The flags are flying all at half mast
The country's at a standstill to see you pass
A day full of sorrow, sadness and pain -
We pray that your death will not be in vain.
You've done so much for the ill, poor and old
You were one precious lady with a heart
of gold
You'll be with us forever - our hearts
we can't mend
For you were one in a million -
our special friend.

Marysia Cheesman

A Tribute To Diana, Princess of Wales

What will we do now you are gone?
How can we possibly carry on?
How will we manage without your sweet smile?
No more to see those eyes that beguile.
Gone that shy look that hid a heart large enough
to cover the world with your caring and love.

You make us ashamed that we left it to you,
Ashamed of ignoring the things that we knew.
The plight of the world, the sick and the poor,
the starving, the homeless and so many more.
Without you to guide us what shall we do?
We'll take a pinch of your courage,
and see your dreams through.

We'll look at these people with kind caring eyes,
That's what you taught us because you're so wise.
We'll help all we can and lift up our voice,
to change what we can and give them a choice.
Your people will miss you now that you've gone,
You did all you could, now we'll carry on.

Pauline Hofstetter

The Spirit Of Life

A Princess of tender years was gently
laid below the ground,
Tears, flowers and waves of emotion will
never again, be so profound.

A Princess who, with her charm and smile
of innocence,
Began to knock down, bit by bit, the walls
of ignorance.

Walls built on fear and years of self-preservation,
Walls that denied the sick and the lame,
any hopes of salvation,

She did not cure anyone with the touch of
her hand,
But filled their Hearts with Hope, that
others will understand,

Her body could stay with us, for only a
short time,
But her Spirit will live forever, in the
People's minds.

J Burge

Britain's Brightest Star

(This poem is dedicated to Diana - the Princess,
the icon, the star, but most of all the mother)

Sweet princess you were unique,
Your exquisite beauty and perfect physique.
You were indeed England's finest rose,
Tackling challenges as they arose.
Just one look I knew from the start,
Your smile could warm the coldest heart.
You loved and cared for everyone,
You shone just like the vibrant sun.
But all too soon you were taken away,
To a land so warm and far away.
It's peaceful there, so lovely and calm,
Where no-one can hurt you or do you harm.

Roxanne Drake (16)

Princess Of Love

She has gone to a higher sphere,
The people's princess at heart
Her memory will always be dear
In hearts though far apart
Love was so profound all over
She needed this and gave it
A great big world to cover
Her arms outstretched to fit
May you rest in peace Diana
Eternal love be yours
Your smile will live forever
Remembered in hearts all over
Their love will always be yours
Sleep on Diana.

Janet L Murray

Tribute To An Angel Of Mercy

An angel of mercy, a tender Princess,
Diana filled lives with immense happiness.
Her love and compassion gave comfort and
cheer,
Her care and concern were so deep and
sincere.

An angel of mercy, beloved and adored,
Affection and kindness she daily outpoured.
She cherished her sons, precious memories
they'll bear
To God we commit them in thought and
in prayer.

An angel of mercy, cut off in her prime,
So much she accomplished in so short a time.
With sadness we mourn - what a jewel we
possessed!
Diana - God bless you. In peace may you rest.

Eileen N Blackmore

Diana

Diana, Diana, our princess so rare
Giving the world your special care
You came within and touched our lives
Lighting the path through your eyes
Always there and constant to show
Your love for us ALL
Was more than we could know.

Our hearts lit up
You were the best
Not deserving all the rest
And now we know
Although too late
God was waiting at Heaven's gate.

Questions come the answers no
Why oh why did you have to go
Now's the time to rest in peace
And while you sleep we will keep
Your love within us oh so deep

Margaret Vercoe

Our World - In Memory Of Diana

Our world was mostly a happy place,
We were so lucky to have had the pleasure of
seeing your smiling face.
Your love and kindness you spread so far,
You were such a wonderful person,
Our very own precious star.

Our world is now a broken place,
We now only have our memories of your
sweet smiling face.
Your love and kindness would have gone on
for years,
Our hearts now seem empty,
We have all cried so many tears.

Our world will never forget you,
You'll always remain in each and everyone's
heart,
And as the years pass us by, we will always
remember that tragic day,
When our world you did so sadly part.

Maureen Hart

Untitled

The death of our dear Princess,
has caused great unhappiness.
The young and the very old
have prayed, kneeling in the cold,
keeping vigils all the long night
until the dawn's first dismal light,
Outside our sombre palaces,
thousands cry, with pale faces,
Flowers in millions are laid there
for our Princess, who's beyond compare.
Many cannot believe she's dead,
She was our icon and figurehead.
She touched all our simple minds,
with the works she did of all kinds.
Throughout the world she was blessed
her ultimate worth cannot be assessed.
When she's finally laid to rest
we know, we've lost the very best.

Ursula Meldon

Requiem For Diana

A light went out
when you went away,
I don't know why
you could not stay.

Someone higher had
plans for you,
he held you in his
arms, and said: he
loved you too.

You were like an angel,
too good for this earth,
but this is only the
beginning, a new rebirth.

I pray you're with the
ones you love,
so sleep sweet princess,
and mingle with the stars
above . . .

Jade Watkins

Diana Forever

Your eyes will sparkle through the stars
Your smile shines through the sun
Your beauty lives forever after
You kind and gentle one.

May Heaven take you with open arms
To guide you, to keep you, to love you
We give you to this resting place
Your loving Dodi too.

Now rest in peace, Diana
Listen as we sing
We hope and pray enormously
That William will be our king.

K Hills

Diana The People's Princess

(When we lost Diana, we lost a jewel in the crown of England. She will always be missed and remembered)

We had a princess with qualities so rare
No-one could ever equal or even compare
She was kind and loving and stood out from
the rest
The people's princess was simply the best,
She travelled the world to people in need,
Just touching a leper, an angel indeed!
People with AIDS, bodies wracked with pain,
Their faces lit up, to see Diana again.
She was like a breath of spring air, so fresh
and sweet.
The nicest person you could ever wish to meet.
She believed in the people who loved her
so much.
She was a 'Queen of Hearts' with that
special touch.
She will never be forgotten her memory
will live on
Such a devastating loss now that Diana
has gone.
Her love for the people shone out in her face.
Such a beautiful princess no-one can replace.

Linda Woodhouse

Diana

Diana
The Dove
Of Love
You have
Reached your goal
And now
Are whole
In Heaven

F Smith

Untitled

All over the world we stood for a minute
For a princess who stood for the people
within it
This wonderful woman walking so tall
A princess, a mother and sister to all
The style, the smile, the twinkle in her eyes
This beautiful princess just lit up our lives
The brightest star that shone through the night
Was Princess Diana's, shining so bright
I felt like I knew you for most of my life
To lose you my princess, it cuts like a knife
I felt so close, as if we had met
This princess so special I will never forget
You brought so much joy. You were Queen
of our hearts
A precious life over but another one starts
We know you are looking down from above
So Princess in heaven still send us your love
A fairy tale ending, words so true
Princess of Angels we will all miss you
As she is laid to rest and we have paid our
respects
To a woman so grand there will be
some regrets
That a princess so great the whole world
through
Was taken so young and beautiful too
But you finally have the one thing you asked
God bless you my princess,
you are at peace at last.

Kenny Page

A Tribute To Diana

Beautiful and kind with a smile serene,
A caring Princess we once hoped would be
Queen,
Our love for you will never die,
You're our brightest star in the night-time sky,
Our Queen of Hearts you will always be,
From now until eternity.

Pauline Gaskell

Diana

Don't seek for I am searching
The answers are not there,
For every day I wonder
Was I wrong to care?

Don't cry for I am weeping
For those I'll never touch,
The sound of my boys' laughter
The things that meant so much.

Be brave for I have courage
For grief is hard to stand,
Reach out to those who need you
Support them, hold their hand.

The path is bright and calling
For me to walk its way,
Fear no longer holds me
I look to God and pray.

Don't weep for I'm not crying
I have my peace of mind,
Look to my two children
And my future you will find.

Samantha Lakehal

Diana

Her light of love has not gone out
For love can never fade,
Although we feel that we
Are left here in the shade.
Her love that shone for all
Will shine upon us still,
And one day we may meet
Beyond some distant hill.
For now it is our turn
To make our own love grow,
To reach all around the world,
Then everyone will know
Her light of love.

Janette Anne Whiting

Diana, Our Princess

It was the last day in August
The sun didn't shine that day
We were so numb with sadness
We heard, you had been taken away.

We were so shocked
The nation cried
The world stood still with sorrow
Now we have lost our princess
How can we face tomorrow?

You were such a lovely person
You brought hope and smiles to us all
At least we have your memories to treasure
And your love, we do recall.

But Diana, you were our princess
And that, you will always stay
You will be in our hearts forever
on this and every day.

J A Dawson

Diana

At peace you lie, in tranquillity
beside the waters deep
On your island, safe and sound
in an endless, dreamless sleep.

Your head on satin pillows
white lilies at your feet
Eyes closed tight in sweet repose
on your own secret retreat.

Far away from prying eyes
no-one to make you cry
Hidden from the world outside
you said your last goodbye.

Sweet Diana, Queen of all our hearts
beside the waters blue
On your island, safe and sound
that's where they buried you.

Leonora Kayes

The More Beautiful A Flower

The more beautiful a flower, the shorter
its life,
At least - that's the way that it seems.
But sometimes - not always - one may
come along,
That will live, evermore, in your dreams.

Slowly, at first, it will open its petals,
Like a nestling unfolding its wings.
Its beauty so subtle, its perfume so sweet,
Your heart feels so full that it sings.

But just as this beauty is reaching its peak,
And your senses can't take any more,
This most lovely of things is snatched
from our lives,
Leaving hurt like you've not felt before.

The physical presence may be gone from
our lives,
But the beauty and love never pales,
It's an honour and privilege to have witnessed
the life
Of Diana, the Princess of Wales.

JWB

Diana - RIP

Elusive butterfly,
searching, searching
For a love
that could never be,
Knowing not - that this was to be
her ultimate destiny!
Painful rejection by Prince of the realm,
Never was he beside her at the helm,
As beautiful as a rose
in its early form
With the dew still on it
in the early morn.
Poor Diana doomed to be
Just a legend in our history.

Maisie Trusslir

Untitled

Please forgive them, Diana,
for what they did when they chose you.
They needed a little sparkle,
to brighten up their Prince.
And you were chosen Diana mostly for
your innocence.
An English Rose, you were perfect
for the part,
Oh Diana, how I felt for you,
Your fate was doomed right from the start.

You gave us so much hope,
You were all we wanted to see
You captured everyone's heart
with a kiss on the balcony.
We really thought you'd brought them
into the twentieth century!
We all saw you blossom, but we
thought you held the Prince's heart.
You looked so good beside him,
we all enjoyed the show.
We couldn't accept Diana that
it was you who had to go.

You didn't need a title
You earned it with respect
You touched the hearts of many
ask anyone you met.
Ask any famous actress
how exhausting it can be,
to perform for the people, a thousand
two or three.
But they wouldn't let you off that stage
they wouldn't let you rest,
That was the price you paid, Diana
for outshining all the rest.

Please forgive us, Diana,
We got used to having you near,
And now you've gone Diana
and you have nothing left to fear.
We'll never see you as our queen,
no more wondering what might have been.

So, sadly, we say a last farewell,
as they lay you down to rest.
To have known you in our lifetime,
we truly have been blessed.

Goodnight Diana.

Alison Wood

Dear Diana - Princess Of Wales

Dear Diana - Princess of Wales we'll miss you
You were a princess so lovely through and
through
You were an inspiration to us all
You stood proud through your troubles -
so tall

We looked up to you in so many ways
We didn't realise then how short a time left
you had to stay
We'll miss you more than you'll ever know
But God decided he wanted you home and
you had to go

Your darling sons will make you so proud
one day
Your nation will look after them
come what may
You were a mum in a million you know
Like your sons we all loved you so

We won't forget you, so much have you done
Each passing day will bring a memory
Of a battle you have won
You were special in so many ways and your
smile brightened up our days

Sleep peacefully now in heaven up above
Keep with you our thanks and all of our love
When the sun shines we'll look up and see
your smile
We'll always remember our special princess
We only had you with us for a little while.

Evelyn Nouhas

Diana - Princess Of Wales

D iana - the name should mean 'Goddess of Love'
I t seems to us she was sent from above
A nd no-one could ever take her place
N one could compare to that lovely face
A nd now Heaven's hand has taken her home

To be with the angels above

P lease say a prayer wherever you go
R emember too the love she could show
I n so many ways she showed how she cared
N ever restricted and never prepared
C aring and feeling for 'everyday' folk
E easing their pain by the way that she spoke
S o unassuming and so down to earth
S o full of humour, laughter and mirth

She's now with the angels above

O ften she suffered, feeling such pain
F eeling unworthy and crying in vain

She'll be loved by the angels above

W hat we would give if only we could
A nd how we would like to send her our love
L etting her know that down here below
E veryone loved and cherished her so
S o sleep 'OUR DIANA' you'll live in our hearts

Back home with the angels above.

Gwen M Harper

Our Darling Diana

Our darling Diana you are simply the best
And now the whole nation has laid you to rest.
Nothing we do will ease the pain
Knowing we will never see you again.
Our modern-day Cleopatra (RIP Diana)
Lovely right to the end.

Irene Russell

Diana, Princess Of Wales

White roses for our princess,
Mother, daughter, sister, friend.
Her love given so freely,
Will the grief ever end?

Laughing with her children,
Always a loving embrace
Made them secure and happy,
As they saw her smiling face.

Even total strangers,
The dying, the sick, the shy
Were given her loving touch.
She would never pass them by.

She died so very young.
There was so much left to do.
There has to be a reason
For what life put her through.

The only good to come
Must come from those still here.
We have to show more love
And not just shed a tear.

There is no point to grief
Unless it helps us grow,
Until we learn to care,
Like the Princess of the Rose.

Pauline Mary Lawrence

To Our Beautiful Princess Diana

Winter is coming but you will be
in the lovely snowflake and all
the thousands of snowflakes will
cover you and keep you warm.
But when winter has gone and
the sun shines in the sky
The snowflakes will turn to tears
and like all the world for you will cry.

Mrs D Smith

Diana (The People's Princess)

A beautiful young Princess
has gone from our midst
One, who by everyone,
will be sadly missed
A shining light in this
troubled old world of ours
Champion of good causes
for the young and the old
To which in her lifetime
she gave many hours.
Tho' shy by nature but in these matters
so brave and so bold
Loving and caring for all with whom
she came in touch
People in distress always evoked
her sympathy and feelings so much
A devoted mother putting
her sons to the fore
Loved and respected
by all the world o'er
A good Ambassador for Britain
performing good works everywhere
May they be carried on in time
and not left 'there'
Bless her dear memory
and may her soul rest in peace
Our 'Queen of Hearts'
for whom our love will never cease!

Janet W Wight
(A loving grandmother and octogenarian)

Diana - Princess Of Wales

God called thee early to thy rest,
With heav'nly love thou now art blest.
Thy work with humankind is done
And blessed peace too soon have won.
The care and love shown valiantly
Has gained for thee thy victory
O'er earthly passion, pain and grief,
And in God's arms now find relief.

J G Ryder

Diana, Princess Of Wales

The shock of losing you has been devastating and cannot be explained.
The tragic way in which you died will never leave our minds.

Your warm hands reached their healing touch all around the globe.
Many more should have expressed their feelings of love towards you when you were alive.
We would rather have you back tomorrow to be by our sides.

Diana, you are seen as our only royal glow and now in our faces this sadness shows.

The flowers lie at a princess's gate a whole world in mourning,
This tribute just for you and the candles in between them light up the now dark sky.
Your memory in our hearts will never ever die.

We pray you have gone to a peaceful resting place so you can never be hounded by photographers in your face.

The charities you helped to change so many lives, will thrive the Diana Fund set up in memory of your life.

And now we grieve and are patient to wait as quoted 'like all good Britons do' to be told the truth behind the mystery that surrounds the death of you.
But will it be truth or will it be lies, will we ever really be satisfied.

A special lady who could bring spring to a cold winter's day.
A smile so greatly missed,' the people's princess' Diana.

Chantel Powell

The People's Friend

The world has lost a friend today
Someone precious to us all
She was a mother to her sons
And a princess to the world.
Her beauty was outstanding
Her heart was full of love
She was as precious as an angel
Sent down to us from up above.
The love she gave to others
Came from deep within her heart
She gave them hope and eased their pain
She gave her hand to all that came.
To her the world was a special place
To the world she was so true
She gave us warmth and love and hope
She taught us how to care.
Today the world has lost a friend
The fairy tale is over,
But the memory of the People's Princess
Will last forever and ever.

A Johnson

The Queen Of Our Hearts

(In loving memory of a dear Princess, Diana)

She was the one, with the golden hair,
Who tried to make the world fair,
She was the one whom we all adored,
Who should have got an award.
She was the one who cared such a lot,
Who did not care what she'd got.
She was the one so independent,
The one so kind and patient.
This heaven-sent angel we all knew,
That blessed the souls of children and adults too,
The person who will be missed world-wide
Princess Diana, now by her maker's side.

Lisa Wheeler (13)

Diana

Tears flowed for Diana,
The nation, stunned in disbelief,
Men and women in their grief
Came to lay their tributes down,
In every city, every town
Tears flowed for Diana.

Tears flowed for Diana,
Flowers for a loved Princess
Helped to ease the deep distress;
An English rose of unique beauty
Brought special charm to every duty,
Tears flowed for Diana.

Love flowed from Diana,
Queen of Hearts she had become,
A ministering angel was to some
Who felt her touch and knew her care
For suffering people everywhere,
Loved flowed from Diana.

Rest in peace, Diana,
Your beauty will not fade or die.
We will never know the reason why,
With mother-love so strong and true
And so much good that you could do,
You had to die, Diana.

W M Stokes

A Priceless Princess

As a bright light, slowly fades away,
Although it hurts, you could not stay,
You touched the world, with your love and care,
The gift you had, was one so rare,
You hugged the sick, and helped them cope,
And filled their hearts, with future hope,
The weak, the lame, you helped them all,
In this world of pain, you stood out tall,
You will be missed by young and old,
The heart you had, was one of gold,
In showing kindness, was your role,
Goodbye Diana, God bless your soul.

Christopher A J Evans

Queen Of Hearts

Our Queen of Hearts is sleeping
God's hand has closed the door,
The photocalls are over
They'll worry her no more.
Her life on earth was pressured,
But through it all she shone
Her light of human kindness,
Her work must carry on.
She had a gift for caring,
No cause was ever lost,
Her critics couldn't stop her
As barriers she crossed.
Her faults were there, but human,
Her married life so sad,
Rejected painfully in love
Who knows what thoughts she had?
She took the love within her
And used it as a guide,
Her boys were her great comfort
A mother's love of pride.
Her life was just beginning
Then snuffed out like a flame,
Sleep on serenely Princess
Free from the binds of fame.

Irene Carter

Diana 1961-1997

They came from near - they came from far
They came with love and flowers,
They came because they felt the need
And stood for hours and hours.

Some queued all night to sign a book,
Some simply wondered why
Their loving caring English rose
Had been allowed to die.

In disbelief they showed their grief
For one so young in years,
And all the world watched silently
As London shed her tears.

Aline Smith

Diana

A light has gone out in the world
Everyone is feeling the pain.
She glowed like a beacon of hope
Life is never to be the same.

Born to be special, born to be Queen
A gift surely given by God.
Helping, caring forever true
Leaving hope wherever she trod.

She came into our lives like an angel
Innocent, sweet and pure.
Married a prince, became a princess
Her duties made her feel insecure.

Her world in turmoil.
We saw her pain and felt her sadness.
Her eyes pleaded for help
But alone she stood, in all the madness.

But from this she drew strength
And from this she did grow
Into the beautiful woman
We all got to know.

A moment's madness causing so much pain.
Changing the world forever.
But remember our loss is Heaven's gain
And her memory is ours to treasure.

Margaret Smith

Tribute To Diana

From this day as time goes by
Our love for you will never die.
We'll remember you for what you've done
For caring and giving and the love for your sons.
With golden sunshine on your face
Up in heaven now your resting place.
With these words a warm embrace
For a lovely princess who'll be hard to replace.

Janet Ann Carter

Diana

It's so sad to watch
True lovers die,
You found your true love
Which you could not hide,
Now you are together
In each other's arms,
Together forever
In all of our minds,

We will feel your tears
When it starts to rain,
We will feel your love
And your pain,
You were taken away
From Willy and Harry,
And your love for them
Just like ours,
Will forever remain.

Love from

Julie Richardson

To Diana, A Very Special Person

(I dedicate this poem to you)

There's only a moment, a second, a breath,
We tread a thin line between life and death,
A lingering kiss, a passionate embrace,
Aim to keep yourself sane in this rat race.

A heartbeat, a pulse, the ticking of time,
We search in our souls for a reason or rhyme,
Happiness and sorrow, laughter and tears
Our memories grasp at the past of
long-gone years,

Yesterday's sunshine and tomorrow's rain,
A capsule of pleasure in a sea of pain,
Close your eyes and imagine the beauty beyond,
Open them again and the vision is gone.

FOREVER IN OUR HEARTS

With deepest sadness, love from

Deborah Chivers

Diana

A devoted mother
A friend to all
A compassionate lady
We came to adore
A vision of beauty
So full of life
You had more than your share,
of trouble and strife
But you held your head high,
for all to see,
With poise and stance immaculately
You were a woman with feelings
and a heart of gold
No better Princess, could this world hold.

Sylvia Brown

The People's Star

A bright new star glows in the heavens tonight
Its name is Diana, Princess of Light,
With golden face shining on people below,
Giving brightness and warmth wherever
they go,
Dance on Special Lady as you journey
the skies,
We will never forget you and your smiling
eyes,
A star filled with sparkle, you are our
leading light.
Sleep well, dear Diana,
God bless and goodnight.

E M Hodges

Princess Of The World

Confusion and disbelief rushed, through my head,
When the news came over the air, Princess Diana was dead.

When the waves of shock had finally settled down,
They laid her body gently below the ground,

People of the world, the wounded, sick and the lame,
Will look towards the heavens and ask, who is to blame?

Her spirit will live forever, in the people's minds,
Because she left behind, the greatest gift, of all time,

Faith and trust in those who will carry out, her dearest wish,
to become, the first PRINCESS OF THE WORLD,
Helping the poor and the sick.

J Burge

Such Silence

Such silence as you passed by
Just the sound of a heartfelt sigh
As you were taken to your final rest
We were saying goodbye to the very best.

Such silence as you passed by
To the place where you now lie
On an island across the lake
We knew our hearts would surely break.

Such silence as you passed by
We bowed our heads and began to cry
We felt as if we'd lost a friend
Would our hearts ever mend?

Such silence as you passed by
Now on angels' wings you fly
Up to Heaven where you'll always be
Forever loved, forever free.

Judith Fletcher

Goodbye Diana, Princess of Wales

A light went out the day you died,
A light went out and everyone cried.
A nation in shock, a family in grief,
Loyalty beyond belief.

A smile so radiant, a heart of gold,
A fairy tale - a story told.
Golden hair - grace and charm,
We couldn't keep you safe from harm.

A gentle smile, a sweet caress,
Giving only happiness.
A special lady - a shining star,
Loved by all, though near or far.

A beautiful angel, only on loan,
She didn't make her last journey alone.
Before she left, she gave us her boys,
To share in their lives, sorrows and joys.

A princess from God in Heaven above,
She did his work, and spread his love.
In people's hearts she will always remain
A Princess of Love - a sharer of pain.

In his wisdom - God thought it best
To take her home and give her a rest.

Sheila Taunton

Diana

D is for your Destiny to make
some dreams come true,
I is for the Inspiration that
always came from you,
A is for the Admiration that
everybody shared,
N is for your kind-hearted Nature
to show how much you cared,
A is for you're always here
I know you'll never part,
And that is why you'll
always be our loving
Queen of Hearts.

Shona Donovan

Princess Of Wales

The sense of my feeling, drained as in me,
Finding myself turning the TV on, and being hit with a tune,
Should this be telling me? That what this word that seemed to say,
Was, how could this be? Princess Di - my friend, died - no way!

I listened without trauma, not really knowing why,
And then, I became tired, shocked, and knew this was the way,
Princess of Wales, died in Paris, my friend I had in my heart,
I could not understand, and still don't know why.

My tears they came, they flooded, they fell,
The shock that I would not meet,
This girl that touched my heart,
When I realised she had died, I remembered,
I remembered the letter, the letter she had sent.

She thanked me, she was grateful, for my thoughtfulness,
She thanked me, for my poem, my poem, that was only my heart and me,
I will never meet her now on this earth,
But, she's in my heart, she left a special part of her heart.

She loved so much of life, she took so much hassle,
But she was a strong person, and I'm glad she found love,
She got so very thin, she became so very ill,
But she gave so much, so much she could give.

She held another's hand, she didn't care at all
Of course AIDS worried others, but care she gave to all,
I am so proud that I knew her, even though at a distance,
Princess of Wales, I pray, that you have found happiness and peace at last.

Mary Jo West

Feelings

(A Tribute to Diana)

The news came unexpectedly
This person was no more,
A heart deprived of beating
Left millions feeling raw

She brushed us with her bearing
She touched us with her thought
Each time she hand-held others
Where warmth was clearly sought

Although I've never met with her
I saw her ways so true
Befriending, caring, sharing
Poor souls she chanced to view

A beacon in her lifetime
That shone above the rest,
We've lived to see her passing
Free spirited and blessed

She knew of sadness often
Yet happiness gave out
A Princess gifting hope around
To people having doubt

Our world is that much poorer
Since now she's slipped away,
'God bless you in your heaven'
These words we pray today.

Sam Royce

Diana

Eyes of azure blue
Pools of compassion,
Seen on every page
Icon of fashion.
Mother, sister, friend,
Caring till the end,
Uniting all in grief
Stunned in disbelief.
She had so much to give
Long may her memory live.

Mona Evans

Goodbye Diana

The town is strangely silent,
All the faces sad,
Inwardly weeping, our Di, lent
To make us glad,
Is in their thoughts, they can't believe,
That she is gone,
In silence they stand and grieve,
Tears shed by everyone,
For this Angel, who lived on earth,
So short was her time,
But she made it count, giving birth,
To sons and in her prime,
Gave us happiness and love; joy
And a great compassion,
A tender caress, a single toy,
This icon of fashion,
Had the common touch, a look,
That healed the broken,
That brought thousands to sign the Book
Of Condolence and leave a token.

Goodbye Diana . . .

Kenneth V Jackson

Diana

Prince Charles of Wales must be
lucky, it is no surprise
For he sees his lovely Diana's face
in his sons' eyes.
She was the people's princess
and nothing more
She reached out and touched
the needy and the poor.
The place she is in is like a savannah
and we all know inside
we all love
Princess Diana

Kirsty Joanne Roberts

The News

The news of your death
Cuts like a knife.
The angels came down
And took your life
The love you gave
Came from your heart
You were our very own
Queen of Hearts

You let us share part
of your mother
William and Harry
She was like no other
Savour each moment
she gave and you shared

Be proud of the world
that loved and cared

Rest in Peace
With your beloved Dodi

Barbara White

A Child's Thoughts

The Queen of Hearts is now in Heaven
Where the angels play
No-one expected her to leave
In such a tragic way.

Her heart was filled with kindness
And every child knew her love
Now she looks upon us
From the skies above.

Sadly missed by everyone
Especially her two sons
We hope you rest in peace now
From two more little ones.

Princess Diana and Dodi
Together forever at last.

James MacDonald

Princess Diana

Princess Diana,
Her death was tragic,
But what she did for the world,
Was truly magic.

Millions of people gather to mourn,
All the comments were good ones,
There was not a scorn.

Before the funeral,
There was a procession,
Making people happy,
Was Diana's profession.

The Royal family,
So unhappy and sad,
Prince William and Harry,
They must feel so bad.

Silence remains,
There is not a sound,
The tears are contained,
As people gather around.

The church bell tolls,
Minute after minute,
The millions of people,
That sit within it.

To tie it up with the funeral,
Where tears of sadness are sure to fall.

Flowers are lying everywhere,
Messages of condolence,
To show the people care,

The choir singing hymns and songs,
The congregation sings along.

The coffin is brought in,
for all to see,
Flowers and an envelope
Labelled 'Mummy'.

Elton John,
He changed his song,
He was a friend of Diana's
All along.

Deep sadness and sorrow,
Is felt by all,
They know there is nothing more they can do,
Nothing at all.

Millions of people gather together,
To pray and remember Diana forever.

Marie Sullivan

An Epitaph Of Love

Diana you found happiness for a short while
You were with the man you loved, and we could see it in your smile
You fought back from sadness, and you never gave in
And you loved your sons, one some day to be King
Ordinary people loved you I know I did
You were absolutely happy, just like a kid
You had a special feeling, for those worse off than you
Compassion pity and love came out of you
Your station in life didn't matter, your humanity showed
And from your radiant beauty it showed
Now God has reached out and gathered you both in
To be enveloped in His love, and to hear the angels sing
Your lover Dodi was with you, on that fateful day
Now you will stay together forever and a day
The sweetheart of our nation
Now part of all creation
Dodi and you were lovers, happy at a fast rate
Then the doors of Heaven opened, and you entered through the gate
Eternity is yours, be happy every day
God bless you Diana and Dodi, this night I pray
Your happiness was short-lived, but you knew it for a while
All the world could see it in that beautiful smile
You will always be OUR Princess, as now with the angels you go
And even God will recognise you by your human glow.

Prince Rhan of Kathari

Queen Of Hearts

(Written with love and admiration in memory of 'an angel' who walked our land)

'Princess Diana' there will 'never be'
another You,
A 'beautiful person' so warm, so true;
Like a star your light will never fade
'You were Heaven-sent',
'You were Heaven-made',
In our hearts you will forever stay,
You brightened up
Our darkest day.
The whole world loved you too.
You were the People's Princess
through and through!
You gave us all more than you
ever took,
With everyone's hand, you warmly shook.
Queen of Hearts is all you ever
wanted to be,
Diana in our hearts you
will reign eternally.

Janet Rose Marsh

Thoughts For The Queen Of Hearts

There will always be Diana no matter where she be
Her name will always be in the books of history
She left behind her heirs and their father to the throne
And the memory to the sons they will never be alone
Diana will never die, she's gone to her castle in the sky
There she will always be but she will never be alone
She will look down from the heavens above from her golden throne
This is life as we all agree
Diana the Queen of Hearts will be in our hearts till eternity

Eugene W Hide

Gone

Early on a Sunday morning without any warning
The Lord took you to his home
He knew that you would fret, because of the death
Of your beloved Dodi who had left you all alone

Up in the sky, were there are no eyes to pry
Your souls together are now complete
Now when you look down, over the crowd
You see our sadness, love and grief.

You served your country, with care and loyalty
Our lives you have enriched
We didn't realise the cost, until our loss
The little things, that will be sadly missed

Your sparkling eyes, that helped you spy
The person who felt left out and down
Your laughter and smile, made it worthwhile
To the public you didn't need a crown

Now you're gone, you have won
The nation's most inner feelings
We poured out our hearts, right from the start
Till it reached the Abbey ceilings.

Eileen King

Diana

The heavens have gained their brightest star
Whom we shall worship from afar.
The lady whom we loved so much,
The Princess with the healing touch.

Her name you'll hear for years to come,
Although not even seen by some.
What beautiful stories we will tell,
About the one we loved so well.

The world has seen its darkest hour,
The earth has lost a precious flower.
It breaks my heart to end this verse
With the words 'Goodnight, goodbye and God Bless.

An Armagh Family

For Our Beloved Diana

Oh Diana, Diana, why did you have to go,
Why did you leave us, when we loved you so,
You were our beautiful Princess,
we thought the world of you.
You were a wonderful mum, we know this is true
Diana, You left us two wonderful boys,
William, so handsome looking just like you,
Harry so inspiring doing what he had to do,
for you,
What will they do without their precious mum,
Who will make sure they still have their fun,
Who will hug them, like you used to do,
If I had my way I would do this, for you,
Prince Charles is their dad and has been
misunderstood,
Things he did were not all bad,
some were very good,
The love he has for his sons shines for all the
world to see,
And Wills and Harry love HIM,
it's very plain to me,
So Diana rest in peace in Heaven above,
Rest assured your boys will have lots of love,
From their families, and the nation, who all
adored you,
But who will love US now you can no longer do?
You, still will Diana, we will never forget you,
Your love will stay with us our whole
lives through
We will pray for you until the end of time,
You were the 'People's Princess'
You were simply divine.

L E Ward

Yesterday

Yesterday, our streets were empty
When I was just a lad.
What has happened? Why is everyone so sad?
My mother said, 'An angel has died.'
And just sat down and cried and cried.
Today our hearts are empty,
And I am just a lad.

Margaret Cooper

Heaven Couldn't Wait

Such a shining light extinguished,
Such a star twinkles no more.
Such a lady adored by people in their millions,
those Lions of dear England have sadly,
lost their roar.

A glowing example to a thousand races,
loved by so many, forgotten by few;
I adored Diana, a wonderful woman,
I'll miss Diana and no doubt, shall you.

From the minefields of Africa to the balcony
of Buck House.
From a yacht on the Med to the
Balmoral Estate,
From the poverty-stricken to the rich and
the famous,
a piece of life has been cruelly succumbed
because Heaven couldn't wait.

Diana, a fairytale Princess,
a caring human being.
Diana; compassionate, misunderstood,
truly tho', a real saint.
Diana; a historical figure, revered by all in every
walk of life.
Diana; now a new star shines in the night sky,
watching over us all in her glory,
our loss is God's gain. . . .

Ron Matthews Jr

There'll Never Be Another One

The grief we share
A light's gone out
The pain we bear
Where can I shout?
Diana once inspired me
As with my son
It was to be
Diana died
And like my son
There'll never be another one.

Melvyn Roiter

Goodbye

On a wet grey morning as we wait to say goodbye
tearful sky rolls back to let the pale blue sky forth, and bright white clouds float by.
People stand and watch with thoughts they remember
The young and old, the sick, the needy, the cuddles and love, given from the heart.
And not just to help and care for the rich but to the very poorest with love and understanding in the way no-one foretold.
People who saw in person the people who saw in pictures, a helping hand and a word or a letter too.
The light of the world the people's friend those who know and those who did not but loved in heart
this day will never be forgotten.
When a family comes down to earth and walks beside the ordinary people who truly love the special woman, and her sons too walk with the common people of the world to say goodbye to a mother and friend 'Diana'.

Goodbye sweetheart goodbye
God bless, we will all remember you this day.

Kath Kay

My Tribute To Diana, Princess Of Wales

Gentle Princess Diana, sent from Heaven above
To spread forth your gift of compassion and love
By supporting the needy the sick and the poor
You strove to end ignorance, to open 'closed doors'.

The Lord lends us his angels to bring love to earth
So you'd come here amongst us to show him your worth
By your loving and giving you'd passed every last test
So he called you home early, to enjoy eternal rest

But the day you departed, earth was left so forlorn
We saw darkness at daybreak, tears of rain in the morn
Then a rainbow was glinting, like the smile in your eyes
And a shimmering sunset proved you'd gone home to the skies.

Now we're left much the poorer, but when grief comes to bear
As empty space fills up each heart, we will offer this prayer -
May we celebrate your life and your courageous deeds thus far
By remembering the magic of your smile in every twinkling star . . .

J Hurst

HRH Princess Diana

The nation's thoughts go out to you
To pass away so sudden seems so cruel
The work and love you freely gave
Will carry on day after day
Smile of warmth
Gave so many hope
A spirit with loving light
Shall shine forever bright.

Alan Jones

Flowers

Diana's gone today,
She's flown to Heaven in a dove-like way
Where the Lady Queen of Hearts
Will rest and stay
Her spirit will return one day,
And dance around the
Lake and flowers that bloom in the sunshine and
Form a rainbow in a colourful spray

RIP

Kevin Tot

Diana

You breezed into our lives in 1981
Bringing a breath of fresh air to a family
that had none
You were young then, and your naiveté it showed
But you won the hearts of many and on us your
love bestowed

You were our fairy tale princess
In your beautiful wedding dress
You were queen of the fashion world
We'd wait for the next gown to be unfurled

You bore the country a fine young heir
Then groomed him to live in the public's glare
You made him as normal as a prince could be
To put him in touch with the people like me

Then followed a brother for the king-to-be
His name you declared to be Prince Harry
The boys, they were lucky to have a mother
like you
It's a shame that you have been taken from
them too

By now you were under considerable strain
To live up to and behold the great Windsor
name
The signs were there, etched deep on your face
The pain you endured increased your
common grace

Your deep blue eyes, as clear as the sea
Were as compassionate as eyes could be
You were light in many's darkest hour
You made the most of your special power

You helped so many with your touching grace
No-one can ever take your place
The world will miss your smiling face
All the people of every race

We had a dream, you'd be our queen
but you never reached the throne
You made it into people's hearts
though you were so alone

Your life was tinged with sadness
sometimes you couldn't bear
You can rest in peace now
life is rarely fair

Today I saw a rainbow, lighting up the sky,
A sign that you are with us even though
you're way up high
There is one consolation, in this
terrible tragedy
And that's that you died happy,
like a woman in love should be.

I know you are still with us
each and every one
Although it's awfully hard to believe
That you are really gone

Princess Diana, a true Royal,
Queen of people's hearts and the world . . .

Rest in peace

Frances Victoria Williams

Diana

Your eyes of meaning,
a touch, a kiss,
our global victims,
will forever miss . . .

Your heart, in a photo,
often caught,
your life, in a lens,
painfully short . . .

Your fairytale beauty,
spectacularly lost,
will the world,
know the cost?

Martin James English

The Princess's Death

Shock, disbelief,
it can't be true,
Now she's gone, we're so blue.
Her heart so warm, gentle, and pure,
she tried her hardest to find a cure.
Her life was in danger more than once,
even when she walked, always with a bounce.
Her beauty, charm and warm loving care,
helped other people not to despair.
The nation loved her for her honesty,
but all she cared about was other people's
poverty.

The tears roll
the children keep low,
Charles travels to bring young Di home.
The papers plastered with her innocent face,
we all know she was full of grace.
As her body is escorted to the Chapel of Rest,
it's a shame she's gone,
the best of the best.

Siân Mills - (Wales)

Diana

The world is now a sadder place
With the loss of your sweet face,
Compassionate and full of grace,
Loving every creed and race.

In your gentle arms you held them close,
The maimed, diseased, you cared for those.
You were dedicated to your cause
Of showing us many of the world's flaws.

Babies felt comfort in your arms,
The young and old fell for your charms
And now you rest in Heaven above
To be forever in His love.

Joan Britton

Two Wonderful Women

Mother Teresa now you have gone,
Your love and your memories will always
live on,
Now you join our dear Princess Diana,
On earth you both did all that you could
Having faith and love from above
May you both now rest in peace,
And all the worldly troubles cease.

J Willson . . .

A short poem by my son . . .

Diana's Children

Prince William and Harry
your mother now gone,
Knowing the world loved her
her memory lives on.
On earth she always did her best,
In heaven dear Lord now let her rest.

Diana, Someone So Beautiful

Only God knows the reason,
But we just don't know why,
He took someone so beautiful,
And made the whole world cry,
A loving heart stopped beating,
It just seems so unreal,
But her smile will live forever,
Her gentle touch we will feel,
And when our hearts are heavy,
And teardrops gently fall,
We'll remember her smile with gladness
And the love she gave us all.
Watch over our Princess, Lord,
And keep her in your care,
At peace at last within God's house
An angel so very rare

Diana.

Sue Ridgeway

A Prince Is Born

(In memory of Princess Diana, for whom the people of the world cried an ocean of tears)

Sometimes in this troubled world
When the future seems forlorn,
The time to be happy - a time to smile
By the grace of heaven is born,
And on a dark and dreary day
There came a ray of light,
And for a little while, it seemed
the day was fair and bright.
A baby prince was born to us,
And some day he will know
That in his tiny hands he held the
power to set our hearts aglow
A welcome royal baby - born in a land
that's free
Where men are not afraid to fight
and die for liberty
A baby born to be a king
Be part of history
May God protect him - keep him safe
And guide his destiny.

M Hemsley

Diana

Sleep, dear princess, rest your eyes
You're with the man you love
The nation mourns, no more lies
As the heavens open above

The tender love you gave each day
Will be missed by everyone
You always had something nice to say
Yet the pain stays now you're gone

The years may pass slowly now
Your memory will never die
You gave so much and yet, somehow
We can never say goodbye.

Brian Macro

The Princess

A true Princess so fair,
her beautiful face, her beautiful hair.
The way she died was such a disgrace,
a tear rolled down the nation's face.

A beloved mother to Wills and Harry,
and ex-wife of a Prince she chose to marry.
A woman full of love and compassion,
but also a trend-setter of fashion.

To us all, she left lasting impressions,
So clearly seen from our mixed expressions.
A nation mourned, and was downhearted,
at the needless way that she departed.

Her legacy can never be measured,
always, and now forever, by a nation treasured.
She always tried to do her best,
now she's found eternal rest.

May the Lord take care of her forever,
Her beauty fadest never.
A gifted lady, oh so rare,
now gone forever, it just ain't fair.

Her legend lives on,
tho' she is now gone.

David Carress

The Queen Of Hearts

She wanted to be the Queen of Hearts
She was demanded in many parts.
But yet she was, a lonely soul
Surrounded always, by protocol.
Until she met Dodi
And fell in love
And was happy for once,
As graceful as a dove.
Suddenly she was robbed of this,
They died together,
And will be sadly missed.

Tiffany Aubrey (12)

Courage

People the world over,
in the depths of despair,
Their angel of courage no longer is there,
An ocean of tears wept,
an endless searing pain,
A catalogue of memories,
by the sound of your name.

A mother to all children, not only your own,
Your beloved boys William and Harry,
now stand alone,
But your legacy of courage will live
on in them,
Even though your shining smile,
will never grace them again.

In God's arms may you sleep fitfully,
And may blessed peace, be granted to Thee,
Sure in the knowledge your
work will continue,
As a world-wide, heartfelt, memorial, to you.

Even though the world, may now seem
cold and dark,
And a world full of tears,
remain in our hearts,
May we all look to the wide horizon, and see,
A beacon of courage, that will burn on
Forever . . . for thee.

Sweet dreams beautiful Princess.

Tracy Bell

A Poem For Diana, Princess of Wales

Diana - the Queen of Hearts you became
The Queen of Hearts you will ever remain
God made a special person and sent her down to
earth
You carried out his wishes for all that you were
worth
Your passing has shown the world how much you
were loved
And we hope that you can see how much from up
above
The good deeds that you did really
were sublime
They will remain with us forever until the end of
time
The good Lord sent you to us from above
To do what you did best - spread happiness and
love
Lots of people living got to know your worth
Because you made a heaven for them
here on earth
Of course there is a heaven and that you are truly
there
And for all the good you have done God will give
you special care
Rest in peace Diana - you made the world a
better
place
You will always be remembered for your beauty,
love and grace.

Sid Speyer

Diana

Diana, our Queen indeed
Always there for those in need,
The sick, the aged, the children, the poor
Her heart an ever open door.
At last she found her true love - BUT -
Would this, in this cruel world endure
For these two people, so caring, so nice?
So GOD took them by the hand
And led them both to PARADISE.

Frankie Betts

God Bless Diana

Her life was a test
and she gave of her best
She fought with her back
to the wall
She laughed and she cried
and tragically she died
A princess whose life
touched us all.

God Bless Diana.

Geraldine Lockwood

31.08.97

God decided to take, into his care
A beautiful princess, so young and rare
A princess so benevolent and grand
Who to poor and weak, gave heart and hand

She had her troubles, like us all
But carried on, both proud and tall
A fine lady, world-wide adored
Now in the house of Our Lord

Free at last from entanglement
For evermore at peace, content
A peace that to us all one day will come
When our sorry life, its span has run.

And God beckons us, to his Heaven above
When all is wondrous, with joy and love
So don't be sad, or frightened feel
When you hear that big bell peel
Or when you hear that beating drum
For now on, only the best's to come.

K Coleman

Diana

The world is so sad we all want
to cry

Our Queen of Hearts has said
goodbye

We hope she knew the love
we felt

As she took our hearts and made
them melt

Everyone loved her, she shone
like a light

But what terrible grief
As we all say goodnight.

Carol Duke

Memories

There is a day to be born, with a day to die.
Our mortal life spans days and nights
That twinkling star or the blink of an eye,
Is not that long, according to our
Lord's rights.

Could I live forever, I hear you ask?
Could I be forgiving, and a princess too?
Could I have a little happiness in
my daily task?
Could I own a little privacy when
I'm feeling blue?

When my days are done and I'm on my way,
I shall look upon you and quietly say
I did my best, what more could I do?
But my memories and spirit will always belong to
you.

Peter Mitchell

If

You touched the common people like none had
done before
You shared in grief and sorrow and still you gave
much more
You showed the world that protocol did not
command your heart
All of this you gladly gave to us.

If all the tears we cry would cause the world to
overflow
And all the pain and grief we feel could somehow
let you know
That all the love we have for you could make you
smile again
Then all of this, we gladly give to you.

If only I had powers to transport you in my
dream
If only this was yet to be and I a time machine
If only I could rewind to before the pain set in
I would, I would, if only that I could.

Audrey Shaw

A Tribute To Diana And Dodi

Such happiness gone, like a leaf in the breeze
Two hearts so in love that have ceased to be.

Such a waste of two lives, with so much
to share
Such joy, that was already waiting there.

Like flowers cut down, as they started to grow
Two lives entwined, with what future
who'll know.

What looked like a future, that could only
be bright
Has now turned into the darkest night.

You have gone dear lovers to a new home,
together
Let's hope that it's better and you will be happy
forever.

Hazel Kendall

Princess Of Light (A Tribute)

Closed now are the eyes that smiled within
Lost is your future that might have been
Taken from us when your world looked bright
We'll never forget our Princess of Light
Although your own happiness was
not complete
Often weighed down by each defeat
You brought comfort and joy to victims of war
With love and kindness to the humbled
and poor
You did not claim to be an angel or saint
Merely a canvas on life which to paint
We all glowed in the light of your fame
Forever young you will always remain
In our memories, in our hearts and minds
A Princess of Light that shone on mankind.

Ivor M Kirstein

An Angel

Princess Diana was an Angel
to those in deep distress
She showed them real companionship
and gave them happiness.

Now she is gone they all will miss
her cuddles and her love
I think this was bestowed on her
from our dear Lord up above.

She was a saint there is no doubt
the way she played her part
She gave ill persons a zest for life
from out a loving heart

The world will be a duller place
without her infectious smile
And many folk will grieve for her
and this will last a while

Lachlan Taylor

The Queen Of Hearts

The world came to a standstill
After hearing the tragic news
No one could quite believe it
Everyone was so bemused.

She was our Queen of Hearts
The people's Princess
Words can never describe
Her warmth and tenderness.

She had the human touch
Showing people that she cared
From the young to the old
A cuddle is what she shared.

So goodnight sweet Diana
Wherever you may be
One thing is for certain
You are in all our memories.

Ian Fowler

Princess Diana (1961-1997)

Her heart ruled her mind
by everything said and done,
captured many hearts
and loved by everyone.

Sunday being a day of church
the nation is in mourning,
something very tragic
happened early this morning.

Killed in a car crash
nothing can take her place,
I know I'll always remember
her charitable loving face.

Thirty-six. So very young,
and her sons grieving for their mother,
so irreplaceable, kind and considerate
princess like no other.

Today outside musky and silent,
may seem like a normal atmosphere,
but really it's the nation's respect
to Lady Diana no longer here.

Diana, I think she did her best
has passed on to a better place,
and deserves a well-earned rest.

Kerry Mason

Untitled

The times you came this way before
The countries you will travel no more
For photos took you away from this land
For this no-one will understand
For we were blind and could not see
It was Jesus that knew and made you free
From all the photos you had to bear
You left us sudden and standing there
Bewildered with thoughts and wondering why
Because you were so young and had to die.

God bless. Love from

Dee Dickens

A World Of Sadness For Its Princess

Unknown you were, when first you came to the world's light,
And for freedom, peace and love you made it your personal fight,
Combining each precious moment with that gift you were bestowed,
For a world's love undeniably did certainly grow.

You gave of yourself, but never the return you asked for,
The camera-man, the press, your plea they did ignore,
Two sons you cherished, now you they are without this day,
But your smile and memory will live with them anyway.

A world of sadness, for it lost its princess the other day,
Now you've gained a freedom from all life's way,
Yet forever in the hearts of so many who held you dear,
May each and every one of us always feel your presence near.

Gladys Moody

Angel

Heaven needed a Princess
The best that there can be,
So Diana the beautiful was chosen,
To care for all who need.
The gift of Love she showed us
Often went misled,
By all the news and papers,
Who tried to 'ruin' it
Was often said,
The brightest star in the heavens,
Must be 'Lady Di'
For there's no other meaning,
Why Diana had to die.

Nicola McNeil

Grieve Not

(This poem was inspired by Diana's love for her boys)

Grieve not for me, for I live
surrounded by the trees
that bear the fruits of happiness,
in the garden of the free.

I'm bathed in rainbow raiments
and see eternal light,
that shines forever skyward
on the darkest night.

So in the springtime of your youth
or wisdom of the old,
I am there to comfort you
in seasons yet untold.

You'll see me in the flowers
touched by fragrant rain
and as gentle breezes kiss you,
you'll know, I live again.

Jean Caldwell

Untitled

Princess Diana, Queen Of Hearts
Loved by all from the very start.
Everything you could possibly do
You did for those who needed you.

You're loved and respected throughout the land.
All it took was a word or a touch from your hand
To change a bad day into one to be treasured,
A memory to share of joy and of pleasure.

You were there for all who needed a friend,
Working for others until the end.
You died so young but left your mark
On a world that's better because of your heart.

Sarah Burke (15)

A Poem For A Princess

'Now out of our reach, but not out of our hearts
You'll look down on us, from your bright shining star.
You're the light of our lives, that has dimmed so much
We're desperately missing your loving touch,
You've shown us just why, we shouldn't give in
And now with your strength,
we can and will win.
You wouldn't go quietly, you wouldn't give in
No matter what was said,
or how we had sinned.
Together with Dodi, you both held on tight,
To the power of Love, that has shown to unite,
The nation and all, together today,
To love and to hold, come what may,
And all because of you, our Queen of Hearts,
May this be, just the start.
More powerful in Death, than you were in life
How we wished Dodi had made you his wife.
Be happy Princess and Dodi too,
For the lessons we've learned
We'll always miss you.'

From a modern-day Mum

Dawn Y J Wright

Diana

Goodbye Diana, Giver of Love,
Take care of your sons from up above.
I wish I could hug them to ease their pain.
Your love for them will never wane.
They will feel your presence wherever they are
You are the brightest shining star.
I hope they are happy in years to come
And people will say 'A job well done.'
You taught them how to live like the rest,
Darling Diana - simply the best.

Love is all.

Helen Clark

Princess Di

The grey skies weep on this sad August day
When all the world in stricken silence grieves
And scarce can credit Princess Di is dead -
A treasure which from each of us is thieved.

Yes! Gone forever from us that shy smile
Which warmed the hearts of many
in sore need;
A loving mother, caring friend to all
With heart which for the poor did intercede.

Some saw her as a headstrong, wilful girl
Born to high status - every whim indulged,
Yet she endured deep grief and suffering too,
And many were her sorrows undivulged.

And I? I see an innocent young girl
Chosen as consort to our future king.
Her marriage doomed to failure from the start
With nothing but a token wedding ring.

And other, no less precious lives were lost
Upon this weeping sombre August day.
All sacrificed to our intrusive lust
For media news. An awesome price to pay.

Marjorie Swindley

Diana's Common Touch

Her small hands touched people
The sick and the lame
Her warm hands touched victims
Of war mines in pain
Her royal hands touched pop stars
Presidents and kings
Her maternal hands touched Harry
And William our future King
Her gracious hands touched flowers
From crowds in their throngs
But only the deaf saw her
soft hands speak out loud
with love.

J C Hall

Goodbye Diana

Miss you, yes, we will,
As we who loved you, all stand still.
Silent, and in prayer, we will stand,
Thoughts of you, with such a gentle hand.

Kind in thought, word and deed,
To help and comfort, those in need.
From those of lowest birth, you chose,
The tiny babe, without a robe.

You were there, in their hour of need,
Among them all, you did proceed.
In countries far, you travelled wide,
You were there, by their side.

The landmines, you did your best to ban,
You saw people, with loss of leg and hand.
You walked among them, their hopes were
high,
Your best you gave, but we saw you sigh.

We saw a tear, on your saddened face,
When you saw such agony, in the human race.
A tribute to DIANA, would be,
To ban all landmines, let this us see.

Thank you DIANA, for all the good you did,
It seems as though, you were too good to live.

V M Foulger

For Princess Di

When we lose a one we love we all say
'If only'
If only we said the things we should have said
'If only'
If only we had done the things we should
have done
'If only'
Perhaps if there's a second time around
We can put things right
'If only'
But time and time again we all will say
'If only!'

J Robinson

Veni Lumen Cordium

(Come light of every heart)

Thanksgiving for the wonderful legacy of Diana Princess of Wales. The People's International Celebrity Star . . .

Creative sustainer, source of compassion,
Vitalising young life with aspiration,
Permeating hearts with mutual goodwill;
Kindle zest, your work fulfil.

For world community of justice and peace,
Brighter hopes, clear vision,
nobler deeds increase.
United Nations aid solidarity,
Pulsing in one fraternity.

Unfathomable Cross shares sharpest pains,
The giver of concord, corruption restrains;
All-merciful Lord vanquishes loss and death.
Providence restores human worth.

Hail faith's victor in Heaven's eternal light,
Upward on the pilgrim way where souls unite.
With happy saints joining raptured harmony;
Friends of every race in cheerful company.

Light and assurance when earth's toiling
is past,
Quickens heartbeats with joy evermore at last;
Infinite delight all gloom and doubts remove,
At home in everlasting love.

James Leonard Clough

To The People

I must say be very careful
What you say for these two
small boys not far away
who've lost their mum in a very
sad way. We know we're hurt
and very sad, but just love
Princess Diana's two little boys.

Rest in peace Diana

Barbara Pearson

For Princess Diana May She Rest In Peace

The whole wide world stood still today,
For just one minute's silence.
Thoughts all turned to one we loved.
No time for hate or violence.

You were, to all, a shining light.
A guide through all our sorrows.
Now you're gone, the darkness looms,
O'er all our sad tomorrows.

The tears that flowed, throughout the world,
Would swell the largest ocean.
Causing waves of deep despair.
All crashing with emotion.

We love you, Di, there is no doubt.
Like none, who came before you.
Every face, awash with tears.
A sign, we all adore you.

The nations rise and nations fall
But you will live forever.
Locked within a global heart,
No guns, nor bombs can sever.

M J Plummer

Princess Diana

You were a lovely angel,
With cries of help
You were always there
With a smile
Now you have flown
To God in the sky
I ask 'Oh why
Did you have to die?'
But you will always be remembered
Your heart of gold
Which will never grow old
For it is an everlasting love
For you had so much more.

S A Mullett

Diana, Queen Of Hearts

A nation dumbstruck by the news
Grief shown in all forms, from the Mall to the Mews
For this would be Royal wonder
Who touched the hearts of the people from the north to Down Under
Public response ever great has stunned the world as we grieve
For Diana the Queen of Hearts, sweet reprieve.
Spurned by the Establishment: The Crown
Who thought her just a jester, just a clown
But the bud in the corner has blossomed and grown
Into an English Rose, the fairest, who is fit for a crown.

The whole human race embraced her
She stood by the cause of the outcast, the depraved
She put value to the lives that she saved.
Think of her as the martyr to those causes

Think also of the part you can play.
The only reward that she asked for was a return of the love she selflessly gave.
Our hearts exude our pride in our princess
These eulogies to her will be endlessly made
For she has bridged the span between Royalty and the common man
Truly a saintly Royal with a miracle touch handed on.

She loved us all: we loved her so much.
In search of true love she oft laid her soul bare
A cue for the media to chide her, to tear her to pieces, oft without a care!
Still, she rode out the turbulence and came out on top
Begging for privacy and that the hounding would stop.

A romance did blossom when she found a true knight
He loved our fair princess right through to the end
Her name and good honour he did defend.
She glowed in the sunshine and sparkled at night.
Respect to Diana, the Queen of our Hearts
She is now a legend, an icon from these parts
Respect is now called for, respect is now due
Not just from me but also from you!

A C Yap-Morris

The Spirit Of Love

The spirit of love, flies on the winged heels of Hermes, and circles our world impregnating every inch of our earth, sky and sea, rebounding and entering the hearts of you and me.

No longer will this spirit of love, stay locked behind closed doors, stifled, pushed down, hidden in dark corners

For a princess, Queen of our hearts, has rubbed the lamp of love, and a genie has emerged, setting the spirit of love free forever more, never to return to the confines of darkness, hidden, unseen.

The Princess of Love has set our love free and 'her' spirit will live on always in the hearts of you and me, she has showed us all how to love, to show compassion, to care, how to heal the world, to make it a better place for all humanity.

So when I see a flower, sparkling in the morning dew, I will remember her, a rainbow, a sunset, the rising sun, the sound of children's laughter, in these things I will see her smile, and give thanks that she was given to us all be it just for a while.

And that she has given us a miracle, in that she has spread the winds of change throughout our land.

Princess of Love,
Queen of our hearts,
I will remember you.

May Strike

Diana - In Remembrance

Events can make you laugh or cry
Events can make you wonder why
In a world clouded over with sadness
and strife
You shone rays of hope to many a life
To people troubled with fear and bitterness
You made all of them smile with happiness
Your presence made the earth seem a
happier place
With your charm, sincerity, honesty and grace
For someone who could bring a smile of joy
to the world
To an untimely fate you were ultimately
hurled.

Your death was such a sad event
Your last journey too, when to Althorpe
you went
To an island paradise at the home you
once knew
A place finally away from the photographers'
view
In the heavens, you and Dodi, will eternally
rest
From this world where you both tried
your very best.
Dearest Diana, we will love you forever
As your tireless work brought people together.
To a happier place now Diana departs
Being forever our Queen of Hearts.
So you will never be forgotten,
although you may not be here.
To listen when we thank God
for the time you were here.

Callum Conn

Diana

A wonderful caring person.
Loved by one and all
Gone now, alas but never
To be forgotten at all.

God rest her sweet soul.

A A Usher

Farewell Princess Diana

You were the Rose of England,
The whole world loved you so.
You gave your all to everyone.
It's so sad you had to go.
You're a saint 'Diana',
True royal of Wales, so
Loving, compassionate,
and sad.
Your smiles, hid your
broken heart.
Thousands light a candle,
and say their prayers for you.
I sat and watched your
cortege on TV
With tears, I prayed for
you and Dodi too.
Banks of flowers laid
in tribute, and great
sorrow for our loss of you.
People lined the streets
of London
Crying - 'Farewell Diana.
We will forever remember you.'
You found happiness with Dodi
Tragic it was short-lived.
Now you are together, as
for a little while you lived.
No pressure in heaven from Paparazzi
driving you apart.
So goodbye Princess Diana
Rose of England
God bless your dear heart.

Doreen Petherick Cox

Princess Diana

People loved you,
Praised your every move,
You knew the truth in people's hearts,
You cared about the world,
You loved smiling and fashion,
You were blessed,
You will be sadly missed.

Kenneth Mood

Our Tribute To Diana, Princess of Wales

Diana was our Queen of Hearts,
Forever to remain,
Nothing was too much for her
with no thought of gain.
She visited both sick and poor
she gave hope where none before,
She was taken, to a far-off shore
she can't be with us anymore.
She is with her Maker,
Her spirit now is free,
And as her works, do carry on,
We will, remember, such a one
Who gave inspiration,
when there was none.

SO LET US REMEMBER OUR OWN
QUEEN OF HEARTS,

May she always so remain in our hearts,
No-one could replace her,
Where could they ever start?
You will always be remembered,
Our own Diana, Queen of Hearts.

God bless you, Diana,
As we do,
There will never be another you.

Pennsworth

Goodbye Diana

Everywhere is silent,
No one says a word,
Trying with all our breaking hearts
Not to believe what we have heard,
And minds are filled by darkness,
While eyes are filled with tears,
For she was an echo of an angel's voice,
That will sound for a million years . . .

Paul James Hurrell

A Tribute To Diana

As we watched you carried down the street
our hearts were filled with pain
there was lots of sunshine
and not a sign of rain.
We looked upon your coffin
and couldn't see your face
we knew this was the journey
to your final resting place.

We looked on with numbness
and total disbelief
how do you sum up one's feelings
anguish shock and grief?
The crowds they were enormous
but this wasn't any treat.
Just an air of sadness
and the sound of horses' feet.

Your coffin lay upon the tiles
there were crowds in every pew
our hearts were very heavy
but there was little we could do.

The Prime Minister read the lesson
with dignity and grace
I think there was a tear
on almost every face.

Your brother read the tribute
one we shall remember
On the day the world will not forget
the 6th day of September.
When he talked about your lives together
he sometimes had to pause
and as soon as he had finished
there was deafening applause.

You have now been laid to rest
at your final journey's end
I'm sure the people realise
that they have lost a friend.
As we think and ponder
the awful question why?
Perhaps it's time to bid farewell
'Goodbye Diana, goodbye.'

Dickie Anderson

Dedicated To The Memory Of Diana, Princess of Wales, 1961-1997

You Princess Di were one of us
For there can be no doubts
That you enjoyed just meeting us
When on your walkabouts

And which is why, when amongst us
We loved you to the core
For your thoughtfulness and kindness
Which we shall see no more.

For in life we adored you Di
And our love for you just grew
And now in your untimely death
We still think the world of you

As you were the Princess of our hearts
Each time you were about
And the flowers, cards and tributes now
Confirm this without doubt

For you Di cannot be replaced
As there is just no other
Who we can love as we did you
A caring royal mother

And as the world now mourns for you
With dignity and pride
Your immense popularity
Can never be denied

Because you were to everyone
A bright and shining star
And now forever in our thoughts
This is still what you are

And cherished memories of you
Will never fade away
As sadly, you are laid to rest
On this September day

For when God calls us home to him
He chooses but the best
To share with him a life in heaven
As his eternal guest

And for you Di, until such time
When we shall meet again
I pray that you now truly find
Much peace in his domain

And though your passing caused much grief
For others and for me
My privilege to have written this
For a much missed Princess Di

Who will always be remembered
With affection and much pride
As you look down upon us now
With God there by your side

And though no words will bring you back
They can express our love
And this you have in huge amounts
In heaven there up above

Yet this tribute to a princess
Has given me no pleasure
Though such sweet thoughts of you indeed
Are now all ours to treasure

Yes, cherished memories for us
Of Diana, a true friend
Whose life at thirty-six years old
Would sadly have to end

But for you Di, Princess of Wales
Our love will never cease
And may you with your Maker now
Forever 'rest in peace'.

Arthur Morgan

Diana

Diana the princess in all of our hearts,
We can't come to terms with the way she departs.
We need some answers, I need to know why
All of that week I just sat and cried.
I've got to do something, I've got to be strong
Elton John, now he sung a song
Her two little princes stood very tall
But the Earl Spencer, he said it all.
I haven't had the pleasure of getting up close
Or touching the hand of our English rose,
But my turn will come at the end of my life
When I meet her up in paradise.

Kerry Colton

Beautiful Creations

When in His goodness,
God made this world,
Flowers and plants, birds and bees,
All living things both great
And small, the earthly joys;
He made a woman:
He made the sunshine,
He made the trees,
He made the thunder,
Its power and noise;
When he stood back to view his work,
He then declared with a trumpet call;
She's the most beautiful of them all.
Looked he into the angel's eyes
He whispered softly,
'Next to the beauty of a woman,
Is the beauty of a flower!'
She's more beautiful than my springtime,
More brilliant than my stars;
More heavenly than my sunrise
In the early morning hour.

George Ponting

A Privileged Nation

Years of unhappiness culminated
In divorce, which some people hated.
And Diana really became our Queen
Of Hearts. Loving, gracious and serene
The subject of the world's admiration
But she belongs to us - the chosen nation.

Then she fell in love, was happy, contented
With Dodi. But the fairy tale ended.
She was tragically, cruelly taken away
To find eternal rest and peace we pray
With Dodi, a privileged man, who shared
the adoration
Of a grieving, mourning but privileged nation.

Carol Liddle

A Tribute To Diana
Princess Of Wales, Queen Of Hearts

A princess of style beauty and grace
No-one will ever take her place;

So caring loving and kind
An inspiration to mankind;

She wore her heart upon her sleeve
For us it was so hard to grieve.

Words cannot describe what we wanted to say
The day Diana passed away;

And when she was finally laid to rest
We knew in our hearts she was simply
the best;

Poor Dodi she will never marry
Our thoughts are forever with
William and Harry;

Our loss is Heaven's gain
Rest in peace and suffer no pain.

Pat and Frank Watson

Tribute To Princess Diana

How little did you know that morn,
That you would never see the dawn.
Your life taken away, too young to die,
No-one will ever understand why.

Two young princes William and Harry,
Your two sons that you doted on.
Having to come to terms with grief,
Missing a mother's love and affection.

You were so thoughtful and so kind,
Your warm personality like a ray of sunshine.
Caring for others, easing their pain,
So sadly missed around the world.

The radiance of your smile,
Was like a breath of fresh air.
Now you dwell amongst the angels,
Peace and comfort in God's care.

Joan Craven

Farewell Princess Diana

Thank you for all the good you've done
For the spirits you lifted in everyone
For all the charities, you gave so much
To the sick and dying, a loving gentle touch
A healing, helping hand.
The warmth you showed inside
As a mother, a friend and to the deprived
You are adored throughout the land.

Like in everyone's lives
You had your own sad times
Like the 'landmines' you try to rid
From the press photographers you hid
Following in your every move.
They just wouldn't leave you alone
Looking for that 'picture' or scandal
they could find
Forgetting all the good things you had done
Through your eyes a sparkle glowed
Within a happy heart
A new love in Dodi you found
Through your smile it showed
What was to be a new start
Again the' paparazzi' hound.
Chasing you to a tragic end.
Died together in horrific pain.
The world mourns for you
And can't believe it's happened
Bowed in shame
Who's to bless: Who's to blame?

Our thoughts are with your family
Especially Princes William and Harry
For Dodi, whom you planned to marry.

As they lay you down to rest
In peace, in a flowery grave
We say thank you, for all the love you gave
As the whole nation weeps
Memories of you in their hearts,
will always keep.

Diana the people's Princess
Once again she'll find happiness
With Dodi the one she loves
Both heaven-sent above.
We won't ever forget how much you cared
And from that crash of despair
Will shine an eternal hope
That without you in our world
We will begin to cope.

Now free from life's sorrows
You gave us strength for tomorrow
Farewell our beautiful Princess
Safe now, God Bless.

Rosalind Archer

Diana - Queen Of Hearts

I see your face before me,
Your wonderful infectious smile,
To have you back amongst us,
I'd walk a million miles.
You were the 'people's princess',
with a heart of purest gold.
That gave so much to everyone,
from the youngest to the old.
You did so much for those in need,
like the helpless and the poor.
The starving and the injured, and poor souls
knocking on heaven's door.
Diana, you gave your time so freely,
to charities galore,
So much money raised so generously,
we couldn't ask for more.
The brightest 'star' in heaven,
now shines down, from up above.
To light the world with radiance,
like a beacon glowing with love.
Now your life is over,
no-one else can take your place,
I wish for you to be here,
to wipe the tears from my face.
My heart breaks for you Diana,
for I'll not see you anymore,
I do believe that God was shocked,
to find 'you' knocking on heaven's door.

Patricia Taylor

In Memory Of Diana, Princess of Wales

You were a shining light in our dull lives,
We found you compassionate, caring
and wise.
You, who led a privileged life, were always
aware of those
Who were sick, uncared for, needy,
without homes.
You brought us sunshine amid the daily grind,
We thought your smile was beautiful and your
eyes kind.
To the 'Establishment' you were a much-needed
breath of fresh air,
You tried to instil into your sons the need
to care.
Your love for children always shone through,
We wanted you to find joy and happiness too.
Though unkind words may have appeared in the
press
For public figures it is a penalty to be met.
You will always be remembered throughout the
years,
Over your death will be shed a river of tears
For the world will become a colder,
duller place
Now we can no longer hope to see joy on
your face,
The joy of finding someone to love and
protect you,
The joy perhaps of a gift of a daughter too.
The legacy you have left to your sons I hope will
remain,
That they will try too to lessen others' pain.
Go with God, Diana, and rest truly in peace,
For you at least sorrow, pain and anguish
will cease.

Christine Naylor

Diana -Woman Of The Decade

Diana - what a lady
Kindness in her mind
Children came to love her
Someone pure and kind

Diana - a graceful woman
With her children - always there
Fun to be with - pleasant
A smile, a look, for prayer

Diana - a working woman
For peace, and so sincere
No-one can replace her
The princess we held dear

Diana - our nation's grieving
We cannot understand
Why - oh why - our sorrow
Grips all across our land.

Mary Hulme

Diana

The white stick man we pass in the street
The deaf who do not hear the beat
The cripple wheeled in his chair
The cancer child with no hair
Diana with all her love was there.

Civil wars which seed such strife
The refugee camps, the loss of life
The little kids with extended bellies
Diana acted - we just watched our tellies.

Landmines destroying life and limb
AIDS sufferers thin stark and grim
The old, the frail the very weak
To all did Diana's love speak.

The huntress hunted has broken wings
A sad lament the nation's soul sings
A million bouquets as the tears swell
Each in our own way now bid farewell.

Richard Keller

Queen Of Hearts

Someone stole the light
that could not be replaced
there seems to be a tear
on everybody's face

A golden sun that kissed us all
slow passes out of view
you live on in the hearts
of everyone you knew

Tiny hands you touched
together pressed in prayer
you meant so very much
to people everywhere

The day the earth stood still
together or apart
the special place you fill
Queen of all our hearts.

J Le Fort

A Tribute To Princess Diana
(who died 31st August 1997)

We have lost such a wonderful lady
Who was a Royal Queen in all our eyes,
Now we face the greatest task of all
Of saying all our goodbyes.

She was dearly loved by millions
From the youngest to the old,
Throughout ages she will be remembered
In the greatest story ever told.

Her touch brought comfort to so many,
Her smile would light up the sky,
Everyone who knew her would say,
'That's our Princess Di.'

Her life cut short, too young to die
She left two boys with a broken heart,
To all of us who remember
She was 'Diana, Queen of Hearts'.

Vera Ewers

The People's Princess

A true Princess has passed on by,
and so we ask the question why?

She gave out her heart and her mind,
because she was so sincere and lovingly kind.

She wished the needy to be well,
her dresses, to charity, she even did sell.

She cared for others like no one could,
because she herself really deeply understood.

Helping others was her way,
even those who'd gone astray.

Everything she did she cared,
making sure her love was shared.

To each and all and everyone,
our hearts were emotionally won.

The shocking news has made us numb,
for which we won't be overcome.

We're all saddened with the grief
and in a state of disbelief.

We'll give our love and sorrowingly pray,
because the pain simply won't go away,
but in our hearts she'll certainly stay.

Nichole Jackman

Diana

No words can express the thoughts
that we feel,
Just a silent prayer for the soul as we kneel.
The sense of sadness and loss and distress,
For a princess who was loved, and one of
the best.

The only words which may bring consolation,
She's out of this world free of tribulation.
There is no hell for hell is on earth.
Heaven's the place where she'll find
her worth.

J Stuart

A Special Star Called Diana

God sent a special angel from heaven
That grew up pretty and bright
She cared about the people on earth
And brought them happiness and delight.
Many people felt deep love for her
And loved her dazzling smile
She often used to take the time to
Chat with them for a while.
A place was vacant in God's city
Called Zion
A special call went out the only person
Who could fit it was Princess Diana,
She was the special one without a doubt
A beautiful star now shines in Heaven
As Diana has taken her place
Her beautiful dazzling smile is there,
on her lovely radiant face.

Patricia G Gray

Untitled

We did not go to sleep
We did not even try
For we alone knew that
We would awake and cry

A day filled with sorrow
A night wracked with pain
How could we face tomorrow
Without you once again?

Slowly dawn came
As surely as it would
You had gone to an island
And taken all that was good.

The tears and the flowers
The scents and the smells
Will live within our hearts
Until our own death bell knells.

P J and A M Stemp

Diana

(For Diana, Queen of Hearts, As entered in the Book of Remembrance, St James's Palace, on 2.9.97)

Oh Princess Diana,
Now we have lost you.
You shone like the sun
In Establishment's power.
In our hearts we still see you
In the twentieth century -
The people's Queen - you'll still be.

God bless and guide William
With emergence of destiny
And help us and guide us
To make landmines history.

Doreen King

Diana

Never before, in the whole of my life,
Have I ever witnessed so much sadness
and strife,
I heard the news on that dreadful day,
It was the day that the angels took you away.

You were full of love, compassion and fun,
I just hope God, knows what he has done.
The good work on earth that you have started,
Will carry on though you have parted.

I'll never again, see your smiling face,
You were someone, just too hard to replace.
From where you are, you can see us all,
But I'll see you again, when I get God's call.

R Delmaine

Diana

A gentle touch, a smile so true,
The kindness in her eyes so blue.
She showered the world with happiness.
Our Queen of Hearts, our sweet Princess.
She had her share of sorrow
Her anguish and distress.
No time alone, no privacy,
Hounded by the press
Her last few weeks she found a peace
A feeling of content
Though met with disapproval
Those weeks so precious spent.

Then a sudden tragedy
A disbelieving end.
The loss of a mother
The loss of a friend
The world especially Britain
Stands on common ground
To mourn a lady so unique
No other to be found.

So let us say our last goodbyes
And unite ourselves in prayer
And hand our precious Princess
To Jesus' loving care

Karen Hutchinson

A Beautiful Angel

A beautiful angel from heaven sent
She wasn't given, only lent
Her short time on earth she gave all her love
Her crown is waiting in heaven above
Our gift is her boys we must show them we care
There are bound to be times, they'll be filled
with despair
But look to the sky, boys, to the brightest light
That's your mum Angel Di saying goodnight
What the whole world is saying is perfectly true
She will always look down,
she will always love you.

RIP Diana, eternally.

I Hunter Nock

Diana

There's not a mountain that is hollow,
but if there was, it wouldn't take a year,
for a nation to show its grief and sorrow,
and overflow it with saltwater tears.

A spectrum holds seven colours of beauty,
yet it disappears when the rain subsides,
not even God can stop this prism of duty,
or the cries of we love you, goodbye our
rainbow sky.

Tragedy and heartbreak,
for you, seemed to go hand in hand,
like the ugly duckling on the lake,
too much, too young to understand.

If I could make a wish upon a star,
a stairway to heaven I would build,
to ask the angels why our lives have
been marred,
and question the reason their little sister
was killed.

Today my heart is broken,
a piece of it gone forever,
truer words from me have never been spoken,
for humanity has lost its greatest treasure.

Sweet dreams, goodnight God's child,
with all our love from ground to steeple,
cradled in God's safe hands, sleep in peace
for a little while,
and may eternal bliss be yours,
our princess of the people.

Keith Taylor

The Best Princess

Diana, you were the world's best princess,
We are going to pray for you every day,
And hope you are happy in heaven,
I never met you but I still love you,
Nobody will ever forget you,
You'll live in our hearts forever.

Goodbye Diana

Tehibah Khan (7)

Diana

Now you are gone
The whole world will mourn
You were the only one to save our hearts
Now you're the Queen of Hearts
We all love you
And we will always love you
You are the best
So forget the rest
Now you belong to heaven
We will never forget you
I have never met you but
I still love you.
Now all the country will shed tears
Because you never let our lives
be ruled by our fears.
We won't ever forget you
You are watching us
We will always pray for you
All the luck we have it's from you
Have a good life in heaven
We'll be thinking of you and
We'll be missing you
DIANA.

Osman Khan (12)

Diana

Our special princess, so unique,
with such finesse
You were taken from us, so tragically
We realised too late, how much you
meant to us
You were known to have a genuine handshake
And with outstretched hand
Everyone's heart you touched
Your good work on earth is done
And rewards await you in heaven
Where! You will be crowned, with a jewelled
head-dress
'Cause! After all you were our
special princess

C Marianne Lyons

Tribute to Princess Diana

Dearest Princess Diana
May you forever rest in peace
Knowing that the world over
The people's love for you will never cease
You always had such dignity
A beautiful smiling face
A warm and charming personality
And such amazing grace
You touched the hearts of many
With the things you've said and done
You brought many people happiness
Where sadly there was none.
God must have been short of angels
When He called you to His side
Dearest Princess Diana
We will always remember you with pride.

Ruth Parfitt

A Tribute To Diana

Diana we will miss your smiling face
No-one else could ever take your place
You loved to talk, hold, and touch,
Diana you were loved so much

Come rain or shine you were there
To show the people that you care
Around the world to different parts
You really were the Queen of Hearts

We can wipe our tears away
But in our heart you will always stay
With everyone you shared your love
Now you shine down upon us from above

Diana, what do we do now
You're not here to show us how
You were put to the greatest test
But you turned out simply the BEST.

R Blackbourn

Diana, Princess of Dreams

In the summertime of her life she left us
with only soft memories and tears.
We will never see her again on earth,
the sad fated princess of dreams.
Her passion for children and the homeless
is nothing now but a sweet echo
and a pain in the heart of every one of us.

She died so young, so full of joy at life,
life, that in its fullness was nearly hers
for happiness was not always her friend.
Poor Diana, who having finally found love
after the dark shadows of the past,
died in the midst of that love, doomed
to be a memory forever in our hearts.

Sleep well, Diana, Princess of Wales,
sweet defender of the poor and defenceless.
Rest in peace, stalwart mother and friend
and know that the whole world grieves
for the loss of such a bright and gleaming star.
For like a star, you will forever shine brightly
in the hearts of the people,
Diana, Princess of Dreams.

Jacki Larcombe

Love For A Princess

There's not enough words to really express
What I feel about the loss of our beautiful
princess,
Diana was a beautiful angel in every way,
And I'm going to miss her in my own
special way.
You can see the sadness on the faces of people
passing by;
We are all going to miss our lovely, darling,
Princess Di.
God bless her and keep her,
as an angel on high
We'll never ever forget you,
our Darling Princess Di.

Elizabeth Chuter-Pride

My Tribute To Princess Diana - An Angel In Disguise

There's sorrow the whole world over
In countries far and wide,
Since hearing of the tragic news
That our Princess had died.
Throughout the world, the people,
can reflect as they mourn,
That she was our Queen of Hearts,
our rising of the dawn,
To me you were a picture,
so beautiful to paint,
You were an angel in disguise and you
died a saint.

You were loved by everyone and you
spread that love around,
To the meek, the mild and humble,
Happiness in you they found.
My fondest memory of you is, when you
held the leper's hand,
To give him comfort and ease his pain,
You brought joy throughout the land.
Everyone will miss you, our angel in disguise,
Now you are an angel in God's heavenly skies,
Your smiling face, your clear blue eyes,
your charisma and your charm,
Why did you have to go away,
you did no-one any harm.

You gave hope, love and comfort
to everyone you met,
You were an angel in disguise,
someone we won't forget,
Wake up, sweet Princess,
your Prince waits for you,
For a marriage made in Heaven, spend your
honeymoon there too,
Be a shining star, a guiding light, now your
spirit's free,
Some day that angel in disguise may
come and visit me.
From that little girl who came to be,
part of the Royal charter,
She was an angel in disguise,
And to me she died a martyr.

P Kinton

Diana

The sound of your laughter
Still rings in our ears
A nation united
by a river of tears
We will always remember
we'll cherish, we'll love
An angel taken from us
to heaven above.

So, God bless our Dodi,
who at last brought you joy
Forever watch over
your two beautiful boys
And go now sweet lady,
in peace you'll now rest
Forever in our memory
our precious princess.

Syreeta Muir

No More Smiles

No more smiles.
no more wave of the hand,
no more the gentle touch,
that made you understand
She cared.

No final goodbyes
to those she loved the best.
No more hurting
now she is at rest
and in peace.

But no peace.
Her image bought and sold
in death as in life.
With many stories told
in her memory.

Remembering her,
a million flowers lay on the ground.
Each one a message from the heart
and those who loved her stand around
in silent grief.

Norma Peckston

Diana 1961-1997

Quiet, yet said everything.
Manic, yet she stayed cool.
Followed and tortured by the press, the focus for them all.
She cried alone and let it out when nobody was about,
then, rose again without a doubt.
She's a light,
She's a star,
She's away, and yet not far.
For her there were no barriers, no line she would not cross,
no hand she would not touch,
For all, a terrible loss.
She asked for nothing, and gave herself not stopping for a breath.
Why is it we realise this only after her tragic death?
In life she was hounded and never left alone.
I only pray, for that giving woman,
that she has travelled home.
She deserved more and has gone to find it,
whilst the nation is left to cry,
for the loss of the 'fairytale Princess'
who never said goodbye.

Victoria Coughlan (15)

Diana's Song

You were the music, that made the world sing.
Your loveliness, your beauty, and everything.
You were the rhythm, that beats in our hearts.
Now your passing, has torn us apart.
But the harmony you gave us; will never die!
It'll grow stronger and stronger, as time passes by.

You came into our lives, like some sweet melody.
The hurt and the lonely, you set them all free.
Though Diana, you did not live very long.
The world will never forget: Diana's Song.

Paul King

The Secret Joy

Like a large white moth she flew
Through the dark winter night,
Silent and sorrowful, ready to fight,
Anxious to feel the safety of our light.

Beating her wings at the light of our door,
We did not see, we did not hear;
So near was she, so near, so near,
But her pains were not seen,
nor were her tears

And so she turned back across the
stormy moor
And flew into the darkness and oblivion, sore
From beating in vain at the light of our door,
Not seeing those of us who adored.

On she went, flying, flying, ever trying,
Never crying, till like a candle glow
He shone through her despair.
In the sleeping world, was a friend, not a foe

Round and round the candle she flew
Feeling the happiness she never knew
Until the coming of the morning dew
Saw the inevitable fate of the two.

The moth was dead, the flame too.

RIP Diana and Dodi,

S Aisha Malik (16)

For Diana

Through your 'being' in our world
You have left our world with the legacy of your essence.
That no-one can ever put in a bottle
It is unique to you.

With your existence in our world
You will always be part of our world
You will always be in our world.
Forever

M Comley - (Windsor)

To Diana

To Diana the Queen of our hearts,
Our world has been torn apart.
From the beginning you've shown us compassion,
Your emotions and love you never did ration.
You were always there when it mattered most,
You were always the perfect host.
You were a perfect lady and a perfect mother,
There'll never ever be another.
You gave so very much, and took
nothing back,
You accepted us all rich-poor-white-black.
We never met and that breaks my heart,
You loved us all from the very start.
You tried so hard to do what was right,
Who now will shine that guiding light?
You might not know it but you taught
us so much,
Wherever you went, you left your
healing touch.
You taught us courage, strength, compassion and
how to care,
Now you're gone it makes me angry because it's
so unfair.
You had so much to give and you found your true
love,
At least now you and Dodi are free above,
You are together forever and they can't take that
away,
Amongst the stars, Dodi and you can dance and
play.
Each night I look up and know you're there,
For evermore you'll be in our prayers.
You're not really far if we look in our heart you'll
be there,
Shine, shine, like a sparkling star,
Shine shine so we know you're not far.

Alan Shine

Diana - Queen Of Our Hearts

Now you've gone, we'll never know
The love you had left to give,
To all the needy, sick and poor,
You gave a reason to live.
For others like us whose lives you touched,
I'm sure you lessened their fears,
All that's left now is an empty void,
In which we pour our tears.

The many that loved our Queen of Hearts
Lost someone special.
The day that you departed,
And now we are without exception
Terribly broken-hearted.
We may not see your beauty again,
Or be able to touch you ever,
But of one thing you can be sure,
You will remain in our hearts forever.

Mark Blackledge

You Smiled . . .

When life had lost all meaning
and desperation near
When all paths seemed unending
and motives seemed unclear
When there was nought but struggles
and nowhere was there rest
When every word against us
and every move a test
When living was existing
and anguish stark and bright
When no one seemed to hear us
and pain gave no respite
When faith seemed lost forever
Like trust for fellow men

. . . You smiled with love and gave us hope
and life began again . . .

Norm Whittle

Diana

No, we never met you in person
So why do we feel like we do?
Why do these tears keep on falling
Wishing the news wasn't true.

It's because Diana, we loved you.
Every hair on your beautiful head,
You brought sunlight to everyone round you
And we just can't believe you are dead.

We are all in some way guilty
For your life being taken away.
We all liked to see you dancing
To watch you at work and at play.

But if only we could change things,
We'd do it now, today.
For one more chance, one more glance
And to take our pain away.

But life goes on without you,
This we know is true,
But the world will be much darker
Now that we've lost you.

A million tears, a million more
Can never bring you back.
But you're free at last dear Princess
And we should take comfort in that.

You are where no-one can hurt you,
With Dodi and your father too.
We know that they will love you
The way we'd want them to.

We'll love you till we die Diana,
And no matter what anyone says
You were our Queen, our guiding light
Ever shining, ever bright.

And so we must now say goodbye,
The hardest word, but we must try.
So, thank you Diana, for all that you did
God bless you, God keep you, Goodnight.

Anne Wood

Diana's Prayer

Remember me
Is all I ask
The way I'll remember you
Mourn a while
Taste sorrow
It's what you'll need to do
But love me
Always love me
I need that more than ever
It helped me through
The darkest days
When I thought I'd cry forever

Remember me
Without pity
I'm at peace with myself now
My path is planned
I must move on
Your strength can show me how
No more sadness
No more tears
I'm anchored in your pain
Paint a smile
For my memory
In time we'll meet again

Remember me
In days to come
When the world blocks out the light
I'm with you now
And evermore
Unseen
Not out of sight

Remember me.

Martin Hickman

Diana

Angels are not ours to keep
they're only here on loan,
they're sent to Earth to earn
their wings
that they may then fly home

Diana earned hers quickly
she also found her soul-mate
Much too soon, to our great
loss
they flew up to Heaven's Gate.

Linda Woods

Diana - The English Rose

(Dedicated to Diana, Princess of Wales who was held in deep affection in South Asia)

A touch, a cuddle, a gentle smile,
by a hospital bedside -
you lingered awhile.
Caring for total strangers,
showing compassion -
light from a burning candle
in a hard and unkind world.

You ran like the wind,
a whirlpool of sadness
heartbreak and sheer joy.
William and Harry -
Your two boys,
kept you focused
on the present.
You radiated love
for your kith and kin.

Then came a cruel twist of fate,
on a Parisian night -
a chase, a screech,
it was too late.
They brought you back -
confined, lost forever.
A Princess, known
throughout India and Pakistan,
from an island in the Maldives
to the foothills of Sri Lanka.
The world cried
as they said goodbye
to an English Rose.

Ivan Corea

Diana's Light

A distant echo, a thousand sighs,
Thinking of Diana, tears in our eyes.
She was a light shining so bright,
Died in France in the dead of night,

The country mourns, her people weep,
Diana's light is now God's to keep.
He will caress her in his arms,
Speak of her good, her wonderful charms.

She touched our hearts, filled a void,
Her sudden death has left us annoyed.
We will miss Diana, ever so much,
Her gorgeous smile, her tender touch.

William, our future King, grieves for his mum,
Walking amongst the people,
there's a silent hum.
Harry walks behind his head held low,
Thinking dear sweet Mum,
why did you have to go?

Diana was wonderful she cared with grace,
Loved all of the people whatever their race.
As the coffin goes by, the crying starts,
Diana, so beautiful. Our Queen of Hearts.

Thomas McCartney

William And Harry

I think of you two boys every minute of the day
Your hearts have been broken and it's for you I
will pray
Your mum was so beautiful, loving and kind
I know you are sad that she left you behind
Your mum had the hands we all wanted to touch
She had the smile that we all loved so much
She helped those in need even when she was down
She was like an angel in a big flowing gown
She left so many memories for us all to treasure
And to you two boys she gave so much pleasure
Everyone will miss her happy smiling face
The way she walked was so full of grace
It's hard to see past the pain and the hurt
The tears that keep falling and wetting your shirt
The private moments you all spent together
Will be carved on your minds forever and ever
The body and soul is like a hand in a glove
The soul leaves the body and watches from above
She will always be with you, helping you through
Your loving father will be there helping you too
Then one day you will find the pain has eased
And you will know that your mum would be
pleased
For one star in the sky will shine brighter than
bright
And she then knows her two boys are alright.

Paula Keating

Diana

Diana you were our Queen of Hearts,
Everyone all over the world will miss you,
You helped lots of people in need,
For that you will be praised.
Princes William and Harry are lucky to be
your sons.
And Dodi's lucky to be your friend,
I wish I'd met you,
Goodbye Queen of Hearts.

Aasim Khan (6)

Diana

(Written back in 1980 when the engagement was announced)

At last all doubt is over
an end to Fleet Street tales
The nineteen-year-old goddess
Will wed the Prince of Wales
And all her loyal subjects
Will look on with a sigh
And ask 'Princess of Wales
Is it Lady Di or Dai?'

Steve Smith

An Angel

God lent us an Angel with a heart full of gold
Whose effortless caring, went too long untold.
Your name was Diana, your smile so renowned
In all of our hearts - our Princess was crowned:
Not just of Royalty but common and plain
You touched the whole world - despite
personal pain.
You tended the sick, the poor and the weak
For all of us Di, your actions did speak
Your strength, love, compassion, your endless
caring ways
Brought hope, love and light to our
darkest days.
Then Heaven called you home, saying your work
here was done,
The hearts of the world, you had already won.
You've left us so very much, especially your boys
To follow in your footsteps, to bring further joys.
Tho' you're no longer with us, our sweet Lady Di
Forever you'll shine, the brightest star in the sky.
So rest now Diana, you've done all you can
to better the world - for your fellow man.
You've earned your title, yes, right from the start
You have and always will be
Queen of all Hearts.

Maria Brosnan

Diana

What a sad day was the first of September
A day the whole nation will remember.
A princess and friend who had joy for
a while
Sadly no more will we see their smile.
Flowers, tributes and respect sent by all,
No-one argues with God when he calls.
It was time to go, it was a shame that way,
But unfortunately we don't have a say.
At least they didn't have to make the last
journey alone.
And they'll be remembered when the
flowers are gone.

Margaret Bajai

Diana

A beautiful lady once crossed a field
And stole the heart of a prince and his shield
Her movements were graceful her laughter
so gay.
He just had to stop from going his way.

A fairy tale started and the world waited
to see
The lovely wedding at St Paul's was to be
Diana looked radiant in ivory and pearls
So proud and pretty on the arm of her Earl.

Then the world was overjoyed of the birth
of her sons
But unhappiness followed and the nation looked
glum
The beautiful Princess was in despair
And all that followed wasn't fair

One day out of the blue, happiness came back, for
all to view
But tragedy struck and that was the end
of a beautiful Princess that was only lent.

In palaces and castles the flowers were strewn
about
The colours wereso lovely it would make the
rainbow shout.
The tears in people's eyes were very hard
to bear
To lose our lovely Princess we all did love
and care.

When clouds go rolling by that darken the sky
There is a light that shines forever and it's where
we said goodbye.
That's where Diana is sleeping until
She meets us again one day

So until then remember her as the sunshine
and its ray.

Edna Dedman

Look What We Have Done (Past Tense)

We read the papers every day
and you were never far away.
It seemed you were always there.
Such beauty, though a gift to share.

We paid our pennies, watched your life.
We wished you well, not all that strife.
Your smile enchanted, every time.
They tried to catch it, every time.

The Powers could not understand.
You touched the heart of common man.
The Press they stalked your every move
hunting for the front page news.

Of fox they say, the chase too cruel.
Why did we let them do it to you?
They chased you to the tragic end.
One world, two princes, now orphaned.

Like a diamond on the printed page,
Like a butterfly pinned in a glass case.
Like a rose crafted with artist's knife.
Your beauty shone much brighter
in real life.

We thought they ought to let you be.
We wished you peace, but now we see.
Our silence only helped condone
so they would not leave you alone.

The Paparazzi at your door.
They had your life but wanted more.
Now you're gone, the quiet grows louder.
The silent majority roars with anger.

Too late.

So we must learn.

Good is lost with mere intention.
For right to win there must be action.
Silence sides with creeping evil.
It's time to act,
and now we will.

For Diana.

Chris Blackmore

A Tribute To Princess Diana

God sent an angel, from heaven above
To come down to earth and show, His love.
Her name was Diana, so fair of face
So full of grace.
She helped the sick, and comforted the dying,
Diana was our English rose, and as you know,
You can't pluck a rose all covered in dew,
Without its fragrance remaining with you.
You can't light a candle without its glow
following you wherever you go.
Oh God! What we cannot understand,
Is why you took our angel
So soon, from this land,
Two sad princes you left behind
But perhaps in time we shall see,
Why this was meant to be.
God bless you Diana, wherever you are,
Perhaps you are looking down from above,
Safe in the arms of Dodi, your love.

Anne Thomas

Tribute To Diana, Princess Of Wales

You came from out of nowhere
Thrust into public view
I saw you shyly standing there
A very lovely you

I never got to meet you
I never shook your hand
But I felt as if I knew you
I know you'll understand

And now you've gone away
And Dodi's gone as well
A dark and tragic Sunday
Your loss no words can tell

The world now turns without you
But you are always near
Your love for people was true
We all still hold you dear.

Robert Hamer

Diana

Even though we'd never met
And our lives were worlds apart
You will always be remembered as
'The Queen of People's Hearts'.

I visited your home on that very sad day
My mummy cried and I held her tight
I've drawn a picture of that now, sad place
Though there were flowers, I've drawn it
in black and white.

You will live on forever in all our hearts
I send my love to Wills and Harry too
You were a wonderful mum and princess
The people of the world, will always love you

At least you had finally found happiness
Rest in peace, Diana.

Lisa Parker and Martin

A Poem For Diana

Diana, Princess of Wales
You will always be in our heart
And though you've been laid to rest
We will never be torn apart

You touched the lives of so many people
We will always remember you
The world cannot believe you're gone
But in our hearts we know it's true

My heart goes out to your two boys
Who will always miss you dearly
And though you are far away
They will see your star shining clearly

So now dear Diana, rest in peace
We know you'll be looked after
We'll remember you the way you were
Your sparkling eyes, your loving laughter.

Katherine Macdonald (15)

Diana

Numb with shock, and in a state of total disbelief,
A nation mourned, with one accord, united in its grief,
But, now with body laid to rest, the soul is flying free,
The time for tears is over, and that's how it should be.
For we move on and, though the parting seems so hard to bear,
The grief must turn to gratitude for the part we had to share
Of a life, just lent, who, journey done, moves on to finer things;
We knew the love and now we feel the heartache that it brings
But those who love and leave us would much prefer that we
Can smile and join with them again in happy memory.
Say not goodbye, bid them farewell, although it be in pain,
For there will come a time when we will reunite again.
Commoner or Princess, many come to serve,
May the Lord reward them with the peace and the joy that they deserve
And may our hearts be joyful for a gift that was God-given
When an angel touched us for a while and was then recalled to Heaven.

Carol Banks

Thank You Diana

Thank you Diana, for all your smiles,
They shone so bright for miles and miles.
Thank you Diana, for the touch of your hands,
They were soothing to all from many lands.
Thank you Diana, for those special words,
They were inspiration to all who heard.

Linda J Russell

Diana

Princess Diana, kind and gentle,
From our midst you've gone away,
But you've left us many memories,
To talk about throughout each day.

We will talk about your beauty,
And of course your lovely style,
And your eyes as bright as diamonds,
And your ever-winning smile.

We will talk about your goodness,
And the kindness you have shown.
To the under-privileged people,
And to those who felt alone.

We will talk about your own life,
Which held troubles hard to bear,
At times you could not hide your sorrow,
Your tears just asked 'Does no-one care?'

In the short life you were given,
You enriched our world with love,
And now we join in prayer together,
May you rest in peace with God above.

Mary Brady

The Bereavement

How sad I was when you passed on,
Diana, I miss you more each day,
Fond memories, I look back upon,
You were my guideline in every way.
I see your lovely face in the flowers;
Roses, lilies, make me think
I am lost and must while away the hours,
So, pen to paper brings me to the brink.
New lives, your children grow
Bring hope and talents, inherited I know.
I cry no more, time passes on,
Dear Diana, I think silent thoughts upon.

Joyce Mary Brodmann

Unequalled Loss

There was no pain, there was no grief.
The sun still shone.
There was no rain, no disbelief.
She was not gone.
Not yet.

There was no crime.
There was no blame.
There was no time.
There was no shame.
Not yet.

There were no tears.
There was no loss.
There were no fears
No blemished gloss.
Not yet.

There was no theft,
Nothing snatched.
We weren't bereft
Of one unmatched.
Not yet.

There was no shade
There were no showers.
Still moments made
the timeless hours.
As yet.

There were no cries.
No hurt endured.
No need for lies.
Nought unassured.
As yet.

Slowly the healing hands of time
begin to turn.
Time enough for all the tears
that can be cried.
Time to let us show that we can earn
The love and years she never denied.

We cannot meet our debt.
Not yet.

Jesse W Walton

Remember

Who is this lovely lady
We all love, so very much
Most people never met her
Others, gifted by her touch

The path of life she walked down
So endless in her aim
To rid the world of senseless things
That hurt and cause much pain

Who is this lovely lady
That everybody knew
The smile we saw so often
Turned grey skies into blue

With endless acts of kindness
And ever loving ways
Her love flew like a peaceful dove
Making people happy
Just by giving love

Alone, the world she travelled
Crossed seas and barren lands
The want to comfort people
To talk or just hold hands

We know your boys will follow
In footsteps that you've made
For they loved you dearly
And all your love is saved

Who was this lovely lady
No-one knows for why
In heaven on earth remembered
Everybody loved you
Your name will never Di

Ernest Tomlin

Diana - The People's Princess 1961-1997

A myriad flickering candles
Glimmered upwards to the sky
As a nation came together
To say a last 'Goodbye'

To a princess they had come to love
Throughout her adult years
Through her triumphs and her traumas
Her happiness and tears.

Her celebrated royal marriage
Her mothering of two boys
Her ordeal of a royal divorce
Her sorrow and her joys.

As she blossomed in her beauty
We saw her caring work unfold
As she touched the lives of millions
Through the sick, the young, the old.

She was the nation's brightest star
A light of charity and love
A legacy she shares with all
Blessed by Our Lord above.

We saw the sweetness of her smile
We saw the gentleness of touch
And portrayed in our hearts
A face we loved so much.

We saw compassion in blue eyes
We saw humanity at best
We saw graciousness and strength
Now our princess lies at rest.

In perfumed bowers of flowers and blooms
Words of longing and remorse
But for those who loved and were beloved
Death is but a pause.

June Pledger

An English Rose

Her endurance did but fill our hearts
this angel of the mist
Our soul does weep for one so young
Our body no more of bliss

Her smile did grace our humble thoughts
this life that lay so rare
Now for us no more to see
Like God she still will care

Another star will shine above
To light our darkest paths
While she sleeps in absent thoughts
Our body and soul will fast

Though our loss her memory reigns
In us in high esteem
We can rest like her at night
Forever in our dreams

Sleep O pretty one sleep
For memories there do lie
Heaven above embalms the soul
Let not the darkness contrive

The spiritual air shall bless her peace
As her eyes occlude to rest
There do she abide but not alone
For he shall be her guest.

W Beavill

In Thoughts Of You, Diana, Princess Of Wales

The sadness of losing you is impossible to bear,
We turned for a moment, you're no longer there.
Your compassion and beauty always shone
through.
Come to us in our dreams,
We'll always be thinking of you.
We watched you bloom from bud to flower,
Your leaving, too hard to devour.
Diana, our Princess - our Special Friend,
Oh! What an Angel God did send.

Joan Fowler

Princess Diana's Visit To Bolton Hospice

We all waited in anticipation
To see a princess loved by the nation.
School children with a small Union Jack.
Wonderful memories they will take back.
Policemen stood so smart and proud.
There was no trouble with the crowd.
On a mobile phone we heard one say,
'The advance party has just left Topp Way.'
The weather was chilly, though it didn't rain.
The sun peeped through now and again.
A car drew up - who would it be?
We craned our necks to try and see.
Officials and dignitaries including the Mayor.
Everyone was delighted to be there.
There was even a crew from German TV,
Who asked why Diana we had come to see.
Two ardent supporters then gave their views.
They may even be on the German news!
Some more limousines - was she here?
The crowd gave out a rousing cheer!
Diana alighted, dressed in pink.
Beautiful and charming, as we think.
Into the hospice - a most worthwhile cause.
By each patient's side she took time to pause.
With staff and relatives she would stay to chat.
So very caring; then after all that
Outside for a walkabout - shaking hands
with the crowd.
She shook my hand warmly - I felt rather
proud.
Continued down the line - then sped away
To carry on with the rest of her day.

Carol Duxbury

The People's Princess

Diana you're gone but your memories remain
In some little way this helps ease our pain
We never would have dreamt you'd leave us
like this
I know one thing for sure you'll be sadly missed
I hope you're in peace where you've gone
In the hearts of your people you'll always live on.

Heather McCann

End Of A Fairy Tale

A
light
was
extinguished
in Paris today,
Queen of Hearts
but never
Queen for a day.
A tragic ending
of doomed fairy tales
Light a candle
in memory of
Diana - The
Princess of Wales.

What then of fame - what of renown
tho' the Princess was divorced from the Crown -
What tragedy for her beloved Royal sons
William and Harry
our heartfelt condolences go to all of her family.
We'll miss her compassion - a personality
remarkable
Life will be dulled without her vibrancy -
her sparkle.
We mourn her now - the tie we'll not sever
She'll live in our hearts for ever and ever.

Lucy Green

A Poem For Diana

God was strolling around Heaven above,
Looking for a new angel who knew how to love,
Looking down to Earth he saw a star
That shone so bright and reached so far.
Your time on Earth had come to an end
God only put you out on lend,
He wanted you back in his own land,
It was time to give God your cherished hand,
We'll miss you Di
Everyone will,
You'll make a marvellous angel,
Always remembered.

J Abernethy

Diana

You touched so many.
You cared so much,
You lifted people's hearts,
You made us smile,
You made us cry,
You even made us laugh.
So many weep,
You weren't to keep,
And oh, so many flowers.
To pay respect and sign their names,
Your people queued for hours.
You shared your love with everyone
All around the world,
And all that love comes flooding back
As this tragic time unfurls.
Forget you Diana, we will not,
Our memories will go on and on,
For all the good you did for us
Your loved ones will be strong.
We'll light a candle in remembrance
And will do so every year,
Nobody can hurt you now,
So rest and have no fear.

C Young

Perfume In The Air
Flowers For A Princess

I still recall the perfume in the air
When I was there.
Sincere expression of a public grief
Beyond belief.
The anger and immeasurable pain
That still remain.
Her caring for the lost, with natural style,
That lovely smile.
Devoted love surrounding her two boys,
Her hopes and joys.
The feeling we have lost a special friend
Will never end.
I still recall the perfume in the air
For I was there.

Irene J Goldsmith

Thank You Diana

I didn't know you
But I thought I did
Your feelings for us
You never hid.

You made it clear
From the very start
All that you did
Came from your heart.

Two boys you have left
They must wonder why
Their beautiful mother
Had to die.

We are united in grief
But we feel so alone
God needed you more
For he called you home.

Thank you Diana
We'll miss you forever
Can we hope to replace you?
No . . . Never.

Lisbeth Webb

Princess Diana
HRH - Her Royal Heaven

I cannot write the words or say
The way the world feels today,
We couldn't believe it when we were told,
You were taken from us with your heart of gold.

No one will ever take your place,
Your smile, your warmth, your loving embrace.

God has taken you into His care
We hope you and Dodi find peace there.
You both have gone to Heaven to rest
We all know God takes the BEST.

M Duck

No Matter What

You will always be in our hearts,
no matter what.
You will never be forgotten,
no matter what.
Your sons will always be looked after,
no matter what.
We'll always be thinking about you,
no matter what.
We'll make sure your sons don't get tortured by the press,
no matter what.
Your memory will always be cherished,
no matter what.
We will always grieve,
no matter what.
You will always be our Queen of Hearts,
no matter what.

Farid and Saeeda Khan

Diana

As we see her coffin
On our television screen
We celebrate the life of Diana
A Princess but never a Queen.

She would always cuddle the sickly child
Hold hands with anyone with AIDS.
A loving mum to Wills and Harry
Her memory I hope will never fade.

But the press made her life a misery.
Just to make the newspaper pay.
If only they had left her alone a bit
Things might be different today.

But Diana was Queen in all of our hearts
May she forever rest in peace.
May God look after Prince William and Prince Harry
And her charity work continue and never cease.

Jenny Bosworth

A Nation's Salvation

On the day of your final journey, when all the world stood still
From the corners of each Kingdom they came to bid you their farewell -
And as the nation's feelings are an emotion that united stand as one
Overwhelming is the silence because their dear Princess has now gone;
Your care was for all God's people, you saw their sadness behind their smiles,
And happiness you gave them, for you made each one feel worthwhile -
Now all the nations mourn you and it seems dark without your light
Because with your wisdom and courage many battles did you fight;
Cherished and always remembered from a great love that travels around
And on this day of your final journey - not one of us should make a sound;
As now that you have 'passed away', then also as our time will pass
For our world in this life to forget you is a seemingly very hard task;
But remembering you is so very easy, because like a saint you became
'The World's Princess' is believed by all of mankind to be a well-deserved name;
'May our memories from the essence of your vibrant personality blessed with a love only true
Paint the grey areas of our nation and world with wonderful colours and fill hearts with virtue';
For you have restored faith in all human kindness, not only God's loving creation -
Diana you became a salvation for the nation, now you are the nation's salvation.

Sarah Jane Deacon

The Day The World Cried

Oh, how we cried when we heard our Diana had died,
The princess of the people, queen of all our hearts,
Gone from us forever, now we are apart.
Oh, how we cried.

If only it had been a nightmare,
So many mourning people and children everywhere,
We queue to write our personal thoughts and lay flowers to show we care
Like a sea of petals and lace,
The people came to say goodbye
It's become a special place.
Oh, how we cried.

Now there's a lump in my throat so big I may choke,
When my little son Adam said 'Di not wake up no more, dead,'
Then when a clip from '93 was shown on TV
'Look, Mummy, Di wake up, Di okay'
He really doesn't understand you see, he's only 3.
Oh how we cried.

Now Diana's young sons alone without their Mum,
Oh God what has the world become?
No more cuddles, kisses and big hugs,
The two young princes have lost their special love,
Oh, how we cried.

No more cameras or intrusions in your life today,
Our shining Star suddenly taken away.
Rest in peace, the world's Princess,
As God only takes the best.
Till we meet again one day
The day the world cried.

Tracy Maureen Claydon

So Gentle

So gentle a Princess,
with compassion that's true.
A heartfelt emotion,
that's indicative of you.

So patient with others,
your love shone through.
Your own pain and suffering,
was kept only to you.

So loving in expression,
in word, a simple deed.
Just a smile or a touch,
was all that they'd need.

So kind . . . oh so kind,
in all that you do.
With gentleness, compassion,
I want to be like you.

My heart broke in two
on the day that you died,
The angels in heaven?
Yes I'm sure that they cried.

But I take comfort in the knowledge,
that I know where you've gone.
To heaven . . . because that's what
all the other angels have done . . .

Paula Baynes

A Much-Loved Princess

Princess Diana we know you are gone,
But your memories will still be with us.
You're smiling down from heaven above,
While we pray for you,
You are the best thing in our lives,
And we will never forget you for what you have done for us.

You will be missed,
People all over the world love you.
Goodbye Princess

Jibran Khan (9)

Queen Of Hearts

A caterpillar plucked from obscurity
With naiveté of a young child
Now enters a world so different
With responsibilities beyond dreams so wild.

A life so different and new
Not knowing what fate has in store
Someone who gave so much
And then gave a little more.

The caterpillar evolves into a wonder
And the world stared on in awe
As the butterfly blossomed and the
Queen of Hearts we saw.

In our hearts we captured her
And her love she did give
But only when unconditional love returned
Did she fail to live.

When one so loved is taken away
Maybe we should join one another
And return the love she gave to us
To two boys who lost a Mother.

Andrea Brisley

O Lovely Princess

O' lovely Princess, now you have left us,
Everyone will make a fuss.
O' lovely Princess, we will cry deep inside for you,
We will always be thinking of you.
O' lovely Princess you have left the whole world upset,
Most of whom you never met.
O' lovely Princess, everyone will miss you and
your lovely smile,
Which could be seen for over a mile.
O' lovely Princess, now we will all mourn,
And want you to be reborn.
O' lovely Princess you will live inside our hearts,
Even when we're playing darts.

Tehmeena Khan (13)

A Tribute For The Princes

I look at your face,
I see a warmth there.
The rosiness of your cheeks,
The gold strands upon your hair,
The beautiful smile, your stance full of grace.
For Princess Diana - your Mother,
lives on in your face.

Cry if you want to, your pain you must share
For your loss is felt widely
Too much for two so young, to solely bear.

Seek comfort in your family
Seek pride from your Mother's grace
You are the children of an Earth Angel
Whose hard work for charity, brought a
Smile to the Nation's face.

You are Diana's sons. Let her strength
and love help you through.
Seek comfort with the knowledge that your
Mother would have sacrificed anything to
share a longer life with you.

RIP Diana.

Love from Tracy Brightman and family

To Diana - Our Lost Princess

Your time with us was all too short
You did not have the time to do
All those things you wished to do
But you lit the path and showed the way
So we could follow and achieve one day
The hopes and ambitions you held so dear
And bring hope and comfort to those that fear.

If come the dawn of a bright new tomorrow
We can create a world devoid of sorrow
Then, Princess, despite the heartaches
and the pain
Your earthly time will have not been in vain.
So look down from the stars on high,
And forgive all those who made you cry.

Gwen Liddy

Diana

You only wanted to find love
and longed for happiness.
We watched as on your wedding day
you dazzled in that dress.

You'd lived the dream of every girl
by marrying your prince.
The 'happy ever after' part
has sadly ended since.

The world demanded you each day.
Life wouldn't be the same.
There was a private side to you
that really hated fame.

You sought the chance to be yourself
and had the common touch.
You met the poor and soothed the sick
with smiles that meant so much.

The mother love within your heart
was always to the fore.
You had the love of your two sons
and millions, millions more.

You were the Queen of people's hearts
and part of everyone,
and now so tragically a cloud
has passed across the sun.

Our hearts go out to all who grieve.
We're praying for them too.
Diana, may you rest in peace.
We will remember you.

John Christopher

Dodi And Di

The gates of heaven opened wide,
The angels stood there side by side,
Dodi then whispered to Di,
Come on darling, let's go inside.

Christine Harvey (14)

In Loving Memory Of Diana, Princess Of Wales 1961-1997

Memories are a keepsake, treasured all life through.
Ours are very precious because they are of you.
A place in our hearts will always be kept for the Queen of Hearts we'll never forget.
As the years go by memories of you will never die.
Time passes and fades away but the memories of you will always stay.
As each day dawns then starts anew, as it closes we think of you.
In between no matter where in our thoughts you're always there.
We'll think about you often we talk about you still.
You haven't been forgotten, by us you never will.
We think of you today, no words can tell,
The loss of the nation a while ago was hard for us to show.
Your passing comes with much regret it's a day of our lives we'll never forget.
The greatest treasure we still retain is your angelic face in a picture frame.
Among the tears and heartache we all had to suffer.
We're glad you chose to be our Queen of Hearts because there will never be another.

Sue Chapman

For All Eternity

(For Diana, The Princess of Wales)

You were the light of the World
Such beauty to behold
You have flown and gone to sleep
And now the World doth weep
In the Heavens far away
Where all the angels play
Is where you will always be
For all eternity.

Nicholas Fletcher

Diana

On the 31st of August
We shed a million tears,
Because we lost our princess
Of only thirty-six years
God sent her down from heaven
To love the old and young,
To care and help the people
As many hearts she won.
With her kindness and her courage,
She helped us all to see
How one can make a difference
And how loved someone could be.
Her beauty and a sense of style
Was watched the whole world through.
To everyone she was a saint
Someone we wished we knew.
To us she seemed so human
Her feeling she let show
She was a perfect mother,
Why did she have to go?
I think her soul was perfect
That's why she couldn't stay
God called her back to heaven
Though we'll miss her every day.
We never will forget you
You'll have eternal rest
Although the pain's too much to bear
God obviously knew best.
Forever young and beautiful
Your work will carry on
And heaven will be a finer place
We know that's where you've gone.
So goodbye our Queen of Hearts
We know you're not alone
With other saints and angels
And a new love of your own.
If tears could build a stairway,
And memories a lane,
We'd walk right up to heaven,
And bring you down again.

Rachel Yetton

6th September 1997
A Tribute To Princess Diana Of Wales

To understand the reason why
Our gracious Princess had to die
In such a way to make all nations cry
Caught almost everyone's eyes.

The blind the sick of every race
Could hear or see about our princess' fate
All in tears and sorrow too
It is hard to know what to say and do.

Lots of people kneel in prayer
For the Princess of Wales we love so dear
Lepers or AIDS, minefields as well
Our Princess of Wales covered them well.

In charities beyond compare
Each one of them received fair share
Her radiant smile we shall never forget
And millions of flowers our Princess did get.

No-one will ever know how Lady Diana felt
When lonely at times in the place where
she dwelt
Her love and affection for her two sons
Has always been there since their lives began

Her brother Earl Spencer and sisters as well
And their mother said all the words that a
tribute can tell.
With hearts full of sorrow and tears as well
Our Princess' tribute was read so well.

After the tribute from outside the Cathedral
Came loud applause heard in the Cathedral
The silence was broken with love
and devotion
For a loving Princess loved from ocean
to ocean.

Goodbye to our Princess of Wales
Along with all those beautiful tales
About all the good deeds which you
have done
And giving lots of people and children lots of
love and fun.

William and Harry our two young princes too
Will always love and remember you
For all the good things that you did all over
the world
And the mother that you were a real 'Queen of
Hearts'.
To all your family which touched our hearts.

Farewell to our Princess of Wales and
Queen of Hearts too
And for all good work which you did do
But most of all just being you,
'a candle in the wind'.
God bless you and keep you Princess Diana
for ever and ever.

RIP

Leslie Blamire

Our Beautiful Queen Of Hearts

You were our light and guiding star
People loved you from near and far
You had a radiance that outshone the rest
To us you were the very best

You were there for the needy
Whether young or old
They felt a warmth from you
As you were not afraid to hold

The sick and the dying
You held to your breast
They felt your radiance
Like they had just been blessed

Your thoughts were for others
We all know that you cared
You are our Queen of Hearts
Because your love you shared.

And now you are gone
And no more to be seen
Heaven's gained an angel
And we have lost our Queen

Our beautiful Queen of Hearts

Sylvia O'Reilly

Ode To A People's Princess

Why do I feel such dark despair,
Princess of Hearts, you are not there
To comfort those in pain and need,
No-one to take your place, indeed.

Your gentle touch, your heart so true,
Innocence and love were all you knew,
Who else will bring your tender touch
To two young boys you loved so much?

Your life at times, filled with despair -
For all our love we were not there
To tell you of the joy you brought
To all of us, in a life so short.

There is no comfort here for me
Expect hope that in Eternity
You find the peace that you did crave,
That led you to your untimely grave.

Goodbye Princess, so full of love,
Sleep peacefully with God above.

Jill Silverman
for the Silverman family

Diana, Princess Of Wales

A day to remember
The 6th of September
So many people came to mourn
The most beautiful princess ever born

Lady Diana is her name
Her love for our country was not in vain

Your name will live forever in our thoughts
For the joy and caring you have brought

As you are finally laid to rest
Peace be with you always
You are the best.

Good night and God Bless

Lady Diana, England's Princess.

Christine Read

To A Princess

Goodbye Diana OUR Princess,
Your heart was filled with kindness,
You reached out and touched those in pain,
You even touched those who were lame.
You sat the children upon your knee,
You travelled for miles across the sea.
You sat with the people and let them talk,
Most of them were unable to walk.
You married Charles when you were young,
And now unfortunately, your time has come.
William and Harry have been so brave,
On the big day they weren't expected to wave.
The people mourned and lay flowers down,
Upon every face there were tears and a frown.
On Saturday the 6th of September,
everyone stood still,
Diana everyone loved and worshipped
and everyone always will.

God bless Diana.

Stacey Buchanan (14)

Diana

Diana, Diana why did you go?
Did not you know we loved you so?
Your beautiful smile
Your lovely face
Your whole body was full of grace
You were unique
You were our queen
The likes of whom no-one had ever seen
What will we do, what will we say
Without you, to help us face each day?
Our great loss, is Heaven's gain
But the world will never be the same
A light's gone out, but we must all try
To reach you in your home up high
So we will hug, we shall smile
And maybe in a little while
The world will be a better place
Because of you.

Iris Allen

In Memory Of Diana Princess of Wales

The pain and the sorrow that is felt in our hearts
The shock and the disbelief
No-one could imagine the sadness we'd feel
As the nation unites in its grief.

Princess Diana has gone up to heaven
A Queen in her own right
No-one will ever come to terms with the shock
Of what happened on that dreadful night

Her life was so tragically taken
Why now? As she started to live
She had finally found herself happiness
Of which she had so much to give.

She was thoughtful, kind and considerate
And our hearts she did deeply touch
She was genuine and caring
We will miss her ever so much

We think of her family, her Harry and Wills
And our love to them we extend
We'll never forget our Diana
A true lady right to the end.

Marion Dawn Priestley

Diana - So Beloved

That beauteous face,
Those eyes full of compassion,
A smile so warm and gentle
No one can take your place.

For your boys we feel such
Special pain,
So many hearts are broken,
From Heaven guide us all with
Your love,
We have lost our precious Lady,
A Nation ne'er the same again.

Mary Lewis

Your Light

The night the Lord put out your light
The furthest star shone ever bright
And as we look to skies above
With hearts of sorrow and with love
We search inside to ask God why
Why He thought it best you die
Perhaps your life was heaven-sent
And God's took back the life He lent
The reasons we will never know
But sleep assured we loved you so.

From all of those you left behind
You fill our thoughts, distract our minds
The grief, the sorrow oh so real
Cannot express the hurt we feel
And as we think of your fair face
We remember you and your sweet grace
At every dawn of every day
We think of you in a special way
For even death could never part
Or take away our Queen of Hearts.

Julie Doran

Ours

Touching hands.
Holding arms.
Were the trademark
Of her charms.
Eyes like stars in pools of blue
Radiant smile for you and you.
What will we do without our Di
Tears still flow from my eyes.
But as I wipe them away,
I hear a voice
So sweetly say.
'Don't pine for me, I know one day
I'll see you all.
So let me lay
In rest and peace.'
And now I know, oh how
We loved 'Diana' so.

Florence Brice

Diana, Princess Of Wales 1961-1997

She was beautiful, compassionate and full of love,
her innocence was there for all to see.
She left the nation breathless on her royal wedding day,
in her diamonds and her dress of ivory.

A princess who was vulnerable, with tender dreams,
a freshness blowing like a summer breeze.
Fragmented by the protocol in time her heart would break,
although she tried so very hard to please.

Drowning in bewilderment she made her stand,
and to the world outside she was a star.
She touched the heart of everyone with sympathy and care,
and gave her all to troubles near and far.

What magical enchantment had surrounded her,
what moments of delight she had to give.
Her smile was like a beacon to the lonely and the lost,
And gave the sick the hope and will to live

But now the light has gone, no glimmer left to shine,
extinguished in a land across the sea.
A nation is in mourning for the princess that they loved,
who will live forever more in history.

Rene McDermott

Star

The brightest star that shines above,
Is called Diana, the star of love.

God loaned her to us, for a little while,
To help us through life, with her beautiful smile.

This world will be a much sadder place,
Without the glimpse of her lovely face.

But we thank you Lord for her charm and grace,
That melted the hearts, of the whole human race.

Now the brightest star that shines in the sky,
Will be with us forever, our beloved Princess Di.

Catherine R Smith

A Tribute To The Queen Of Our Hearts

You enriched our lives with your presence
And the love and care you displayed,
You have left us all with memories,
Too precious to ever fade.

You would embrace the sick and the needy,
Your smile could brighten the darkest night,
You showed the world who was suffering
And asked for help in their plight.

You inspired us all with your sparkle,
Your naturalness, your care, your touch,
I wonder if you knew, Princess Diana,
How we loved you so very much.

Our nation has lost a Princess,
Your sons have lost a best friend,
There is no sense or reasoning in
Why your life should tragically end.

An ocean of tears have fallen,
Floral tributes are being laid,
In the length and breadth of the country,
Millions of people have prayed.

The world wasn't ready to lose you,
But in a place that our eyes can't see,
You have been granted eternal life,
And from suffering you'll always be free.

We are privileged to have lived in your lifetime,
What more is there left to say,
Except we will miss you Princess of the People,
More than words could ever convey.

Joyce Sprason

A Guiding Star For Our Nation

On the first of July, nineteen sixty one,
A beautiful guiding star was born.

Descending to earth, she shone on our nation,
Spreading rays of love, compassion and inspiration.

We embraced this star, and followed her light,
A country transfixed on such a celestial sight.

Yet to be modest and unassuming was her only aim,
And to spread the human message, is the reason why she came.

So proud was this nation, to accept her common touch,
But, we knew she was special and loved her so much.

As the years progressed, and her radiance had grown,
She became admired by many, if only she had known.

But, on the 31st of August, nineteen ninety seven,
This nation lost our star as she was taken back to heaven.

Who could have imagined, the power of this being,
To affect every one of us in the ways which we have seen.

United in grief, our land became one,
Shocked to believe our beautiful star had gone.

But so powerful was this presence, her light will never fade,
Her warmth is in our hearts.
The warmth DIANA made.

Julie Leonovs

A Tribute To 'The Queen Of Hearts'

You lived your life, with so much potential,
You travelled the world, your love so remarkable,
Your name defined hope, 'Queen of Hearts',
Your life has ended, before it could start.

Your work so tireless, now you're laid to rest,
An ambassador of freedom, you were simply the best,
Now the world is weeping, a nation filled with grief,
Touching the lives of many
a fresh summer breeze.

Problems were down to earth,
a candle in the wind,
Two children seek an answer, losing a mother and a friend,
No one can comprehend, and you will never know,
Just how much you meant to us,
your memory shall ever glow.

Simon D Cook

A Tribute To Diana

In a darkening world your candle burns
Reflecting realms of peace
A beacon lighting paths of joy.
A glow . . . you have released.

Into way beyonds your hands have reached
And into the extremes,
Stirring the pillow of our hopes
And colouring all our dreams.

You scrolled for us a fairy tale
Following throughout the years
Alas the ending now is scarred
By grief and sorrowed tears.

Malcolm Wilson Bucknall

Our Queen Of Hearts

Our Queen of Hearts has passed away
But in our hearts she'll always stay
She helped the poor and all in despair
A unique lady remembered everywhere
A wondrous love she showed us all
Around the world she played her role
Angelic charms, giving endless attention
Remembered to all with love, not to mention
Wills and Harry her two loving boys
Who filled her heart with love and joy
Who feel the pain from the loss of their mum
Our hearts go out to them one by one
Our English Rose with the radiant smile
Who captured our hearts from far and wide
Diana we love you from all over the world
Now gone from us to God's return
Our Queen of Hearts you'll always remain
The English Rose forever to reign.

Jacqui Comeau

Diana

The world's greatest star
You helped all of those around you
No matter how near or far
The help you gave to those in need
Shone out like a sparkling star
You brightened the lives of others
Their faces shone so bright
Even through a dreary day
They brightened up at night
I am sure your work will be continued
After this our saddest day
With William and Harry. We are with
Them all the way.
You will never be forgotten
In the country and afar
God Bless You forever
Diana our brightest star.

George Moneypenny

Diana

There's so much to say
there as you lay
Your soul must be tendered
as it is sacred today
We mourn your fate
that was determined by some
Your heart was full of grace
and your status was grander
to us your disciples.
The people will change of this day
and stamp out the vile,
reap out the juices of fair game
You did so much good
with style and heart
which will not be forgot.
We'll never be apart,
the world is at a halt
mourning for you this day
In our hearts you will always stay
So rest in peace
our Princess Grace
for you were the cream of
the human race.

Helen Vesey

Poem For Princess Diana

Diana you are the Queen of my Heart
So suddenly why did you have to part?
When you look down with your smiling face
You will see that no one will ever take
your place.
The pain and sorrow is too hard to bear
Myself and others will always care
The tears I've shed could fill the sea
It's like I've lost a part of me
Although now you are able to rest
I will miss you Diana, you were the best.

Rest in Peace
our Queen of Hearts.

C Wilcock

Sleep Children Sleep

(Dedicated to the memory of Diana,
Princess of Wales and Dodi Al-Fayed)

Sleep Children Sleep,
This earthly night is over,
And we are left alone,
Within our hearts to wonder.

Sleep Children Sleep,
Returned to God, His treasure,
You gave the world your love,
And gave the world such pleasure.

Sleep Children Sleep,
Hand in hand together,
Always in our prayers,
And in our hearts forever.

Sleep Children Sleep,
And whilst the world is weeping,
Your souls will be as one,
Forever in God's keeping.

Mike Smith

Diana - Princess Of Wales

So sorry for the loss
Of our beautiful Princess,
She radiated love
Like none other could possess
She's died much too soon,
I can't believe she's gone
Our beautiful Diana,
Where did it all go wrong.

Our world has lost an angel,
But her soul lives on elsewhere,
You have been taken from us early
Because God wants you over there.
May you rest in peace Diana,
Your good work here is done,
You will be loved and missed forever
By all and everyone.

Julie Struggles

Inspiration

Today when grief is rife,
In this land of ours.
When the palaces of the capital,
Are all, bedecked by flowers.
I see a new thing happening,
For once the world is one.
As we share such great emotion,
For a Princess who has gone.

Her life though prematurely taken,
Cannot have an end.
For all the seeds she's sown,
For broken hearts to mend.
And though we all grieve deeply,
Let her legacy grow.
For still there is so much of her,
For each of us to know.

She was pure inspiration,
She has touched so many hearts.
Even when sorrow enveloped her,
She still played her part.
For she knew of God's goodness,
Submitted to his plan.
Learned from her emotions,
To benefit fellow man.

Janet Parry

Princess Diana

This is a peace giving
to Princess Diana
our beautiful one
with great power
She gives her heart to everyone
to loads of people with none
She did not deserve to die this way
I wish you love in all I say.

Abé Struggles (10)

Loss Of A Princess

When one loses that special person
Hurt and pain, crying, being uncertain
Frustration unable to control the loss
Keeping one's mind active to be the boss
Pain will not abate or go away
But in time, eventually heal one day
Two people in love, gone together
Now at peace, floating like a feather
A Nation consoling its grief
All together in total belief
That God looks after all those who care
Bringing all people close to share
A special moment in history over our land
Peace should reign like a wand or hand
Helping all those in need of help in a time
Unable to control pain and suffering to climb
That mountain of a healing period, past
Coming to terms with it all at last
Final journey to her resting place
All of us walking at a slow pace
Never to be forgotten in history for less
Diana, The Nation's, loss of a Princess.

Anthony Higgins

Diana

You are gone now gone from our view
But Oh Diana how the people loved you
No one can hurt you anymore
They say you understood the poor
You had so much love to give away
Your kindness did the masses sway
In this world of trouble and strife
You did not have too happy a life
But you gave to others a smile and a promise
And you tried your hardest landmines
to abolish
Oh the tears that have been shed since that
terrible day
Now forever for you will we pray
Rest softly Diana you're coming home to rest
At Althorp in peace at your father's breast.

June Clare

Diana

D id the stars shine in the heavens
did the sun shine in the sky
or was it only since we knew you
they shone down from up on high

I n a world of fear and darkness
you let your light shine through
you gave your love to others
who couldn't help but love you too

A ll through your private sorrows
as you trod a lonely path
your sons brought joy and comfort
their love you'll always have

N ever in this world before
has someone cared as you
the dying, sick and needy
all put their trust in you

A s your light of love and caring
from this lonely world departs
your love will shine forever

Diana, Queen of Hearts.

Sarah Lightbody

Diana, Princess Of Wales

Goodnight sweet Princess
You have earned this rest and more.
A welcome awaits you
Behind Heaven's door
It's time for us to say
A silent goodbye.
We do this oh so sadly
With many a tearful eye.
You were the kindest Princess
So lovely and sincere
You cared so much for others
Which made you so very dear.
We shall always love and miss you.
No-one could say less.
Sleep now, sweet Princess
Goodnight and God Bless.

Mary Wiggins

Diana

You were an English rose so fair
That will bloom forever more
Your voice a distant whisper
Of the waves upon the shore
Your touch was a gentle mist
That fills the valley and hill
No person could deter you
No voice could change your will

You laughed with many people
That had shed many a tear
Met strange unhappy persons
That loved you very dear
Shared with their food and drink
That lived on far-off shores
Helped them in troubled times
Knocked on so many doors

Your life was an open book
Showed so many on a lonely path
How to take another look
It's not always been easy
The way you worked and played
You had so many good friends
On the short journey you have made
God bless you, Diana

C B Cundell

In Memory Of The Princess Who Became The Queen Of Hearts

We only had you for a few short years,
and now we cannot hide our tears
You were someone so full of love and joy
and special to every girl and boy
For people who were most in need
You stood up and took the lead
The Queen of Hearts they said of you
and this will be forever true
For all the hurt and love you shared
Will always be remembered by us who really cared.

Anne Sayer

Farewell To Diana

I stood in line in London,
sunshine flickering through the trees.
The streets were filled with flowers,
heady, sweet perfume clinging to the breeze.
The book sat there before me,
Whatever could I say?
Mere words could never express it.
The sorrow of that day.

I ran across a cornfield,
the colour of your hair.
The September sun was shining,
but such sadness in the air.
Along the motorway we stood,
in silent admiration,
of a shy and lovely Princess,
the sweetheart of our Nation.

Diana, you have filled our hearts,
with your beauty and compassion.
How could you go so suddenly -
still the epitome of glamour and fashion?

You meant so much to all of us,
how will we carry on?
September was the saddest month,
to so abruptly find you gone.

But though September's lingering sun,
is slowly drifting past,
the memory of all you meant to us,
is truly bound to last.
The love you showed, the kindness too,
compassion never-ending.
May you rest in peace, eternally,
your memory never fading.

Linda Willis

Farewell, Queen Of Hearts

Tears weep
Our crying eyes.
Sadness engulfs
Everybody's lives.

A nation mourns,
Bad news has broken.
A fairytale is lost,
The whole world is shaken.

You touched precious hearts.
Many were all alone.
Revealing lost sadness,
Highlighting the unknown.

Goodbye, Princess Diana.
May your spirit be free.
Enjoy eternal happiness,
Now you hold Heaven's key.

Your beautiful aura
Will outshine our sun.
Treasure your journey . . .
As Spirit . . . Heaven become one.

Farewell, Princess Di.
A new legend begins.
Farewell, our Queen of Hearts . . .

. . . Goodbye

Simon Mills

Summer's End

P aragon of beauty, she who
R eigned o'er hearts, in death lies sleeping,
I rretrievable; such loss will
N ever fade from memory's keeping.
C ruel fate un-lit a star, left
E arth in sorrow's sadness steeping.
S haken nations now unite as
S ouls, once torn, are joined in weeping . . .

Susan Devlin

Diana's Poem

P is for the people, for whom you've done so much,
R is for remembering those whose lives you touched.
I is for immortal, which you really should have been,
N is for never leaving us, remaining to be seen.
C is for your compassion, shining like a star;
E is for everyone who loved you from afar.
S is for sadness which now fills up the world,
S is for supporting us, women, men, boys and girls.

O is for officially the world's most photographed face,
F is for finally being at peace, in your final place.

W is for William and Harry, who have lost a mother,
A is for although they'll pray, they'll never have another.
L is for the lessons that can be learned from all you've done,
E is for the extreme loss felt by everyone.
S is for speaking on behalf of and for the nation,

This poem for you Princess Diana is a lasting dedication.

A W Marsh

They've Taken Diana

They've taken Diana, it feels so wrong.
She wasn't with us for very long.
The grief, the heartache and terrible pain
Is our sad loss and Heaven's gain.
Those loving cuddles and gentle touch.
Oh Diana, we miss you so much.
Our hearts go out to Wills and Harry.
For the terrible pain they have to carry.
An erected monument to: Diana our star
As we look up, we hope you're not far.

M Ford

An Inspiration

Where there was despair in life
You brought hope
Where lives were torn apart in life
You showed courage
Where there was no love in life
You gave yours freely
Where people felt alone in life
You made them feel significant
Where there was sadness in life
You brought joy
Where illness isolated those in life
You touched
Where there was darkness in life
You shone
For those less fortunate in life
You showed compassion
Where others dare not tread in life
You placed yourself

So much for so many
You did with such care
With beauty and elegance
A kind of magic so rare
Although we cannot see you
You'll never be far from here
For you're everywhere around us
Our Queen of Hearts we'll hold you dear
We'll miss those unforgettable eyes
And your beautiful smiling face
But may we follow in your footsteps
And make this world a kinder place.

Jayne Lee Whitton

Diana

Dear to our hearts you'll always stay
In our thoughts never far away
An angel in Heaven now you'll be
Never again your lovely smile we'll see
Although Diana we never met, I feel so sad and upset.

Jennifer Johnson

Our Own Princess

When death struck like a thunderbolt, its swift and powerful force
Did snatch away a life that should have run its natural course.
Our routine day was shattered, in the blinking of an eye,
And millions round the world were left bewildered - wondering why.

You touched our hearts in many ways; more than we realised.
Now our minds will hold the image of your smile, and sparkling eyes.
You REALLY FELT the suffering of the sick, and those in need;
You deplored the way the world was ruled by selfishness and greed.

At times your heart did rule your head, more often than it should,
When confusion, mixed with turmoil, made you so misunderstood.
But your caring, loving presence, and your influence and your worth,
Will be felt for years to come, in all the corners of the earth.

Georgina D Harrold
(on behalf of all at Phosco Lighting)

For Your Boys

I know it's hard to accept that I've gone
But I am the verse in the lines of your song
I'll be with you always, my family I'll keep
I'll walk beside you, I'll watch while you sleep
Your memories of me, you'll pass on and on
With me in your heart, I'll never be gone
So if you feel sad, try not to hide
I left my love for you inside.

Elaine Gaudin

A Dedication To Princess Diana

Whenever death is fated to come, it will come,
But such a cruel death only comes to some,
For one so kind and good, an ill-deserved fate,
But that you found joy can our pain alleviate.

You were the star that shone in front of our
eyes,
Now you are the star that twinkles in the skies,
Our eyes search, our arms reach and our
hearts call for you,
Our borrowed angel, gone back, much to
our rue.

Diana

Unforgettable, unique and irreplaceable.
May God rest your soul in peace.

Ranjana Chowdhury

Heart Of Gold

A diamond, a sparkle, in the sky
A shining light, which blinds the eye.
many gathering from afar
Joining together to form a star.

A jewel, a tear, from the eye
A glitter, so bright, passes by.
Standing, listening to words which are spoken
Mourning crowds, hearts which are broken.

A Queen of Hearts, a heart full of Gold
The warmth which was given for others to hold.
Silently suffering, events from the past
Enjoying the present, happiness at last.

A burning candle, a blooming flower
Spreading to others the love and the glamour.
Tragically shocked, a fall from the nest
Our Fairytale Princess is now laid to rest.

Rebecca Murby

So!

So many people so many souls,
So much love, achieving same goals,
So many flowers, so piled high.
So many tears, for our Lady Di,
So many children, playing at school,
So much heart-aching, seems so cruel,
So much good, owed to one girl,
Such a big oyster, and she was the pearl.
So many people, cared so much,
Our Lady Diana, with angels' touch,
So many people, flowers they lay,
And how they united, together to pray.
I stood there silent, at the side of the road,
With thousands of people, as past she rode,
Such a Loss. The world now knows,
That so many people, cherished one rose.
So many times, she held out her hand,
To heal the suffering, throughout the land,
A fairy tale princess, oh, so true,
An angel from heaven, through and through,
Now your island's your fortress, safe at last,
From prying eyes, that haunted your past,
God bless you Diana, we love you so,
Our hearts are sent with you,
to the place that you go.
And I treasure the time when we meet again
For I know if I'm hurting,
that you'll heal the pain.

God bless you

Steven Eastwood

Diana

Once in a lifetime
An angel appears,
To touch people's hearts,
To dry children's tears.
To comfort the weak,
The sick, and the dying.
Can you wonder why
A whole Nation's crying?

J L

Ode To Princess Diana

Our loss
Is Heaven's gain
But in our hearts
she will remain

A Princess with a heart of gold
Endless stories . . . of good are told
She was not afraid to help the poor
And those in need
Set apart from selfish greed
She cared so much, She cared so much
A Princess with a loving touch
It's so hard to think she's gone
Darkness falls . . . where light has shone

A legacy of love
Is what Diana gave
Her love and light shine on
Past her island grave

Words cannot express
Exactly how we feel
But the sadness deep within us
Is very, very real

A legacy of love
Is what Diana left
A legacy of love
To comfort the bereft

Queen of our hearts
You'll always be
A shining light . . . for all to see
So do not stand at my grave and cry
I am not here . . . I did not die.

Mark Tann

To Dear Diana And Dodi

God took you to his heavenly place
No words or thoughts can ever convey
How much we miss your smiling face
You were both so full of life together
We are going to miss you for ever and ever.

You are bright stars shining above
As free as two loving doves
He made you happy for such a short while
The tears I have shed have
dampened my smile.

God Bless you both.

Ruby McClelland

Fate Of A Princess 1997

A long fight began and
For two long hours in the presence of hope
Oh - the fate of a true Princess
Two Princes are left to cope.

Shock in abundance came
One sad Sunday morning in Britain,
As people woke to tragic news
They'd have preferred not to listen.

For events that have led
To this tragic end of lovely life,
The sorrow - for indeed, why could
She not have remained a wife.

But blame is easy and
Convenient - is often unfair,
For who would NOT pursue this woman
When, if they saw her somewhere.

News unbelievable
A whole nation feels pers'nally bereaved,
This sad day that August brings, is just
One more Rose God has achieved.

Long will be her mem'ry
Intensive spotlight at her funeral,
The people, united in grief
Diana, who made a world feel tall.

Barbara Sherlow

Our Sweet English Rose

Our heart-warmed thanks to you, our Princess,
For your loving smile and youthful zest,
Your humanity and compassion an
encouraging glow,
Your untimely death was a devastating blow.

We all loved and admired you wherever
you went,
Every moment of your life was a
moment well spent,
You will never know how much we miss you
down here,
You were kind and understanding, but
overall were sincere.

You were our Queen of all Queens, an example
to us all,
And never in all eternity from grace will you fall,
To your life on this Earth we give you applause
For your unselfish devotion to every cause.

And now sweet Princess we bid you goodbye,
Now in your sanctuary, at peace may you lie.
Our love for your life so strongly it flows,
So sleep peacefully now, our sweet English Rose.

Marcus Tyler

Untitled

Diana the one we most love
you're like a gleaming white dove
winging its way to the heavens on high
For all our tears we've shed for Di
You will always remain in our hearts
and in our minds.
Christmas time will be sad for some
Like William and Harry who will
have no mum.
God bless you William and Harry
and all your grieving family
Especially your father who I know
will take good care of you both.

Andrea Nicole Boyd (14)

Eulogy

The dreadful news one Sunday dawn
Left a nation, stunned, to mourn
The passing of too short a life -
Princess, Icon, Mother, Wife
As had been, indeed many faces
To many people in many places.

Yet 'though your life was often fraught,
Through your heartfelt care you sought
Those by your word and deed, who thought
You were beyond their call.

And caring, you gave without measure,
Bringing so much joy and pleasure
To many - a smile for them to treasure,
A lesson for us all.

We shed our tears; we laid our flowers;
We said our prayers in those dark hours.
We came to stand, to wait, to sign;
A never-ending sombre line.

But in our hearts, your sun will never
Set, although you're gone forever.
Those who'll miss you can but be guessed;
And on the day you were laid to rest,
A bell tolled in Westminster steeple.
Farewell, Woman of the world;
Goodbye, Princess of the people.

David Willis

Diana

Princess Diana was our one and only.
Who was indeed at times very lonely
God made her wait
Until she went on a date
With Dodi her soul mate
They went together
Hand in hand
To remain in God's kingdom forever

RIP

Sheila Woollacott

Diana A Ribbon In The Sky For Your Love!

Oh Lord so long for this night I pray,
That a star would guide Diana back our way,
If for life may I touch her hand,
So she can once again grace the land,
There's a ribbon in the sky for her love,

Even though your sight is clear in Heaven above,
Your heart remains as pure and gentle to us as a dove,
There's a ribbon in the sky for your love,

For with you we've got on our side,
We'll find strength from each tear we cry,
From now on your soul will never die,
There's a ribbon of love in the sky,

Diana you are not alone,
We will always be here for you,
And each day from your depart,
Your smile of love will grow fonder in our hearts.

God will protect you now and forever,
So you will sustain through life as a bird of a feather,
But we know from the Lord above,
A ribbon will shine in the sky forever for your love!

Natasha Brown (16)

Love Will Never Die

Our love for you will never die,
All we do is sit and cry.
You were taken in a tragic way,
Now all we can do is pray,
For your sons so sweet and kind.
I'll never forget the day I saw you in the crèche all day.
Looking down on the purity of a child,
So young, so pure and mild and kind.
That's you, Princess Di.

G Fletcher

Goodbye Diana

I couldn't cry
Now you've gone to the
Paradise in the sky
I don't know why
You've done a lot for others
In their hour of need
Hounded by the Paparazzi
Only for their greed
We'll miss you Diana
Your happiness
Your mood
Always kind
Never rude
Goodbye Diana once again
I hope your work was not in vain.

All of the heartache
You've suffered
All of the pain
So goodbye Diana
Once again
Rest in peace
Amen

S Baillie

In Memory Of The People's Princess Diana

You were so very special Di
You never were afraid.
You even spent time with lepers
And with people who had AIDS
We are all heartbroken
That you had to die
At last you are left alone
To be an angel in the sky
God bless you Diana
Our Queen of Hearts
RIP.

Kathleen Jones

Diana Princess Of Wales

A bright English Rose, that's just a cliché.
You brightened our lives in many more ways.
You brought in the sun when you entered
a room,
You chased away darkness dispelling all gloom.
You brought hope to the helpless, around
all the world,
To cripples and lepers, to boys and to girls.
And just when it seemed that your life was
going to plan,
You were taken away from the family of man.
A family you lifted a family you loved,
God needed your presence in Heaven above.
Diana, this world is a much poorer place,
Without you to help all the poor and displaced.
We will always remember that bright
shining star,
Our Queen of hearts, wherever you are.

S R Firth

A Special Star

As I looked into the sky last night
I saw a star shining so bright
It seemed to twinkle straight at me
And set my troubled spirit free
It must be Diana, no one else
has the power or the love
To spread her magic round the world
Thank God, on high, above
She gave everyone a special star
To pin their hopes upon
Turning tears to laughter, despair to joy
The most unique icon
But the most amazing thing of all
Which has left the whole world reeling
Is that she never came to realise
The impact of her feeling
She left us without knowing
The effects from near and far
Of how her loss would shatter us
She is a very special star.

Corinne Tuck

Angel On Earth

Angel on Earth,
None of us knew,
how much you really cared.
God sent you here to do His will
and filled you with love which you shared.
He gave you a task that wasn't easy
and sometimes very unfair,
but for all the people that needed you,
you were always there.

Now you have left this Earthly place,
your goodness is shining through.
You have united the world,
which is very hard to do.

As for us you've left behind,
great sadness your passing brings.
Now you're an Angel in Heaven,
and you have earned your wings.

Deirdre Layton

Diana

No more sunshine,
or rain
No more joy,
or pain
At last you have found your
true domain
In our hearts and minds, where
you will forever remain
A symbol of hope for the weak and
the lame
A shining light for the strong and
the urbane
None of us will ever forget
your name
Diana, Queen of Hearts.

John Parker

Our Diana

The sky at night
May it shine so bright
Lives have been left open
Many say they are broken

How do we go on and live
Knowing you can no longer give
The presence of your life

You were there
Yes you always cared
about people not the same as yourself
You gave them hope
Lifted their heads.
Not once would you gloat
Yes Diana you really cared

The angels have come
Took you and a loved one
Now you are gone
From our world forever

No more must we grieve
Live life let us succeed
In the hopes and dreams
of our Diana.

Dawn Howarth

Hearts And Flowers

The day you appeared, all coy and serene,
On my television screen
I sat spellbound and starry-eyed,
As you emerged, the blushing bride.
But the media's love allowed you to upstage
Your shy husband on every page.
And as the world's press was bowled over,
I sensed instinctively it was over.
But today, when I was told you were gone,
The brightest media star that ever shone.
I sit stunned . . . silently, crying,
With the world and its sick and dying.

Betty Lightfoot

Diana

Diana you were one of the best
Far too young to be laid to rest
But I believe in God above
He only takes the ones with love
So much love you had to give
Perhaps that's why you could not live
If all the tears that flowed for you
Had all been saved I'm sure it's true
Another ocean made for you above
In remembrance Diana the 'Sea of Love'.

My brother David was young like you
Just one year younger that is true
But my belief the good die young
Words say it all when Elton's song was sung
So Diana if you ever get a chance to meet
My brother up in heaven, you're in for a treat.

Elizabeth Ann Middleton

Tranquillity

A willow bends its weeping head,
Beside her resting place,
For here lies our own Princess,
A Lady of such grace.

A willow sighs, a sigh for all,
At a loss so hard to bear,
Dark clouds will bring our teardrops,
For the beauty sleeping there.

A willow sways, as if in dance,
A celebration of her caring heart,
A Nation silent, at one in grief,
A pain not known, until you part.

A willow sweeps its foliage low,
As if to kiss goodbye,
To a life that was in all too brief,
A beautiful soul, called Di.

Eileen M Bailey

Princess Of Heart

Diana the Princess of Heart
Her death has torn a Nation apart
For what she had done
Her memory will live on

So tragic this tragedy
Full of energy
Who could help but notice
Her work was tireless

Especially with children
Her arms were always open
The love she showed
Radiated and glowed

For God in His wisdom
Has taken the Princess to a higher Kingdom
The Nation will not forget you
Because your attitude just grew and grew

To us the people you turned
We salute you as respect you've earned
From a nobody
In our hearts you became somebody.

Walter Mottram

Sorrow

The pain we have
Will never go
Our tears of sorrow
Will forever flow.
The wisdom you taught us
Through all that you did,
Will keep you here
And your legend will live.
But now that you're gone
You'll always be near
For you captured our hearts
That's what made
You so dear.

Teresa Webb

For Two Lost Boys

Look up at the sky
and you will see your mother there,
on every cloud, in every star
to help your sorrow bear.
She is not really gone from you
she's in each gentle breeze,
just listen and you'll hear her,
and your aching heart she'll ease.
Her body lies by a peaceful lake
at rest and out of pain,
but don't, for one sad moment
think you'll not be close again,
for her arms will e'er enfold you
when you're lost and set apart,
and her love will always be with you
forever in your HEART.
So look up at the sky, the trees,
the breeze that rustles through,
and remember, with each passing day,
your mother's still WITH you.

Margaret Hanning

Diana

I can't understand this feeling of pain
For someone who never even knew my name
I never knew how my heart could ache
My thoughts one person could so overtake
I never knew how much you had done
All I knew one day a King would be your son
You were so good so thoughtful too
Is it too late to let you know I love you
I will try to be good try to be kind
And if I falter I will bring you to mind
I hope your good work will carry on
I hope the love of the common
People will pass to your son
And most of all now you are free
I hope by your side Dodi will be.

Patricia Winter

Our Princess, Our Angel

We had a special Princess, Diana was her name.
And now we have not got her, the world won't be the same.

She had an angel's smile, and the touch of feather down.
So tender was her heart, oh Lord who let her down.

Our hearts are slowly breaking, the tears just fall and fall.
The Heavens have stole our Princess, we'll miss her one and all.

We will never see our Princess, never ever again.
Oh help us dear Lord, help us through this pain.

We love her very very much, she had a heart of gold.
Now she'll walk the streets of Heaven, so slender, smart and tall.

We feel so empty so sad and blue, we walk not knowing what to do,
We've lost a special angel, Diana it is you,

I wish I could wake up and find, it's not true.
We've cried so many rivers, this I'm sure is true.
We've lost a special Lady, Diana it is you.

Rita Wall

Diana

Diana you had a heart of gold,
For the sick, the homeless, the young and the old.
The world will be a much sadder place,
Without the presence of your face,
You had so much love and kindness to share,
You showed the world how much you cared,
But now Diana you have gone away,
We always thought you were here to stay,
Perhaps God decided you needed a rest,
And everyone knows HE only takes the best.

Catherine Radcliffe

Princess Diana

She came to us like a bright new dawn
Unsullied and full of vibrant life,
She dearly loved the Prince of Wales
So soon to become his lovely wife.

She emitted such joyful radiance
On the day her father, full of pride,
Gave her to Charles to have and hold,
A beautiful Fairy Princess Bride.

The following year her son was born,
Prince William was her pride and joy,
And when Prince Harry came along
She adored another little boy.

She guided their lives with all her love,
She carried out duties far and wide,
She gave great comfort to young and old,
And we shall remember her with pride.

To her we've now had to say farewell,
Be it said in poetry or in prose,
She will live forever in our hearts
Our beautiful perfect English Rose.

Jean Eyre

Princess Diana

Princess Diana you've gone above
And left behind the ones you loved
The day you left we felt such pain
But now you're free to love again.

They say God only takes the best
Safe in his arms, I pray you rest
In a land that never sees the rain
Free from all the grief and pain.

When the sun shines down from up above
We'll know you're sending all your love
To ease our sorrow down below
Why God took you, we'll never know.

Susan Fraser

Saint Diana Spencer HRH

I hear ten billion holy notes
Herald the saint of human-kind
In that sweet mood when pleasant thoughts
Bring sad thoughts to the mind.

In her good works did God's hand link
The humane soul that through her ran
And much it grieves my heart to think
Of her short life-span.

To every child she was a fan
She showed the world she cared
About the common man
Their grief she kindly shared.

If this grief from heaven be sent
If such be God's Holy Plan
Have I not reason to lament
The tireless media man!

The cherubs have spread out their wings
To guide her up to heaven
Where choirs of angels sing
She's gone to meet her king!

Denise Russell

Diana

You brought light and hope wherever you went
Your time for the people was freely spent
Now the world feels empty and sad.
Too late we have realised just what we had.

You came to us for such a short while
With your lovely face and beautiful smile
You touched our hearts, you eased our pain.
We will never know your special kindness again.

Now you have gone to Heaven above
for God to keep you in His love
One day we will all be together again,
and there'll be no more tears, and no more pain.

L F K Missen

Diana

Diana you were a royal princess in every way.
Your beauty came from deep within
So full of compassion and grace,
A treasured gift to the human race.

You taught us how, to show that we care
Your example has been an inspiration to
millions,
Your sense of duty and self-discipline to be
admired.
You were no stranger, to suffering and pain,
But you used this experience to help others gain.

To Wills and Harry we send our regard,
And pray that their future, will not be too hard.
We do not want them to keep asking why?
But to heal themselves and find time to cry.
Your sons' fine qualities are a credit to you.
A result of your love and tenderness,
Which will always enrich their lives.

Diana, we love you, we miss your face
There will never be another to take your place.

Your sons are royal, long may they live.
Let us never forget, how you taught us to give.
It's so hard on them, that you had to die,
But He will resurrect you, in the twinkling
of an eye.

Caroline Lester

Diana, Queen Of Hearts

No more flashes
No more pain
Now our lives will
never be the same.
Reporters here, reporters there,
They followed our Queen of Hearts
everywhere
Such grace, such beauty, she gave us all,
Now none of us are standing tall.

Sharon Norris - (London)

Diana

'From the green vales of our England,
To distant stormy shores,
All hearts are filled with mourning,
At the wilting of our rose,
And although the sun shines brightly,
And the flowers gently sway,
A sadness is prevailing,
That locks all light away,
There are countless who will miss you,
As our days turn into years,
Each star in heaven's ocean,
I'm sure will share their tears,
But surely as the dawn will come,
And amber sunlight rise,
Our memories and most fondest thoughts,
Will one day dry our eyes,
So farewell to you Diana,
As our paths must sadly part,
Your golden smile and healing touch,
Made you Queen of every heart.'

Granville Jones

She Cared

She cared
And had so much love to give

She cared
About how the world would live.

She cared
About the sick, the lonely and the dying,

She cared
And tried to ease their crying

When she needed comfort
Where were we?

Too late we came to care,
Like she.

Sylvia D Lee

Princess Diana

Di was young and beautiful
Adventurous and bold,
Princess Diana
Of this we were told.
Who went out of her way
To help all those in need.
Princes Di, showed the way
By doing these countless deeds.
She was the mother of
Two young wonderful boys.
Princes William and Harry
Who were her pride and joy.
A princess and a mother
They loved very much.
Also, a daughter - a sister
With that warm and common touch.

Then that day we all remember,
When we heard she was gone.
For she brought a nation together
As we all felt that bond.
For she had helped the young,
The poor, the old and the sick.
Princess Diana was the one
That God had picked.

Eddie Biggins

Diana

With tears in our eyes
Our hearts full of sorrow
Your tragic death touched our lives
But we must grieve less tomorrow.
For your caring we must remember
The good in people that you saw
Your smile so warm and tender
The hope you gave to the sick and poor.
Our prayers we know you're hearing
As you walk in heaven's paths
In return for all your giving
We crown you Queen of Hearts.

Rhoda Jacobs

The Loss We Feel!

I smile when I think of your beautiful face,
and pray that you're in a wonderful place,
These memories also make me cry,
especially when I think I couldn't say
goodbye.
I feel your presence; I know you're still here,
with us catching every tear.
A crying shoulder for each other we lend,
I wish we could see you once again.
The sorrow shows we miss you so,
the memories we'll keep and never let you go.
They're buried deep within our hearts,
where I know we'll never part.
There's so many things people had to say,
before you were cruelly taken away.
Although we are far apart,
close you'll be inside our hearts.
You made so many people so happy,
you're everything I wish I could be.
We want you back to touch,
we love you Diana, we do so much.

Denise and Jaime Stock

Diana: Princess Of Wales

Diana, every life you touched,
You brought a smile of joy
For this we will miss you
More than you will ever know,
Our Queen of Hearts, we love you
But now was the time for you to go.
God needed you now to start your work above
We will miss your smile, that lit up the sky
Also the sparkle in your eyes
But you will be with Dodi, high up in heaven
Where your two souls will be joined as one
Looking down from above
Watching your sons William and Harry
Growing more into the men they shall
one day become.

Helen Christine Bladen

Diana

(Dedicated to my later brother,
David Antony Marks - 1925-1947
Who was killed in an avalanche in Austria)

Princess Diana, of the fairest face
I miss your lovely soul,
I miss your smile, I miss your grace,
Losing you was so cruel.

Princess Diana, you had such style,
You had a heart of gold,
I shall never see that lovely smile,
Like you, my body is now cold.

I want to speak so many words
to bring you back alive,
I cannot face this saddest loss,
The tears I shed, they so often arrive,
But I went to church and had comfort
from the cross.

Goodbye, lovely lady, I was always
on your side,
I hope, gently, heaven does hold you,
Because I cried and cried,
But I'll see you in the flowers
and morning dew.

Anna Parkhurst

Diana

God lent to us an angel
To walk upon this land
To comfort troubled people
He gave her healing hands

She touched the lives of many
The dying, young and old
To keep her strong and beautiful
He bathed her heart in gold

One day he closed her lovely eyes
It brought us pain and sorrow
To return to him - Diana
The angel we did borrow.

Shirley Eatough

Diana, Princess

Once, so like a shy gazelle
Sheltering arms of children seeking,
Nations fell beneath your spell -
Those graceful looks, that charm
in speaking . . .

You brought new ways, refreshingly,
To deal with Royal tedia,
Your natural loving tenderness
Made hunters of the media.

Happy as a butterfly,
Your last days of romance
Who could guess that you would die
By a cruel mischance?

Greed and speed and frantic chase
Damages most cruelly
Through this tragedy make haste -
And learn to love more truly!

Julia Kampmeier

Saying Goodbye

We didn't get to say goodbye
And that really makes us cry
You brought so much love
In our hearts
That love for you will never die.

In our hearts you'll still be there
Locked inside our loving care
Miss you more than you'll ever know.

If tears could build a stairway
And memories a lane
We'd walk our way to heaven
To bring you back again
You'll be loved in our hearts
for always.

Mel Leggett

Diana

Diana, Diana my heart is aching
With love
With sorrow
With pride
Your pain and anguish pushed aside
Whilst reaching out to hearts
Worldwide
The sick the dying the pain-filled
Lives of families and all mankind

Black or white rich or poor
There was no difference there
You looked you listened you touched
And made their lives worthwhile

We've learned a lesson
From your life
To love to help not hate
You gave us strength
To do these things
Thank God it's not too late.

Susan Davies

For Diana

Our Lord asked for my return
I leave, think joyfully
Your love will last forever
Love is not less, eternally

Weep not, that unseen I am
With Our Lord, I lay my head
For He called me back to Him
I only sleep, I am not dead.

Know only that He sent me
If only for a while
To do this work and love you
Be not sad for me, but smile.

Rejoice at all the happy times
And hold them in your heart
I am not dead, but waiting
For Love cannot depart.

Lynne Diane Moutter

My Everlasting Poem to Princess Diana

How can a woman we hardly know,
hurt friends and us common folk so?
We watched her grow, from timid girl,
to tear our hearts with grace and twirl.
A startling beauty, a wicked smile,
her young life, edited, put on trial.
She spoke her mind, we backed her cause, leave her be, she's no real flaws.
A heart of gold, courageous, bold,
a loving mum, a joy to behold.
Hold my hand, don't be afraid,
another friend made, never betrayed.
Just what is it about Di, the rebel,
that multiplies her fan club, treble!
Maybe a touch, a call, a grin,
helped so many take it on the chin.
An aristocrat, with special powers,
who giggles a lot, and brings you flowers.
A lady, who deals the common touch,
that makes her loved so very much.
Irreplaceable, by way of caring,
a valiant heart, a little daring.
How can someone so really good,
be so very misunderstood?
And now the world's brightest star,
going home, in a Mercedes car,
Finally lost her marvellous life,
no longer a lover, mother, wife.
No-one understands this mood,
a mourning shown by flowers, strewed,
Rest in peace, you will be missed,
forever by our memories kissed.

And now you are in heaven
The stars call out your name
Surely this Mother Earth of ours
Can never be the same
Your island home at Althorp House
Is carpeted with flowers
The continuation of your good works
Is now not yours, but ours.
Your gentle heart has made its mark
The world has no choice
The feeling's there, it must go on
That is the people's voice.

Your legacy to us is clear
Two sons you'll always cherish
Love like yours, so strong, so sweet
Can never ever perish.
We know you don't want sainthood
Your method was grass roots,
But no one in the whole wide world
Can ever fill your boots.

All your family showed their love
In London, Earl Spencer said it all
The world admired those sons of yours
For they did walk so tall.
In death, you've made an everlasting mark
With the magic that you weaved
Normality is coming back
It's so hard to achieve.
Each day, with effort, your work goes on
'A Candle In The Wind' by Elton John.

Valerie & Brian Hurll, Dawn and Richard

A Dedication To Diana Princess of Wales

If I could make a wish come true,
'Diana' I'd give my wish to you,
So you could guide your sons from above,
To show them the way with your wonderful love,
To show them through this terrible plight,
To love and hold them when they cry in the night,
I only wish you'd had the time,
To hug and kiss them one last time,
Help us through this terrible pain,
Of wishing you were here again,
We all remember your beautiful smile,
To sit and think, just once in a while,
Of all the goodness you have done,
And won the hearts of everyone,
So I dedicate this wish to you,
And hope my wish for you comes true.

Mavis Foster

Diana

So beautiful you were, Queen of our Hearts
Why did Our Lord let you depart
From this world where you did so much
For the homeless, the needy and ones
badly hurt.

You were helpful and caring and so very kind
You spoke to the ill people and eased
their minds
A dying child you held with so much
love and care
When a friend was in trouble you were
always there.

Your two little boys will miss you so much
They are so full of pain and full of hurt.
May the Lord ease their sorrow and
their pain
Life without their Mum will never be
the same.

The earth will miss your smiling face
You were full of beauty and of grace
Be happy above the sky so blue
And I do hope 'Dodi' is there with you.

Irene Joan Blair

Diana Queen Of Hearts

For a very special lady
Who will never be replaced
You showed such loving and caring
To whatever problems we faced

So as we sit and wonder
And will never understand why
That someone so very precious
Was far too young to die

But only God He knows the answer
As He watches from above
So our hearts and thoughts go with you
But most specially goes our love.

Jenny Lyndall

Goodbye Diana

Shush! Shush! An angel's sighing.
Down below the world is crying
They've come to London, all in distress
To say goodbye to their princess
Amidst a mighty sea of flowers
A million folk have stood for hours
At Westminster Abbey, choirs are singing
Muted bells will soon be ringing
Elton John as candles glow
Gives his greatest ever show
Diana's brother with indignation
Lays the blame, in his oration.
Those outside who hear his voice
A great ovation is their choice
Inside the Abbey, the great and good
Do the same, they understood.
Forgive Diana from up above
Those who doubted all your love
For we don't recognise the worth
Of someone till they've left the earth
When my mother died, I stayed dry-eyed
I loved her so, but I never cried
For I'm a man so big and strong
To shed a tear is really wrong.
But for you Diana, who I never met
I joined the world without regret
Goodbye Princess, your love so strong
Forgive all those who did you wrong.

Doug Sharkey

Diana

A beautiful lady to us God sent
Taken so suddenly - she was only lent.
Her life on earth was so worthwhile
Her gentleness, kindness, that lovely smile
Those memories of her can never fade
Let her rest in peace where she is laid.

Brenda A Tuck

Diana

Although we never knew you,
You were a queen to us.
A statuesque figure.
A Princess to always love.

You reached out and touched the
hands of others
Which no-one ever did
The poor, the needy and the sick.
Your work was legendary.

The time you spared to help us
Your love you gave to friends
The kindness you showed to others
This nation will mourn a legend and mother
and a friend.

There are no arms to hold you
Or words that we can say,
But rest assured you will be missed
Each and every day.

We hope that you may now be happy
Wherever you may be
And know that we all miss you
Our Princess, Queen of Hearts.

Cheryl Watson

Diana

I never got to meet you
I never held your hand
But I feel the same as everyone
From each corner of the land.

The shock has stunned the nation
We cannot understand
You spread your love like magic dust
Then left without goodbye.

Our tears could fill an ocean
There will never ever be
Another like our 'Queen of Hearts'
Who left so suddenly

'Rest in Peace'.

Valerie Darling

Our England's Rose - Diana

Diana, our very own Princess of Hearts
People adored her right from the very start,
A loving mum to sons William and Harry
Memories of her forever they'll carry,
From above she'll watch over them with pride
There for all time close by their sides,
Charity work was her passion in life
Campaigning tirelessly throughout her
young life,
She'd found happiness at last but it wasn't to be
She died in the arms of her precious Dodi,
Angels came and picked our flower
Now we mourn her finest hour,
God called her home with Him to rest
Proving again He only takes the best.

Dorothy Madeline Corlett

Untitled

MUM please hear my cry for help
A tragedy has happened
They've sent our lovely PRINCESS DI
To join you up in heaven
Care for her as you would me
And take her in your home
And give her lots and lots of love
As if she were your own

This lady's like a diamond
Unique in every way
And everyone she met
She brightened up their day
Two years ago you went from us
And why! We never knew
But now I know from in my heart
There's a job you had to do
You made your home up in the sky
And waited for our PRINCESS DI
Above the world TWO ANGELS rest
For you two simply are the best.

Jackie Hyde

To Diana

You first came into our hearts
and raised Britain's smiles
Back in 1981
On your wedding day to Prince Charles.
Since that day and from then on
Continuing through the years
You reached out to Britain's people
and helped them through their fears
You gave our husband two sons
And Britain an heir to the throne
Although born into strong traditions
You made sure they were not alone
Finally when the marriage was over
and it was time to part
Britain still stayed with you
Pulled you closer to its heart
'I won't go quietly'
Was a line you once said
We knew you wouldn't during your life
and we won't let you now you're dead
As everyone is crying
and Britain's in a mess
the question why? Is still unanswered
while we mourn our own princess.
Although we'll never see you once more
We want you to know how much you meant
Watch over the ones that loved you from
heaven
the place from which you were first sent.

Dale Short

Diana

Diana we miss you and we always will,
For the kindness you showed to the
sick and the ill,
Your radiant beauty and kind smiling face,
Is something that nobody can ever replace,
You're now with the angels in heaven above,
So rest in peace sweet Princess.

We all send our love.

Adrian Porter

Diana - Our Own Queen Of Hearts

Princess Diana, you were a lovely girl
to cope,
You were loved and respected and gave
people hope,
It's heartless the way that you had to go,
But the world has seen, how it was so.
We know that you're aware of the sorrow
And heartache, that was brought on
that 'morrow
And now know just how much you had love,
As you sadly look down from your new
home above,
You may have lost your HRH label,
But to everyone the world over, you're
still able,
To bring, tears, love, prayers and flowers,
In return for the work you did, for this
country of ours,
We hope you find peace at last,
And settle with your loved one,
away from your past,
May God bless, and help your
dear boys now,
To cope as you did, as only they know how.
The whole world will miss you, and your
tasks will cease,
But now from this horrific fate,
you will find peace.

E Harrod

Untitled

I walk along the beach and sigh
And think of our Princess Di
Although I'm very far away,
I mourn for her each coming day.
At night my thoughts relive her past
Her deeds, that were all good - so vast!
Then - as my footsteps mark the sand
They vanish as by magic hand
But memories of Di will stay
No ocean-wave can wash away.

Ursula Chaplin

Princess Diana

You are our Queen of Hearts,
Loved by all the nations.
Helping every kind of people,
You are their salvation.

It didn't matter where they lived,
In countries far and wide,
Your hands outstretched to help them,
You were always by their side.

High or low, you helped all people,
And a wonderful mother too,
Bringing up two lovely princes,
To be loyal, brave and true.

We will always miss you,
In heartache, sorrow and tears,
But we will never forget you,
Through the future years.

As the 'Candle in the wind' was sung,
So was your life right here,
Burning brightly for your people,
With hope, happiness and cheer,

So God bless you brave Diana,
There is a new star in the sky,
It will shine upon your people,
So you'll never die.

Nancy Scott

Diana - The People's Princess

A gentle touch laid on the head
Of a child sick, upon her bed.
A lovely smile, her eyes so warm
Upon those folk, who were forlorn.
A soothing word, a pretty face
Often a tear, but full of grace.
All this because, she was so kind
So caring, with love in her mind.
A mother with her gentleness
For her two boys, now in distress.
They can take solace in a prayer
Because she's now, in God's good care.

Joy Baker

Diana, Princess Of Wales 1961 - 1 September 1997

On Sunday morning
The world turned cold
When the announcement was made
Diana would never grow old.

Throughout the day
The people felt numb
Unable to believe that
her time had come.

To touch a small child
or in a dangerous place
Always the same
familiar face.

A friend to the people
A shoulder to some
But to two young boys
She was their mum.

The nation they mourn her
The world alongside
To William and Harry
Part of their world has died.

To you both, feel the love
of the people unbound,
As the tears of the world
Fall to the ground.

Lesley J Beard

Diana Queen Of Hearts

You're so modest and kind
The humanitarian torch you carried,
Will forever shine
Upon the less fortunate among mankind
To whom you devoted your precious time
Helping them to dismiss their insecurity
By contributing so much to charity
May God be with you in eternity.

Prince Marley

A Tribute To Diana

Our hands were tied we did not care
in your hour of need.

They took your life away from us
just to feed their greed.

You touched our hearts, you gave us hope
to live our lives as one.

How sad for us we did not know
till now that you are gone.

We weren't there that morning
the day you passed away.

We'll never get to tell you
the things we want to say.

Your lovely smile we all will miss
your gentle tender ways.

Our hearts do ache the pain we'll bear
through long and lonely days.

If we all cared as much as you
the world could all unite.

Through thick and thin we'd think of others
we too could see the light.

You grew and blossomed so beautiful
and nurtured as a mum.

But all too late you slipped away
the damage has been done.

So no more tears and no more pain
Dearest Diana 'We'll meet again.'

J Buckley

Diana

It broke our hearts and brought us low,
Before Our Lord, we stand and bow,
Now sanctified, the nation cheers,
A mingled crowd of pain and tears.

We wait in thankfulness to God,
Our homes secure, our hearts at rest,
The outer zest, the inner tear,
All hearts and minds in sorrow share.

I A Johnson

Diana

Sunday 31st August
It was a dark and gloomy day
Why did you have to leave us
And leave in such a way?

You touched our hearts,
Our People's Princess you were
We admired you so much
Diana, you really cared.

These precious years we knew you
You really showed the way
A warm and friendly person
What else can we say?

Always in the limelight
Life's been hard for years
Never having privacy
It's brought you many tears.

You found true love at last
Dodi was so special to you
With plans for your future
So much, so much to do.

Rest now in peace
Nobody to harm
A life for you
Will be so calm.

Now in heaven
With Dodi you will be
Goodbye, God bless
Sleep peacefully.

Jackie Patterson

Diana

You came into our lives so shy - and really not so long ago.
We watched you as you spread your wings
And gave us joy and all those things
We took delight to watch and see - such grace and beauty
Oh your poise! - and yet you giggled with girlish glee!
That showed us you were human - free

The light which shone around your head - is gone
And we are left to miss you so, and try to understand the why
Of such a sudden dreadful death

And when the sharpness of our grief has mellowed
With the passing time - we'll think of you and smile and try
Within our lives to touch and care - to reach out
When we have a chance - in memory of one
Who shone - so bright.

R Simpson

Forever

Do not weep for me as in paradise I roam
So release your heart from its sorrow and pain
For my mind is free from its troubles known
And my soul at peace in this garden where I'm lain.
The lessons I have taught you I hope you've learned well
And look to the future and on the past do not dwell
I leave you these words in remembrance of me
Forever young, forever loved, forever home, Forever free.

S Powell

To The Queen Of Hearts

I'm in a nursing home again
Seeking a cure for this awful pain
I look through my window and what do I see?
Tall leafy trees and grass that is green.
A few horses neighing and some woolly sheep grazing.
A world at PEACE with no need for crying.

But when I look at my TV screen
I see only sights that make me grieve
A nation is sighing and the world is mourning
The death of a princess without any warning
From north to south, east to west
People are sobbing and cannot rest.
A modern Cinderella is being driven away
Lost to the world with so much at bay.
God gave her to us, but now takes her away
On a journey to Heaven on a flowery road
She leaves us in sorrow and hearts that are torn.

In sinister silence her boys join her at the Mall
Two tragic figures brave William, brother Harry so small
With their heads bowed low we prayed they wouldn't fall
How they must have suffered on that long long walk
With the one loving MUMMY absent to their call.

Two lonely Princes having lost the love that counts
Alas, must now climb life's cruel and steep mounts
Please love them if only on my account
Would be Diana's only sad and mournful shout
The world embraces them in their final farewell.

S I Williams

Diana - The People's Princess

Remembering how you touched our hearts,
how your smile could dry a tear,

Remembering how you tirelessly fought,
to raise funds year by year,

Remembering how you gave your time,
to see us ordinary folk

Remembering how you'd add a personal
touch by sharing with us a joke.

Remembering all our tributes, to try and show
how much we cared

Remembering how the world was full of grief
and sorrow, when it heard

We'll remember how a light in our lives,
was abruptly smothered

We'll remember what we should have said,
but alas had never bothered

We'll remember the multi-coloured fragrant
carpet spreading all across the land

We'll remember because you were loved and
adored, and our words now seem ever so bland

We'll remember all you stood for and how there
will never be another

A more caring, compassionate, generous princess
and not least a more caring mother.

Diana you will be in our hearts forever
May you rest in peace.

J Berry

Untitled

Though brief the flame
that was her life
with love she many singed,
a billion eyes a crying
tears of reality's tide.

Buried princess, buried dreams
eternal smile, eternal grace,
the rebirth of a legend . . .
the Lady of the lake.

Marcus Throup

Diana You Are Love

Diana you are love.
Your two royal sons you loved the most;
Very sad they've lost their mother,
Yet all the needy you did love
As if you were their mother.
Your marriage had to break down;
Protocol was put before you,
You were forward looking and
Had a forward view.
The love you showed to children
Started in your early years,
Then it spread to everyone
As your love released their fears.
It spread beyond our country,
It spread throughout the world;
Even now it stays with you
In the after-world.

Your death was so untimely
And a shock to everyone;
But still you live,
Love you'll still give
In the world where you have gone.

When you were down here with us,
You sought to ban landmines
And sought to house the homeless,
Plus help of other kinds:
That help was not forthcoming
The powers all turned deaf ears.
I wonder if they'll listen now;
Now you are, not with us.

L Andrews

Diana - Princess Of Wales

This is a week in all of our lives
One that we'll never forget
As the Princess of Wales is laid to rest
To her we owe a great debt
She touched the hearts of everyone
In countries far and near
It didn't matter what race you were
She was loved so very dear
She had a raw deal of that there's no doubt
But always came smiling through
Her smile we'll remember for the rest
of our lives
And forget her we could never do.
Her life was cut short in such a tragic way
She didn't deserve to die
But now she's at rest in the arms of the Lord
It's now time to say our goodbyes
Life goes on but memories stay
But our love for Diana will not go away.

Olga Giblin

It All Makes Sense Now

Diana, you were a highly sensitive person,
I don't know if you knew,
This may be the reason that you often felt so blue.
You often felt misunderstood,
Sometimes you felt shy,
People trampled over you,
And made you want to cry.

But now you know I'm sure,
That your struggles weren't in vain,
Your sensitive perception helped ease a lot
of pain,
Your heart was filled with love,
Your intentions always pure,
People strove to copy you, to capture your allure.

Forgive all those people who weren't so sensitive,
Hopefully your death will change the
thoughtless way they live.

J Boitoult

Ode To Diana

'Faith, Hope, and Charity,

The greatest of these is Charity'
Kindness, benevolence, giving to the poor!
One small word involves all these things,
That small word is surely LOVE!

The whole world has shown and given love
At the end of a short life's span!
She stepped out bravely with help from above,
Long-honoured be her name!
Never an 'also ran'!

Candles have burned, gradually to diminish,
Stacks of flowers wither and fade,
Worthy acts and good deeds will never finish,
She lit the torch, we must back up and aid!

Her beauty and humility live on in our hearts,
We cherish the love, she bestowed in all parts,
The candle in the wind!
The English Country Rose
Now rests with Our Lord in sweet repose!

Mary Dearnley

Princess Diana

With tears I shed I look to the sky,
Like the whole nation I wonder why?
But Heaven is the place I know you'll be,
An angel like you will have the key.

So don't be afraid as God takes your hands,
Look over your shoulder and Dodi there
stands.
Together forever, with the love that you share,
One hug and one kiss and finally a pair.

Now with true happiness you've finally found,
Please take one look back down at the ground.
The whole world is in mourning, you'll be
sadly missed,
A treasure like you, we've all been kissed.

With love,

Carol Wood

Our Beautiful Diana

Our Princess
Our shining light
Loved by all
Your star burns bright
You opened your heart
You shed some tears
You gave us joy
Throughout the years
You were so sweet
And oh so kind
You filled our hearts
You filled our minds
Now taken from us
And spirited away
We will always miss you
As we kneel and pray
You were an icon to us all
And now Heaven has
The most beautiful
Angel of all.

Paul R Nevett

Why

We find it hard to understand
Where are you Mum
Please take our hand,
Two days ago we laughed and cried
Where are you Mum
Don't try to hide,
They're trying to tell us
That you've gone
To Jesus?
That must be wrong,

But now we've seen you lying there
You never spoke
We touched your hair
We waited for that little smile
Where are you Mum?
Talk for just a little while,
Please tell us what we have to do
We are scared, and are missing you,
We have been told we must not cry
But Mum, you never even said goodbye.

Christine Franks-Brown

Carpets Of Flowers

Carpets of flowers stretch for miles
Covering the world in piles and piles
Bearing messages of love to a special one
Princess Diana - who has died and gone
Carpets of flowers began to be laid
Last Sunday morn and people prayed
At the sudden death of one so young
Grief touched us all and firmly clung
Carpets of flowers have steadily grown
Especially in London where people are drawn
To attend the funeral of the Queen of Hearts
As a nation from Diana parts
Carpets of flowers are seen everywhere
Being woven with such love and care
A week of sorrow - a time to remember
Princess Diana - God Bless her.

Hilary Bratton

Princess Diana

The light will always shine on her
as it did in life
her vision of beauty a camera could not resist
her love will always be there,
as it was in life,
her laughter and sense of humour will
not be forgotten,
and most of all, her concern for those
who were homeless,
she came to them like a glorious
angel at night,
and in her time of sorrow
her tears were there for us all to see,
her love for her children so strong,
such an adorable loving mother full of grace
Diana, a supreme human being.

Kathleen Keating

A Tribute To Diana

So many tears have been shed,
So many words have been said,
Now we have to let you go,
Your radiant smile we'll see no more.

We've shared your joy, we've sensed
your pain
We've watched you fight back,
again and again.
The courage you've shown;
your smiles and your sorrows,
We'll cherish them now and through
all our tomorrows.

May your sons learn well from the lessons
you taught,
May they be true to your memory in deed
and in thought,
We've followed your life - in its many parts,
No need for a crown, you are
Queen in our hearts.

Jean Harrison

Diana

Although we never met,
Your kindness touched me deeply,
I know I'll never forget
The way you smiled so sweetly.

You were with us such a short while,
Showing compassion worldwide
But there was sadness
Behind that smile
And now there are tears
I cannot hide.

So farewell Princess Diana
We know that you have gone
As we look up to heaven
We'll see the light you shone.

Jeanette Snook

A Tribute To Diana

No passing, with a useless sigh
Nor seeking secret place to cry
For homeless, dying, weak or sick
No pause in mind, but action quick
A comforting hand, a warming smile
Some kindly words and stay awhile
Not duty call, and briefest stay
Or unctuous words, then let us pray
But love from heart, overflowing
With goodness, kindness and knowing
All feel pain, joy and sorrow
A Queen today, yet clay tomorrow
Born in the gutter or the sky
We are all but born to die
No man's greater than his brother
As final breath makes all discover
Knowing this whilst still alive
Ensures a memory to forever thrive
And a million mourners who will cry
As at the passing of our DI.

L Wilkinson

Diana

WHY oh why did she have to die?
She was loved by all, we want to cry.
We have never known one so caring,
She was always there helping and sharing,
She helped the sick, the aged, the dying,
She did not care if you saw her crying.
The People's Princess we all called her
That she will be although we've lost her
She was so caring she was the best
Millions will cry when she's laid to rest.
She used her life to help and support
Why did her life have to be so short.
The world will miss her, we'll cry and we'll fret.
You can rest assured we'll never forget
We won't forget her, we won't even try.
Why oh why did she have to die?

Len R Le Page

Diana

This day, I felt, so sad inside
God's Heaven, seemed to open wide.
The clouds, they all, stood to one side
And I saw, a pathway, in the skies.
My eyes were shining, bright with tears
As I remembered through the years.
I held a sweet rose to my lips
A petal, for each year, I kissed.
Then on the pathway, there I saw
A face so beautiful to all.
An angel, God had sent to us,
Diana, Princess, Queen of Love.
She looked so happy, and serene
The sweetest smile, that I had seen.
She touched my rose, of petals bright
And spoke so gentle, and so right.
She sent a message to the world
To thank us, for the love we shared.
A rosary, of prayers she toyed,
A prayer, for us, and for her boys.
DIANA.

Barbara Flamson

'Diana' - 'Princess Of Wales'

Oh, Guiding Light, though now asleep,
Forever youth, your image keep.
The image, that with us you shared,
Portrayed to all, you really cared.
The chord, you struck in every heart,
Surely from none, will ever part.
May the legacy, you left behind,
Of friendship, caring, love and kind
Forever stay, with everyone,
And so continue, now you're gone.
So may we all, your gifts portray,
As we journey on, from day to day.

Edna M Dolphin

Diana

In death as in life your star shines bright,
Even though you are physically out of sight,
Your work will go on through others I know.
Even though we wish it was you, not them -
and so
Your love you have given will be returned
Because it was real, not false, or learned.

So many people have grieved on your day
Not knowing at times what to say,
Because you have touched so many inside,
When grieving is done, your love will not hide.
Your love has made so many people strong,
Including your sons, proving loving's not wrong.
Your spirit will go on through the years
Making people smile, even through their tears.

D iana you knew happiness at times
I n giving to people, enriching their
lives
A nd making the world a better place,
N ot stinting your time, your beauty,
your grace.
A nd so you will never be forgotten.

Patricia Baker

A Tribute To You Diana

Diana you became our Queen of Hearts
Your death has torn us all apart,
You will always be the apple in our eye
We ask the Lord why did you die?
Your kindness you kept on giving
The sick, you gave courage, to keep on living.
You nursed our children, giving hope to us all
Helped, pick us up, when we did fall.
Your smiling face, and physical reactions
Were just a few of your many attractions
You touched the hearts of an entire nation
You were truly God's own creation
And in our hearts you'll always stay
Oh Diana, why did you go away?

J Rollo

Diana

I'll always be with you . . .

I am the rainbow that smudges grey sky,
I'll always be with you, I did not die.
I am the gentle breath of the wind,
I am the golden sunlight that kisses the morning dew.
I am the silent teardrops of rain
That shimmer like jewels on the windowpane.
I am the sweet scent of flowers, the soft flutter of wings,
Each precious petal that opens and
song thrush that sings.
I am the glistening pearly snow
on the mountains,
The sway of emerald grass, and glint on sapphire sea,
I am the stream of the river as it rushes
with me.
I am the shadows of moonlight, the echoes
of night.
I am the tears on your pillow,
the whispering light.
I am the twinkle of stars in the heavens above
Your guiding light shining with warmth from my love.
You reach out to touch me, you know
I am there.
I am the gentle breeze that strokes your
soft hair.
And so my sweet princes as you drift into sleep
I'll always be with you, so please do not weep.

Marilyn M Fowler

Diamond Diana

Britannia's First Lady
Queen of the Mall
Adorned, as a Goddess
Oh, what a gal!

God was her Maker
Jesus her Guide;
The fact that she lived here
Bursts us with pride!

In the eyes of the world
No other, so special
Has ever, been here, to reside!

Kevin Setters

The Queen Of Hearts

The Queen of Hearts had many parts
To play upon our earth
Compassion love she gave to all
The length - the breadth - the girth
A lovely Angel from above
Was sent from Heaven to spread her love
Her lovely face her radiant smile
Was with us for such a little while

Administering love wherever she went
Giving her all until her lifetime was spent
Diana, Diana oh how we loved you
There is no-one can take your place
now it is true
Far too young and lovely to die
No wonder we all have a tear in our eye
A cruel twist of fate, a call from above
And now we have lost the princess we loved

Like the Messiah you touched the lepers
Embraced the sick and the dying
Dear Diana you were goodness itself
No wonder our hearts are all crying
A special Angel from the good Lord above
Who ministered a really caring love
How on earth will we manage without your
sweet smile
Our thoughts will be with you for all
of the while
We know you have gone to heaven above
To reside with the Lord and all His sweet love.
Our Diana our sweet English rose
Rest now in peace in heavenly repose.

Eleanor Brandes-Dunn

Diana

You didn't know me
though I knew all about you
Your image was everywhere,
always on view.

Your smile touched the world
you were everyone's friend,
You lit up our lives,
No-one thought it would end.

A bright light went out
on the day that you died,
The world was in darkness
and everyone cried.

Your name will live on
we will never forget.
We all thought we knew you
though we never met.

But now you are gone
to a far better place
the memories live on,
in pictures of your face.

The sky's lost a star
we were privileged to know,
but our affection for you
will continue to grow.

Rest in peace, Diana.

JH

Diana

How we grieve for Britain's Princess
For a life tinged with sadness
For a love that gave much gladness
Lost now in a moment's madness.
Now she has gone, a shining light.
The void now dark, which should be bright.
Surely as night transcends into day, sweet
English rose - in our hearts you will stay.

Jean H Fox

The People's Princess

P rincess Diana you saw the pain and trouble
and deep despair
R eaching the world to make us aware

I nside and out your beauty shone

N obody could compare with you
There could be only one
C aring for William and Harry, your
motherly love shone through
E each day you made others happy and the
people's love for you just grew
S omebody so special you can never be
replaced
S o we'll always remember our
'People's Princess's face'.

D iana you reached both young and old in
every land
I n offering a friendly helping hand

A nd trying in all ways to understand

N o greater gift could you give mankind

A nd kindness of your heart brought peace of
mind.

'For in our hearts she'll be living still
As years go passing by.'

Love

Margaret, Philip, Peter, Jonathan,
Matthew & Philip (Jnr) Diamond

Treasured Memories Of Lovely Diana

Each one thread with gold
They never tarnish or grow old
If only our prayers were answered
And dreams would come true
We would not need memories Diana
Because we would still have you
Rest in peace Diana, so dearly loved
and sadly missed.

E Warren

Diana

So, sit with me and think a while
of all that we have had

If we had never seen her smile
would we now feel so sad

If she had not caressed a child
in such a special way

Would there have been the river of tears
that we have shed today

So, sit with me and think a while
of the Diana we have known

And give thanks to the Lord above
that she was ours on loan

Give thanks she did not die alone
but had Dodi by her side

Joined together eternally
in Heaven she'll be his bride

So, sit with me and think a while
think of Diana and Dodi and smile.

Carol Jackson

Princess Of Wales, Queen Of Hearts

Her fairytale had fallen apart
So she became a Queen in our Heart
Warmth she spread to young and old
A brand new fairytale to be told
Of Princess fair, so misunderstood
Who defeated hurt to do such good
But happy ever after was not to be
Our Princess now at last is free . . .

RIP.

Linda Fish

My Island

Here on 'My Island'
With trees standing high
The sun goes a-sailing
Across the blue sky
I see a small stream
Neath the shade of a tree
That blossoms forever
Each flower for me.
The rambling roses
Of colours divine
Send our their beauty
To the clinging vine
A place of contentment
A place to belong
This 'haven of silence'
This place far beyond
What a place to surrender
As my memories unfold
Here on 'My Island'
I have treasures untold.

F Davies

A Tribute To Diana

As nights draw in and days go by
Have you ever wondered why
We have lost our wondrous pearl
Whose last few days where just a whirl
For our Diana was always the light
Who shines so brightly now by night
She was the diamond of them all
But wasn't that clear before the fall
Of our gracious Princess now asleep
To all the world as we now weep
Love from the world to heir and son
For the loss of Diana your beautiful mum
So look to the stars above the steeple
There you will see the
'Princess of the People'.

June Watson

Death's Dark Veil

Diana Princess of Wales,
sunlight of our hearts,
hope and joy,
from this world departs,
truly, for God knows why.

If the stars in the sky could
shed tears and grief,
they would tell a countless tale
of mourning and disbelief.

As the clouds at night cover
the shining moon,
a veil of darkness, crowds our minds,
with death so terrible and so soon.

No place was too high for this champion
of people, an heir to the throne,
work, charity, love,
conceals tragedy, fear, loss,
for the heavens above.

Colum Donnelly

Diana

A tender smile
A loving touch
A princess who meant so very much
Now she's gone
To Heaven above
With her goes
All our love
No words can ever really say
What we feel on this sad day
A shining light
From us has gone
But her memory will linger on.

P D Darragh

To Diana . . . Princess Of Wales

Goodbye my dear, our sweet Princess
May the angels reach out with a soft caress.
You cared so much for the sick and the poor
No human on earth could have wished for more.

A simple hug . . . a gentle smile
Your 'common touch' stood out a mile.
A Lady born, beyond compare
Compassion there for all to share.

Another like you? The answer is nay
Not if we wait until Judgement Day.
Our Queen of Hearts you will always be
Remembered forever . . . with Majesty.

Now you're at peace with the one you love
God Bless you and keep you . . .
in Heaven above.

C H Boon

Goodbye Diana

Diana may you rest in peace
Something you have rarely known
Now may you take your rightful place
Upon God's heavenly throne.

It's there for all the world to see
The love that you once gave,
And we know that you will pass it on
From within your peaceful grave.

To us you were the Queen of Hearts
The legend of a nation
A lovelier person still to be born
Out of God's own creation.

We will call the new ocean Diana
An ocean made from tears
An ocean that will glitter and shine
And last a million years!

Kirk Nichol

Morte Dans Paris

(Composed in memory of Dodi and Princess of Wales)

Every century there is a Romeo and Juliet,
Lovers whose lives touch a generation.
Young, charming, sincere love, not to forget,
whose hearts and minds received ovation.

Theirs was a love in which the world rejoiced,
whose innermost secrets made angels smile.
A tale which belonged to Byron's poetic voice,
immortal love that never faced human trial.

And now the grief of a nation joins in unity,
to remember their Romeo and Juliet's love.
World leaders and members of the
lower community,
united by funereal flowers, and a
peaceful Dove.

Now at eternal rest, Dodi, the people's Leander,
With Diana, his Hero and earthly soul mate.
Whilst above the mortal coils of earth meander
two new stars, whose love, their
constellation make.

Peter Everett

To Our Princess Di

Dearest Lord in the Heavens above
We ask you to give Diana your deepest love
Taken from us and now in your loving care
Where she can bide in peace with you there
She was kind and loving, and deserved
the best
You saw it time to take her, give her peace
and rest
Peace from those who would not let her be
You took her away. You let her go free
She did so much good, touched everyone's heart
Then sadly from this life she did depart
A loving princess to us, and a loving mother
Upon this earth like her, there be no other
And even though she be from life now gone
She will always be remembered by everyone
Many will pray to you each and every night
That Diana be a special star of yours -
Forever To Shine Bright.

April Denham

The Princess Of Wales

The radiant star that lit our world,
The smile that lingered in our hearts,
The soothing comfort of her hands -
This troubled soul of many parts.

Oh yes she's gone, but not too far,
For mothers always stay so close
To all their young, with Love that holds;
She will be active in repose.

To the distressed she was a friend,
A hopeful beacon and so bright;
A Rainbow that stood out to cheer -
A dawn of Joy to sweep the night.

W Henry Jones

Everyone's Princess

Everyone's Princess
Loyal and unique
A wonderful legend
Fond memories, we keep.

Elegant and pretty
Charming and kind
A heart full of warmth
A smile so divine.

You were the nation's favourite
The world adored you too
You'll stay forever in our hearts
Because Diana, we all love you.

Denise Hemingway

William & Harry In Memory Of Mum

We've all got a mother, we
hold dear to our hearts.
We want her there forever
and we never want to part.
But when she's taken from us
it brings us so much pain,
And it's so hard to carry on
when so much sadness still remains.
I have sadly lost my mum
so I know how you must feel.
But though it may be hard to cope
one day your pain will heal.
Your mummy is your best friend and
she helps you through your day
And it may seem hard to cope
when that's taken away.
I am so much older,
with three sons of my own
And I feel only sadness
that you've been left so soon.
But you have so many memories
that mummy left behind.
Her strength, her love, her courage
She was one of a kind.
She changed so many lives
with everything she did.
And showed so much compassion,
and a special love for kids.
She's left a lasting memory
for all the world to see.
A kind and loving mother
As we would like to be.
And as she sits in heaven
With Dodi by her side.
She can have the happiness
she sadly was deprived.
She was a special mummy
but you already know.
And I know it made you sad
that she had to go.
But just remember one thing
when you think of mum.
The whole world saw the love
she had for her special sons.
So be happy in the knowledge,
that your mum's love for you
Will always be the one thing that
helps you both get through.

Lynn Brown

Diana

Thou has from innocence been plucked by nature's hand
To bloom so beautifully a radiant flower grand.

With colours floating through the gardens of our life
And touching hearts with petals soft and gently laid

Though storms have lashed and beaten out their rage within thy heart
Never hast thou wilted through the pain.

E'en courage made thee blossom more
And spread thy floral blankets cross the desert sands

To reach a heart far from the bounds of love and now begin
When cruelly were thee trodden to the ground by man's own greed and self demand
And so to bloom again with the promised land

You have left a scent so sweet it could never be forgotten.

David Green

Diana

Where has she gone, why has she gone
Up in God's world, in heaven above,
There's hurt and pain and never-ending tears
But we still have for her, a lot of love.

God must have had a reason, what for and why?
But Diana, Diana, your name will never die
Without you the world will feel colder
but you'll be like an angel on our shoulder.

You'll be here in spirit and in our memories
Our thoughts for you will never fade
All your people gave their last words
As they all bowed down and prayed.

People have given all their prayers and thoughts
Given by us for you to receive,
Everything has been torture, which shouldn't
have happened
But we have to take it in and have to believe.

But we know now that you're at peace
To be around and to be free
Not covered by cameras or a microphone
And now you're above to be left alone.

You could make a miracle or a dream come true
For your people in need and their problems too
They gave you their love, respect and thanks
Now everything's disappeared and just gone
blank.

How could we let a miracle go away
We have to live without you day by day
From anger and depression there were tears
We have to try and fill our hopes and fears

There are now two sons without a mother
They've lost their fun from you and each other
They won't have a mum to see them grow up
They'll strongly stick together brother by
brother.

They'll both have good memories of her
to keep them going
As they've lost the biggest piece from their lives
Now she's just in their hearts and their thoughts
Also in their dreams, which seem so alive.

But we all have to accept that she's gone
Let's not forget Dodi who made her happy in life
Let's hope they'll be above us always and
together
As we will never forget you Diana,
always and forever.

Natalie Hill

Always Remembered

So tragically taken our darling princess
What would have been, then we'll just have
to guess
When I see against the sky a beautiful
church steeple
Your final farewell, and the power of
the people.
When I hear hymns and voices lifted on high
Our hearts so broken as we said goodbye.
A garden of roses, scented and sweet
The many you helped, with so many more left
to meet.
The colours of springtime, a promise of
new life
Perhaps finding happiness as Dodi's new wife.
The summer sun glinting upon the sea
I'll cherish your light that will forever be.
When autumn blazes with fire and splendour
Your spirit shining so loving and tender.
When moonlight bathes the night-time frost
Thoughts of how you sparkled, and your life
so sadly lost.
When I see a lawn spangled with morning dew
The tears that we cried, in loving memory of you.

Stephen Denning

A Letter To Diana

It is so hard to find the right words to say
How I felt when I heard the news on that fateful day.
Disbelief and grief at the tragic loss of one so kind,
One so misunderstood by some, by the ones who were blind.
Blind to the meaning of your feelings for those suffering alone
And as I heard of your tragic death which none could condone,
I cried deep in my heart for that which could never be,
For the happiness you had fought for but would never see.
You tried to teach us all to love, to care for human kind
But your life will not be in vain, for you have left behind,
The greatest legacy of love the world will ever know,
May your image and your goodness in my heart forever glow.

Thinking of you always,

Irene Smith

Diana

We still cannot believe the news
So sad - it's hard to bear
To lose a Princess in this way
Our grief the whole world shares

Since entering our gloomy world
Your smile and kindness shone
The happiness you brought to all
Will linger on and on

Fear not, Diana, for your sons
Like you, they're loved by all
One day YOUR King will rule this land
YOUR double, strong and tall

So farewell Diana and Dodi
May you enjoy everlasting love
You'll be the brightest stars shining
In the dark skies up above.

Sylvia Kelly

Tribute To Diana, Princess Of Wales

You were the People's Princess, the Queen of Hearts,
In our lives you played a special part,
You gave love to those in need,
Who were homeless and had a mouth to feed,
Those who were injured through landmines,
You gave them a cuddle and were ever so kind,
You were so unique, so special and strong,
It seemed nothing you did could ever be wrong,
Forever you will remain in our hearts and thoughts,
For our attention you always caught,
Happy images of you we'll always keep,
Whilst you lay in Heaven and peacefully sleep,
May God look after your two sons,
Who have been robbed of a wonderful mum,
Never at all will we forget about you,
As all good things said about you were absolutely true.

Emma Robinson (14)

A Tribute To Diana

Thirty-six, a life so young, the flames no longer glow,
This sweet young girl, no longer there, to see her children grow.
A beautiful girl, of regal line, her traditions deeply burned,
Fell in love with a princely knight, but found her love was spurned.

Two sons had she, this loving wife, before this love was dead,
The future of our Royal House, was in these two sons bred.
But then it came, the awful time, for the Princess, all alone,
And stripped of rank, her hopes all gone, the Rose walked on her own.

We watched the love, the mother gave, to nurture both her sons,
And through the sadness, came great joy, of hope without the guns.
She touched the hearts of lesser souls, held fast within her arms,
Touched the sick with outstretched hands, worked magic with her charms.

This gentle Soul, no longer here, the nation mourns her fate,
And thousands shown respect with awe, and remember far too late,
The deeds on which this young Princess, firmly took a stand,
And how deserted by the few, now millions join their hands.

Janet Allen

Diana, Princess Of Wales

Born to beauty, wealth and fame, her destiny was set
To bring compassion to a world of sorrow and regret;
To know the pain that comes through loss, her young sons now must face;
To overcome the media lies of infamy and disgrace.

Many would have broken with the pressure that she bore
Many would have turned to hate, that deep emotion raw.
Diana found the inner strength and faith to rise above
The pettiness and sham and fake, and transmute it with her love.

She spoke with truth and showed her care through laughter and through touch
(Those simple acts that people fear, and yet which mean so much)
Leaving gentle thoughts and joy to linger when she'd gone
By caring for others, and bringing relief, her spirit shone.

For all their life upon this earth her sons must wonder why
This soul that shone so brightly was extinguished from their eye.
No mortal man can cause her harm, no-one can do her ill
Though from this plane her form has gone, her love shines still.

Jennifer Densham

Diana - Queen Of Hearts

We look back upon your wedding day
Oh the joy and merriment!
Seems like only yesterday
This fairytale event
But the marriage didn't last
Seems we loved you more than he
Too shy for the pressures of public life
And the strain of publicity
But you worked through all your troubles
And you began to smile once more
You found joy in helping others
And became our Ambassador!
As you helped the sick and the needy
Our admiration grew
You won the hearts of thousands
I just hope of this you knew!

'The Best Roses are always the first
to be picked!'

With love,

Ruth . . . xxx

The Rose

Of all the roses in the garden
Fragrant in the morning dew
Blooms a rose that's called 'Compassion'
Princess Di that rose was you
Deep within your heart you cared for
Sick and lonely girls and boys
Held their hands, smiled,
hugged and kissed them
As you did your own small boys
Now in heaven you walk in safety
Rest in peace you were adored.

O Roberts

For Diana . . .

Words can't really tell you
Of the pain I feel inside
The grief and tears keep flowing
They will not be denied

I hope the words bring comfort
For I write them from the heart
Of my love for a beautiful Princess
From whom we've had to part

I never, ever met you
Yet I adored you just the same
My personal precious memories
Of you will always remain

The thoughts of your compassion
Your tender caring ways
You gave so much to everyone
Yet never wanted praise

All you ever really wanted
Was to love and be loved in return
Yet why did pain, not pleasure
Come from those things you yearned

But then suddenly your happiness
Was there for all to see
For a while we shared a romance
Fate decided wasn't to be

Princess Diana
I hope God will let you know
The world you've left behind you
Is grieving for you so

Thank you for being our Princess
Our 'Queen of Hearts' for sure
Rest in peace in a world of love
That is yours for evermore.

Valerie Ann Allcock

Diana Princess Of Wales

Diana Spencer born a lady
Also, had this special gift of love and affection
Throughout her short life, day
By day she used her skill and attention
To help others in great need.

Never thoughtful of herself
Always full of careful thought
For the people of the nation itself
Ever watchful to do, what she ought
No matter what it cost!

A true loving mother of her sons
Will and Harry, they were her pride and joy
Ever wanting them to be like other little ones
Taking them to shows and funfairs
like Billy and Roy
She's to be praised for her mother love.

Her life has been blighted with sadness
But she never let it darken her soul
Forever lifted her head to the brightness
Of life, by helping charities as a whole
Many of them will remember her well.

Diana Princess of Wales will always
Be remembered as the Queen of Hearts
The nation's most loved lady, her days
In life spent mostly to help others
at home and in foreign parts
She will never be forgotten.

May Diana, your happiness shine in
Heaven above
No sadness now to endure each day
But sheer love and delight with your new love
You, will be forever in the nation's prayers
Come what may! Amen to a wonderful lady.

Alma Montgomery Frank

Diana

We miss you dear Diana
So very very much
We miss the feeling of love
Brought by your tender touch

The young, the old, the sick and dying,
Even lepers too
You gave them all such kindness
Those people never knew.

I feel that I know you
Although we never met
I'm sad that you have left us
We owe you a great debt.

I like the name we call you
The Queen of Hearts it is
Forever we will think of you
And all the good you did.

Christine Jephcott

Precious One

'Up above our heads you fly
Just like a butterfly'.
Diana was your name
Our Queen of Hearts you became
We will never forget the day
we lost you in that tragic way
Our hearts will never mend
Your memory will live on
until the very end
We will always remember that
lovely shy smile
Those electric eyes said it all
loving and caring most generous
of all.
We hope you have found the happiness
you deserve.
You will always be our princess
Rest in peace precious one.

Roger Hutt

The Sunflower - Diana

People stand in awe of her,
trying to look into her face.
They have never seen anything so beautiful
and full of grace.
She grows with a ferocity
and determination of mind
And nothing will stop her,
until she reaches the skies.
What is this desperation to grow so tall
When everything around her is so small.
She battles on, no matter what the weather
Sometimes tired and at the end of her tether.
The sun sees her struggling
and takes care of her plight
He beams down on her, with all his might.
They face each other, the flower and the sun
She's done her work and reached the skies,
She smiles at the sun, drops her seeds,
bows her head, and gently dies.

Kelly Mitchell

Tribute To Diana

What a beautiful Princess you were
An angel among the living
So thoughtful, so kind and always giving.
Your heart reached out to the human race
You did it with style, poise and grace,
You leave a picture in everyone's mind
People will remember you were so kind.
Now you are in the garden of love
In the arms of God above
You will never be forgotten by anyone
You will always be remembered,
We will cherish your memory forever
We will forget you never.

Phyllis Russell

Diana

Our sweet and loving Princess
Was laid to rest today.
Though why and for whatever reason
only the Lord can say.

Her smile full of radiance
She shone just like a star.
She touched the hearts of many
She helped both near and far.

Diana we all love you
and pray for you today.
And in our hearts remember
your caring loving ways.

M C A Fuller

A Nation Weeps

We stand around in disarray,
In shock and utter disbelief.
Throughout the days that lie ahead,
The whole world will unite in grief.

For we have heard the dreadful news,
Princess Diana has died today.
Such needless waste of her young life,
Her radiance gone, taken away.

She worked so hard for her beliefs,
When things seemed wrong and so unfair,
No matter what the cause may be,
If she could help, she would be there.

Reaching out to those in need,
Dying, sick and homeless ones.
How sadly now she will be missed,
A loss so great, for years to come.

This Nation mourns a Princess who,
Had for us, the common touch,
Her lovely smile and special way,
By young and old, was loved so much.

Farewell, the people's 'Queen of Hearts',
May the dear Lord hold your hand,
Your love, compassion, countless deeds,
Forever, remembered in this land.

Margaret Ashman

From A Princess

'Don't cry,'
Step forward
Wipe your tear away
Instead, reach out,
Touch, smile, love,
Make someone
Happy
In more than
Words can say.

Nadine Johnston

My Boys The Princes William And Harry

Two young boys in true Brit style,
Walked their longest lonely mile,
Their shoulders heavy hung with grief,
No tears to ease, to give relief,
Maybe their mother's voice was nigh,
Helping, urging, do not cry,
For in the coffin that you see,
My body's there it is not me,
For I am walking by your side,
As ever I am full of pride,
I may have left this earthly plane,
But you'll still feel me ease your pain.
A mother's love and guiding hand,
Between heaven and earth can still expand,
For both of you are part of me,
So I'm still here though not to see,
Your lives must sail their chartered course,
Your Royal births you must endorse,
And when your lives to death succumbs,
I'll be there waiting, 'my boys'
my darling sons.

Lynne-Elizabeth Hawkes

Golden, Shining Star

You did bless me with your light,
Smiles of love,
You gave such heart,
Some goodness,
Only children saw.
So cruel the void,
So dark our hearts,
So beautiful, thoughts of time.
To love, then lose,
You have to go,
Eternity,
Now your joy.
God blessed you,
Precious one.

Sheridan

Our Lovely Flower

In our thoughts you'll always stay
Queen of all our hearts.
Your sons will always be with you
Although you're far apart.

You taught them how to love and care,
To give as well as take.
They will never let you down,
As you watch them from the lake.

Your last few weeks were oh so good,
Such happiness you found,
You and Dodi shone like stars,
Pretty flowers all around.

So Queen of Hearts now you're in heaven,
Like a ship that sails and sails,
You'll always be a lovely 'rose',
OUR PRINCESS OF WALES.

Evelyn Criddle

Untitled

There was no warning, no reason why your life came to an end. One so young and full of joy, and compassion, 'The People's Friend'.

Your death was so untimely good work is left undone, and people with heartfelt intentions say 'This work will carry on.'

You gave wealth to the poorest, the dying, sick and lame. A wealth of love, a wealth of hope, no other could do the same.

The brightest star in the heavenly sky will shine with radiance tonight. While we, 'the common people' will say
'God Bless, Diana, and goodnight.'

Jacqueline Jones

Diana

A child was born into our world
and nurtured tenderly
No bells rang out nor clarions
heralded that day
But soon her destiny unfurled
for everyone to see
A light grew bright within her heart
A love she chose to share
with lepers, commoners and Kings
A quality so rare
Her too brief life on Earth
Embodied all human frailties
But through it all unselfishly
She gave herself to others
Bringing joy and comfort to
the sick and maimed
To babies and their mothers
Jesus' love shone through his pain
And now we've seen it once again
For Diana's love has stood the test
And all whose lives she touched are blessed
And though her Earthly body
This empty world departs
The brightest jewel within the Crown
Will shine forever in our hearts.

Edward C Fairweather

God Bless You Diana

God Bless you Diana
We love you my angel, we do.
Never a day goes by
When we are not thinking of you.
God has taken you to Heaven
To reign with Him above.
We know one day we will meet you up above.

Philip Evans

The Queen Of Hearts

A young child prays in silence,
In a state of shock, from unexpected news.
An angel has gone,
Now a candle in the wind.

Churches and parks, full of gifts,
Mountains of wondrous colours,
With each different species of flower,
Everyone sent, with love and affection,
Strong devotion of respect to a
people's princess.

We miss your radiant smile so much,
That raised such hope for so many.
Hospital visits to children in need,
Help to AIDS and cancer worldwide.

Great care and feeling of concern
always shown,
Millions mourn in despair, for courage
so rare,
Tears of sorrow, enough to fill a lake,
Engulf a nation so deep in grief.

Union flags fly at half mast,
Candles burn shining bright,
Till like Diana,
The light goes out.

An eternal flame she becomes,
Observe the night sky,
Thousands of stars are joined by one,
An oasis in a desert, rises into Heaven,
Laden with untold sentiment,
A saint could not ask for more.

Messages of comfort, cover your coffin,
One small bouquet, MUMMY it read.
To us you will always be
Our very own English Rose
Diana we love you so.

Thoughts of kindness remembered,
As you depart from this life,
God Bless,
May you rest in peace,
The Queen of Hearts.

N Astell

Diana

Diana you were England's Rose
Your smile gave us hope and grace
You were our only 'Queen of Hearts'
Whom no-one can replace

You were the jewel of my crown
The sparkle in my eyes
You gave us all the love
That will never ever die.

On Earth you shone out your love
Like you thought you must
Now you're a ray of sunshine
That shines from dawn till dusk

I'll look at the sky every night
Thinking of you 'the best',
And see your beautiful star
That outshines all the rest.

Flowers may die
And time pass by
But Diana you'll be in my heart,
Until the day I die.

Diana, you were my true friend.
The day you died, part of me died too.
R.I.P. Always in my prayers.
It seems England is nothing without you.

Emma Gardner (13)

A Rose And A Thorn

Sweet of fragrance
And sharpness of mind
Her strengths were petals of love
Which blossomed with every
Heart she touched.
Mother of two
Out of the world were her tears.
Tired and forlorn
Were the wings of her steed,
But on she went
Until the coming of dawn.
If heaven and earth
Be the isthmus
Then Princess Diana
Will be 'reborn'.

David John Smith

Diana

The vision never witnessed,
Till the lady held a hand,
A smile of warmth gave hope,
Broke down the walls of shame.

As the beating heart waned,
We heard the angels sing,
A special soul, released,
Delivered to the king.

Tears of millions flowed,
A river of hope now born.
Rain raised up above us,
And spread around the world.

Now laid to rest forever,
Upon your island of dreams.
A country's unique treasure,
Never one the same.

Paul Copland

A Flower Of Love

In a manor house long ago
An English rose was born,
A child of natural beauty,
A rose without a thorn.

She grew into a woman
Much loved by everyone,
Her beauty and her presence
Outshone the summer sun.

She was everybody's princess
Right from the very start,
With love and understanding
She stole everybody's heart.

Now beneath a carpet of flowers
Under a canopy of green,
Rests our beautiful Diana,
Who we wanted for our Queen.

Marlene S Browne

Diana

Deep in our heart
Your beauty is kept
To love to cherish
And never forget

No verse, no flowers
No words can say
How much we'll miss you every day

As each day dawns
And starts anew
As each day ends
We'll think of you

And in between
No matter where
In our thoughts
You will always be there.

Ian MacQuire

Diana Princess Of Wales

The sea is still,
The twinkle has gone from the stars,
There's no salvation left in the army.

There's no movement in the trees,
There's no warmth from the sun,
The birds do not sing anymore.

A Guru has left fashion,
A maker has gone from news,
A British treasure has been lost.

Our hearts are heavy with sorrow,
Hope has left our lives,
Love has left our hearts,
No more giggles,
No more tears,
Just an emptiness.

We will remember,
We will never forget,
You touched our lives so briefly,
We unite in our grief.

Our beloved Diana,
Queen of Hearts,
Find eternal happiness,
And may you now rest in peace.

K Rands

Diana

The young girl walked down the aisle
with pride,
The Prince she loved by her side.
The fairy tale was not to be,
Her love had strayed, he set her free,
A Queen of Hearts for you and me.
Compassion, love and humour too,
She gave to all straight and true.
Touched our hearts we felt her pain,
Two lovely sons our country's gain.
A Princess in Heaven, I am sure she
reigns supreme to weep no more.

Rosemary Lake

A Little Girl Cried For Diana

My little granddaughter Debra phoned me
She's only five years old.
She said 'Are you crying Nannie
For my Princess Diana has passed away
I want her back for she's my friend
Nannie when will we see Diana again?

I want her to come back' she sobbed
'Take me to Heaven Nannie to get Diana
back'
This brought a lump into my throat
To hear a child sobbing for Diana
'Nannie are you wiping your eyes with
a tissue?'

She asked me how she got to Heaven
I said she rose from the earth
into heaven
'How do I get up to Heaven
So I can bring back my
Friend Diana?'

Janet Brown

Death

No one can make any sense of death,
No matter how hard they try,
People pretend that they're alright,
When inside they want to break down and cry.

Instead of letting their feelings out,
They keep them bottled up inside,
They don't realise that the thoughts get easier,
For the loved one that died.

Sooner or later time heals the pain,
But the feelings will never go,
For Diana, who has gone,
'Cos we'll always love her so.

Joanne Bailey (14)

A Tribute To Our Beautiful Princess Diana

We have lost our beautiful Princess
Our beautiful Princess Di
Why oh why should such a thing happen
Only God knows the reason why.

There will never be another like her
So good, so kind, and so true
Thinking nothing of herself
But only what she could do

To help others she travelled the world
Giving hope to those in need
Something only a chosen person could do
And you must be special to succeed

Hugging the little black children
Who had lost their limbs with the mines
Talking and sympathising to those with AIDS
Made them feel much better for the time

Shaking hands with the lepers not many would do
But our beautiful Diana has done it
And to all the other charities she helped
She had the nation's love, and she won it

To Mother Teresa she could be compared
As they had most things in common
With the love and care they shared

Today that shining light has gone out
Our beautiful Princess had gone
And it must be straight to God above
Whilst the nation is shedding tears and tears
But they are not tears of water
They are tears of love.

Mary Warnock

A Poem For Diana Heaven Above

When you look down from Heaven above
You can see all those that you love
When we look up to the sky at night
We can see you. Your star shining bright.

You are missed each passing day
Although we know you are not far away
We know that there is none fairer
Because you were the world's greatest carer.
We know that there will be no other
You treated the sick as though their mother
You helped the needy and the poor
Until you could give no more.

I feel sure all of your great work
Will not be in vain
And that a hospital will be built in YOUR name.
Then we can look up to the Heavens above to say thanks to Diana
The one we all love.
God Bless You.

George Moneypenny

To Princess Diana

The day you died,
The whole world cried,
Why did it happen?
Why did you have to go
And leave behind so many people who loved you so?
You cared, you loved, you comforted so many, always with a smile or a sigh.
Rest in peace now, your memory will never ever die.

D Ridings

A Wonderful Mum

(God bless a truly remarkable woman
who will be sadly missed but never forgotten)

Diana, how can you ever be replaced,
With a smile that lit up your pretty face,
Those sparkling eyes and lovely blonde hair,
Life without you is too much to bear.

Our love for you will always grow,
Much more that you'll ever know,
A princess you were, but you didn't care.
To the poor and sick you were always there.

A mother you were, two healthy boys.
You gave them love and played with their toys.
You shared their stories and happiness too,
Their world was better because of you.

It's hard to believe now you are gone,
A daughter, a friend, a wonderful mum.
Memories of our Queen of Hearts we'll
always keep.
Rest in peace Diana, in eternal sleep.

Mandy Walsh

The Love Of Life

Seize the moment, take the chance,
for life never waits for the weak
or faint-hearted!
Grasp it, and hold it forever,
whatever it may be, drink it in,
and savour the moment, the second,
for it will never return again.
That is all your life, forever,
lived in that one brief idyllic
moment of joy, be it sight, sound
taste or touch or smell -
Oh, take it, and embrace it in your
soul, and in your memory, before it slips away,
forever gone, in the blink of
an eye, in the catch of your breath.
That is the love of life.

Iris A Gooderham

Diana, Princess Of Wales

D iana you graced our earth
I n times of sorrow and despair
A n Angel lent from Heaven
N ever relenting in your quest to care
A shining example to us all

P ray for her soul tonight
R est in peace our Angel Queen
I n you we've seen the light
N o one can ever replace you
C ompassionate, kind and adored
E qually, in your fine sons live you
S ecure in the love that you poured
S o many people now grieve for you

O ur hearts touched deeply worldwide
F or now you are the people's legend

W e'll always remember you with pride
A candle in the wind now extinguished
L ong before your time was due
E ternally your presence will linger
S o much the whole world loved you.

Elaine Eke

Diana

Your lovely smile and beautiful face
Will no longer be seen
But the wonderful memories
Of all you have done
Will stay forever green.

The love you so freely gave
The understanding and comfort so great
Will now be felt by everyone
You meet at Heaven's gate.

You may no longer be on earth
But the love you left behind
The caring and beauty of your dear heart
Will live forever in our mind.

E Anderson

Gone Too Soon

(For Princess Diana - the Eternal Queen of Our Hearts)

You were just like an angel from
Heaven above,
The light of your face shone upon us all;
Your heart had so much to give,
I'd weep tears of joy to recall.

Why did you have to leave us so soon,
When you bore a warm heart's
devoted aid?
You may not be with us now,
But your light of love will never fade.

'Twas sweet to see an unselfish heart,
As every glance of yours revealed;
You were no stranger to pain yourself,
But your destiny was not to yield.

Yet, though we cannot see thee more,
In our hearts you will remain;
I know we will rejoice always,
Thanking God that you came.

Julie Byfield

Jewel In The Crown

A diamond that shone
in a world full of strife
So much pain in her short sad life
With much love to give
kept locked in her heart
A jewel that was hidden alone in the dark.
The world stopped for a moment
a sigh swept over the land
People were numbed - couldn't understand
We wept unashamed - loving her -
and wanting to know
why! Oh why!
Did God want her so?

G Tominey

Diana . . . The Queen Of Hearts

A tribute paid to our Princess Di
This Sabbath morn we say goodbye
You helped the people you've done your best
But now you're taken and laid to rest

Flowers are left in your respect
You are a person we cannot forget
In lots of tasks you got involved
Your aim it was the problem solved

For the world you did your best
Angola, Bosnia and all the rest
Charity work, yes, here and there
For the elderly you really cared

The Royal Family you played your part
The nation loved you with all its heart
The grief is shown with family and friends
Their love for you will never end

A charity worker, the Queen of Hearts
For everyone you played your part
The people upset, lots of crying
They all loved you, there's no denying.

Dougie Nelson

Diana And Dodi

D oting mother of the world
I nsuring that it be known caring of the
sick and needy
A ffection for those you met worldwide
N ever have the British been so proud
A Queen of Hearts you hear them say

A nd now that's what they pray
N ow you have gone
D isaster is an awful thing

D reams come dreams go
O nly together you did go
D ismay and tears now you have found
happiness
I n love together Diana and Dodi go.

Michaela Tucker

Diana

Then her Spirit departed
and entered the Kingdom of Heaven
Diana the beloved and true-hearted
gone to stay in the Kingdom of Heaven
for evermore.
And now she sits and gazes at us
with those deep and tender eyes
And looks upon the people
united in their grief.
Your end was too sudden Diana,
your thoughts unknown,
but you left the nation,
memories proud to own.
Part of you will live on forever
in both your sons, William and Harry.
Your life was not in vain,
although a nation is left in pain.
Goodnight sweet Princess
your life on earth is past
but we as a nation will love you
dearly until the last

Rest in peace Diana for evermore.

Margaret Kinghorn

God's Angel

God was short of an Angel
But why did he choose you
When God was short of an Angel
He said only the best will do
Now God has got his Angel
and Heaven is a brighter place
but earth has lost its brightness
Except for her light in our hearts.

Gwen

Diana

Diana was our Princess
But sadly she has gone
Her beauty both inside and out
Is still with us, after that tragic dawn.

Our Princess had a troubled life,
Which often left her blue,
But she always had compassion,
Love and laughter, for all mankind
This she gave, to me, to you.
No-one was beneath her,
the needy, the sick, the dying,
Her arms she'd wrap around you,
As only she could do.
Most of all she was a mother
With two sons she loved so dear.
'My boys William and Harry,'
those words still linger here.
When history books are written
I hope it shall be seen.
Diana you blessed us with your
presence, you will always be
our Queen.

Vera Barrett

A Tribute To Diana

You were our emblem
Now you are gone
No other flower
Can take your place
You were our lovely rose
We will remember
Through the years
As you scattered your petals
Across the land
Now there's nothing left
But a river of tears
And a sea of sand.

J Boyle

Our Princess

You came into our lives touched us with
your love
Now you are with God up in Heaven above,
With your warmth and charm you were special
And you did so much for us the people,
So caring, thoughtful, compassionate
and kind,
You have left a lot of sad people behind.
A precious gem, a treasure and so unique
In our thoughts memories of you
we will keep,
Our sadness, grief and tears all express
How much we miss you our Princess,
With your bright shining eyes and
radiant smile
We thank God we knew you, if only
for a while,
Everywhere we go we see your smiling face
No other could ever take your place,
We still can't believe that you have gone
And the light is out that once always shone,
Never to be forgotten we will love you forever
OUR one and only beautiful
Princess Diana.

Linda Roberts

For Diana

On this day of great grief, and disbelief
The house - and the land -
observe a minute's silence
Only my singing finch is not silent
But trills a song of such joy, and light,
and laughter,
Which is in itself a very fitting tribute.
And afterwards I play Ravel's beautiful
'Pavanne For A Dead Princess'
For our own beautiful, dead princess.

Sue Garnett

A Tribute To Diana Princess Of Wales

Diana, you were so human
With such a beautiful soul
that you were chosen to play a
special role
You showed us all the way we should be,
Kind and compassionate to those
less fortunate than we
You gave hope to the sick, weak and old,
The homeless people out in the cold.
With a sunny smile, a touch of the hand,
You made them feel the most special
in the land.
Then suddenly you were snatched away
That was a dark and dismal day
Our shining star taken above to
shine down forever with eternal love.
Now when we look up to the sky at night
and see a light twinkling bright
It's you our Diana making sure
we're alright.
Goodnight sweet Princess.

Irene Mellowship

Diana

Your life was snatched
away that night,
The pain's so hard to bear,
It's cruel and doesn't seem right,
It really isn't fair,
The world needs someone
like you,
The Queen of all our hearts,
Your love was sweet and
oh, so true,
In all your many parts,
As mother, carer, sister, friend,
Whatever guise you wore,
You did your best until the end,
Dear Princess, we adore.

Sue Gemmell

Diana

As a child you were a tomboy,
Climbing trees, as children do,
Far away from worldly troubles;
Nothing ever bothered you.
As you grew the real world prodded,
Subtle hints that life was hard,
You sensed that things weren't easy
Out there beyond the yard.
In your teens you cared for children,
Little knowing how your care
Would become almost a legend
For the suffering everywhere.
You became our 'fairy' Princess
When you married Charles of Wales,
But though the fairy tale turned sour,
You're still special in the Vales.
Born a Lady with a title;
Truly regal from the start,
You became a Royal Princess,
But a 'Lady' from the heart.

Angela Rowlands

Diana

Your ornament of beauty and respect
God took you in your prime
But your name we won't forget
As bells of Cathedral chime
People stand with crying eyes
You're now a princess of the skies
The people's Princess you were to be
You were gentle and caring, people could see
The 'Queen of Hearts' you will remain
In loving memory we mourn your name.

Dee Rhys Jones

Untitled

She had a gift so very rare,
To help all who were ill or lonely,
It did not matter who they were,
She listened and talked to them,
Helping many people.
She must have been a wonderful mother
To William and Harry.
They will be lost without her,
But she left her two sons to carry on
Her caring ways,
She was the people's Princess
And will be forever remembered.
Why did it happen?
We shall never know,
Her life was cut short
Just when she found love with Dodi,
She was the 'Queen of Hearts'.

I W Burnell

Requiem For Diana

Oh the silence on this saddest day
The crowds they mourn ten deep along
the way
And yet again the silence as the millions
weep and pray
It's DIANA! DIANA! DIANA!
All that they can say
Oh fairest one so well beloved
The million hearts that you have moved
Sleep well sleep deep at peace at last
And now the flag flies at half mast
Homeward homeward you are bound
To lie at peace in hallowed ground
And know that you have left a
legacy divine
But peace and joy at last are thine.

June Clare

Diana - Our Princess

You had so much love to give,
And so much life to live -
You and Dodi, in peace at last,
Where all the hurt is in the past.
Together forever, in a better place -
You were an example to the human race!
They tried to break you,
they pulled you apart -
But everything you did was from
your heart!
A greater person, we'll never know
As compassion for others we will all
try to show.
Your memory will go on and on,
As we remember you with a song,
'England's Rose', the 'People's Friend',
The happiness you gave will never end -
Mother Theresa died the same week,
And of that event we have to speak.
She died of a broken heart, that's true -
I believe it was because of you!
Your destinies are forever entwined,
Even if only in my mind -
My own mother died so recently,
That I know how tragic your sons'
Loss will be -
You never think sorrow will come to
An end -
But what comes after this life is your
Best friend - Happiness at last.

June Lillingstone

Ocean Of Tears

There are not enough words to express our
sorrow.
Our tears flow yesterday, today and tomorrow.
May the ocean of tears for Diana strengthen
William and Harry forever!

Brian W Zelley

Diana And Dodi

Diana and Dodi you made us smile
You finally found happiness for a
short while
We heard of your love and prayed it
was true
You had found Dodi, perfect for you
A light was now shining in both of
your eyes
To the world this had come as
no surprise
Then your lives were taken so untimely
and sad
You were the most wonderful Princess
the world ever had
I miss you so dearly as I know
your sons do
May God give them strength so they can
pull through
Now the time has come to say goodbye
As you take your place with the stars
in the sky
Goodbye Diana and Dodi
Together now for eternity.

Emma Moore

Tribute To Diana

This English Rose from bud to bloom
Gave us love and laughter
This world has never seen.
Her smile and tears were from the heart,
Her touch and smile were worlds apart.
We will miss this Lady and friend
of ours,
So God bless you Diana,
For touching our hearts.

N Jones

Diana Princess Of Wales

(I was inspired to write the verses below within hours of accepting the terrible news of Diana's death)

I scarcely could believe
my ears, as I awoke today,
I heard that our Diana,
had sadly passed away.

My sorrow I share with
all, I know,
For that dear lady,
we loved her so.

The life that she led was
so full of care.
She had plenty of love
that she wanted to share.

The children, Red Cross,
and people afar,
Will all have read about
that terrible car.

Her devotion to others
was clearly seen,
To me, she'll always be
my queen.

Her devotion to others
can't be upturned,
She'll be in the place
that she's rightly earned.

Where we all wish to go
when our lives cease.
Next to God in lasting
peace.

Les Ball

Diana

O Diana you've gone and left us
Gone up to your home above
Where the Lord was waiting for you
To fill your heart with love

He said your work is over
There's no more to be done
So I took your Dodi with you
Then you both could be as one

They took your title from you
They tried to bring you down
You did not need their title
Nor did you need their crown

Your boys will never forget you
They will think of you with pride
They will hate the day they lost you
And the awful way you died

Whenever they are lonely
And feel the need to cry
They will know that you are near them
To help them say goodbye

So rest in peace dear Diana
And never more be sad
You are with the two that love you
Dodi and your dad

So farewell my Fairy Princess
On Earth you did your best
That's why the good Lord called you
To let you have your rest.

Rita O'Brien

My Poem Is . . .

'Please God, in Heaven above,
Look after our Princess,
And give her our love.'

Marie Yates

In Loving Memory

So many of us have lost,
Ones that we love,
When God calls them,
Up to Heaven above,
The golden gates are open,
Our loved ones,
Once again walk through,
Our hearts are filled with sadness,
In this sad time of despair,
They say that in time our pain
disappears,
All that we have are memories,
To keep through the years,
Memories are for keepsakes,
I know that's very true,
But we never wanted memories,
Lady Di, we wanted you.

With love and may
God bless you now
and always

Ayshea Ahmed

Princess Diana

You were an angel
that came from Heaven,
You always cared,
and smiled for all to see,
You gave us your heart
Helped us, to believe,
You offered us hope,
for you were an Angel.
we truly believe
God's gift for all to see.
Now you're in Heaven
and at peace. God bless thee.
We will always remember
those gifts you gave
for all those in need.
For you had so much love to share,
How wonderful is thee
Princess Diana our pretty Queen.

Giulietta Pecchia

A Princess Lost To You And Me

A great tragedy has occurred
Gone for ever her loving tender spoken word
The nation shocked beyond all belief
Filled with mourning so full of grief
The light it has been extinguished
From England's pleasant shores
The star that shone so bright
Has now passed through Heaven's open doors!

No longer will she with her presence grace
No more to see her loving tender face
But the memory of what she used to be
Will remain for ever deep inside you and me.
At last you have found tranquillity and peace

Safe in God's arms
Diana,
You now can sleep.

J Barnes

My Tribute to Diana

Diana was like a flower
Her petals were her hands
They reached out far and wide
Because she could understand
The centre was her heart
She opened to everyone
And just like a flower
She soon was dead and gone
For us we will remember
This flower our English Rose
What we will do without her
No-one really knows
She will live in all our memories
She will be at our side
Because we will never believe
Our English Rose has died.

Janet Dronsfield

Princess Diana

Gone from Earth to Heaven above,
A Princess whom all the world did love,
With a cheery smile a touch of her hand.
Even though her own life didn't go
as planned.
She knew heartache, pain and tears,
Putting this aside she helped all around
her forget their fears.
A loving mum to both her sons,
We'll remember you laughing with them
having fun.
Now in Heaven in God's arms so
gently lay,
To be remembered every day.
I have no more words to send.
Just God Bless Diana
Goodbye and Amen.

Sylvia Reeve

O' Night So Dark!

Oh night so dark, oh morn so bright.
Our Queen of Hearts has taken flight
Muffled bells toll, with oceans of tears
As the six black horses draw slowly near.
Silence, deep grieving silence falls.
While strong shoulders bear the people's
Princess tall
Mountains of flowers to soften her path.
Golden sunrays her chariot will craft
To carry her high to the eternal place.
Where the love of the people, attire her
in grace.

Dennis East

Why Take Away . . . ?

Diana the people's princess
Beautiful, caring, serene
Her life so cruelly taken
'Why take away our queen?'

We wept and sobbed heartbroken
Laid flowers and cards to rest
Signed pages of condolences
'Why take away the best?'

The streets were lined with people
Who loved her so very much
Who treasured her as a jewel
'Why take away her touch?'

Her sons, William and Harry
Our hearts go out to them
Oh God what were you thinking
'Why take away their mum?'

Her brother, The Earl of Spencer
His emotions running high
His speech so moving, so angry, so real
Why take away his Di?

Let's not forget her Dodi
Another family's son
He gave her untold happiness
'Why take away this one?'

On an island in a tranquil lake
Close by, a star was born
Diana, just to let you know
You'll never be alone
And may you and Dodi rest in peace
Your souls in heaven above
May all us mourning, left behind
Remember and cherish your love
As we ask today, 'Why take away . . . ?'

Sue Elliott

Diana

Of all the rest
Put to the test
Princess Diana
Was the BEST
Her feelings for others
Were always there
Because, she really did care.
A heart of gold
A smile so sweet
For everyone, that she did meet.
She was a real Mum
Who loved her boys
They were her two greatest joys.
She cared about people in distress
And for them, she did her best
She was the Nation's Princess
She is still.
Forget her, we never will
God has her in His keeping
We have her in our hearts
A tribute to the Princess of Hearts.

L Ashton

In Memory Of Diana, Our Princess

You left us so suddenly,
When we didn't expect,
Such a wonderful Lady,
Full of love and respect.

You cared for your country,
Like a mother for its child
You were loving, caring,
And remarkably kind

Oh how we'll miss you,
Our sweet English Rose,
You are now in Heaven with Jesus
Goodbye England's Rose.

Linzi Jones (17)

Our Queen Of Hearts

A tragedy occurred on Sunday
the last day of August
Diana was taken away from us
The question I ask is WHY?

Why did God take you away from us
It's only Him who knows
I'll always treasure your memory
And support the charities you chose

I never thought this could happen
To someone so special and caring like you
You were the people's Princess
And the Queen of my heart too

I've seen you on the TV
And in the papers too
My dream was to have met you
Now this won't come true.

Rachel Taylor

Diana - Princess Of Wales

She came to us
So young - so shy
Dear Lord, why did she have to die?

She gave the world
Such love, such joy
She also gave this land
Two boys.
The nations of the earth have cried
A river of tears since she died
Lord give her peace
In your golden land
It will take us a lifetime to understand

Tonight a bright star
Shines in the sky
We know it's for you
Our own Princess Di.

E M Tucker

A Tribute To Diana

In life we loved,
In death we weep,
And mourn we shall at your passing,
Your candle burned bright, though
Snuffed out too soon
The memory of you will always be true
And the loss we felt at your passing.

Donna Brown

Diana

The loss of a Princess
The final farewell
The rose that will never die
The tears of sadness
The tears of a Nation.
God bless Diana our Queen of Hearts.

Amy Davies (14)

Diana, Princess Of Wales

You were loved for your compassion
Your ability to love
The sick, the sad, the needy
Inspired by your touch.

May your soul be free and happy
On the wings of a white dove
Watching over William and Harry
Encompassed by your love

Your memory will live forever
In the words of Elton's song
In the hearts of the British Nation
Just where you belong!

J Bowrey

Diana

You came into our gaze at such
a young and tender age,
You learned to live as such a Lady.
The press harassed you looking for
anything shady.
They always tried to run you down,
But you were seen happy and joyful
With never a frown.
Your sons that you loved and cherished,
Gave your eyes that sparkling glow.
And those two boys will always know
How much you loved them so.
But now we've lost a beautiful woman,
In this world no-one can take your place.
Because of the press you tried not to face
I hope you're in a nicer place, because
We've lost a beautiful face,
You will always be in our thoughts
and hearts,
Because to the Nation you were the
Queen of Hearts.

Paul Kirk

Our Shining Star

When we think of our beautiful
Princess Di,
Our thoughts will remember, and try
not to cry.
A special kind of Angel, sent down for
us to love,
God has taken her back to His
Heaven above,
Thank you dear Lord for the beauty
you sent,
Only here for a short while just to be lent,
When we all look up into the stars
at night,
The Princess of Wales will be beaming
down bright.

Janet Merrick

Diana

I was lying there just listening, to my radio in bed,
The news came on and startled me, what was that he said?
I turned the radio louder, I thought it can't be true,
Such a shock it gave me, I felt depressed and blue.
It's only people just like me, who die in that sad way,
Not someone sweet like she was, what will the papers say?
Lots of pictures everywhere, people crying in the street,
Laying flowers at the gate, in rows and rows all neat.
All the world in mourning, and boys without a mother,
And Saturday the funeral, the earth will be her cover.

Barbara Callaghan

Diana Princess Of The People

Princess of the people,
That is what she was called.
For wherever she went to visit,
The people were enthralled.

In this her very own country,
And in countries far away.
The children she did cuddle,
Which really made their day.

She showed so much compassion,
For the sick, and for the poor.
And as she went to meet them,
Her they did adore.

She seemed to understand their problems,
No matter what they were.
She did not just go touring round,
But showed she really cared.

Iris Covell

Diana

Rest in peace Lady of the lake,
Only the Lord knew the path you would take,
In hours of happiness you were gone
But for many years forward your name will live on,
To some a smile, a word, a touch,
Some never showed they loved you so much, with the aid of a flower loved your coffin alone.
Carpets of bloom in reverence born
Words were spoken, songs were sung,
With muffled tone bells were rung
A day long remembered by young and old
For many years the story told
Of the Lady of the lake who touched each one,
Sleep on Princess, may your legend go on.

Sarah Watson (13)

Dear Diana

Although I did not know you,
You were often in my thoughts,
Now you're not a Royal,
I know it hurts, of course.

Now Wills and Harry need you
They must be asking 'Why!'
Now you and Dodi are together,
At peace, up in the sky.

God Bless you Dear Diana,
I'm so sad that you are gone,
Maybe one day I'll join you,
And we all can be as one.

Barbara Nelder

Never Forgotten

The Princess of Wales
Diana by name.
There will never be a woman
The same.
Who captured the hearts of the nation.
She was special, unique, just one,
Creation.
She was kind and considerate,
Gentle and shy.
Why did she have to die?
The Princess of Wales
There will be no other
Who cared and shared
Like a mother.
Your sons shall miss you
More than we will ever know
You were their inspiration
To help them grow.
But you'll never be forgotten.
You're a symbol across the land.
And the day will come, when you
And your sons can walk, hand in hand.

Sylvia Mellon

For The Queen Of Hearts

Like a ray of sunshine you burst
through the clouds
We were touched by your fragility
Your shyness tugged a chord in
our hearts
We felt your vulnerability
When times were black and
moments hard
The power of your love came
shining through
When suffering reared its ugly head
We shared the troubles with you
And in return you showed us how
to touch the sick to hold the lost ones
so forlorn
You gave them hope when all was dark
Your love reached out a wave of warmth
The gifts you gave we can't repay
however hard we try, or what we do
Diana on the day you went away
a part of the Nation's heart
died with you.

F Booth

A Tribute To Diana

I didn't know you Diana
Though like many others I feel I did
You touched our hearts
With your unique personality
In so many ways and for so many people
You will always be remembered . . .
As a continual burning star
Always shining from afar
May you rest in eternal peace
As a guardian of Humanity . . .

Moira Westfall-Harvey

Diana, A Tribute From Nidderdale

On Ashfold edge one Sunday morn
I thanked the Lord that you were born.
The early sun gave off warm rays
There was no cloud there was no haze
The birds were singing; o' such praise,
The gorgeous heather on the hill,
The whispering stream, my heart was still.

And on Ashfold edge that Sunday morn
I thanked the Lord that you were born.

salut d'amour

Gerald Finlay

Princess Diana, Queen Of Hearts

There's not many people in this world willing to give a helping hand to those in need
Many are just too scared, others too cruel to open their eyes and see.
All it takes is to show a little tender loving care to those around you
it really does make a difference even though you may not see it.

There's only one person who really made a difference
Someone we all knew and admired very much
She cared for everyone, no matter who or what they were.
In her heart we were all the same.

She met people less fortunate than ourselves
People who were dying, even people who'd lost limbs
She treated them as normal people when others wouldn't
Holding hands with AIDS victims, she really made a difference.

Her smile, her special touch was well-known to people
It was as though she healed people mentally and forever.
No-one else could ever do that, not now, not ever.

She may be out of sight for now
Although she's not out of mind
She's left us two precious gifts behind
and her work will never cease

No-one will ever be able to take your place Diana
'cause you were very unique indeed
Your candle burned out long before your legend ever will
You'll always be our Queen Of Hearts . . . forever . . .

Denise O'Donnell (17)

Diana, The People's Princess

She brought comfort where there was sorrow,
Joy where there was grief,
Just meeting her, and seeing her smile,
Was a blessing beyond belief!
She helped others overcome their troubles
Despite problems of her own;
Giving them strength in difficult times
And encouragement to carry on!
Diana brought light into so many lives
With her compassion and love;
She will always be remembered as
Someone special in this world!
Our hearts go out to her beloved sons
And the Royal family;
May God bless and strengthen them
In their sadness and grief!
Let them feel Your love surround them Lord,
And of Your presence be aware;
Knowing You are a God of comfort
And all their burdens You share.

M Skirrow

The Princess And Her People

You walked by, you smiled,
And kissed our tiny child's hand,
You're not just a Princess,
But also our friend,
You have gone to travel,
The heaven above,
But you're our Diana,
And you'll always be loved,
William and Harry will be OK,
As the nation of people make sure,
Our love will be with them each day,
So our dear Diana, this we will say,
Our dear Lord Jesus, will help you on your way,
To be a sweet Angel, now you are above,
And your star will burn brightly,
On the people you love.

Barbara Moss

Diana, Princess Of Wales
The Fairytale Princess

The 31st August 1997 will go down as one of the most tragic days in our history when the nation learned of the death of LADY DIANA, PRINCESS OF WALES.

The fairytale Princess who touched the hearts of the people when she courted then married PRINCE CHARLES.

The shy Lady Di blossomed into the beautiful Diana and became the PRINCESS OF WALES. The tireless work she did for the Red Cross, Human rights and humanity.

Her heart and arms reached out to all the people suffering in the world.
The gays, AIDS, HIV positive and lepers.

She even found a way through the landmines in war-torn Bosnia and Angola to try and bring them eternal peace.

The shock of how she died will live with us forever. We can only hope and pray for her sons Princes WILLIAM and HARRY, so they can draw from her strength and become one of our future kings.

The final tributes have now been paid.

She is our candle in the wind! And millions of people can't be wrong.

She is now laid to rest on her paradise island, away from the crowds that held her so dear. She is asleep waiting for Prince Charming to wake her up with a kiss, then take her to Heaven's door. A sight so beautiful and rarely seen before. She is now Heaven's brightest star where she can look down on us all below and the world that loved her so.

In peace she rests, our Queen of Hearts, the 'FAIRYTALE PRINCESS, LADY DIANA, PRINCESS OF WALES.

K Pendlebury

Untitled

God gave us a flower, so radiant and fair,
A rose sent from Heaven, who showed love and care.
They named her Diana, this person so sweet,
Showing love and compassion to all she did meet.
The sick and the homeless, the young and the old,
So special, so precious, with a heart made of gold.
Giving to others what matters so much,
A kindly word, a human touch.
Lighting our lives each and every day,
Comforting all that she met on her way.
Now summer has ended, our flower has died,
On the last day of August, a whole nation cried.
We will miss you Diana, we won't forget you
Or the way that you loved us, and we loved you too.
We'll always remember your smile and your tears,
Such an inspiration through all your short years.
No we won't forget you, or all you have done,
Diana your memory will always live on.

Thora Elaine Dodds

Diana

You are the friend I never knew,
Oh Diana, how I miss you,
The tears I cry are not in vain,
They help to take away my pain,
'Thank you' for all your love and caring,
Your understanding, thoughtfulness and sharing
Diana I will love you till the end,
Goodbye my princess, saviour and friend xxx

Jayne Spooner

The Angel - Diana

God gave the world an Angel,
To walk upon the earth,
Her destiny decided,
From the moment of her birth.
To marry into Royalty,
And give the land a King,
Of very special qualities,
That only love can bring.
She never knew the happiness,
That lesser mortals find,
For when God creates an Angel,
He has bigger things in mind.

She held her arms out to the world,
Helping where she could,
To show us in her special way,
The path to right and good.
To all the sick and needy,
To the hearts that break in two,
To the lonely and forgotten
Her loveliness shone through.
Now our hearts and eyes are open,
Thanks to an Angel's love,
And God has called our Princess
To her resting place above.

But her spirit lives in all of us,
For she showed us that we can,
Hold out our hands in friendship,
And help our fellow man,
So for what Diana started,
We must carry on the same,
And build the world she dreamed of,
In the memory of her name.

Carole A Pearson

Diana - Full Of Style, Full Of Grace

On a special day that year
God did put an Angel here
With a happy, caring face
Full of style, full of grace

At the age of just nineteen
Finally the world had seen
A Lady that would come to us
And fill us with such happiness

On that day in eighty-one
To the people she did come
On the balcony, with that kiss
To the world, she brought such bliss.

To the world she did bring
William, our future King
The next to the world she did carry
Was the bonny, Prince Harry

In the public eye each day
But in her very caring way
She would help the sick and needy
She herself was never greedy

In the people she had pride
Her feelings she did never hide
In this world she had a part
Truly 'The Queen of Hearts'.

In this life we now lack
An Angel whom God has taken back
Now in the sky, as a star
Which we will look at from afar

Diana a friend of you and I
Her memories live, they'll never die
To her sons, we do cast
A love so strong, it will always last.

Lynette Hobbs

A Minute's Silence

Those amongst us who did not know you
Admired you as you grew in beauty and in grace.
We recognised a mother's love so strong
and true -
Felt the joy and gentle radiance -
Were brightened by the smile that lit your face
As you daily braved your purpose through.

You wrenched compassion from your
inner self
To comfort the rejected and cast down.
We witnessed the anguished look, the
troubled frown.
Delight and colour celebrate your memory.
Your gifts were not measures of
material wealth:
Our fragrant bouquets of flowers adorned your
crown.

In realisation of the price you paid for
loving care
We yearn to see your laughter, eagerness and
sense of fun.
You were no stranger either to suffering
or despair
But - sharing, rejoicing in life - all our hearts and
minds have won.

Sarah Mansfield

Untitled

God gave her to us for a while
To spread happiness and a smile.
She took away some of the world's despair
She was genuine, she did care.
Diana would never have meant to make us cry
But guardian angels do have to say goodbye.

L Morrison

From Diana Our Princess

(Dedicated to the memory of Diana,
our very dear Princess)

Lay me to rest in some quiet spot,
Where the sound of water is near;
Where songs of my childhood filled the air
And all that I held dear.

But now I bid you, weep no more,
For I am now at Peace;
But turn to those whose need is great,
That their hearts may be at ease.

And look to all the little ones
Who are orphaned, hurt, distressed;
They need the care of loving arms
To feel that they are blest.

Make a channel of peace in your hearts
Where the unfortunate may find rest;
Then you will find great peace of mind,
Knowing you've done your best.

Edith Cartwright

In Loving Memory Of Princess Diana

You were our beautiful Princess,
With a heart of gold.
You had time for everyone,
The sick, the young, the old.
The sick you made feel better.
The children you made glow.
You brought joy to pensioners,
The whole world loved you so.

But now the world's in mourning
For our beautiful Princess,
I feel the need to say goodbye,
Sleep peacefully,
God Bless.

Irene Durston

To Our Sweet Princess

Just a little poem
To one we all so miss
Diana, Princess of Wales
Our sweet, sweet Princess
Your love will last forever
Your warmth and tenderness
The burning light of Britain
Now so tragically deceased.
Elton John changed the words
To such a famous song
To be sung in your memory
So it will live on and on,
We hope your little Princes
Have learnt from your strength
To care, love and cherish
The less fortunate.
If they carry on your work
as a testament to you,
Perhaps we'll love the Royals
As much as we loved you,
An English Rose in bloom
There is no finer sight
And now she's gone to Heaven,
With all her guiding light
As you lay there in the sky
With Dodi by your side
We thank him for the happiness
He brought back to your smile.
Rest in peace
Diana and Dodi.

Alan Breeze

To Diana

If only God had spared you
Just for a few more years
To watch your precious sons grow up
And see them through their fears
But fate stepped in and took you
To a place the best by far
And when we look up, we'll see you
You'll be the biggest brightest star.

Joyce McArdle

Diana

It's so hard to believe you have gone,
And that we'll never see you again.
You touched the hearts of millions,
Not a foot could you put wrong.

Without you things will never be the same,
No-one can replace you ever.
You were one in a million,
But then life is just a game.

To many you were the 'Queen of Hearts',
And that no-one can deny.
You changed people's lives,
In so many different parts.

You broke down barriers through,
Your charity work,
For that you were admired.
You showed a sense of compassion
In the never-ending murk.

Your love of people, won you
many friends,
Who saw you as a shining light.
You were a 'People's Princess',
Not a better image could you send.

You'll live in our hearts, always
and forever
As Diana our Princess.
Your memory will never fade
We'll forget you never.

Laura Hunt

Diana's Love

Diana's light shone so brightly
around the world,
And for all her good works
Her memory will go on timelessly,
The whole Nation mourned her tragic passing,
And we hope her dear love
Will go on throughout the world
And be remembered forever.

P Rowe

Her Smile

And when she smiled, the whole wide world
seemed like a tiny nutshell
where love and joy and perfect peace
would settle happily in the unity of marriage
where lives became a meaningful existence,
where hurt became a joy in spring
where suffering snuggled in the arms of God
and the poor and wretched felt rich in love
where the dying felt hope for their tomorrows
and death no longer a darkened tunnel

And when she touched or held a hand
all sorrow melted into a candyfloss
of joy and gladness, to know someone cared
Then into a world of dreams we'd be taken
as we gazed into the depths of her eyes
which held such softness, yet hid so much hurt
but there was a flourishing, unabated love
which surged so freely in a kindred soul

And to us all, she was our Queen
who captivated and won our Hearts
the grace of a feather on a silent breeze
or a swan on a bed of ivory petals
To the Nation she became a hope for tomorrow
a hope for today and hope for the future
To the Nation she became a hope of all dreams

Yet now all we have is her memory and Spirit
which lives on the petals of the whispering wind
and dances in the midst of the snowy
white clouds and listen . . .
to her laughter in the chorus of the waves
see her smile in the waking of the golden sun
let her love now rest in the beds of our souls
and her beauty reign in the memory of her smile
let her joy ride us forth
into the future
of peace, of hope, of love

Esther Austin

Diana

God saw your new-found happiness
when you walked hand in hand
The look of love upon your face
Yes, He could understand.
He knew through pressures in your past
when all had seemed unfair
and pressures in the future
would certainly be there.
So to keep this new-found happiness
To let your love survive
He opened up the gates of Heaven
and took you both inside.
But that has caused a Nation
to cry and wonder why
He took from us this precious one
Our Darling Princess Di.
Please help us Lord to understand
when life seems so unfair
that your love will guide and lead us on
through depths of dark despair.

Joan Smart

The Queen Of Hearts

She comforted the sick and the poor
She travelled the world to do much more
Diana Spencer was her name
But now she is gone. It's not the same.
No-one can take her place
Her warmth, her smile, her charm and grace
The world is sad now she is gone
This saint of a lady has travelled on
The gates of heaven will open wide
To let an angel step inside
The Princess of Wales may be gone
But the memories of the Queen of Hearts
Will live on.

J Saunders

Diana

Silence fell upon the world
When you were laid to 'Rest',
We all know now
You surely were the 'Best'.
Forgive me Di for doubting you
throughout the early 'Years',
A candle by my side,
Tissues, to wipe away the 'Tears'.
Forgotten are the rumours, the Tabloids
and the 'Lies',
I saw you cradling a sickly child,
and all the sadness of this world,
Was mirrored in your 'Eyes'.
Sleep in peace with Dodi
and 'God Bless',
I wish I could have touched you,
even now, in 'Death'.
Last night I had the strangest dream
I saw you in a coffin made of glass,
God's influence on the human mind
is 'Grace'
and for a fleeting moment gazed upon your lovely
'Face'.
Those eyes are closed 'Forever',
but we'll forget you 'Never',
Gracious Diana.

Elfi Maria Hill

A Tribute To Diana

The whole world will forever mourn
A princess who like a radiant light
Gave hope and courage to those who had borne
The sufferings of disease and the wounds
of fight.

Plucked from life before her time
We need to ask the reason why
Was it God's will - if not 'tis a crime
We will not forget her - she was our 'Di'.

Bill Bridgman

To Princess Diana

Dear Diana an angel here on earth,
Now you have left us they really know
your worth.

Your radiance shining forth like a beacon
in the night,
On the ill and injured in their sad plight.

God rest your soul in glory you were our
Queen of Hearts,
May your memory live forever among
your patriots.

Farewell my Rose of England to thee
I vow my grace,
To a beautiful happy countenance your
lovely smiling face.

S W Frost

To A Princess

Beautiful as a sunset
That fills our skies
As lovely as a flower
With mischief in your eyes
As wise as any other
As loving as can be
The ability to smile
No matter what you see
God's given gift to all of us
And spoiled by our hand
But still you go on shining
Right across our land
The gift of love you gave
In every place
The kindness and humility
Ever in your face
Thank you gracious princess
For being who you were
For shaking up your world
For teaching us to care

Mrs Sheppard

Dedicated To Diana, Queen Of Hearts RIP

Our Princess Diana a shining star,
a princess beyond imagination.
Someone who cared for the world.
A true princess people loved her, I love her.
An angel in our hearts,
a true Queen of Hearts.
As people mourn my heart is filled
with pain and shock. Her beautiful face,
her smile.
Those sparkling blue eyes.
Why did God take her away from us,
her wonderful life cut short.
A kind warm loving person to all of us
in England.
London won't be the same without Diana.
God has taken Our Princess,
Queen of Hearts away.
Our country has lost a remarkable woman.
I can't understand the pain for Harry, William
and Prince Charles.
I write this poem, with hurt and pain.
Sympathy for all the Royal Family.
We will all miss her so much.
She was our angel from God.
Taken away. I try to come to terms
with what has happened but I can't
but we will in years to come.
Diana would like life to go on, so would I.

Dean Berg

Diana

Diana, the girl who became
Princess, with eyes so blue, heart
of gold, whose compassion touched
each and everyone from poor and
rich to young and old, her life
will enrich us all.

G A Pocock

Tribute To Diana

My sweet Diana you will never be forgotten
No matter where you are
Your radiant smile lights every candle
So it glows like the sun
Unfortunately you have to die before
You know we care
Life will never be the same for anyone.

You were taken from us in the prime
of your life
No reason, nothing, we have to believe
You left behind two children, and your new love
Dodi, who was gaining a wife.
You were the happiest then, but God decided it
was time to leave.

Oh dear Diana you have to leave your humble
subjects full of grief
Flowers and cards that honour you on the tragic
day.
But what happened on this fateful day, left
everybody in disbelief
Now you have peace from the press for which
they have to pay.

Rest in peace - God Bless.

Keith Regan

Diana

I cannot believe the news today,
That our princess has been taken away.

A tidal wave of tears we have wept,
An ocean of messages and flowers we have left.

Something good comes from something bad,
Something happy from something sad.

A memory we'll carry ever onwards in our hearts,
A world united, let nothing ever part.

You touched our hearts in different ways,
And now we wish you peace and love always.

Kerridwen Jeffery

To A Lovely Beautiful Princess We All Loved

It's hard to part with the
Princess
We all love,
It will be harder for the
Whole nation
To say goodbye.
It will be harder still for her
Sons
To say these words
'We will always
Love you
Mummy
Until we die.'

Princess Diana will never walk alone,
Dodi will always be by her side.

Sadly missed by her own family,
Mother, sisters and brother Spencer
Her sons William and Harry

May you walk in peace, Diana.
God Bless you.

Vera Peters

Our Diana 1961-1997

Time stood still the day you were taken,
Never again will you awaken.
Your wonderful smile, your loving charm,
How you welcomed with open arms.
You conquered your goal including fashion
Your lovely touch and compassion.
Your lonely face, sadly missed,
Upon faces you once kissed.
You had a way, a kindly manner,
Oh how we'll miss you our Diana.
We never met, or spoke or saw
We'll not have a chance anymore.
The ill, the sick, the lame, the blind,
All were healed by your marvellous mind.
And now you are gone, we remember you,
Through the hearts of your beloved two,
Your shining stars, William and Harry,
Your spirit is theirs, for them to carry.
We miss your kind heart and your manner,
Goodbye, our sweet Princess Diana.

Steven Lee (13)

Untitled

A truly Royal Princess,
The genuine caring kind,
You'll always live forever
In everybody's mind.
Not just the British people,
We will not be alone,
For right across the entire world
They all made you their own.
God bless you sweet Diana,
Our love will never dim
And may He take great care of you
Now that you dwell with Him.

A Grant

A Brave New World

Thank you Diana the people say now
you are in a brave new world and
then you look and say I am only round
the next corner.

Our hearts have broken but we all
know that you will repair them all
in your brave new world.

As we all see the world ever so
different without you and your smile
your light will never die.

Michael Hallam

Dedicated To Princess Diana

Diana,

You're as precious as a rose,
as delicate as their petals,
soft and gentle, and as beautiful
as their scent.

Each petal that you carried
FLOWED LOVE.

You cared, you dared, you
showed us how to LOVE,
you brought happiness
wherever you trod.

But now, that stem has been
broken and all our hearts have
been broken,
now sadness does occur.

But my thoughts of you will
never fade, as my love for you
will be forever great.
You're the Angel in heaven,
so PLEASE be happy, we will all
meet you there one day.

By the gates of heaven, you'll
greet us all there.
RIP

With love

Lorraine Waggott

Untitled

You were an angel in disguise
You won our hearts with those
Loving eyes
Your kindness we shall always
Treasure
Our love for you will go on
Forever.

D Lindsell

Tribute To Diana, Princess Of Wales

Chorus: You are now and forever,
Queen of our Hearts.

Your memory we will treasure,
For the rest of our lives,
You gave us so much love,
You were ruled by your heart,
And not by your head,
For now we must grieve,
And show it with flowers.

Chorus: You are now and forever,
Queen of our Hearts.

And may your candle continue to burn,
With a bright shining light,
Through the days and the nights,
From summer to autumn.
And winter to spring,
With the joys that you did bring us,

Chorus: You are now and forever,
Queen of our Hearts.

George Barr

Princess Diana

'Special' is a word that is used to
describe something - one of a kind.
Like a hug, a kiss, a smile or a sunset.
Or a person who spreads love
with a wondrous smile or
kind gestures, a special touch.
'Special' describes people who act
from the heart, and keep in mind
the hearts of others.
'Special' applies to something
that is admired and precious
and which can never be replaced.
Special is the word that best
describes you dear Diana.

Patricia Streich

The Angels' Choice

The sweet little angels of Dunblane,
They played in Heaven, safe and free from pain.
But somebody was amiss, things not
quite complete.
A person unique, loving and sweet.
Their choice was made, they told our Lord,
'Please bring her home from abroad.'

Jesus looked into His angels' eyes, knowing what
Grief would result in her early demise.
'But she has children of her own, two boys
That love her, an heir to a throne!'
'Our need is greater' all children cried.
Sadly the Lord agreed and our princess died.

Now Diana is in her paradise found,
No longer shackled and establishment-bound.
As Queen of Hearts, she reigns with love,
And guards her children from above.
When sorrow fades, her memories live on,
William and Harry, they are your legacy
Now that she has gone.

Jean Doran

To Our Dearest Princess

Endless people needed to show
their feelings from the start.
Countless eyes shed tears of sorrow,
cleansing the grief from broken hearts.
A part of us was taken from us,
the pain is hard to bear.
We didn't stand alone today
with all the millions waiting there.
A show of loyalty, love, affection,
caring, sharing, everyone.
Anger, despair, and desperation
that our princess has really gone.
Prayers and compassion for all her family,
especially her boys.
May we ever remember, her love and
laughter, tears, heartache and joys.

Sandra Houghton

Landmines - The Enemy

Landmines were used to keep the enemy away
When they were put below the earth
No one gave a thought to
How they would kill the innocent
And maim young limbs as well
This saddened all the world
But there was nothing they could do

Then along came Diana Princess of Wales
Who cared about what was happening
She visited the victims personally
And gave both comfort and support
Where it was wanted most

But most of all she cared enough
To try and see they were removed
So that people no longer had to walk in fear
That they could be at peace again

Now that God has got Diana in his care
Please can her dream and wishes
That all landmines be removed
Become a thing of the future
So that all the good things
She did in this cause
Can be a living memory to her name
Diana may you rest in peace

Pamela Jewell

Diana

Whole nations weep and mourn for you
Our princess gone, her loved one too
Women and children and brave men wept
As over us all the sadness crept
Flowers we bring and other gifts too
Showing how much we cared about you
Who cared about others - victims of strife
And illness and other blights of life
Your concern for others has shown us all
How we can help all those who fall
Compassion worldwide in all its parts
God bless you Diana Queen of our Hearts

Brian L Sellwood

Guilty!

For gain they lied and twisted you to the core
For one last frame they can use you no more
For the last snap of flashlight, for the last
iris close
Was it worth it, was it worth it - only they know.

I don't need the pictures to know who you were
If I were blind, would a difference be there
I knew you by deed, I knew you by love
I knew you in my heart and that was enough.

They can justify their reasons,
They can justify their greed
But they can never justify the way
They took you from me

Now, they have taken all their pictures
They have deceived us with their facts
They have taken the largest prize of all
And they can never take it back

Jackie Thompson-Hedley

Untitled

The saddest day in all our hearts,
Is a day we will remember,
The day a light went out, on the dawn,
Of the first day of September.

Born a lady fair of face,
A princess in the making.
She came to be a symbol for,
The people of all nations.

Diana, fair of face, full of grace,
Loved by all the people,
You touched our lives, and gave us all,
Your love and tender feelings.

A lady, a princess, and then a queen.
A truly golden girl.
Not just a Queen of Hearts Diana,
But a Queen throughout the world.

K M Firth

Goodbye To The Queen Of Hearts

I cannot explain my feelings
When on the news I heard,
Of Princess Diana's awful death
I could not speak a word.
Diana had just found happiness
All the world hoped it
would last,
Because no-one was
more deserving
She'd had a really
troubled past.
She gave so much pleasure
To everyone she met,
Young or old, rich or poor,
The people won't forget.
I know that God will care
for her
In everlasting life,
She'll never know
more heartache
No loneliness or strife.
I know the grief we're feeling
Is tearing each of us apart,
But we will always remember
Diana, the Queen of Hearts.
God bless you Diana

A Fulham

Diana's Star

There's one more star in the sky tonight
It's called Diana, Princess of Hope and Light
God put it there as a mark of respect
When he heard how the whole of Great Britain
had wept

It twinkles so brightly overhead
Just like you did Diana before you were dead
It shocked us all as never before
When we heard that our Princess was no more
But we can find comfort in the sight
Of that new bright star in the sky tonight

Jennifer Walker

The Lady Of The Island

Beyond the land and water dark
The lady lies
In rest eternal - she the cherished beauty
Never dies.

In flame and flower, in town and country
She will dwell.
The mention of her name resounds
In Heaven, not Hell.

In vigil kept, in crowded streets
Is untold grief.
The People's Princess now a memory,
Her life all too brief.

Her goodness, scattered petals
On a fevered land.
Her treasure, freely given
From an outstretched hand.

And those who share the outpoured grief
Catch all the tears
And so anoint each other
To allay the fears.

The Lady of the Island
Sleeps the sleep of peace,
Though never for a moment
Shall her beauty cease.

Ann Chandler

Untitled

The rain is God's tears as we hear about Di's death,
The sun is the flowers we lie on the ground.
The water in the ocean is all the people's tears.
The world was Diana, now it's shattered.
Diana was the world, now it's shattered.

Stephanie Woods (10)

Goodnight To Our Angel

Thirty-six years ago when God was not too busy.
And He hadn't got too much to do
He decided to create an angel and send her down to earth
So here is what He decided to do,
He took her eyes from the stars in the skies
And her smile from the sun He took
He made her hair from a whispering breeze
And her voice from a tinkling brook.
He gave her a sweet loving nature
And a friendship warm and true
Yes! God knew what He was doing thirty-six years ago
Because that angel Diana was you
You were a wonderful loving mother
Giving your sons
such tender care
When they needed a shoulder to cry on
You were always there
For others too you gave kindness
To people from near and far.
You helped to cheer the wounded
And took the young sick in your arms
But now God has taken our angel
We are left to mourn her alone
God needed our angel in Heaven
So now He has taken her home.

Grace Wozencroft

Darling Diana

Darling Diana why did you go
all the people loved you so.
To everyone you were sweet
and kind I just can't get you
out of my mind.
Now rest in peace you
beautiful one.
To your two boys you
were a lovely mum.

Barbara Ann Belcher

Beautiful Diana

Beautiful Diana Queen of
hearts and love.
You have gone from this sad
earth up to Heaven above
You were treated badly while
here on earth below
But you gave only love
and hope everywhere that you did go.
And helped people who
needed love and kindness of
this you freely gave
May you now find
peace and love as you
sleep in your grave,
Rest on beloved Diana you've no more
need to frown
For up in Heaven I'm very sure
that you'll have earned your crown.

Margaret McKeand

Diana

There was sudden excitement in Heaven.
The angels just couldn't suppress,
Their joy at the news of the coming,
Of a beautiful mortal Princess.
When she walked through the gates they were dazzled,
By the aura of beauty and grace.
And they welcomed her into the Heavenly Host,
Where she surely had earned her right place.
The Cherubims flocked all around her,
While she giggled with them in their mirth.
They were drawn to this lovely new Angel,
Just as children had been on the Earth.
The Heavens could hear the Earth crying,
In sorrow and anguishing pain.
And the saying was given fresh credence -
EARTH'S LOSS IS NOW HEAVEN'S GAIN.

Isobel Cook

Our Beautiful Princess

A shining star
The brightest light
Glowing out into the night
With so much trouble staring her in the face
She still made our lives a better place
She was so caring, loving and sweet
Only just finding her own feet
A life tragically cut short
In circumstances we could never have thought
She changed our lives with her selfless grace
No one could ever take her place
Our Queen of Hearts, our guiding light
She understood each person's plight
A daughter, a sister, a friend, a mother
Nothing more important to her
than the welfare of others
We are all so saddened, angry and shocked
At the loss of our beautiful
princess whom we loved a lot
Through the selfish acts of greedy yobs
All who loved her have been cruelly robbed.

Hazel Ogden

A Treasure Lost
'Diana' Princess Of Wales 1961-1997

A flame that like a star shines bright,
With such life it dances.
Offering comfort, offering warmth and light,
The darkness it enhances.
Suddenly flickering, all too soon gone is that light,
Leaving only memorised glances.
Its spirit curling heavenward and from our sight.
A treasure lost but never forgotten,
Within our hearts, forever burning bright.

Sheila V Baldwin

The People's Princess

A wonderful person
Has just passed away
But our memories of you
Will be here with us to stay.

You were always smiling
You'd leave your troubles behind
Because if it was raining
You'd always bring sunshine.

You made so many people happy
Even if by shaking their hand
Or comforting sick children
And waving to your fans.

You were a wonderful mother
To your handsome young sons
You enjoyed each other's company
And had lots of fun.

You're the people's Princess
And that's who you'll always be
So goodnight and God bless
To Britain's finest lady.

Marie Alderman

A True Angel Of Mercy

You were on this earth, so few years,
Giving love, where there were only tears.
You were an angel to behold,
Whatever your duties, you played the role.

Loved by millions, all over the world,
Wherever sick children, there to be held,
Paupers, lepers, some with AIDS,
You walked among those, of whatever trade.

A Royal, yes, so human too,
A Princess of the people true,
That radiant smile, that always shone,
A light has vanished, now that you are gone.

The eyes of the people, all are wet,
As we watched your last journey, on TV set.
We loved you Princess, for what you were,
If help were needed, you did not deter.

All over the world, they will never forget,
Our Royal Princess, your duties all met.
God bless Diana.

A E Powell

To Diana

A bright star burst on
our world.
She shone for 16 years.
To the sick, the sad, and the
hopeless a light.
Dear Diana has left us now.
To live in love above
And is the brightest star,
To shine down from the
myriads in the sky above.
Shine on Diana,
you have left a
lesson and legacy of love.

G Haslam

Diana

Not Goddess of Hunting,
But Goddess of Love
Diana's now an Angel
Up in Heaven above.

She showed us the courage,
She showed us the way,
To keep on trying always
Day after day.

Please stay with us forever
And we will stay with you.
In God's care and His keeping
For an Eternity,
Or two!

Julie Hicks

Diana

(Full of compassion, style and grace,
A real English Rose with a beautiful face.
This was Diana)

Your sad, short life
sometimes left you in tears,
We're thankful you found
happiness in your later years.
Your visits to the sick,
AIDS victims and such,
Showed us you cared and
loved us so much.
We'll never forget you,
our darling Di,
Now home at last and at
peace where you lie.
Queen of Hearts you'll
always remain
We'll never see your like again.

September 6th
The day you left us,
we all said goodbye,
We cried together for
our Princess Di,
Your boys escorted you,
it made you feel proud,
As they walked together
Through the London crowd.
Forever in our thoughts.

J M Barber

Angel Of Love

You captured our hearts with your kindness
and love
An angel of mercy sent from above
To give hope to the needy, the sick and the poor
Who on this earth could ask for more?
We can try and ask God why you had to go
But only He will ever know.
A place in our hearts you will have forever
Wonderful memories to always treasure.

Jean Carswell

Our Shining Star

Why did our beautiful Princess Diana have to die,
Without a chance to say goodbye,
Oh! Why? Did she have to go,
When everyone loved her so,
Please take her in your arms dear God, we pray,
And keep her safe both night and day.
Could it be her work was all done,
So she was taken away from everyone.
But why? Oh! Why? Did she have to go,
When we all on earth loved her so.
But one day we may understand,
Why God took her by the hand.
She did her best for both young and old,
Yes! She really had a heart of gold.
All her pain and suffering has now gone,
And she has left us all to carry on.
She would not wish for fuss or tears.
Just remember her in the future years,
Her loving and caring ways,
We will all remember for the rest of our days.
May 'Diana' rest in peace with God above,
That's where we will all send her all our love,
Just look up into the sky at night,
It's there you will see Diana's star shining
so bright.

Zena Williams

My Tribute To Diana, Princess Of Wales

Lady Di, you were so cool,
You visited hospitals, youth clubs and schools.

The lepers, the AIDS sufferers,
Their hands you would hold,
You were so warm-hearted,
You had a heart of gold.

From your family and the world,
You have had to depart,
You may not live as a person,
But you live on in our hearts.

Amy Maddix (12)

Cloak Of Sadness

With outstretched arms and radiant smile,
You stayed and talked with us a while
Easing our hurt, our sorrow and pain,
By your gentle touch, compassion and care.
Removing all barriers of class, race and creed,
Giving warmth and love to those in need.

Snatched from us cruelly on that dark day,
Now gone is our precious sunshine ray.
The pain of our loss is so hard to bear,
A cloak of sadness we will always wear.
But in our hearts you have a special place,
We will remember your compassion,
your beauty and grace.

Diana now with Dodi you will always be,
Together through all of eternity.
Cradled lovingly by angels with tenderness,
Your soul is now free, peacefully at rest.
A floral carpet has now been laid
Our memories of you will never fade.

Bless you Diana our Queen of Hearts.
May you have sweet dreams.

Susan Clarke

A Special Princess

I couldn't believe it, when I heard that day,
Princess Diana, had been from us taken away,
Diana was so special giving to one and all,
And when she was pulled down, she still
walked tall,

From early life, love she tried to somehow find,
But to others' needs she never was blind,
Giving all, all she could possibly truly give,
And happiness she found, the press wouldn't
let it live.

William and Harry, two princes, how do
they go on?
Their memories will help, but never take
her place,
For there was no-one with her style and grace.

I think there'll never be an end to this goodbye,
For many people will always shed tears and cry,
The strength of love I saw, showed how much
we did care,
And this special princess's memory will always
be there.

Cheryl Drakeley

Diana Princess Of Wales

It's fitting that the heavens should cry
When one so young should sadly die;
Diana's life cut brutally short!
For what was precious life so bought?
The world is humbled, wracked with guilt
For all the pain and sorrow built
Around an image; obsessed we preyed
And laws of the pack our minds obeyed,
Forgot the human soul inside
Who lived and loved and hurt and died.
Somewhat numbed we pass the day
While her family faces their personal fray.
And so the skies steadfastly weep
While Diana sleeps her deepest sleep!

Wendy P Frost

A Critic's Lament To Diana

Diana, how our hearts cry out to you,
We didn't give the love when it was due,
And now, too late, we only have the pain,
We realise, we'll not see you again.

We can't go back in time, re-live the past,
But now your motives are more clear, at last.
We thought you did it all to gain the fame,
But now, without you, nothing is the same.

We're sorry that we judged you out of hand,
But we still loved you dearly, in this land.
We know you set so many hearts aglow.
We'll love you for all time, we hope you know.

Gwendoline Andersen

First Friend And Best Friend

My thoughts and prayers are with you
William and Harry
As your future must look very bleak.
Seeing the anguish etched on your faces,
As you appeared on TV that sad week.

You have lost your first friend and best friend.
Who can never more be by your side.
But your unique mum Princess Diana.
You can remember now with love and pride.

Your mum would not want you to be unhappy
for long.
As her goal in life was to bring only joy
and she won.
When grief overwhelms you, find comfort in this.
Knowing she would have wanted nothing
less for her sons.

Now remember the happy times you shared
together.
Don't let her memory ever die.
Talk to each other and share your grief.
Never be ashamed, when you often will cry.

When your grief is unbearable and you near
despair.
Turn to the Lord Jesus, and ask Him in prayer.
To comfort and guide you, through these
difficult days.
He promises, if you ask Him, to be with
you always.

Jean Monteith

Queen Of Hearts

You gave so much love in your short-lived life
Even when you hurt so much inside
You were one in a million, so hard to replace
No one will ever take your place
Sleep in Peace
Our Queen of Hearts.

Joanne Airnes

A Shining Light - Still Shining Bright

A Princess for The People she was from the start,
from the moment we saw her - She ruled our
hearts.
As a nation we know she had the human touch,
ever radiantly beautiful - She was needed
so much.
You reap what you sow, the bible saying goes,
she reaped so much more - Than she'll ever know.
It's hard to take in that she's left us so young,
a dedicated heroine - And so often unsung.
Her courage and strength we humbly applaud,
her great legacy to us, are the boys she adored.
An immense void is felt by all Dads and Mums,
as a tribute to her - We must cherish her sons!
A nation veiled in grief - We're united by love,
this will surely bring peace to our Princess above.
She's a shining light that will always glow,
and our respect for her will eternally show.
She's irreplaceable, to the hearts she touched,
'til the end of time - She'll be missed so much.
As Queen of Hearts - Her beauty, elegance
and style,
will be captured forever in our Historian Files.
'So Diana Our Princess - Our love will never cease,
you're a Beautiful Angel who can now rest
in peace!'

Val MacFadyen

A Memory Of Diana

God has taken Diana to His haven of rest,
And transferred her love to His angels instead,
The night has a thousand eyes;
The day but one, yet the bright world
dies with the setting sun.
The mind has a thousand thoughts,
the heart but one,
Yet light from a young life dies and her
love is done.
With the dying of the sun, we will remember.

Ethel Smith

To Diana

Why it should happen
We'll never know.
It seems so unfair
That you had to go.

We can never forget tho'
Your special flair
In your short lifetime
You showed us you cared.

Wherever they came from
Whoever you met
You treated them all
With equal respect.

Such kindness and love
By word or by touch
To so many people
You meant so much.

All the sick children
You made feel better
Whether by visits
A card or a letter.

We knew you were special
Right from the start
Without a doubt
Our Queen of Hearts.

We all now must take
A leaf from your book
If only we gave more
Rather than took.

The job that you started
We must now face
Let's make this world
A much better place.

Sue Reilly

Goodbye Beautiful Diana

She was the brightest light of the world,
She brought hope into the hearts
of every boy and girl,
I will miss her presence in this world
that must carry on
Her beauty created poems and now
a special song.
Goodbye beautiful Diana, may
you rest in peace,
And maybe one day again, this
world will be at ease.

Goodbye beautiful Diana, the
world has shed many tears,
You were so special, you will be
remembered for years,
May your family find comfort in
what I've put into words,
I miss you already, there is even
a hush amongst the birds,
It really feels so strange without
you in our lives.

There was so much joy and hope
When we looked into your eyes,
Why did your time come so soon?
Why did you have to go?
Was it because someone else
above needed you so?

Goodbye Diana

With love from Susan xxxx

Susan Thompson

Princess Diana RIP

Death strikes in many ways
We can only question why
You touched everyone
Thank you for sharing in our lives
We all have a pathway to take
Not knowing what lies ahead
Never again to see your smile
Our lives will never be the same
Your lovely sons we share
Their grief, their pain.
In Wills we see your smile
Your shyness you are so alike
In Harry, we see your outgoing ways
The world grieves for you Diana
You had truly found happiness again
The stars in the sky
Shine so very bright
Yours will shine on everyone
Candles burning in the night
Dodi brought back your laughter
Eased your ache, your pain.
Brought back your sparkle.
It was lovely to see again.
Love was there for all the world to see.
Now in heaven, love for you both for eternity.
We loved to see you in the press
Papers brought for a glimpse of you
What can anyone say we all grieve
(Not anymore Diana) of you to see
When you lost your HRH.
You were still HRH to all of us
(Rest in peace Diana).
'You were ours' one of us
So sadly missed by the nation
God now has you in His keeping
Diana our Queen of Hearts
Thank you Wills and Harry
Your mother was a very special lady
Our thoughts and prayers
Are with you today and always
God bless and keep you safe.

I Kerswell

Diana, Queen Of Hearts

Diana - Queen of all our Hearts
How can we bear to let you go?
Your kindness and compassion
Is why we love you so.

Your beauty, both inside and out
Made you our Shining Star,
You never spared yourself
To help others near and far.

You didn't confine your efforts
To just a nearby few,
You tried to help humanity
And this the whole world knew.

So for all the help and love you gave
Your death was felt worldwide,
We in Great Britain loved you dearly
Our Princess - our Nation's Pride!

Your life was often troubled
You were rarely given peace
But your love for Wills and Harry
Will never, ever cease!

We're sure that you'll continue
To guide them from afar
Just as you care for all of us
Our Princess, our Shining Star.

Diana, for your sake we're happy
That you finally found love
Not on earth to enjoy it
But in Paradise above.

Goodbye Diana.

June Thorington

Diana

Diana you define
The United Kingdom

On the first of July 1961
An angel was born a babe
Diana was her name
Sparked now an eternal
Light that would lead the way.
Who could have known
From a bloom you were
To become a beautiful bouquet.
A princess soon you were
Titled and so you were
Required to mount the
Royal pedestal for all
The world to gaze.
And so we saw your
Sparkle, a princess you
Were our queen
Whose beauty was
Astonishing.
Your shyness not to be
Ashamed.

Your heart was soon
To be broken
Thanks to God it did not
Last.
For one could not deliver
So much love without
Reclaiming some one day.
This gift you gave to
Others could not have
Been for your own pain
Endured and fought to pave
The way to quench and ease
Another's day after day.

It reminds me of a
Figure the most important
In all times.
The Lord Jesus Christ
Who sacrificed His life
For mine.

And so there came a
Calling for an angel
To depart, from a world
That loved her dearly
And whose love had
Etched an English rose
On every needy heart.

You've made us feel
United like the grand title
Of our isles.
This United Kingdom
Must now succeed to lead
The world in forming an
Everlasting PEACE!

T S Pryor

Diana, Princess Of Wales 1961-1997

God sent us an angel
from the heavens above
She showed us how to care,
showed us how to love.
She helped with the sick,
needy and the poor
Young and the old
and many, many more.
Her presence surrounded us
she captured our hearts
Our thoughts and our memories
she will always be part.
Only God forgot to tell us
this angel was on loan
No sooner was she here
then she had to go home.
We had no time
to say our goodbyes
But the feelings of love
will always be a part of our lives.
So goodbye our sweet angel
goodnight and God bless
Heaven is so lucky
to have our Princess.

Lisa Penney

Forever Young

Forever young you now will be,
Forever young eternally.
Your life has been snuffed out like a flame,
Our lives are never to be the same
And your two boys - how they must feel,
So young to face life's toughest deal.
We think that what we feel is grief,
What they must feel is beyond belief.
So hard to believe that you've really gone,
When this nation's heart you had clearly won.
Who would believe it would end this way,
Was it meant to? Who can say?

And now the stage is finally set,
For your greatest ever performance yet.
As millions will follow your final appearance,
It will be such a tragically moving experience.
But our memories are loyal and never will fail.
The joy that was you,
The Princess of Wales.

Sally Hales

Diana

Our Queen of Hearts God Bless your name,
As in us all you will remain,
Our love and thanks could not convey,
How we feel for you today,
You gave to us such faith and hope,
You showed the way and helped to cope,
With your warm and loving care,
That was always there to share,
Your heart was full of gold,
Just waiting to unfold,
Young or old, sick or frail,
You always gave the right portrayal,
Now our hearts feel for you,
As we say a prayer or two,
So now in Heaven our sweet Princess,
Rest in Peace, goodnight, God Bless.

Dale Gibson

Tribute To Diana

Diana! Diana! So full of grace.
Beautiful smile, beautiful face.
Although she was hurting so badly inside.
She thought only of others, her pain
she would hide.
Happiness started to come her way.
Until her life ended on that fateful day.
Shock! Spread through the nation
She was loved so much,
She reached out to her people
With her soft gentle touch.
Her boys will remember all
The love she gave
And the millions of
People who mourned
at her grave.

Margaret Thornton

Diana 1961-1997

A heart of pure gold
The kindest eyes
The warmest smile
For both young and old

Just a touch of her hand
Would light up your life
Make you forget
All your trouble and strife

Reaching out to lepers
Embracing AIDS
Never was she daunted
Never was she phased

A woman so fine
Good to the core
To live on this earth
Never, no more

God bless and keep her safe Diana.

Lynne Blackham

Diana The Fairy Princess

When we first saw you, you were quiet and shy,
With a sparkling smile and deep honest eyes.
You were to be the wife of the future king,
With all the royal ties.

We saw you as our Fairy Princess.
You looked so innocent, so happy, complete,
In that beautiful dress on your wedding day.
For us all it was really a treat!

You had two lovely children,
Gave your life totally to their care.
A devoted mother who loved them completely.
They knew you were always there.

At times you were deeply unhappy,
With a haunted look behind that smile.
But you went ahead, loving and caring,
And suffering all the while.

You cared so much for ordinary people,
For the elderly, the sick and the children.
We thought you could go on forever.
We couldn't believe it, when

You were taken away on the last day of August.
Such a cruel and sudden end.
We all knew we loved you when you were alive,
Didn't realise how much until then!

You've gone to be with Jesus
To the Palace in the sky.
Where you'll find true love and be cherished,
The apple of God's eye.

Lea Wright

Dearest Princess

You have left us
But in such a tragic way.
How, if ever are we to get over you?

You were special, unique in a way no-one could ever describe.
Your loving touch, your caring words and your beautiful smiles are no more
But will be remembered for always

Why did you leave us Diana
So soon, and in such a tragic way?

You did what no other has ever done before
You touched so many hearts
Changing lives forever

But, darling Princess, when you finally found true love.
Little did you know, that it would take your life.

I pray that may you finally rest in peace
with your beloved Dodi.

Naila Shah

In Memory Of Diana, Our Queen Of Hearts

You gave so much, you gave your all
To people in countries large and small

You reached out a warm and loving hand
And spread your kindness all over the land

The world is a much sadder place
Without your beautiful, smiling face

You touched our hearts and we loved you so
Much more than you could ever know

You will live on in our memories for ever
Our Queen of hearts whom we'll always treasure

Shelley Hewson

It's The Good That Die When Young

She helped some worthy charities
The whole country was her fan
But now she has passed away
And her work only just began.

Her fame helped promote charity
But it killed her in the end
The gap she left upon this earth
Is one that'll never mend.

I hope to God her two sons
Will follow in her wake
'Cos if we had more Diana's
A better world we'd make.

The odds were stacked against her
Her looks attracted the Press
But if only they'd left her alone
We'd never have had this mess.

Now the Princess of Wales
Whose praises we've all sung
Has showed us once again
It's the good that die when young.

Kim Prince Wilkerson (14)

A Thought For Diana

Flowers speak in one voice
petals shed as tears,
our English rose has risen
the one we've loved for years,
her legacy left within compassionate
hands,
as every heart she touched became
a friend.
Her memory remembered in one song
of a rose that flourished, now
she's gone.
We must not weep for that empty
space,
but find solace in a loving
spiritual grace.

Hilary Anne Bannister

Thank You Diana

You have shone your light on the world
and made it a better place.
You have charmed us with your radiance,
your elegance and your grace.
Beauty far beyond 'skin deep',
your heart is solid gold
and yet it has been broken
and you've suffered pain untold.

You have loved the unloved,
given hope where there's none,
with compassion and kindness
what wonders you've done.
But you left us without warning,
now the world pours out its grief,
in despair, in shock, in mourning
and total disbelief.

But though you're gone, your light shines on
in your boys and through each nation.
We'll remember you forever
with such love and admiration.
You're in a better place now,
in perfect peace, it's true,
this world was never meant
for one as beautiful as you.

Sandra Lewis

For Diana

When I see the brightest star
I shall know just where you are
Watching from the skies above
Looking down on those you love.

The kindness you showed
Your love truly shone
We all have our memories
Which will always live on.

Miranda

Diana

You'll never know, how loved you were
How sorely missed, now gone
But you'll live on in all our hearts,
As will the words in Elton's song
Diana, Queen of Hearts were you
Your gift of love was free
Rest in peace forever more, at Althorp,
home of thee
We see the pain in your sons' eyes
Their sadness, bravely borne
We pray that God will comfort them,
And help them as they mourn.
God lent us his angel, for such a short time
To show the world, how to love
But sadly he called her, too precious to stay
To rest in his heaven above.

G Read

Our Precious Diana

The night began so happy for me,
But, later it ended so sad,
How, oh how could it possibly be?
Our lovely Princess was dead.

The world will grieve forever
For, this sweet loving lass,
Forget her, we can't - no, never,
The mourning, at no time, will pass.

It's her two boys I worry about,
Can they really ever be free
To do as she taught them, laugh and shout,
Happy, as she'd want them to be.

I hope, sincerely, they'll see clear,
Compassion and love for all other,
Poor, ill and maimed they'll help to cheer,
With hearts as big as their Mother.

Bonnie Parker

Diana

Always in our thoughts,
With so much love to give.
Never a cross word were you to say.
Our love of you, will always stay.

Always to remember.
No more to take.
Her life so hard,
Full of heartache.

The love has not gone.
She will never be forgot.
Always remembering.
Our lovely Queen of Hearts.

She gave so much.
Yet asking so less.
With this tragedy that happens.
Our pain so immense.

We loved her so much,
Or so it seems.
But how could this happen,
To our would-be queen.

Her family so strong.
Learning to know,
That the world and everyone
Did love her so.

Goodbye dear friend
You were constantly loved,
And because of this
We were all so touched.

Diana you're with us always
Even when in rest
So to our dearest Queen of Hearts
Goodnight God bless.

Louise Brown

A Tribute To Princess Diana

Diana, Queen of Hearts why did God take you away?
Turning our nation into grief.
The grief grows day by day.

Through all the pomp and prejudice
It mattered not to you.
You were Princess of the people,
With a gift so rare, but true.

You helped the poor and dying,
And touched the hearts of men,
Your beauty so undenying,
Your love came from within.

In a dreary Paris underpass three lives
Were lost that night.
A shining star amongst them
And that star still shines so bright.

You have brought us all together,
And as we mourn you in pain.
A legend in our lifetime,
We never shall see again.

Now when my life is over,
And I'm stood in Heaven's queue,
If an angel comes to fetch me,
Diana let it be you.

Martin Clohessy

She Did Not Judge

Diana did not judge a person
by their race,
Or a race by a person
She judged a person as a
Person.

Kevin Hibbert

An Angel Of Mercy

An angel of mercy she proved to be
So full of faith and constancy
No task undertaken, whether great or small
She did with love in her heart
She gave her all
She brought hope to the sick
She comforted the dying
She dealt in kindness and love,
Left the rest to the Lord above.
No-one ever understood
All she wanted to do was good.
They ostracised and criticised
But her smile was her passport to the world.
Now she's gone her memory lingers on
So when in future years we talk
Of this Rose cut from off its stalk
We can but say, that God knew best
When he took you home 'Diana'
For some peace and rest.
To wear his crown of glory
Our beloved Princess.
Rest asleep in Jesus. Till we meet again.

Vilma Ira Steel

Goodbye Our English Rose

Goodbye to our English Rose
We'll never see the like again I suppose.
Never see your radiant smile
A Royal who stops to talk awhile.
Never see your great joys
One who gave us two fine boys,
Never more will your kindness bring
Now only William to be our King.
Never more to feel your love
You are up in Heaven far above.
Never more to see such grace
Never more to see your face.
Each day the heartache grows
For DIANA our ENGLISH ROSE.

Colin Allsop

A Poem For Diana, Princess Of Wales

You're a star in the sky
And a star in our hearts.

You're the Princess we care and love
And your life of which we played a part.

You were an angel on Earth
And now an angel above.

We're all going to pray for you
And send you our love.

Princess of Wales we care for you so dear
We're all going to miss you and cry
millions of tears.

We all join in one
We all join together
Our love for you Princess Diana
Will live in us all forever and ever.

Andy Watts

31st August 1997

'A star fell from heaven:
dusk fingered it,
dawn put it out' . .

The click and snarl of Mammon
Long had ceased,
While you, dear Shade
Were forced to quench
The brilliant fires of Truth
Which, too late we'd come to see.

But our soaring surge of tears
Washed away the obscene
Grey glare of Death
And we prayed for more time
To get to know you, while our hearts roared
In the silence . . . now profound.

Bruce Pinkard

Tribute To The Queen Of Hearts

I was born to be a princess
And a queen never to be.
Though the title of the 'Her Royal Highness',
Was for a while given to me,
I was not regarded as such by all.
No difference, I made between great or small
The same between the rich and the poor,
For any of them I would open my door.
I was considered naive and ignorant
My life was not so brilliant,
Sometimes full of sorrow and agony.
I took time to feel your misery
The grief and pain I went through
Was unknown and not understood by you;
Being rejected, ignored and betrayed
Makes me understand others more;
So I learned to love you just as you are.
I seek your comfort by comforting,
Your love by loving,
Your comprehension, but instead
Criticism was poured out over my head.

Today, that I am no more with you
Many speak of my kindness and love
But very little about me they knew.
Except for my Maker who is from above
When I was followed and harassed,
By so-called human beings, I was chased
Like a fox, no-one was there
To defend my cause, the greedy
Took over for the love of money
Like me there are many today,
Who are passing the same way
Instead of trampling over them, try to
understand,
Don't pull them down but give them
your loving hand.

One can only love the unlovable
And can touch the untouchable,
When his heart is filled with the love of God.

Therese Valsin

My Princess

Is it true what I heard about Heaven last week?
They needed a Princess, so you they did seek,
They whisked you away to be Queen in the sky,
So soon, so sudden, we'll never know why.

Why you had such beauty, is easy to understand,
For love and respect, 'twas yours to command,
But now that you're gone, our love still remains,
And you'll always be 'The Princess of Wales'.

Now you lie on a lake, in pastures green,
Sad though it is, never to be seen,
A beautiful girl, who's happy at last,
But sadly now, that's in the past.

So lie there and rest, my Princess so sweet,
As these candles and flowers I lie at your feet,
To know you I long, but never did meet,
But lie there and rest, my Princess so sweet.

Paul Coates

Diana Queen Of Hearts

Diana you were born a Queen
A Queen of all our hearts
You were the end of every Rainbow
Where the loving starts
You gave light where there was darkness
And hope where there was none
And you never ceased in your endeavours
Until the deed was done
You gave young and old a purpose
You gave sick and dying hope
And with your strength and compassion
You taught us how to cope
You were the people's Queen of Hearts
And in our Hearts you'll be
No one can hurt you now Diana
In Heaven you are free.

R.I.P.

Christine Hervin

Goodbye Diana England's Rose

Goodbye Diana England's rose,
Why you were taken no-one knows,
You understood, both sadness and pain,
The likes of you we'll never see again.

When you were born and put on this earth,
You grew to such stature the people knew
your worth,
An heir you produced who will certainly
do you proud,
For when he becomes king, he'll surely
lift a cloud,
He will be a ray of sunshine just like his mum,
And Harry will be there - his very best chum.

So keep looking down on us and the sun will
always shine,
And we hope, in the near future we will do
without the mines,
You did such a brilliant job and you did it all
with love,
You can see your good work carrying on as you
look down from above.

So rest in peace now Diana with Dodi by
your side,
You can at last enjoy yourself, as you no longer
need to hide.

God bless you and all your family.

J A Jackson

A Tribute To Diana

No more will we see your smiling face,
So calm, so kind, so full of grace,
You stretched out your hand to one and all,
You lifted their spirits and made them feel tall.

Now we must take heart from the legacy you left,
We must try to uplift the poor and bereft,
To pass on your care and compassion,
To strive, to feel, with a passion,
That makes this world a better place.

Margaret Ann Monteith

The Light Has Been Extinguished

They turned out in their millions
Just to watch the hearse pass by
To watch the final journey
Of an angel known as 'Di'
Tears were streaming down their cheeks
Their faces filled with pain
They knew that they would never see
The likes of her again
From north to south,
From east to west
The silence filled the land
Not a single noise was heard
Just peace on every hand
Every land throughout the world
Has joined us in our pain
I doubt if we shall ever see
The likes of this again

'The light has been extinguished'
From the candle in the wind.

David Smyth

Diana

Though we've never seen you or looked upon your face.
I know that in my heart of hearts you're in a special place.
You left us with that smile of yours,
That touched so many folk, young and old,
Sick and lame
You always had a joke
Now you're up in heaven
Showing angels what to do
God bless you our Diana
The world will always miss you.

George Goldsworthy

Princess Diana

Regal and charming;
Dazzling and bright.
You shone like a star,
In the blackness of night.

For young and old,
Your love was sincere.
Once you were shy,
But became dignified and bold.

Your smile I will always remember.
It was like the sun in the sky.
Shining its warmth to everyone.
Why did you have to die?

There is a saying,
That the good die young.
God wanted you in his care.
But your legend lives on.
For people in the world to share.

Linda Webster

Diana, Princess Of Wales - 1961-1997

Awake and sleep no more,
Come join the crowd's applause;
See how the heavens adore,
Fair one who lived for cause!
Drop care from heavy lids,
Ignore our weeping,
Now you are sleeping,
As the gods did bid,
In shadows deep!

Crushed in gentle sleep,
Let rest restore the soul;
The setting sun did weep
So well you played your role!
Arise, be with us all -
We beg your cordial greeting,
Anticipate our meeting,
Evermore - a star reborn!

Nola B Small

Princess Diana

Lady Diana Spencer Born 1st July 1961,
Her mother, father, brother, sisters -
Couldn't have imagined the love she held;

In the beginning a childlike bride of twenty,
Full of life with innocence and grace,
Mark this day! - Her Royal Highness,
The Princess of Wales,
Duty followed welcoming -
Prince William her first-born,
An image of Diana - the future king!
A second, a brother for the heir Prince Harry,
Diana's love and devotion -
For her sons - knew no bounds,
As time passed admiration for her grew,
Her compassion for great causes -
Around the world within many a state,
The suffering of sick children,
Agonies of the homeless,
Victims of landmines - scared forever,
Many more the Princess held up close,
Her Royal Highness now -
An ambassador of people's hearts,
Strength filled as she caressed those in need,
Her smile touched those around,
Her beauty throughout stunned - she sparkled,
Her voice echoed giving unlimited courage,
Determine a being - an ambassador of humanity,
Good deeds that she undertook,
Monitored through the public eye,
No movement made unnoticed,
Boundaries of intrusion the press crossed,
The Princess - England's rose,
Radiant with beauty - her humour dazzled,
Through her enchanting smile,
Joy she embraced within her private life,
On the verge of happiness,
Suddenly . . . tragedy struck,
The beloved Princess of Wales -
Was breathless of life,
Denial filled across the nation,
We couldn't comprehend - what's happened!
A life taken so young - she was but 36,
Anger overwhelmed by grief,
A nation in mourning - pining,
For our caring Princess
Searching for hidden answers,
But in truth Her Royal Highness,
Touched deep within - indeed Diana,
Of hearts was the queen,
Her memory marked by her tragic death,
The nation joined in grieving -
For a woman who gave inspiration,
Not forgetting her brave growing sons,
Prince William - Prince Harry who possess -
Part of Diana - God bless them both.

For although England has lost -
Our Queen of Hearts,
They have lost their mother!

Karenanne Nelsey-Brown

Diana
A Tribute To Our Duchess Of Cornwall

You were the one who shone the torch,
For the rest of the world to see.
You gave compassion and comfort,
Held out a hand to those in need.

You broke down the barriers,
The stigma of leprosy and AIDS.
You witnessed so much heartache,
And started the landmine campaign.

You visited the homeless and sick,
The elderly and the young.
You showed us all,
How the world can unite as one.

Your love shone through Diana,
Through your eyes we could all learn.
The wonderful love you had for your sons,
A mother of affection and fun.

And all too soon our Queen of Hearts,
To the happiness you've finally found.
You're a legend that will always live,
God bless our very much loved Princess.

Audra Ann Murphy

Diana

Diana,
I may have never met you,
And in life it's now too late,
Until I get to heaven,
I can, but only wait.

I hope that you are happy,
Looking down from up above,
Knowing that your children,
Are surrounded with so much love.

William and Harry, have grown from boys to men
In a week we all regret,
Their strength, their courage, their sadness,
No one will forget.

The world is now in mourning,
Feels like you were a friend,
We're going from day to day thinking,
'Will this pain ever end?'

One good thing to come from this,
Is that, that you are free.
Now Diana, do as you wish,
Be who you want to be.

As our tears, continue to fall
Diana please know, you were loved by all.

Derek Wilson

The Day The World Stood Still

The 6th of September
A day we shall always remember
As the Day, the World stood still
in silent prayer, for one who is now at peace.

She was our most precious jewel,
so cruelly taken away,
now shines down, forever and a day.

God bless you, our Princess Di,
Forever in our hearts, and memories,
You will lie.

René Lucioni

Thank You

Thank you Princess Diana so very much
For all the people you ever touched.
I hope you know you will never be replaced,
We will always think of your lovely face.

Thank you also for your determination,
This will be remembered throughout all nations.
Your work for charity knew no bounds,
People felt special when you were around.

Prince William and Prince Harry have lost a mother,
They will feel empty, needing to rely on each other.
I pray one day the sun will shine again for them,
I am sure people will agree and add their Amen.

So farewell Diana and God Bless,
You will always be our Princess.
You reached out to people in their pain,
Now earth has lost but Heaven has gained.

Jane Kenny

Ode To Diana

Diana was a Princess we all know,
With hair so fair as the snow.
Elegance never seen before,
With a smile we grew to adore.

She was a cut above the rest,
As a Royal she was the best.
All the good she did for all,
This classy Princess so tall.

God needed you more than us,
That's why there was a sudden rush.
Here today, gone tomorrow,
Leaving us with all our sorrow.

Her memory will live on,
Like the shine from the sun.
It will never go away
Hence we need a 'Diana Day'.

J Stevens

Diana

Princess of our Hearts, your life is over
But your presence in our hearts
Still lingers on.
You brought into our lives a ray of sunshine
Reviving hopes, where hope
Was all but gone.
Your passing cannot dim our feelings for you,
Your death is but a closing of a door,
And though 'tis one we never can re-open,
Still yet, in death, your loveliness shines on.

You put the spotlight clearly on the people
Intent on taking more than
Was their share.
You took control of adverse situations,
And brought to our attention how unfair
Some people's lives could be . . .
Doing your best
To change in some small way, another's need.
Oh! Princess, how in death the nation
mourns you!
The pain is more than anyone can bear.

There'll never be another to replace you,
For no-one holds such charm
To captivate; nor yet to emulate
Your smile. Which like a beacon shone
so brightly
Calling us to love, instead of hate.
Our hearts just cannot comprehend the sorrow,
We find it hard to keep reins on our grief
But pray - as each day passes by - tomorrow
Bring some small measure wherein we find relief.

Rosylee Bennett

Diana - Princess Of Wales

God reached out a hand and swept you away
No time for goodbyes and kisses just a hand
along the way
You were the Queen of Hearts and admired
for so long
Is there any truth in the saying 'That only the
good die young'

Whisked away at 36 years of age - you had so
much to give
Always a friendly smile - always the will to live
Cards and flowers no matter how fitting could
never take your place
A worldwide stage so big that only you
could grace

Since your death, life feels strange, something's
quite not right
The days never even get going, it's a sad and
dreary sight
Missed by everyone from all different walks of life
The tragic news on Sunday morning cut just like
a knife

The flowers outside Buckingham Palace are
beautiful, quite an array
Simple little gestures all with cards which say
'Diana - Princess of Wales - gone but not
forgotten'.
You'll live on forever, for all the good work you
have done

Every living soul knew who Diana was
The most photographed woman in the world and
all because
She married into royalty at an early age
Now she's gone forever - just another empty page

A lady who cared with all her heart, yet never
reached her peak
A lady so graceful, a priceless gem, a lady
so unique
Rest in peace - there's no-one to touch you now -
you led a tangled life
Rest in peace Diana - Ambassador - Angel,
Mother and Wife.

Leigh Smart

Beautiful Princess

Into this world a child had come
A source of joy to Dad and Mum,
They knew not then that you'd become
A Beautiful Princess.

You lived through childhood young and free
Then went to teach at nursery;
Still no-one knew that you'd soon be
A Beautiful Princess.

The nation then forgot its strife
The day you came into its life
And you became a Prince's wife,
A Beautiful Princess.

Throughout the world you soon found fame
And to this nation you became
A Royal beauty to acclaim,
Our Beautiful Princess.

And to the Prince you bore an heir,
A handsome boy with flaxen hair,
The image of his mother fair,
The Beautiful Princess.

Then two years later came another
Just as handsome as his brother,
Both sons cherished by their mother,
The Beautiful Princess.

And then the family parting came
The Royal title left your name,
But in our hearts you stayed the same,
Our Beautiful Princess.

Through days of illness, racked with guilt
A million tears you must have spilt
But still we backed you to the hilt,
Our Beautiful Princess.

When health returned, you then resumed
To comfort those whose lives seemed doomed,
And once again your beauty bloomed,
Our Beautiful Princess.

You sold your robes, a selfless deed,
And gave the funds to those in need,
And showed the world you were indeed
A Beautiful Princess.

Your reputation grew and yet
Compassion in your heart was set,
You touched the lives of all who met
The Beautiful Princess.

And then your heart a new love found.
As you and Dodi travelled round,
The pressmen came to haunt and hound
Our Beautiful Princess.

And as upon that fateful day
The paparazzi chased their prey,
The angels came and took away
Our Beautiful Princess.

Then as the truth upon us dawned
The press throughout the world was scorned
As nations grieved, and nations mourned
Their Beautiful Princess.

Your people came from far and near
To lay their flowers and shed a tear
For one so loved, for one so dear,
Their Beautiful Princess.

Some kept a vigil through each night
And slept on streets by candlelight
For they had lost their star so bright,
Their Beautiful Princess.

Until upon that final day,
It seems the whole world came to say
'God bless, God speed you on your way,
Our Beautiful Princess.'

Now that the world has said 'Goodbye.'
Our hopes upon you sons will lie
That they may serve as well as Di,
Our Beautiful Princess.

As your last earthly home you make,
Upon an island in a lake,
We pray the Lord your soul to take
Our Beautiful Princess.

When safe in Heaven, free from pain,
As Queen of Hearts and Love you'll reign,
In mortal hearts you'll e'er remain
OUR BEAUTIFUL PRINCESS.

David R Williams

To Diana, Our Princess

How we prayed it wasn't true
When news came you had died.
Our dear Princess was gone from us,
And people from all nations cried.
You were with us for such a little while
We can no longer see your smile.
You cared so much for those in pain,
You rejoiced for those made well again.
The sick, the needy, too many to name.
The old, the young, you loved them the same.
Your two young sons, you loved them so,
You won't be here to watch them grow.
You left them memories to share,
You taught them how to be kind and fair.
We on Earth needed someone like you,
To show us the way, to be good and true.
Your pain is ended, your worries are gone.
Here, our lives will still go on,
Sleep sweet Diana, we remember you with love.
May your light which shone so bright on Earth
Live on in Heaven above.

J E Cooke

Queen Of Hearts
Love To Diana A Poem Tribute

We never knew you
But we all loved you
Came from God one of His angels
You took pain away from people's faces
You only wanted to be good
And help others
You were the best Mother to your boys
William and Harry
You could have been a good Queen of England
But I think God blew the wind
And you were called back to Heaven
We won't forget you ever
Love from all of us to you
Queen of our hearts, Diana.

Steven Knight

Diana, Heaven's Angel

God loaned to us an Angel
just to see how we would fare
She had the sweetest countenance
the bluest eyes and golden hair.

She went about her duties
with so much charm and grace
and those fortunate enough to meet her
will not forget her smile or face

She had her fair share of ups and downs
just like you and me
but she lived in a giant goldfish bowl
laying bare her sadness for all to see

Still she cradled sick and dying children
ridding the stigma surrounding AIDS
she fought hard to abolish landmines
seeking only compassion and love,
not accolades

She has taught us all a lesson on life
and one that we should heed
we are all equal in God's eyes
and should practise love and caring,
not greed

It is said God moves in mysterious ways
His wonders to perform
Now He has claimed His Angel back
We owe it to her memory to reform.

June Jackson

Diana

I will never forget this August day,
When you were so sadly taken away,
The powers of evil have finally won
A very sad tragedy that cannot be undone.
So unfair and painful your life has been
Now at last your soul can be set free
To Rest in Peace with your love that came to be.

All Our Love,

Vanessa Barlow

Diana Princess Of Wales

Snuffed out like a candle
In the best years of your life
Mother of two Princes
Once a Royal wife

You spread joy and happiness
Everywhere you went
Your beauty and your smile
Were surely heaven-sent

When first you came among us
So quiet and so shy
But always in the background
Was that twinkle in your eye

You blossomed like a flower
A beautiful pink rose
Your petals soft as velvet
A Princess down to your toes

But angels cannot live on earth
And this is surely true
If ever there was an angel
It was surely you

So sleep well my sweet Princess
In that peaceful, tranquil place
And always you will be for me
The Lady of the Lake

B Walby

Diana

D is for dear, to all of our hearts,
I is for icon, right from the start,
A is for always, we will never forget,
N is for natural beauty inset,
A is for angel up on high,

Diana, we love you. Goodbye xxx

S Brehaut

The Life Of A Princess

The life of a Princess,
Diana's her name,
Without her on earth,
Just won't be the same,
For seventeen years
She was part of our lives,
From the day Prince Charles met her,
And made her his wife,
That kiss on the balcony
How we all swooned.
Then we all watched
As she budded and bloomed,
She became a mother
With pride and with joy,
Princes William and Harry
Her beloved two boys,
She worked so hard, night and day,
Supporting charities, home and away.
The years that went by
Saw laughter and tears.
But still she remain strong,
Through those unhappy years,
Caring for others, and sharing their fears,
Then came the day, her life came to an end,
The People's Princess, everyone's friend,
And now sweet Princess
You're in Heaven above,
With Dodi beside you
At last she found love,
While down here on earth,
We will always remember
The Queen of our Hearts,
For always - forever.

Sarah Jolley

On The Death Of Diana Spencer

The sky was appropriately black and overcast.
Flashlights of lightning splintered across the sky
and a clap of thunder revelled with my hangover;
last night's wine was now clawing
at the back of my eyes.

A woman's distant voice outside
says 'She was such a pretty girl', and asks
when it happened? 'Just after midnight'
comes a gentlemanly reply.
Someone has died, I conclude, probably a child
another rape, strangling
whatever, the facts can wait
and I attempt to turn my splitting head
into an acheless pose and recapture sleep.

Headache wins over sleep and I arise.
Frail and slow I move on narrow cottage stairs
down to find my wife and her father
standing side by side,
staring out of the porch door
at the sinister blackness of the sky.
The house lights are on
at half-past ten in the morning.

What's happened I ask, and my wife turns
and there is redness in her eyes,
the signs
of which I know that she has cried.
Diana and Dodi Al Fayed have been killed
in a car crash late last night.

The vision of Diana comes in an instant;
her coy beauty, the way blues set off her eyes
and even if I did not move a muscle at that time
my mind recoiled from the words
that disbelief say I've misheard.
But Sandra's face says it all
and finally,
gripping the reality
My words come out 'Oh what a shame'
and then a flash of irony, and I exclaim
She was reported to have said
'The next thing I do will shock the world.'
Of course, she couldn't have known,
but she has.

The morning remained gloomy not just
because of the dark clouds and thunder
and the frequent cascades of celestial tears
but the news rooms have been up all night
editing bits of Diana's life
together this way and that,
comparing her to Princess Grace,
exploring every single fact
of her and a nation in shock.
Time and time again Her face is shown
and every time I see her, I want to cry.
But I don't.

Father-in-law's off home
and wife and kids do a Sunday shop
leaving me alone with my hangover
And TV on which I find the Waltons easy-
going on my heart, ears and eyes.
Until John boy, an aspiring writer, reads aloud
to two old spinsters the story of
one of their lost loves of days gone by.
The scene is brilliantly scripted and the words
of his love story moves them all to tears
and finally enough emotion has been accrued and
I join with them and shed my tears for Diana.
Then briskly wipe away the evidence.

With the afternoon came the winds.
No ordinary winds, they were very much
out of place
It seemed like a wind of anger tearing
across our land
thrashing the branches against window pane,
ripping the blossom off late summer flowers
and casting their colourful beauty aside.
They were the sort of winds that made you feel
(along with those deep black skies)
that the very chemistry of the earth
has changed and this could be
the beginning of the end.
They were the sort of winds that intuition says
it's best to stay inside.

The village, usually with a golden glow
as sunlight strikes the Cotswold stone
today is sombre grey and still,
sorrow hanging in the air.

The kids have heard a princess died
but for them there is no sadness
for surely very soon, they say,
a passing prince
will wake her with a kiss.

It feels the whole world is canopied
with the shock and sadness
and Yogi Bear videos,
although cheerful sounds emit,
do not impart their happiness.
My dwindling headache moves me
to reduce the sound on our PC
so kids can play their favourite games
without blasting into other rooms
and tearing at my dehydrated brain.

A call for dad to come and see
what's happened to our new PC,
Windows '95 has crashed,
and three hours later the machine
still will not re-boot and Amy cries
because she thinks it's her fault.
So I console.
And it strikes me that
this is the second crash today to touch
my life with sadness.

That night we ate
a memorial Chinese take-away.
And after a hair of the dog I'm
beginning to feel human again.
Digesting all the information
broadcast throughout the day
I am left with these thoughts.
Why has no one yet said
that although Diana is dead
she did at least die 'in love' and perhaps
her last thoughts or even her last cry
was Dodi, are you all right?
Because that's what she would have done,
cared about someone else, and not herself.

I turn to sleep at ten o'clock
and still with sadness reflect
on the future of the monarchy
now Diana's left.
Sleep comes easy in spite of the gloom
in my soul which is shared by my wife, I know.
Although she has said little
on the subject.
I know her quiet way.

So here it is then, a few words,
a sentiment to record just how I felt,
an aid to memory, with JFK and Presley
to answer the question in years to come
'What were you doing the day
Diana Spencer died?'

Philip L Baskerville

Princess Diana, Our 'Queen Of Hearts'

Princess Diana you are revered and loved by all,
You had to leave us when you heard 'His' call,
So tragic your death, but it just had to be,
To bring home to everyone, a great loss to see,
Your eyes and your smile, you were an Angel
on earth,
Sadly only some people realised your worth,
The whole world thanks you for your courage
and care,
And for all your good work as we say
our prayers,
But in spite of your commitments you never
neglected your Sons,
You gave them loving cuddles and lots and
lots of fun,
We thank you Prince Charles for choosing your
wonderful Bride,
So your two lovely Sons can remember their
'Dear Mother' with pride.

Jan Graver-Wild

A Beautiful Princess

A beautiful princess so full of fun;
Such a joy to have with us as bright as the sun.
The compassion, the beauty, the love that
she gave.
Showed us joy to all people, and that
she was so brave,
Deep down inside a great sadness, she hid.
But she showed love and duty, in all that she did.
She helped so many people in her very short life
Although a mother, a princess and a wife.
We were all so sorry that she had to depart.
Our lovely princess with the golden heart.
She was loved by us all, her new life just begun.
This great lady of cuddles kisses and fun.
She helped lepers, the needy, also the blind,
Their attraction to her was her way.
We'll remember Diana, was a special kind
For forever and ever a day.
Her grand smile will be missed, her loyalty too.
She was a very rare person we found.
Taken from us, her work, still left undone.
But our Queen of Hearts' love,
was shared all around.
We will always remember Diana by name.
As for us, there is no-one who can e'er
be the same.

Gwendoline Fields-Fitzpatrick

Island Of Dreams

We did not think you
would be left on an island,
but then it is your very own.

But you are a beautiful
English rose, left to
flower on in our lives,
roses are still beautiful yet.

But we will remember
you always especially
when the roses bloom again,
Diana.

Sheila Hunter

A Princess Lent From Heaven

God lent you to us for just a while,
A beautiful princess so tender loving and fragile
He could not promise how long you would stay.
We knew he would call you back to him
some day.
Our hearts tore apart when we heard of
your death
God came to you as you took your last breath.
Now you're with angels that can only
but stare at the most beautiful Princess
that we all did share.
You will always remain
Queen of our hearts, and now I must go
and let you depart.

GOD BLESS.

Jackie Desilva

Sun Moon And Stars

(In memory of Princess Diana)

I looked up at the night sky
And what did I see?
A 'Diana' star shining for me,
There was a half moon out as well
I could see,
On that beautiful July evening as clear
as could be,
For God created all these wonderful
things did He,
The universe, the heavens, you and me,
And are our dead relatives gone
We wonder don't we?
Why! They are up in the heavens
Like stars we can see.

Madelaine Thomas

Sisters Of Charity - 7.9.1997

(A tribute to two ladies who died within the same week, and from whose example we have much to learn, and give thanks for.)

Lord, how slow we are to learn our selfish acts
can hurt another,
When thoughtlessness deprives the Royal children
of a Mother.

When people with a lust for news of worldly
glitz and glamour
Can soon reduce to dust the lovely girl
who was Diana.

And many thousand miles away another
flame expired,
A saintly life of selfless love which all
the world admired.

That noble Mother of the poor, whose workplace
was the gutter
Is elevated now on high,
Teresa of Calcutta.

These sisters have both left this world,
transcending time and space;
They meet together, and behold their Maker,
face to Face.

This is a time to dedicate our lives
to God anew,
To think, before we act or speak -
'What would Jesus do?'

Lord, stir compassion in our hearts,
to give the helping hand,
That peace and hope and love will flow
in this and every land.

Help us bring out the best in folk,
and not to knock them down,
For all who bear the name of Christ
shall wear a Royal Crown.

Dorothy Lloyd

Britain's Fairest Rose

Many thousands flocked to the capital
for that funeral day,
Floral tributes everywhere - Diana would
pass that way.
Even in death she was the mother of
a future king
And for Wills one day Britain's church bells
will ring.

Her sons followed the cortege, both standing
proud and tall,
Wills and Harry wondering why their mother
died at all.
I hope that in heaven her soul finds peace
and rest
And that she shares with Dodi in
eternal happiness.

Diana lives on in her sons, so her life was
not in vain,
But we will never see the likes of
Diana Spencer again.
Elton John dedicated a song to Britain's
Fairest Rose,
While resentment against Royalty in the
people grows.

I never thought I'd see such crowds on the
roads or motorway
As Diana's funeral cortege passed slowly
along that day.
Diana brought comfort to many, right across
the land
But when she died so cruelly there was no-one
to hold her hand.

She has left such memories that time will
never dim
And I hope she finds Dodi, and spends eternity
with him,
God bless you lovely Princess, I never realised
your worth,
But you will live on forever in our hearts,
here on Earth.

Janis Old

Untitled

I was driving along in Paris,
when I saw a shining bright light.
I followed it, it led to Heaven.
I was now out of sight.
I then saw the gates of Heaven,
so walked gracefully in.
This place was so genuine,
here there is no sin.
It was then I saw Dodi, looking so upset,
For he had left his family,
I told him 'Do not fret.'
Then as I turned and looked around,
I saw faces of angels so plain,
Then I realised I had seen them before,
they were the children of Dunblane.
So this is the reason I had been taken,
it now seemed kind of fair.
Someone needs to look after these children,
I will make it my duty to care.
So take care of one another my people,
I may be gone but we are not apart,
I want you to always remember me as,
'Diana, Queen of Hearts.'

Kelly Maddison

My Dream

No more to weep
No more to roam
Diana you are going 'Home'
So young you were
To leave this way
Unfortunately you had no say
I can but dream
When I look above
That your smile
Reflects in the sun
The clear blue skies
Become your eyes
And that you are smiling down
On your two boys.

P A Kennard

Princess Of Our Country

Princess of this country you were
Loyal, loving caring you were
Love you gave to everyone
Your name is on every tongue
We speak of you, your love you shared
You showed your people
You're the Princess who cared
Everyone is crying out for you
Our world so suddenly torn apart
You were our only 'Queen of Hearts'
It will never be the same again
Now that you're gone
That wonderful light that came with you
Has since not shone
No more Diana to see
But live on . . . your name will be
In William and Harry
And in books of history.

Nirmala Singh

Blithe Spirit

Blithe spirit of England,
Princess of the isles,
You still walk this land,
The hills and green valleys,
The town and city ways.

Lithe fountain of life,
Cascading showers of joy
Over man and child,
Your infectious glow
Warming hearts anew.

Caring hands of love,
Translucent smile
Lighting the shadows of life,
Lingering bitter-sweet,
Diana - blithe spirit.

Esme Francis

Legacy Of Love

Goodbye, Queen of Hearts,
Your country worships you,
You are a shining beacon
For all that's good and true.

The brightest star in Heaven
Now bathes you in its light,
The warmth of our affection
Your pillow for the night.

We came from all over
To share your funeral day
Something drew us to you,
You were special in that way.

Your memory lives on now,
In William, your eldest son,
The love you poured into him,
Your wicked sense of fun.

He will be a great leader,
A king to make us proud,
A man for all the people,
A Royal for the crowd.

Sleep now, 'beautiful lady',
Secure in your dreams.
The people truly loved you,
You really were our queen.

Gary Hodgson

Farewell To Diana

Princess Diana's life was so short
It is with deep regret
Her love and joy within her heart
Her determination will be met

The places where you visited
With the people always kind
Your smiles were warmly welcomed
With cheerfulness on your mind

With bouquets of flowers left side by side
To the Princess whom we love
The messages to the one so dear
With God's Blessing from Above

Two Princes left behind to mourn
No Mother's love to share
But one day they will meet her
In her Saviour's Tender Care

Princess Diana we say goodbye
A sad time to remember
As you were driven slowly by
On the sixth day of September

Princess Diana 'God Bless You'
As your memories linger on
You will never be forgotten
For the duties you did perform

Ivor Wilson

Tribute To Diana

Amidst the traumas in a troubled world
Your presence was a shining light.
With your thoughtful, caring ways
Intent in putting wrong to right.
You achieved so much in your shortened life
The memory of you will always remain,
A true Princess, giving so much love,
Rest now in Peace, in Heaven above.

Jinty Wicks

Diana

There was a young lady called Di
The apple of everyone's eye
Her death was so shocking
It left us all rocking
And now she's at Peace in the sky

S Harwood

Diana

Saturday the 6th was a day of sadness
She was a much loved person who brought much gladness
Diana had so much love to give
It was a shame her life was to be short-lived.

Her smile and laugh were a treat to see
As I watched the funeral on TV
Millions of people turned out for the day
They lined the streets as she went on her way.

Inside the Abbey the coffin lay
As the closest to her had their say
They spoke of a sister whom they did love
Who was at peace like the bird the dove.

Hymns were sung and prayers were said
People couldn't believe our Diana was dead
Her two boys whom she gave her heart for
They couldn't believe they'd see their Mum no more.

The final hymn was sung out loud
We paid our respects with our heads bowed
As she made her way to the Great West Door
Diana will live in our hearts ever more.

As she made her final journey and was laid to rest
A song came to mind she was 'Simply the Best'
No-one can express what a sad day it's been
To me Diana you were a Queen.

Rest in Peace
The People's Queen of Hearts

Ann Penrose

A Prayer In Verse For Princes William And Harry

Your mother is gone but please don't grieve
She'll watch over you awake or asleep
She can't be replaced, just remember her love
Especially for you but also for us.

When you need a cuddle, a hug, or a squeeze
Just turn to your dad, I know he'll be pleased
He'll share in your sorrow he'll share in your fun
and he'll share in your sadness at the loss of your mum.

Mabel Wakefield

Princess Diana - 1961-1997

If anyone deserves to go to Heaven, Diana who died August 31, 1997.
This little girl, when she was born,
Her young life, was a torment, from then on,
Because her parents, helped to play a part,
Her unhappiness, when they decided to part.
As she grew, a Princess she would be,
That day, she married into Royalty,
Now that beautiful Princess, a Mother of two,
With her two sons, alone, at home,
Rumours were her husband Prince did roam.
What a wonderful British Queen, Princess Diana, would have been.
To this young lady, circumstances forced,
Against her will, her divorce,
An angel she was to those in need,
Children, the old, the ill, the diseased,
'When she knew', innocent children, deformed, or killed,
By landmines, buried by a foe,
She 'pleaded to nations', landmines, must go.
Her quest to find happiness, in her young life,
Then, such a terrible death, she did suffer,
Harassed by those for Front Page cover.
Everyone who loves her in this world will mourn today,
Of a caring Princess, whose life was taken away,
In a car crash, on a French motorway,
The compassion for all, she has shown,
Her 'elder son' may now acclaim our Throne . . .

Brian Marshall

Diana Queen Of Hearts

Our Queen of Hearts
Now dead and gone,
Her charity work must carry on.
Diana Day sounds good maybe.
Thirty-first of August, in her memory.
No one woman will ever do
The work Diana preferred to do.
Her shy joyful face
Her comforting arms,
Never to be forgotten, so many charms.
Thinking of others no matter what
Creed or colour she loved the lot.
Travelling the world, ache in her heart to see
People who suffer, it could be you or me.
Diana found time to sit and talk,
To the end of the earth she would walk,
Harder the task, more determined her aim
To stop the world's fighting, suffering
and pain.
Diana, an angel from heaven,
God-sent, loved, from the beginning
to the end.

Patricia Firth

About Our Caring Princess

She always had a lovely smile
For everyone she met
And she touched all our hearts
Which we will never forget

Also the many lives she cheered
Giving hope to patients too
For she gave them all her love
Which was so very true

She was our loving Queen of Hearts
And that she will always be
God took her to her Heavenly home
Where now she is at Peace.

I Thirkill

Our Lady Of The Lake

Gone is her smile
Gone is her kindness
Pictures and memories
Left here to remind us
Of a beautiful lady
Just past her 36th year
Who filled the world
With goodness and cheer

Gone too is her hurt
Gone too is her sadness
She is now freed
From a world full of madness
Her last months on earth
Were her happiest ones
We thank God for this
And her beautiful sons

Gone is her wisdom
Gone is her leading
We are left here
Our hearts are bleeding
We must carry on
With her charity work
To end all the suffering
And help those who are hurt
So be kind to others
For everyone's sake
For Princess Diana
Our Lady of the Lake

Elizabeth Blair

Diana, Goodnight

Each flower placed upon the ground
Symbolises your good deeds,
For despite your confusion
You cared for others' needs.
Never in all of history
Did so many people weep
For the nation lost their Princess
The night you fell asleep . . .

Joanne Gough

Diana - A Princess Loved

The flame of life extinguished, Diana you
have gone,
To your final resting place, but your memory
will live on,
Your beauty and grace are world renowned,
Both to the rich and to the poor,
Your fight for the homeless, also leprosy
and more,
All people worldwide love you,
Some though, you've never even met,
Others know Diana, your love they shan't forget,
AIDS sufferers everywhere know they too have
your love,
A love which is now in heaven, with the Lord
above,
For little children everywhere, Diana. you're
a star,
Up in the blue, blue heaven, shining from afar,
A waste of life, still filled with love,
A love which will last for evermore,
Your fight for the landmines is one we
can't ignore,
Diana, lovely Diana, now heaven is your home,
I hope you find true happiness,
Through this very sad release,
Our 'Princess of the People',
Diana, 'Rest in Peace'.

John Webb

Diana - The People's Princess

(Rest in peace - England's greatest rose, my thoughts are always with you)

Beyond the stars and universe
May your soul be laid to rest,
The moon will rise, the sun will set,
I for one, shall never forget!

Chris Quelch

Diana 'Princess Of Wales'

Like a Princess in Sleeping Beauty
You were born with a silver spoon
It stirred up for you much sadness
And ended your life too soon
When in your early childhood
Your life was torn apart
You showered on your baby brother
The love in your tender heart.

As your teenage years were passing
'Twas hard to believe it was true
Every girl's dream of Prince Charming
A fairy tale real for you
A princess you took your place
Charming and shy and full of grace
Your cup was filled with happiness
When with a son and heir you were blessed

With your children you often played
Crushed and broken your love betrayed
Your world had crumbled round your ears
Causing you much grief and tears
We stood aside and criticised
Unaware how you felt inside
You rose above it and showed your worth
Leaving your stamp upon the earth

You went where angels fear to tread
Upsetting many a dignified head
Even on a landmine scene
You dared to challenge the whole regime
You touched the untouchables
You held their hand
Cared for the old and young in the land
May the work you started never cease
As you walk hand-in-hand with
'The Prince of Peace'.

Margaret Annette

Diana - 'Queen Of People's Hearts'

People's hearts throughout the years are
filled with happiness, yet sometimes tears,
we've not the power to make the choice
between being sad or to rejoice.

It all depends on chance itself, which at
times doesn't seem to be quite fair, a sequence
of events will mostly cause the change from
total happiness, which often can be so rare,
to a feeling of complete despair.

A pretty girl demure and shy, became a
princess and caught the people's eye, from
then till now and how those years now seem
so few, that lovely girl in stature grew.

She knew those changes within her heart
like us, throughout those years from total
bliss to unhappy tears.

Perhaps it was because of that she did avow to
make, not knowing then the difference to the
world she would surely make, to little children
most in need, to those with HIV or AIDS, the
homeless and many other kinds even getting
heads of states to ban the use of landmines.

She little knew when very small that
at her end she would stand so tall,
or that when from this world she departs
she would live on in memory as a Queen of
People's hearts

We know now that if she were here today
these are the words she would surely say
'Be understanding of another's needs and with
gentle words and love help them their fears allay.'

She has shown us all by what she did to help the
world to be rid, of fear and cruelty and not at
least of all blind bigotry.

So if through her we have learned a thing or two
and whilst we may not always have the power to
change what life may have in store for us, by way
of happiness or tears, by her example we may
learn to take it in our stride,
get on and make the best of things as we live on
through the years.
Then if by this we realise her life, was not in vain,
and while now her tragic passing causes us much
pain, in time that pain will gently ease and our
normal life restarts, we will remember always
lovely Diana,
Queen of People's Hearts.

Larry Dean

Diana

(From all the staff at Medway)

Our voices here are one
We'd like to send this money for all the things
you've done
Whoever needed help or just a shoulder to cry on
You were the one they turned to that someone to
rely on
You didn't care what cause it was, what colour or
what creed
You were there for everyone, a true friend indeed
We'll never know your like again or the power
you imparted
All we know is now you're gone we're left
broken-hearted
Your photos they were gold dust to the media and
the press
Whether just wearing jeans or in full
evening dress
Your two sons they will do you proud in all that
they aspire
For they will have your boundless energy, drive
and desire
So as you gaze down on a people lost without
your smile
Think of those who miss you, your wit
your charm your guile
So sleep soundly now Diana for you have
found repose
Our ever-loving, ever-giving,
lovely English Rose.

Martin Kerrigan

Dear Diana . . .

I was a quiet, shy, twelve-year-old
When you first came on the scene
You seemed shy and quiet too -
But so elegant and serene.
You became a role model for fashion
With frilly collars and that 'Di' hairstyle
From then on, I wanted clothes
and hair like yours
Even spotty socks that stood out a mile!
If there was a special occasion,
Be it by day or by night
Just follow our Princess's example
For she always looked 'just right'.
But gradually things began to change
It was more than your looks that inspired
Your strength, kindness, compassion and love
THESE were the things that we admired.
Oh, Diana, you taught me so much
In so many different ways
It truly feels as if a friend has been lost
In these terrible, nightmarish days.
We were worlds apart, we never met
But you were there as my confidence grew
More than that, you inspired my
generation to care . . .
And for that, we will NEVER forget you.

Thank you, Diana, for EVERYTHING.

A Casey

Diana

Diana, Queen of the people's hearts
We all loved you so,
You shone a light around the world
With a warm and tender glow.

For children and the sick you cared
Your love will never die
Now with the Angels high above
A 'diamond' in the sky.

Pam Griggs

For Diana

The whole world is weeping,
Sour tears of disbelief,
Our Princess, gone for ever
A nation torn with grief

Let the bells of the land, ring
Chimes of the joy you brought us,
Let the birds, in the sky, sing,
The song of wisdom you taught us.

You touched our lives with your kindness
Warmed the hearts of all you met,
Gave hope in a world of cruelty,
I pray we never forget.

Our farewell is brimmed with sadness.
Too soon for us to part.
Left with only sweet memories.
Queen of our Broken Hearts.

Reneé Foulger

Our Lovely Di

So young, so shy, our lovely Di,
Then like a flower she grew,
Her petals unfurled, as she travelled the world
Her beauty and grace shining through,
Our lovely Di.

With love and compassion so freely given
To the sick, the dying, and the living.
Her beautiful smile, her gentle touch
To one and all, it meant so much.
Our lovely Di.

Her life with us was all too brief,
But as we come to terms with grief,
We look for the star with the brightest light.
And shed a tear as we say goodnight.

God Bless, our lovely Di.

Heather Wood

Queen Of Hearts

On a tranquil little island,
A serene and quiet spot,
Dear Diana 'Queen of Hearts', lies sleeping,
Never to be forgot.

Her love of life was enormous,
The love of her family too,
You will never be forgotten, Dear Princess,
We thought the world of you.

No more hugs and kisses,
Or a gentle touch you chose,
Indeed you were Dear Princess,
A very special English Rose.

Goodnight, God Bless, Diana,
Your work is finally done,
The 'Queen of Hearts' you truly were,
Your memory will live on and on.

Joyce Norton

Diana

You were a candle in the wind,
You went from place to place,
Country to country, giving your love.

You touched so many people,
With love and warmth for all,
You held hands with AIDS victims
You also held the hands of lepers,
And all the wonderful children,
You gave hugs and kisses to,
Will never forget your kindness.

You will be remembered for years to come,
You were beautiful and irreplaceable.
Rest now Diana, your work is done,
On your island in the sun,
With a gentle breeze,
And a pathway of flowers,
We will remember you.

V Leeks

The People's Princess

She never sat upon a throne
But was Queen of Hearts in every home.
She lost the title of Her Royal Highness
But the whole world knew she was the finest.
She started off so very shy
But her confidence grew as years went by.
A great ambassador for the nation
Faced with all kinds of situations.
Reaching out to people there
Our Diana showed that she did care,
Wiping the tears of a crying eye
The people's Princess was Princess Di.
Little children she did love
Embracing them with a hug
The poor and sick she couldn't ignore
Supporting charities ever more.
But the terrible shock that hit us all
Was when a car she was in, lost control,
The pain of sadness and tears now shed
Was when we heard the Princess of Wales
was dead.

For out of a tragedy such as this
Robbed the whole world of the people's Princess,
So as her body is put to rest
It's goodnight Diana and God Bless.

Maureen Burns

Diana, The People's Princess

Diana the People's Princess,
A lady with beauty beyond compare.
Mother, daughter, sister and best friend,
With love for all, her time she would spend,
With the sick and poor,
No-one could have given more.

Our angel sent from heaven above,
To teach us how to care, how to love,
United in grief we stand together,
In our hearts she will live forever,
We pray to you Lord above,
Hold close the Princess we love.

Carol Stannard

Heaven's Gain

A smile to melt
a million hearts,
The train to
Paradise departs,

The train arrives at
Heaven's door,
With floating clouds
and harps galore,

The angels queuing for
a chance,
Just to ask?
For that last dance.

To see the girl
we idolise,
They now see for their
own eyes,

So look above
A starry night
And you will see a
majestic sight.
The brightest star is
looking down,

Dear Lord, watch over
our Diana,
For she is surely,
'The Jewel in the Crown'.

Alan Barilli

For Diana

Like a light you came into our life,
And suddenly you were taken away,
We all sobbed that day,
Although your life was full of strife
You always showed a happy face.

You will be sadly missed by your sons too
We know you were devoted to them
Happiness came at last but it eluded you,
For you the heavens hold a place
Where you can meet your love again in haste.

Joyce Rose Phillips

A Light Has Gone Out

(Compassion, not indifference.
Expression and warmth, not 'stiff upper lip'.
Vulnerability is strength)

'A light has gone out in the world', that's true,
But if we look to the skies at night
You are there, Diana,
Shining still, from all the stars of Heaven
Shining with love on this troubled world.
You are with us, I feel it,
The playful wind,
The rustling leaves,
The dancing water
Hold gently your singing, ringing soul.
You dear, kind lady,
Without you, we sit by a sea of tears and flowers,
Flowers in the shape of a cross.
By day we think of you and sigh,
But go to work,
Hug our children, friends, families,
And say prayers for your boys.
At night candles flicker
As shrines to your beautiful memory
And talk and tears are quietened in sleep.
I haven't slept much
Since that dreadful Sunday, Diana,
So I'll look to the skies
And see you smiling in Heaven,
As God guides the world,
Sleeping and turning in your blanket of stars.

Goodbye Diana,
Love from

Naomi Sachs

Untitled

There is not a day goes by, but what a baby is born
To hear that first cry, is an unbelievable joy
It's a pity that they have to grow up
But grow up they must
With their fathers' and mothers' trust
One day a special child was born
Although no-one knew at the time.
Whilst growing up, she was a shy little thing
But all that time, happiness she would bring
The years passed by, then came along
A prince, who wooed her to belong
To him and be his Queen forever
They married, to be parted, no never,
But, not like all the fairy tales, it had a sad ending
They went their own ways, but remembered
They had two little boys, who needed love from both,
This story could go on forever and ever
But, alas, one night we lost our precious Princess
The boys, their mother
Never again to smile, shake hands,
Be there, when wanted, by family and friends
But our Princess will never grow old
As the likes of us who mourn
When she left us, our hearts were torn
She will never be forgotten as long as we live
Our memories will always remember the Princess who loved to give.

Olive Wright

Diana

You were like the sun
Shining and radiating round everyone.
You were like the sun
Warm and open, shrouded by rays of light
Making people's lives very bright.
You gave it all, you did not hold back
Although lots of things you found hard to hack.
But you never gave up, oh no, not you.
You were one of God's chosen few.
You did your job and you did it well
And everyone knew you were really swell.
Now in God's place you've gone to dwell
And what a tale you'll have to tell.
Your love will continue wherever you are
Shining down like a brilliant star,
Because that's what you were
And that's what you are
A shining Princess sent from afar.
'Diana'.

Janet Elizabeth Scott

A Rare English Rose

Diana, Princess of Wales bloomed
A rare and beautiful lady;
Growing from a tiny bud,
To a tall and regal princess.

As a tiny child she was nurtured
Like a rare and tender plant,
Until she grew and matured
Caring for those in great want.

Wind, rain and storms crossed her path,
But, struggling on she braved it all.
The tender plant grew stronger and stronger,
Till in the end she towered over all.

A rare and beautiful rose,
Came to a sad and sudden end;
Leaving behind a fragrance,
That will linger forever and ever.

Sr M Dominic Aherne

A Tribute To Diana - Princess Of Wales

The world unites in sorrow
At the loss of your bright light
Taken from us in an instant
Gone forever in one night

But remembered always
In the hearts and memory
Of a whole world who loved you
And mourned this tragedy

We are sorry you were taken
Our grief is plain to see
Our own precious People's Princess
We will miss you desperately

So goodnight sweet Princess
You will forever be
Our own Rose of England
A beautiful memory

Lin MacDonald

Beautiful Princess Diana

D is for Devoted to William and Harry
I is for Intelligent
A is for Angel
N is for Nanny to every child
A is for Always will be a part of us
as she looks down on us from Heaven.

God bless you.
May you live in peace
Forever in Heaven.

Alana Jones

Diana Of The Last Century

Diana our Princess of the realm
Such a lovely lady, always at the helm
She roamed around the world
Helping others with a smile and a touch
Never before in the last century
Has anyone helped the country so much
That August day she was called away
And left the whole world in dismay
We can only pray for Diana - our Queen of
Hearts.

S R Woollacott

Beautiful Memories Last Forever

We felt the pain on that sad morn.
When from our lives you were torn,
Your smiling face we won't see again,
But in our hearts you will remain.

A loving mother, with a caring heart
Too soon your life just fell apart
But in God's care you are now at rest
Princess Di you were simply the best.

Sadie Darragh

How Much You Meant To Us

The flowers upon your gravestone
Show how much we really care
The loss of a special person
The pain we cannot bear.

The love that you gave us
Will remain in all our hearts
Even though we may be now
A million miles apart.
The flame of your candle will
Burn on this earth eternally
We'll put it in the high heavens
For everyone to see.

And the flowers upon your home ground
Show how much we really care
The loss of a special person
The pain we cannot bear.

Your smile brought to our lives
Friendship, hope and grace,
You were our only 'Queen of Hearts'
Who no-one will replace.
We'll always feel cheated that
You went so soon and suddenly
But we must be grateful
That you came along for us to see.

And the flowers upon your grave
Show how much we really care
The loss of a special person
The pain we cannot bear.

You were our English rose
You're the affection of our love
You were the happiness of our lives
You are the peace of the dove
And now you're an angel in heaven
Sending your warmth and love down
Your wings are lined with gold
And upon your head, heaven's crown.

And the flowers upon your island
Show how much we really care
The loss of a special person
The pain we cannot bear.

And the flowers upon this great earth
Show how much we want you near
The whole nation is weeping
Now we know that you're not here.

Emma Gardner (13)

A Lovely Lovely Lady

The most beautiful flower to bloom on
Earth. Alas! - The petals fall too soon,
Shines now the brightest light in Heaven
Dwarfing the stars, the sun and the moon,
Scintillating brighter than all the gems
of every size and hue.
The only jewel in the crown
Diana that was you.
Our rainbow after a thunderstorm
A dove whiter than any other.
A Princess, daughter, sister, friend,
but most of all a mother.
Sleep on dear Diana in God's kingdom above
Our love for you time will not sever.
You did not quite make it on Earth as
'The Queen'
But you will reign in our hearts forever.

Ann Elizabeth Laws

A Poem For Our Princess

Out of all the lovers in the world,
It was Dodi that you chose,
and to follow that you had to die,
our lovely English Rose.

From all of us you're sadly missed,
as a nation our grief shows,
we watched your funeral - taped it too,
why did you have to go?

Clare Sellar (13) &
The Sellar Family

To Diana

A flower-like face, erased in full bloom
Blue eyes sparkling like a sunlit sea
Shadowed, when clouds hide the moon
Never again the sun on her face
The gentle wind tossing her hair
Her lovely smile, lost forever, one, yes, one beyond compare
Never to see her beloved sons grow into manhood and maturity
To be there with love and pride to praise them both for doing well, whatever path they choose to take
To laugh with them, to hug, to tease in moments of hilarity
So many things, she planned to do, to help the sick, the needy too
So little time to see it through
Her vision to help make it come true
The whole world mourns, so deep the pain
Our great loss, is Heaven's gain
Rest in peace, may happiness you find
In such great measure, you left behind
An English Rose, a Princess too
Our hearts are full of love for you.

Frances A Corcoran

A Tribute

An English rose has died today,
The music has become, muted and deep,
As we strive for loving words to say,
We too, turn for comfort and weep.

The sparkle in your eyes has now been stilled,
Yet memories will abound in time,
But my rose your destiny has been filled
Now we too must make ours for thine.

The laughter in your smile has now passed us by,
Your touch so gentle and kind,
If we can only reach out once and try
We too will have peace of mind.

You left behind a lot of love,
And memories to cherish and keep,
Two fine sons, a legacy from above
Millions of hearts will always miss a beat.

An English rose has left us and gone,
To a place of everlasting peace,
If ever one lesson has been learned, from you the beautiful one
Is the loving gift you gave to our disadvantaged and weak.

Tony Heenan

Angels Upstairs

Climbing the tranquil stairs
A candle dances in the coldness
Now you have been called away
Cared for by the angels upstairs
Where voices are cloud soft
Sunshine smiles with radiant charm
Matching your serene beauty
A temporary gift placed on Earth
Now in the hands of angels upstairs
Living in Heaven's garden
A face painted on every flower
Coloured by graceful hands of angels upstairs
A Princess remains in our thoughts
As a smile and a light.

Neil Mason

Our Princess Diana

Diana was our brightest star
Much loved by all, near or far
From the sick to the very poor
Their pain touched her to the very core
Diana reached, out to ease their pain
She understood, no need to explain
Her own life was touched with sadness and strife
But Diana still laughed and got on with life
Sadly God took her away
We miss her so much, wished she could have stayed
No second chance did she get
But her love, charm, goodness, we will not FORGET.

P M Youngs

Peace To A Golden Rose

Happiness like beauty is a transitory thing
given on loan
Often snatched away before it fully blossoms
Leaving behind a trail of emptiness,
Pining for the past which cannot be reclaimed.
Wishing hopelessly it were a bad dream
Yet realising it is true.
Diana Queen of Hearts this is how we think
of you.

Beautiful flowers strewn across the land
So gratifying to us the living,
We feel we have played our part
They mean nothing to the dead
Diana is gone she can smell them not,
Though forever she will live in our hearts.
For the people's Princess true love
came about
With the handsome Dodi Al Fayed
Their tragic death was fate that goddess
of destiny
That flicked their candle out.

Goodbye English Rose Elton John sang,
Deep pangs of grief and sorrow
Passed through the crowds that listened then,
A Princess young and lovely had left this world at
dawn
Driven to her death by a drunken chauffeur
While the night-clubs of Paris blared on.

I am sure the angels hugged you Diana,
praising your good deeds
Compassion and kindness to anyone in need
You did not have to mix with those less
fortunate than you,
It was your wish to do such work
A gift bestowed on you.

Beyond death's dark horizon,
After winter comes the spring,
Our hearts call out 'Diana'
The seeds you sowed have reaped we sing,
You worked endlessly for charities
Now two willing hands are still.
You have gone to Heaven's mansion
There, resting at God's will.

Kathleen McSorley

The Sound Of Silence

A bright light has been extinguished
Princess Diana has been taken away,
A much loved and respected Lady
Our world is much poorer today.

A little boy placing some flowers
Had some words of comfort to say.
'God decided that He needed her
That's why He took her away.'

Diana's children William and Harry
Have lost a jewel from the crown.
They were the apple of her eye
God - give them strength and courage
As the days go by.

Diana's bedside manner was unique
She gave faith and hope to the weak.
A pebble of beauty in a sea of drabness
Her presence in a room, turned misery
to gladness!

The whole world mourns your passing
No-one can take your place.
You were a wonderful person Diana
Full of elegance and grace.

Norman Desmond Humphreys

Diana

Diana you were so sweet and kind
You left a world of love behind.
You always thought of others' needs
You were so good you did good deeds.

We only realised when you were gone
All the good works you did, which must now go on.
All the charity work that you did start
Is now forthright in everyone's heart.

All the love you gave your boys William and Harry
Will make them grow strong, full of love and one day marry.
They will miss their mother so very much
They will always remember your love and your tender touch.

You were an angel sent from above
To show everyone how to give love.
You will now be happy in Heaven above
Now all the angels rejoice in your love.

Sandra Ingham

Tribute To Diana

We cannot believe that you have gone,
it is so tragic and so wrong.
To take away a heart of gold,
makes us all feel very cold.

Helping others was in your soul,
Helping the young and helping the old.
You were a light within our world,
our protector and our shield.

Our world will never be the same again,
because your loss, is our pain.
As a nation we are lost in grief,
Finding it hard to believe.

Knowing you are no longer here,
Wiping away another tear.
Only your star in the galaxy above,
our Diana, the one we all love.

Tina Downham

Diana - The English Rose

(Dedicated to Princess Diana who was held in deep affection in South Asia)

A touch, a cuddle, a gentle smile,
by a hospital bedside -
you lingered awhile.
Caring for total strangers,
showing compassion -
light from a burning candle,
in a hard and unkind world.

You ran like the wind,
a whirlpool of sadness,
heartbreak and sheer joy.
William and Harry -
your 'two boys',
kept you focused
on the present.
You radiated love
for your kith and kin.

Then came a cruel twist
of fate,
on a Parisian night -
a chase, a screech,
it was too late.
They brought you back -
confined, lost forever.
A Princess known
throughout India and Pakistan,
from an island in the Maldives
to the foothills of Sri Lanka.
The world cried
as they said goodbye -
to an English Rose.

Ivan Corea

Diana, Princess Of Wales

To Diana, Queen of all our Hearts
Gone forever, now apart
Lost from our touch at the break of new dawn
Your body has died but your spirit lives on.

In a life full of sadness and heartache and tears
Just as you had begun to dispel all your fears
You were taken from us in the blink of an eye
Too quick for us even to say our goodbyes

In your life, you never knew the extent of our love
We only hope you are watching, and smiling above
Simply irreplaceable is what you are
But we're too late to tell you for you've gone so far.

Forgive us, Diana, for the things that we said
For we did not realise until you were dead,
How, for us, you were a beautiful, unforgettable song
At peace, now with the angels, where you have always belonged.

Sarah Fox (16)

Dear Diana

These words were in my heart but I didn't want to write them for I knew if I did it would be true . . .

Maybe if I didn't write it it wouldn't be then I would wake up and it would all have been a terrible dream.

But it is true and you're gone.

A hush fell over the world when we lost you,
A hush that has made everyone examine their conscience . .

Our hearts ache without you and for all those you so dearly love;
Rest in the arms of God at peace knowing you did not die in vain.

Barbara Petrow

Farewell To Diana

On Saturday morning I got up
And turned the TV on
A funeral had begun for someone
Now forever gone.

Princess of Wales, Queen of our Hearts,
The one that everybody admired.
Your memory will live on forever,
Even though your great life has expired.

The funeral cortège going down the street,
The nation shedding tears.
We never thought that you'd leave us so soon,
Only living for thirty-six years.

My family down now to watch the parade.
It's now coming up to half-way.
My mum goes out into the garden,
But it was silent out there that day.

She comes back into the house, which
Is just as silent and still.
She watches the Abbey doors open,
Her eyes now starting to fill.

The people there singing hymns of praise,
Earl Spencer's speech to his sister.
Now standing still for a minute of silence,
The world will sorely miss her.

The funeral over but people still mourn,
They sit there and silently pray.
I definitely think that this must be
The saddest of all Saturdays.

Lauren Parrott (10)

The Love We Have Lost

You know that we love you,
You know that we care,
You know that we miss you,
With this pain we cannot bear.

These tears that we are crying
are full of feelings that are true,
We know that you loved us
and you know that we love you.

Sara Long (15)

Princess Of Hearts

My wedding day - a magic celebration!
A reason to rejoice across the nation.
The sound of peeling bells that
sparkling morning
Heralded a brand new era dawning.
The years were full of promise, stretched
before me
Yet, I did not foresee a sadder story.

I may have been the daughter of an Earl,
But inside, I was just a British girl.
A British girl, but now Princess of Wales!
It seemed to be the stuff of fairy tales.
I didn't know my life of fame and glamour
Would dazzle me with all its noise and clamour.

Then, what went wrong? I wish that I could tell;
My marriage had become an empty shell.
I kept my smile and played my Regal role,
But no-one seemed to see inside my soul.
The crowds would see me, cheer and wave
a banner
They could not see ME - childlike, hurt Diana.

My deepest joy was touching the unloved;
The first Princess to reach with hands ungloved -
To care for those that others had rejected;
To comfort them and see hopes resurrected.
Of all my work accomplished in this land,
The most important - stretching out a hand.

Here lies my coffin at the Abbey door.
A silenced shock. The Princess is no more.
My sons, I speak to you now from my grave,
You must be noble and you must be brave.
And, as I lie beneath this hallowed steeple,
I urge, you, sons, go out and love the people!

Jacqueline Lopez

A Tribute To A Princess

God only knows the reason why,
Our beautiful Princess had to die.

His guidance he gave her, using her heart,
Her soul he filled from the very start.

The world knows the example she set,
Our fearless Princess, her duties she met.

In Diana's image, our young Princes will grow,
True love avails all that's what they know.

Look down Diana from Heaven today,
Listen and hear what our world has to say.

A tribute to you the stars they sing,
In your son you have left us
A special King.

Ruth McGibbon

Diana

Most had never met her
But she crept quietly to our hearts
A pretty sweet shy girl
She spoke she looked she smiled
She had us in a whirl
So gentle so kind was she to all
Rich and poor young and old
She cast a magic spell around
Her caressing hands knew no bounds
No-one will ever take her place
She was an Angel on Earth
So full of grace
Diana you were too good for us
We did not appreciate your worth
And so God took you from us
You outlived your time on Earth
Goodbye sweet Lady
Your beauty will never fade away
Rest peacefully beneath your flowers
Perchance we meet one day.

Rose

The Fragrance Of Eternity
A Tribute To Diana

The name 'Diana' your parents gave to you
means, 'The Roman goddess of Moon'
But, Alas! You departed from us so soon.
Your angelic name is now inscribed
deep down in our hearts and souls.
You were the Princess of Hearts and mind,
So sweet, wonderful, radiant and kind.
Whenever you trod on any road or street
The celestial stars, the moon and the angels
bowed to you and were keen to greet.
The Princess of many millions of hearts
No-one ever wanted you to depart
From this world at such a young age
Your glorious name is now written
in every book and on every page.
The fragrance of thy name and soul
will spread everywhere like heavenly
perfume of Sandalwood,
Oh! Fragrance of Eternity we'll never
forget you, because you were so kind and good.

Gulshan Khanna

Princess Diana

Dear Lord you know what
Pain we were going through
Our Princess Diana was killed
She's been taken from us
Now all we have of Diana
Is all those memories

She was so young
At 36 years
Her eyes would sparkle
Her smiles on her face
She held her hands
To help you all on your way

She will be missed by those
little children
The old folk and the sick
The AIDS victim and leprosy
And who else she would visit
She is our Queen of Hearts.

Sharon Brown

Diana

Diana, when you came to us,
You were so very shy,
But you blossomed like a flower,
As the years went by,
Into an English Rose,
With your own special style,
And a very loving mother,
With a wonderful smile,
The people grew to love you,
For all the good you've done
And also for your beauty,
And your lovely sense of fun.

You were so very versatile,
You knew just what to say
To the people that you visited,
Both here and far away.
You could dance with the best of them,
The film stars and the pros,
And you looked just like a model,
As everybody knows.
The children love you madly,
You're their fairy-tale Princess,
But, you did not deserve to be,
A prisoner for the press.

We felt the loneliness you suffered,
When you only needed love,
And believe me you have got it,
Though you're now in Heaven above.
So now my dear Diana,
As your new life starts,
We will remember you forever
As our own sweet Queen of Hearts.

Josie Love

Tribute To Princess Diana

None of us could believe the news that came
one Sunday.
Princess Diana had her young life suddenly
taken away.
To people all over the world she was
a leading light.
Good causes like landmines she backed with
all her might.
To people with many a serious illness
Diana was so kind.
Such compassion and caring will be very
hard to find.
A most beautiful woman but also a
very loving mother.
To William and Harry she will never be replaced
by another.
The people their tributes for a long time
will send.
Most people for certain feel that they have lost
a good friend.
Our thoughts and respects most definitely
with her family too.
Diana a little space is reserved in everyone's
heart for you.
We like to think that with Dodi, Diana really
found true love.
Now always thinking of them together with the
good Lord above.

Elizabeth Ann Allingham

Princess Diana

Is life meant to be this way
As we tip-toe gently into another day
Breathe the early morning air
Everything seems so clear.
Climb upon a rainbow with me
Your love will last eternally.

Trevor Smith

In Memory Of Diana, Princess Of Wales

A blank sheet of paper stares at my grief
for a Princess I have never even met,
though I share in her first Christian name.
Finding the words to sum up the pain
is like stepping through a field of landmines.
Pictures flash through the mind, of a mother
whizzing down a flume with two laughing sons
who have now lost the person who let their spirits
sing. How alien their funereal solemnity,
William's head bowed in a parody of Diana's
coy shyness and Harry gazing straight ahead,
as if he could not believe his mother was dead.
'Mummy' on the wreath brought tears to the eyes
of even the childless like me. She was so loving
to so many children with disabilities or cancer.
One squeeze of the hand of victims of leprosy
or AIDS banished the ogres that plagued
their healthy compatriots. Her country
mattered profoundly as she carried out duties
often hard for a timid young creature to bear.
Most of all, I miss her vitality, that ebullience
that makes us all rebel against the idea
that beautiful Diana lay stone-still in that coffin
shrouded by the stuffy, age-old royal standard.
How could one so alive have died? It makes
no sense. Shock stunned the nation, which shed
its tears in an ocean of flowers for her and
for Dodi. It seemed she had found
true happiness at last, but the car crash
snatched that away - or did it?
Her children will mourn her forever, surrogate
and real, but she and he form a new constellation
their wedding hymns sung by the angels.
There's more space in heaven for a girl of her
gifts than the overcrowded earth could ever
afford, far away from all paparazzi, where Diana
can take revenge at last, as her namesake did
on Actaeon.

Diana Stow

Oh Diana

Diana you gave this world new life and hope
At this tragic news we just cannot cope.
Every man woman and child shall shed a tear
In a world of sadness now that you are not here.

Deep down in all our hearts we feel the pain
Will we ever be happy and smile again
Your warmth and kindness you shared with the world
Embedded in our hearts your memory will be held.

You devoted your life to those worse off than you
You spread love and happiness in all you had to do.
You gave a glint of hope where there was none before
You made people laugh and smile in the aftermath of war.

Now your life has come to an unhappy end.
We have lost a wonderful Lady and a personal friend.
So this is now where your new adventure starts
Diana, you will always be our Queen of Hearts.

Ian G Lewer

A Tribute To Diana Princess Of Wales

Can the sun ever be as bright above
Now that we've lost the Princess of love
Huge was her impact in this world of ours
Like bursts of sun between the showers

Quite lucky were those who knew or met her
And in a way it's even better
For extolled with zeal by the media
Millions knew her causes and charisma

Oceans of flowers were fitting tribute
For with beauty and grace they follow suit
Bright and colourful their message is strong
Despite all the odds she went along

Individually we've not her style
But all our efforts would be worthwhile
So do your bit lessen pain and sorrow
And ensure a brighter tomorrow.

H C Derx

Diana

I cannot believe this has happened
I cannot believe this is true
I cannot believe the world has lost
A wonderful person like you

The loss that I feel is enormous
The grief in my heart will not mend
Though I never was honoured to meet you
I feel like I've lost my best friend

In life you felt all emotions
Happiness rejection and pain
But if you knew how the world has grieved for you
You would never feel lonely again

If our tears could give you back to us
You would be here today
For the tears the world has cried for you
Will never fade away

A child a wife and a mother
You carried them out with such pride
Your children will grow and live through you
Your love held cherished inside

If there could be some consolation
Now that you're in Heaven above
It's that the love of your friend has died with you
Embracing you in eternal love

And so with these words I will leave you
A Queen a Princess and a Friend
The compassion and love that you gave from your heart
Will stay with me right to the end.

Linda Weeks

To Diana, Princess of Wales . . .

. . . You came into our lives a shy young lady
with much hope in the world.

On your wedding day, a day many would have
been petrified of,
you looked so beautiful and confident.
A picture which will always remain in
our minds.

Gradually, you turned heads, wherever
you went
but eventually this would be your downfall.

People judged you, condemned you,
while all you did was good.
While all you did was to help.

You gave us the gift of a King, a gift
which will
live on although you have gone.

I pray that William and Harry have your
strength in future years although I am sure
you will keep a watchful eye on your 'boys'.

If I had one wish, I would wish that you could
live again.

If I had one day I wish it could be the day you
entered our lives.

If I had a choice I would choose you any day.

I have always felt that you, Diana, were
a figure England
could feel so proud of and now you
have left us.

You enabled many to see the way.

You gave many the confidence to carry on,
to do things they had felt impossible.

And now, our Princess, you have gone.

We all feel such love for you. All you need to
do is open your eyes and see.

You will never be forgotten and will live on
in our memories always.

God bless you and may you rest in peace . . .

Heather Burberry

Diana Of The Caring Heart

Clouds gently kiss the mourning hills
Whilst weeping rain floats like a banner
As fields of grain sway in the breeze -
They curtsy to the name - Diana.

In every town and village
Hamlet or castle tower
The union flag - at half mast -
Bows its head at this sad hour.

Diana was the Princess
of people - low and high -
A star who shone - with caring love
Oh - far too young to die

For those who suffered - she fought hard
All dangers cast aside.
The ill and injured - were her cause
Little children - her great pride.

Princess of Wales - Diana,
From her beloved sons - she parts
Remembered till the end of time -
As our own dear Queen of Hearts.

Idina Mary Miller

To Diana

In Medieval countries
Thousand upon thousand centuries ago
Stretching back in time who knows how far
The worship of Diana, huntress, Goddess of the moon
She who helped the unfortunate, the wanderer,
Saved the mariner from shipwreck and disaster
As he sailed out to find new lands
Over the sum of the world.
Guided by sun and moon and stars
In fragile craft on perilous seas.

And laughing boys and girls
With vine leaves in their hair
And flowers in their hands
Came playing on the piper, dancing to the shrines
To honour the goddess Diana
In far off Pagan times.

In nineteen ninety seven
On this day of her funeral
Throng from the east from the west the people -
Stand silent in the streets like corn in the fields
Waiting - as the hearse slowly passes of Diana the hunted
Princess, worshipped as a goddess, so young to die.
The Queen of Hearts.

Mary Sage

Poem For Diana

You touched our lives
You touched our hearts
And we can't believe you've gone
But our love for you will never die
It will always carry on

You were so beautiful and kind
A very caring soul
You really did love everyone
To you it wasn't just a role

You shone a light upon the world
Made us all unite
I hope you are at peace now
Sweet Angel, goodnight.

J Larkin

I Will Mourn For You, Diana

I will mourn for Diana, for Diana, alone,
But not for the others in the public zone.
For Kings and Lords I will not cry,
When to be born they have to die.
Only for Diana, our Lady of Shallot,
For you, Diana, I'll cry a lot!

When I saw your star go by,
In the dark of a velvet sky,
I wasn't quite sure of what I'd seen,
Just a brilliant flash inside in my brain.
Stayed in my mind, stayed in my sight,
Diana - I'll mourn for you all right!

I mourn the hurt your loss will bring,
To all who loved you, and to you would cling.
The cause of your death, people are asking,
Greedy people, avaricious for gain,
Stabbing our hearts with unspeakable pain,
That their shining star is forever gone!

There is a tale I never resist,
About a lady, through time and the mist,
Alone in her castle in solitude,
Loved by her people be they lofty or rude,
And when she drifts down through the barley and rye,
Covered in flowers she never will die.

Farewell Diana! From the hearts of us all,
The rich and the poor, the great and the small,
Your gift for compassion, for pity and love,
Bird of peace, hunted dove,
Sleep on your own, Lady of the lake,
Until God calls you, at his day break.

Tom Ritchie

Princess Diana

Princess Diana and her friend Dodi Al Fayed
have left us with hearts of lead
together soaring through the heavens above
secure and happy in their love
they leave us with our rivers of tears
we pray to 'God' and hope He hears
our prayer for her darling sons
that they remember their mother's fun,
her compassion, beauty and wonderful smile,
we all miss her, it will take a long long while.

Diana's brother, the Earl Spencer, very bravely
defending her name
told the world we're all human and the same
with sensitive feelings and we all feel pain,
her charm and beauty not her only assets
but love and charity, one of the many facets.

Nobody else can replace this girl
she was the real gem, the rare pearl

Take comfort in all the nation's grief
we hope it affords you some relief
knowing of our genuine love
and hoping she's looking down from above,
we've cried and cried, but the tears still flow
Princes William and Harry we just wanted you
to know
She didn't want to leave her boys
it wasn't her that made the choice

May Mummy, Diana and Dodi rest in heaven's
peace.

Shalom

Shirley G Piazza

Diana Our Precious Princess

Diana beautiful and so very kind
Precious to every living kind
She helped the sick and the poor.

Jennifer Youngs (8)

Diana

To the dearest Princess that this world
ever knew
Diana mania, it just grew and grew
You were vibrant and loving and
so full of care
We would wait for hours with an excited air
to catch a glimpse, to see how you dress
You truly were our greatest princess
The most glamorous woman, you shot
up our charts
and you quickly became the queen
of our hearts.
Your love and compassion always
shone through
To help anyone, you'd do all you could do
For the sick and the injured, the lonely
and poor
You touched every life, even those troubled
by war.
The charities you helped, the good work that
you've done
Your the Queen of the nation, you're our number
one.
Not a person in need, by you would
be shunned
But your life has been ended, as a nation we're
stunned.
We can't understand it, or believe that
it's true
Everyone's grieving, we really miss you.
We're sorry for the problems and
unbelievable stress
Placed on your life, especially by the press.
Things were starting to look up, what more can
be said
You'd found a dear friend in Dodi Al Fayed
We're glad you found happiness, before your life
had to end
You'll always be remembered as the world's
greatest friend
Dodi and you are in peace together
and your memory lives on forever and ever.

With love from

Melinda-May Wells

Diana, Princess Of Wales

How we do weep on this poignant day
Words can't express what we want to say
The nation is grieving for you beautiful Princess
So young, so vibrant, so caring, so tragic
The people's Princess you touched all our lives
Our nation has lost one so exquisite
You cared for the poor the ill and the needy
Your tenderness there for each and everyone
Your love for your children always put first
They will never again have such tender devotion
Your charisma and charm always shone through
Whatever the task you had to do
Your work with AIDS and leprosy victims
Your compassion and concern was clear to see
Today our nation will shed an ocean of tears
Not only for you but for Harry and Wills
Tonight we will look to the shining new star
Glistening in the sky so near yet so far
Goodbye Diana we all loved you
If tears could build a stairway the beautiful flowers a lane
We could walk right up to Heaven and bring you back again.

Dawn Mardlin

Diana

You gave love, and hope, to so many, in sickness and despair
A tender smile, a loving touch, a gentle stroke of hair,
I write with deepest sorrow, the whole world shares my grief.
God has you in his keeping, that brings me some relief.

Rita Downs

Untitled

Diana, Princess of Wales, we mourn
For your tragic death, your sons forlorn
For lives snuffed out in a single flash -
An appalling crash

You drew attention to things of import
To AIDS, to landmines - the justice you sought
Yet your public acclaim gave you much distress
Our media Princess

The sick, the dying, the old and young
You helped all those you went among
You touched our hearts with your tenderness
Our loving Princess

We'll strive for your work to continue
And this will be our epitaph to you.

R Sen

Remember Princess Diana

A new star in the night has been born
And she's telling all people not to mourn
But to remember the life she once led,
And that the hungry need to be fed.
To remember the people that can't talk
And encourage the lame and help them to walk.
Also that AIDS can't be passed on by touch
What she asks us to do isn't much!
Just to help the people and not ask 'How?'
And to do what she would be doing if she were here now.

All my heart is with
your two boys
God bless them.

Louise (16)

An Ode To Diana

While most of us were fast asleep
God took Diana's soul to keep
And as the day began to dawn
The whole nation starts to mourn
Oh no, dear Lord this cannot be
To take Diana unto thee
She is so young we need her so
She's two young sons who need her more
Their sweet mother they adore
She made the world a better place
With her kindness and her grace
The tears of all begin to flow
We love you, Diana, as you will know
The nation, carpets of flowers strew
They did not know what else to do
And when her coffin was in sight
We realised our sorry plight
We had not time to say goodbye
Or your brave sons standing by
We'll not forget when you're above
You taught the world the ways of love
No-one was too humble
You reached out to foreign parts
The whole world will remember
Our lovely Queen of Hearts.

Ann Cornish

Princess Diana - A Prayer

Candles are burning
For you today
In a little church
Where you used to pray,
And as we light them
We thank God above
For we know
He is sheltering
The one we all loved.

God bless you and keep you
Our Angel above.

Frances Thompson

Heartfelt

(Dedicated to Universal Motherhood and Sarah my eldest daughter, whose compassion is a guiding light)

Oh Heart,
Of my nation's heart, how beat you so -
Yet still!
The forfeit of your soul - surrendered - to His almighty will.
Whence, on that August Sunday, He whispered to the dark,
Come, My child you're needed, you've made your earthly mark.

Fear not,
My gentle Mother, you filled your nation's need.
Who served as a tabernacle, to the House of Windsor's seed.
Through love and pain of labour, my will - you have decreed,
In trust - the throne of England - Your bloodline to accede.

Ask not,
In mortal quandary - that - I still, so pure a heart.
Such pain as yours - Remembered, When My Son played His part.
Suffering only by your trespass, her need in Me Repose.
My Kingdom's need, a Princess, at peace - Your English Rose.

Your Sun,
That sets in sadness, on a millennium of years.
Will rise again in gladness, from the shadow of your tears.
In the dawning of that era - Her truths will be acclaimed.
In the warmth of her Beatitudes - mankind - will be enframed.

RIP Diana
In purpose - ask - if she did - but touch your heart

Sean F

To Diana Princess Of Love

A nation cries, the valleys mourn,
Deeply saddened our hearts torn.
Sweet Diana, our Princess of love,
Now an angel in heaven above.
Taken away in your prime,
You had found happiness at this time.
Wonderful woman, so full of grace,
With such a beautiful face.
Comfort for the dying, help for the living,
To charities always giving.
Caring for little children, trying to ease their pain,
Helping them to have courage and to smile again.
You treated us all as equals,
Touching and shaking hands,
There will never be another like you,
In our valley's land.
You endured so much heartache and sadness,
Always to surround us with gladness.
Diana and Dodi at peace together,
You will live in our hearts forever.
We will miss you very much
Your laughter, joy and gentle touch.
We will always remember your kind ways,
We will always love you Princess of Wales.

Carol Rees

Diana

D Dearly loved
I In our hearts forever
A A great person
N Never to be forgotten
A And rest in peace our dear Princess.

Karen, Rosemary & Kelsey Muxlow

Diana

You taught the world how to care
You gave all of your love
in times of despair.
You held out your hand to those who had AIDS
Reducing the stigma
Breaking down barricades.

The plight of the homeless
a forethought in your mind
Giving hope to so many
And a new peace of mind.

Your presence, your touch and that
beautiful smile
Left your mark the world over
As you lingered a while

Diana, you taught the world how to care
In our hearts you will stay
You will always be there.

Doris Moss

Her Royal Heart

Your radiance and charisma will
be an everlasting memory in our lives.
You were a brilliant new light,
showing by your own example,
a different way to live
and how to treat others,
especially the sick, handicapped
and homeless, and those who were
shunned by others.
You were the Queen of our hearts.
Cruelly fate stepped in
and cut your life short,
and now the aura that was you remains
forever frozen in time.

Margaret Dawson

Silver Shoes

The soul of Diana in ballet shoes
Down Whitehall joyfully danced,
Past Parliament Square and the people there
Who stared as if entranced:
For past them on a carpet of pearls
Diana joyfully danced!

An angel fair in silver shoes
Danced along a London mile,
Freed from her cage, beyond Earth's rage
In captivating style,
And freely was she laughing, laughing -
Oh laughing all the while!

In celebration of her sweet Life
We watched, sour Death to offend;
Of those she met, none would forget
For each one was her friend:
With each and every one she danced -
And the dancing will never end!

The soul of Diana in ballet shoes
Through Hyde Park joyfully danced,
For the huddled throng in silent song
Who stared as if entranced;
And past them on a rainbow of love
Diana joyfully danced!

Leslie E Thomas

Diana

The world has lost a Princess.
Diana was her name.
She was kind and beautiful.
Her death was such a shame.

They would not let her live in peace,
They watched her day and night.
They made her life a misery,
To keep her in their sight.

They left her dying in a wreck,
No comfort did they give,
They walked away with their photographs,
Do they realise what they did?

She had found happiness at last,
She had found her one true love,
Paparazzi sealed their fate,
Now they are both gone from us.

There is no one to replace her,
No one to show they care,
Diana you will be missed,
Now that you're not there.

She leaves the world so stunned with grief,
We cannot believe she is gone.
So many hearts are broken,
Now we are left to mourn.

Maureen L Laird

The People's Princess

A beautiful Lady her love shone out
She gave her all to the people without
She became our Queen without a crown
She loved and hugged those that were down
Her light was so bright it lightened the night
Her smile was so real and she acted so right
The people they mattered to her our Di
We love you so much it's so hard to say 'Bye.'

E M Paternoster

Diana

This world will be so dull without you.
A bright light went out with your death.
You still had so much to give this world
What will we do without you,
You will be loved forever more
And my heart goes out to all who loved you.

Joy

Diana

You were caring and loving
and oh so fine
You helped the unfortunate
You were one of a kind
You were full of confidence
and very strong
Whatever happened you always
went on
But now you are gone up past the sky,
All it does is bring tears to my eyes.
My thoughts and my heart
lies with your two sons
Your friends family everyone.
Now the world is sad we all weep,
Our beautiful Princess
We wanted to keep.
We hope you are happy,
But we hate to part, and you will
always be the Queen of Hearts.

Diana you will be dearly missed.

Vanessa Johnson (12)

Diana

Diana was a shining bright star,
Loved by thousands from here and afar,
She walked with such style and grace,
A much loved person of this human race,
She didn't care about what colour or creed,
She cared for everyone in real need,
The stars will be shining
brighter in the sky,
Because of the presence
of wonderful Di,
Her smile was lovely,
she could talk with her eyes,
The memories of her will never die,
Her sons have lost a great chum,
She was truly a special mum,
Diana's compassion had really grown,
Another love like hers will never be known,
So goodnight Diana have a lovely rest,
Because God only takes the best. RIP.

Margy Walmsley

In Memory Of Diana Princess Of Wales

Such love, such grace,
making the pieces, come falling into place,
Break through the darkness, turns on
the light,
Making blindness give way to sight,
Your love has conjured, all who loved you,
Helping the wounded, holding their hand,
Such love, so gracious, we can't understand
Walking among the lepers, and people with AIDS
Diana Princess of Wales, was not afraid,
She sat amongst, on the floor,
Such love, such grace, such peace for evermore.

E Lilly

The Brightest Star

Last night I looked up to the sky.
A star came into view.
The brightest star I ever saw.
And at once I knew,
That star was you Diana.
Twinkling bright and clear.
As if to say, please don't cry,
I'm really very near.
You were the Queen of all our hearts.
A Princess true and fair
So rest in peace, free at last from
Life's trouble and from care.

Colette Collins

Diana Princess Of People

Diana, in person, you are with us no more,
You have entered the gates of Heaven's door,
Your memory will always be in our minds,
Of helping people, all colours and kinds.
No problem for you was too big or too small,
You lived for the people, you loved us all.

Happiness was what we wanted for you,
You found it in Dodi and your children too,
A wonderful woman, a wonderful mother,
on a pedestal, you were unlike any other,
now an angel of the heavenly skies,
we have to say our last goodbyes.
Forever embedded in all of our hearts,
God bless 'sweet Princess', now
your freedom starts.

Sadly missed, greatly loved.
Forever my inspiration.

Traci Stirling

Diana - Princess Of Wales

You truly were an Angel here on Earth,
Caring and compassionate, your people knew
your worth.
You helped the poor and suffering, sat with
the sick and dying,
Your caring heart saw their pain, it sometimes
left you crying.
You touched the hearts of many by your
loving ways,
Your beauty, and your spirit,
set the world ablaze,
To have lost someone like you,
we cannot comprehend,
We feel as though we have lost
our dearest friend.
Diana, Princess of Wales, our Queen of Hearts.
You will live forever in our memory and in
our hearts.

P Hall

Star In The Velvet Sky

On that dreadful day, when the news came
filtering through,
We will all remember where we were and what
we were about to do.
There was a numbing silence, paralysed
in disbelief,
But no matter what race or creed, we became
united in our grief.
That night, in silent conversation, I looked to
the velvet sky
And there, outshining all the stars, was
brightest one so high.
'Princess Diana, thank you for being you,
I will celebrate your life each time that star
comes into view.'

Lesley Pimm-Jones

Ode To Diana

Diana you craved for love
You did not get

Those who loved you, will never forget

Men big burley men heads bowed
Crying, openly in the streets
Women, moaning holding their men in grief
Children sobbing, they maybe, knew not why.
They all looked and saw what made their
parents cry.
It was your cortege, slowly passing by
We all have our memories of Princess Di.
We who never saw her, remember her with pride.
She left a legacy of love which, no-one
ever denied.

B Gardener

What's Happened In London?

What's happened in London,
all these people I see
bringing beautiful flowers,
are they grieving for me?

I've known pain and sorrow,
but happiness too
all you people in London
must believe this is true.

There are others who suffer
almost all of their days
their trials and hardships
never cease to amaze.

What's happened in London
to make it appear
I alone have known sorrow
Heartache and tears.

Your love for me strengthens
my faith in mankind
now channel your grief
for the needy and blind

There are people in countries
who are dying and maimed
give your love and attention
to these victims unnamed.

What's happened in London
will bring sunshine from rain
my life though now over
has not been in vain.

John Charlesworth

Diana

D evoted to the people,
I rreplaceable you are,
A ngel of goodwill,
N ature's shining star,
A lways precious, our Queen of Hearts.

Karin Edwards

To Diana

A shy little girl when she was small
Living at Althorp's lovely hall,
But this unknown girl achieved great fame
When she married into the Windsor name.

Maturing into a woman of guile
She gradually became an icon of style,
Royal jewels and Versace gown
Adorned this figure of high renown.

We saw her daily on every page
As she twinkled across the world, her stage,
But beneath the glamour was a caring side
Grieving with those whose loved ones had died.

She cuddled lame children just for a while
And made them feel well by her sunny smile,
She visited sick people across the land
Extending warmth with a touch of her hand.

But Diana's life - so tragically brief -
Has brought out love amidst the grief,
One legacy, her sons, with amazing pride
Followed her carriage with manly stride,
And if people still care now she has gone
Her other legacy will carry on.

Maisie Cottingham

In Remembrance Of Diana, Princess Of Wales

No more flowers to gather in England
All the gardens were bare.
Each lovely head bowed in sorrow,
Joined in terrestrial prayer.
They softly surrendered their essence
That woeful day in September:
Some blossoms are pressed in Bibles
For the world is wont to remember.
Hears broke like the stems of the flowers,
Such homage ne'er before seen.
The fingers of time will underline
Second Corinthians Nine: Fifteen.

Nina Cox Rynear
Lake Wales, Florida

Diana

You were a fairytale Princess,
beautiful naive and shy,
You were our Queen to be,
the wonderful Lady Di

As the years passed on,
You got used to your Royal life,
The public's love for you grew,
You were no longer just Charles' wife.

Then you gave us an heir to the throne,
a young son, the image of you.
And as William grew older,
He was joined by Harry too.

The next thing we knew is that you are ill
that life is being cruel to you,
no-one could believe that such a picture
of perfection,
could be bulimic and insecure too.

Life dealt you another awful blow,
a separation, then a divorce,
but as to whether the country still loved you,
the answer was yes, of course.

We loved your beautiful smile,
your blue eyes, your golden hair,
your never-ending compassion,
your qualities were all so rare.

You suffered pain from this love,
you were endlessly pursued,
by newspapers and paparazzi
This hurt you more than we knew.

You were still a Princess,
even though you had no Royal status,
You were our Queen of Hearts,
You cared for what really matters.

You gave your life to others,
to your sons, who you loved so much,
You made those in suffering feel better,
with a look or even a touch.

Then at last we heard you were happy,
and that made us all smile,
You had found a new love called Dodi,
and were in the papers all the while.

So image our horror and sorrow,
when we awoke one day to find,
that you, our saviour from Heaven,
our beautiful Princess had died.

We're consoled by the thought that
you're happy,
our pain is not quite so harsh,
But Diana we'll never forget you,
We'll always remember the day of the crash.

And now a nation is sad,
and aching at your loss,
we feel for your sons and family,
and at the press we're cross.

I look up at the stars,
And just for a moment I see,
that old twinkle in your eye,
and I'm glad you're free.

Emma Louise Wellington (15)

For Diana, Princess Of Wales

As our summer died, so did a Royal gem;
A sparkling precious stone of vibrant hue,
That all who gazed upon could breathe anew;
Their spirits lifted from the gloom
Of life's banal and ordinary tune.
She conjured up a magic light,
Embraced our hearts both far and wide;
She gave her soul before she died -
Her glance could heal a thousand wounds,
Heart and mind, frail body too.
Now the incandescence of those eyes of blue,
And that tortured spirit laid to rest,
Shall we remember? Time will test,
Though never can we thus forget -
When blooms have died,
Her kindness lingers yet.

Lynda Dickson

Silence Everywhere

Click of the hooves of the horses,
I heard silence everywhere.
Not a word was spoken.
Just a charm of a bell in the background.
The soldiers walked silent behind
There were lilies round her coffin,
They handled the coffin so gently
The crowds bowed their heads
With tears.
Not a dry eye to be seen,
Prince Charles and his two sons,
Began to walk behind the coffin.
Heads bowed to hide their tears.
The choir sang to the angels,
I should think Diana would hear.
Elton John made up a song,
It made my tears flow,
Earl Spencer her brother,
Spoke from his heart
I will never forget his words.
I can only say she is at rest,
And on an island of her own.
I only know she'll be a Queen,
of Hearts' and always doing good.

Jean Rickwood

Diana

The whole world loved Diana
She was our English rose
Whatever she did, wherever she went
She looked stunning in any clothes.

She was kind and caring and thoughtful too.
Everyone's friend, like me, and you.
Young or old, rich or poor,
Her love for the people grew more and more.

Everyone loved her in a different way
For her looks, for her caring
And for things she would say.
Sometimes when she walked
With that little wiggle,
What I loved the most, was her
Infectious giggle.

Now she has gone
And we miss her so much
To that place up in the sky.
The star, that shines the
Most each night
Will be our Princess Dia.

Joyce Jones

Diana

You came for just a short time
To give us all your love
Your strength and understanding
Engrossed us like wings of a dove

You have left us now
But still you're here
We feel your presence strong
And hope some day
That we may be
With you where we belong.

Scarlett Parker

Princess Diana

Princess Diana we love you so much,
The children you helped will miss
your gentle touch,
It's such a shame you left this
way,
But don't worry you'll be OK
You've got big blue eyes that
shine so bright,
We will miss seeing them, they
were a wonderful sight.

Hayley Bunclark (12)

Nothing To Fear

Diana, it is hard to believe you're not coming back
The world seems empty and black
You were so kind
And will always be on our mind
You were so compassionate
Your death was the deepest cut
You had such beauty
Helping others was your duty
Cut down in your prime
It feels such a terrible crime
You were our Princess
A gift to honour and bless
The nation cried
When you died
You cared for the forgotten
Those the world tried to shun
You helped the sick
Meeting you did the trick
To cure them when they were ill
You worked better than any tablet or pill
Now there is just shock
To your shrine we will flock
You have left a wonderful legacy
To care and love was your plea
You helped crusade against landmines
And comforted those in bad times
Your understanding was the key
As you helped those suffering leprosy
Our grief was united
Our tears were not hid
All colours and races
Laid flowers at your places
Black and white, rich and poor
We grieved at your door
You are a saint
Because you showed tolerance and restraint
Your death is so difficult to bear
Because it's for you we deeply care
We won't see that bright smile beam
We wish it just was a bad dream
You were the brightest light
Put out on that dreadful night
You gave people hope
But without you, we won't cope
You will always be in our prayers
As you climb heaven's stairs
You were our treasure
Your huge kindness we cannot measure
You gave us so much
Because you had that special touch
We shall not forget
That we owe you a tremendous debt
You were simply magic
And your loss was simply tragic
Now you are at rest
Diana - you were simply the best
To quote a favourite line
From a Chris Rea song so sublime
'I see you dancing
Your song is clear
You've got to show me, got to show me
There's nothing to fear
Nothing to fear'.

Tariq Ali

A Poem In Memory Of Diana, Princess Of Wales

You were our shining star,
People loved you from near and far,
Your love and compassion for young and old,
Did not know any limits,
You gave hope to millions of people,
I wonder where you got your endless love?
Was it because of your own sadness in life?
No-one will ever replace you,
You were a bright and shining star, our hope,
But now that light has gone,
Now sleep our Princess,
You are forever in our hearts,
You were our Queen of Hearts.

Ghazal Reid

The Crossing

Oh the British are great.
For mourning in their millions
From every town city and village
they paid their
respects to a lady.

The British are great
For covering the ground with flowers.
So genuine the grief when they placed their
bouquets together for the world.

The British are great for extending the route
of the procession.
Making the police worried
By the amount of people waiting to say their
last goodbye to the lady Princess Diana.

Days and nights people stayed out.
To be near the Abbey and the funeral
procession.
Taking their chance to see a lady of the earth
one more time before she departs forever.

Oh the British are great.
For letting go of Diana.
The silence is deafening as she moves towards the
light and begins the crossing.

Look after our friend.
Who gave good to the world.
Was kind to all the salt of the earth.

Halo for a friend.
Who would need no teaching.
Being one when she was here with the living.

P A Beavon

Diana

A nation's heart broken today
No words for feelings can convey
Far mightier men have failed to be
A little girl changed history.

E Seagrave

Love Conquers All

An old garden lay in need of care
Until a young shoot was planted there
She grew so strong despite the weeds
And bloomed though no-one knew her needs
In time two smaller shoots appeared
She was so proud, although she feared
The weeds would twist and stunt their growth
Keeping sunlight from them both

She had no thorns upon her stem
Designed to love and comfort them
A stem so strong it stood erect
Incapable of showing neglect
To her young offspring she so cherished
Always loved, always nourished
All life's true meanings they would see
And thus a stronger flower would be

The garden now so rich with love
Blossomed with colour, and from above
The sunlight shone so warm and bright
That flowers grew and won the fight
To keep the cruel weeds at bay
And so all future fears allay
That darkness would again unveil
Its cruellest side and thus prevail

The flower with all its petals unfurled
Then spread its love around the world
With style and grace and loving care
Planting goodness everywhere
It grew so widely and gained such fame
The sick, the needy and the lame
All recognised the fact she cared
Rejection she both knew and shared

She died so suddenly one day
The darker side had got their way
Her death a tragedy, great shame
The 'Queen of Hearts' had been her name
She'd brought such hope to those in pain
Never shall we see again
The love that seemed to know no fear
'Amor Vincit Omnia'.

David Wilkinson

Diana

Goodbye Diana,
Your love is still here,
Still in the hearts of many,
Shed by a tear,
You were respected,
A Princess who cared,
Stripped of your title,
Your words are still heard,
You found your love,
At the very end,
Your heart was true,
Was Dodi a friend?
Publicity, press,
That's what you feared,
They ruined your life,
Or so it appeared,
Who would take a life,
Of someone adored?
Your love, care and compassion,
Goes on evermore.
Respect of the nation,
That's what you gained,
You must have felt sadness,
Though you never complained.
Goodbye Diana,
Your words will be heard,
Acted on and followed,
From the Princess who cared.
There is a new star,
In the sky tonight,
Dedicated to you,
In heaven . . . goodnight.
You were so young,
It left us confused,
So long forever,
What a Princess, did we lose!

Rebecca Thomas (14)

Letter To Diana

I never met you, Princess Diana,
Though I felt I knew you well.
I watched with interest of your travels,
Heard the tales you had to tell.
I was proud when you showed such
compassion
To those in so much pain,
And the love you showed for those with AIDS
Over and over again.

I loved to see you with your children,
Special outings, having fun,
Turning up at school sports day
Showing your boys that YOU could run!
The visits that you made to people
Just quietly, behind the scenes,
Showed those of us that loved you
The makings of a Queen.

I wept with you when times were hard,
At the sadness that you showed,
Rejoiced at the sparkle back in your eyes
With promise of a happier road.
But now - suddenly, you've gone from us
And left a hole on earth,
An empty space, just lacking love,
Compassion, beauty, mirth.

Have no concern for your boys dear Princess.
They'll be loved as we've loved you.
The nation will watch and care for them
In everything they do.
So rest in peace, our Princess,
You've earned your early rest,
And be assured we'll not forget you.
You really were one of the best!

June Bootle

Earth Angel

God needed an angel that's for sure
He chose you Diana with your
innocent appeal
Queen of our hearts for evermore.

You crept out at night visiting the sick
and the poor
In this life you were dealt a rough deal
God needed an angel that's for sure.

Escorting princely sons through the
beggar's door
With your street-wise knowledge and
nerves of steel
Queen of our hearts for evermore.

You were never afraid of the leper's sore
Your suffering enabled others to heal
God needed an angel that's for sure.

Your aim was to clear landmines left from war
While your courage and beauty shone serene
Queen of our hearts for evermore.

Love for humanity were the robes you wore
From princess to angel at the turn of a wheel
God needed an angel that's for sure.
Queen of our hearts for evermore

Elizabeth Boultwood

Tribute To Diana - A Nation's Loss

London is silent, there's sadness in the air,
A nation mourns a tragic loss,
They place their flowers in the sign of a cross.

A gun carriage rumbled, on
cobblestone streets,
Mumbled sound of voices, a clatter of
horses' feet.
A nation stands traumatic as her coffin
passes by,
We all ask the same question,
'Why did Diana die?'

A bell tolls at intervals, silence to shatter,
Behind their mother, two sons walk proud,
Oblivious of the watching crowd.
London is silent on this sad day.
A nation paid respect each in their own way,.

Carpets of flowers, candles that gleam,
Who was this princess? No one need ask.
She could have been queen, a worldly task.

Her caring attitude needed no praise,
helping people in many ways.
We watched a nation openly cry,
All asking the same question
'Why did Diana die?'

Dorothy Slater

Tribute To Diana

Today we shed a silent tear
Knowing you Diana are no longer here.
So beautiful and full of grace
One we can never replace.
You were so full of magic
Your death was so tragic.
You cared for people in distress
Truly the people's Princess.

A Daraban

Diana

Goddess of the chase,
And how she was chased,
To her death in Paris.
Dear beautiful lady.
Loved so much and now
We mourn.
Princess of our hearts,
How we miss you.
Diana.

S D Peacock

Diana - Princess Of Wales

As in the old time fairy tales,
A shy young girl met the Prince of Wales.
He made her his Princess, his blushing bride,
To travel life's journey, side by side.

Folk welcomed her with great delight,
The People's Princess, her future so bright;
She enchanted us all with her friendly smile,
And how we envied her fashion style.

She personified loving motherhood,
As her sons grew, she did so much good
As patron to numerous charities,
Helping the suffering, their problems to ease.

The fairytale marriage came to an end,
Then it was Diana who needed a friend.
But she travelled afar, found the will
to succeed,
Bringing help and compassion to all who
had need.

One fateful morning we awoke to sad news,
The death of a loved one, too young to lose;
The scale of our mourning hitherto unseen,
Not just a Princess - in our hearts a Queen.

If you see a new star shine in the night sky,
It may be Diana - at peace now on high.
To honour her memory we must do all we can
To fulfil her dreams for the welfare of man.

Doreen E Roberts

Untitled

Queen of our hearts, so gentle and kind
Another like her we'll never find
Her death made us sad, it made us cry
Why oh why did she have to die?

The way she was treated, so very wrong.
When her love for others so very strong.
Just a look, then her gentle touch.
To ordinary people meant so much.

An Angel and we loved her so
We did not want to let her go,
Memories of her will always be there.
Her smile, her love, her endless care.

Margaret Whitehead

Diana

Diana, Queen of people's hearts
that's what you longed to be.
You touched the hearts of many,
that's clear for all to see.

You went about, doing good,
reached out to all you knew,
You comforted the needy ones
their love just grew and grew.

You were so sweet, so very young,
you touched so many hearts,
You will be missed of course you will,
you played so big a part.

Yet, there's a man who did the same,
in fact He did much more,
Lepers healed, made blind eyes see,
and all our sins He bore.

Christ healed the lame, made dumb lips speak,
raised people from the dead.
Gave such comfort to the sad,
just by the words He said.

He did so much for everyone,
He died for you and me,
He suffered there in agony,
Upon Mount Calvary.

And still His love goes on and on,
His love for all mankind,
But you are very special,
and, you're always on His mind.

S Palmer

It's Too Late To Say Sorry

Like a fly caught in a web, you were always in a trap.
They photographed your every move, there was no turning back.

Helping others was your aim, you travelled round the world.
But though you were a woman, you had the heart of a little girl.

You gave such love and happiness, with every little smile or touch.
The love that you craved for yourself,
Well, you never had that much.

Your marriage ended and you were sad, by
Then you were feeling the hurt.
When you tried for happiness again, the
Tabloids just dished up the dirt.

I must confess, once or twice, I wondered about some of your work.
Like some others, thinking that way, well I was such a jerk.

You gave everyone so much happiness,
never asking much in return.
You left us too, your two lovely sons, so
From them we will continue to learn.
DIANA
I made mistakes, so did you.
I was wrong but you were wronged.
SORRY.

Carol-Anne Lewis

A Tribute To Diana Princess Of Wales

You will always be our shining star
People have worshipped you from afar
You did a lot of good work all for mankind
Another person like you will be hard to find
To the young and elderly you held out your hand
To all of those people it felt so grand
The memory of you will never fade
From all of those lovely friends you've made.

R Warrington

Princess Diana

Our Diana, the people's Princess,
loved by all, she was a success.
Throughout her work, her short-lived days
she was so caring she had that way.
An elegance within her
fate never deterred her,
always putting on a brave face.
Her small, side smile
a known figure, an idol
full of compassion and grace.
Now our Diana has gone
her spirit lives on
her memory still burns bright.
She took us so far, yet now we have to go alone
without her guiding light.
I don't think she knew how much she meant to us
a worldly love, a worldly trust.
A devoting heart
always doing her part.
A Princess with such a charismatic manner
The people 's Princess, our dear Diana.

Gemma Bruley (15)

Princess

Diana, the grief today, tomorrow,
for evermore.
Untold love from far upon this planet.
Nations, cities, towns, villages people unite
to this unfolding tragedy.

Our tears falling now like children, pure innocent
thoughts joining these multitudes
to say

'We are so sorry. We'd all want it to be yesterday.'

With time to see once again your courage, joy
and just to believe in you, Diana.
Princess of all our lives,
Goodnight.

A Cornish Farmer, August 31 1997

The People's Princess

She was a Fairy Princess,
Whom many came to see
Wed her Prince in Holy matrimony.

She bore two sons,
Her joy and her pride,
Happy she seemed, with her Prince by her side.

But all was not well,
behind the scene,
Our Princess was not as happy
as she should have been.

Her marriage ended, it was all so sad,
The Prince wanted another,
She understood,
So she turned her attention to doing good.

She held the hands of the sick and the lame,
She raised money too
To help combat their pain.

She saw mines left around to explode,
Human lives to endanger,
The maiming and the killing
filled her with anger,

So she started a campaign,
to remove all these things,
She saw the misery poverty brings,

She talked, she helped,
She cuddled, and kissed,
She was loved by all,
By all, will be missed . . .

Daisy Ellen Jones

Princess Diana

God sometimes sends to earth an Angel
To show us how to love and care
We all know you were that Angel
Now that you are no longer there

May God grant you eternal rest
In his Heaven above
With all his other Angels
Surrounding you with love.

Rest in peace.

Diane Walker

What's In A Name?

Diana the Baby
Diana the Lady
Diana the Bride
Diana the Worldwide

Diana the Princess
Diana the 'Her Royal Highness'
Diana the Supermum
Diana the Number One

Diana the Star
Diana the Godmother
Diana the Ambassador
Diana the Saviour

Diana the Best
Diana the Fairest
Diana the thoughtful
Diana the Immortal?

Diana the Queen?
Diana the 'may have been'
Diana the Quaint
Diana the Saint

Diana the Great
Diana the Late
Diana the Memory
Diana Eternity.

Diane Smith

Reflections

How could I fail to remember
Those poignant days in September
So many grieving hearts, laid bare
As thousands bow their heads, in prayer

Oh! What respect for you, was shown
You'll never, ever, be alone
Silence speaks volumes so they say
If that be so, it spoke today.

Oh! The pain in everyone's face
No-one could ever take your place
Pavements were made gardens just for you
Words of condolence written too.

You had a message, you wrote the script
Since you read it you were worshipped
Yes, the tears ran down thousands of cheeks
But hurt in their hearts will last for weeks.

You were blessed with a heart of gold
Love of you shall never grow cold
Tho' your coffin has now been laid
The memory of you shall not fade.

To me you were the English Rose
The flower that every lover chose.

William J Hall

Diana (1961-1997)

Your pain was starting to subside
and conflicts now were few,
the love you gave so willingly
was being shown to you.

The anguish that had shadowed you
was always swept aside,
by helping those who suffered most
you gave them faith and pride.

You lived among the privileged
this wealth set you apart,
but all the riches you possessed
were held within your heart.

Your children suffer from your loss
a nation shares their grief,
and shows that love above all else
has set your troubled spirit free.

In peace you rest beside a lake
by summer rose and willow tree,
your life an inspiration
your early death a tragedy.

Jean Pedder

Poem For Diana

To millions she was a
beautiful Princess
To thousands she was a
caring one,
To hundreds she was a special friend
But most of all to two
Young boys she was a
loving mum.

C V Chant

A Prayer For The Princess Our Thoughts!

As we held one minute's silence
We remembered how she gave;
Even putting herself in danger:
Other lives to save!
Taking so much interest in others,
With ALL ages she shared
Their sorrows, grief and troubles;
The 'People's Princess' cared!

Denny Rhymer

The Day The World's Heart Broke

The sun shone jewel-like in the sky!
Then dark clouds gathered and did cry -
Tragic news! Our beloved Diana
Princess of Wales has died.

My husband woke me with morning tea
'Twas he who broke the news to me!
Dodi had died in a bad car crash
Diana, seriously injured in the same smash.
They fought to save her life - in vain,
She'd left for Heaven and knows no pain.

Farewell courageous Princess!
With Dodi rest in peace.
Flowers shall be laid by millions
The world's tears shall never cease.

The clouds cried - as did I,
That September Sunday morn
When the Queen of all our Hearts did die.

RIP

Patricia Cairns Laird

Diana - The People's Princess

If things had been different
It has to be said;
What a queen of the people
You would have made.
Your caring and loving
Has set you apart,
You will always be queen
Of the great British heart.
Such weeping and mourning
All over this land,
For 'Diana' was loved
Because she took a stand,
Unique and appealing
Your deeds must not cease,
So you our dear Princess
Can rest now in peace.

Rena Johnstone

Diana Princess Of Wales

You filled me with love
You filled me with glee
You filled me with sadness
When you left so suddenly.

But do not be afraid
For I will not forget
The love you gave to others
That I have not yet met.

But when we all do meet
In that Heavenly sky above
We will all be at peace with ourselves.
And that's all because of your love.

Judith Faulkner

In Remembrance Of Diana Princess Of Wales

Our beautiful Princess Diana,
Our Angel taken from this Earth, from us.
Now truly beautiful place resting,
Near to those who love her.
Heaven has our Angel Princess Diana,
Who's with Dodi her love, and others.
To watch over beloved William and Harry
Sisters, brothers, and the whole family too.
Will always remember
Big hearted Princess Diana.
Your love's lifted me.
Rest Peacefully.
God bless always princess Diana.
Her beloved William and Harry too.

Rosemary Sheridan

My Lovely Memories Of Diana (An Angel In Silk)

Your wedding day Diana, was so sunny
and so fine.
I shall never forget it as it was a day before mine.
I will always remember your sweet pretty face.
Smiling at the crowds, like a doll dressed in lace.
The month we chose to marry was a lovely time
of year.
When all the little creatures are buzzing around
out there.
The birds were singing, the bells were ringing.
Oh what a lovely summer sound.
The sun was gleaming, the people
were screaming.
To get a glimpse of their Princess, in her
beautiful silk gown.
You came into our lives, on that most
precious day.
And like a dazzling butterfly, you have
flown away.
We miss you Diana, and may you rest in peace.
Because our love for you will never ever cease.

God Bless.

Vi Toms

For Diana - And Dodi Al Fayed

Were I to die young
Let me be beautiful
And adored
Let me be with the
One I love, and who
Loves me
Let me have mountains
Of flowers, and armies
Of mourners
Let me, let me.

Vivienne Lorimer

Diana Spencer

P eople's Queen of Hearts, may you
R est peacefully
I n Heaven, where you belong,
N ever shall we forget the
C are and love,
E ncouragement, help and
S upport you have shown and
S hared around the world.

O ur deepest sympathy lie between our
innermost
F eelings and thoughts far beyond living
memory.

W hat happiness came your way, with
loyalty from
A l Fayed, your best friend, lover and
companion, has
L eft endless remembrance of true love,
E nvied by those who gave grief and
S orrow until the arrival of two innocent deaths.

Shabnam Yasmin

The People's Princess

Diana and Dodi were lovers.
They will never be parted again
Although they never got married
Together in death they will reign

She can now be a queen in heaven
Dodi will stand by her side
Although her boys will miss her
They will think of her always with pride

She is gone but never forgotten
And even when apart
The nation will always remember
Diana
The Queen of their heart.

Keena

Diana - A Princess - Loved By The World

A look of compassion
A heartfelt touch
For young and old
The sick and the maimed.

Plagued by the media
No privacy allowed
The price has been paid
Long life not allowed

We know that speed kills
The young and the old
Too many lives lost
As fast cars fill our roads

A sad realisation
Her boys far away
In her own English country
Her in France - far away.

Elizabeth M Jones

Diana

We had a Princess
Diana was her name
She looked so lovely
Just like her name

She was so magic
And cared for all
She died so tragic
We now all mourn

Diana left two jewels
Their names we are in awe
William and Harry
She loved them most of all

Now we mortal people
Are left with an empty space
We can only hope in Heaven
God gives Diana, a very special place.

Maureen Metcalfe

How I Wish

How I wish you had not gone
For you were such a special one
Your presence lifted any gloom
A special smile lit every room
Your soul was taken from that car
Is in the sky now, the brightest star
You are all together in the sky
Your beloved Daddy, Dodi and Princess Di.

Violets are blue
Roses are red
The sun will shine no more now
As Diana is dead.

Joyce Matthews

Our Queen

Princess Di you were our queen,
The best our country's ever seen,
You filled our hearts with love and joy,
Your love you gave to every girl and boy,
But now you're gone to God above,
To share around your special love,
This place will give you no more stress,
Or will you be hounded by the press,
But in our hearts you'll always shine,
Our true princess, Princess Di.

To the princess who will always be sadly missed
by all the nation, rest in peace,

love,

G A Mayley

A Mother For Heaven's Nursery

Our Lord gazed around His Heaven,
In serene Paradise above,
His need was for someone so exceptional,
Who was caring and filled with love,
So He calmly glanced upon our earth,
And that very special person He did see,
Her name, Princess Diana, of Wales,
The perfect individual she would be.

He knew how it would break all of our hearts,
For He had to take Diana, our princess
so quick,
But He had a very important role for our
Queen of Hearts,
Tending His children and babies, who had been so
very poorly and sick,
The children had to leave their beloved parents
behind,
So they now need to be showered with love,
Our Lord has ended each child's suffering,
Making them well again, to reside in
Heaven above.

So with all your radiance and beauty Diana,
He has now also taken you there,
To bestow all of your love and affection,
on all our babies so innocent,
for whom you care.
For in Heaven's nursery you are now tending,
A mother's love you will always replace,
With hugs and kisses for our angels,
A loving mother, they will see always,
As they look at your beautiful face.

As you enter you shall light up the nursery in the
darkness
For a love such as yours, will chase away
any fear,
Calming words from your lips, erase
any anxiety,
As your tranquil presence shall always
be near,
God has chosen well, His stand-in mother,
With such sincerity, perfection and great care,
No more tears will ever tumble, on our
babies' cheeks
For Diana their own special Princess will always -
be there.

So as the night draws in the nursery, Diana,
Please kiss my baby each night for me,
Take her in your loving arms,
and sit her on your knee,
Read her a story up in God's Heaven,
And tell her not to cry,
For her Princess will look after her,
And sweetly sing her a lullaby,
Please sit with her Diana,
Until her little blue eyes decide to sleep,
And so in our lovely Princess Diana's care,
She is now, and Diana's love she may keep,
All the children in God's Heaven,
Are now sheltered from this world's pain,
For although we had to lose you
'Our Queen of Hearts'
Just look what our children did gain.

Beverley Wood

Why Did They Take You?

Your beauty was enchanting,
Your heart overwhelming,
You mind was charitable,
Your bravery commendable,
Your ability was unbelievable,
Your happiness was noticeable,
So why, did they take you?

Niki x

Diana, enjoy that you are now free, and please don't worry about those astounding young boys of yours, they are in the hearts of billions of people all around the world; they will be safe from hurt and hatred.

With love from
all my family,

Niki x

Diana -Why You?

Somebody pinch me, say it is not true,
God has really taken you?
Your life, so much of it we shared
You may not know, but WE really cared.

We cared that you had so much pain, and
admired at how you came back again.
You brightened up the dark despair
Reaching out to another, holding hands,
being there.

You gave us hope when there was none
It is hard to believe such good has gone.
THEY criticised you, said you were misguided
Your work to help others, quite often derided.

They took your picture everywhere
and in its profits they all did share
Their pursuit of you remained unbounded
They were never happy until they had
hounded . . . You

Beautiful Diana, another chapter
about to start
Happiness found with Dodi, and his
loving heart.
He would have loved you for yourself
Despite the 'baggage', the PRESS,
your own wealth.

If we can take solace in knowing,
The joyous way your life was going.
Your style and popularity soared
Your new self-confidence we did applaud.

You looked so happy and carefree
But your life was to be taken so tragically.
Just one more photo, one more chase,
This time the hunters won the race.

We watched in silence as you came home,
With your sisters and Prince Charles
you were not alone.
In gentle respect the tributes came,
Millions of flowers and cards all bearing
your name.

Saturday, the 6th of September
A date I feel we shall always remember.
The day we knew you had gone forever
You left such dazzling memories
to treasure.

We loved you Diana, it is very plain to see,
Our thoughts, now with your sons,
Princes William and Harry.
The intrusive treatment you had to endure,
Will never befall them, your Brother is sure.

I still shake my head in disbelief
Like everyone else, I'll come to terms
with my grief.
Ironically, THIS TIME, what the media say, is
TRUE.
GOD has a new ANGEL because
He chose YOU.

Maureen Fryer

Untitled

You acted by touching and careing
we watched
You gave your ears and listened to many
we heard
You would smile softly with your eyes
we smiled
You wept, tears falling on your cheeks
we cried

But we did nothing

You died

Only then did we show what you
meant to us

God forgive us.

Jennifer McIntyre

Ode To Diana

A loving woman a caring mother,
She had a heart like no other,
She nursed the sick and helped the poor,
Life will be hard with her here no more,
A priceless pearl, a unique touch,
Her love was worth very much,
Her work on earth is done,
Her heavenly duties have just begun,
Picked from others because of her splendour.

For some time she walked alone,
But in our hearts it was she who held
the throne,
She will be forever our shining light,
That will be eternally bright,
An earthly Angel who is at rest,
She was without doubt the best,
Picked from the pack our Queen has gone,
But her love will linger on,
So in our hearts she will stay,
And will be remembered each day,
As our very own 'Queen of Hearts'.

Layla Brinson

Butterfly Di

I think of Di as a butterfly
Taken in the summer of her life
Never to know an autumn's day
Harsh winter will not come her way
Butterflies need sun and flowers
Not winter's cold and sleety showers,
Maybe she would be flying yet,
We all helped to make the butterfly net.
So now we can wail, and we can cry
It will not bring back our butterfly Di.

Heather Kirkpatrick

The World Mourns

Today I saw a Nation weep,
whilst a Princess lay in Eternal sleep.
In sorrow the World now bows its head,
For a caring Princess now is dead.
Over the World the sounds of grief,
Yet from life's pain she's found relief.
Openly we shed our tears,
Caring not if anyone hears.
Tomorrow for us the sun won't shine,
For she'll be in your thoughts and mine.
We wonder what life's all about,
For a Light of God has just gone out.
In life she suffered many a barb,
Each painful thrust in her heart did stab.
Now God has set her Spirit free,
To dwell in His House till Eternity.
So to God we now do plead,
Comfort her sons, in their hour of need.

M Muirhead

Diana, Princess Of Wales

In life, she was full of beauty, charm and
tenderness.
She was a well of love, pity and kindness -
And most precious to the forgotten and
rejected.
She was everyone's sister, mother and friend;
She was so close to so many.
And then, in the space of a few moments,
Amidst needless carnage and sorrow,
Her life began to ebb, drop
By drop, away from us all -
And we were left to wonder -
Would her memory be immortal?

David Houston

Our Princess Di

My mother broke the news today,
To take it in, I really try.
I light a candle and try to pray
But all I can do is cry.

God has sent us a lovely gift
In you, our Princess Di.
To give the poor and needy a lift,
Wipe the tears from a little child's eye.

To diseases like leprosy and AIDS,
You blew the old myths right out of the way.
You held all sufferers in your arms,
You brought the sunshine into their day.

Last night in Paris, your time came,
God called you and Dodi too.
The world will never be the same,
May God bless both of you.

The cold dark nights are setting in,
With heavy rain and blustery gales.
It's just the way our hearts feel within,
Without you Diana, Princess of Wales.

Nobody will hurt you again our dear Di,
Tears of despair, they have no place
Where you are now in that heavenly sky,
Only joy will show on your angel face.

Susan Ann Kelly

To Diana, Princess Of Wales

No words express the loss we feel,
A loss which only time can heal.
You gave your help to those in need,
Regardless of their colour or creed.
You showed compassion, gave love so rare,
A caring love, beyond compare.
You gave us hope to carry on,
That hope will live on, now you've gone.
Farewell, brave heart, may you rest in peace,
Our thoughts and prayers will never cease.

Jessie Stewart

Lady Diana

She gave so much to others
She put smiles upon their hearts
Her giving, caring spirit, she certainly
made her mark!
She was loved by so many people
She was open in all she said,
Her beauty, charm and shyness
always went ahead.
With deep compassion she reached out,
to lepers and people with AIDS - and
people whose bodies had been torn apart,
from the mining fields of late.
She trod where others didn't,
She held out a loving hand,
She offered help and understanding
in the hearts of people over all the land.
We don't know where she stood with
God, but it's not for us to say.
But I hope she asked Jesus into her
life - so she can rest in His love today!

Jeni Stanley

Diana - Loved As A Mother

The people whose lives were lacking, followed you
around,
Yet, you befriended the homeless, who slept upon
the ground.
Cardboard cities you'd visit, often late at night,
A shining star, sympathising their plight.
You touched the sick and you held their hand,
Healing emotions rippling round every land.
Your grace and beauty shone through all
your pain,
Queen of our hearts, you will always reign.
Overflowing with compassion, we will remember
you,
But most of all, you were the loving mother of
William and Harry too!

Denise A Johnson

Rest In Peace Princess

Rest in peace oh sweet princess, on the island full of flowers.
The water of the lake will sing you sweet lullabies, the trees will watch over you like almighty towers.
The sun will rise and set over you, the birds to you will sing their song.
The world didn't realise just what it had lost, it did you so much wrong.
You showed such pity and compassion to those that were in need.
All that you had you shared so willingly, you didn't have any greed,
Your beauty wasn't just on the outside, you had a loveliness from deep within your heart.
Your virtues are too many to mention,
I wouldn't know where to start.
Your warmth reached out to so many people, your radiant smile, your gentle touch, just little gestures but they meant so very much.
You too had many problems, but still with others your time you shared, you gave so much but took nothing in return, you showed people that you cared.
To the young man with AIDS you gave hope to carry on, and to the leper you gave dignity when he thought pride and dignity had gone.
The day you died so tragically, it broke a million hearts around the earth.
Your short life wasn't wasted, you gave joy and love from the moment of your birth.
It was said at times you felt so very lonely and longed for someone on whom you could depend,
God must have heard you call in Heaven, for he gently took you in His arms, and said, 'Come unto me I will always be your friend.'
You're safe now with God, our sweet princess, free from suffering and pain.
God is looking after you, until with your loved ones you will meet again.
The next world that you will live in, will be full of love right from the very start.
Until then you will be remembered in a million people's hearts.

Melinda Evans

That Beautiful Butterfly

A beautiful person was Princess Di
Tall and slender with a twinkle in her eye
She was full of grace and goodness too
And was always nice to those she knew
She was very good to those in need
But had little time for pomp and greed
She wasn't treated as she should have been
For she would have made a splendid Queen
She was just like a butterfly among the trees
Floating around on a summer's breeze
With wings spread wide to embrace
The unfortunates of the human race
She was such a friend to the crippled and ill
And will be hard to replace if she ever will
She would talk to them with that lovely smile
And they would forget their pain for a while
God sent her to us to do his work
And though sad at times she did not shirk
Now her work on earth is finally done
And we all know that she has won
A special place in God's Heaven
That she has made her final haven
So fold your wings, sleep, don't cry
For we all love you Princess Di
Goodbye butterfly.

Angus D McEachran

Diana
Our Very Own Queen Of Hearts

Diana our very own Queen of Hearts,
The best Queen we never had,
The one who gave joy to everyone,
And never showed when she was sad.

In all who loved her kindness,
She truly is a saint,
Her place now is in heaven,
With God whom He first sent.

An English rose can't be replaced,
An ever-loving mother,
Do not fret Diana,
We'll look after your sons forever.

No more heartbreak,
No more pain,
No more hurt,
Life on earth has been a strain.

Always loving, always true,
We will always think of you,
When we reach heaven, and call your name,
We know that you will be the same.

J Eldridge

Diana

You came for just a little while
So beautiful with a lovely smile.
With a heart full of loving and giving.
Dear World this is how we should be living.
This was the message Diana was sharing
With her love and compassion and caring.
Was this her destiny her fate
To bring our world right up to date?
How many ears will now listen?
How many eyes will now see?
How many hearts wil now open?
Because of Diana's destiny.

Margaret Whittaker

She Who Was Always

She was always

D edicated (devoted) (Direct)
I n
A ll
N eeding
A id (Aid) (Assistance) Attention)

She tried to help the human
race.
She met them personally face
to face.
She helped to settle their pain,
their fears.
Their love to gain, to wipe
their tears.
And now their Princess's life
has gone
In their hearts her memory
shall always live on.

D McNiven

Collecting Angels

Dear Lord

You called away our princess
Mother Teresa too
Only you can tell us why
you do the things you do
Is there a special reason
that you've taken them away
to leave this world a darker place
and break our hearts today
I search my heart each minute
and now I know the reason why
You must be collecting angels
Tell them we said goodbye.

From The Edis Family
Nottingham

A Poem For The Princess Of Wales

Born to be a Lady - soon to be a Queen
A look, a glance, a friendly smile, not all that
it would seem.
So young and free so full of love,
The love she gave was ours to share
She showed us how to spread good cheer,
Yet now alas she is not here
A nation lost a personal friend
This shock, this grief, will never end,
The love she gave we'll always cherish
Her charitable works will never perish
Within her life her love imparts
She was indeed our Queen of Hearts
Wills and Harry her 'two boys'
Will always be her pride and joy.
So through all the grief which carries pain
Within our hearts she will remain
A Queen without an earthly crown
is part of what we'll miss
She showed us love, she showed us
care the children she would kiss.

M Thomson

Goodbye Di

Princess Diana was surely a Queen uncrowned
Her beauty, loving and caring were world
renowned
The nation has lost a most precious pearl
She took to our hearts as an ordinary girl
Her lovely looks and radiant smile
Captivated all along with her style
Now she has gone and no longer here
Who can but shed more than a sorrowful tear
Now in Heaven and in everlasting peace
Our love for her will never cease
An eternal legend forever Diana will be
Never to be forgotten by the people of her
beloved country.

S W Jones

Untitled

I am yet frail, but show strength.
I choose not to grieve
But to smile with great length.
I wish to live in eternal peace.
I choose not to suffer
But in love let time cease
I walk in the hills in solitude
I choose not to hate
But still through soulful eyes allude
I choose not to weep
With the wind, rain, and sun I move.
I choose to love.
My aura shining bright does this prove
I choose to dance
My lithe graceful figure in flight
I choose to sing
My gift of loving still in plight.
I choose to live
Not in darkness but in light.

Kerry-Anne Hollins

In Memory

Princess princess sleeping deep
Yours is your beauty now to keep
Everlasting eternal, in our hearts you will stay
Never forgotten, not even for one day,
Your dreams we will treasure
Your dreams we will chase
Landmines from our world we will try to erase
To the homeless we'll give shelter
To the Red Cross we'll give aid
As an ambassador for our country
You were the best God ever made
You're gone now never to be forgotten
In our hearts you will always live on
God bless you Princess Diana
Your work will never be done.

RIP

Andrea Ogden

A Tribute For The Late Princess Diana

Through her young life on this earth,
Lady Diana helped the lame and poor
God guided her from strength to strength,
as she called at the sick man's door,
She did fulfil the good work that was prepared,
through each guided step
When Princess Diana worked for charity,
in every word of respect.

She never thought about herself, but her thoughts were cared for all
And gently held young children close to her, never to feel that appal
She spoke to those around her, as though they were her own
No pride had she felt, no high opinion had she sown.

Loved by all the world, and will surely be well remembered
For the future to come, and perhaps for many years ahead
They say Princess Diana, was irreplaceable, this of course was so,
But, life always goes on, even if spirits feel low.

Believe Princess Diana is in spirit, her beauty will behold,
Never to let that flame go out, not even for wealth or gold
Even those cares Lady Diana shared, were perhaps a witness for the Almighty God of Love.
But, the greatest richness is always there, if we believe in God above,

So let Princess Diana's kindness and compassion, be an example to us all,
Through the goodness she did fulfil, especially through God's call,
Sadly she left those gifts behind,
but, her footsteps could follow on,
Through the testimony, of all the good work, that she has so willingly done.

Rest in peace, Princess Diana, who was the fairest in the land,
Rest with loved ones in Paradise,
under God's gracious, and caring Hand.

Jean P McGovern

Farewell To A Princess

The sun was shining brightly
But our hearts were dark and sad,
As a nation joined in sorrow
To mourn the brightest star we had.

Diana, Queen of all our hearts
Was being laid to rest,
Everybody's favourite Royal,
She was truly loved the best.

We all felt that we knew her,
We'd seen her smiles and tears,
We felt the love she gave to all,
We shared her joys and fears.

A truly special Royal,
She had the common touch,
She was the people's Princess,
We all loved her so much.

She was an inspiration to us all,
Sometimes her life was tragic,
But she overcame all obstacles
With her own special kind of magic.

For all of us who loved her
Her death has left a gaping hole,
Nobody can replace her,
She was this country's soul.

A gifted, warm and tender person
We shall not see her like again.
Diana, the people's Princess
Will always in our hearts remain.

June Stokes

Diana

To one who bore the sweetest name
The world will never be the same
The people's Princess has gone to rest

The world is weeping it is almost
Like the world is sleeping

Everything is so quiet and still
Our thoughts go with Harry and Will

The world has lost its greatest friend
She did not look down to people
She treated everyone as equal

She was loved by everyone
All over the world
England, France, America
To name but a few.

I'm sure you'll all agree
There's a space in all our hearts
Where Diana the Queen of Hearts will always be.

Andrea Meek (14)

Diana

Words cannot express, the death of our Princess,
For on that night she died, every nation cried.
It will take ten million tears, for 100 years,
This will not bring her back, from that flash attack.
You brought joy to young and old,
and warmth to people cold.
Helping the sick and poor,
looking stunning in everything you wore.
Diana always the brave,
chased to an early grave.
Just like Marilyn Monroe,
a life without sorrow.
So when we look up to the skies,
you'll be immortal in our eyes.
Always in my dreams, I confess,
I'll miss you - good night - God Bless.

Darren Peary

Diana

The days have passed,
The tears still flow.
Queen of Hearts,
You'll never go!
You're the one that we love!
The world will mourn
For the sweet smile
You always adorn,
So farewell to a Princess,
One of a kind
You were so very special,
To all mankind.
'The best way to mourn the dead,
is to look after the living that belong to them.'

Lee Bromley, Lisa Cook,
& Chantal Davidson

Diana

A night could never be as dark
as the shadows that swept around
her heart.

The sun could never be as bright
as the smile she gave chased
away the night.

Soft hands that reached for young
and old
and poured out love instead of gold.

No rivers here could run as deep
as eyes that now forever sleep.

Golden girl whose days have run
and chased the rainbows of the sun.

Wendy Ann Carter

Diana

An angel came from Heaven
To live with us on Earth
Her name Diana Frances
Was given at her birth

Her life was often troubled
She took it in her stride
Life often gave her laughter
Life often made her cry

She took her chosen path in life
To be a Prince's wife
She bore a perfect family
And gave them a quality life.

Others meant so much to her
She had precious time to share
With lots of underprivileged folk
She was an answer to a prayer

God called on her so suddenly
The world is still with shock
Diana was an angel
That cannot be forgot.

Elizabeth Aulds

Diana

So suddenly and sadly
You were taken away
Leaving the world
With such utter dismay!

The grief and the sorrow
No words can express
As we mourn the loss
Of our beloved Princess!

Your life was cut short
When God made his call
But you will live on
In the hearts of us all!

Barbara Reeves

Goodbye Princess Diana

Goodbye Princess Diana from a nation in tears,
Forever we shall remember you through
the years.
Goodbye Princess Diana from a world in grief
and pain,
Perhaps it was God's wish that we'll never see
you again.
Goodbye Princess Diana friend of mankind
To the leper, the poor, the cripples and the blind.
Goodbye Princess Diana Queen of hearts
sleep on,
We'll miss your sweet smile and beauty now that
you've gone,
Goodbye Princess Diana God's gift to mankind
A Saint, legend so sweet and kind.
Goodbye Princess Diana in Heaven's garden
you rest,
Who can blame God for taking the best.

L Hillary

We Will Remember

When we waken up tomorrow
and we see the droplets of rain,
We will remember all your sorrow
and your heartbroken pain.

Then, when we see a child smile,
we will remember how much you cared
and how you would, stop for a while
until all your love was shared.

When we look at the rising sun
We will remember your radiant face,
and as we watch the swallows fly
We will remember you beauty and grace.

As long as day follows the night
and compassionate needs must be met,
'Queen of Hearts' you may be lost from sight,
But your people, will never forget.

Mo Lyon

Di

As the end of September '97 draws near
A Mother and Princess died, that's clear
This world is in mourning, states the news
Press have their 'Headline', what have they
to lose?
Quite a lot by the sound of stories on TV
'Cos they caused the accident you see
Did they think of the consequences as
they pursued
Di and her fella on motorbikes, they
should be sued.
Harry and William, her sons, what of those?
They've lost their 'Mum' but there's 'Dad'
I suppose.
Boycott the papers, what good will that do?
It won't bring them back, but hanging
won't too.
Normally I do not care about the Royals
But when the 'vultures' of the press are involved,
my temperature boils.

'Together they have found peace
Death being their tragic release.'

Samuel Newsom

A Million Hearts

A million hearts are aching
For a Lady gone away,
So many tears have been cried
Since the news that sad, sad day.
If only we could turn back time
We could erase the past,
We'd still have a Princess Di
And your happiness would last.
Our hearts are aching for your sons,
Whose lives must seem so bare,
For the only consolation is that
So many people care.
While a nation grieves so bitterly,
The whole world feels such pain,
The hardest part is knowing
That we won't see you again.
The smiles, the love,
They are all gone,
But your memory will always
Linger on.

Caroline Brown

Diana And Dodi

There was a princess
so kind and true,
Everyone thought the
world of you.
Just when you seemed so
happy at last
This terrible tragedy
happened so fast.
It's so unfair that you
have gone
Let's hope you'll both be
reunited as one.

God bless.

Doreen Cupit

Why?

Why did you have to go?
Why did you have to leave?
You were so special,
So very fragile,
Very important.
You did a lot when you were here,
But now you are gone,
You have left a gap in our lives.

We will always miss you
You will never be forgotten.

Elizabeth Alexander (10)

Dear Princess Diana
Our Queen Of Hearts

There on an island in the sun
Lies a place of solitude, entirely homespun
Where rests in Peace a Princess bold
A Princess blessed with a heart of gold

A Princess worshipped by the masses
Ordinary everyday lads and lasses
She was truly an inspiration to behold
Her compassion we all must uphold

Dear Princess Diana, you were much too young
to die
But our Dear Lord needed you in Heaven on high
For only the very good die young, it's true
Love and compassion must continue and flourish
in memory of you

Dear Princess Diana, so beautiful and refined
Who else but you could have been so kind
who else but you could have done what you did
And at all times remained impeccably vivid

Dear Princess Diana, our Queen of Hearts
With you we shall always and forever impart
For no-one really dies whilst someone
still remembers
You will always be in our thoughts and
forever remembered

Dear Princess Diana, you didn't need a crown
Your very presence dried even the tears
of a clown
You gave people hope, you eased their pain
Dear God, please allow her sparkle to have not
been in vain

Princess Diana is now at home serenely at rest
There's no denying she was simply the best
She was righteous, she was human
She was the people's good Samaritan

Princess Diana was the people's Princess
Glowing with fervour and finesse
Princess Diana was also the people's
Queen of Hearts
She was the number one on their
popularity charts

God bless you your Highness, we'll pray for
your sons
Don't you worry, for these sentiments
are everyone's
We all loved you, we always will, we'll
never forsake
Rest in Peace Princess Diana, on your island
on the lake.

Albert Horsman

Happy Resurrection

Jehovah's Witnesses foretell, one day
there's going to be,
A happy resurrection of friends and family,
Who've passed away but really are
worthy of His test,
To live on Earth for evermore,
They'll be back to join the best.

There isn't any doubt Diana will be
one of those,
Chosen by Jehovah to return though
I suppose,
We must, just be patient, wait for
Jehovah's day,
Then along with all the others Diana
will be back to stay,
Then with one tremendous voice
The whole world really will rejoice.

Jehovah promises to take away the
pain and this world's sin,
Replaced with everlasting love, a new
world will begin.
We must all promise then to love
our neighbour and,
Show love to Jehovah, then we'll
understand,
There'll be no more dying, just a
happy life for sure,
Where we can share the best of
everything for evermore.

Eileen Southey

My Tribute To Diana

Always loving and always true
these tributes Diana are for you
Compassion and beauty also share
in these compliments of one so rare
A Lady in every way respected
By people from all walks of life
For the good you did! When unexpected
visiting the sick who were fighting for life.
Your smile will never be forgotten
it brightened up many a room
and now that you are up in Heaven
'Dodi' and you will be Bride and Groom.
You deserve the happiness
which you gave to others
just by caring and being kind
such a devoted and loving mother
You'll be a legend till the end of time.

Jean E Twist

Diana Princess Of Wales

A heart of gold stopped beating
Our hearts cried out in pain.
You were a Rose lent to us.
And an angel full of life.
God took you back, he needed you.
He sent a beautiful glow of light.
To say it's time to go.
My heart goes out with sympathy
For the boys you left behind.
I hope you have found peace at last
In God's beautiful garden of rest.
You and Dodi can find happiness.
Which was denied you here on earth
Look after them Lord as they rest in peace
Give them all the love you can.
As our light has gone out now.
Now it glows in Heaven above.

R Budworth

Diana

Her beautiful, radiant, smiling face,
That cheered our lives, our breathing space
Has gone in sleep - true peace at last
But always remembered as our Queen of Hearts.

The lovely Diana, who entered our lives,
Had dreams of happiness that sadly expired.
But in spite of her sadness, helped others in need
She showed great compassion, let us follow
her lead.

The token gloved handshake was never her way
Each touch, hug or cuddle always made
someone's day.
And never again will anyone replace
Her beautiful, radiant, smiling face.

J Down

Lost Princess (A Prayer)

However young and beautiful,
However good and kind,
It is never quite the right time
For the cleverest to find
That life and love be taken
From this world to Heaven's Realm -
Angels bear our Princess gently -
Dear Lord, you're at the helm,
And though we cannot understand
This loss of our Princess so dear,
Please have her soul in Your keeping,
Away from doubt and fear,
And one day at the last trump
May ordinary folk like me
Meet, with those very special ones,
Who went early to be with Thee.

S R Alton

Angel In Our Eyes

Can't seem to find
the words to say
About the day
you went away
A life so short
with so much pain
There'll be no sadness
in your life again
You were always an angel
in our eyes
And now you've flown
back to the skies
To be with angels
up above
Shining down upon us
with all your love
Wearing a halo of hearts
around your head
A nation in mourning
our Queen of Hearts dead
You did so much
for our human race
And never again
will we see your face
Your eyes so blue
that smile so shy
A heart so true
and we wonder why
Your life is gone
just taken away
Now for your children
we must pray
Through them your life
will live on
That's how we'll know
you're not gone
For them we must
pave the way
As they will bring
a brighter day
Out of sight
but not out of mind
There'll never be another
of your kind
We love you Diana
a princess so sweet
And I know again
someday we'll meet.

Amanda Rawlings

Diana - Our Fairy Tale

The announcement came on that
Sunday morning,
They said you died just as day was dawning,
The birds stopped singing
flowers bowed their heads,
Stunned and shocked - you just can't be dead.
You loved, you cared even when you were down,
You were our Queen of Hearts
and so deserved your crown.
I never met you but felt you were a friend,
Now in heaven with Dodi
your broken heart will mend.
How we wish we could turn back time,
We loved you too much, that was our crime.
As the world keeps turning your vision is clear,
We'll treasure your boys as if you were here.
Our fairytale has ended now that you're gone
We only have pictures and a heart warming song.
But when the candle flame dies
and the tears stop flowing,
Your memory will stay here
and keep on growing.
Our world is now poorer without our Princess,
Goodbye, Diana be happy, find peace and God
bless.

Lynn Howlett

A Star So Bright

I sit and cry,
And I wonder why
Our Princess Diana had to die
It seems so unfair that
you should go,
I and so many others loved you so.
At night I look up to the sky
I find the brightest star and I
smile and think of you,
If I could have just one wish
It would be to have you back
on Earth again,
I know that could never be,
I know that you have gone to
a special place
Where you can look down on
your beloved boys
Your light will always shine from
that brightest star,
No-one will ever forget you,
You were so special,
Life has to go on for us all
We'll never get over it,
Each day will get better,
But I'll never forget the
beautiful Princess we lost,
On August 31st a date I'll never forget
I felt compelled to write about you,
to me it seemed the natural
thing to do.

V Anderson

Diana Our Princess

Diana our Princess
You simply were the best,
How we shall all miss you
Now you're laid to rest.

Your nature was compassionate
You had the gentlest touch,
All the world over
We loved you very much.

Expression is beyond words
For the loss of you our flower,
A personality pure and bright
We'll miss each passing hour.

Jayne Bailey

Diana

Your lovely face, your tender touch,
To so many you gave so much,
Our love for you will never cease.
May you and Dodi rest in peace.

In sorrow we mourn,
No time for goodbyes,
Our memories are precious,
There are tears in our eyes.

We will miss you Sweet Princess,
And have shown how we care.
Your light shining forever,
In tribute we share.

The world stopped still
The day you died.
Bereft of an Angel
With no place to hide.

We couldn't foresee
That terrible day
When our treasured Lady
Was taken away.

Your last precious weeks
In happiness spent,
The twinkle in your eyes
Showed a love that was meant.

We wished you so well,
Hoped you're happy at last,
Now your work is unfinished,
The flag at half mast.

We see your face in every flower,
Your voice in the birds above.
An English Rose, yet still in bud,
Ever to bloom in our garden of love.

Hazel M Bown

Missing You Diana

We miss you more
than words can say,
You're in our thoughts
each passing day.

You showed the world
how much you cared
The love you gave
was evenly shared.

You really were a special Mother
For your two boys they'll be no other,
Hope they turn out
just like you
Loving and caring in all they do.

But now it's time to say goodbye,
Although we still may need to cry,
You're in our hearts forever more,
Until we join you through God's door.

L Evans

Tears For A Princess

All for the sake of a front page story
the paparazzi try for a moment of glory
but disaster strikes in the midnight hour
as the cameras click, it all turns sour.

The whole world stands in dismay and in shock
they just don't know whether to believe it or not
the Princess is dead, that's what they say
our hearts hit the floor on this sad August day.

A beautiful Princess, all she wanted was space
but they wouldn't allow it, what a disgrace
they wouldn't give in or give her a chance
they were all cashing in on her new romance.

She touched millions of hearts
in such a few years
now everyone's eyes have filled up with tears
Diana we'll miss you, we loved you so much
we'll all miss your smile and your tender touch.

Gordon Stewart

Our Diana

Our Diana is Royalty and does what she wants
to do
She smiles with her eyes when she speaks to you
And moves around with loving care
We always know when she has been there

She has started to go to countries over sea
For they have heard of her loving care you see
And they followed her wherever she went
They thought she was an angel God had sent

Our Diana and her lover have gone
Up on high to their Heavenly home
With myriads of Saints they will sing
Heavenly praises to their Lord and King.

William Howarth

Princess Diana

A mangled mess of Mercedes
Was there for all to see.
Then Diana, Princess of Wales
soon set her spirit free.
A Sunday too, a sad, sad day
for folk like you and me.
May her soul now rest in peace
and soon grieving cease to be.
Instead, give thanks for her special life
and all she tried to do.
The uncrowned queen of people's hearts
and fashion icon too.
A mother proud, of two royal sons
starting life anew.
Such worldwide fame
and true acclaim,
Gained by the chosen few.

Thelma J Town-Clear

The Queen Of Hearts

The day is dark.
The rain has never stopped.
Absent is the sun;
It too mourns her loss.

She was . . .
Witty, warm, compassionate;
With a natural empathy;
A rapport with the people;
A truly devotee.

A Queen in people's hearts.
A crusader of her time.
She broke down barriers;
Enhanced our lives

Beautiful, vulnerable;
Lonely Princess.
Your privacy denied;
By the hounding of the press.

Unique, yet not immortal;
Still it's hard to believe she's gone.
More human, than human;
The brightest star that ever shone.

Julie Ann Sloan

Diana

Diana, you were classed as the Queen of Hearts,
For your charity work and caring side,
It's sad when people have to die,
And nobody will ever understand why.
People will always remember how
You showed compassion towards the
sick and dying,
We all wish you were here now
So we can all stop crying.
Now you're the brightest star in the sky
You'll shine and sparkle so bright,
And when we look up every night,
We'll be saying Diana goodnight.

J England

Diana RIP

The world stopped turning when you
passed away,
We were numb and heartbroken, our lives
in disarray,
Millions cared enough to write their
tributes down,
The love you craved was finally all around.

Love is really far too small a word,
Diana you were worshipped and adored,
With flowers and words we paid our final dues,
We feel there's no-one fit to fill your shoes.

You were a shining light with a heart of gold,
A legend many generations will be told,
You touched the hearts of all you came upon,
Despite your struggle to be loved by 'one!'

Thanks for your life so sorry it was cut short,
So many lessons your good example taught,
If Britain's Monarchy is to remain,
Our hope is that King William soon will reign.

Linda Weston

To Diana

Why do I feel guilty
Why do I feel wrong
The wings of a butterfly
Are just like Elton's song
The light that you put in this world
Was your love all aglow
And you were never frightened
To let your feelings show
Your boys are very proud of you
As I am sure you'll feel
The candle in the wind that blows
Will burn forever real
Why do I feel guilty
Now, I think I know
I have to write my feelings down
Because my love is hard to show.

J Ferrier

English Rose

A sea of flowers rim the edges of special places.
Places of remembrance, places that signify then and now.
Colours, reds, greens, yellows, all combined,
Pile deep, a pile that remains to flourish and deepen.
Mourners pay respect, many too confused and angry to understand.
Many know it is an unforgettable day,
Not until now did we realise how needed one person could be to a nation.
Notes of goodbye and love, scribbled onto weathered pieces of small white card.
Gradually buried amongst heavier showers of love and great sympathy.
Some places are shrines made by the people,
Portraits, familiar yet now much more meaningful.
Poems and letters of farewell and grief.
Strange to us all it seems, that as a nation mourns
An unfamiliar feeling of everyone together is also experienced.
An unfamiliar sight.
Queues of inconceivable length stretch so far
That it is like a puzzle to reach the end, almost impossible.
The greyness of the ending day and the coldness of its air
Do not deter the ever-expanding array
Of flowers and tributes, or the growing crowds.
Huge and overwhelming.
Old and witness to parts of history that are remembered forever, one of which is today.
Its presence almost cold yet one which has and will outlive us all.
It overlooks a mass of grief.
This, a palace yet a shrine to all the people, a place to publicly mourn.
The road, edged with metal barriers, people fixed against them waiting quietly.
Everyone with the same thoughts, the same facial expressions,
And the same grief.
Police, scattered evenly, some on horseback
Raised noticeably from the grey yet lightly petal-covered floor.
So many police, so many people and so many flowers.
So many people saddened at such a loss
But maybe also unsure if such expectations could ever be met again.
The crowds never seem to lessen, and even young children stand and queue,
With their gifts of pictures and letters.
Along with the old and the frail,
And those who have come from far and wide
To pay their condolences to someone whom they probably never met,
But loved and admired so much.
Some of the captions inscribed on cards are simple yet significant.
'Born a Lady, became a Princess, died a Saint.'
As you make your way through the crowds to the front,
In an attempt to lay your own tribute
And see for yourself what you have been watching in your own home for so long,
You notice the silence more.
As no one really speaks, and everyone stands,
Thinking about the same person,
Who has begun to bear the name as our 'English Rose'.

Zita Stockbridge (15)

In Memory Of Your Mummy

Dear Princes, William and Harry
Please do not cry
For in this life you just pass by
Your mum has gone to Heaven's best
And there she'll have eternal rest
One day you'll meet her in God's own home
And never more will you be alone.

Margaret Brown

Princess Of Love

Our Lady Diana, the people's
Princess, who brought us such
caring, love and sweetness.
Who gave to her people her smile
and her heart.
Our Lady Diana, The Queen of
our hearts.
She felt for her people,
She suffered their pain,
She comforted the dying,
Those ill and the maimed.
No matter what colour or religion or race.
Her love was the same,
wherever the place.
Our Lady Diana our England's Rose.
Her beauty brought sunshine
wherever she goes.
Her smile and her laughter
brought happiness and love.
Our Lady Diana you gave us your love.
You reached for all children, with
cuddles and hugs.
Our Lady Diana you gave them your love.
First and foremost, you were a mother.
Loving your sons like no other.
William and Harry your pride and joys.
Your love will live on, in your precious dear boys.
Lady Diana, Princess of Love,
Your star is now shining in Heaven above.
The world is in mourning, with sadness
and tears
Lady Diana will be remembered for years.

Janet Davidson

Your Tears

Your tears pulled a string in our hearts,
Your final happiness a smile to our faces,
For only you, with our hearts broken in two,
Will be remembered in our world's places.

When you left our world
The world stood still
The silence the grief and despairs
The joy you brought to the people you loved
Will be remembered for many years.

Sue Voce

Oh Diana!

Oh Diana what have you done?
You spent August sitting in the sun
Perhaps it was all good fun
being with a rich man's son.

But you were so very precious
and the nation was all very anxious
As the mother of a future king
Your actions you knew you should carefully
think

Your judgement you did let slip
and your safety you let out of your grip
You let go your own bodyguard
and without him you were caught off guard

Now you are gone for ever
And the nation will mourn for ever
But your memory will linger on
and your work will continue on

Without you it will not be the same
but will not diminish your fame
The charities in your name will flourish
which the nation as a whole will cherish

We know you ended up loving
but will never know what you intended doing.
Was it only a 'Shirley Valentine' thing
or perhaps you planned a wedding?

Whatever it was, you can rest in peace
Take life out there with ease
You left a mark on the whole world
with your wish to have a 'Heart of Gold'.

Albert Moses

The Princes

You walked through the crowd,
your head held high,
your father beside you, I started to cry.
Your mother's strength, I felt through the pain,
I knew her presence was by your side yet again.
Your life she filled, with laughter and fun,
Don't let no-one undo all the hard work she has done.
She trained you to be king, for that is your fate,
She wanted you to enjoy life, before it was too late.
The people's king, she would want you to be,
Not stuck in a palace, for no-one to see.
When the wind blows softly and ruffles your hair,
You'll know it's your mother, letting you know that she's there.
But do not whisper, or say it low,
Shout to the world, how much you loved her so.
We cannot imagine your suffering or pain,
But we know for certain, you'll meet her again
By heaven's gate, with St Peter at her side,
A smile on her face, and her arms open wide.
Walk in her footsteps, you'll never go wrong,
With love in her heart, she made this world strong.
Her compassion for others, was there for all to see,
And very proud of your mother, you surely must be.

Catherine Smith

Farewell To A Star

From Heaven we were sent a star
to help others both near and afar
This you did with a beautiful smile
And stopped to chat for a while
You gave so much love.
Now you are gone as an Angel above
And will shine down upon us
in the sky from above.

Janice Plevin

An Ode To Diana, Queen Of Hearts

In nineteen-eighty-one, a shy and pretty thing,
But there you were ready, set to marry our future king.

Then you had your first son, William was his name,
You knew then, he'd have to cope with the fortune and the fame,

Then came your second son, you decided to call him Harry,
You also knew the burden and troubles he'd have to carry.

Your illness came and took its toll, the troubles and the strife,
Trying to be a good Princess, a mother and a wife.

Then one day it was announced that you and Charles had parted
And all the nation felt for you, we could see you were broken-hearted.

You busied yourself as before, helping charities,
Even though you were so lonely, only others you tried to please.

But then along came Dodi, you found true happiness,
With everything that you'd gone through, you deserved nothing less.

The thirty-first of August in nineteen-ninety-seven,
God decided to take you back and now you are in heaven.

God had only loaned you to us for a little while,
But I will never forget your shy and demure smile.

We also know upon that day the world was torn in parts,
But to everyone around the world you were the . . . Queen Of Hearts.

Delice Morris

Diana

Diana, you were the Queen of our hearts
You spread your love to the world's many parts.
Our world will now be a poor, sadder place
No longer we'll see your sweet smiling face.

You cared for the dying, the needy, the sick.
You helped the young homeless,
their beds made of brick.
You reached out to touch a leper's
hand and hugged a man with AIDS
To let then know how much you cared
and to show you weren't afraid.

Children from around the world you
were especially fond.
The less abled and less privileged
you held a special bond.
You cuddled tiny babies, their mums
addicted to cocaine.
And kissed away a young child's tears
crying out to you in pain.
You always had time for children
whatever their colour or race.
Just a touch of your hand or one
of your smiles would give hope and
bring joy to their face.

We'll never forget you Diana for all
that you have done
To make our world a better place
for our future's daughter and son.
Thank you for all the love you brought
For the kindness and compassion that
you taught
And for telling us all not to be too smug
We all sometimes need a kiss and a hug.

We're really going to miss you
You were special to us all,
You'll make a lovely angel
So elegant and tall.

Rest lovely Lady, now in Heaven above
Your Dodi is with you, you'll share eternal love.
We'll watch over your boys on this earth below
And shower them with the love that
for others you'd show

Look down on us Diana, help us
all to be,
More caring towards others and a better
world we'll see.

Goodbye, England's Rose, sleep safe in
Heaven's peace.
May the special love you left us
help all our wars to cease.

Margaret Rhodes

Diana

Here I am writing with tears
In my eyes,
Our Queen of Hearts has
Gone up to the skies,
She was loved and honoured
In every way,
We're going to miss her
Every day,
Two lovely sons she left behind
That's something I just
Can't understand,
She was such a beautiful
Southern girl,
Who cared for people around
The world,
She was such a wonderful
Lady we will always remember,
But would like to forget
That day before September.

James McBeth

Diana Our Princess, Queen Of Hearts

Today our world, is a very sad place.
We have lost a Princess, so full of grace.
She, was like the cool breeze,
on a summer's morn,
Out looking for homeless, at the crack of dawn.
She took time for her people,
both young and old,
She made sure no-one, was left out in the cold.

The sight of a poor leper, was once taboo,
Diana changed all that,
and for AIDS victims too.
She saw many a child, who had lost a limb.
Even when knowing, their chances were slim,
Diana, picked up that child,
and gave it a cuddle,
She tried so hard,
to get the world out of this muddle.

Then came that very fatal crash,
As from the paparazzi,
our Princess and Dodi did dash.
Tears were shed, across the land,
From the rivers to the sea, soaking into the sand.
A thousand years may pass us by,
Our people will still talk of our darling Di.

Those horrid landmines,
she fought so hard to stop,
Oh, please Lord, don't let her good work stop.
Diana was British, through and through,
She united this world and converted them too.

M Buxton

Diana

The world has lost its princess
Through no fault of her own.
All she did was fall in love
With Charles, heir to the throne.

They went on to have two children
And brought them up splendidly.
Cracks started to show in their union
It would seem the marriage was not to be.

The divorce was the end of a fairytale
That the world had seen begin.
Charles and Diana went their separate ways
To start their lives over again.

When, at last, Diana found happiness
The press insisted on playing a part.
They hounded her at every moment
As they had done right from the start.

A quiet night out with her boyfriend
Was all it was meant to be.
A photographer's flash went off once too much
And the night ended so tragically.

The nation was stunned by the news the next day
Their beloved Diana was dead.
The angel we had for the people on earth
Is now an angel in heaven instead.
Goodnight, God bless, Diana.

Anita Harwood

Tranquillity

Flowers bare their petals;
For an English Rose
They weep.
Only tranquillity disturbs
The Princess of Wales -
Asleep.

Robin Pearcey

Diana

Queen of Hearts, our hearts
are broken,
your radiance, our hope,
how will we cope,
let your spirit guide us,
let us feel you walking
beside us.

R John

Shine On In Heaven

On September 6th ninety-seven,
our beloved Princess, was laid to rest in heaven
Drawn through the streets of London,
by the magnificent black horse
Such a fitting ceremony, yet so full of remorse
A picture in London,
the world had never seen before
Her people publicly weeping,
for a princess they adore
Down through Westminster Abbey,
our Diana's love, from heaven shone
Through the heart and soul of Elton John
He sang deep from his heart,
right down to the core
From this fine singer, you could ask no more
He sang of England's greenest hills
to touch the hearts of Prince Harry and Wills
Diana's brother stood before us, so full of grief
His words brought the nation,
some kind of relief
You could actually feel this young earl's heart
open and blister
We've lost our princess, but he lost a sister.
Rest in peace Diana.

F G Chapman

Dying, She Saw . . .

The flash of cameras killed her joy,
Even with her first-born boy . . .
She could not escape the cruel intrusion,
Royal immunity became an illusion.
Stung, she rebelled and lost her 'cool',
And ceased abiding by The Rule.
This led, in turn, to deep distress
For all concerned: a Royal mess.

Once alone, she roamed the world;
The Great Compassion now unfurled.
This was a magnet to the ghouls
Pursuing through hospitals and schools.
Emotionally starved, she sought to impress
With greater extravagance in dress.
The difficult liaison spelt her end:
Dire repercussions it does portend.

Dying, she saw the flashing still:
And even her hearse with impious light,
they fill . . .

But somehow, a different light was shed
And will not cease, though she is dead.

Margaret Clary

A Tribute To Diana

With tears still flowing I write this verse
To express our feelings of our dreadful loss
Our green fields have faded in the Emerald Isle
Our shamrock won't grow without your
wonderful smile
Diana! Britain's Princess you will never die
You are now 'God's Royal Angel'
Way up in the sky.

You are deeply mourned in Ireland.
RIP.

Betty McCabe

Diana

Diana you were so very special,
This world just could not hold.
God took you by the hand
And led you to His fold.
The world is now a lonely place,
Without your smile, your lovely face.
So please God up above,
Shower her with all our love.
Diana you loved Dodi with all of your heart
Now you are both in heaven
You will never be apart.

E Webster

The Star That Glows

Diana called herself - the Queen of People's Hearts,
She captured the nation's interest right from the very start.
And now our lives without her will never be the same,
We carry on with everyday life, but we cannot stop the pain.

Remembering all her charity work as she tried to help raise funds,
We can all remember her forever as she now lives within her sons.
It's for those we grieve the most as they've not only lost a mother,
They've lost the best friend they'll ever have and they'll never have another.

The nation's still in shock as we cannot understand,
Why you went so suddenly and left our beautiful land.
You lived your life for others of that we can all agree,
But it was time to live your life for you, time to be set free.

Time to live for Diana, for William and Harry,
And maybe Dodi was the man for you,
We would have loved to see you marry,
To see you make a brand new start
and live a happy life,
You would have made so many people happy and for Dodi a lovely wife.

Now all we have are memories,
memories and dreams,
But I think we've all learned from this that nothing's ever as it seems.
Just live your life day by day as it's only ours to lend,
and nobody knows how suddenly it's all going to end.

so rest in peace Diana and watch us from above,
You can see the nation grieving, you can see how much you were loved.
Our lives go on without you but will never be the same.
We'll remember Diana with fondness every time we hear her name.

Diana Princess of Wales, Queen of People's hearts,
We'll carry on your good work, we've already made a start.
Please look down on us Diana, and if you're happy let us know,
all the stars shine brightly but we want the Diana star to glow.

To shine the brightest in the sky will surely let us know,
We're doing what you would have wanted, we'll all try to have a go.
Your boys will miss you so very much no-one can replace their mother,
our thoughts will always be with them,
but for now they have each other.

There's nothing left for me to say,
Words cannot put things right,
but please shine brightly in the sky
and guide us with your light.
You'll be missed so much by everyone,
More people than you'll ever know,
This dedication I've written is to let your name live on, and flourish and grow.

Emma Jane Soule

Despair

Who can say as a nation
We cannot share our grief.
Look at our people,
There are so many of us who weep.

United we stood, in despair and doubt,
Where is our queen?
Wake her please,
She cannot sleep.
There are so many people weeping,
So many I can't count.

It's getting frightening now,
Too much to bear.
I'm waiting to wake Diana,
Hoping you'll still be there.

The tears we've shed
Are not all in vain,
You did so much in your short life,
We will meet again.

So don't worry about William and Harry too,
Because deep down in our hearts,
We know you'll watch over them,
And don't despair dear Diana, because we
will too.

C Travers

Diana Queen Of Hearts

Diana oh Diana
You were the Queen of Hearts
Diana oh Diana
How we all loved you so
We loved you so
You brought love, you brought healing
You brought joy into our lives
Diana oh Diana
Sweet love of ours
Sweet love of ours
You were taken oh so early
to that glorious realm above
Now Diana oh Diana
You are the Queen of love
the Queen of love
Now Jesus he enfolds you
He enfolds you with His love
Diana you're safe in his care now
In that glorious realm above
that glorious realm above.
Diana, we won't forget you
For as long as we shall live
Diana, oh Diana,
In our thoughts you'll always be -
The Queen of Hearts

Stephen Dews

Diana, Queen Of Hearts

Diana, Queen of Hearts, you were a star
We all worshipped you, some from afar
We remember you like a radiant sun
You were here for everyone
spreading happiness and light.
Now day has turned to night
And we all mourn you, now your
life has ceased
May you always rest in peace.

M Jones

God Looked Down

God looked down on Diana
and gave her a few weeks of love,
Then He took her and her lover
to the peace in heaven above.
No one will ever part them
together they always will be
Two bright stars in the heavens
that will shine for eternity.

Patricia Lindsay

Rose Of England

Rose of England and symbol of love
Carry on blooming in heaven above
Your roots are the lifeline you gave to the world
Your stem - the support for those cast out
in the cold.
Look down on your people and there you will see
Your compassion and goodness have left a legacy
That will not fade when the winter comes
But will live on in your memory in your beloved
sons.
No matter that the petals of the sweetest rose
of all
Are not pure perfection - but are still beautiful
when they fall.
The scent of this rose will float down on the
breeze
And mingle among us - forever to please.

Madeline Wrigglesworth

Diana Memories

Lovely sweet Diana
Just like my lovely Laura
Twenty-six Laura passed
To God's glory
Beautiful souls in Heavenly grace
The love of God shone on your face
We remember you with your lovely smiles
And your gentle ways,
Giving peace and joy
To many people's days
Not forgotten are these moments
By many a weary soul
You walked beside us through the world
Now angels' wings they are unfurled
To bid welcome to souls
To God returned.

Dorothy Davies

To Our Princess Diana

May the Lord lift up our hearts
And shine the brightest star,
So we on earth can say
Thank you to our Princess Di
May he ever keep us near
To someone who was treasured here.
You were our saviour in hours of need,
Oh! How we miss your good deeds.
Goodbye dear friend, we will meet again,
When Heaven's doors say come to them,
My tears are many; they will not stop.
So please help me to be strong to carry on,
You were too young to pass that way,
But our loss on earth - is Heaven's gain.

Alma Diment

Diana

D evoted, caring, mother of two,

I nspiring them, to care for me and you,
instinctively reaching, loving, more than we
can say

A n angel of light, you showed us all the way,
Queen of hearts, that's plain to see,

N o-one ever cared as much, about you and me,
no-one will ever replace you Diana, you were
just you,

A beautiful, caring, loving Princess is what we
all had
all the world is now stunned, heartbroken
and sad.

Ann Jones

A Public Life

Early days, awkward and shy,
Engaged to Prince Charles
Was the young Lady Di.
It caused headlines we winced at,
'Di-lightful', 'Di-licious'
We waited for pressmen
To start getting vicious.
But as it developed
We followed the story -
Watched you become Princess.
A blushing bride fitted
To wed future kings.
A fairy-tale romance,
The wedding dress - glory!
The world will never forget such a thing.
The press had a ticket
To re-invent prices
For photos and gossip
From 'friends' old and new.
Yet each accusation
Just strengthened the feelings
that we - that's Joe Public -
Had forged for you.
A son came, another,
The monarchy flourished.
The burgeoning family's new generation,
Yet still the press dug, and they delved
And they furrowed through poor dirt
For stories that mention
Your vaguest connection
To someone in scandalous straits.
We could wait
To find out the truth about your indiscretions.
Here it is, it's another.
A woman who stole his heart before you ever
Came onto the scene,
Approved by the Queen
As a fitting companion for our future King.
But there must have been knowledge of his
real feelings
And considerable Machiavellian dealings
Before such a suitor was found.
Did you feel, at any time,
that you were part of a deal.
An innocent, far removed from the ways
By which kings of old kept their wives
Strapped in stays,
Unhappy and silent,
Child-bearing, dependant
Upon the goodwill of the people
To stay at the top of the list
For a fight or a cause,
You did so much good.
You may yet change some laws
That will protect your children.
Even at the point of happiness,
Even as it came to a close,
You may have committed the press not to the
desecration,
But to the protection,
Of a gentle, if much maligned, rose.

Robert Malcolm

Our Tribute To Diana

God lent us His messenger
to show the world true love
Now God has called her to his side
to dwell with Him above
Unhappiness and sorrow
of these she had her share
But through it all her gentle smile
came through which said 'I care'
'Suffer little children'
our heavenly Father said
'Succour the minefield victims
attend each patient's bed
Hold out your hand to lepers
AIDS sufferers and such
Goodbye our own Princess of Hearts
to you who gave so much
We give back to God an angel
who showed us all such love
May you now find your peace with God
at home with Him above.

Dennis & Lilian Partridge

Epitaph To A Floored Paragon

You were slain, yet 'twas not the paparazzi
your bane,
but the bluff of those who harvest emotions,
the so-called 'Creator gods' promotions.
Diana translates, in the sacredotal tongue,
Senscar, Language of Light of the Throng
(Spirit Nation), the original song,
as Transcendental compassionate One:
You were all of that, sent from the All Highest
In the constellation of love, Cygnus,
beyond the Tuat;
from whence 60 winged angels,
traffic with spirits going home
to highest heaven -
for assuredly that is your goal.
That you have left us bereft in soul
surprised some, the
Unfeeling, for you touched
not just hearts and minds
but our lives
with a warmth unsurpassed, uncontrived.
'I know what you are wishing for love in a
peaceful world'
was said of another
but you had the same Avatar's courage,
to rail against the slaughter of children,
by invidious landmines that killed them
So they (scions of warmongering)
cut you - The Inviolate
- down, by subterfuge,
scapegoating others to drown.
Your memory will always live,
as long as the earth
for though the millennial
cyclic cataclysm to come
may efface parts of England your worldly home,
you will be remembered by all,
souls who saw unmitigated compassion in action
with your nurturing of the dispossessed
When the New World Order, the powers that be,
had proscribed Spiritual Liberation,
except in scattered enclaves, tribes.
God speed selfless Princess of the Ineluctable,
Spirit Child of the Indestructible,
May your sterling example never pall
may your kindness to foe
and friend inform us all,
May you stay forever young
May you now know peace sprung
From God of Everlasting Peace
The One who bids all hatred
cease, as your shepherd, Home.
One day the collective dream will come true
and this world will be one of peace for you
Thank you for being with us like a sister,
thank you for not
being a twister, thank you, Woman, Goddess,
Angel, Child
for a resilience, a smile, a flight,
that conspired to foster
healing light within those wearied of their plight.

Will Wagglejavlin

Dulce Diana

Unfairly, another philanthrope dies
So young; and yet I hear the sound
Of cynics sharpening scythes
To hack and pluck; and suck
The life from an idealist's cries.

Take heed you realists
Lest you never understand.
The ass-like stance that hides your fears
Is written in sand;
To be blown away
By a single wave from an altruist's hand.

The day Diana died was real
As our shivered breast revealed.
And each tear shed on run-red cheeks
From red-welled eyes, fell for her ideal.

For the day Diana died, the world was denied,
A mother
And a friend.

Gavin MacBain

Blame

It wasn't me, said the paparazzi,
Shutters clicking,
Flapping in to catch the picture,
Make the millions,
Loud abusive and persistent,
Vultures on their prey.

It wasn't me, said the editors,
Chasing circulation figures,
All condemning paparazzi,
Buying pictures,
Showing close-ups,
Blurred beyond all recognition,
Fat cats out of sight.

It wasn't me, said the owners
Sanctioning and giving orders
Just fulfilling their agendas
Satisfying public intrest
Safely bolstered by their power
Unrepentant in the backlash
Full of pious cant.

It wasn't me, said the Family,
Strangling in their protocol,
Ostracising, agonising,
Failing in their understanding,
Trapped in a well-meaning muddle,
Cushioned from reality,
In their castles of despair.

It wasn't me said the chauffeur,
Vilified beyond description,
I just followed
Given orders,
Turned from hero into villain,
Scapegoat made to take the blame.

It wasn't me, said the Princess,
Reaching out to touch the heartstrings
Of the sad and aching people
Who mirrored her despair,
Seeking frantically for solace,
Building tragedy relentlessly,
As the adoration grew.

It wasn't me, said the public,
Unrelenting in their interest,
Grabbing juicy
Bits of gossip,
Justifying tabloid claims,
Seeking to devour the princess,
They had taken for their queen.

But above all, without question,
Guilty though they all may be,
I am sure because I must be,
It was not me,
Not me,
Not me.

Paddy Lease

Your Presence

In 61 you came to us,
In 97 you left.
For thirty six years you were on loan to us, now
God's taken you back to rest.

You touched this world with your presence,
and how much you will never know,
But the people will continue to pray for you,
and never let your memory go.

Please God hold Diana close to you
as in your arms she rests,
You really don't know what you took from us,
but you took the very best.

This gift of light you gave us only you could take
away,
We are all so sad you did this in such
a tragic way.

Barbara Richards

Reflections On The Death Of Diana

In the midst of life we are in death,
And whilst yet breathing there is no breath,
But in the middle of this mourning
We see an understanding dawning:
That whatever outer garb we wear
When the heart is finally laid bare
Revealing what is really inside,
It shows that many of us have lied
About what is worthy and what is not
Applauding the false, the truth forgot.
And we see the ugliness of sin
And recognise the state we are in.
Slaves to technology, gain and wealth,
Grabbing, not heeding those in ill-health,
Doing our own thing, swathed in our ease
Whilst many are rotting from disease,
Homeless, rejected, starving, alone.
And now does the inner spirit groan,
For those dark hours of waste and of strife
The sorrow in Diana's anguished life
Oh please let it not be lost, dear Lord,
Since for us all, Your blood was outpoured,
And no repentant sinner is lost
For us all You came to count the cost.
And now may the nation search its heart,
To know how each may yet play a part.
Severing from the past as with a knife
Longing to care for every broken life,
Not just to give them cursory thought
But what to do as we really ought,
For each must have a specific task
Well concealed beneath their outer mask.
So ,may we all with one accord
Seek a pure direction from the Lord
And let's not seek for a greater token
Than, as her brother Charles has spoken
Words of great courage, honour and truth
Keeping from traditions bonds aloof,
Tribute of truth graciously measured,
Note the family pledges to uphold
The causes for which her life was sold.
Do not lose sight of any one of these,
The old, the poor, and the amputees.
Remember in prayer each precious son
Whose calm bravery our hearts have won.
May they never fear to laugh or weep,
And in public their emotions keep,
But following in their Mother's path
Know it's not a sin to weep or laugh,
To know that the nation wants them real
And to share with us the way they feel.
Let the guilty now say they were wrong
And we shall see the weak become strong.
Diana's death is expressed in the nation's
pain,
Let us see that it never happens again.

Pearl A Kumar

Diana

We are the people
Who brought the flowers
Who loved Diana . . .

We are the people
Who brought the flowers
Who signed the books
Who mourn Diana . . .

We are the people
Who brought the flowers
Who signed the books
Who weep on the streets
Who miss Diana . . .

We are the people
Who brought the flowers
Who signed the books
Who weep in the streets
Who bought the papers
Which hurt Diana . . .

We are the people
Who brought the flowers
Who signed the books
Who weep in the streets
Who bought the papers
Who paid the photographers
Who killed Diana. . .

Kay Toms

Thirty Six Short Years

When the 'Spencers' gave birth, to new daughter
DIANA in 1961
It was no earth-shaking event,
But - little did the future sick - the lame - and the
handicapped realise
That her arrival - was heaven-sent.

At nineteen - she married Charles -
Prince of Wales
In a fairytale wedding - that we watched on TV
She was shy - young and pretty -
we adored her
Our future Queen would be an asset - to the
Monarchy.

Sadly, the path of true love - seldom
runs smooth
After the birth of William and Harry - came
separation and eventual divorce.
But - the public love for Diana never faltered
At her public appearances, they would cheer, and
shout themselves hoarse.

Now - freed from Royal duties
The world began to see - the real Diana,
Visiting and comforting - so many poor
unfortunates
In her own inimitable manner.

With her wonderful smile - a touch of hands -
or a cuddle
This Princess brought hope to the terminally ill -
with leprosy or AIDS
They will always cherish - that wonderful moment
of contact
Before time - and memory fades.

Visiting the sick or wounded in Bosnia
or Africa
Her arrival - always seemed - to bring
out the sun,
Our Princess - was a modern-day
Florence Nightingale
Plus Mother Teresa - all rolled into one.

In the summer of 1997 - she found a short-lived
love - but
Tragically - in a Paris tunnel - came her last
'Ride of the Valykrie'
Our dearest Diana - we will never forget you
From the first day - when you drove past
our balcony.

Paul Gold

Tears For A Princess

Forgive us Princess if we cry.
You really did not deserve to die
Hunted and hounded like a fox
Heaven has gained but we have lost
I hope now your boys can live in peace
And public pressure means photographs cease
So you will not have died in vain
And they need never know that pain
Then as you wished they would be free as a
bird
That is if the public has been heard
No-one could take your place we know
But they can be protected as they grow
Your caring compassion will ever be
Imprinted forever in our memory
Never selfish always so kind
What beautiful memories you leave behind
Sleep peacefully Diana you did your best
You were a cut above the rest
A angel with a friendly smile
God lent you to us, just for a while
To teach us all to love and give
And learn the way our lives to live.
Then He took you home to rest
Goodnight Diana and God Bless
May the charities in your name increase
And God grant you eternal peace.

June Rose Gilbert

To The People's Princess

How could our beloved Princess suddenly pass away,
We want you back, your people say,
Why couldn't the press just leave you be,
Showing us pictures you didn't want us to see.

You've left behind a trail of grief,
How could such a generous person live a life so brief,
Your love seemed endless, it went on and on,
And you always shared it equally
between everyone.

Millions have come to lay their flowers,
Drawn together by your powers,
They are there because you are so loved,
You shine out above the rest like a glowing white dove.

The country's flags all fly half-mast,
To show we will never forget the past,
People queue for hours to sign the books,
There was always something special about your looks.

Now we shall never again see your pretty face,
Or your pretty dresses made of silk or lace,
Except in photos they all took,
Which now is where we will have to look,
To see the lady who's made people's dreams come true,
There was no-one anywhere quite like you.

Will our happiness ever restart,
Rest in peace our Queen of Hearts.

Sarah Pizan, Jacqueline Scott & Sarah Ingham (13)

My Last Day

On my last day, I rose and dressed -
I chose the gown which faired me best
I bathed, and made myself look good
For the one who cared, and understood.
For the one who gently took my hand
And said no more than, I understand.
He loved me, and it seemed at last
That I had put away my past . . .
On my last day, I dined at the Ritz
An elegant place and brightly lit
A fairytale - a bit like me -
Is that what paparazzi see?
Did paparazzi see the face
Escaping from that dreadful chase?
Through Parisenne streets we drove and dashed
Too fast - too fast - my dreams all crashed . . .
On my last day, they snapped and clicked
Their cameras, to make them rich . . .
I didn't mind that, for a while,
The odd 'Hey Di - give us a smile!'
But sometimes it would make me sad
When I felt low, and still they had
Their pound of flesh, from me, and mine
Their cups overflowing with my wine.
My life, it seemed, was in their hands
And did they care, or understand?
On my last day, though I tried to live,
I gave up all I had to give.
My love, my family, my sons
And all for what? Events may run
Away with us, but does it make it right
To make each day an endless fight?
But never mind, all that is done.
No more pictures. For I am gone.

A L Griffin

Diana, Diana

(1961-1997
The Queen of People's Hearts)

Diana Diana you came into the light
you gave us your love almost overnight,
Your sorrow and pain we all did share
We always thought you'd always be there.

Diana, Diana you always came through
the love of a king was never true,
you laughed you smiled you put on a face
the beauty the style even the grace.

Diana, Diana they took you away
ripped from our hearts never more to play,
the world has a silence worse than fear
the world is so sorry now you're not here.

Diana Diana we loved you so true
the life the love you never knew,
why oh why did you have to go
when the world, yes the world, loved you so.

Diana Diana you rest up above
arm in arm with the one you love,
together forever in God's great world
she deserves better that sweet little girl.

Diana Diana the Queen of Hearts
the love of a princess never to part,
your memory goes on in all of our minds
now and forever till the end of time.

Diana Diana goodnight our princess
now you're an angel always at rest,
a star will be born in the sky up above
made from tears and joy with so much love.

To say goodbye always means pain
from the disaster that struck us what shall
we gain?
To the people that killed her may they
burn in hell
in God's great kingdom never to dwell.

JJH

Welcome Home

Golden gates opened and arms outstretched
Said Dodi to St Peter, 'Look who I've fetched.'
St Peter looked at the two with a frown
on his face,
'Stay here I must talk this over with
His Grace.'
The Angel went off to talk with the Lord
To lose this martyr Earth could not afford.
He explained to the Lord how he felt
about this.
The good she had done and how she would
be missed
The Lord looked at St Peter and said
with a smile
'I only lent her for a while.
She laid a trail of good and love, I guided and
helped her from here above.
I gave her warmth from my summer sun.
Gave her wit from my garden of fun.
Gave her strength from my silver streams
and gave her love from my sweetest dreams.
To this I added the grace of a swan
and an enchanting smile with which hearts were
won,
her compassion touched each corner of earth.
Her work was done to all its worth.
Then what she needed was love and rest
I gave her Dodi, he was the best.
So let them in and make them one
Their work on earth has all been done.
Oh! Peter don't look so worried dear one,
her work will go on through her
beautiful sons.'
Peter went to the gate, where they stood hand in
hand, and said 'Welcome to this
heavenly land.
Go to the garden, take in the hue
There's a place reserved there for you two.'
And as they entered with wonderful grace
She looked back once more
. . . that smile on her face.

Sara Gwilym

God's Fairest Flower Princess Diana

God had it planned dearest Princess Diana
When He chose you, the fairest flower that ever grew
For He knew, you had so much love and compassion to share around.
You blow your sweet fragrance all around, to let mankind know your worth.

For you dear Princess Diana, like God you touched the sick and the lame,
You helped so many charities, not one of us could do it like you.
At times you put us to shame.

Your sons were truly blessed,
Your hugs, kisses they will miss, but God will watch over them
For you, now your good work, on earth is done.
You'll meet us all one day on God's golden shore
We too will give you hugs and kisses for evermore.

You're the brightest jewel in God's crown
God bless you Princess Diana, you have earned your rest,
We know by your love you were truly blessed.

You, dear Princess Diana, left a legacy no-one can touch,
God had it planned for He loved you so very much.
Goodnight, God Bless.

Lucille Hope

Diana

A butterfly who simply touched the flowers with kisses,
Our Princess, who caressed the souls of so many.
Candles shimmering, symbols of hope,
Blurred only by tears,
Dazzled by love
Now you are gone.

Jan Truan

31st August - 6th September 1997

Shock, disbelief, it just cannot be,
This to happen to someone as lovely as she.
I won't believe it, please bring her back,
See the flowers pile high,
sorrow the family wrack.

Oh Lord, make it a nightmare dream!

On the 6th September, the world stood still,
hearts shattered by grief, and
concern for Princes Harry and Will.
A million love flowers towered
like a stair to the sky,
And the tears flooded down
For our Princess Di.

For once - Ireland united,
bonded by grief,
Oh Lord! Please make it a
permanent peace.
Old ones and young ones,
the whole world through
felt she was family -
someone they knew.

Her vulnerable frailty,
and the light in her heart.
This made her so special
in this world so dark.
She will always be near
to guide tender hands,
Uniting by love,
The world and its lands.

Jane Darnell

Diana

There's an extra light in heaven,
A star called Princess Di,
Her body may be earthbound,
But she's looking down from high.
Her spirit's all around us,
And when the wind blows she sighs,
Just like the rest of us,
She's thinking why why why?

E J Cassettare

Queen Of Hearts

Born a Spencer fit to be a Queen
Why of why did they treat you mean
You were young and fresh so much to give
But in a loveless marriage you had to live.

The people at last found a Royal to love
No more handshakes through the hand of a glove
But for one man you would be Queen
Throughout the world would still be seen
Why oh why did he treat you mean?

Struck down were you in the prime of life
Never to feel time's ugly knife
Beautiful and graceful you will always be,
may God look kindly down on thee.

Why did this happen one has to ask
If only this man had stuck to his task
to find a young bride so beautiful and fair
to love her forever with tenderness and care.

Your people woke up with sheer disbelief
and the world is still quaking with
inconsolable grief
Why oh why did she have to die, can't angels
live here on earth as well as the sky?

Sunday 31st August will forever remain
in our hearts for Diana really was the
Queen of our hearts
We will feel her passing the most while
all the Royals will be proposing a toast
for they think they won but I think they lost.
Her life was the price and that's what it cost.

S Reeves

Diana

You'll never know how much you're missed.
Your beauty no longer can caress.
Compassion and warmth will always flow.
An ebbing tide of love will grow.
Little children will never know your kiss.
You'll never know how much you're missed.

Sharon Dodd

Dedicated To William And Harry

I really don't know what to say
To write or what to do
But I had to send this poem,
Just for the two of you.

I couldn't believe it when I heard
Your wonderful Mother had died
My heart went out to both of you
My tears for you I cried.

For I too - have lost a parent
So I know just how you feel
You just can't seem to take it in
You can't believe it's real.

Don't hold your feelings back
If you want to cry then cry
For just like me with my parent
I didn't have a chance to say goodbye.

Your Mother will always be with you
To share your sorrow and joys
And I know for certain in my mind
She was proud of her wonderful boys.

But it gives me some relief
To know you have each other
To cuddle and to share your grief
Over the death of your dear Mother.

Your world will seem so empty now
You life won't seem the same
But lift your head with dignity
When you speak your Mother's name.

Carol Mead

Princess Star

Twinkle, twinkle princess star,
Children loved you near and far.
Pretty, kind and sparkly too,
Princess Diana we all miss you.
Twinkle, twinkle princess star,
We will always care for you.

Maple Infants' School
(Turquoise Class Y1 Aged 5)

Love Is All Around

(You will always be with us Di in William and Harry)

The light has dimmed, the candles glow
there's silence all around.
People in their thousands,
so still, without a sound.

Your inner beauty taught us all
We know it was so hard - Alone
To put your shyness to one side
with no-one there to call your own.

It was so cruel - the way you died
So sudden, without warning
We know you were so happy - then
but you've left a nation mourning.

You left us all a precious gift
A legacy so rare - your darling
Wills and Harry
and we'll treasure them with care.
And if Charles can cast away his doubts
we'll be waiting for him too
Your precious boys will show the way
because in them there's you.

We'd love to think you're happy
with Dodi by your side
Mother Teresa came as well
I'm sure to be your guide
For all of those who loved you
your family, your boys and your friends
for Dodi who made you so happy
there's only one thing we can send -
A commitment to you and your loved ones,
to cast stubbornness and hate to one side
in its place we'll put love and compassion
and in your boys - put all our pride.

Karen Hodge (13) and Mom

Diana And Dodi

'Look at all the flowers my love,
Who are they for? Can you see?'
'They are for the Queen of Hearts my love -
And some are meant for me.'

'Look at all the tears my love,
Who are they for? Can you see?'
'They are for the people's Princess, my love -
And some are wept for me.'

'Look at all the books my love.
What is written? Can you see?'
'Love and kisses and grief my love
For you, Will and Harry - and me.'

'Look at all the people my love.
Why are they here? Can you see?'
'They are here to say goodbye - my love
To their Queen of Hearts - and me.'

'Your body rests on an island
And mine in a cemetery
But our spirits go to the Summerland
Where at last we can be free.'

Diana and Dodi may God bless you both always.

You are just a whisper away . . .

P V Taylor-Marshall

Untitled

Would walk a million miles,
to hear that voice and see that smile.
Yes I'm getting on in years,
Still can shed many tears,
To turn around and find someone gone,
We did not have her long,
Yes that was our Princess Diana
Queen of our Hearts
Like Jesus none will ever fill
their places.

Evelyn

To Princes William And Harry

When we heard of your sad loss, how sorry we all were,
How can one truly express their sorrow when they have not the pain,
The life was taken of one so pure. 'Why? 'It cannot be explained,
To take the life of one so young, so happy so sincere, and full of joy.
It did not just affect our land, it made the whole world cry,
In Heaven now, your Mother has gone to save a place for you.
A place without sin or pain worthy of so few.
As hard as the pain on earth will be throughout the coming years
Remember that our hearts are with you when memories turn to tears.
Safe in the arms of Jesus your Mother will wait for you,
And when the time comes for you to join her, you'll know just what to do.

I am deeply sorry,

Andrew Crowthorne.

Diana

Hounded Huntress
Impressed Princess
Driven to earth by baying pack
Queen of Hearts, a life so ransom'd,
Death defines your paying back.

Your path enticed
With diamonds iced
Slipp'ry the slope of love's incline
Though your lover seemed so handsome
In his hands were Fate's landmine.

Cards shuffled,
Bells muffled,
Aces high and Jokers wild
Knave of Arts who stole your heart,
Cheated life and lost our child.

Sweet hart chased not
For princely profit
But for rags to riches score
Drink, don't drive, the warning tells us,
And now 'Belt up'! for evermore.

Joan Woolard

Diana

In August '97,
You were taken up to heaven,
Your death left our hearts broken,
and our words so softly spoken.
Oh sweet Princess how we cried,
that fateful day on which you died.
But on the 6th September,
the saddest day we've seen,
when we threw the flowers,
we were crowning you our Queen.

Fiona Smith

Victims

Homeless, leper and HIV,
Victim of war - the amputee,
A princess went where many fear to go
She touched and spoke her love to show,
So remember to give of yourself more
When someone knocks upon your door,
Do without a cigarette or drink -
That money might bring victims back from the brink,
Self-sacrifice is what we need,
So look at Diana's life and take some heed.

Gillian Ackers

Diana's Legacy

Fate was cruel for taking one so young,
From your beloved people and cherished sons;
Leaving us all bereft and in pain,
At the loss of never seeing your sweet
face again;
As our Queen here on earth - it just wasn't
to be,
That likelihood ended when Charles
set you free;
But I'm sure the good Lord, in His wisdom and
love,
Has already made plans that you reign
from above.

You will guide your two sons along the
right path,
Ensuring with time, they won't forget
how to laugh;
And when the Crown is placed on dear William's
head,
He'll remember his Mother and all that
she said;
With a loving heart and a thought for
the poor,
He will make a fine King, of this I am sure;
And with angels on high, you'll be so
full of joy,
As you look down with pride and whisper
'That's my boy.'

Harriet E Bognar

Our Queen Of Hearts

Tears on our pillows
pain in our hearts
The night Diana died
our world fell apart.

Everyone knows the heartache
that no-one could bare to hide
for our Princess who had died.

All the world could do was
to break down and cry
the day they heard their
Queen of Hearts had died.

Life will be so grey without
her here, words cannot express
the sorrow and pain, this world
will never be the same.

Keep your arms around her Lord
and give her special care
make up for all she has suffered
and all that seemed unfair.

May you always walk in sunshine
and receive the happiness you deserve
May the winds of love blow gently
and whisper so you will hear how
much this world will always love
and miss you and wish you were here.

Joanne Duncan

To Diana, Princess Of All Time

With eyes of blue and hair of gold,
Oh! How the memories begin to unfold.
The day that we met I shall never forget,
Not a cloud in the skies, the sun shone bright,
On this beautiful lady, what a radiant sight!

'Twas in Glasgow town on that fine summer's
day
With infinite charm, she went on her way.
The crowds were delighted, ecstatic with glee,
A more kind-hearted beauty they never would
see.

I followed your progress, I shared all your tears,
In joy and in sadness, down through the years.
It's so sad to accept, our dear Princess has gone,
But in all of our hearts your name lingers on.

Margaret McHarg

To Princess Diana

None of us will ever understand
why God took you away on that sad night.
But when you died
the world lost a true shining light.
A caring soul,
always so energetic and full of fun,
Yet God decided
your life's work is now done.
We must now learn to live without you,
your beauty, your wit, and your charm.
At least we know you're now safe
from the press and can come to no harm.
That doesn't mean
we won't miss you so very very much,
Because you were a true Princess,
yet you possessed the common touch.

D Ridings

Tribute To Diana

Although she may not be here right now
She knows she will always be loved.

She was a blessing sent from God -
For us from Heaven above,

She only wanted happiness, care, peace
and love,
She was a human being in the form of a great
white dove;

She knows the world will miss her,
But she would probably say,

'Don't cry, don't worry, be happy,
Because I'm not too far away.'

Paul A Baird

An Ode To Diana

Dear Diana,

The people's Princess you are called
When we heard of your injuries, we were
appalled!
We never knew, that you would come to so much
harm,
We will always remember your oh,
so shy charm;
You would always stop and pass the time
of day,
Shun protocol and go your own way,
The rich and the poor and also the famed
They all chose, to pay homage to our
English rose

Sheila Thompson

Got To Forgive - 1997

God, You've just got to forgive Diana
For WE can't find it in our heart,
She suddenly has left us
In a hurry to depart.

Oh God, we feel our right arm is gone
It's all so unforgivable,
Her death does seem so senseless
A person so loveable.

Place her under Your wing God, and please know
Our prayers for her are consistent,
But I can't help adding, that,
Our sadness is persistent.

Now Diana's divorced from US too
Our world's a little emptier,
Gone is she and privileged
Are we for having known her.

Her caring is boomeranged at her death
For caring is what she did best,
Hard worker and survivor
Diana is now at rest.

So, God, now she is in Your keeping and
This WE are unable to forgive.
She'd at least have waved goodbye,
Had she been allowed to live?

Barbara Sherlow

Why Did You Leave Us?

Diana, you had a heart of gold
Helping people young and old
From next door neighbours to travelling far
Collecting cheques, cash from a jam jar
Why did you leave us?

Landmines, AIDS and lepers too
These are concerns which belonged to you
Your life so full of grief and pain
Yet you shared your love all the same
Why did you leave us?

For just one moment you found love
Cupid shone from high above
Although you're not of mind and body
It is OK as you're with Dodi
You still should not have left us.

You're in a place where you can rest
Free from tabloids, free from press
You touched our souls with words you've spoken
Indeed Great Britain's heart has broken
Because you left us.

Jason Rorbach

Light At The End Of The Tunnel

When you think the world has gone to pot,
With no feelings, and young children shot,
Drugs and muggings being rife,
What has happened to our life?
You don't feel safe to walk the street,
You don't know who you're going to meet.
It took one lady to change all that,
Sadly, she had to die, to bring about.
Her name was Di, Princess Di,
Her mourning has brought together,
Young and old, rich or poor, black or white,
All over the world, they gather together,
To show their emotions and feelings forever.
In a tunnel she died,
With her true love by her side.
May they both rest in peace,
And the rest of the world, live in peace.
Like a star in the night,
Let that light shine bright.

Stanley Burdis

A Tribute To Princess Di

Dear Diana,
Privileged you may have been,
We thought one day you'd be our Queen.
But fate was cruel; they thought you a fool!
But with a strong mind of your own
A force in you had grown
To speak out for the weak and ill.
You obeyed God's stronger will
To help and love humanity
(Not hiding behind royal vanity).
Your sons must always be proud,
As all in Britain, whose heads have bowed.
You were lovely, bright and caring.
We've lost you now: heartbreak and grief
we all are sharing.

H M Birch

Mourning The Morning

A nation grieves
A nation mourns
A nation filled with sorrow.
Now for you this whole nation
Must strive for a better tomorrow.

You warmed my heart
You warmed my soul
You gave when no-one cared
Now, that you have to depart
We're so very glad you shared.

Ray Levine

A Life Of Joy And Pain

(Tribute To Diana (1.7.61 - 31.8.97)

I heard of Diana's accident and started to pray
My final conclusion was Lord have your way
The Princess had found true happiness
Which was reported in all of the press.

The confirmation that Diana was dead
Sent a mixed message into my head
At first it was a feeling of disbelief
Then this feeling turned into grief.

The death of Diana was around 4 o'clock
This was a horror and a great shock
The Princess was suddenly taken away
But in our hearts she'll always stay.

Thirty-six was the age Diana died
At this great loss the whole nation cried
The Princess' life has gone to waste?
Because the Mercedes was involved in a chase.

The paparazzi were given the blame
Whatever the case things won't be the same
Some say the driver had too much to drink
But it is irrelevant whatever we think.

Princess Diana was a shining star
In the night sky she is now very far
In the eyes of the world she provided a spark
And with warmth and kindness she left
her mark.

The funeral was held on the 6th of September
This is a day to always remember
Diana has now found perfect rest
We will miss her for she was simply the best.

Diana's life demonstrated joy and pain
Let this be a lesson for those who remain
Live right and do good from this day on
And remember God Almighty is number one.

Colin Hines

Diana - Friend To The World

You came from nowhere as Lady Di, so young, so beautiful and very shy.
You betrothed yourself to our future king, and the nation waited to see your ring.
Then your wedding day came, and we all watched with glee
As you married your Prince, 'twas Prince Charlie.
Your face was a picture, exquisite your dress,
You were no longer a Lady, you became a Princess.
It wasn't too long before William arrived, he's so much like you - a beautiful child.
And then followed Harry, he's more like his Dad.
Two beautiful sons - we were all so glad.
The nation adored you, you'd won all our hearts
With your kindness and love; that you gave without thought.
Then with sorrow we learnt of your separation
The people were shocked, and your friends and relations.
You didn't look well, your happiness gone; a very sad time for you and your sons.
But through the darkness you came, back into light,
And started to live again, you rebuilt your life.
You gave all your time to others in need, you worked very hard; a true saint, indeed.
And then we all heard of the man in your life,
It was Dodi Al Fayed, would you be his wife?
The rumours were raging, the press were relentless
They followed and chased and photo'd and pestered.
Your life's not your own now, they all want to know
Will you marry this man; the one who's your beau!
The truth of the matter is we'll never know
As before you could tell us; fate dealt a sad blow.
We all heard the news with such disbelief,
The nation was devastated and full of much grief.
We couldn't believe what they told us was true
But alas, it was. There would be no more You.
We shed many tears as we watched all the news, the photos and films of your life through the years.
From a babe to a girl to a mother and friend,
Just thirty-six years from beginning to end.
Your funeral day dawned, so sad from the start,
The whole world grieved, it broke all our hearts.
A song was re-written and dedicated to you,
a beautiful song, the words were so true.
You were taken back home to your family estate,
and laid to rest there, on an isle, near a lake.
Although you are gone now from this earthly plane,
Your friends and your family, you will meet again.
But life must go forward, we must all progress,
And we'll always remember our special Princess.

Dianne Pike

For 'Diana'

To a beautiful lady, a Princess named 'Di',
We didn't always see eye to eye,
Still, no-one is perfect, I have to say!
If we were all angels, Heaven's empty today!
There were times that you liked to be
On the front pages for all to see,
And yet you needed too, to hide
From the press, (their time they'd bide).
You cared so much about all that's wrong,
Those with AIDS, landmines, the list's long!
You were so natural in all you did,
Your love for your sons you never hid:
You'd run to them with open arms,
This, the most wonderful, of all your charms!
The world stood still the day you died,
There were not many who hadn't cried:
The loss is greater to the lucky few
In this great world who had met you!
Now you are with the Lord above
Who gave you that abundant love,
For you to share with everyone,
Now, alas, your young life's done!
So Charles, the Prince, must do the same
For 'Wills' and 'Harry'! LONG LIVE YOUR NAME!

D J Baldwin

More Than A Beautiful Princess

Diana was so beautiful charming and full of grace
Within the hearts of every human, she will always hold a place
Her qualities were endless as a princess and a mother
Within the days of our lives ahead, there will not be another
She will always be a fashion icon, to appeal to every age,
Accompanied by models and popstars she would unknowingly upstage.
She shook hands with an AIDS victim, cuddled ill children as if they were her own,
No mummy's hugs for Wills and Harry now, they must feel isolated and alone.
In the past month or two she was really glowing from within,
She found real happiness with another man, was this such a sin?
We were all keen to buy the papers, on which their faces would appear,
Little did we know the final price paid, would be so very dear.
They are now together eternally, as Angels overlooking from above,
It would have been some consolation, if they had declared their undying love.

Sharon Outram

Ode To Diana

I'll remember you for what you've left
Your inspiration was the best
You've touched the hearts of all the world
In spite of sufferings now unfurled.
Your wedding was a great sensation
Until we heard the revelations
You can still assure us of your love
And pray for us from up above.

Mary Tickle

Our English Rose - RIP

Awoke that morning, turned on the telly,
Diana, the Princess of Wales dead,
my legs turned to jelly.
My brain could not surmise the terrible news,
Gone forever, cannot amuse.
Chauffeur, Dodi, beloved Diana, all had died,
Paparazzi had followed the car,
Accused, I can't say who they are,
Crash disaster the vehicle's a wreck,
Bodyguard fortunate to be alive, able to trek,
Drinking and driving is a dangerous game,
Lady killed, Diana, Princess of Wales her name,
Millions in mourning, tributes galore,
Cuddly toys, flowers, covered the floors,
William and Harry, our Princes lost their mum,
Strode behind her coffin, faces glum,
Future king, so very young,
Elton John played piano and sung,
Service electrifying, Earl Spencer expressed his grief,
A wreath, a card 'Mummy' a word so brief
Sons broken-hearted, still in shock,
Memories their brains will lock,
Gracious Lady, feeling for all mankind,
Loving, caring, characteristics specially designed,
Beautiful features, a special smile,
Designer clothing was her style,
Tall and slender, full of grace,
Those in Heaven can see her smiling face,
Laid to rest in her family's ground,
Our English Rose, a Lady of Renown
RIP.

Alice Harrison

Diana

That wor nobbut a bairn when tha 'married in'
Chucked in at t'deep end an' left ter swim.
Tha's shown 'em since as tha worn't flaid.
By, Diana, wor a queen tha'd a made.

G M Gibbs

Diana

A light's gone out, a bright, warm human gleam
That penetrated mankind's darkness with its love,
And in compassion's name brought forth a stream
From erstwhile arid earth, warmed by a human sun above
To illuminate a crop of petty daily cares
That concealed the deeper needs of human hearts,
And brought man everywhere to kneel in prayers,
For a brief time leaving all the surface arts
Of ordinary life, and bending all his thought
Towards the greater depth of man's real needs
For which in vain throughout the years he's sought
While in his vanity worshipping too many creeds:
But now the lost lightbeam has shown the way
He should pursue to bring him to his kinder day.

Rannoch Melville Russell

Diana

You were a wonderful lady
Always helping folks
You were kind, sympathetic and gentle
And laughed and loved good jokes

Everybody loved you
You were a loving mother
You called out to help people
You taught us to love each other

And then one night your car went crash!
The ambulance came in more than a flash!
They worked away with syringe and knife
But try as they might, they couldn't save
Your life

And now the burden that we bear
You are no longer smiling here
We'll miss you, Princess of our Hearts
Our lives will go in stops and starts.

Sophie Louise Reed (9)

Diana

She was the jewel in the crown
The whole world knew that
She left us with such sorrow
To heal we must wait for tomorrow
With her tenderness, her loving ways
These will endure through historic days
She lit up a cover
She lit up a room
We all know she had an art
With her radiant smile she could light up hearts
We'll always remember this beautiful person
Walking amongst landmines, comforting children
The hurt in the world was overbearing
For one young woman
She was so caring
She gave so much, she needn't have
She had found happiness at last
Under love's flag
It seems that tragic event just had to be
But she left us with the image of her and Dodi
Sailing the sea for all eternity.

Joan Bartlett

Princess Of Love

Princess of love, Queen of Hearts
Love and tenderness flourish
With passionate feelings within
For each and every being.

We all loved you dearly
Your good work will forever live
Memories of you will live on
The smiles you put into everyone's lives.

The happiness you placed in every heart
Made many a merry and brighter day
You helped the sick heal their pain
A touch a smile their sorrows fade.

R Joseph

Diana Queen Of Hearts

If you do wonder if it's really worthwhile,
To pass on a kind word, and a gentle smile
Just remember Diana, the Queen of people's
hearts,
And how she passed among us,
And with her love did part.
Remember all the pleasure we all did receive,
By this special person's kind thoughts and
thoughtful deeds,
Look around you to the next person there in line,
Can you hold their hand and give them Diana's
smile?
And if each and everyone of you
Could just be more like she,
Can you all imagine what a good life this
would be?
If we would help our fellow creatures,
Who for no fault of their own,
Have found themselves lonely and without a
home,
Or illness has struck them either in body or in
mind,
Or they live in foreign countries
That're plagued with troubled times.

As millions have all amassed, to show how
much they cared,
You know how much you could change the world
If like her would share,
Just a little kindness, just a tender smile,
Please now don't waste her life make it all
worthwhile,
For no greater or lasting tribute could any of
us display,
Than to make life better for all across this world,
That would make Diana's day.

Rotha Muluihill

Diana

The world in sorrow woke up and wept,
As across the world the shocking news swept.
The people's princess has gone,
And so the world longs,
To see her smiling face.
No more a Queen of Hearts,
As the news shot through our hearts like a dart.
So now it's time for her to rest,
Princess Diana you were the best.

Caroline Madden (11)

A Tribute To Diana

If only it was a dream
My heart would not be so sore,
For I would wake up with a beam
Knowing your heart's music is ever faithful,
ever sure.

But alas! It was no nightmare;
Diana our Princess is dead.
Why this sudden call I'll never know until . . .
Most likely I never will.

O Diana my heart bleeds for you
So radiant were you and so full of life;
Even the butterflies and bees adored you
For you were beauty itself, every man's dream,
So ethereal, so like a goddess
Yet you were such a natural
Born to give the labourer rest,
Indeed we've lost an opal.

You have gone Diana
But never from our hearts
For you've become the water we drink,
the food we eat,
the air we breathe.
We know you're with us in spirit
Watching us in open and secret mourning
Your natural desire to console, ever burning.

In our hearts
You are forever alive,
Compassionate and loving,
Generous and caring,
Beautiful and noble,
Down-to-earth and affable.
Shine Diana shine,
And show the world that you're alive!

David Carvalho

The People's Princess

She touched our hearts at the royal wedding
To marry Prince Charles was such a blessing
Her heart reached out to a caring nation
She gave us back what the monarchy had taken
The love and laughter which shone out
Helped the needy and sick with what life was about.

She has two sons, William and Harry
Her love for them will undoubtedly carry
Her spirit lives on, to let her star shine through
Of all the good Di intended to do
Her loving boys we now consider
For the hurt and grief of losing their mother
We mark this time in disbelief and sorrow
A nation in shock, with no outlook for tomorrow.

That fatal morning on the 31st of August
Came to us all without a purpose
Our loving Princess and companion Dodi
Were killed in an horrific car crash
They were hounded and chased by the paparazzi
No peace they ever were given
And to her death, the national press surely must have driven.

Now peace and happiness be with them both
For a couple, they deserve much more than most
We say our prayers and shed our tears
But you'll not be forgotten for many years
And in our hearts you'll always remain
Our Princess of the people.

S J Barnett

Our Special Rose

She was very colourful and vibrant
Her fragrance smelled so sweet
Her arms were like outstretched petals
Always open and ready to greet.

Her figure was shaped so perfectly
Like a stem so slender and sleek
But her smile that was so radiant faded
As she suddenly fell asleep.

She was, and will always be our special flower
So soft like velvet to touch
But now her petals are closed forever
In our hearts we'll miss her so much.

There is a peaceful garden now
Where our special flower can grow
She can stand high above all others
Because she's our special English Rose.

We can visit her each and every day
Touch her petals of velvet and weep away
Smell her fragrance that we'll always remember
And silently pray to our rose forever.

This special rose was our princess and friend
We loved her dearly until the end
If ever we could choose another flower in bloom
That flower Diana would always be you.

Goodbye our dearest princess
Thank you for your loving care
But the thing we'll miss about you most
Is you not being there.

Janet Elaine Hill

Untitled

Diana, a beautiful Rose
only lent,

To bloom again in
HEAVEN.

F V Brown

Poem For Diana

Dynamic Di, with chic physique,
The contents of this world can be so rotten.
You'll never be forgotten.
Above in the sky, your place of rest,
Wishing right now you were my guest.

Juliette Clarke

Lady Of Light

A black shadow has been cast across our land, grief and despair shrouds us.
I hold out my hands and I close my eyes and still I see the vision, the Lady, your light, how it dazzles me.
You were the light that lit up this world, still my mind it will not heed. Everywhere I am so is she.
Mortal man has once again quenched his thirst for greed.
I am now in a river of souls yet so frighteningly alone and no-one can comfort me.
A child's cry of innocence can be heard, unknowing of the wolves that lurk waiting in the dark.
In a world where so much violence and evil reigns, a light came among us and gave hope to those in despair and love to those in grief.
The light lit up this miserable world where violence and greed creeps through the very veins of the civilised world to spread the disease of destruction.
This light was tormented by the greed of leech-like beings called civilised man. I thank the Lord that there is more good than evil.
The light grew stronger with the passion to fight for the crusade that no other human being possessed this holy shroud.
To me this light is and was the same power and energy as the last crusader that walked our earth.
We didn't learn then, so why should the human soul learn now that the light visits us once every two thousand years and still we do not do it justice.
We weep for the loss of this light knowing full well that we will not see the likes of this light again.
It is only in our own deaths that we will feel the naked energy. This power is within us all but only one has given solace to the humble man of this world. The grief and loss that now spreads through our world will reach out and up to touch the very soul of the universe. Man will continue to spread his violence and disease through the very veins of the world. Man should sit up and cease his evil and violent ways so the lights of the universe may shine for all time.
For you my lady, your light will be forever lit in this mortal world.
You have changed the way people feel. How precious life is and you have shown us how to give that most precious gift - love.
Your light shines within me and I feel the pain of loss.
You my Lady of Light - the ultimate sacrifice has been made.

M Woodhouse

Diana, Queen Of Our Hearts

This lady had compassion,
How can that be wrong?
She opened up her heart to us,
It helped to make us strong.
In this cruel world we live in,
She showed how much she cared,
To change this place, whatever race,
Unfairness, she laid bare.
Throughout this land,
Throughout this world,
We weep her loss, as one,
It's broke our hearts,
We've lost our soul,
But we must still journey on.
So let us now with one accord
Join forces, in her name,
To care and share, in gentle strength,
And let compasssion reign.
Let's keep alive her legacy,
This Princess of our hearts,
Let's follow her example,
We too can play our part,
In simple tasks, in ordinary life,
In everything we do.
Evil can be overcome,
She had her troubles too!
So what more fitting tribute,
To this gentle golden dove,
Than strive for good, as she did,
Our Diana, Queen of Love.

Pat Weeks Goodridge

Diana

Diana, a royal English rose, you've whispered
your last goodbye,
Travelling on, a spirit freed, to rejoice with
heart and soul,
The Lord will embrace you gently and quietly
console,
As you tell Him very softly of the trials you've
had to face,
Your sons you loved so dearly and the elusive
dreams you chased.
You tell Him of the sadness you found in foreign
parts
And how you tried to ease the pain in so many
desperate hearts.
The Lord in time will touch your face with a
tenderness much like your own,
Place a well-earned crown upon your head and
lead you to your throne.
He knows you will be greatly missed and can
never be replaced,
And yet He smiles and whispers 'Home at last,'
With your new-found love - and the elusive
dreams you chased.

Peggy Richardson

Our Princess

Bye bye Di
with your lovely smile
and heart so full of love.
Now you're gone
we must all carry on
the work you did
for the poor and needy.
You were born a child of the 60's
with that modern approach
to give the young hope,
and the old a lasting memory
of your kindness to cherish.
Your spirit will live on in all of us,
rest in peace princess.

Helen Barrie

Diana

We hear almost daily of tragedies
that are perhaps none of our concern,
But now there is one from which
there is so much for all of us to learn.
There's a limit to what a person
can be submitted to
before the cracks will show.
It varies with each one of us
and with some it's difficult to know.
So many wicked things
are happening in the world,
that it calls almost for a crusade.
In fact someone came along
to change a great deal,
and so a plan was laid.
This Queen of Hearts no doubt had no idea
of what life had in store.
For in such a humble way she gained
the love and affection from everyone,
it would seem for evermore.
The world needs an example
set against all that should not be
And despite setbacks and unhappiness
the way was shown to you and me.
We'll never know why there must be sadness
it's just a mystery,
But the short life dedicated
to caring and compassion
will go down in history.
This life will not have been in vain
if those causes get support.
And although much
has already been achieved worldwide,
imagination has also been caught.
The fact that one person
can so affect everyone
so that they have felt a personal care.
Is unique
and it will no doubt lead
to every one of any denomination,
or in their own way
To want to say a prayer.

Reg Morris

Tell Me It's Not True

Tell me it's not true
What I have seen on my TV
Beautiful Princess Diana is dead
For all the world to see
Tell me it's not true
As I look at my 6-year-old son
And that we will never see her smile
Again or her sense of fun
Tell me it's not true
As I cry myself to sleep
Come back and make me smile again
'Cause all I do is weep
Tell me it's not true
As I look at her lovely face
Full of warmth and beauty
She never fell from grace
Tell me it's not true
As I think of William and Harry
And only hope that as time goes by
Their loss will be lighter to carry
Tell me it's not true
As another day just starts
Diana Princess of Wales
Will always be in our hearts.

D J Farrow

Like Argante Or Igraine You've Become

At the heart of the rose
Lies the Goddess of Love
Like Argante or Igraine you've become.
A lady of the lake
Shining brightly in our eyes
Like Brigid or Britannia you've become.
Your barge across the water
Was prematurely set in motion,
To join with the Company of Avalon,
you are one.
You arise in people's dreams
From the light cast by the moon
Like the everlasting Goddess you've become.
Made immortal by the masses
Sainted by the (so called) sinners
Our sacred sovereign sister, you're the one.
Watching over your blessed isle
Strewn with flowers and ringed with trees
Britain's mythology you've entered,
you've become.
Arthur's everlasting bride
Merlin's counsel sought by you
In heritage revealed
Our mythic one.

Alex Langstone

Diana

Your joy was our joy
The way you cared
In all you did
In so little time

We cherish your memory
For now, forever
Our lives will go on
In our hearts is your song.

Horizon Domino

To Diana

When you were sad, you put it aside
To give your love to the sick, worldwide
So when we look up in the sky,
We will always remember you, Princess Di
Because, up there, shining in the night
There will be a shimmering light,
Because, you were the best by far
You'll always be a shining star.

Sarah Ellis

A Princess Among Gods

This poem I write in remembrance to your plight,
everyone's favourite Princess they say
but now you've gone away.

Flags at half mast
and pictures in the windows
shows how much respect and admiration
you've gained from this nation.

Already a song's been made,
many times it's been played,
like a sharpened blade
it cuts into our hearts
and that's where remembrance truly starts.

No-one shall forget you,
too many things you've done,
too many hearts you've won.

Now you're a princess among gods.
Forever rest in peace.

Karl Cox

Sleeping Beauty

Resting on a beautiful island
In the middle of a lake,
Lies a very special angel
'Twas God's decision to take.

A world woke up to a tragedy
And was left to wonder why
Heaven had a greater need for
Our beautiful Princess Di.

The world went dark that Sunday
Nobody noticed the August sun
No longer to light the world with her smile
And so much of her work left undone.

The beginning was as in fairy tales
Brought to us with a prince's kiss
If only that kiss could wake her up now
We wanted a happier ending than this!

Shirley Dixon

Bye Bye Di Di

Although I never met you
I think it's only right
That I should come and say goodbye
Before I sleep tonight
Mum and Dad they tell me
That I'm a lucky boy
And that William and Harry your children
Gave you so much joy
I have often asked my Mummy
Who is Princess Di?
And as she turns to answer me
There's a twinkle in her eye
I know my Mum is saddened by this
So I try to make her feel better
And seal her with a kiss
So goodbye Di Di
I will put you in my prayers.
As I hear my Mummy say to me
'Come on get up those stairs.'

Russell Farrow (6)

To Dodi Al Fayed

To show you're not forgotten
Our grateful thanks we send
For making our princess happy
If only at the end

We pray that you're together
In that paradise in the sky
Where everyone is happy
And our angel will no longer cry

So once again we thank you
For the happiness you brought
You had the gift she needed
And most gratefully sought.

We who also loved her
Thank you very very much
You gave the love she needed
You had that special touch.

Enid M Tanner

What Is A Princess?

A princess is caring and compassionate
She has so much love to share
A princess is a person we cherish and admire
She wears a smile that lights up all our lives
She is as beautiful on the inside as she is
On the outside
When she is around all our problems disappear
She turns rain into sunshine
She turns cold into warmth
She has that certain look in her beautiful eyes
A princess touches so many hearts with her
kindness
She touches so many lives by her presence
She is gentle
She is everybody's best friend
A princess is you Diana
God bless you
The world is a lesser place without you
You will always be loved
And never forgotten Diana
Goodbye our Princess.

Adrian Hattersley

Princess Diana

P retty as a picture
R adiant as a star
I nterested in everyone
N ear and far
C uddles for the children
E ver in your soul
S oftness in your touch
S plendid in your role!

D arling of millions
I ncredible girl!
A lways for the people and those who were ill!
N ow you're in heaven with angels above
A lways remembered - remembered with love!

B Wapshott

In Memory Of Diana, Princess Of Wales, A Shining Light

'She is irreplaceable,' Lord Archer said
It was then I knew Diana was dead
So cruelly taken on a summer's night
With her love Dodi by her side.

And as the tears streamed down my face
The world became a sadder place
As we cried for Princes William and Harry
We thought of when they were all happy.

Your boys, Diana, are a credit to you
They have been so brave in public view
There is so much of you we'll miss
Your smile, your tender look, your kiss
Will we ever recover from this?

In your short life, Diana, you cared so much
You really had that human touch
The best tribute of all would be
For us to help each other, please.

Claire Black

Ode To Diana

Our dear princess
We will miss your smile
Your zest for life
Your care, your style
We lost a star
That shone so bright
Oh cruel fate
That was not right
You left us crying
Full of regret
But your good deeds
We will never forget
All the world is mourning for you
Now the angels will rejoice
You will charm them too!

N Wilson

Heaven Has A Queen

So young and beautiful
So much to achieve
So little time to spare
So many people to show
How much you care.

'Tell the boys I had to go
Tell the boys I love them so
I had no time to say goodbye
As an angel I had to fly
So much charitable work left undone
For that reason my many friends will carry on
All the good work thatI had begun.'

Why she had to go
Only God will know
An English rose in her prime
She left this world before her time
She touched all our hearts.
In a way a part of the British people died that day
On that fateful early Sunday morning,
Leaving a chasm that could never be filled
By all the flowers in the world.

England mourns the loss of a princess,
Heaven is rejoicing for they are gaining a queen,
All at the cost of the nation's emotions
There she will remain elegant and serene.

The aura that surrounded her was visible
Through the kind compassion that she gave
And felt towards everyone she came in contact with
Even those she didn't know could feel the love
Reverberating through our TV screens.

Untiring and industrious in her nature
Her undaunted drive
Had captured the hearts of the world
Her undying love for sick children
Will never be forgotten.

Never before had the world united as one
The day Diana left for heaven.
She will be accepted and loved as we the world
Took her to our hearts.
Forever more rest in peace
Where she will suffer no more hurts.

Peter Hollands

Tribute To Diana Princess Of Wales

Daughter, sister and a wonderful mother,
For all of us there'll be no other,
The 36 years of her short fulfilled life,
You've inspired us in your doing and in all of your strife.
The pleasure's been ours - to have had this dear lady,
As our patron, our Princess, and a Spencer baby,
We'll never forget all the good things you've done,
Your faith in your work, the affection you won.
Your peaceful departing to pastures anew,
To rest near your father, where your family first grew.
The love and affection she so openly shared.
Was her way of showing to us that she cared.
Diana, William and Harry too,
A unique family bonding, just shared by a few.
A love for their mother that they never hid,
Their devotion to Diana in all that they did.
Remember her smiling, remember her life,
As our Princess, a daughter, mother, once wife.
Cherished are the memories all of us share,
We'll always remember, because all of us care.
Diana, Diana, your memory lives on,
The world can't believe,
that you really have gone.

Caroline Bone

Diana RIP

Diana was the Queen of Hearts
Who tragically died
She will always stay
In everyone's heart
As a kind and gentle
Queen of Hearts
No-one can ever replace her
No-one could ever be like her
She was a wonder woman

The paparazzi got their way
Got their photos got their pay
They chased and chased until
Everything went their way

Poor William and Harry
They haven't lost a Princess or a
Queen of Hearts
They have lost a mum
Their mum

Diana died with the man she loved
Happy they were
Now they're up in heaven
Happy forever
We pray
Diana Princess of Wales.

1961 - 1997

Karen Pearson (12)

Diana

Almighty God the Lord above,
Sent you down for us all to love,
He knew that you were one of the best,
You shone above all the rest.
You showed the world that you cared,
Your hand held out to those who were scared,
Your hand touched many, many hearts
And your smile lit up a thousand stars
Thoughts of you will live forever,
Your memory will last forever and ever.

Rachel Meese

Diana

I had to pay this tribute
as tonight I cannot sleep
thinking of you on Saturday
and the date you have to keep

Your sons have both decided
to walk with you through the crowd
You can't cuddle them or hold their hands
But they'll make you feel so proud

We know you're in a better place
and Saturday is just for the living
but we wanted to give you something back
for your lifetime full of giving.

The happiness you gave us
in your short stay here on earth
Will live on in us forever
remembering your worth

You carried yourself with dignity
With elegance, style and grace
even through your sadder times
when a camera was stuck in your face

You stunned the world with your fashion
you made sick children smile
you spent a lifetime helping others
and would 'walk the extra mile'

So happy before you left us
with the love you had finally found
though never to become our Queen
nor ever to be crowned

May you be together in happiness
with the man you truly love
and see how much you meant to us
as you look down from above

You leave us such a legend
and in our hearts we hold a banner
to one incredible lady
simply known as 'Our Diana'.

Debbie Watkinson

A Tribute To Lady Diana Spencer

You did not fear those who were cast off
by the world,
The impoverished,
The wretched sea of humanity,
No to you they were your constituents,
You fought for them,
You loved them,
and drew attention to their plight.
You helped them to keep life's flame alive
and to continue in their fight.

You moved mountains, crossed the deserts,
and even spanned the sea
To show people and governments
how best to play their parts,
And that is why my dear one lost,
You have been crowned by us as Princess Di
'The Queen of all our Hearts'.

What we saw we loved,
We saw ourselves in you,
vulnerable, insecure.
A desire to do good,
But alas with all the frailties of a mere mortal,
Yet you were gifted with a love
that was so deep and hauntingly true,
Your swanlike grace, your human touch,
Your beauty along with poise,
Will be sadly missed by all of us,
But especially by your two young boys.
Yes your inner beauty was unmistakable,
Your smile was even more,
your compassion was legendary,
and will carry on,
Leaving us with sweet memories of you,
and our own hearts to explore.

At long last you found some happiness,
with a man who showed he could love you,
and who showed that he could care,
Who could reach inside that protective shell,
and rescue you from your despair.
He was your prince, your shining knight,
Someone who would wipe away your tears,
Someone to hold you close,
To love you
and chase away your fears.

Yes! You gave so much,
You showed how much you care,
while you battled your own private demons
deep in the devil's lair.
But through it all you showed
the common touch to folks like you and I.
And that is why you will
Forever dwell in our hearts as the
irreplaceable Princess Di.

Whose life was like a painting
of love and vivid colour,
That continues even now to grow.
But alas the brush is still,
The painting lies unfinished,
And the rest we will sadly never ever know.

William Douglas

Diana The Perfect Rose

You are the brightest stars
That light up all our skies

You are the sun that shines
Upon the earth
The rain when heaven cries

You are the waves that gently
Rock the seas
And the butterflies that dance
Upon the breeze

You are the perfect rose that blooms
But its beauty never dies
And the sweetest songbird that
Flies across our skies

God's precious gift, that's what you were
But sadly lent, not given
Now all the love you gave to us
We give to you in heaven.

Lynne Hall

Queen Of Hearts

August 31st was a very sad day,
It was then that you sadly passed away,
In every heart on every day,
We'll miss you Di in every way.

We'll never forget your smiles and charm,
'Cos you never ever done no harm,
You helped everyone in each and every way,
Your presence here we believe will stay.

You remind us of a little white dove,
So young and pure, the one we love,
We'll miss you Di forever and ever,
For now Dodi and you can be together.

You'll never be forgot our Queen of Hearts,
For here our Princess your life just starts.

We all miss you Di the one the only
Queen of Hearts.

Wayne Baylis

Diana

Who could take her place,
Now that she is gone?
Wouldn't it be a shame,
If, of all her good works, only memories remain?
A hundred charities she did help
in her short lifetime,
Is there anyone out there who could hold up
to that claim?
Would she have wanted us to help,
As she had always done?
The poor, the starved, the AIDS victims,
The poor downtrodden ones.
Her death left an awful gap, that may
never be filled,
But the spirit of her good works
Will not be left to die,
For with a little help from all her friends,
It shall lift its wings and fly!

Pauline Uprichard

Diana

Your spirit was beautiful,
Your caring heart immense.
Why your life was cut so short,
Just does not make any sense.
You were taken from us,
In such a cruel way,
And we'll never know why
Till our dying day.
But your soul shines on
In grace and love
Throughout this land.
So let us go forth and reach out our hands
As you did for others,
Without hesitation.
And may we be proud to show
We can be one loving nation.

Lynn Suzanne Finch

Diana

Why do I feel so empty, why
do I feel so sad.
I only knew you from a distance
with admiration for your strength
when things were bad.
How you seemed to draw your happiness
helping others in need,
Maybe it made you feel to give your
love and kindness it filled the lost and
lonely gap inside your heart I'm sure
you had.
Goodbye Diana, hopefully you will
find peace love and contentment in
the heavens above
With your partner and love in life
and in death Dodi Al Fayed.

Eileen Walsh

Tribute To Diana

Palms were laid at Jesus' feet,
Flanders' poppies soldier on.
Now flowers for Diana
Will bloom still, though she has gone.

Massed flowers for Diana
Will forever link her name
To carpets deep with flowers
- Whilst, still more, the flowers came.

Such tributes from the people,
For the people's Princess Di,
Spontaneous their gesture,
Heartfelt sorry was their cry.

Unprecedented action,
An outpouring warmth and love,
For one who showed compassion
To the lowest, from above.

She cared, she showed it, acted,
To alert the world to blame
And showed how love responded
When the hand of friendship came.

Her death was sealed with flowers
- Our tribute as she died,
But as she died, remember
Her, our English rose, with pride.

Michael Harris

Images Of Remembrance

I thought I saw your face today
I can't quite remember where.
I know,
I saw it in the face of a crying baby,
arms reaching out for love.
No, wait.
I saw your face looking up through
the eyes of a beggar asking for pity.
Then again it may have been in that
dying woman whose hand reached
out for compassion.
It's hard to say really.
For you are reflected in all of these images.
A gracious lady who was able to express
love, pity and compassion.
Even as the sky itself joins in our tears,
and the wind echoes our cries of grief.
Still, a single ray of sunlight shines
through.
If we can seek to imitate all that
you were.
If we could give what you gave
just once a day.
Then the shining light that was
you Diana
Will never fade away.

Laura McHale

September 6th, 1997

The Queen-that-never-was sleeps on her isle
Guarded by rocks and roots and stones and trees.
Bereft now of her presence and her smile
Her people mourn, awash with memories
Of one whose light so luminously shone
Before the Seine became the Acheron.

DMC

Prayer For Diana

Dear Lord,
For all the love, joy and kindness,
That Diana gave to others,
May she be given eternal blessings,
In heaven.
Amen.

Nicky Westover

To The Queen Of Hearts

I am in a nursing home again
Seeking a cure for this dreadful pain.
I look through my window and what do I see?
Heathered mountains and grass that is green.
A world at peace with no cause for grief.

But when I look at my TV screen
I see only scenes that make me grieve.
A whole nation is sighing a whole world
is mourning
The death of a princess without any warning.
From north to south from east to west,
People are sobbing and cannot rest.

A modern Cinderella is being driven away
Lost to a world with so much at bay.
God gave her to us, but now takes her away
Her journey to heaven on a flowery road
Leaves us in sorrow with hearts that are torn.

In a sinister silence her boys tread The Mall
Two tragic figures, brave William with brother
Harry so small
With their heads bowed so low we feared
they'd fall
How they must have suffered on that fateful walk
With no loving mummy to answer their call.

Two lonely princes having lost the love
that counts
Alas must now climb life's so cruel mounts.
Oh please love them if only on my account
This and this only would be Diana's mournful
shout.

Sadie Williams

God's Garden

God came and plucked our English rose
He also took the man she chose
To be together in God's garden in heaven above
And there to share a wonderful
peaceful love.

M M Cook

Diana . . . Lady Of Love

What a terrible twist of fate
happened on that day,
The grief of all the world was with us
on that day of tragedy.

A noble Lady, so sweet and kind,
The world lay at her feet.
Why she had to die so young
when she gave her all to meet.

The sick, lonely, disabled, people in trouble,
to help the people all over the world,
especially those who lived in filth and rubble.

Yet the Lord must know what is best
for each and every one,
And that is why he gave to us
His own beloved son.

Like the Princess of Wales . . .
. . . He too died young,
And His life had only just begun.
So we all have to pray and be content
to know a victory for Heaven has been won.

Maybe who knows she will have a great part,
in Heaven as on this Earth,
and bring the understanding of all nations.
. . . what everyone is worth.

So pray for Diana and let her soul be free,
and remember forever with pride and love,
what she did for all the world to see . . .

Edna Jones

Once Upon A Time

Once upon a time, there was a beautiful princess
She loved all the people and the people loved her
She married a prince, but happiness was not
to be,
So God took her home to rest eternally.

Rest in peace, Diana.

Annie Robinson

Diana

You were a ray of sunshine
in this bleak and sad old world.
Your kindness and compassion
brought hope and happiness untold.

You know how badly you'll be missed
whilst watching from above.
We know that you'll continue
to spread your serenity and love.

Your good work will continue,
with ever-growing speed.
You were sent to us in order
to plant the caring seed.

Your sons will miss you most of all,
a fun and loving mum.
Their overwhelming sadness
is like shutting out the sun.

May God embrace you and Dodi
with an ever-open arm.
Be happy together for always,
secure and out of harm.

So, with a prayer, we give you back
to the place from whence you came.
You touched our hearts and gave us hope -
the World will never be the same.

Carole Wallis

Diana

A perfect angel who was heaven-sent,
not ours to keep, she was kindly lent.
Lent by God from up above,
she came to fill our lives with love.

But his skies were dark without her light,
so he wanted her back to make them bright.
God claimed her again to turn her into a star,
so her love can continue to shine from afar.

Our lovely lady we loved you so,
none of us ever wanted you to go.
Our perfect princess, our number one,
so sadly missed now that she's gone.

We shan't forget that fateful day,
when God decided to take her away.
He left us all with tears to weep,
and precious memories we'll always keep.

Helena Devai

Diana

On the 31st of August I got out of bed
Put on the TV to hear Princess Diana was dead
It doesn't seem fair that you had to die
We all keep asking ourselves
'Why Diana why?'

That radiant smile and beautiful face
The way she walked with such style and grace
The whole world could see
how happy you'd become
At last you'd found happiness,
Dodi was the one?

Now no-one can trouble
you, you're in a safe place
It's God's turn now to share you style and grace
He called you up above,
He knew the pain had to cease
So now the time has come
For you to rest in peace

But now the whole world will never be the same
For the memory of Diana will always remain
We all took a liking to you
Right from the start
Because Diana you're our Queen of Hearts.

P Yates

Diana's Day Of Farewell

It's sixth September Ninety-seven
The time is 6 am,
It's the day of Diana's funeral
Crowds are a multitude, without mayhem.

London looks unbelievable
With oceans of flowers,
Parliament Square is inadvisable
Pavements choked up, crowds defying the hours.

Some are still sleeping at present time
In their warm sleeping bags,
The mood is one of deep warmth so sincere
Camp site in Hyde Park, people display
black tags.

The police look out of their depth today
On this sad occasion,
Can hardly be spotted in this vast crowd
A train provides temporary accommodation.

Martin Lewis is narrating here
Studio lily-decked,
Another lovely picture of Di
Hangs there where all can sit back and reflect.

Sadly now, this is the morn to mourn
She watches from the sky.
From the crowds respected quiet is observed
Millions waking to say goodbye.

Barbara Sherlow

The Resignation Of Diana's Love

Money is not the answer
To mend the crippled bones
It was money that killed - the tombstone
of all impersonal mines.

Don't let her death now be in vain
But carve her name with pride
On a little piece of white paper
Banning all impersonal mines

And let the Princes grow with pride
While we crown them with her love
Her two sons - her inspiration
Now the resignation of her love.

Helen Darlington

I Have A Dream

I have a dream
And in my dream I see
Diana, Princess of Wales.
She stands before the heavenly throne
And God addresses her in kindly tone;
'Who speaks for you, Diana?'
She with a roguish twinkle in her eyes,
Raises her head and quietly replies,
'A loving friend, who seeks not wealth nor fame,
Mother Teresa of Calcutta by name.'
God hesitates, then summons up his tried
And trusted courier, Gabriel to his side.
'Go bring me Mother Teresa of Calcutta,
Where she's rescuing the poorest from
the gutter.'
Then Gabriel, his appointed task complete,
Leaves Mother Teresa before the Master's seat.
Diana's wish to her is then declared,
That she should speak for her for whom
she cared.
'May it please you, Lord,' Teresa says
with feeling
'This lady's hands were dedicated to healing,
The homes of poor and lowly she has graced,
The outcasts of society she's embraced
And deprived children, conscious of her charms,
Have known the comfort of her loving arms.'
'As you describe her,' God says with a smile,
'You could be quoting straight from your
own file.'
To these good ladies God then gives his blessing,
Angelic choirs proclaim their songs of love,
Now two new stars pass through celestial
portals,
To shine forever in the heavens above.

Edward Farren

Tribute To Diana

The people's princess, so very true,
I can't find the words to do justice for you,
You've done so very much for others,
but little for yourself,
They must be so grateful,
those people you did help,
The children from Angola, Pakistan
and our London too,
What people have you not touched
with your love?
I believe only a few.
You touched my heart,
and I'm still young in years,
If I can cry young,
Then the old will shed many tears.
People called you the Queen of Hearts
And those people are now silent,
As you so sadly depart.
Everyone will remember you Diana,
In their own special way,
And so the world stays silent,
With no words left to say.

Natalie Astbury

Born To Give

In awe, the world looked across the sea -
and cried,
Sorrow for their Queen of Hearts -
who died.
She cast away the destroying toys of self -
and
Entered a new era of care and love
Guided by God's Son, Jesus Christ above,
the real King.
In dignity and truth, followed in His
steps.
And joined all those, who were inspired for good
by God, for He is Love.

Love is kind, exalteth not itself
Really cares for others in their needs,
Stoops to tend their wounds which bleed.

Love faileth not and
God is Love.
And love is to care for one another,
As a faithful sister or brother.

R M Stephens

To Diana And Teresa

I shed a tear when we lost Diana
and also Mother Teresa. How sad
that they both left this world when
they were loved so dearly. I knew
their homes at Kensington, also
at Calcutta. Though miles apart,
with one thought in mind they
shared their love in common to
help the sick in this sad world,
they played a leading role and
both will be remembered when
the good Lord calls his role.

F J Wright

For Diana And Dodi

Deep in our hearts you will always stay
In people's thoughts every day
A tragic end to a beautiful star
Nations miss you near and far
At peace in heaven away from harm.

Diana loved you with all her heart
On that black day you were never to part
Dark days ahead in every land.
In heaven you will walk hand in hand.

Goodnight God bless

J Fisher

To A Unique Lady

France was the unhappy host
Who took Britain's most precious jewel.
What did really happen?
Which man broke the rule?

The only thing in common
Was they did not understand
The grief and hollow feeling
Suddenly inflicted on this land.

Diana, you were not perfect,
What your brother said was true,
But you were a compassionate human being
And we loved you for being 'you'.

Your charisma and your natural charm
were well beyond compare,
Your lovely smile and caring touch
made all who met you so aware . . .

They'd met a unique and loving person
who though regal and full of beauty,
exuded such love and compassion
far beyond the realms of duty.

And some sick who'd felt so abandoned
realised, perhaps all was not in vain
and somehow found the courage
to strive to live again.

Yes, London watched with bated breath
on that tragic day,
and silence reigned as did the tears
as you passed on your way.

The people stood in disbelief
There was a deafening silence in the air.
Your sons were such a credit to you
Their pain so hard to bear.

But tenderness reached out to them
from thousands of hearts in the grieving crowd
as they bravely followed behind you
Their strength would have made you proud.

You died at such an early age,
Our country is wracked with sorrow.
France took away our most precious gift.
She took away our tomorrow . . .

Why didn't she take enough care of you
on that fateful night?
You were our 'candle in the wind'. . .
and she put out the light.

Sue Browne

Not For Us A Faded Rose

God, to us, works in mysterious ways,
Measuring out our span of days,
Sometimes we cannot understand
And should not try
To reason why
When someone in the midst of life,
Someone who is needed, loved,
Someone spreading happiness, comfort and joy,
Is suddenly broken like a valueless toy -
Leaving a nation to grieve,
Finding it hard to believe
In a God of love and compassion -
Until, we stop to think
Of the good that lives on,
And will live on,
Long after we ourselves are gone.
This is God's plan.
Diana, Princess of Wales,
The Queen of Hearts,
Her work here done,
Moves on somewhere out there
Beyond the moon, stars and sun,
To continue her spiritual climb
Into a happier realm
Of love, and a peace sublime.
God will bless you, Diana,
And those you love.

Thomas C Ryemarsh

Diana

The bloom of youth at its height
The way forward seeming clearer,
So many problems to set straight,
In the nation's heart becoming dearer.

But she, on this island, alone.

With love and compassion she reached out,
Showing the qualities Our Lord preached,
But evil men cannot let good have its way,
For their god is money and is paramount,
So hounded in life they never left her.

But she, on this island, alone.

So young to be taken,
So tragically too,
So much potential,
So much left to do.
They bore her home along people-lined streets,
Flowers in her pathway,
A nation in grief.

But she, in that island, alone.

Marina Robbins

Diana - My Tribute

God gave you on loan, for thirty-six years,
Then took you away and left us all in tears.
He gave you the feelings that not many share
A true sense of giving, compassion and care.
He gave you a heart so much bigger than most
Then made you a princess, a remarkable post.

You gave it your all, and then some more
You showed us the way, you opened the door.
By touching and caring you opened our eyes
To a world that was hidden, been put in disguise.
A leper, the dying and many with AIDS
The care in your heart was shown in your gaze.

You did so much good in your short life,
It makes me ashamed, when I moan of my strife.
You once said sorry for words that caused stress
But there was no need, you were the people's princess.
Diana, though we were always worlds apart,
You will always remain a Queen in my heart.

Barbara Smart

Untitled

A jewel in our hearts
The good work you have done
Nothing was out of your reach
Bringing joy to everyone
The touch and your arms enfold
The smile you gave
Both to young and old
We will never forget
The kindness in your heart
You gave to everyone
Your smile said everything
We will never forget you
You will always be with us
God bless you Diana
Our English rose.

Ivy Blades

Your Smile

Your smile, your warm embrace,
Lit the light on everyone's face.
You reached so many people
With your loving touch,
It seemed you had to leave us,
To reach the whole world
And make us cry.
You did this all alone
Without any help,
So God be with you
To take care of yourself.
You will be remembered
For evermore,
And worshipped by everyone
With a loving call.

John Gold

Diana

My heart is breaking and my mind is numb,
Two young lads have lost a special mum.
A world is grieving for what has gone,
The sorrow and heartbreak will go on and on.
You were plucked away in the prime of youth,
What you were promised was not the truth.
A beautiful girl, full of goodness and cheer,
Was used and abused by those she held dear.
The torment you suffered, the tears and the pain,
But your love and compassion never did wane.
They never realised just how precious were you,
They showed you no love, did not hold you true.
A soft summer breeze, a new flower in spring,
A gentle snowfall or a bird on the wing.
So many things that will bring you to mind,
And we will remember you were one of a kind.
Some part of us all was lost on that day,
The pain and the hurt just won't go away.
The tears may subside and life will go on,
But the memory of you will always be strong.
The most wonderful angel full of goodness and love
Has been taken to be with the angels above.
My heart is breaking and my mind is numb,
A nation's mourning has only just begun.

G Hockerday

Our Princess

A light has gone out of this world,
A beautiful candle snuffed out,
We wonder why and we can't find the answer,
We can't realise what all this is about.
She was the defender of good causes,
With her loving and all her deep caring,
It wasn't a mere gesture,
It was her whole life she was sharing.
She brought comfort and joy to the sick,
With a touch and a word of good cheer,
She couldn't take away all the pain,
But she told them what they wanted to hear.
There is no doubt of her love for her sons,
She showed them a far simpler life,
The pride for them shone in her eyes,
But she told them of life's struggle and strife.
When happiness seemed to be blossoming,
And Cupid was sending his darts,
The stormclouds angrily gathered,
And took Diana the Queen of our hearts.
Now all that is left are just memories,
Which we will always treasure,
The pleasure she gave us on earth,
Will live in our hearts forever!

Edith Antrobus

Our Diana

It is four weeks now, since we lost our Di,
Oh why, oh why, did you have to die?
Our hearts still ache, the tears still flow,
Our dearest Di, we miss you so.
We miss your beauty, and your smile,
The hands that touched, the sick, the blind.
A heart that was, oh so kind,
Another Di, we will never find.
So please, dear Lord in heaven above,
Take care of Di, and give her our love.

Patricia Boylett

Tribute To Princess Diana

There was a lady
Who shone so bright,
As though she had
An inner light.
Now that light
Has been extinguished
And never will
There be a lady
Who shone so
Bright as she.

Lisa Haynes

Goodbye Diana

Stunned at first with disbelief,
Someone pinch me, so I can wake with relief.
But the news reports continue to say,
Our beautiful Diana has been taken away.

A week passes, almost in the blink of an eye,
And now it's time to say goodbye,
To someone so gracious, sincere and true,
And that of course, Diana, is you.

The sobs of heavy hearts can be heard
for miles around,
As the tolling of the muffled bells sound.
But heaven's bells are ringing clear,
For the person we all held so dear.

Now as your new life's about to start,
May you forever live in the nation's heart.

Sarah Staples

For Princess Diana (RIP)

Diana sweetness, kindness
and light,
cruelly taken from our sight,
Candles have burnt on through
the night.

Kensington Palace is where
we all came -
to feel your presence and
hear your name -

Poems and tears have flowed
for you,
If only we had let you know,
When you were with us on
Earth below -

'Good night sweet Princess.'

Kathleen Brosnan

Diana
1961 - Princess of Wales - 1997

Your tender touch and your caring smile,
We wanted you to stay a while.

You gave hope and joy to the sick and needy,
We want you still, are we being greedy?

As you stroll in God's beautiful land,
Take the angels by the hand.

They knew you weren't like any other,
Our sorrow is deep, we feel it will smother.

You gave the world beauty, style and grace,
You made it seem a better place.

Look down on us Princess, smile and wave,
You taught us to love, with the love you gave.

Gloria Cornish

Diana

On the thirty-first of August
nineteen ninety-seven
Diana Princess of Wales
ascended into heaven
The nation united in their grief,
They heard the news in disbelief,
She stole the hearts of everyone
with her beauty and grace
Everywhere she went in the world
with a smile upon her face,
To Diana people mattered
whatever their ailments were,
May we through her example
show that we too care,
Ours is not to reason why
one so young should have to die.

Valerie Hessey

Diana

As the Queen of Hearts,
You became part of all our hearts.
Never, ever discriminating,
Always so radiating.
Time for everyone,
But now you're gone.

Never causing any harm,
You were flowing with charm.
tireless work for those in need,
With no feeling of greed.
so many years still to live,
And still so much more love to give.

A leader in fashion,
You lived life with passion.
Keeping your problems to one side,
Never given a chance to hide.
You deserved your new found happiness,
but were hounded by the press.

Goodbye, God bless,
Now you will get the happiness,
And the peace you deserved on earth,
But you were never given.
Your memory will always live on,
In our hearts, minds and souls.

God bless you, MAY YOU NOW REST IN PEACE.

Russell D Thomas

A Fond Farewell

You left without a word
Our grief is hard to hide
God took his shining star
To be right by his side
You've left a void so deep
That no-one else can fill
We miss you lovely Diana
And we always will.

N Carruthers

To Our Lovely Princess

You came to us some years ago,
a shy young girl nineteen or so.
Through the years we watched you grow
into the woman we all loved so.
You gave us two lovely boys
and filled their hearts with love and joy.
You brought love and happiness
throughout the land and
always had a welcome hand.
We all loved you so very much,
your gentle smile, your caring touch.
Like many of us you had your share
of heartache and despair,
but you came through
to smile again, to show
the world you were their friend.
And now you are gone
we say goodbye,
God please take care
of our 'Lady Di'.

John Aylen

Untitled

The Lord looked down
From His promised land,
And took Diana by her hand,
Of all the angels He has above
He knew she was special.
She was a martyr for us all
Her kindness shone like a star.
She was loved by all afar
And in death, she's still with us
In many different ways.
So we kneel and say a prayer
As Jesus leads you up that stair.

C Alder

Princess Lament

You've left the sunshine
The flowers the foliage
on the trees
When you left the
world behind
Whether raining or
sunshining
The world knows 'tis true
You've had your day
You're on your way
This world you're
passing thro'
We miss your smile
We miss your charm
That you gave us
You made us sigh, you made us cry
You made us all feel blue
They're congregating
Openly stating
They all love you Di
National flags unfurled
As you're passing thro'
this world
You've left the sunshine
The flowers, foliage on
the trees
Everywhere people care
you've got them on
their knees
When you left
the world behind.

B Croft

Diana

Heaven has an angel
Diana is her name.
We will always miss her
Life will never be the same.

Heaven has an angel
With kindness, love and care.
One day we all will join her
And we will meet her there.

C Neve

Diana, Queen Of Our Hearts

Diana, the Queen of our Hearts,
Diana, Princess of Wales,
We look to the sky, with tears in our eyes,
For what happened that night, words just fail.

You made the sun shine so bright,
When it was not to be seen in the sky,
And all we can think since the time you
were gone,
Is why, oh why, just why?

Why did a person so kind and so true,
Who did nothing but good all around,
Suddenly be gone, like a dream in the night,
But I hope now, a better place you have found.

Now Heaven has a new angel,
I hope it is a place where you can rest in peace,
And any hurt you may have felt, while here
on Earth,
Be gone, may it just cease.

I hope that in Heaven you have taken the love,
I am sure you felt, and you knew,
All the love from your family and from
your friends,
And all the people, like me, who never knew you.

So, Diana forever, Queen of our hearts,
You earned the title with ease, never fear,
We never really knew how much we loved you
and what we had,
Until suddenly you were gone, and no
longer here.

Andrea Michelle Hodgson

Queen Of Our Hearts

You were the light that shone in our hearts,
You were the smile on every child's face,
You were the wind beneath our wings,
You were the beauty in every growing thing.

As beautiful as a butterfly,
That shone in the night sky,
As radiant as the sun,
You could reach out to everyone.

After marriage came two children,
You gave them love and affection,
But then the marriage was sadly ended,
And your heart was now unattended.

On holidays you were followed,
Your life had no privacy,
Always hounded by the press,
Because they knew you would be a big success.

Our people's Princess is gone forever,
The space in our hearts will never be filled,
And we now have to say our last goodbye,
To our most beautiful and caring Princess Di.

Kellie J Martin (15)

A Tribute To Diana

Look beneath the surface,
You'll see a heart of gold,
Look beneath the surface,
You'll see a treasure unfold.

Look beneath the surface,
You'll see a diamond so rare,
Look beneath the surface,
You'll see it all there.

Look beneath the surface,
You'll see a life so strong,
You were born to prove a purpose,
And a memory lingers on.

Diana, may your death be a lesson,
To those who turned away,
That your only ambition,
Was to show us the way.

Pat Vieyra

Diana

Dearest Diana, Princess of Wales,
You touched our hearts, because you cared.
You were special, by just being there,
Someone so kind, so giving, so loving.
Lost forever, only our memories remain,
Taken from us so quickly, no-one can believe
The tragic way your life was to end.
So much love is sent to your family and sons,
Your boys have shown courage, having borne so much sorrow.
We all together mourn, with pain in our hearts,
No words can express, this feeling of emptiness.
Our world has lost a guiding light,
Your boys have lost a mother who brought them delight.
Your short turbulent life, no-one can imagine,
The anguish and torment you had to endure.
Fate intervened, and you were gone.
Memories now are all we have to make us strong
We are now left to continue your fight,
Your life was not in vain, so much goodness is in sight.
Princes William and Harry, gain strength as each day does come,
With pride and love in their hearts, that you were their mum.
Lost from this world, you united a nation,
Sadly peace on earth for you was never granted.
Dodi brought you happy days, together you were taken,
Together may peace and love be eternally yours.
Princess Diana, you were Queen of our hearts,
Fondly remembered today and always,
Forever in the thoughts of your grieving nation.

A Sackey

Diana

Well they say the good die young!
I'm starting to believe it now.
What can we do without you,
We need your HELP!

No more kisses, no more hugs Why?
She went without a goodbye Why?
She lived a short but pleasant life.

She helped the poor,
She helped the wounded
And she helped us!

God has taken her back.
She had a place in everyone's
heart and she always will.

She was the Queen of
Hearts and the people's
Princess, the Princess of
Wales and a mam too and
she always will be!

DIANA REST IN PEACE
WE LOVE YOU
FOREVER!

Sharlene Kennedy

Diana The Special Star

D iamond ring you showed to us with a shy smile
I n St Paul's a beautiful bride walked down
the aisle
A loving caring mum you became
N ation's Queen of Hearts you will remain
A lthough Diana now you are gone,
your memory will live on and on.

T he brightest star in the sky,
I s our lovely Princess Di,
A nd that special star up above,
I s sending down to her sons
A mother's special spiritual love.

Alice Haddington

Outside Looking In

On the outside looking in
At a fairy story about to begin
Bringing smiles to all around
Loyal wishes abound

Soon celebrating two bundles of joy
A young mother now not so coy
Then there's pressure to perform
But this Princess would not conform

Dire warnings came and said reject
Unkind words took their effect
An ideal world fell apart
As media wolves were eager to chart

Like a comet coming close to Earth
You sprinkled everyone with your mirth
But then you turned and went away
Leaving us all to cry and pray

On the outside looking in
At a funeral about to begin
Bringing sadness to all around
Loving memories abound.

K Deacon

6th September 1997

This day we have laid to rest
Our only true-blooded English princess
We know she is in heaven above
Leaving behind a legacy of love
And on this bright September morning
The whole world is in silent mourning
And the new title she must now take
She should be now 'The Lady of the Lake'
And now she is passing away the hours
Amid the trees and natural flowers
And Dodi and Diana did both meet
When their loving hearts ceased to beat
We know now that they will never
Be apart, but be together forever.

P F Kett

Farewell To Our Princess

This cool day in September
I shall never forget
I was down there in London
To pay my final respects.
I sat in Hyde Park
With thousands of others too
All there for the same reason -
YOU:
Diana, you were such a warm
And compassionate human being
Those stunning pictures of you
We never tired of seeing.
In your final hours
It proved one picture too many
Now the world has to cope
With not seeing any.
We'll remind ourselves
Each once in a while
By looking at old pictures
And remembering THAT smile.
We'll ignore all the stories
Not take in all the lies
We'll just take a minute
To remember THOSE eyes.
You were knocked so many times
But never did you fall
And you did not need a title
You proved that to us all.
You continued your work
You continued to live
Though much was taken away
You always managed to give.
That's how you'll best be remembered
Caring for another
And the dedicated love
You showed as a mother.
The crowd spoke softly
Of 'ifs' and 'whys'
But then it fell silent
Bar the weeps and cries.
You were taken to Althorp
Your final resting place
Lie in peace
Our Amazing Grace.
The day we buried Diana
Was so tragically sad
We lost The Greatest Queen
Britain never had.

Natalie Bennett

A Shining Light

She was a light, that radiantly shone
To be missed by so many. Now she has gone.
Maybe in the heavens, a star will shine
Welcoming Diana by our Lord divine.

For the abolition of landmines, she worked
Venturing near minefields, where danger lurked
Diligently working for a world ban
Of inhumane contraptions, invented by man.

Diana, Diana with much love and charm
As limbless young children she held in her arms
Helping them to gain courage, face up to life
After losing limbs by the surgeon's knife.

Diana, Diana gave courage to so many
Not only the rich, but those without a penny.
Amongst AIDS sufferers, she did go
Strength and courage from her did flow.

Diana, Diana who dressed in style
A beautiful young lady, with an infectious smile
Loved by the rich, the sick and the poor
A lady welcomed, through any door.

God bless her now, she is up above
For the way she ungrudgingly shared her love
Giving hope to many who had lost their way
Preventing so many from going astray.

So many Diana, will never forget
And for a long time will sadly regret
Your early departure from this life
That cut through Britain like a knife.

She was a light that radiantly shone
To be missed by so many, now she has gone
Maybe in heaven, a star will shine
Welcoming Diana by our Lord divine.

Albert B Lewis

Why Di

And as I listened to the people cry and shout
That across the world a shining light has
gone out
Oh Lord why did you have to take our Princess Di
Now all that is left for us is to weep and cry

She could reach and touch
A heart in pain
A quality so angelic, yet so perfect
Will we ever see the likes again

She cuddled the untouchables
And the down and outs
She gave them heart to shout out
Look we are human beings too

She taught us how to love
And care for each other
The way we were taught by you
Our father and mother

Now can you hear the people crying
Can you see the sorrow on their face
It's for you sweet Di
Our only true member of this human race.

Leslie Rogers

Diana

Maybe if we had adored you just a little
bit less,
And cared just a little bit more,
You'd still be here on this so sad day,
But there again, who could be sure?

The whole world thought the world of you,
It now unites in grief,
Your very life now stolen
And shock echoes with disbelief.

The simplest tribute
That there could ever be,
Is for us to care as much as you
For all our world to see.

Margaret Burgess

Diana - Our Queen Of Hearts

Diana, you meant so very much
to each and every one,
We've heard the news,
but still we can't believe that you are gone.
The gift you brought
was happiness and unique healing powers,
In death your people honour you
with tears and many flowers.

Our lives will never be the same
without your smiling face,
We all respected you so much,
your honesty and grace.
Today our sorrow knows no bounds,
we are lost without you here,
It's taken death for us to show
how much we held you dear.

And so you've gone to rest with God
and his chosen ones,
We hope that your legacy lives on
through both your sons.
The pain I feel is not for me,
but for that of my two boys,
I'll tell them all about your life,
your sorrows and your joys.

We will never forget the way you touched
our lives so very deep,
I only hope you now rest with God
in eternal sleep.

Jane Clayson

Diana

You-beautiful, Princess,
now-you've-left, our-world, to cry.
The-light, of-the-world,
why-did, you-have, to die?
You-mystical, lady,
who-brought-a-smile, to-all-faces.
And-narrowed, the gap,
between-all-nations, and races.
Your-wish, was-for-fighting,
and wars, to cease.
Your-dream, in-this-world,
was for harmony, and peace.
O, Diana, shine-down,
from-your-heavens, above.
And-continue, to spread,
all your kindness, and love.
You've-comforted, the poor,
and-held-hands, with the dying.
I-won't-believe, it's-you,
in-this-coffin, I see lying.
Why-do, all-the-good-people,
get-taken, away?
When-it's-the-bad, that-should-go,
and the good, that should stay.
You'd, make-roses-bloom,
on-a winter's, day.
You'd-make-suffering, and pain, fade away.
So-under, the moon, I-began-to-pray.
That-your, precious-soul's, not-too-far, away.
For-hand, in-hand, with Dodi, you-did-fly.
To-that-paradise, called heaven, up-in, the sky.
Flowers, are laid, around-every, church-steeple.
As-the-news, has-saddened,
the-lives, of all people.
Your-riches, were-present,
on-the-day, of your birth.
So-what, would-you-want,
with-the-riches, of earth?
Like-a-magnet, you-drew, everyone, to your side.
For-your-beauty, astounds-one, as did, your pride.
You, were-created, from-very-special, seeds,
of love.
For-they, were-hand-picked, by-Jesus-in-heaven,
above.
You-now, wear-a-crown, of-thorns, on your head.
As-with-Dodi, side-by-side,
you-both, lay dead.
But-with-your-soul, up in heaven,
and-your-body, laid to rest.
Believe-me, Diana, you-were-one, of the best.
At-least, you-died, with-your-love, in your heart.
Although, you've-been-buried, miles, apart.
But-no-one, will-hurt you, anymore.
They-are-all, now-shut-out, by heaven's door.
And-your-worldly, goods, have-been-taken, away.
Now-you've-been-given, a-room,
in-God's-heart, to stay.
People-only-die, when-their-memory,
goes-down-stream.
But-you'll, go-down-in-history,
and remain, in-every, dream.
The-short-time, that-you-spent-with-us,
made-an-improvement, to-this-earth.
Now, you've-gone-and-left-us,
we'll-really-know, what-you, were-worth.

Linda George

Untitled

To lose a star who shone so bright
To lose a person who was so nice
A saint, a winner, a people's princess
Is a great sadness and a loss

If ever there was anyone else
Who shone as bright,
They still could never match
This person who just lost the fight.

Through all the years that she was here
So much joy and happiness gave
But now the star has left this world
She will never grow dull or fade away
And never will she be replaced.

Diana rest in peace.

Marie Thornton

Diana

Just a little poem
So simple yet so sad
To help us to remember
The Princess we once had.

Her caring ways were noticed
Her work was never done
We took it all for granted
But one thing, our hearts she won.

Her life was full of ups and downs
But she didn't stop to blink
And what she did in her short life
It makes us stop and think.

Today we have no Princess
And it's very hard to bear
But even so in her short life
Diana - taught us how to care.

So it's just a little poem
And it's simple and it's sad
But it helps us to remember
The Princess we once had . . .

Ann Nother

Untitled

I pray for you Diana,
My sister, my friend.
Your life, taken from you,
Before it should end.
So vibrant, so youthful,
Cut down in your prime.
Taken so soon,
Before it was time.
Taken to heaven,
To rest up above.
And there, we shall meet
If like you, I am good.

Jayne Biggin

In Remembrance Of Diana

She came down from the heights of her
Royal station;
this remarkable girl gave her heart to the nation.
Like the early life of an obscure Carpenter
She rose a bright star through the darkness
and gloom.

Overcoming her sorrow, ignoring Royal protocol,
She dwelt on the edge of God's love
and compassion
For the poor and the outcast and those
without hope,
Touching hearts young and old with her beauty
and love.

Then in death she became that lost
spiritual dimension
of this once God-fearing nation then known for
its honour,
whose inner soul has been lost through
rejection of Christ
Who gave homage to Diana to release
profound grief.

This emotional response of a heartbroken people
Unable to express their deep need for a Saviour;
Rediscovered a hidden urge of wanting to pray
Not understanding that God, works in
mysterious ways.

Yet Diana was lost like the rest of our nation,
Still searching for Truth and the reason
for living.
She had her faults and oft lost her direction
But she gave a short glimpse of God's
perfect way.

For Christ is our Life, our Truth, and our Way.
The Way we should follow that leads not astray.
He alone is our Saviour, the Lord God Creator;
Where in His Love, Peace and Joy forever
we'll stay.

Nina E M Parsons

Diana, Queen Of Hearts

A tragic car accident,
cutting life's fragile thread,
And leaving a world stunned to learn
the people's princess was dead,
Bringing an outpouring of grief,
that, in the coming hours
Saw literal rivers of tears
become vast oceans of flowers.

Of a loving mother two young princes
now sadly are bereft,
And this troubled planet
a much darker place has been left,
As it comes to terms
with the reality that has to be faced -
We have truly lost a princess
who can never be replaced.

With her elegance, her beauty
and those stunning blue eyes
She captivated, entranced
and deeply mesmerised;
Being vibrant, fun-loving,
exuding vitality,
But primarily a lady of great humanity.

The shy, young girl
who became a fairytale princess,
But whose concern for others
was so pure and selfless,
As she loved ordinary people
in a manner so unique -
The needy and the dying,
the unloved and the weak.

She hugged people, she touched people,
she felt, and she shared,
And it was apparent to all
she genuinely cared,
Explaining why she was loved
so very, very much,
For, although she was a Royal,
yet she had the common touch.

She never stood on ceremony, choosing instead
To be guided by her heart,
rather than her head;
And with all that she met
she so easily could relate,
Although her love for children
was especially great.

Devoted to her darling sons,
whom she loved passionately,
And to her favoured charities,
which she served tirelessly;
Alerting the world to landmines,
with their awful human price,
And breaking down taboos,
dispelling fears and prejudice.

She identified with the suffering,
and gave them dignity,
From those dying of AIDS
to the victims of leprosy;
And, by just being with people,
she made them feel better,
Remembering those she met
through many a thoughtful letter.

The champion of causes
unpopular and neglected,
But, with a magnetic appeal,
that saw her much respected,
Transcending colour, class,
creed and nationality,
As she touched and warmed hearts universally.

To the sick, the disabled and to the despairing
She brought so much comfort
with her unique brand of caring,
And to both young and old,
throughout an entire generation
She was both a living legend and an inspiration.

Her untimely death can but make us wonder why
Our precious jewel, at such a young age,
had to die,
Leaving an aching void
in the countless hearts she had thrilled,
And great future potential, tragically unfulfilled.

I'll always remember where I was
on the day that she died,
And, though a man,
I'm not ashamed to admit that I cried;
For her life spoke compassion
through its every endeavour,
Gone far too soon,
I will love and miss her forever.

Yes, she was a lady I loved,
though we never had met,
A blazing beacon of hope
the world ne'er will forget;
And what joy, tinged with sadness,
her memory imparts -
The Princess long ago crowned Diana,
Queen of Hearts.

Ian Caughey

A Legacy

Diana was only lent to you and me
her life had a meaning for all to see
She felt sadness, pain and happiness too
She considered others who tragedy
and despair knew.

Although her time was only short
to others happiness she brought.
She loved her children as we could see
but also cared for you and me.

For other people's suffering played a part
after her short life she now lives in many a heart.
We know she's left behind a legacy
for all mankind.
Now her message is complete
she's sure to have a heavenly seat.
Like a star in the sky you will be shining bright
sharing a part of God's heavenly light.

Marjorie Edwina Ashley

Tribute To Diana, Princess Of Wales

Your beautiful face we will miss today,
Your smile brightened the darkest of days.
The love you shared in your short life
You struggled through all the strife.
The courage you had won't be lost
The price you paid, such a cost,
Never to see you, taking part,
In the plight of others, straight from your heart.
The work you did will go on and on.
Never to stop, now you are gone,
Today I kneel and pray,
Help me Lord, walk a better path,
Open my eyes to someone out there.
Who needs a moment, someone to care.
The smiles of happiness, tears of pain,
Her life and work not in vain.
Deep in our hearts, forever to reign.
God Bless.

Ruth Newlands

Diana

Your smile was full of sunshine,
Now our tears are like the rain.
Together we make a rainbow,
Though our hearts are filled with pain.
We will never forget your kindness
You truly were the best
Perhaps everyone will be kind to others
When you're finally at rest.
The kindness and compassion will give
William and Harry the strength to
carry on.
Knowing the love, for their Mother,
will live on and on and on . . .

Sylvia McGillivray

The Last Farewell

Oh what a week that was
Princess Diana and Mother Teresa
Departing in such sad sad ways
All in the space of a couple of days
On hallowed ground now
they can be found two of the best
There laid to rest.

Lady Di, went early Mother T, went late
Now only Heaven knows their fate
Two angels of mercy side by side
Leaving this world in a great divide,
The people laid their flowers for hours
And hours and days and days creating
A scented perfumed haze, sharing
Each other's fears and shedding the
same sad tears, you can be sure
When the Lord come calling, there won't
be any time for stalling.

Two good women who helped
the poor, the sick, and the needy
And laid the blame on the door
of the greedy, with passion and
desires they tried to quench
the sadness fires. With all
downtrodden folk, they would listen
softly when they spoke, trying to
ease their pain and never for a
gotten gain.

God has granted them highest estate,
He'll let them sit either side of
Heaven's gate, wearing their shrouds
Looking down, and saying thanks,
To all the crowds, celestial
Bells are still ringing their tolls,
for two such fine souls.

They showed us a Christian teaching,
Without ever preaching, they got the
world to take heed, when your fellow
man is in need, so let's say goodbye
And don't ask why, a young Princess
And a kindly old nun could lighten
up our world as bright as any
shining sun.

Maria T Moore

Diana

The Princess we had, we have no more.
Took from us in a flash,
The cameras and the paper trash.
She left her mark on all of us,
But when she was alive she gave us a buzz.
Kind and true to ill and poor,
The Princess we had, we have no more.
Her sons live on to fight the cause,
The needy the sick and all the crew
Will live on in all of you.
She was happy for a while
And we saw Diana smile.
It wasn't to be, oh what a shame,
We have cried tears like falling rain.
Her short life has left its mark,
But the days ahead seem very dark.
The candle lights the way ahead,
To follow the light is what she said.
Before the flame died out
We had the best without a doubt.

Marilyn McKinley

The World's Princess

The love, the caring, and happiness too,
Around the world it came from you.
With no conditions, you gave it free,
With that added smile and touch for thee.

The hearts you've touched the world over,
The help you gave shall never be over,
You have shown thoughts with love and care
To all who needed and in despair.

The work, the tasks you took in hand,
The distance travelled throughout the land
You always smiled and took the time
To speak and laugh without decline.

In this short time you achieved your goal,
From in your loving heart and soul
You have shown an example in your short life,
How we can love instead of strife.

The love you gave your family too,
The happiness they shared with you
The love for them it shone from you,
With that magic smile and eyes so blue.

At this sad time and forever more
The whole world loves you more and more
The inspiration you have gave us all
Thank you Di from one and all.

George Duncan

The Birth Of William

Oh! Woe is me, a child is born,
Into a world, so old and forlorn,
A world that is wicked and often vile,
This small infant to defile.

Oh no! My friend, this is not true,
To this wee babe, it's all quite new,
And look who is holding that tiny hand,
One of the fairest in the land,

A Princess no less, with a Prince at her side,
Sharing a love which they cannot hide.
With this start in life, there's not much to fear,
For this little Prince - a breath of fresh heir.

Elizabeth Roch

Tribute To Diana

Rippled by the breeze, symbolic flies, the Union
Flag, half mast, against grey skies; crowds in
Silent reverence line the route the gun-carriage
Now takes, in last salute; flowers pave the way,
As on it goes, tribute on tribute, to our English
Rose; you captured many hearts, by your good
Deeds, your kind, compassionate ways, to those
In need; you reached out, with such loving hands,
To sick and suffering, in many lands; you
Walked with Kings, yet had the common touch,
You asked for little, but you gave so much;
'Candle in the wind'
Your flame burned bright, now quelled forever is
Your shining light; as stalwart Guardsmen lift
You, shoulder high, before the altar, solitary,
To lie; fine speeches made, the sound of prayer
Is heard, we will remember every spoken word;
Choirs sing, resounding trumpets play, to give
Thanks for your life, on this sad day; two
Princes stand, in sorrow, side by side, while
In the shadows, other members hide; the pomp
And ceremony soon is o'er, the flag-draped
Coffin reaches the West Door; out of the Abbey,
In September sun; Westminster's muffled bells
Are softly rung; with tearful faces, waiting
Crowds amass, in fervent tribute, quietly, as
You pass; sincerely comes the sound of their
Applause, approval of your every worthy cause;
'Goodbye Diana', sadly, you have gone, but
Evermore your legend will live on, and in God's
Garden peacefully you'll sleep, from all your
Cares and sorrows, now released.

Dorothy Neil

A Prayer For Diana

God sent you to this world of need
A Princess so precious to every creed
Barriers were broken by your gentle touch
So few have ever done so much
To reach the sick, the lonely and sad
Memories to treasure, each heart you made glad.

The day you were called to your heavenly rest
We all felt pain no words can express
Your love had no limits,
Those in need you'd embrace
To give fresh courage, their troubles to face
The only tribute worthy of you
Is to follow your footsteps all life through.

Taken from this world, we wonder why
God will tell, when we meet him by and by
Rest in him Diana your life was not in vain
Our loss here below is heaven's gain
Your loved ones in prayer to the Lord I commend
To guide and protect them through to the end.

N Cowie

Tear Of Hope

An English Rose
We'll never replace
Her heart touched
Many with grace

A Princess with a
Heart of love
A fairy tale
From God above

She looks down
On the weak and the poor
With tears of hope
A smile for sure.

Diana looks down
From above
With a prayer for
All of us.

Nigel Thomson

Our Caring Princess

It was not only today God sent the sun,
To shine as Princess Diana did on everyone,
She was sent to show you and make you realise,
You can see the world through another's eyes,
Our caring Princess did so much good,
She took many risks we know she never should,
She was so sincere, and gave so much love,
We know now she's being blessed up Above,
The good Lord chooses His helpers to do
His work,
And He chose the Princess, and she never shirked,
Cancer, AIDS, cripples, lepers, and of course
babies,
She even took risks in minefields, but was loved
by all ages.

Jan Graver-Wild

Tribute To Diana

Diana you taught us so much in your short life
Lessons to cope with trouble and strife
Bringing us love in this world full of hate
Showing us people for whom 'life' was too late,
Caring for lepers, the sick, lonely and sad
Teaching us 'hugs', making them glad.
Always reminding us 'time' somebody cares
Swept us along totally unawares
Suddenly you are gone, plucked out of sight
Lord, we miss you Diana, as a nation might.
We love and adore you for showing us how
To care for others and we need to right now.
Truly an angel this Earth to treasure
Reminds us to help others in good measure.

Diana Curtis

Poem For A Princess

I've written many poems in my life
But this is the saddest one YET
I'm writing a part of history
That no-one will ever FORGET
August 31st 1997
A normal Sunday MORN
Unaware of the tragic events
That happened at early DAWN
My daughter phoned me up
Shouting 'Mam put on the TELLY'
Princess Diana has been killed
And my legs just turned to JELLY
No, no it can't be true
It's someone playing a bad JOKE
Things like that don't happen to Royalty
Just to us ordinary FOLK
I'll never forget the time
I'll never forget the PLACE
The look of disbelief
etched upon my FACE
I'd never even met you
Or even shook your HAND
Just like millions of others
Right across the LAND.
To me you were a soapstar
Even though you lived in a PALACE
You could outshine all the glamour
We'd seen in 'DYNASTY' AND DALLAS'
In your earlier years
You once said you had a DREAM
How you thought you and Charles
Would really make a great TEAM
But circumstances took over
And it was never meant to BE
So you found your contentment
Sitting children on your KNEE.
You really had compassion
None of it was FAKE
You were determined to help others
Despite your own HEARTACHE.
Although true happiness deluded you
Right till the very END
We who have lost you
It's as though we've lost a dear FRIEND.
It was to be a 'UNIQUE' funeral
It wasn't like any OTHER
I've never cried as much
Since the death of my dear father and MOTHER.
Crowds of grieving people
Grown men were seen to WEEP
And outside every Palace
The flowers were knee DEEP
The streets became deserted
The Country came to a STANDSTILL
I've never seen the likes in MY lifetime
In fact I don't think anyone ever WILL
The Royals stood outside the gates
Even protocol was BROKEN
The silence fell over the crowd
And not a word was SPOKEN
You were the sister
Your brother Charles ADORED
And when he gave a speech
It really struck a CHORD
Because you called yourself
'A rebel with a CAUSE'
The people couldn't control themselves
And just started to APPLAUSE
The tearful final tribute
Was played by Elton JOHN
Singing 'Candle in the Wind'.
Your memory will always live ON
It had only been out one day
And has gone to the top of the CHARTS
Which just goes to show
You really are the 'QUEEN OF HEARTS'
It's only been a matter of weeks
And yet I still need to hear your NAME
There's just an awful emptiness
Life will never be the SAME.

Eileen Glenn

Untitled

You are in Heaven that I know
Because God only takes the best
So dear Diana rest in peace
We all miss you and love you so.

R Danks

Unforgettable . . .

Diana, you were the nation's unique heroine,
Your death has united us all in grief,
We, regrettably, demanded your vibrant presence,
Now we all look on in disbelief.

The news was exceptionally surreal,
It all occurred so fast,
Your flame now shines brighter,
The flags now fly at half mast.

You profoundly influenced the nation,
We gave you unconditional admiration and love,
Now God requires your compassion,
To assist the loving angels above.

The flowers signify your beauty,
The tears signify our pain,
Your appeal will be with us forever,
We realise you did not die in vain.

Diana, Princess of Wales, you will
eternally remain to be our
unique, compassionate, beautiful
and exceptional Queen of Hearts;
we think of you always.

Scott Burns

Diana

She touched my life
Tell the tears of my sorrow
Lost without you
I find myself loving
You more

We never even met
And yet precious memories
From pictures take rhyme
For such beauty there has been
Whose life touched our hearts
Like a dream.

Paul Just

Diana

On the last day of August, in ninety-seven,
a Princess, took her place in heaven.
Not just a Princess, a fairytale dream,
a hope for the future, a 'Someone Believes'.

Her beauty, integrity, love from the heart,
were to be the ingredients that set her apart.
The call on world leaders, to listen, to act,
placed the whole world beside her, to pray for a pact.

When she plucked from the table, of weary heart's feast,
someone was whole, for a short time at least.
And though hearts will sadden once more, from life's pain,
just to savour that magic, brings comfort again.

And who would have thought from this shy young girl,
we would witness this sadness all over the world?
But for each individual, that bathed in her light,
a darkness has touched them, remembered, for life.

Steve Percy

To Our Diana

We hope you and Dodi are at peace,
Watching over your two boys,
Away from all the pressure,
Away from all the noise.

You are our bright and shining star,
Twinkling in the skies,
We'll miss the beauty of your smile,
We'll miss your sparkling eyes.

You are our lovely angel in Heaven
Shining down on us from above,
We thank you Di, for all you've done.
We say it with all our love.

J Greenwood

Diana

A light has gone out in the world today,
For a star has ceased to shine.
A day of sadness truly felt,
In your heart and mine.

For Diana was taken from us,
Our Jewel in the Crown had gone,
And the work she tried so hard to do
Could not now be done.

There surely must be a reason,
She could not have died in vain,
To leave us broken-hearted,
With naught from her life to gain.

So we must do as she did,
By showing compassion and care.
Never forgetting the joy she gave us,
Here was a life we're happy to share.

With eyes as blue as the deepest sea,
And a smile a joy to behold,
Her kindness came from deep within,
It counted for more than gold.

So rest in peace, Diana,
May the Lord watch over you.
And as you sleep eternal sleep,
He will guard your young sons too.

Margaret Turner

Our Princess Diana

Her smile was like the first spring day
Her beauty rich as summer.
Her warmth like golden autumn leaves.
Her death - like darkest winter.

Deborah Sheppard

Goodbye Diana

She really was so beautiful
A princess she became
A night out turned to tragedy
In Paris, what a shame.

She touched the lives of everyone
And gave out love, the Queen of Hearts
A people's princess, gone forever
A sense of caring she imparts.

The normal busy bustling Mall
Was the centrepiece for today
Silent, but for the horses' hooves
As they trotted down the way.

On down past all the palaces
They took the traditional way
That monarchs for centuries went before
And Diana then did today.

The coffin was lifted off the gun carriage
It was heavy and lined with lead
Eight six-foot men carried it
Into the Abbey - oh if only she was not dead.

In the background Big Ben struck eleven
As they entered the great West Door
All stood for the National Anthem
Tears of sadness were flowing out more.

The whole world came to a standstill
They stopped and each bowed their head
A gesture of love and of loss
For Diana - oh if only she was not dead.

She made her final journey home
To her old ancestral place
Mid applause from all the people
Who'll never forget her face.

Her mother thanked God for the gift of Diana
For all the loving and giving
She now gladly gave her back to Him
With Him her soul will be living.

Florence Linton

Diana

Diana you were so special
I could identify with you
You had a very sad life
And I have had one too.

Your eyes just told the story
Being the gateway to the heart
But you were loved by millions
Right from the very start.

You helped the down and outcasts
You had a heart of gold
And you brought so much pleasure
Both to the young and old.

Now you have gone to a better place
With the angels up above
And they'll give you what you longed for
Yes they'll shower you with love.

And we are very lucky Di
We've got William and Harry too
Two very special nice young men
You've left us part of you!

You've also left us a legacy
On how to care and love
You know that we still love you now
As you look down from above

Nora St John O'Shea

Cradled In Your Arms

You reached out to touch children,
You reached out around the world,
You reached out with inspiration
A saint upon the earth.

You brought life to the dying,
You brought a smile into their eyes,
You brought hope and understanding
The light of humankind.

Diana you brought happiness,
The Queen of people's hearts,
You gave your gift of love to those
You cradled in your arms.

Eily Tatlow

Princess Ours!

Sweet Princess, ours, a precious gem
within the Royal Crown;
You no longer walk amongst us
but from heavenly home, look down.
We have watched you grow and flourish
from bud to glorious bloom;
A bud so slowly op'ning,
then snatched from us too soon!

Your eyes held much compassion,
your hands, a healing touch;
your smile brought joy to thousands;
your tears, meant oh so much.
From within, there glowed a radiance,
a shining beacon bright;
You touched our hearts with gladness,
and brought to darkness - light.

You brought hope where there was sadness,
you cheered us on our way;
If only God had spared you,
just a few more years, to stay!
In such short time you taught the world,
your feelings you expressed;
Your example we must follow, helping all,
Sad, lonely, sick, depressed.

With your Love, the heavenly paths you'll stroll,
With love, your hearts will brim;
The years will never dim your light,
your beauty, with age, never dim.
Time will heal all pain, 'tis true,
and you're forever blessed,
God grant you life eternal,
give you solace, peace and rest.

Margaret Scothern

Diana

God gave us a gift of an angel,
a gift so precious and rare.
A shy unassuming young person,
whose purpose in life was to care.
She cared for the poor and the homeless,
sick children she took to her heart.
She carried out her duties regardless,
even when her own world fell apart.
She campaigned against evil landmines,
which cripple so many each day.
To us she brought home the full horror,
of atrocities in lands far away.
She brought hope and compassion to many,
a thing rarely seen in this day.
Though the press would often deride her,
she would not let it stand in her way.
Her smile could stop eyes from crying,
with a young man she once shared a joke,
And though he had AIDS, and was dying,
she held his hands firm, as they spoke.
And just when her troubles seemed over,
when in Dodi a new love she'd found.
True happiness she seemed to discover,
but the press once again had to hound.
And now the whole world is in mourning,
the news we find hard to believe.
Our tragic loss is just dawning,
as a whole nation begins to grieve.
Now the people's princess is in heaven,
we will not let her good deeds cease,
Diana, an angel among angels,
we pray that you've found perfect peace.

Janet Ashcroft

Diana

Our dearest delectable Di,
At first you seemed so shy,
But then a rosebud did bloom
And was picked far too soon
And it's left us all wondering why?

Pamela Jean Ann Hornby

Farewell To A Princess

With everyone in mourning,
For our beautiful Princess Di,
In that fatal crash in Paris,
The whole world is asking why.

At only 36 years old,
Her life was taken away,
The 31st August 97,
Was that terrible sad Sunday.

Just when she'd found happiness,
And her future looked so bright,
After all the years of heartache,
When her life seemed to be going right.

With all the good she had to do,
For which she didn't boast,
Her smiling face and friendly touch,
To those who needed it most.

As people flocked from miles around,
And all did their own parts,
To say farewell to a Princess,
Our very special 'Queen of Hearts'.

All the flowers placed in memory,
And the people there on the day,
Just shows how people loved her,
In a very special way.

As she made her final journey,
With the crowds lining the way,
The two Princes and mourners walked behind,
With their final respects to pay.

She was laid to rest in privacy,
Away from all the press,
With just her family round her,
She would have wanted nothing less.

An extraordinary special funeral,
As the country came to a close,
With Elton John's great tribute,
To say 'Goodbye to England's Rose'.

Katy Jane Illingworth

Diana

She came into the world like an ordinary girl
but she was special like an oyster's pearl.
She grew up known as Earl Spencer's child
witty, sweet, quiet and mild
The nation came about her when she met the Prince of Wales
it was the beginning of paparazzi tales
They got engaged and then were married
Diana HRH was the name she now carried
Princess Diana gave Charles two baby boys
the nations of the world were filled with love and joy
The marriage then deteriorated
Diana then had a new life created
Soon her and Charles got a divorce
but for the cameras a smile was forced
The papers talked of her and men
the minds kept working of the devious pen
Diana carried on helping charities
from fatal illnesses to disabilities
Another of her topics was to ban the landmine
She saw victims who'd had a terrible time
She helped children of all kinds of races
never forgetting one of their faces
While all of this occurred
more rumours by the papers were stirred
Diana's title was taken away from her name
it was plain and simple all over again
At last she met Dodi who was the one
they went on holidays to the sun
the papers followed and Diana preached
'I'll surprise you lot in a couple of weeks'
She did that all right one morning in France
it was the paparazzi's last chance
With Dodi she got into a black car
but to their destination they went not, not by far
The car was chased along by the River Seine
into a tunnel the chase went, but car did not come out again
The black car crashed and killed Dodi dead
while Diana was rushed to a hospital bed
She died in the morning around three
the black Mercedes was a deathtrap you see
The news travelled across the land
no-one could understand
The floors of London were carpeted in flowers
while the queue for the condolence book went on for hours
Everyone across the world has the same question in mind
why does God always take the kind?

Keren Collins (14)

To Diana, Queen Of Our Hearts

To think, to care, to see, to feel . . .
Is not a lot to do.
It only becomes 'very special'
When you do it for other people,
and not just . . .
For you.

The very special gift you had,
I'm sure you never knew.
It was just ordinary,
The right thing for you to do.

A gift so rare,
You can't compare with those who rush around.
Not thinking of the others,
Who stood on shaky ground.

You stood amongst the mighty,
The royalty and the great.
But still not losing touch with us . . .
The whole of the human race.

Di did it without thinking,
It was the right thing for her to do.
She wasn't out there gaining points,
She never needed to.

She never knew how people felt,
About the things she did.
The peace she gave . . . her gentle touch . . .
To all of us it felt so much.

Her loving care where'er she went,
Not too proud she stooped and bent.
To meet us all along the way,
This very proud lady is in our hearts . . .
To stay.

Christine Fincham

Diana - Always In Our Hearts And Souls

To Lady Diana, Princess of Wales - England's glistening diamond - please listen dearest Princess:

The world will never again be the same
as our great beauty, dearest Diana has gone
forever will be lasting your fame
we will make you immortal dear England's Rose.

It was a great honour for us to have you on Earth
Diana, we will always keep you in our hearts and minds!
A unique mother for the two boys to whom you gave birth
we will make you immortal as an embodiment of love and care.

You let your actions be lead by your heart
and touched many people's lives with your caring soul
but when did you seek your own happiness for a start?
We will make you immortal as our candle in the dark.

Tributes we pay to our beloved Princess
we cry in the nights and bring flowers on the day
a sad place the world now is without your tenderness
we will make you immortal as an inspiration for doing good.

Diana, it brings us to tears: we miss you so much!
now for William and Harry we open our hearts
twinkle down from Heaven - we can still feel your touch
we will make you immortal as our lady with the golden heart.

To have an open ear for all the needy was your goal
dearest Princess we thank you so much for being with us
with your death reality took us and pierced our soul
we will make you immortal as an icon of true felt love.

Stefanie Ricker

A Butterfly In Flight

I watched this beautiful creature
Spread its wings and flutter away -
Alighting on each flower and bush,
As if to say - 'Let's play'!
Like our Princess it persisted
In its quest to find a friend,
A game of happy 'make-believe',
Which turned to 'let's pretend'.
Its wings were those of compassion
As it wended on its way,
Children admired the fascination of this beauty
Flying up and far away.
It flew from us, sadly, one very last time,
Not out of mind, but out of sight
When we were asleep, one very dark night,
Right up to heaven's safe-keeping,
Resting in peace and quietly sleeping,
Leaving us sad and gently weeping.
An extra star now twinkles above,
Brighter than most -
Exuding great love!
Guarded by angels and a beautiful dove!

Freda Ringrose

Princess Of The People

Say it with a flower
Show it in a card,
To the people's princess
Send a fond regard.
For there won't be another
To stand so straight and tall,
And angels bow before her
As she enters Heaven's hall.

Her heart was ever-caring
Her mind full of good deeds,
A shoulder strong to lean on
For those so much in need.
No-one could ever slight her
She gave her everything,
Her short life she devoted
For happiness to bring.

Princess of the people
We speak your name with pride,
Within our saddened hearts
Forever you will abide.
Diana how we miss you
Your warm embracing smile,
And forever to your memory
We will e'er stay loyal.

Sweet 'prima inter pares'
How great your wondrous ways,
A sovereign in the making
Though clouded were your days.
But through each storm and tempest
You held your head on high,
And walked the road to glory
As you gave the world great joy.

Now you've gone and left us
And tears may swell the sea,
For your beauty and your kindness
We never again shall see,
And in your new-found kingdom
Regina you will reign,
And all of Heaven's people
Your office will ordain.

Princess of the people
We send a sad farewell,
May God love and protect you
And all your deep fears quell.
You'll always be remembered
Though tears like rain will flow,
For we'll never find another
As good as you - we know.

Len Fox

Faded Flowers

Somewhere in a city
The faded flowers weep
Crying for a soul
We all wished to keep
She touched a life
She lit a soul
Now she flies
Through death's darkest hole
She left a tear
A memory
Give her love on
Her last journey
In our hearts
She was a Queen
Now all we have
Is a shattered dream
The light has gone
The joy, the charm
But rest assured
She's in God's arms
So rest in peace
Our beloved Di
For all that remains
Is for us to cry.

P Keetley

In Loving Memory Of Diana

You came into our lives,
you brought peace and love,
The fragrance of a beautiful flower
sent from heaven above.
You lived your life for others,
you were so calm and so serene
You really were Diana, of our hearts the Queen.
You didn't ask for fame or fortune,
you only wanted love,
And yet you gave so much,
now you are in heaven above.
Nothing can harm you now sweet English rose,
No-one can hurt you,
Jesus saw your sweet eyes close.
We shall never forget your sweet smiling face,
Your eyes so full of compassion,
your tender gaze.
You shook hands with the lonely,
the sick and the sad,
You made many an aching heart feel glad.
You loved the little children
as our Saviour did of old,
You will always be cherished for your heart of gold.
Now your loving heart is stilled to beat no more,
No more will your lovely face
look on the sick, the sad and the poor.
Be happy now sweet Princess
for earth was not your home,
The Lord had better plans for you
He came and took you to His home.
So sleep in peace and take your rest,
For you Diana were one of the best.
Sleep in peace with the one you love
May you both be happy in heaven above.
I never even met you and yet I felt I knew you,
The day you died it felt as though
we all died with you.
Why did you have to go like that?
You didn't deserve to die,
Your lovely face your look of love is gone,
we wonder why?
I pray for your loved ones
that they may know God's peace,
That they may find comfort in His love
which will never ever cease.
Your memory will linger on like an eternal flame,
Shining in the darkest places
we shall always remember your name.

Jean Parkey

To Diana

Weep not for me when I'm gone
but listen to the sweet bird song,
beneath a tree so strong and high
whose branches reach up to the sky.
There rest I,
Among the leaves so fresh and green
all Heaven's beauty can be seen
Springtime's soft and gentle showers
bring alone the summer flowers.
Then in autumn leaves will fall
ducks will swim and birds will call,
While water laps against my shore,
Weep not for me when I'm gone
as at last winter's snows will come
I'll be here in my childhood home.

Margaret Vinall-Burnett

Diana, Princess of Wales

Diana, Princess of Wales
was a person so special
and caring with a heart
of gold.
She has left a void
which can never be filled
The Heavens are richer.
for her star
The work she did should
carry on
By people left behind
to make the world a
better place.

N A Callear

In Memory Of A True Princess

Dear Diana, who gave so much,
We'll miss you with your loving touch,
You walked right through the barriers to,
Make people aware of your points of view,
How you cared, and how you shared,
You clarified where others blurred.

You were a gem, so rare indeed,
You shone your light for those in need,
So many things have come to light,
That touched with love, upon their plight,
You touched upon so much it seems,
And now we are left with shattered dreams.

For a while you made us smile,
You were so lovely down the aisle,
We watched you grow in stature too,
As from the ashes you rose and grew,
Like someone reborn, you came successfully through,
Bulimia, anorexia, despair, and lost love true.

On these things and more, you opened the door,
To open the mind, to where we were blind before,
You paved the way as a pioneer might do,
And shed your light upon these points of view,
Yes, you walked and talked, how we'd listen to you,
Because we knew, what you said, was true.

The sick, the dying, the afflicted and lame,
You loved them all, and felt their pain,
And the tears of joy, when they heard your name,
As you held them in your arms again,
And had them laughing their pain away,
How they will miss you, no words can say.

In hospitals you had them laughing again,
You mended hearts together, and then,
At home and abroad, with so many children,
Who will never forget, who they met, and when,
Your legacies will live on and on,
In your memory, now that you are gone.

Lepers too, you held to say,
Look it's wrong to keep them hidden away,
They are human beings, treat them that way,
With love, and acceptance, show you care today,
And you showed the world, without a doubt,
That this was what it was all about.

Your laughter was a joy to see,
Spreading happiness with your empathy,
You could relate to others who,
Were amazed with how they took to you,
Like a breath of fresh air, where e'er you went,
That's a part of our memory, that will never be spent.

In the USA, where they held AIDS at bay,
In a way, no words can say,
You took one look, and held this man's hand,
And without a word, said I understand,
You made that man, laugh and cry,
And forget that he was going to die.

Putting people at ease so easily,
You made it seem simplicity,
Like a Queen of Hearts, you touched the soul,
Now we're bereft, left with a hole,
That we, now, don't know how to fill,
I wonder if we ever will.

R C Strong

Diana

I've never been so upset,
Although we've never met.
I have cried every day,
Since you went away.
I wish you could see all of the flowers,
And the people queuing for hours.
Millions are signing condolence books,
I can't get over their saddened looks.
You're the most loved person of my times,
I will think of you every time Big Ben chimes.

Pete Martin

To You Diana

(My tribute to Diana and Dodi, loving you forever, greatly and deeply missed but I shall never forget you nor shall this world. Loving you forever and ever)

It's not fair, in the world,
What's going on?
People are dying, one after one
And even at more of a rate
As the case may be
Here's looking at you
'Cause I'm looking at me
There's some things in life
That you cannot foretell
If only we could
You'd make matters well
Before the time of things
Had a chance of going wrong
My heart and my soul
Go out to you Diana
With my song.

This is, my song
And its name, is 'Diana'
Diana, our Diana
A lady, for all
Her strength, stood her tall
Diana our Diana
Top of the best
Above, all the rest
Diana, our Diana
She was an inspiration to many
Showed the world, we can, agree
Diana, our Diana
Her love, and her passion
And her love, for the latest fashion
Made her Diana, Princess Diana
Diana, our Diana
All her love
For charity and voluntary work
Made Diana, what she is
But, it was not just that
She always, loved to give
Diana, our Diana.

Such a loss to the world
Our emotions are filled
Filled with sadness
Filled with tears
We remember all the good about Di
What she has done over the years
Diana, our Diana
What she stood for
What she represented
She mixed with all classes
And ages of life
That included the kids
Colour, creed, religion, disease
Didn't come into it.
Whatever Diana had she would
Always willingly give it.
Diana, our Diana.
That's what made her special
And very dear to our hearts.
She's a legend to us all
Loved forever in my heart
Diana, our Diana.

She mixed with the rich
But, yes, also the poor
The work that Diana did
Cannot be ignored
She also stood up for those
Who could not stand up for themselves
She brought things to light
Where other people had failed
Diana, our Diana.
A great loss, gone, gone, from us all.
She'll never be forgotten
Just like football.
Inspired the world over.
Bigger than any king
The nicest thing about Diana
She did her own thing,
Diana, our Diana.
Her love, our Diana's
Will never be lost
When you talk of Diana
You cannot put a cost
Diana, our Diana.

She was loved by the young.
Loved also by the old
Princess Diana
Had a heart made of gold
Diana, our Diana.
Many a royal had
Come before her Lord
But Diana was the one,
The one we adored
Diana, our Diana
My Diana, your Diana
Our Diana, Princess Diana
A people's Diana, everybody's Diana
May her soul, and memory
Live on forever.
Diana, our Diana
Diana, if one and one
Really, make two
Our world, this nation
We all love you
You found love, and happiness
With Dodi
I shall always remember
You and he
Diana our Diana.

But now I finish my song
With a big sorry,
Sorry for the Spencers
For the whole family
Thinking about you William
And you Harry
Charles is their father
So do the right thing
Open your heart
And with your mouth, sing
Diana our Diana
Mr Fayed,
We're sorry for what's happened
My thoughts are also with you
As I look through the wind
Such a tragedy, and loss of lives
A forever, lasting pair, to us all
Girls, boys, fathers and wives
Teenagers, family
And the Earl Spencer
You were closest of all to Di
Very dear
And the Queen,
It's not been easy on you
You are the Queen of the country
Now what do you do?

Not forgetting you're a
Grandmother as well
We wish you all the best
Now our Princess has fell
Diana our Diana
An awful fall
That we could not foretell
We know they must be at peace
As one, in Heaven and no, not in hell.
Their love, always shining
Through and through
Devoted and caring, our Diana,
That was you.
William and Harry will have
Part of their mum's genes.
Carry on her good work,
Fulfil Diana's dreams.
I know Diana would have wanted that
Such a special lady
And these are the facts.
Diana, our Diana.

September 6th 1997
Will be an everlasting memory to us all.
No matter how big you are,
No matter how small.
The lowering of a flag,
Waving a scarf or banner
A thought for the little girl
Who asked 'Mummy, are all
These people here, for Diana?'
Diana, our Diana.
This little girl, no I haven't met her
The question she asked her mum was
'Are all these people here today to
Make Diana better?'
I said this needed to be right
Right down to the last letter

She looked up at mum and asked
'Are all these people here today
To make Diana better?'

My heart pours out, and with my soul, sings.
It is always children who say the
Most moving things
Diana, our Diana
Your life will live on forever,
We loved Diana
She is the 'People's Princess'
Because she treated everyone the same
As an equal, as a person, as people
Diana our Diana
Ambassador of the people
For the people.
Diana our Diana
The Princess of Hearts
The Queen of Hearts
Diana.

Simon Peter Dennis

The Tunnel

Bosnian dreams,
Landmine Queen,
Light amidst one tunnel.
Kindness, care for those in doubt,
Given hope, dark tunnels.
Her tension's rife,
A shattered life,
A still Parisian tunnel.
No end in sight, cold street lights,
Now candles light her way.
In many minds, and hearts with pain
Her epitaph remains.
Conscious of the need to give -
Sad loss,
Although tears, life gained.

Barrie W Neate

People's Poetry

Real poetry written by real people. Editors at Anchor Books believe that poetry should be easy to read and enjoyable for a wide range of people.

Anchor's books of verse are about the things that concern ordinary people in their daily lives. In some books the poems are of a serious nature, addressing issues that are important to people. In others, the verse is light-hearted - expressing the humour to be found in the world around us.

Poetry is for sharing. A poem which communicates with its readers can share an experience, an insight, a feeling, or simply a comment on life that makes the reader smile.

If you would like more information about Anchor Books and other Forward Press publications send for a free copy of the latest 'Poetry News' from Forward Press. Write to:- FP Poetry News, Forward Press Ltd, 1-2 Wainman Road, Peterborough PE2 7BU.